THE
GOOD
HONEYMOON
GUIDE

LUCY HONE

Second edition researched and updated by
NICKI GRIHAULT

includes
WHERE TO GET MARRIED ABROAD

The Good Honeymoon Guide
First edition 1997; this second edition 2002

Publisher
Trailblazer Publications
The Old Manse, Tower Rd, Hindhead, Surrey GU26 6SU, UK
Fax (+44) 01428-607571
info@trailblazer-guides.com
www.trailblazer-guides.com

British Library Cataloguing in Publication Data
A catalogue record for this book is available from the British Library

ISBN 1-873756-51-8

Text © Lucy Hone 2002
The right of Lucy Hone to be identified as the author of this work has been asserted by her in accordance
with the Copyright, Designs and Patents Act 1988

Photographs © as follows:
Cover: © Paul Steel/Corbis; facing p48, top: © KTA International (Antigua & Barbuda), bottom: © Ladera
Resort St Lucia, BGB & Associates; facing p49, top: © The Cocobay Resort, KTA International (Antigua
& Barbuda), bottom: © Curtain Bluff/Ken Maguire; facing p64 © Kiwayu Safari Village, Cheli & Peacock
Photo Collection; facing p65, top: © Seychelles Tourist Office, middle and bottom: © Hotel Bora Bora;
facing p96: © Lemuria Resort of Praslin (Hotels Constance); facing p97, top: © Lemuria Resort of Praslin
(Hotels Constance), bottom: © River Club, Victoria Falls, Zambia/Outposts; facing p112: @ Luttrellstown
Castle Limited; facing p113 top: © Relais & Châteaux, bottom: © Villa San Michele; facing p208:
© Henry Stedman; facing p209 top: © ZFL Châteaux Lake Louise, middle: © Hotel Salto Chico, bottom:
© Hayman Island Resort, McCluskey & Associates; facing p224 top: © La Mamounia, bottom:
© Governors' Camps, Loldia; facing p225: © Tortilis Camp, Cheli & Peacock Photo Collection, bottom:
© Matusadona Water Wilderness, Zimbabwe/Outposts; facing p272: © Bryn Thomas; facing p273: © Bryn
Thomas; facing p288 top: © Amanresorts, bottom: © Rick & Jane Field; facing p289: © The Peninsula
Hong Kong, bottom: © Governors' Camps, Il Moran

Editors: Henry Stedman and Anna Jacomb-Hood
Series Editor: Patricia Major
Typesetting: Henry Stedman
Design: Bryn Thomas
Layout: Anna Jacomb-Hood
Index: Jane Thomas

Every effort has been made by the author and publisher to ensure that the
information contained herein is as accurate and up to date as possible. However, they are unable to accept
responsibility for any inconvenience, loss or injury sustained by anyone as a result of the advice and information given in this guide.

Printed by
Kelso Graphics (☎ 01573-223214), The Knowes, Kelso,TD5 7BH Scotland

THE
GOOD
HONEYMOON
GUIDE

LUCY HONE

Second edition researched and updated by

NICKI GRIHAULT

includes
WHERE TO GET MARRIED ABROAD

Authors

Nicki Grihault Abandoning belly dancing as a career, Nicki set off to live, work and travel abroad. After jillarooing in Australia, teaching English in Rome and tour repping in the Indian Himalaya it was perhaps inevitable that she would become a travel writer although her degree is in psychology. She has worked both for Wanderlust magazine and Culture Shock! Guides and has published *Working in Asia* (In Print Publishing, 1996).

Nicki is currently travel editor of *Executive Woman* and assistant editor of *Woman Abroad* magazines; she is frequently abroad and always on the lookout for romantic destinations around the world.

Lucy Hone Born in London, Lucy comes from a family of travellers. Her first major trip on her own started with a six-month stay in Southern Africa in 1986. In 1987 she moved to Scotland to study at Edinburgh University from where she graduated with an MA in History. Since then, both before and after her marriage, she has been all over the world in search of places offering romance, luxury or uniqueness. In the process she has tested beds, beaches, resorts and restaurants, seeking out the best honeymoon destinations each country has to offer.

Lucy currently lives on a farm in Dorset, working as a freelance writer for a wide variety of national newspapers and magazines.

Acknowledgements

From Lucy Many thanks to the following people who between them contributed in no small way to the insight and detail of the first edition of this guide: Philip Grierson, Kate Theobald, Katrin Holtkott, Erika Schule Grosso, Elizabeth Martin, Jane Roche, Toni Anne Leyland, Vanessa Janion, Edward Paine, everyone at ZFL and countless people at the various tourist boards, for allowing me to constantly pester them with queries; to Esther and Chris Henry, Andrew and Caroline Blatter, Tubes and Tan Thompson, Anthea and Biddy Fahey, Tre Petrie, Ian and Roo Cross, Miller Edwards, Doughlas Lochhead, Lizzie Howell, Tim Carter, Katie Stockton, Rodney and Vicky Theobald, Jess and Malcolm Wren, and Nige and Lizzie Walley for their much appreciated contributions; to Jane and Rick Field for the photo opposite p288, to Camilla Blood for her contacts and Scot McRae and Sally Blofield for the workspace.

Thank you also to the countless number of honeymooners I interviewed, for all their comments, tips and insight, and especially to those who made a special effort to take notes for me while they were away!

Thank you Gabby for coming to my rescue when I needed it most, and to Roo and my mother for their unfailing support, enthusiasm and interest.

But most of all I'd like to thank Andrew and Caroline for introducing me to Bryn and the idea of *The Good Honeymoon Guide*, and Trevor for always being there for me, in the good times and bad.

For this edition: many thanks to Nicki Grihault and everyone who helped her update this guide, and to Henry Stedman, Anna Jacomb-Hood and Bryn Thomas at Trailblazer for transforming the text into a book.

From Nicki Thanks to Lucy Hone for her guidance and to both Lucy and Bryn for entrusting me with the project. I am grateful to everyone who helped with this second edition: the countless hotels, public relations' managers, tour operators, tourist boards and others, in particular Small Luxury Hotels of the World and ZFL PR Agency, as well as the editor 'the travelling Hen,' and Anna Jacomb-Hood. Most of all, though, thanks to Paul for his love and support.

A request

Every effort has been made by the author and the publisher to ensure that the information contained in this book is as up to date and accurate as possible. However, the quality and prices of resorts can change very quickly so we would welcome any constructive comments from readers (postal address on p2; email: lucy.hone@trailblazer-guides.com).

Cover photo: Sandbar, Great Barrier Reef, Queensland, Australia © Paul Steel / Corbis

CONTENTS

PLANNING

1

Your honeymoon is a holiday to look back on all your life. It is your chance, after all the hectic wedding preparations, to spend some time alone together: a time to enjoy one another and experience something together as a married couple. But, just like the wedding, it also requires some serious research and planning: it always amazes me how many couplers spend months arranging every last detail of the wedding and then rush into booking a honeymoon. No wonder so many couples get it wrong! Do your homework, consider all kinds of options and you'll be guaranteed a holiday that is truly special, something to cherish in years to come and dream about on boring days at work.

ONCE YOU'VE GOT ENGAGED

The first thing to do once you get engaged is to decide who is going to book the honey-moon. Although most couples choose to plan this important holiday together, there are those who still believe in the tradition that it's a man's job, especially in Europe. As one husband-to-be said to me: 'Melissa is sorting out everything else, I just want to have something that I can say is totally and utterly mine. She hasn't got a clue where we're going, but as soon as I saw it (in a brochure) I knew it was just perfect for the two of us and I am having such a great time planning it all in secret'. If you do decide to go it alone, note the Surprise Honeymoon section on p8.

The engagement is the hardest bit, once you've asked and she's said yes, the rest is easy. You can start having all those conversations that you wanted to have before but didn't dare. **Andrew Blatter**

Whatever you decide it's essential to get straight on with bookings as the best rooms, the best views and the best deals are the first to go. Look through the Contents List at the start of the book ticking off countries that appeal. Even if one of you loves the sound of Costa Rica or Morocco and the other hates it, tick it: you might be surprised at the kind of honeymoon you could have there. The golden rule of honeymoons is to go somewhere that neither of you has been to before as there's nothing more tedious than being given a blow-by-blow account of a holiday one of you enjoyed, or even didn't enjoy, with someone else.

Each chapter of the book is structured so that you can quickly tell whether or not the country is right for you, starting with the best time to visit. The Practical Information box tells you, amongst other things, approximately how long it takes to fly to that destination.

Flights are a big consideration when booking your honeymoon as you are going to be pretty exhausted after the wedding and may not necessarily feel like hours cooped up on an aeroplane. Don't think that romantic necessarily has to mean distant, it doesn't. Having said that, if you've absolutely set your heart on a country and a hotel that is thousands of miles away why not take the plunge? After all this is probably going to be the biggest holiday of your life.

WHAT KIND OF HONEYMOON DO YOU WANT?

Presumably you know each other well enough for it not to be a problem working out what your dream holiday comprises. But there are a few things to bear in mind: however much you long to flop on a white sandy beach and do absolutely nothing, it's a good idea to check that there are things to do when you decide it's time to venture off the lounger. The aim of this book is to inform you exactly what there is to do at or near each hotel: but check with the hotel or travel agent exactly what sports facilities are available at the time of year you are visiting and whether or not they will cost extra.

Take care to build plenty of time for rest and relaxation into your itinerary if you are planning an active honeymoon with touring, sightseeing and adventure activities. You will be amazed at how tired you are after the wedding, and even more so if you've got jet lag after a long flight. Consider having three days lying on the beach or in a mountain hideaway before you hit the trail; that way you'll both get much more out of the holiday. You don't have to dash around and see every single highlight of your chosen destination, even if you have decided on a really alternative place for your holiday. Tour operators, particularly the specialist ones, tend to push people into doing too much. You don't want to be exhausted, you're here to enjoy it: besides, you can always go back for more another year if you loved it that much and felt there was more to see.

SURPRISE HONEYMOONS

Surprise honeymoons are great. They are romantic, dreamy and exciting – as long as you both feel that way. So do check that your other half is genuinely happy to go ahead with the plan before you take the ball into your own court. And check again a week or two before the wedding, and once more a day or two before the big day, that they are still happy to hang in there until the departure lounge. Bear in mind that half of the romance of your booking the honeymoon is that you've taken the trouble to think about what your partner would like, so there's nothing wrong in telling them a few days before you leave. This option often leads to a great deal of relief on both parts. Many people also find it difficult to get excited about a holiday they cannot visualize.

That aside, the key is to think about your partner and decide honestly what you think they would want. Don't book a trekking holiday in northern Thailand if all your fiancé(e) wants to do is lie on the beach. Perhaps best is to plan a two-centre honeymoon with something for you both: for example, a few days on the beach at either end and a few days in the middle for trekking, white-water rafting, canoeing, diving, looking around ancient temples or going on a safari. A good way to get an idea of where your partner would like to go, while still allowing you to keep it a surprise, is to get them to tick the countries they are interested in, on the Contents List. That way there's still plenty of scope but you know they'll approve of the basic destination. Some tour operators will provide an all important packing list (without giving the game away) to the partner who is going blind, so to speak.

COPING WITH TIREDNESS

Most couples are extremely tired after their wedding. I can remember waking up the morning after and physically struggling to lift my head off the pillow, and I'm a morning person. It really does hit you: the emotion, the supreme effort that you've both put into the big day, and the excitement. All you'll want to do is flop, so bear this in mind when making your departure plans: try not to travel the very day of your wedding and consider whether you can both cope with a long-haul flight.

COSTS

One thing you must get straight, right from the start, is how much you think you should allocate for the honeymoon. There's nothing romantic in talking about money and budgets, least of all for your honeymoon, but there's also not a great deal of romance in starting married life broke. You simply won't enjoy a honeymoon if you end up scouring the cocktail menu trying to find something you can afford each time you're thirsty, or getting to some wildly exotic country and feeling you actually can't afford to go on the dug-out tour up the river to see the orang-utans' sanctuary. So talk about it and decide together what makes sense – which could of course involve the dreaded marital notion of **compromise**!

Make sure you think about all the expenses you are likely to incur, including extras such as airport tax, service charges, tips, and shopping sprees. On your honeymoon, try not to go mad and spend way over your budget: I've talked to couples who are six months into their marriage and still paying crippling credit card bills – hardly the way to start married life.

Bridge the World in the UK is one company that is part of a new trend in giving 'Honeymiles' – contributing to the honeymoon fund instead of buying a wedding present. People can buy you a particular experience such as a Sydney Harbour Bridge climb, or two or three days' car hire, depending on what you list.

It is worth noting that the room rates quoted in this book are rack rates only. These are the rates you would be charged if you walked into the hotel and asked for a room for one night only, and as such will very rarely apply to your honeymoon. A good travel agent or tour operator should be able to get a sizeable discount on this rate. For example, leading UK tour operators can expect to obtain discounts of 40-50% off the rack rate, depending on the time of the year and the length of your stay. The Internet of course is a great place to search for bargains, and with 'visual tours' you'll know instantly whether you like the look of the hotel and can pick the room you like best.

Order your foreign exchange and travellers' cheques at least a week before you leave and try to have some small change for taxis, tips on arrival etc. In many countries it's a good idea to have some US dollars in cash, as well as cash in the local currency. If you are not on a package tour it would be worth checking how you should pay your hotel bill: some hotels do not accept credit cards and they may even refuse to accept the local currency, or charge an extra premium for doing so.

Throughout this book, prices are given as much as possible in both US$ and the local currency: where only a US$ rate is shown this is the principal currency used by tourists in that country.

MAKING A BOOKING

Travel agents and tour operators around the world work in very different ways. You can book your chosen hotel **direct** by using the phone, fax or toll-free number, or email address, given for each hotel listing; through an **international booking agency** such as Small Luxury Hotels of the World, Relais & Châteaux and The Leading Hotels of the World; through a **travel agent**; or by using a **specialist tour operator** which has a range of hotels in a particular region with which its employees are well-acquainted, so you should get really expert advice and can organize getting there as well.

I have tried to give the names of travel agents or tour operators through whom reservations can be made, for every hotel listed in this book. A large proportion of these tend to be UK-based tour operators as they often get the cheapest rates. Once you have decided which hotels you are interested in look at the companies listed below: they are grouped according to the country they specialize in. Do give a tour operator or a travel agent a call before you book direct, you might end up saving yourselves a lot of money, even if it costs you an international call. Using a travel agent or tour operator is also incredibly time-saving, something you'll be grateful for as the wedding approaches; it's nice to know that your dream holiday is being taken care of.

WORLDWIDE OPERATORS

Abercrombie & Kent: UK (☎ 0845 070 0610; 🖹 0845 070 0608); USA (☎ toll-free 0800 323 7308, 🖹 630-954 3324); Australia (☎ 39-536 1800, 🖹 39-536 1805); Hong Kong (☎ 2865 7818, 🖹 2866 0556); 💻 www.abercrombiekent.co.uk

Air France Holidays: USA (1-800-2-FRANCE); 💻 www.airfranceholidays.com

American Express Vacations: USA (toll-free ☎ 1-800-346-3607)

Bales Worldwide: UK (☎ 0870 241 3208, 🖷 01306-740 048); 💻 www.balesworldwide.com
British Airways Holidays: UK (☎ 0870 242 4245); USA (toll-free ☎ 1-4A-VACATION or 1-877-428-2228);
  Australia (☎ 2-8904 8810); 💻 www.baholidays.co.uk
Elegant Resorts: UK (☎ 0870 333 3380, 🖷 0870 333 3371); 💻 www.elegant resorts.co.uk
Hayes and Jarvis: UK (☎ 0870 898 9890, 🖷 020-8741 0299); 💻 res@Hayes-Jarvis.com
Hideaways International: USA (☎ 877-843-4433); 💻 www.hideaways.com
ITC Classics: UK (☎ 0870 751 9300, 🖷 0870 751 9419); 💻 cc@itc.com
JMC: UK (☎ 0870 555 0440); 💻 www.jmc.com
Kuoni: UK (☎ 01306-740 719, 24-hr brochureline 0870 0745 8664, 🖷 01306-744 222); 💻 www.kuoni.co.uk
Nomadic Thoughts: UK (☎ 020-7604 4408, 🖷 020-7604 4407); 💻 www.nomadicthoughts.com
Qantas Holidays: UK (☎ 020-8222 9129, 🖷 020-8748 7505); Australia (☎ 1300-650 729);
  USA (toll-free ☎ 1-800-682-6017, 🖷 310-535-1057); 💻 www.qantas.com.au/qantasholidays/
Scott Dunn: UK (☎ 020-8672 1234, 🖷 020-8767 2026); 💻 www.scottdunn.com
Seasons in Style: UK (☎ 0151-342 0505, 🖷 0151-342 0516); 💻 www.seasonsinstyle.co.uk
Sunset Travel: UK (☎ 020-7498 9922, 🖷 020-7978 1337); 💻 www.sunsetfaraway.com
Tailor Made Travel: UK (☎ 01386-712 046); 💻 www.tailor-made.co.uk
Thomas Cook Ltd: UK (☎ 01733-418 450); 💻 www.tcholidays.com
Travel Impressions: USA (toll-free ☎ 800-284-0044)
Tropical Places: UK (☎ 0870 727 7077, 🖷 01342-822 364); 💻 www.tropical.co.uk
Virgin Holidays:UK (☎ 01293-617 181); 💻 www.virginholidays.co.uk
Western & Oriental Travel: UK (☎ 020-7313 6600, 🖷 020-7313 6601); 💻 www.westernoriental.com
Worldwide Journeys & Expeditions: UK (☎ 020-7386 4646, 🖷 020-7381 0836);
  💻 wwj@wjournex.demon.co.uk

CARIBBEAN SPECIALISTS

Abercrombie & Kent: UK (☎ 0845 070 0610, 🖷 0845 070 0608); USA (toll-free ☎ 0800-323-7308,
  🖷 630-954-3324); Australia (☎ 39-536 1800, 🖷 39-536 1805); Hong Kong (☎ 2865 7818, 🖷 2866 0556);
  💻 www.abercrombiekent.co.uk
Alken Tours: USA (☎ 718-856-7711, 🖷 718-282-1152); 💻 www.alkentours.com
American Express Vacations: USA (toll-free ☎ 1-800-346-3607)
Caribbean Concepts: USA (☎ 206-575-0907, toll-free ☎ 1-800-777-0907); 💻 www.caribbeanconcepts.com
Caribbean Connection: UK (☎ 0870 751 9500, 🖷 0870 751 9419); 💻 cc@itc-uk.com
Caribbean Islands Club: UK (☎ 020-8232 9781, 🖷 020-8568 8330); 💻 www.vch.co.uk/villas/
Caribtours: UK (☎ 020-7751 0660, 🖷 020-7751 9030); 💻 www.caribtours.co.uk
Caribbean Vacation Planner: USA (toll-free ☎ 1-800-356-9999, ext 304)
Crown International: USA (☎ 201-265-5151, toll-free ☎ 800-628-8929, 🖷 201-712-1279);
  💻 www.crown intmark.com
Discover the Bahamas: UK (☎ 01737-218 803, 🖷 01737-362 341); 💻 www.discover-the-bahamas.co.uk
Elegant Resorts: UK (☎ 0870 333 3390, villas 0870 333 3340, 🖷 0870 333 3371);
  💻 www.elegant resorts.co.uk
Harlequin Travel: UK (☎ 01708-850 300, 🖷 01708-854 952)
JMC: UK (☎ 0870 555 0440); 💻 www.jmc.com
Kuoni: UK (☎ 01306-740 719, 24-hr brochureline 0870 0745 8664, 🖷 01306-744 222); 💻 www.kuoni.co.uk
Nomadic Thoughts: UK (☎ 020-7604 4408, 🖷 020-7604 4407); 💻 www.nomadicthoughts.com
Ralph Locke Islands, Inc: UK (toll-free ☎ 0800 894 057); 💻 www.caribisles.com;
  USA (toll-free ☎ 800-223-1108, 🖷 310-440-4220)
Sandals Resorts: USA (toll-free ☎ 1-800-SANDALS or ☎ 1-305-284-1300, 🖷 1-305-667-8996);
  Canada (☎ 1-800-545-8283 or 1-416-223-0028, 🖷 1-416-223-3306); UK (☎ 020-7581 9895, 🖷 020-7823
  8758); Germany (☎ 603-177 2526, 🖷 603-172 5081); France (☎ 1 55 57 93 93, 🖷 1 55 57 93 94);
  Italy (☎ 31-242 105, 🖷 31-262 085); Spain (☎ 91-630 7318, 🖷 91-630 7312); Japan (☎ 3-3591 3828,
  🖷 3-3591 3810); 💻 www.sandals.com or www.beaches.com
Seasons in Style: UK (☎ 0151-342 0505, 🖷 0151-342 0516); 💻 www.seasonsinstyle.co.uk
Tailor Made Travel (Fiji): UK (☎ 01386-712 073, 🖷 01386-712 071); 💻 www.tailormade.co.uk
Thomas Cook Ltd: UK (☎ 01733-418 450); 💻 www.tcholidays.com
Tropical Places: UK (☎ 0870 727 7077, 🖷 01342-822 364); 💻 www.tropical.co.uk
Travel Impressions: USA (toll-free ☎ 800-284-0044)
Unique Hotels/CaribInns: UK (☎ 01242-604 030, 🖷 01242-602 262); US (toll-free ☎ 0800-317185);
  💻 www.unique-hotels.com
Virgin Holidays: UK (☎ 01293-617 181); 💻 www.virginholidays.co.uk

INDIAN OCEAN SPECIALISTS

Abercrombie & Kent: UK (☎ 0845 070 0610, 🖷 0845 070 0608); USA (toll-free ☎ 0800-323-7308,
  🖷 630-954-3324); Australia (☎ 39-536 1800, 🖷 39-536 1805); Hong Kong (☎ 2865 7818, 🖷 2866 0556);
  💻 www.abercrombiekent.co.uk
Carrier: UK (☎ 01625-547 030, 🖷 01625-547 830); 💻 www.carrier.co.uk
Colours of the Indian Ocean: UK (☎ 020-8343 3446, 🖷 020-8349 3439); 💻 www.partnershiptravel.co.uk
Elegant Resorts: UK (☎ 0870 909 5301); 💻 www.elegant resorts.co.uk

Elite Vacations: UK (☎ 020-8864 4431, 🖷 020-8426 9178); 🖳 www.elite-vacations.co.uk
ITC Classics: UK (☎ 0870 751 9502, 🖷 0870 751 9419); 🖳 cc@itc.com
Nomadic Thoughts: UK (☎ 020-7604 4408, 🖷 020-7604 44070); 🖳 www.nomadicthoughts.com
Seasons in Style: UK (☎ 0151-342 0505, 🖷 0151-342 0516); 🖳 www.seasonsinstyle.co.uk
Somak Holidays: UK (☎ 020-8423 3000, 🖷 020-8423 7700); 🖳 www.somak.co.uk
Sunset Travel: UK (☎ 020-7498 9922, 🖷 020-7978 1337); 🖳 www.sunsetfaraway.com
Susie Freeman (Mauritius): UK (☎ 01488-668 821, 🖷 01488-668 706)
Thomas Cook Ltd: UK (☎ 01733-418 450); 🖳 www.tcholidays.com
Tim Best Travel: UK (☎ 020-7591 0300, 🖷 020-7591 0301); 🖳 www.timbesttravel.com
Tropical Places: UK (☎ 0870 727 7077, 🖷 01342-822 364); 🖳 www.tropical.co.uk

INDIA SPECIALISTS

Abercrombie & Kent: UK (☎ 0845 070 0610, 🖷 0845 070 0608); USA (toll-free ☎ 0800-323-7308, 🖷 630-954-3324); Australia (☎ 39-536 1800, 🖷 39-536 1805); Hong Kong (☎ 2865 7818, 🖷 2866 0556); 🖳 www.abercrombiekent.co.uk
Colours of India: UK (☎ 020-8343 3446, 🖷 020-8349 3439, 🖳 info@fdb-partnership.demon.co.uk)
Cox & Kings: UK (☎ 020-7873 5000, 🖷 020-7630 6038); USA (toll-free ☎ 800-999-1758, 🖷 813-258-3852); 🖳 www.coxandkings.com
Elegant Resorts: UK (☎ 0870 909 5303); 🖳 www.elegantresorts.co.uk
Greaves Tours: UK (☎ 020-7487 9111, 🖷 020-7486 0722); 🖳 www.greavestvl.com
Hayes and Jarvis: UK (☎ 0870 898 9890, 🖷 020-8741 0299); 🖳 res@Hayes-Jarvis.com
Indian Explorations: UK (☎ 01993-822 443, 🖷 01993-822 414); 🖳 www.explorationcompany.com
Nomadic Thoughts: UK (☎ 020-7604 4408, 🖷 020-7604 4407); 🖳 www.nomadicthoughts.com
Worldwide Journeys & Expeditions: UK (☎ 020-7386 4646, 🖷 020-7381 0836); 🖳 wwj@wjournex.demon.co.uk

NORTH & SOUTH AMERICA SPECIALISTS

British Airways Holidays: UK (☎ 0870 242 4245); USA (toll-free ☎ 1-4A-VACATION or 1-877-428-2228); Australia (☎ 2-8904 8810); 🖳 www.baholidays.co.uk
Carrier: UK (☎ 01625-547 040, 🖷 01625-547 840); 🖳 www.carrier.co.uk
Cathy Matos Mexican Tours: UK (☎ 020-8492 0000, 🖷 020-8446 4044)
Connections Worldwide (US/Can): UK (☎ 01494-473 173, 0161-835 3655, 0141-332 1311, 🖷 01494-473 588); 🖳 www.connectionsworldwide.net
Cox & Kings: UK (☎ 020-7873 5000, 🖷 020-7630 6038); USA (toll-free ☎ 800-999-1758, 🖷 813-258-3852); 🖳 www.coxandkings.com
Destination South America: UK (☎ 01285-885 333, 🖷 01285-885 888); 🖳 www.destinationsouthamerica.co.uk
Elegant Resorts: UK (☎ 0870 909 5306); 🖳 www.elegant resorts.co.uk
Exsus: UK (☎ 020-7292 5050, 🖷 020-7292 5051); 🖳 www.exsus.com
Journey Latin America: UK (☎ 020-8747 8315, 🖷 020-8742 1312,Manchester ☎ 0161-832 1441, 🖷 0161-832 1441); 🖳 www.journeylatinamerica.co.uk
Kuoni: UK (☎ 01306-740 719, 24-hr brochureline 0870 0745 8664, 🖷 01306-744 222); 🖳 www.kuoni.co.uk
Last Frontiers: UK (☎ 01296-658 650, 🖷 01296-658 651); 🖳 www.lastfrontiers.co.uk
Metropolitan Touring: Ecuador (☎ 02-464-780, 🖷 02-464-702); 🖳 www.ecuadorable.com
Nomadic Thoughts: UK (☎ 020-7604 4408, 🖷 020-7604 4407); 🖳 www.nomadicthoughts.com
North America Travel Service: UK (☎ 020-7938 3737, 🖷 020-7937 0508, branches in Mancester, Leeds, Nottingham and Barnsley); 🖳 www.northamericatravelservice.co.uk
Reef and Rainforest Tours: UK (☎ 01803-866 965, 🖷 01803-865 916); 🖳 www.reefrainforest.co.uk
Roxton Bailey Robinson: UK (☎ 01488-689 702, 🖷 01488-682 977); 🖳 www.roxtons.com
Scott Dunn: UK (☎ 020-8672 1234, 🖷 020-8767 2026); 🖳 www.scottdunn.com
Seasons in Style: UK (☎ 0151-342 0505, 🖷 0151-342 0516); 🖳 www.seasonsinstyle.co.uk
Ski Independence: UK (☎ 0870 555 0555, 🖷 0870 550 2020); 🖳 www.ski-independence.co.uk
Sunny Land Tours: USA (toll-free ☎ 1-800-783-7839); 🖳 www.sunnylandtours.com
Sunvil Discovery: UK (☎ 020-8758 4774, 🖷 020-8758 4711); 🖳 www.sunvil.co.uk/latinamerica
Tim Best Travel: UK (☎ 020-7591 0300, 🖷 020-7591 0301); 🖳 www.timbesttravel.com
Trips Worldwide: UK (☎ 0117-311 4400, 🖷 0117-311 4401); 🖳 www.tripsworldwide.co.uk
Thomas Cook Ltd: UK (☎ 01733-418 699); 🖳 www.tcholidays.com
Virgin Holidays:UK (☎ 01293-617 181); 🖳 www.virginholidays.co.uk
Worldwide Journeys & Expeditions: UK (☎ 020-7386 4646, 🖷 020-7381 0836); 🖳 wwj@wjournex.demon.co.uk

ASIA SPECIALISTS

Abercrombie & Kent: UK (☎ 0845 070 0610, 🖷 0845 070 0608); USA (toll-free ☎ 0800-323-7308, 🖷 630-954-3324); Australia (☎ 39-536 1800, 🖷 39-536 1805); Hong Kong (☎ 2865 7818, 🖷 2866 0556); 🖳 www.abercrombiekent.co.uk
Asian Affair Holidays: USA (toll-free ☎ 1-800-742-5742)

LEADING HOTEL ORGANIZATIONS

THE LEADING HOTELS OF THE WORLD
⌨ www.lhw.com
Australia: toll-free ☎ 1-800-222-033
Canada: toll-free ☎ 1-800-223-6800
Germany: toll-free ☎ 0800-8521100
Hong Kong: toll-free ☎ 800-96-2518
Japan: ☎ 3-5210-5131
New Zealand: toll-free ☎ 0800-441 016
UK: toll-free ☎ 0800 181123
United States: toll-free ☎ 1-800-223-6800

RELAIS & CHATEAUX
⌨ www.relaischateaux.com
Australia: ☎ 2-9299 2280
Canada: toll-free ☎ 0800-735 2478
France: ☎ 0-825-32 32 32
Germany: toll-free ☎ 00-800 2000 0002
Italy: ☎ 055-239 6168
Japan: ☎ 3-3475 6876
Spain: toll-free ☎ 00-800 2000 0002
UK: toll-free ☎ 00-800 2000 0002
United States: toll-free ☎ 0800-735-2478

PREFERRED HOTELS & RESORTS
⌨ www.preferredhotels.com
Australia: toll-free ☎ 1-800 143762
Europe (inc UK): toll-free ☎ 00-800 3237 5001
Hong Kong: toll-free ☎ 800-96 3365
Japan: toll-free ☎ 00531-65-0002
United States: toll-free ☎ 1-800 323 7500

SMALL LUXURY HOTELS OF THE WORLD
⌨ www.slh.com
Australia: toll-free ☎ 1-800-251-958
Canada: toll-free ☎ 800-525-4800
Europe: toll-free ☎ 00-800-525-48000
Hong Kong: toll-free ☎ 001-800-525-48000
New Zealand: toll-free ☎ 00-800-525-48000
UK: toll-free ☎ 00-800-525 48000
United States: toll-free ☎ 800-525-4800

STERLING HOTELS & RESORTS
⌨ www.travelweb.com
Australia: toll-free ☎ 1-800-655 147
Hong Kong: toll-free ☎ 852-2576 5888
Japan: toll-free ☎ 0120-266 500
New Zealand: toll-free ☎ 0800-442 519
Singapore: toll-free ☎ 65-788 5333
France: toll-free ☎ 0800-91 72 32
Germany: toll-free ☎ 0800-182 22 20
UK: toll-free ☎ 0800 252 840
United States: toll-free ☎ 1-800 637 7200

DESIGN HOTELS
⌨ www.designhotels.com
Australia: toll-free ☎ 1800-995 654
France: toll-free ☎ 0800-904 076
Germany: toll-free ☎ 0800-337 4683
Hong Kong: toll-free ☎ 800-337 4633
Singapore: toll-free ☎ 001-800 33 74 46 33
UK: toll-free ☎ 0800 169 8817
United States: toll-free ☎ 800-337-4685

British Airways Holidays: UK (☎ 0870 242 4245); USA (toll-free ☎ 1-4A-VACATION or 1-877-428-2228); Australia (☎ 2-8904 8810); ⌨ www.baholidays.co.uk
Carrier: UK (☎ 01625-547 020, 🖷 01625-547 820); ⌨ www.carrier.co.uk
Colours of India: UK (☎ 020-8343 3446, 🖷 020-8349 3439); ⌨ www.partnershiptravel.co.uk
Elegant Resorts: UK (☎ 0870 909 5305); ⌨ www.elegant resorts.co.uk
ITC Classics: UK (☎ 0870 751 9504, 🖷 0870 751 9419); ⌨ cc@itc.com
Kuoni: UK (☎ 01306-740 719, 24-hr brochureline 0870 0745 8664, 🖷 01306-744 222); ⌨ www.kuoni.co.uk
Magic of the Orient: UK (☎ 01293-537 700, 🖷 01293-537 888); ⌨ www.magic-of-the-orient.com
Nomadic Thoughts: UK (☎ 020-7604 4408, 🖷 020-7604 4407); ⌨ www.nomadicthoughts.com
Seasons in Style: UK (☎ 0151-342 0505, 🖷 0151-342 0516); ⌨ www.seasonsinstyle.co.uk
Sunset Travel: UK (☎ 020-7498 9922, 🖷 020-7978 1337); ⌨ info@sunsettravel.co.uk
Symbiosis: UK (☎ 020-7924 5906, 🖷 020-7924 5907); ⌨ www.symbiosis-travel.com
Thomas Cook Ltd: UK (☎ 01733-418 450);⌨ www.tcholidays.com
Tropical Places: UK (☎ 0870 727 7077, 🖷 01342-822 364); ⌨ www.tropical.co.uk
Western & Oriental Travel: UK (☎ 020-7313 6600, 🖷 020-7313 6601); ⌨ www.westernoriental.com

AFRICA SPECIALISTS
Abercrombie & Kent: UK (☎ 0845 070 0610, 🖷 0845 070 0608); USA (toll-free ☎ 0800-323-7308, 🖷 630-954-3324); Australia (☎ 39-536 1800, 🖷 39-536 1805); Hong Kong (☎ 2865 7818, 🖷 2866 0556); ⌨ www.abercrombiekent.co.uk
Africa Archipelago: UK (☎ 020-7471 8780 or 020-878 05838, 🖷 020-7384 9549); ⌨ www.africaarchipel ago.com
African Explorations: UK (☎ 01993-822 443, 🖷 01993-822 414); ⌨ www.explorationcompany.com
Africa Tours: USA (☎ 212-563-3686, 🖷 212-563-4459)
Art of Travel: UK (☎ 020-7738 2038, 🖷 020-7738 1893); ⌨ www.artoftravel.co.uk
Best of Morocco: UK (☎ 01380-828 533, 🖷 01380-828 630); ⌨ www.morocco-travel.com
British Airways Holidays: UK (☎ 0870 242 4245); USA (toll-free ☎ 1-4A-VACATION or 1-877-428-2228); Australia (☎ 2-8904 8810); ⌨ www.baholidays.co.uk
Carrier: UK (☎ 01625-547 010, 🖷 01625-547 810); ⌨ www.carrier.co.uk
Cox & Kings: UK (☎ 020-7873 5000, 🖷 020-7630 6038); USA (toll-free ☎ 800-999-1758, 🖷 813-258-3852); ⌨ www.coxandkings.com

INTERNATIONAL HOTEL GROUPS

OBEROI HOTELS
🖳 www.oberoihotels.com
Australia: toll-free ☎ 1-800 55 41 76
Canada: toll-free ☎ 800-5-OBEROI
France: toll-free ☎ 0800 90 86 07
Germany: toll-free ☎ 0130 82 42 22
Hong Kong: toll-free ☎ 800 96 2595
Japan: toll-free ☎ 00531-65 0003
Singapore: toll-free ☎ 65 232 5958
UK: toll-free ☎ 0800 962096
United States: toll-free ☎ 800-5-OBEROI

MANDARIN ORIENTAL
🖳 www.mandarinoriental.com
Australia: toll-free ☎ 0011-800 2828 3838
Europe (inc UK): toll-free ☎ 00-800 2828 3838
Hong Kong: ☎ 2881 1288
Japan: toll-free ☎ 00531-65-0006
Singapore: ☎ 65-222 4722
USA/Canada: toll-free ☎ 800-526 6566

FOUR SEASONS HOTELS
🖳 www.fourseasons.com
Australia: toll-free ☎ 800-142 163
Canada: toll-free ☎ 800-268-6282
Europe: toll-free ☎ 00-800-6488 6488
Hong Kong: toll-free ☎ 800-96 8385
Japan: toll-free ☎ 00531-65-0011
New Zealand: toll-free ☎ 0800-44 9286
United States: toll-free ☎ 1-800-332-3442

HYATT HOTELS & RESORTS
🖳 www.hyatt.com
Australia: ☎ 13-1234 (local call cost)
Canada: toll-free ☎ 800-233-1234
France: toll fee ☎ 0800-90 8529
Germany: ☎ 180 523 1234
Hong Kong: ☎ 852-2956 1234
Japan: ☎ 0120-512 343 or 3-3288 1234
New Zealand: toll-free ☎ 0800-44 1234
UK: ☎ 0845 758 1666 (local call cost)
United States: toll-free ☎ 800-233-1234

REGENT INTERNATIONAL HOTELS
🖳 www.fourseasons.com
Australia: toll-free ☎ 1-800 022 800
Canada: toll-free ☎ 1-800-545-4000
Germany: toll-free ☎ 0800-180 8197
Hong Kong: ☎ 800-96 8384
Japan: toll-free ☎ 00531-61-3333
New Zealand: toll-free ☎ 0800-440 800
UK: toll-free ☎ 0800 917 8795
United States: toll-free ☎ 1-800-545-4000

SUN INTERNATIONAL
🖳 www.sunresort.com
Japan: toll-free ☎ 00-70-800-881-489
UK: toll-free ☎ 0870-5300 200
United States: toll-free ☎ 1-800-207-6900

Elegant Resorts: UK (☎ 0870 333 3370, 📄 0870 333 3371); 🖳 www.elegant resorts.co.uk
Farside Africa: UK (☎ 0131-315 2464) 🖳 www.farsideafrica.com
Frontiers International Travel: UK (☎ 020-7493 0798, 📄 020-7629 5569); USA (☎ 724-935-1577, toll-free ☎ 1-800-245-1950, 📄 724-935-5388); 🖳 www.frontierstrvl.com
ITC Classics: UK (☎ 0870 751 9503, 📄 0870 751 9419); 🖳 cc@itc.com
The Legendary Adventure Company: USA (☎ 713-744-5244, 📄 713-895-8753); 🖳 www.legendaryadventures.com
Nature Encounters: USA (☎ 323-733-6622, 📄 323-733-6623); 🖳 www.nature-encounters.com
Nomadic Thoughts: UK (☎ 020-7604 4408, 📄 020-7604 4407); 🖳 www.nomadicthoughts.com
Okavango Tour & Safaris: UK (☎ 020-8343 3283, 📄 020-8343 3287); 🖳 info@okavango.com
Roxton Bailey Robinson: UK (☎ 01488-689 702, 📄 01488-682 977); 🖳 www.roxtons.com
Somak Holidays: UK (☎ 020-8423 3000, 📄 020-8423 77000); 🖳 www.somak.co.uk
South African Affair: UK (☎ 020-7381 5222)
Theobald Barber: UK (☎ 020-7723 5858, 📄 020-7723 5417); 🖳 tbsales@miljam.co.uk
Thomas Cook Ltd: UK (☎ 01733-418 650); 🖳 www.tcholidays.com
Three Cities Hotels (Botswana, Zimbabwe, S Africa): UK (☎ 020-7225 0164, 📄 020-7823 7701)
Tim Best Travel: UK (☎ 020-7591 0300, 📄 020-7591 0301); 🖳 www.timbesttravel.com
Tropical Places: UK (☎ 0870 727 7077, 📄 01342-822 364); 🖳 www.tropical.co.uk
Virgin Holidays: UK (☎ 01293-617 181); 🖳 www.virginholidays.co.uk
Worldwide Journeys & Expeditions: UK (☎ 020-7386 4646, 📄 020-7381 0836); 🖳 wwj@wjournex.demon.co.uk

AUSTRALIA AND NEW ZEALAND SPECIALISTS
Abercrombie & Kent: UK (☎ 0845 070 0610, 📄 0845 070 0608); USA (toll-free ☎ 0800-323-7308, 📄 630-954-3324); Australia (☎ 39-536 1800, 📄 39-536 1805); Hong Kong (☎ 2865 7818, 📄 2866 0556); 🖳 www.abercrombiekent.co.uk
Austravel: UK (☎ 020-7734 7755, 📄 020-7494 1302); 🖳 www.austravel.net
Bridge the World: UK (☎ 0870 444 7474, 📄 020-7734 6455); 🖳 www.bridgetheworld.com
Elegant Resorts: UK (☎ 0870 909 5305); 🖳 www.elegant resorts.co.uk
Hayes and Jarvis: UK (☎ 0870 898 9890, 📄 020-8741 0299); 🖳 res@Hayes-Jarvis.com
ITC Classics: UK (☎ 0870 751 9504, 📄 0870 751 9419); 🖳 cc@itc.com

CAR RENTAL WORLDWIDE CENTRAL RESERVATION NUMBERS

AVIS
UK (☎ 0870 606 0100); USA (☎ 1-800-230-4898); Canada (☎ toll-free 1-800-272-5871); Germany (☎ 01805-5577); Japan (toll-free ☎ 0120-31-1911); Australia (☎ 136 333); see 💻 www.avis.com for a full listing of numbers worldwide.

HERTZ
UK (☎ 0870-8484 848); USA (☎ 800-654-3131); Canada (☎ 800-263-0600); Germany (☎ 01805-333-535); Australia (☎ 3-9698 2555); Japan (toll-free ☎ 0120-489-822); see 💻 www.hertz.com for a full listing of numbers worldwide.

BUDGET
UK (☎ 01442-276 000); USA (☎ 800-527-0700); Canada (☎ 416-622-1000); Australia (☎ 39-206 3666); Japan (☎ 8191-281-0543); Germany (☎ 3733-179-031); 💻 www.budget.com

Newmans South Pacific: USA (toll-free ☎ 800-351-2323); 💻 www.newmansvacations.com
Nomadic Thoughts: UK (☎ 020-7604 4408, 🖨 020-7604 4407); 💻 www.nomadicthoughts.com
Qantas Holidays: USA (toll-free ☎ 1-800-682-6017, 🖨 310-535-1057); UK (☎ 020-8748 8676, 🖨 020-8748 7236); 💻 www.qantas.com.au/qantasholidays/
Swain Australia Tours: USA (toll-free ☎ 1-800-22-SWAIN); 💻 www.swainaustralia.com
Tailor Made Travel: UK (☎ 01386-712 073, 🖨 01386-712 071); 💻 www.tailormade.co.uk

EUROPE SPECIALISTS
Abercrombie & Kent: UK (☎ 0845 070 0610, 🖨 0845 070 0608); USA (toll-free ☎ 0800-323-7308, 🖨 630-954-3324); Australia (☎ 39-536 1800, 🖨 39-536 1805); Hong Kong (☎ 2865 7818, 🖨 2866 0556); 💻 www.abercrombiekent.co.uk
American Express Vacations: USA (toll-free ☎ 1-800-346-3607)
Argo Holidays: UK (☎ 020-7331 7070, 🖨 020-7331 7065); 💻 www.argo-holidays.com
British Airways Holidays: UK (☎ 0870 242 4245); USA (toll-free ☎ 1-4A-VACATION or 1-877-428-2228); Australia (☎ 2-8904 8810); 💻 www.baholidays.co.uk
Crown International: USA (☎ 201-265-5151, toll-free ☎ 800-628-8929, 🖨 201-712-1279); 💻 www.crownintmark.com
CV Travel: UK (☎ 020-7591 2810, 24-hr brochureline 0870 603 9018, 🖨 020-7591 2802); 💻 www.cvtravel.net
Elegant Resorts: UK (☎ 0870 333 3370, villas 0870 333 3350, 🖨 0870 333 3371); 💻 www.elegant resorts.co.uk
European Rail Services: USA (☎ 877-268-3316, toll-free ☎ 1-800-782-2424); Canada (☎ 416-695-1449, 🖨 416-695-1453); 💻 www.dertravel.com
French Affair: UK (☎ 020-7381 5222); 💻 www.frenchaffair.com
Greek Islands Club: UK (☎ 020-8232 9780, 🖨 020-8568 8330); 💻 www.greekislandsclub.com
Harlequin Travel: UK (☎ 01708-850 300, 🖨 01708-854 952)
Ireland Vacations: USA (toll-free ☎ 866-433-6007); 💻 www.ireland-vacations.com
InnTravel: UK (☎ 01653-629 010); 💻 www.inntravel.co.uk
Invitation to Tuscany: UK (☎ 020-7603 7111, 🖨 020-7610 4175); 💻 www.invitationtotuscany.com
JMC: UK (☎ 0870 555 0440); 💻 www.jmc.com
Magic of Spain/Italy: UK (☎ 0870 027 0400/0870 027 0500, brochureline 0990 462 442); 💻 www.magic travelgroup.co.uk
Mediterranean Experience: UK (☎ 020-8445 6000, 🖨 020-8445 7111); 💻 sales@themed.net
Meon Villas: UK (☎ 01730-268 411, brochure 01730-230 370, 🖨 01730-230 399); 💻 www.meonvillas.co.uk
MLT Vacations: USA (☎ 952-474-2540, toll-free ☎ 1-800-328-0025)
Qantas Holidays: UK (☎ 020-8222 9129, 🖨 020-8748 7505); Australia (☎ 1300-650 729); USA (toll-free ☎ 1-800-682-6017, 🖨 310-535 1057)
Seasons in Style: UK (☎ 0151-342 0505, 🖨 0151-342 0516); 💻 www.seasonsinstyle.co.uk
Spain at Heart: UK (☎ 01373-814 222, 🖨 01373-813 444); 💻 www.spainatheart.co.uk
Spanish Affair: UK (☎ 020-7385 8127, 🖨 020-7381 5423); 💻 www.spanishaffair.com
Simply Travel: UK (☎ 020-8541 2206, 🖨 020-8541 2280); 💻 www.simply-travel.com
VFB Holidays (France): UK (☎ 01242-240 340, 🖨 01242-570 340); 💻 www.vfbholidays.co.uk

PLANE TICKETS AND SEAT RESERVATIONS
If you are travelling independently ring several airlines or travel agents and look on the Internet to get the best deal. Before you actually book a long-haul flight, you may want to look at the airline's seating plan and think about where you'd like to sit (some seats have extra leg-room). The travel agent may have a copy but if not ask the airline

to send you their timetable. These timetables state the aircraft used on the flight and show seating configurations.

It's not always possible to book seats in advance (particularly if you are on a charter flight) but do make sure the airline knows you will be on your honeymoon. I've talked to honeymooners who were told at check-in that they weren't even sitting together: most airlines do all that they can to keep newly-weds together, even if they won't let you book seats in advance. You must specify any special dietary requirements in advance, however. Check in early, particularly if you're non-smokers and don't want to land up near the smoking section.

It's always worth getting someone responsible (perhaps the groom's mum) to confirm your outbound flight 24-48 hours before departure, just to be on the safe side.

PASSPORTS, VISAS AND INOCULATIONS

Some countries require proof of citizenship, **visas** etc, so check with your travel agent or the tourist commission that you've got everything you **both** need as soon as you book, as it can take weeks or even months to get through the bureaucracy.

Take your marriage certificate with you if your plane tickets and your **passports** are in different names. Alternatively, arrange for your passport to be amended in advance. This is possible in Britain, but you can apply only three months before the date of your wedding and your passport will be valid only from the date you marry. Make sure you allow plenty of time for your new passport to be processed. Check out the procedure in your own country and again leave plenty of time for paperwork.

Consult your doctor about **inoculations**. Some countries require vaccination certificates and will not permit you to enter without one.

If necessary, make sure you take **anti-malaria pills** (prescribed by your doctor) both before and after your return from holiday and use **mosquito repellents** liberally at dawn and dusk. Drinking bottled water will help to avoid diarrhoea – not a wonderful honeymoon accompaniment.

Lastly, stock up on *all* necessary **prescriptions** (including contraceptives). Leave these in their original bottles and take a copy of the prescription, especially if you're going somewhere really exotic, so that you don't have them confiscated by Customs.

PACKING

Have a really good think about what you want to take a good month before: this particularly applies to the bride of course, as not only are you likely to be more concerned about what you are wearing on your honeymoon, but the last few weeks will be so hectic you'll hardly give a moment's thought to life and your holiday after the big event. In fact, most of the hints below apply a great deal more to the bride than the groom.

Take a suitcase, even if you are a die-hard sailbag or rucksack type, because it protects clothes better, thus cutting down on the ironing.

Decant all big bottles of shampoo and toiletries into small containers or pick up trial sizes which are available in most pharmacies, so that these don't take up valuable space and weigh a lot. You could even get one of those gift-with-purchase cosmetic packs which have miniatures of everything from mascara to moisturisers. Before you pack your hairdryer, call the hotel to check if they have one. Take plenty of sunscreen and insect repellent if required, both of which may be more expensive abroad. Put all bottles in a sealed plastic bag, even if they are brand-new, as some plane holds aren't pressurized and you don't want anything leaking on your clothes. Pack extra camera batteries and buy films before you leave to avoid having to pay costly resort prices.

Most guides tell you to 'think twice' about that extra T-shirt, dress or jacket: 'do you really need it?' they chastise, well I think you do. What the heck, this is your honeymoon, and even if you normally make a point of travelling light, make the most of the fact that for this one holiday you may want to wear something different every night, with shoes to match. Obviously this philosophy is not relevant if you're trekking through the jungle but you could leave the bulk of your clothes and your suitcase in a hotel while you go off trekking.

JET LAG

If you do opt for a long-haul flight, there are various ways of easing jet lag. Some countries have homeopathic pills designed to guard against jet lag. In New Zealand, for example, you can buy No Jet Lag pills, which are taken every four hours through-out the flight and have really helped me in the past. Aromatherapy oils are a good idea – some airlines and hotels are now using them. Ginger tablets help quell travel sickness. You can buy all of these in health food shops and some chemists.

FEELING ODD AFTER THE BIG DAY?

Having put so much effort into planning their wedding and their honeymoon many couples feel a little strange or end up rowing over nothing when they first get away: mainly it's the anticlimax of the big event being over and a feeling of guilt about not making the most of their 'holiday of a lifetime'. It does happen ... so don't feel that you are odd or ill-matched if it happens to you, you're not alone. As Jessica Wren, a good friend of mine admitted: 'When people talk about honeymoons, you always hear about holidays of a lifetime, but we both felt very weird for the first week, and this was made even worse by feeling guilty because it was supposed to all be so special. It was the first time we'd had that much time and space to be together for ages, plus we'd just done the massive thing of getting married. Looking back it was kind of inevitable that there'd be a getting-used-to-the-idea stage, and it did only last about four or five days. But it would have helped if someone had warned us, that way it would have taken some of the weirdness out of it.'

ISLANDS

2

The Caribbean Islands
(BEST TIME: NOVEMBER TO JULY)

The name 'Caribbean' can't help but conjure up romantic visions of dreamy days spent on secluded, white sandy beaches; watching the sunset with the sound of the ocean lapping near you; sailing from island to island, stopping to snorkel over coral reefs teeming with fish; and enjoying beach barbecues in the evenings with the rum punch flowing.

There are a lot of places in the world offering this kind of idyllic picture but there is one aspect of the above description that you won't find anywhere else in the world, and if you do, I guarantee it won't be quite the same or come anywhere close to having the magical ambience that it exudes in the Caribbean. That one unique aspect is, of course, the rum punch. It may

---

THE CARIBBEAN ISLANDS
The ultimate tropical islands, some livelier than others, but generally offering great watersports and lovely sandy beaches
When to go: Peak season is between mid-December and mid-April, but the weather is usually just as good right through until the end of July and from November onwards
Average maximum temperatures °C

	JAN	FEB	MAR	APR	MAY	JUN	JUL	AUG	SEP	OCT	NOV	DEC
Barbados	29	29	30	30	31	31	30	31	31	30	30	29
BVI	25	25	25	26	26	27	28	28	28	27	26	25
Anguilla	26	26	26	26	27	28	28	27	28	28	27	25
St Kitts/Nevis	26	26	27	28	29	30	31	31	30	29	28	27
Antigua	26	27	27	27	27	28	28	28	28	27	27	26
St Lucia	28	29	30	31	32	33	32	31	31	30	29	28
Grenadines	29	29	31	31	31	31	33	33	33	31	30	29
Tobago	29	30	31	31	32	31	31	31	31	31	31	30
Jamaica	30	30	31	31	31	32	32	32	32	31	31	31

Capital: Each island has its own capital
Flight times: to Barbados from:
    New York: 5 hours
    LA: (via Miami) 9 hours
    London: 8½ hours
    Sydney (via LA and Miami): 20½ hours
Approximate exchange rates: Antigua and Barbuda, Anguilla, St Kitts and Nevis, St Lucia and St Vincent, East Caribbean dollar (EC$) – £1 = $EC3.84, US$1 = $EC2.70; Barbados (BB$) – £1 = BB$2.74, US$1 = BB$2, A$1 = BB$1.03; Trinidad and Tobago (TT$) – £1 = TT$8.76, US$1 = TT$6.16, A$1 = TT$3.20; Jamaican dollar (JM$) – £1 = JM$64.87, US$1 = JM$45.45, A$1 = JM$23.37
Time difference: GMT minus four hours for most of the Caribbean
Voltage: 110/220v
Combine with: If you want a two-centre holiday combine two Caribbean islands as they tend to differ quite markedly from each other
Country dialling code: Barbados ☎ 1-246; BVI ☎ 1-284; Anguilla ☎ 1-264; St Kitts and Nevis ☎ 1-869; Antigua & Barbuda ☎ 1-268; St Lucia ☎ 1-758; St Vincent & the Grenadines ☎ 1-784; Mustique ☎ 1-784, Tobago ☎ 1-868; Jamaica ☎ 1-876
Further information: Caribbean Tourism Organisation (UK ☎ 020-7222 4335) 🖳 www.doitcaribbean.com)

SAILING IN THE CARIBBEAN

For some of the very best sailing in the world look towards either the **British Virgin Islands**, the world's largest yacht charter playground, or the **Grenadines**. Both areas provide interesting sailing around beautiful islands with only short day hops from anchorage to anchorage and lots of great bars and restaurants to discover each night. There is nothing quite like the freedom of a boat; if you don't like what you see when you arrive at a new island you can up anchor and find somewhere you do like. Sailing also enables you to see more of the islands and how much they vary from one another. The 15-20 knot Easterly trade winds are just perfect for easy and exhilarating cruising, although you can expect more squalls and gusts between June and November. Avoid August and September when there is a serious possibility of tropical storms and hurricanes.

There are essentially three ways to sail in the Caribbean. Charter a yacht through companies such as **Sunsail** (UK ☎ 02392-222 300; USA ☎ 410-280-2553, 🖷 410-280-2406; www.sunsail.com), or **Moorings**, (UK ☎ 01227-776 677, 🖷 01227-776 670; USA ☎ 888-952-8420 or 727-535-1446; 🖷 yacht-charter@moorings.co.uk), or **Horizon Yacht Charters** (☎ 1-284 494 8787, 🖷 1-284 494 8989, 🖷 info@horizonyachtcharters.com; PO Box 3222, Road Town Tortola, BVI). Voted 'Best Charter Company in the Caribbean' by sailonline.com, Horizon's boats are immaculate, the staff really friendly (and experienced) and surprisingly good value for money. All these companies have boats of varying sizes and cover the BVI and the Grenadines, either on a bareboat or crewed basis.

Charter a crewed yacht through professional agencies such as UK-based **Caribbean Connections** (☎ 0870-751 9380, 🖷 cc@itcuk.com) or **Elegant Resorts** (☎ 0870-333 3390, 🖷 www.elegantresorts.co.uk), or **Camper & Nicholsons** (UK ☎ 020-7491 2950; USA ☎ 561-655-2121 Palm Beach; ☎ 1-954-524-4250 Fort Lauderdale): each company has yachts with every kind of comfort, from air conditioning to professional cooks, and an itinerary made personally for you.

The third option is to go for one of the 'sailaway holiday' packages offered by many Caribbean hotels involving time in the hotel and a few days on a boat. Hotels that offer these kinds of deals include **Petit St Vincent (PSV)** and **Young Island** in the Grenadines, **Biras Creek** and **Peter Island** in the BVI, **Anse Chastanet** in St Lucia, and the **Cotton House** on Mustique (all are featured in this guide). Rates vary a great deal but start from around US$1419/£998 for a week's bareboat charter of a yacht in the BVI with Moorings.

If you are sailing in the Grenadines try to pick up the yacht at **Marigot Bay** in **St Lucia** so that you can sail 'down' through the islands – it's much easier and is more fun than travelling northwards upwind.

Sample itinerary

Day One: Marigot Bay, St Lucia to the Pitons (lunch in Soufrière Bay at the Hummingbird Restaurant and pre-dinner drinks at Lord Glenconnor's Bang Between the Pitons).

Day Two: Exciting ocean sailing to St Vincent. Lunch overlooking St Vincent's volcano, lush mountains, rivers and remote fishing villages. Anchor in a secluded bay, snorkel and explore by kayak.

Day Three: Snorkel the 'bat cave' then set sail to Bequia, visit the turtle sanctuary, laze on the beach and potter around Port Elizabeth's excellent shops, eat at one of the waterfront restaurants and try Maranne's home-made ice-cream.

Day Four: Scuba dive in one of Bequia's top dive sites, then set sail for Young Island, St Vincent. Visit Kingstown – a bustling West Indian town – and the botanical gardens.

Day Five: Tour St Vincent Island with a rainforest hike and swim in a secluded waterfall. Relax in a quiet bay with cows on the beach and fireflies in the trees.

Day Six: Sail to St Lucia arriving in time for a late lunch. Take a mooring between the dramatic Pitons and snorkel from the beautiful beach.

Day Seven: Breakfast early to allow time for a final snorkel at Anse Chastanet – a marine park with the best variety of underwater life in St Lucia.

sound ridiculous, but there is something particularly special about a rum punch served in the Caribbean. It has a lot to do with the people of course, the wonderful bar men and women grinning away at you as they conjure up their glorious concoctions nodding their head in time to the inevitable reggae music. It also has a lot to do with the rum: not its intoxicating strength, although that surely does play a part, but the very taste of Mount Gaye golden rum is in itself quite unique. The place is also special because of the West Indians themselves: there is something about their character, their music, their hot spicy food, the taste of coconut, and their laid-back attitude that will stay with you long after you've washed the sand and salt out of your hair.

The peak tourist season runs from the middle of December through until Easter. Although this is when the Caribbean really swings and when it attracts its most glamorous and style-conscious visitors, it is also much more expensive. If your wedding happens to fall after the middle of April you'll find the prices drop significantly – sometimes by as much as 50% – while the weather stays pretty much the same until the middle of July, and to be honest I think it's much nicer when the beaches, bars and waters are quieter, making it feel that little bit more exclusive. I would avoid August and September as this is when the hurricanes and rains tend to hit, October is usually mixed but by November you're back into long sunny days and reasonable prices again.

Renting a Caribbean villa

Creative Leisure (US toll-free ☎ 800-413-1000, 💻 www.creativeleisure.com) has one-bedroom villas with ocean views on Virgin Gorda, Grenada and Tortola starting from US$318 a night. Many come with full-time staff and swimming pool. Also worth a call are US-based **Condo & Villa Authority** (US toll-free ☎ 800-831-5512, 💻 www.travelsource.com/villarental.html) and **Villas & Apartments Abroad** (US toll-free ☎ 800-433-3020, 💻 www.vaanyc.com).

The **Caribbean Islands Club** (UK ☎ 020-8232 9781, 📄 020-8568 8330, 💻 www.vch.co.uk/villas/) operates a similar programme of villa rentals in the British Virgin Islands (BVI), with one or two properties just perfect for honeymoons and weddings. Ask in particular about **Sugar Mill Plantation House** on **Virgin Gorda**: it was designed by the same architect that Richard Branson used on his famous Necker Island nearby. The house is set in its own private gardens above the sandy beaches of Spring Bay, a five-minute walk away. The house is octagonal and has large open-plan living areas opening out on to a wide shaded balcony which encircles most of the property. It is beautifully decorated with rattan and cane furniture, ceramic floor tiles, high pyramid ceilings and huge wooden doors. Of the 21 rooms, there's one double bedroom with his and her bathrooms, each with a shower, and one villa. People come back year after year for the cuisine – candlelit dinners and a menu that changes nightly. One week's rental, including flights, transfers, taxes and maid service, in Sugar Mill Plantation House (June to October) costs from US$2298/£1616. Also ask about the intriguing **Toad Hall**, and **Vista Del Mare** at **Leverick Bay** which can be rented for exclusive use and has a double waterbed and a stereo that can be channelled to all parts of the villa.

SANDALS

Sandals run all-inclusive resorts all over the Caribbean, each designed as the perfect couples-only holiday, which means they make extremely good honeymoon destinations. Sandals won't appeal to everyone for the very fact that they are so popular with couples getting married abroad and with honeymooners – they claim they invented the 'Weddingmoon' (wedding complimentary for anyone booking more than four nights). However, they certainly do have their benefits, and by paying up front at least you can start saving for your holiday well before and not have to continually dig into your pockets for that extra ten minutes' water-skiing or more rum punches.

There are 16 Sandals and Beaches Resorts across the islands of Jamaica, Antigua, the Bahamas, St Lucia, Cuba and the Turks & Caicos islands. **Sandals Halcyon, St Lucia**, is regarded as the most romantic and pristine of their 10 couples-only Caribbean resorts. De luxe rooms cost from US$3780 and Honeymoon Beachfront rooms from US$5250 per couple, per week.

The newest of the Sandals collection, **Beaches Royal Plantation** in **Ocho Rios, Jamaica**, which opened in the former Plantation Inn after extensive renovations in December 2000, promises to be the most elegant and luxurious: De Luxe Ocean Front JR Suite from US$4340 low season; Imperial Ocean Front Suite from US$9800 per couple, per week.

Reservations direct through Sandals toll-free numbers worldwide or through most tour operators and travel agents specializing in the Caribbean (see p10).

UK-based **CaribInns** (UK ☎ 01242-604 030, 🖹 01242-602 262, 💻 www.unique hotels.com) is a select group of small hotels and villas which capture the spirit and charm of the Caribbean. The accommodation ranges from traditional guest houses to exclusive villas and the old-world charm of plantation inns. The group has properties on the following islands: Anguilla, Antigua and Barbuda, the British Virgin Islands, Dominica, Grenada, Montserrat, St Kitts and Nevis, St Lucia, and St Vincent and the Grenadines. For example **Plantation Beach Villas** (Trinidad & Tobago ☎ 639 9377, 🖹 639 0455, 💻 villas@wow.net, PO Box 435, Scarborough, Tobago) are a collection of private villas nestled high on a hillside looking down to the beach: they can be rented from US$280 a day, plus 20% tax.

For the ultimate in luxury go for the extraordinarily beautiful and quite unique **Cove Castles Villa Resort** (Anguilla ☎ 497 6801, 🖹 497 6051, or in the US through Ralph Locke Islands, toll-free ☎ 800-223-1108, 💻 www.caribisles.com), PO Box 248, Shoal Bay, Anguilla. These incredible looking white villas are an intriguing cross between traditional Moorish architecture and something out of the future. They are, however, expensive, costing either US$525 a night plus 18% tax and service in the low season or US$3000 for a five-night Summer Dream Package which includes breakfast, champagne, two days' car rental, sunset cruise, three dinners, tax and service, transfers, and de luxe accommodation in a beach house.

BARBADOS

Barbados is a great place to go if it is your first visit to the Caribbean because it is big enough to give you lots of variety as well as a really good taste of Caribbean life. It stands on its own about 1610km out in the Atlantic, east of St Vincent and the Grenadines. Spanning 34km by 23km it has some of the most stunning beaches in the Caribbean as well as a selection of hotels to suit all pockets. The west coast, known as the millionaires' playground, is home to some of the finest and most expensive hotels in the Caribbean. While the island's British heritage was responsible at one time for earning it the nickname Little England, British influence over the island has waned considerably since it gained independence in 1966. American influences now dominate, as is typical of most Caribbean islands. Because Barbados is a relatively large island and one of the most developed in the Caribbean with lots to do and see, it may be a good idea to combine a week on Barbados with a week somewhere quieter, such as the nearby Grenadines.

Coral Reef Club

Beautiful and very secluded, the Coral Reef Club is set amidst 12 acres of beautifully landscaped tropical gardens on the west coast of Barbados. Run by the O'Hara family and their loyal staff for forty years, and a Small Luxury Hotel of the World, it is renowned for its special ambience.

Greeted by wicker furniture and sofas spilling out onto the beach, the Club has a colonial charm within a traditional Caribbean style. Traditional island-style vil-

---

CORAL REEF CLUB
(☎ 422 2372, 🖹 422 1776, 💻 coral @caribsurf.com), Holetown, Barbados, West Indies
Reservations: Small Luxury Hotels of the World toll-free numbers (see p12) or UK tour operators such as Caribtours and Elegant Resorts (see p10)
Getting there: Taxi from the airport costs BB$60
Accommodation: 85 rooms/cottages and 4 plantation suites
Amenities: Dry cleaning, complimentary water-skiing, sailing, snorkelling and kayaking; golf can be arranged at the Royal Westmoreland golf course
Dress code: Elegant casual in the evening but no jacket or tie required
Weddings: Can be arranged
Minimum stay: None
Rates: Double rooms from US$300 to US$830; Plantation suites from US$865 to US$1900
Credit cards: Visa, MasterCard, American Express
Taxes and service charge: 5% Government tax is added to all room, food and beverage charges, 10% service charge

las and individual cottages offer a perfect romantic hideaway. The open-air lounge and restaurant offer creative and sumptuous cuisine, and the O'Hara's weekly cocktail party on the terrace provides a good excuse to mingle with the other guests.

The individually-styled, spacious rooms are named after the trees and flowers in the garden. All have a hairdryer, fridge and toaster so you can make your own breakfast or enjoy a late night drink. But the four new Plantation Suites provide the ultimate honeymoon hideaway. Each suite has all the mod cons including a CD player cleverly hidden in the elegant furnishings of the West Indian style interiors. The suites also have their own wrap-around terrace with a fully stocked bar, dining area and mosaic-tiled plunge pool with a spectacular view.

If you fancy something active there are two large mosaic pools in the gardens, floodlit tennis courts and a gym. Complimentary watersports include water-skiing, snorkelling, windsurfing, kayaking and sailing. A masseuse is also available to ease away those post-wedding tensions.

Cobblers Cove

Cobblers Cove has a wonderful English charm to it with all the amenities and sport facilities you would ever need. A member of the prestigious Relais & Châteaux grouping, Cobblers is located on the north-west coast of Barbados, near **Speightstown**, further up the beach from the other hotels on this famous stretch of coastline.

On arriving at the old stone fortress-style reception you are greeted with a big smile and a 'Cobblers Cooler' cocktail. Guests walk through the beautiful garden, a tropical paradise full of hibiscus flowers and tiny hummingbirds, to their suite. Complimentary bottles of wine, flowers and a big basket of exotic fruits are provided for honeymooners.

Having a surprise honeymoon and secretly thinking you are going to Canada is one thing, but finding out on the flight you are going to Barbados and then arriving at Cobblers Cove is another story – it was heaven! I couldn't have asked for a better honeymoon hideaway and I will definitely want to have my first anniversary back there!
Gabby Rance
Choosing a honeymoon place was going to be difficult as my wife to be is not only fussy, but well-travelled and spoilt too and likes to be in control, but Cobblers Cove seemed to be the place and it was! **Hugh Rance**

Surrounding the old pink and white colonial building are 40 comfortable and spacious suites. Each suite has its own sitting room with a balcony or French doors opening directly onto the garden and looking towards the sea. The bedrooms are tastefully

THINGS TO SEE AND DO IN BARBADOS

The best way to tour the island is to hire a **Mini Moke** (an open-sided jeep). Mokes can be rented for about US$50 a day from Dear's Garage in Bridgetown (☎ 429 9277). Make sure you take a good road map as signposting on the island can be a bit haphazard.

Start by visiting one of the old plantation houses, the **St Nicholas Abbey** (built in 1650), where sugar cane is still farmed, then go across to the district of **St Andrew** which takes you into the farming community and the old Bajan culture. Further south along the coast is **Codrington College**, a beautiful school perched on the cliffs; from here one can go to **St John's Church**, then head back down to **Bridgetown** and experience some lively evening entertainment!

If you don't want to do much touring around **taxis** can be useful, but agree a price with the driver before you get in as there are no meters and prices can vary considerably.

Tours of the island can be organized through your hotel but you could also try L E Williams Tour Company (☎ 427 1043) which has a reputation for organizing good day trips to Scotland in the north of the island for around US$50 including lunch.

If you want to learn to **scuba dive** or complete your PADI open-water certificate, Hightide Watersports (☎ 432 0931) offer competitive deals and very professional courses. **Barbados Tourism Authority** (💻 www.barbados.org) is a good source of wedding and honeymoon information.

COBBLERS COVE
(☎ 422 2291, 🖹 422 1460), St Peter, Barbados, West Indies
Reservations: Relais & Châteaux world-wide reservation numbers (see p12)
Getting there: Taxi from the airport
Accommodation: Forty suites including eight ocean-front suites and two de luxe suites, the Camelot and Colleton
Amenities: Terrace Restaurant, dry cleaning, complimentary water-skiing, windsurfing, sunfish sailing, snorkelling; scuba diving and private yacht may be arranged for an additional charge; air-conditioned gym, Royal Westmoreland golf course 15 minutes drive away, car hire arranged
Dress code: Smart casual in the evening but no jacket or tie required
Weddings: Can be arranged
Minimum stay: None
Rates: Double rooms from US$255 to US$1750
Credit cards: Visa, MasterCard, American Express
Taxes and service charge: 7.5% Government tax is added to all room, food and beverage charges, 10% service charge

decorated in colourful fabrics and have a fan and air conditioning. The bathrooms are all marble with twin basins and plenty of towels – blue towels for the pool or beach are also provided. A great addition to each suite is a spacious kitchenette which enables you to add your own bits and pieces to the already full fridge and make tea or coffee when you want. Wicker-covered ice-buckets are filled up twice a day to keep those drinks cool.

Two sumptuous, beautifully-appointed suites, the Camelot and Colleton, are both found on the top floor of the main building and have four-poster beds, private plunge pools and of course, a wicked view. These are the rooms to go for, for those who want to have the ultimate in luxury and privacy on their honeymoon.

The hotel has a wonderful terraced restaurant and bar right on the beachfront: both are open from morning until late at night. Complimentary afternoon tea is served by the pool every day – a selection of sandwiches, cakes, and of course scones and jam, but don't eat too much because you also get delicious hors d'oeuvres with your pre-dinner drinks. The menu is of an exceptionally high standard and is prepared by a team of French-trained chefs, who take advantage of the local fresh produce and fish, and yet successfully serve up the kind of dishes that would have you believe you were actually in France! The five-course dinner menu is changed daily, or you can choose from an extensive à la carte menu and, if you still have room, fresh ground coffee is served with petit fours in one of the lounges. Light Caribbean music is played some nights but this is always low key and unobtrusive. The manager, Hamish Watson, gives a weekly cocktail party: a great way to meet some of the other guests – after a few rum punches everyone seems only too happy to exchange stories.

This is the place for those who just want to relax on holiday, and also for those who want to relax and be active. Cobblers Cove has its own private beach, a pool and air-conditioned gym, a floodlit tennis court and a good range of all-inclusive watersports facilities provided all day long. Golfers can take advantage of concessionary rates on the famous Royal Westmoreland golf course.

Other recommended hotels
Sandy Lane (☎ 444 2000, 🖹 432 2954, 🖳 reservations@sandylane.com), St James, is one of the longest established hotels in the Caribbean and has been the epicentre for Barbados' élite for decades. A member of Leading Hotels of the World (see p12), this Grand Dame on the best beach in Barbados underwent a complete rebuild in 2001 and is now open again.

THE BRITISH VIRGIN ISLANDS (BVI)
Right up in the north of the Caribbean lie the Virgin Islands, both British and American. The BVI, as they are known, are much less developed than the US Virgin Islands where international hotel chains have developed sky-scraping resorts. So, if it's unspoilt islands you are seeking, go for the BVI.

Little Dix Bay

Little Dix Bay has to be one of the slickest, most stunning resort hotels in the Caribbean. To me it's one of those places with so many exciting things to do that when you first arrive you hardly know where to begin: do you pour yourself a large tumbler of the complimentary rum and coke; head straight for the beach and take a float out to sea; relax in a hammock; take part in the amazing array of activities on offer from the afternoon round-robin tennis, to diving or sailing; or simply sit at the beach bar watching the world go by?

This beautiful, spacious hotel was built by Laurance S Rockefeller in the early 1950s as a place where guests could relax comfortably amongst great natural beauty, without having to sacrifice the island's conservation in any way. The original architect was careful to use local materials such as stone, red cedar, purple heart, locust wood and mahogany. The hotel has recently been refurbished and is now looking its very best.

The focus of the hotel, apart from its huge crescent-shaped beach, is the main dining Pavilion which, supported by large purple heart beams reputed to weigh more than 1360kg, looks more like something in Thailand or Malaysia than a typical Caribbean resort. The views through the shaded arches of the Pavilion looking out over the brilliant turquoise sea in the Bay are quite incredible.

Little Dix is one of those hotels in which you could happily stay for a long, long time. The facilities are great but best of all are the gardens; they make a wonderfully refreshing change from the beach and for me really made the hotel.

The beach is awesome – it is certainly long enough to ensure that guests never feel cramped. In fact the whole hotel is very cleverly designed so that even when it is full the layout of the gardens and the length of the beach ensure that you'll have plenty of space to yourself. Every kind of watersport you could imagine is available on, or from, the beach, from sunfish and laser sailing, to kayaking and snorkelling, while a fleet of motor boats are on hand to take you water-skiing or scuba diving. The accommodation is spread out right along the beach with cream and dark wood two-storey cottages set about 50m back from the shore, amidst the mature gardens. The beautiful hexagonal premium rooms have lovely big balconies with views through the gardens straight out onto the beach and the sea stretching beyond.

The bedrooms are exquisitely decorated but quite simple in style – there's no great swathes of material or chintzed bedclothes. Instead, most of the furniture is made of

LITTLE DIX BAY

(☎ 495 5555, 🖷 495 5661, 🖳 rosewood@rosewoodhotels.com), PO Box 70, Virgin Gorda, British Virgin Islands

Reservations: Through Rosewood Hotels & Resorts US (toll-free ☎ 1-888-ROSEWOOD) or through the website 🖳 www.rosewood-hotels.com; Leading Hotels of the World toll-free numbers worldwide (see p12) or in the UK through tour operator Caribbean Connection (see p10)

Getting there: 20-minute transfer by private motor launch from Tortola's Beef Island airport, check-in is on board accompanied by rum punches

Accommodation: 97 rooms: 4 garden view; 16 ocean view; 13 de luxe; 16 premium; 4 suites

Amenities: Limited room service, hiking trails, early morning aerobics, Activity Centre for TV screenings of major sporting events, library, games room, seven tennis courts, complimentary watersports, dive centre, private yacht for overnight and day sails, sunset cruises on motor boats, private beaches for picnics à deux, three restaurants including a beach bar, once-weekly picnic at Spring Bay, car rental, health and beauty parlour

Dress code: Resort casual which means closed-toe shoes and trousers for men in the evenings

Weddings: Little Dix is very popular for weddings and usually does about three each weekend; receptions for up to 200 people can either be in the hotel's main dining room or at the beach house; the hotel will do its utmost to accommodate all your requests – brides can even pick their own bouquet straight from the beautiful grounds!

Minimum stay: None

Rates: Doubles from US$275 to US$800; suites from US$800 to US$1000

Credit cards: Most major

Tax and service: 5% service charge on all food and beverages; plus a 5% surcharge and a 7% sales tax on the room

bamboo, rattan and pine, the walls are stone on two of the six sides with wood panelling and wide, shuttered windows on the other sides. The premium bedrooms have a walk-in closet and a good sized bathroom with shower and a turquoise tiled double basin, lots of wonderful toiletries (including the hotel's celebrated mango-coconut soap), new white cotton bathrobes and white fluffy towels.

Each room has a fridge, hairdryer, an ironing board and iron, in-room safe and phone, as well as two comfortable rattan armchairs, a desk, and balcony furniture.

Biras Creek

Biras Creek amazed me. After staying in lots of hotels you tend to get immune to hotel furnishings. But then, once in a while, you stumble upon a special place, which not only makes you feel at home but you find yourself wishing your home was more like this. Biras is just such a place. It's not just the hotel's unique setting – it occupies a 56-hectare isthmus of land stretching out between the Atlantic Ocean and the Caribbean Sea – but the feeling of space and the hundreds of little details that make it so special and ensure that it sticks in your mind forever.

Having arrived by motor launch you'll be whisked around the hotel for a quick tour in a Mini Moke, before being shown your room. There are 33 suites at Biras, 21 overlooking the ocean and nine with garden views, as well as two spacious and wonderfully romantic Grand Suites with panoramic views of the sea and sunken baths. The Premier Suite is along the water's edge.

But this is not a hotel where you have to have a premium suite to ensure a good room and view: the ocean view suites are fabulous and just perfect for a honeymoon. They are all one-storey semi-detached cottages but are laid out at an angle and are totally soundproofed so that you'd have no idea there were people staying next door. All the suites have three rooms: a sitting room with wicker sofa, an armchair and a rattan desk, as well as a small refrigerator which comes complete with complimentary beer, soft drinks, sparkling water and a bottle of wine; a bedroom which is both air conditioned and naturally cooled by the wind coming off the sea – although there is also a ceiling fan; and an en suite bathroom with alfresco shower.

But it's the furnishings that really make the rooms at Biras so special, from the cheeky green wooden frog lolling on his back acting as a door stop to the large cool terracotta floor tiles, the colour-washed doors and shutters painted in aqua and lilac, and the hand-painted fabrics which are designed and

---

BIRAS CREEK
(☎ 494 3555, 🖻 494 3557, 🖳 www.biras.com), PO Box 54, Virgin Gorda, British Virgin Islands

Reservations: Through UK tour operators Carrier or Caribbean Connection; from US and Canada through Ralph Locke Islands (US toll-free ☎ 800-223-1108, 🖳 www.carib isles.com)

Getting there: The hotel has a complimentary private launch that will whisk you from the dock at Beef Island Airport, Tortola, directly to the resort in about 35 minutes or by helicopter from Antigua

Accommodation: 33 suites: 21 Ocean view suites; nine Garden view suites; two Grand suites and one Premier Suite

Amenities: Alfresco dining room, library, terrace bar, freshwater swimming pool, private beach at Deep Bay with beach bar and complimentary watersports, guest towels, two floodlit astroturf tennis courts, full-time watersports instructor, a bicycle for each guest, a 44ft luxury sailing yacht and small motor boats for one's private use, heli-tours

Dress code: Shirts with collars for men and evening resort wear for women at night

Weddings: Biras does both wedding and honeymoon packages; the weddings can be held outdoors, or on the resort's luxury 44-metre yacht, but you must be on the island three working days prior to the ceremony

Minimum stay: None

Rates: Garden view suite from US$525; ocean view suite from US$625 which includes all meals and complimentary watersports, plus every seventh night free; a seven-night Sailaway plan including two nights on board the private yacht and five nights full board at Biras Creek costs from US$750 per couple per night

Credit cards: Most major

Taxes and service charge: 7% government tax and 10% service charge

made locally. Everything has been done so tastefully and with such attention to detail that you'd never know you were in a hotel room.

The resort is spread out all over the isthmus: the cottages are lined up along the Atlantic Ocean with its ripping surf and the outdoor swimming pool is set about half-way between the cottages. The beach on the Caribbean side and its bar are right on the edge of the isthmus along a sandy track (accessed by your personal bicycles). The resort's small fleet of motor boats and yachts are anchored off the pier on the opposite side of the isthmus overlooking the **North Sound**. The main hotel buildings are arranged on many different levels in what almost looks like a small castle, connected by a stone pathway spiralling up the hillside, with incredible views on all sides.

The hotel's facilities are just what you'd expect from a first-class resort: two floodlit tennis courts, a private beach with chaise longues scattered around under thatched huts for shade, a covered open-air pavilion and bar, as well as complimentary watersports such as windsurfing, sailing, snorkelling. There is also a fleet of complimentary small motor boats for guests to explore the North Sound on their own. Refurbishments in 2000 meant redesigned bathrooms, and a helipad to enable guests to take heli-golf tours, heli-shopping tours and – most importantly – for hassle-free airport transfers from Antigua which will land you directly at the resort.

Lunch varies from beach barbecues served on the tranquil Caribbean beach about one kilometre away from the main body of the hotel to three-course meals in the dining room; there is tea in the open-sided Arawak Room looking out over the North Sound, while early morning coffee and pastries are served by the freshwater pool, and full breakfasts and dinners are offered in the dining room.

If you want the full-blown resort, with a big splashy hotel feel, you may find Biras a little too quiet, but this is the place for you if you want to switch off and enjoy the odd drink or chat with other guests and staff. You may well find the general manager topping up your coffee at breakfast or the sales manager joining guests for a night-cap.

Peter Island Resort & Yacht Harbour

Peter Island Resort is a 720-hectare private island located just south of Virgin Gorda. Recently extensively refurbished, the hotel offers superb accommodation in an idyllic island setting.

Because the island is so big there is lots to keep you busy for a couple of weeks, as well as plenty of perfect beach spots on which to do nothing but gaze out over the varying shades of turquoise sea and the shadow of other islands in the distance.

Peter Island has five lovely sandy beaches ranging from the huge semi-circular **Deadman's Bay**, the main beach and the

---

PETER ISLAND RESORT
(☎ 495 2000, 🖷 495 2500), PO Box 211, Road Town, Tortola, British Virgin Islands
Reservations: Through Peter Island Sales and Reservations (US toll-free ☎ 800-346-4451) or luxury operators to the Caribbean (see p10)
Getting there: 25 minutes by guest boat from Beef Island Airport
Accommodation: 52 rooms, plus two villas: 32 harbour-side rooms, 20 beach-front rooms
Amenities: Two restaurants, two bars, including beach bar; four tennis courts, fitness centre, swimming pool, extensive complimentary watersports, five beaches, Dive BVI centre, bicycles for guest use, heli-pad, gift shop, library lounge, masseur, laundry service, free ferry service to Tortola, picnic lunches, island tours and walking trails, deep-sea fishing and sailing trips organized locally
Dress code: Shirt with collar and smart trousers required for dinner in the Tradewinds restaurant; no swimming suits allowed for meals at Deadman's Beach Bar and Grill
Weddings: Wedding ceremonies are very popular at Peter Island and will be costed according to your requirements
Minimum stay: None
Rates: Garden view from US$515; ocean view from US$490; beachfront from US$595; rates include all meals
Credit cards: Most major
Taxes and service charge: A 17% tax and service charge is added to the room rate; guest pays separately for tax and service on beverages

base for all the watersport activities, to **Honeymoon Beach** where a lone thatched hut and two chairs occupy the small and intimate beach, or **White Bay Beach** which overlooks **Norman Island** and where the snorkelling is so fascinating you'll find the fish friendly enough to eat out of your hand. Guests are dropped at White Bay in the morning and left alone with a picnic: when they are ready to come home they contact the hotel via the two-way radio located on the beach.

There is a dive school on the island, as well as complimentary snorkelling equipment, sunfish sailing, hobie cats, sea kayaks and windsurfers, four tennis courts, a basketball court, a fitness room, and bicycles for guest use. There are also boats to charter and deep-sea fishing is available at local rates.

Deadman's Bay also has one of the best beach bars in the BVI, serving fabulous cocktails all day long, lunch between 12 and 3pm, and evening meals every night from December to May. After 1 May, the beachside restaurant is open only on Monday nights, which is a shame as it definitely has a much more convivial atmosphere than Tradewinds, the hotel's main dining room.

Right next to the swimming pool is the main Tradewinds restaurant, where shirts with collars, shoes and smart trousers are required of men in the evening. Reception, Dive BVI, the restaurant, pool and the 32 harbour rooms are on the harbour side of the island. On the other side of one of the island's many peaks are three of the beaches and the 20 beachfront rooms.

The harbour rooms are housed in eight concrete two-storey houses with shiny white A-framed roofs. I would definitely go for the beachfront rooms as they are much more natural looking, though both are nice inside. Each room has an en suite bathroom with lots of towels and full-sized bottles of toiletries, a fully-stocked minibar, a hairdryer and iron and ironing board, a phone, radio and a good sized balcony or terrace with wooden loungers and table and chairs.

The interior decoration of the rooms is in classic Caribbean colours – seagrape green, plantain yellow and cloudless blue – the air conditioning is great, the bed extremely comfortable, and the en suite bathroom facilities impressive. The views of Deadman's Bay from the beachfront rooms are also wonderful, so it is not surprising that Peter's has recently been voted one of the 'Best Places to Stay in the World' by Condé Nast *Traveller* Magazine.

ANGUILLA

Regarded as one of the most romantic places in the Caribbean, Anguilla is a truly undisturbed haven for escapists. Only 26km long and 5km across at its widest point, you won't find any casinos here but you will find the best white sand beaches in the Caribbean – 30 of them in all. A must for visitors is a trip to one of Anguilla's offshore deserted islands where all you'll need is a picnic and a snorkel and mask.

Cap Juluca

If you are looking for the best beaches, full-on luxury and real exclusivity look no further than Cap Juluca, where the hotel's white pavilions shimmer against a turquoise sea like something out of the Arabian Nights.

Spread over 72 hectares, Cap Juluca boasts some of the Caribbean's most stunning beaches, with a garden stashed full of glorious palms, orchids and frangipani. But perhaps most telling of all is Cap Juluca's one-to-one ratio of staff to guests – we're talking serious pampering.

Cap Juluca, named after the Arawak rainbow god, was built in accordance with the Anguillan law that no building should be taller than a palm tree. The result is a stunning array of whitewashed Moorish-style villas lining the perfect curve of **Maunday's Bay**, looking across to the mountains of the nearby French enclave, St Martin.

Rugs, stoneware, inlaid mirrors and leather articles from the Moroccan souks combine with cool white walls, Italian floor tiles and exotic fabrics to create a feeling of effortless chic inside the suites.

The rooms are truly enormous, ranging from 67 to 198 sq metres. They all have private walled terraces for sunbathing with panoramic sea views and some even have their own private or shared pool. There are king-sized beds, air conditioning, ceiling fans, in-room safes, fully stocked minibars with refrigerators and ice makers.

The 30 beachfront junior suites are the best rooms at Cap Juluca, largely due to their Italian marble bathrooms. In most of the large marble-and-glass bathrooms, one whole side – the one near the pillow-edged double bath tub – is a sheet of clear glass looking on to your own walled garden patio. What's more, the glass wall has a door in it allowing you to step straight from the double bath tub into the privacy of your own garden for sunbathing au naturel. Most bathrooms have a separate shower, bidet, dressing area and double basin; all have a hairdryer, bath salts and Molton Brown of London toiletries.

Anguilla is also known for the quality of its food and Cap Juluca offers guests three restaurants to choose from. **George's on the Beach** is great for full breakfasts, tasty light lunches and dinners. It also serves refreshing tropical drinks or cocktails. Most people look forward to a sumptuous dinner at **Pimm's**, which hangs right over the water and where French and Asian cuisine reign supreme. Those who are looking for something less formal head for the new, international **Kemia** which serves delicious bite-sized delicacies such as sushi, satay, Dim sum boxes and seafood tapas. Kemia has a romantic bar to catch the sunset and is open for both lunch and dinner.

CAP JULUCA
(☎ 497 6666, 🖷 497 6617), PO Box 240, Maunday's Bay, Anguilla, Leeward Islands, British West Indies

Reservations: Direct US toll-free (☎ 1-888-858-5822 or 1-866-858-5822), through Leading Hotels of the World reservation numbers worldwide (see p12); or tour operators Abercrombie & Kent, Caribbean Connection, Elegant Resorts, Caribtours (see p10)

Getting there: Via scheduled air service from Antigua (35 minutes) from San Juan (50 minutes) or St Martin (5 minutes), guests are met at the airport on arrival

Accommodation: 12 two-storey 'hotel villas' housing 58 luxury rooms and junior suites, seven suites and six pool villas with their own private or shared full-size swimming pool

Amenities: Three restaurants: Pimms, Kemia and George's; early morning coffee and pastries available in the main house library from 7 to 10am, otherwise breakfast is served on your terrace or at George's; live music several nights a week, movies shown nightly, three omni-turf surface tennis courts (two are flood-lit) plus professional coach, croquet lawn, junior Olympic-sized swimming pool, complimentary watersports including sunfish sailing, snorkel gear, kayaks, windsurfers, water-skiing; deep-sea fishing, scuba diving and day sails can be arranged at local rates; fitness centre with personal trainer, spa, golf on nearby island, boutique and sundries shop, car rental

Dress code: No jacket or tie required

Weddings: Yes

Minimum stay: None, except at Christmas/New Year, Thanksgiving and Easter

Rates: Doubles from US$325 to US$500 per couple per night in summer season; one-bedroom suites from US$620, ask about special programmes

Credit cards: American Express, Visa, MasterCard

Taxes and service charge: 10% government tax and 10% service charge will be added to your bill

Other recommended hotels

CuisinArt Resort & Spa (☎ 498 2000, 🖷 498 2010, 🖥 www.cuisinartresort.com, PO Box 2000, Rendezvous Bay, Anguilla) is a new, Mediterranean-style luxury hotel designed to awaken your senses. Set in lush, tropical gardens full of bougainvillea on a wonderful secluded stretch of coral limestone beach, it has the first full service spa on Anguilla and a delectable restaurant where you can see the Mediterranean and island fusion cuisine being prepared behind walls of glass. You can relax in splendour and seclusion around the negative-edge swimming pool, play tennis at night on one of three illuminated tennis courts, or enjoy a variety of watersports. Of the large and lav-

THINGS TO SEE AND DO ON ST KITTS AND NEVIS

Nevis is just 15.54 sq km and is quite mountainous which makes it all the more dramatic. If you are feeling energetic it's possible to climb **Mount Nevis**, but the climb is pretty tough, made more so by the dense rainforest: it's wise to take a guide.

Horse-riding can be arranged through the **Hermitage Inn** (☎ 469 3477), who will take you for an exhilarating gallop through the surf.

If beaches, not climbing or horse-riding, are your thing head for **Oualie Beach** on the north of the island, not far from Newcastle Airport: it has fantastic golden sands, a good beach bar and lovely views over to St Kitts. **Pinney's Beach** is the island's largest, stretching an amazing 6km which makes it a perfect place to stretch your legs, especially as there's a good selection of beach bars should you feel like the odd rum punch!

If you fancy a night out in true Caribbean style book a table at *Miss June's* (☎ 469 5330), where fantastic hot spicy food is served in a superb atmosphere.

A good way to see Nevis is to do a four-hour tour into the rainforest with either Jim Johnson, Michael Herbert or Lynell Liburd –

these can be booked at your hotel. The houses in wonderfully-named villages such as **Gingerland** and **Cotton Ground** are brightly painted, while **Charlestown**, the capital, is a lovely port and especially worth visiting on a Saturday for the market. From here you can hop on a ferry and make the 40-minute journey to St Kitts for the day.

Basseterre, St Kitts' capital, is much busier than Charlestown, with its pavement cafés full of blaring music and its own shopping mall. Hop into a taxi and go to **South Friars Bay** where there is a lovely secluded beach, plus a vantage point from where you can see the choppy Atlantic on one side and the serene waters of the Caribbean Sea on the other. A good way to see the island is through an organized tour which includes **Brimstone Hill** and visits to the crater of **Mt Liamiuga** – talk to **Greg's Safaris** (☎ 465 4121). Bear in mind though that the walk to the crater is hard work and will take you all day.

For further information visit 🖳 www.stkitts-nevis.com, the Tourist Board's website.

ish 93 guest rooms, 84 are suites and all have large, modern bathrooms. Doubles cost from US$260 to US$695, suites from US$450 to US$1900 includes continental breakfast but excludes 8% tax and 10% service charge. Reservations through The Leading Hotels of the World numbers worldwide (see p12), Caribbean Connection in the UK and most luxury tour operators to the Caribbean (see p10).

ST KITTS AND NEVIS

After a week of beach-filled activity on some of the bigger islands, such as Antigua, time out on these smaller islands can provide the perfect contrast. St Kitts and Nevis are *the* islands to relax on. Spend long languorous days here in a totally unhurried environment that is filled with old colonial charm. The dense, tropical forests surrounding the summit of St Kitts' now-dormant volcano contrast with the more cultivated, fertile valleys below. These islands seem lost in a dreamy past where the pace is slow and the best hotels are former plantations run as house parties where visitors mingle over cocktails and canapés in the evening.

Montpelier Plantation Inn

Montpelier, which nestles into the shoulder of Mount Nevis, is built on the ruins of a sugar plantation 195m above sea level. Today's hotel is famous as the wedding place of Lord Nelson and the young and well-off widow Frances (Fanny) Nisbet back in 1787 and is still just as romantic.

The Great House is reminiscent of a grand country manor run along the lines of an intimate house party, and while you certainly don't have to mix with the other guests it would be a shame not to as the convivial atmosphere is very much part of the hotel's endearing charm. The 17 West Indian-style cottages each have their own trellised balcony with views out to sea and the bedrooms are wonderfully simple and clean, almost minimalist in tone.

Apart from having one of the prettiest pools in the Caribbean, guests can enjoy long lazy days down at the secluded private beach where sun loungers and small wooden gazebos are provided for guest use. You are dropped off at the beach each morning by the hotel's minibus which then picks you up again in time for afternoon tea. The watersports facilities are slightly limited – essentially this is a place for relaxation not activity; those who want full resort facilities can head for the nearby **Four Seasons**. The kitchen will happily prepare you a sumptuous picnic, featuring the much-written about lobster butties, so that you can spend all day down at the beach, after which you'll really look forward to returning to the cooler hills in the evening.

Owned and run by old Etonian James Milnes Gaskell and his wife, Celia, Montpelier has the most wonderful laconic and relaxed atmosphere that confirms it as an established institution.

Nisbet Plantation Beach Club

Also on Nevis is Nisbet Plantation, the family home of Fanny Nisbet, now a wonderful country house retreat offering accommodation in 38 bedrooms in airy cottages set around the grounds which are truly romantic – right down to the hibiscus petals scattered liberally over the bed for your arrival.

The hotel is the epitome of luxury and good taste: once there you can enjoy both the secluded half-mile sandy beach with its beach bar and snorkelling and the old-world charm of the Great House where fabulous teas are served in the afternoon on the veranda.

Reports of the food at Nisbet are really good – it has been described as innovative, elegant and delicious. Dinner by candlelight on the veranda of the Great House is excellent.

There are mountain bikes for those who feel energetic, and hammocks, a drawing room full of paperbacks and board games for those who just want to relax.

ANTIGUA

For years Antigua has promoted itself as the island of 365 beaches, one for every day of the year. While this is somewhat of a romanticized cliché that has gradually lost its sparkle, the beaches certainly haven't.

MONTPELIER PLANTATION INN
(☎ 469 3462, 🖷 469 2932), PO Box 474, Nevis, West Indies
Reservations: All leading Caribbean-specialist tour operators and travel agents worldwide (see p10)
Getting there: Flights to Antigua, Puerto Rico or St Martin and then LIAT or Windward Air to St Kitts or Nevis; taxi (19km) to the hotel approx US$20
Accommodation: 16 rooms, one small suite
Amenities: Private beach, swimming pool, nearby golf course, tennis court
Dress code: Smart casual
Weddings: The hotel does arrange weddings and has a set package from US$750, plus a photographer at additional cost (from US$200)
Minimum stay: None – three working days minimum for a wedding
Rates: Double room from US$240 per night
Credit cards: Visa and Master card
Taxes and service charge: Not included

NISBET PLANTATION BEACH CLUB
(☎ 469 9325, 🖷 469 9864, 🖳 nisbet bc@caribsurf.com), St James Parish, Nevis, West Indies
Reservations: Direct or US toll-free (☎ 1-800-742-6008), through Caribtours or other tour operators and travel agents specializing in the Caribbean (see p10)
Getting there: Scheduled flights to Antigua, San Juan, St Kitts or St Maarten and then take a short flight with Nevis Express, LIAT or Windward air to Nevis, taxis available
Accommodation: 38 cottages: 16 superior rooms, 10 de luxe suites, 12 premier suites
Amenities: Dining room, beach bar/restaurant, swimming pool and sundeck, tennis, croquet, snorkelling, scuba diving, sport fishing, sailing, horse-riding, eco-rambles, mountain hiking and golf
Dress code: Daytime – casual; evening – smart casual, no jeans, t-shirts or shorts in main house after 6pm
Weddings: Packages from US$995
Minimum stay: None – two working days minimum for a wedding
Rates: Superior from US$290, de luxe suite from US$370, premier suite from US$390, all half board
Credit cards: MasterCard, Visa, American Express
Taxes and service charge: Government tax 8%, service 10%

Antigua also offers fantastic watersport facilities making it an ideal two-centre honeymoon combined with a week on Anguilla, St Kitts, Nevis, or even the BVI. If, however, you want to submit yourselves utterly to the Caribbean way of life why not just stay in Antigua, giving yourself time to see some of its most beautiful beaches, maybe do a few days' chartering and really start to unwind in true Caribbean style.

Curtain Bluff

Curtain Bluff has long been regarded as Antigua's best hotel and is often included in the area's specialist tour operators' top three hotels in the Caribbean. Perched on a strip of land that juts out between two sandy beaches, one calm and tranquil the other windswept, Curtain Bluff is a resort hotel with a much more glamorous feel than quieter hotels included here.

Curtain Bluff is the ideal place for people who like impressive but laid-back resorts where guests want for absolutely nothing and enjoy feeling safe in the knowledge that they are on a private estate. It is also perfect for sport lovers who can take advantage of the complimentary sailing, water-skiing, windsurfing, snorkelling, ketch sailing, deep-sea fishing, and even scuba diving if they are qualified. On top of this there is tennis, squash, a gym and large swimming pool, and an 18-hole golf course nearby.

The hotel has everything you could possibly want including the most spectacular views of the sea from each of the 70 rooms and suites, all of which are decorated in pastel shades and have marble floors and huge en suite bathrooms.

Curtain Bluff's restaurant has a solid reputation, thanks to its resident chef of 30 years, Reudi Portman, and the hotel's awesome wine cellar, which is said to have over 25,000 bottles. Dining is consequently an important part of each evening starting with cocktails and canapés on the terrace before moving into the open-air restaurant, where there is music for dancing each evening. It is also a formal affair: men are required to wear a jacket from mid-December until April except on barbecue nights, so don't choose Curtain Bluff for your honeymoon if this kind of attitude is going to annoy you, especially as the hotel operates a full board policy.

> **CURTAIN BLUFF**
> (☎ 462 8400, 🖷 462 8409), PO Box 288, St John's, Antigua, West Indies
> **Closed**: Between mid-May and mid-October
> **Reservations**: Direct, or through tour operators specializing in the Caribbean such as Harlequin Travel in the UK (see p10)
> **Getting there**: 25 minutes by local taxi from the airport
> **Accommodation**: 70 rooms and suites; 5 standard rooms, 39 de luxe rooms, 26 suites
> **Amenities**: Complimentary sailing, water-skiing, windsurfing, snorkelling, ketch sailing, deep-sea fishing and scuba diving (if qualified), four tennis courts, squash court, aerobics, gym and large swimming pool; there is also an 18-hole golf course nearby
> **Dress code**: Jacket required after 7pm during the high season
> **Weddings**: Curtain Bluff is popular for weddings, particularly in the garden gazebo
> **Minimum stay**: None
> **Rates**: Doubles from US$725 per night in the peak season (mid-December to mid-April) and from US$555 mid-October to mid-December and mid-April to mid-May
> **Credit cards**: American Express only
> **Taxes and service charge**: 8.5% government tax, plus 10% service charge

Jumby Bay Resort

Jumby Bay Resort is on a privately-owned 120-hectare island just 3km off the east coast of Antigua. This stunning resort is perfect for honeymooners and is quite unusual in that it operates as a very stylish, all-inclusive resort.

Jumby Bay is a place of utter peace: there are no cars on the island, just golf carts that collect guests for dinner, and the white bicycles with a good-sized pannier assigned to guests on arrival for ferrying themselves around.

Although the resort does boast some of the finest facilities of any Caribbean hotel it is first and foremost a place where people come to do nothing and to get well and truly away from it all. To help you do so there are no phones or TVs in the bedrooms and the island is kept utterly private. Snoozing under a thatched umbrella or lying together in a hammock is how people spend their day at Jumby Bay Resort, punctuated only by the occasional swim, snorkel, or a game of tennis. There's also plenty of pampering on offer in the 'Wellness centre'.

The word 'immaculate' just about sums up this slick resort: the staff are unobtrusive but attentive and the immense main beach is perfect. For the energetic there's plenty to do – 7km of hiking trails (which are suitable for the resort's bikes), a putting green, two all-weather tennis courts and a professional coach, and numerous water-based activities including water-skiing and sailing.

At the heart of Jumby Bay is the Estate House, an old English sugar plantation manor dating back to the 1700s, where guests gather for high tea on the veranda, candlelit dinners in the downstairs dining room or outside on the terrace if they prefer.

Upstairs, the hotel bar, better known as the Library, is well stocked with reading material to keep you going through the day. Breakfast is either served at the beach pavilion or delivered to your room.

JUMBY BAY RESORT
(☎ 462 6000, 🖷 462 6020), PO Box 243, St John's, Antigua, West Indies
Reservations: With leading tour operators and travel agents specializing in the Caribbean (see p10)
Getting there: Guests are met at the airport, a five-minute drive and six-minute cruise to the island
Accommodation: 27 junior suite-style cottages and 11 villas
Amenities: Bicycles for each guest, hiking/cycling trails, three tennis courts with professional coach, large selection of watersports including sunfish sailing, water-skiing, floats, pedalos, windsurfing, snorkelling, and sailing on the resort's yacht *Moonshine*, weekly sunset cruise, plus swimming pools, both shared and private, wellness centre
Dress code: No jackets required
Weddings: The resort caters for both weddings and receptions
Minimum stay: None, except for Christmas and New Year
Rates: Doubles from US$650; luxury villas from US$1195 per couple which includes all your meals, drinks (apart from bottles of wine) and activities; ask about special honeymoon packages
Credit cards: Most major
Taxes and service charge: 7% government tax and 10% service charge will be added to your bill

Guests can stay in the 12-unit Mediterranean-style complex, 27 junior suite-style cottages or one of the 11 villas scattered along the beach and around the pools. The island also has an array of two- and three-bedroom luxury villas and several spacious private manor houses for rent. All the suites are truly luxurious, decorated either in fresh white to contrast with the terracotta floor and dark wood louvred doors and ceiling, or in Caribbean tones of turquoise, coral, green and yellow. Most suites have king-sized four-poster beds. They all have a separate seating area with rattan armchairs, ceiling fan, hairdryer, in-room safe, and wet bar (minibar). The wonderfully opulent bathrooms are something else with their open-air showers and pretty cream and turquoise tiling, Hermès toiletries and bathrobes with your names monogrammed on – which the resort sends to your home address when you leave.

If you view your honeymoon as the ultimate chance to see just how far you can both unwind and do nothing, this has to be one of the most beautiful islands on earth to do it. Day after day of lying on the beach, strolling through the gently lapping turquoise sea and staring up at the starry sky night after night tends to do the trick.

Galley Bay
With its electric mix of old West Indian charm and Gauguin-inspired Tahitian architecture, Galley Bay is a haven on the east coast for honeymooners seeking an unobtrusive retreat. An unassuming elegance permeates the atmosphere, and casual island life and luxury go hand in hand.

On 40 acres of tropical gardens, ablaze with bougainvillea and complete with a lagoon and bird sanctuary, are 70 luxurious low-lying rooms and cottages arranged along a secluded palm-fringed beach. Designed with unrivalled comfort in mind, all rooms have air conditioning, ceiling fans, custom-designed rattan and bamboo furniture, wooden louvered windows and terracotta tiled floors. They are decked out with all the mod cons such as hairdryers, coffee machines, bathrobes, in-room safes, private baths and showers, and king-size bed, and have a balcony or patio.

There are four different room categories to choose from at Galley Bay. Gauguin Cottages on the edge of the bird sanctuary lagoon – as little as 50 yards from the beach – consist of two unique, separate, thatch roof rondavels (connected by a covered patio) with cool, whitewashed walls and high-peaked ceilings. Superior Beachfront rooms are traditional, single level rooms which offer a 'three seconds from bed to sea' guarantee and breezy patios on the seafront. The well-appointed De Luxe Beachfront rooms have big bathrooms. First-floor rooms have large patios with beach showers while second floor rooms have private balconies with spectacular ocean views. Built in 1999, the Premium Beachfront Suites are the same as the De Luxe Beachfront but have beautiful imported Polynesian furnishings, elegant fabrics and oversized bathrooms with tubs in 700 square feet of space.

When you've had enough of relaxing on the sunloungers by the free-form freshwater swimming pool with its cascading waterfalls, you are bound to find a secluded spot under the palms somewhere on the 3½-mile stretch of beach. Complimentary watersports on offer at Galley Bay include windsurfing, sailing, snorkelling, hobie cats and kayaking and there's tennis or a new fitness centre should you want it.

Hors d'oeuvres are served in the cone-shaped, thatched-roof **Teepee Bar** by the beach around 5:30pm and this is a favourite gathering place to sip sundowners as you watch the sun slip into the Caribbean. The ease of an all-inclusive resort means there's no deciding where to eat – just let yourself be enticed by the exotic flavours of the Caribbean at the resort's two beachside restaurants: **Sea Grape**, the award-winning à la carte restaurant serving Creole and Euro-Caribbean cuisine, and the smaller, more intimate **Gauguin Restaurant** offering grill-type fare. Then you're just steps away from a moonlight stroll on a white-sand beach.

GALLEY BAY
(☎ 462 0302, 🖹 462 4551, 💻 www.clas sicislands.com) PO Box 305, St. John's, Antigua, West Indies
Reservations: US toll-free (☎ 800-345-0356); through UK Caribbean specialist Caribtours and most leading tour operators to the Caribbean (see p10)
Getting there: The resort is a 25-minute drive from VC Bird International Airport and a ten-minute drive from the capital city of St John's
Accommodation: 70 guest rooms in five categories: Gauguin Cottages, Superior Beachfront, De Luxe Beachfront, Premium Beachfront Suite
Amenities: Sea Grape Restaurant, Gauguin Restaurant, Teepee Bar and Lounge Bar; freshwater swimming pool, table tennis, horseshoes (the game!), croquet; open-air fitness centre, tennis court, library, bicycles, games room, resort boutique, complimentary non-motorized watersports, walking trails around bird sanctuary lagoon, at extra charge; island excursions, golf, rental cars and massage
Dress code: Smart casual
Weddings: Yes – with a choice of romantic locations; wedding package costs US$600 (free for stays of 13 nights)
Minimum stay: None
Rates: Gauguin Cottage from US$550, Superior Beachfront from US$610, De Luxe Beachfront from US$650, Premium Beachfront Suite from US$730 all-inclusive
Credit cards: Most major
Taxes and service charge: Included

Other recommended hotels
Blue Waters (💻 www.bluewaters.net, PO Box 256, St John's), nestled in 14 acres of tropical gardens with its own private bay boasting two beautiful white sand beaches, is one of Antigua's most secluded tropical escapes.

THINGS TO SEE AND DO IN ANTIGUA

A couple I talked to recently were so enamoured with their Sunday night trip to **Shirley Heights** that they insisted I should recommend that anyone going to Antigua organize their entire holiday itinerary around ensuring that they get at least one experience of this incredible event, if not two.

Shirley Heights, the old English garrison fort high up on the hill above English Harbour, commands the most incredible views of the bay and over to distant **Montserrat**. The weekly 'jump up' at Shirley Heights has become so popular with locals, resident yachties and visitors alike that this sundowner party high on a hill looking down on English Harbour has now become a Caribbean institution. You can either walk up, which takes about half an hour from the Dockyard, or phone Ivor (☎ 460 1241 or on his mobile ☎ 464 0118) the local taxi man who will be happy to drive you up there and collect you later. Make sure you get up there for about 5pm so that you can order your rum punches and barbecued burgers before the 21-piece steel band kicks off and the crowd go wild. And they do! After the steel band finishes at around 7pm live reggae keeps the crowd entertained.

Because Antigua is one of the bigger West Indian islands it's great for couples who think they might get frustrated on tiny islands such as the Maldives. There's plenty to see and do in Antigua to keep most people happy for a fortnight. The best thing to do is hire a jeep and see the island for yourselves, getting a real taste of what Caribbean life is like for the locals. The road system is good enough to find your way round but rough enough to make it quite an

entertaining adventure as you pass stunning coastal views and tracks through the rainforest.

The interior is very arid, quite flat and not that beautiful but the beaches are just magical. **Half Moon Bay** is reputed to be Antigua's most beautiful beach, where the surf gets quite high at one end of the beach but remains flat and tranquil at the other. There's also a good bar set back off the beach itself. Closer to English Harbour is **Pigeon Point** which is a great place to go if you are looking to get away from other tourists, as it's usually used by friendly locals and the crews from the yachts in the afternoons.

For a fantastic one-hour walk come out of the Old Fort and walk up and over the ridge between the English Harbour and Falmouth Harbour across to Pigeon Beach: you just need to follow the white ribbons attached to the trees. You'll get stunning views of both harbours and the Caribbean Sea.

The *Admiral's Inn* (☎ 460 1027) and the *Copper and Lumber Store* (☎ 460 1058) are two historic hotels overlooking Nelson's Dockyard. They are both lovely places to enjoy a cocktail, or even dinner, and are easy to get to if you're coming from English Harbour. Both hotels offer reasonably priced accommodation in a really beautiful setting and the food is apparently really good.

You don't have to have done much sailing to enjoy a few days cruising around Antigua, perhaps over to stunning **Green Island** or down to **Harmony Hall**.

For further information visit 🖵 www.antigua-barbuda.org.

Originally established some 35 years ago and now completely refurbished the all-inclusive Blue Waters combines unique personal service and attention to detail with a classic Caribbean experience. Honeymooners have a choice of 77 air-conditioned luxury rooms, suites or beachfront villas. All have sea views from their balconies, king-size bed and chaise longue, satellite TV, telephone, safe, hairdryer and most have complimentary minibar.

Blue Waters boasts two freshwater swimming pools, a gym, tennis court and complimentary non-motorized watersports and anything from sailing excursions to helicopter tours can be arranged. In the evening there is a choice of dining in the outdoor Palm Restaurant, or treating yourself in Vyvien's air-conditioned à la carte restaurant, equal to any fine dining restaurant in the world. Given notice, Executive Chef Massimo Bertela will even prepare your favourite dish.

A Superior Hillside double costs from US$395, De Luxe Beachfront double US$430, Luxury Suite and Beach Front Villa both from US$750, all-inclusive but excluding 10% Service and 8.5% Government tax. Book in the US (toll-free ☎ 1-800-557-6536) or UK (☎ 01327-831 007), or through leading tour operators to the Caribbean (see p10).

Cocobay (☎ 268-562 2400, 🖹 268-562 2424, 🖵 www.cocobayresort.com, Valley Church, PO Box 431, Antigua) is a colourful collection of gingerbread cottages scattered across a gentle hillside close to St John's, sloping down to a choice of three white sandy beaches. It offers barefoot luxury in beautiful surroundings at a good price. The 42 cottages are decorated with delicately carved Antiguan furniture and offer uninterrupted breathtaking views of the turquoise waters of the Caribbean Sea from their private verandas and wooden shuttered windows. The sea-facing bathrooms allow you to bathe 'alfresco' in the privacy and seclusion of a flower-enclosed deck.

The restaurant has magnificent views and serves a creative selection of authentic local and international cuisine together; meals are prepared by British chef, Nigel Martin. A horizon swimming pool and Wellness Cottage, as well as a variety of watersports, complete the programme for unadulterated pleasure at Cocobay. For something a bit different, guests can take walks with Antigua's 'Medicine Man' Dr Amu through Orange Valley, an old plantation estate rich in indigenous, medicinal plants.

Seven nights sharing a cottage all-inclusive (breakfast, lunch, afternoon tea, dinner, drinks, house wine by the glass, taxes, gratuities and watersports) costs from £839 per person with UK tour operator Virgin Holidays (☎ 01293-456 789).

ANSE CHASTANET
(☎ 459 7000, 🖷 459 7554, 🖳 www.anse-chastanet.com), PO Box 7000, Soufrière, St Lucia, West Indies
Reservations: Most tour operators and travel agents specializing in the Caribbean (see p10)
Getting there: The hotel can arrange transfers from the airport, costing approx US$45 from UVF, the international airport, and US$75 from George Charles airport (SLU) in the north, per car each way – it is best to try and share with another couple
Accommodation: 49 rooms: 6 premium hillside rooms with open-sided views of the Pitons; 12 open de luxe hillside rooms with Piton or ocean views; 12 de luxe beachfront rooms; 14 superior hillside rooms with wrap-around balconies; four smaller hillside rooms
Amenities: Two restaurants, two bars, complimentary snorkelling, mini sailing and windsurfing, full service spa and exercise equipment; art gallery and mountain bike rental for 10 miles of exclusive biking trails
Dress code: Elegant casual, men must wear trousers or long shorts at the Tree House restaurant in the evenings
Weddings: Wedding and honeymoon packages available
Minimum stay: Three nights in winter and seven to ten days over Christmas and New Year
Rates: Double rooms from US$440 including breakfast and dinner from mid-December to mid-April; Premium suites from US$790
Credit cards: Most major
Taxes and service charge: 8% government tax and 10% service charge will be added to your bill

ST LUCIA

Imagine lush valleys covered in bananas, tropical rainforests, towering palms, lime trees, bushes covered in exotic flowers, and two green volcanic peaks, and you're imagining St Lucia. This, the most exotic of all the Caribbean islands, is renowned for its friendly islanders and a climate that is so warm you'll want to skinny dip under the stars at midnight.

Anse Chastanet

Anse Chastanet offers the classic honeymoon experience. Whenever people ask me where they should go for a few days of total and utter relaxation at the start of their Caribbean honeymoon it's always top of my list.

This 200-hectare hideaway is wildly romantic, with bedrooms that seem to have been carved into the hillside they are so much part of the dense jungle surrounds. What makes this hotel so special is its premium rooms which have been designed so that there is nothing to impede the fantastic view over St Lucia's famous Pitons.

The higher up the hillside you go the better the rooms are, and needless to say, the views. While some guests have complained about the long hike up the many stone steps, when they were initially shown the room, they all seem to rapidly change their minds once they've seen the view. It really is quite staggering and most guests at Anse Chastanet seem to find themselves sitting for hours on end staring at nothing else.

The best rooms of all are those beginning with No 7 (particularly 7F); these are

THINGS TO SEE AND DO IN ST LUCIA

Just 15 minutes outside **Rodney Bay** by car or a lovely rural walk to the north-eastern tip of the island will take you to **Cas en Bas Estate**, where there is a superb windward beach on the Atlantic side. This off-the-beaten track beach is perfect for windsurfing as it is protected by a reef. You can also arrange mountain biking, horse-riding, walking and sea kayaking here from your hotel.

The *Bistro Restaurant* at Rodney Bay Lagoon is a perfect spot for a romantic, waterfront dinner. The food is excellent, lots of fresh fish, fantastic cheesy garlic bread and there's also a good wine list. **The Late Lime**, a five-minute walk away, is the hottest nightclub on the island.

Pigeon Island, bordering Rodney Bay, is a national park with well-kept grounds, lots of interesting early naval history and superb views from the lookout points – there's even a small pagoda where you can get married.

Don't miss Friday night's regular carnival or 'jump up' in the fishing town of **Gros Islet**: it was traditionally a small celebration for fisherman but has expanded into one big party for everyone.

From Ladera there are some wonderful walks down to *Bang Between the Pitons*, a great bar owned by the famous Englishman,

Lord Glenconnor, who seems to be permanently in *Hello!* magazine. It's also worth visiting the **Tropical Botanical Gardens** in Soufrière and the mineral baths, which are unusually well kept for the Caribbean. If you go into **Castries**, St Lucia's capital, visit the wonderful colourful market on the harbour front, particularly on a Saturday morning where, as well as lots of exotic fruit, vegetables, herbs and spices, you can find some good souvenirs such as T-shirts, baskets and sarongs.

Make sure you do the boat trip to explore the golden coastline starting at **Marigot Bay**, one of the most secluded anchorages in the Caribbean where *Dr Doolittle* and *Superman 2* were filmed and where the charter crowd now put down their anchors; yacht charters are offered by Moorings (St Lucia ☎ 451 4256; UK ☎ 0800-220 763). From Marigot Bay you'll sail to Soufrière, the oldest town lying beneath **Petit Piton**, which was named after the nearby volcano. Here you can see the world's only 'drive in' volcano. Close by are the hot springs which feed the mineral baths on the Diamond Estate, where you can lie back in the warm water amongst waterfalls and botanical gardens.

Visit the St Lucia Tourist Board website for more ideas: 💻 www.stlucia.org.

universally regarded as some of the Caribbean's most romantic bedrooms, where two whole sides are open to the view. Although unwanted wildlife might take advantage of the open walls you can both snuggle up under your mosquito net for protection. The alfresco bathrooms in suites Nos 7A to 7F are equally well known for their open-air experience: imagine rinsing away the beach sand and sea salt looking out upon the magnificent setting sun, as the sea turns gold and purple to match the sky.

The rooms are decorated with the bright madras-checked material that is the traditional dress of the local St Lucian women. Combined with the wooden roofs, terracotta floor tiles, and whole rows of wicker lamps, the overall effect is natural and stunning. Apart from the wicked views, the rooms all come with patios or balconies, fridge, tea- and coffee-making facilities and hairdryers.

Although there are some beachside rooms at Anse Chastanet they only have garden views and are not nearly as romantic as the hillside extravaganzas. The beach, which is volcanic and therefore has blackish sand, is the scene for complimentary watersports such as snorkelling and sunfish sailing. Best of all are the scuba diving opportunities with the PADI dive school, which operates daily dives for the experienced and runs courses for beginners.

Other recommended hotels

Perched high up on a hillside, 300m above a lush valley with magnificent sea views below, is **Ladera Resort** (☎ 459 7323, 📄 459 5156, US toll-free ☎ 800-841-4145, 💻 www.ladera-stlucia.com, PO Box 225, Soufrière). To my mind it is one of the most romantic hotels in the Caribbean. The bedrooms are open-sided so you can lie in the four-poster bed shrouded in mosquito netting and stare for hours on end at the totally uninterrupted view of the sea and the stars, and when it gets too hot you can take a dip in your own private plunge pool on your terrace. Days are spent relaxing on the superb wooden terrace by the horizon swimming pool, looking out over tropical rainforest to the awesome Pitons towering either side of the blue ocean beyond. An extremely tranquil hotel, and well cared for, Ladera is the perfect place to flop for a few days in the mountains before moving on to a beach resort. A luxury pool villa costs US$820 in peak season from mid-December to mid-April and then goes down to US$565 between June and September plus 10% service and 8% tax. Ladera also offers three-night honeymoon packages which cost US$2460 in peak season and US$1545 in low season. Book through UK tour operator Caribtours (see p10).

Jalousie Hilton Resort and Spa, (☎ 459 7666, 🖹 459 7667, PO Box 251, Soufrière), set in more than 325 acres of lush rainforest, is a 114-room resort that has been designated a rainforest nature sanctuary by St Lucia Naturalists' Society.

Jalousie, set smack between the glorious Pitons, commands one of the most beautiful locations in the entire Caribbean. It has beautifully appointed individual villas with plunge pools and the added bonus of a glorious beach and five-star spa offering a vast range of treatments. Jalousie's special honeymoon package includes chilled champagne, plantation flowers, fruit basket and hors d'oeuvres in your room on arrival, hand-embroidered bed linens, candlelit dinner for two in a secluded location, Caribbean massage for two, a selection of activities, transfers, use of all non-motorized sports including snorkelling and sailing equipment, tennis, golf and spa facilities, Jacuzzi and sauna.

A Villa Suite with ocean view and private plunge pool costs US$695 January to mid-May; US$595 16–31 May, 1 Oct–30 Nov and US$495 June to September. The Honeymoon package costs US$550 per couple per stay as a supplement to any room rate. Book through leading tour operators to the Caribbean (see p10).

ST VINCENT AND THE GRENADINES

Petit St Vincent

Petit St Vincent, or PSV as it is affectionately known, is the most romantic island of the Caribbean. If you've always fancied yourself as a castaway this is the place to do it, especially if you don't want to forgo the basic luxuries fundamental to any honeymoon.

Some 64km off St Vincent, PSV is luxurious but not opulently so; instead the 22 private cottages are rather low key, letting this 113-acre private island's beauty speak for itself. The low level cottages, built from local Bluebitch stone, are dotted all over the island, some on the hillsides, some set into the sides of cliffs, others set back from the beach.

All are rustic in style with a living room containing two day beds, a bedroom with two queen-sized beds, dressing room, bathroom

---

PETIT ST VINCENT
(US ☎ 513-242-1333 or 800-242-1333, 🖹 513-242-6951, 🖳 psv@fuse.net), PO Box 12506 Cincinnati, Ohio 45212, USA
Closed: August to November
Reservations: Either direct (see above), through The Leading Hotels of the World reservation numbers worldwide (see p12) or leading tour operators to the Caribbean such as Caribtours and Caribbean Connection (see p10)
Getting there: Via 50-minute private charter plane from Barbados to Union Island (US$160 per person one way), then hotel launch to PSV (a 25-minute journey)
Accommodation: 22 luxurious cottages
Amenities: Open-air dining pavilion, convivial weekly barbecue, sailing trips to nearby islands, snorkelling, scuba diving, deep-sea fishing, hobie cats, windsurfers, sunfish sailing, tennis court, afternoon tea, room service
Dress code: Casual
Weddings: Guests can be married in Petit St Vincent, but you have to have been there for three days before you can fly to St Vincent for a licence; and you have to pay for a minister to fly to PSV to perform the ceremony, approx US$810 before flowers, photographer etc; wedding receptions cannot be catered for
Minimum stay: None
Rates: Full board: doubles from US$550 to US$860; ask about summer packages
Credit cards: Most major
Taxes and service charge: 7% tax and 10% service charge will be added to your bill

and a stone-encased deck with two canvas beach-back chairs, two chaise longues and a hammock. Toiletries, bathrobes, beach towels, insect repellent, hairdryers, irons and an ironing board are also found in each room. Whichever cottage you choose, the views are spectacular from the private patio and you're never far from a beach since the whole island is practically encircled by pure white sand.

This utter seclusion is what makes PSV so special, an aspect of the hotel exaggerated even further by the cunning use of red and yellow flags to tell the staff either that you don't want to be disturbed or that you require room service. Communication has to be by like this as there are no phones in the cottages at PSV – it's very much a no phone, no TV, no newspaper kind of place. Even when room service comes you don't actually have to be interrupted, as notes of requests are collected from your mailbox, which means it would be possible, if you wanted to, to spend your entire stay on PSV without seeing another person.

However, that would deprive you of eating in the spectacularly-located hilltop restaurant which looks down over the harbour where a lunchtime buffet is served daily. If you do ever tire of whiling away the time in your hammock there are watersports such as snorkelling, windsurfing, hobie cats and sunfish sailing, as well as sailing excursions to nearby islands. Have a look at 🖳 www.svgtourism.com, the tourist board's website for other ideas.

Other recommended hotels

Young Island (☎ 458 4826, 🗎 457 4567, 🖳 www.youngisland.com, PO Box 211, St Vincent) was one of the first 'whole island' resorts. Small, hilly and covered in lush vegetation and palm trees, there are only 30 wood-framed cottages with louvered windows, whitewashed walls decorated with colourful stencils, long cream calico curtains, and an open-air shower surrounded by bamboo walls and huge banana trees. The best is cottage number 10, one of the two luxury cottages on the beach: it has a sitting room opening out onto your own patio, a plunge pool and a gazebo looking over to Mustique Island from where you can step straight down on to your own private beach. Meals are simple and cocktails are strong.

Double rooms from US$325 half board – ask about 'lovers' packages from US$2800 for seven nights; wedding packages US$650 per couple; sailaway packages are also offered. From the US reservations can be made through Ralph Locke Islands (US/Canada toll-free ☎ 1-800-223-1108, 🖳 caribisles@aol.com) and through UK tour operator Elegant Resorts (see p10).

Palm Island (☎ 458 8824, 🗎 458 8804, 🖳 www.palmislandresorts.com), a short boat ride from Union Island in the Southern Grenadines, opened in 1999 after a complete refurbishment and under the same ownership as Galley Bay on Antigua. One of the smallest islands in the Grenadines with just 135 acres, Palm Island is private, intimate and all-inclusive and offers some of the best snorkelling and beaches in the Caribbean. The 40 guest rooms are nestled on the beach or set back in the foliage, decorated in tropical motifs and with hand-crafted rattan furniture. Seascapes painted by the island's resident artist decorate the walls and wherever you walk or look there'll be palms swaying in the breeze. No children, no chits of paper to sign for watersports or hors d'oeuvres – this is the place to sling a hammock between two of them and just relax. Your own private island doesn't come cheap of course. Beachfront doubles are from US$610 in summer, US$730 in winter all-inclusive. Weddings can be arranged in a gazebo overlooking the sea from US$600. Reservations can be made in the US (toll-free ☎ 800-345-0271), in the UK (☎ 020-8350 1001), or through UK tour operator Caribbean Connection (see p10).

Plantation House Hotel (☎ 458 3425, 🗎 458 3612, 🖳 www.hotelplantation.com, PO Box 16, Admiralty Bay, Bequia) is a charming hotel with a very relaxed atmosphere. The hotel is centred around the beautiful colonial Main House which has five double rooms, 17 cabanas (thatched huts) and eight ocean-view rooms set amongst 20 acres of fragrant tropical gardens. Bedrooms are decorated in simple fresh-looking Caribbean style and are air conditioned with good in-room facilities. If you're not into glitzy hotels and are looking for a quiet place to relax, Plantation House and Bequia itself as an island have immense charm. Doubles in a cabana from around US$245 to US$995 in high season per night with breakfast.

Both Plantation House and Young Island take advantage of their superb location in the Grenadines and offer sailaway packages to other islands and meals on board. A word of warning: don't take an overnight sailaway if you are not familiar with sailing – seasickness could ruin the honeymoon! This proviso aside, a sail to Mustique is worth it to see the island of the superstars and mingle with the rich.

THE COTTON HOUSE
(US ☎ 456-4777, 🖷 456-5887, 💻 www .cottonhouse.net) Mustique, St Vincent, West Indies
Reservations: toll-free in the US/Canada (☎ 877-240-9945) or through The Leading Hotels of the World toll-free numbers worldwide (see p12) or UK tour operators Caribbean Connection, Elegant Resorts
Getting there: Fifty-minute daily flights from Barbados to Mustique with private charter company SVG Air (book through the hotel); Mustique Airways or Trans Island Air (TIA) for US$280 per person round trip; complimentary 5-minute transfer to the hotel
Accommodation: 16 rooms, 4 suites
Amenities: One formal restaurant, pool café, boutique, spa with massage and aromatherapy; hotel car and driver; two tennis courts, swimming pool; complimentary watersports snorkelling, kayaking, windsurfing, except scuba diving; horse-riding, catamaran excursions to neighbouring islands and fishing at additional cost; golf nearby
Dress code: Elegantly casual
Weddings: Weddings arranged in the picturesque grounds overlooking the Caribbean for £727; receptions for up to 12 people
Minimum stay: Usually five nights – a minimum for weddings
Rates: Grenadine cottages from US$530 to US$1250 per couple for an ocean-front suite in high season, half board; honeymoon package includes five nights in an Ocean Front Master Room or De Luxe Suite half-board with VIP welcome tray, champagne on arrival, a body massage each and two days' jeep rental for US$3650; all rates include à la carte breakfast and dinner, afternoon tea, cocktail party, non-motorized watersports, minibar soft drinks, unpacking and pressing service upon arrival
Credit cards: Most major
Taxes and service charge: 10% service charge and 7% government tax

---

MUSTIQUE

Located in the unspoilt region of St Vincent and the Grenadines, Mustique is a secluded 1400-acre private island retreat of barefoot luxury popular with the jetset and a peaceful setting where one can rest, recuperate and indulge on the many heavenly beaches. Britannia Bay is the focal point of the island and home to the famous Basil's Bar & Restaurant (where you may find the likes of Mick Jagger at the next-door table).

The Cotton House

Originally an 18th-century coral warehouse and sugar mill, the Cotton House was carefully restored by the talented British theatrical designer, Oliver Messel, and transformed into an intimate, refined, plantation-style retreat in 13 acres of beautiful, unspoilt surroundings. The hotel is close to two beaches – 200 metres from the Atlantic and 30 metres from the Caribbean Sea. Mustique is simply one of the most exclusive private islands in the Caribbean and this is the island's only full-service hotel so, unsurprisingly, it has long attracted the well-heeled traveller, celebrities and royalty.

Owned and managed by Parisian-based GLA International, the little details are taken care of at Cotton House. When you arrive you can relax on your private patio while your clothes are unpacked and pressed, make a leisurely choice from the pillow menu which includes everything from goose down to latex and then head for an aromatherapy pick-me-up massage in the mini-spa.

The 20 rooms hint at a graceful past with their antiques, louvred doors and elegant furnishings.You have a choice of whether to stay in the Cotton House or the Coutinot

House, steps from the ocean. Elegant De Luxe Suites in the Cotton House have private sitting rooms, king-sized beds, raised tubs and individual terraces with garden and island views; Messel rooms nestled on the hillside have large private wrap-around verandas or corner terraces for dining alfresco. Grenadine Cottages, seconds away from the swimming pool, are the most private, with their own entrance and some have partial ocean views from the balcony. All the air-conditioned rooms are stocked with books and magazines from the hotel's library and luxuries including a complimentary minibar where you can sample the local rum, CD player, hairdryer, fluffy bathrobes and Contemporel toiletries.

Most people opt for a room in the beautiful Coutinot House, which even has a stunning suite in the Historic Tower. All of the five rooms have large terraces with spectacular ocean views, bathrooms have separate shower and bathtub, a Balinese-style writing desk, armoire and full dressing room and wrought-iron four-poster bed draped with mosquito netting.

All watersports except scuba diving are complimentary and private sailing charters can be arranged. Horse-riding and tennis are on offer along with nature hikes and beach strolls. Although you can opt for the hotel's private driver to take you around the island to gaze at the fantastic villas, renting a mule (motorized buggy) or jeep is a fun way to get around, stopping off for a beach picnic and at the famous Basil's Bar.

Hors d'oeuvres and champagne are served at the weekly cocktail party in the aptly named Great Room, the heart of the house, where the chances of meeting a celebrity or two are high. Traditional afternoon teas are served on its veranda and so are the memorable candlelit dinners prepared by the French chef. The Cotton House is a peaceful and relaxing, highly civilized yet informal spot to drink in the magic of glorious Mustique.

TRINIDAD AND TOBAGO

Located right at the southern end of the Caribbean chain of islands, just off the north-eastern coast of Venezuela, Trinidad and Tobago, although politically related, couldn't be more different.

Trinidad is a large, lively island, where the capital Port of Spain, is much more commercialized and cosmopolitan than the capitals of most of its Caribbean neighbours. **Tobago**, on the other hand, is totally laid-back: the numerous deserted sandy beaches along its rugged coastline make it the perfect place to unwind after a wedding. It's an unsophisticated island which, unlike many of its neighbours, is relatively untouched by tourism. Instead, peace and harmony reign, making it the best choice for couples in search of the 'real' Caribbean.

THINGS TO SEE AND DO AROUND TOBAGO

Pigeon Point, the beach on all of Tobago's post-cards where the water is bright turquoise, is a great place to watch the sun go down from the pier, armed with the ubiquitous rum punch, while nearby **Turtle Beach** is also worth a look.

Some of Tobago's most isolated and perfect beach coves can be found from the coastal road on the island's northern shore, so make sure you hire a car and find your very own private beach.

A drive through the island's densely jungled interior is also a must, taking you through rickety shanty towns where men sit all day at the side of the road waiting for nothing in particular.

If you want to experience a taste of local nightlife, then head down to **Buccoo Bay** for a bit of 'Sunday School' – the name given to the all-night party every Sunday.

There will be very few tourists there, but it's a real piece of Tobagan life, with the air heavy with the smell of marijuana, jerk chicken on the barbecue and popcorn. The music is loud, and mostly a mix of reggae and soca – a blend of reggae and calypso native to Trinidad and Tobago.

For further information visit 🖳 www.visit-tnt.com

Blue Waters Inn

It's worth going to the north of Tobago, not just for the beaches, but to stay at Blue Waters Inn. Located at Speyside, this lovely moderately-priced hotel has a really personal character.

This is one of the world's most classic hotels, not because it's big and flashy or even over the top in the luxury stakes, but somehow it has a magical feel that you'll always remember. It will appeal particularly to British couples who will appreciate the understated tone and the family-like atmosphere. When we stayed there one Christmas we ended up mixing our own cocktails from behind the bar and raiding the fridge late at night to make cranberry and turkey sandwiches. If that makes you think, 'Well, why didn't room service make them for you?' then the Blue Waters isn't for you.

The hotel is situated in one of the most beautiful bays in Tobago, well away from the island's main tourist area in the south. There is a superb beach and a PADI diving school which takes guests out to the numerous nearby dive sites to see incredible coral corridors, as well as manta rays at the right time of year.

BLUE WATERS INN
(☎ 660 4341, 🖷 660 5195, 🖳 bwi@blue-watersinn.com), Batteaux Bay, Speyside, Tobago, West Indies
Reservations: Through US tour operators Caligo or Into the Blue; UK tour operator Hayes & Jarvis or Harlequin (see pp9-10)
Getting there: Transfers can be arranged, airport taxi costs US$40 one way
Accommodation: 38 rooms, including three bungalows with full kitchens, four self-catering units, 31 standard rooms, all with ceiling fans, balconies/porches
Amenities: Scuba diving, kayaking, windsurfing, basketball, boat trips, health club, tennis, deep-sea fishing, bird sanctuary and hiking tours, car rental, restaurant, bar, recreation/TV room
Dress code: Informal/casual
Weddings: Can be arranged, price depends upon requirements
Minimum stay: None
Rates: Standard double from US$90, self catering from US$130, bungalows from US$205
Credit cards: Most major
Taxes and service charge: Included

JAMAICA

Strawberry Hill

Strawberry Hill, nestled high up in Jamaica's **Blue Mountains**, is the perfect colonial retreat. This wonderfully romantic hotel is the most idyllic place to unwind after a long flight and a hectic wedding, before moving on to a beach resort for a little more action once you are ready for it.

STRAWBERRY HILL
(☎ 944 8400, 🖷 944 8408, 🖳 www.islandoutpost.com), Irishtown, Jamaica
Reservations: UK Island Outpost (☎ 020-7440 4360); USA/Canada toll-free (US ☎ 800-OUTPOST), 🖳 ukreservations@islandoutpost.com; or through UK tour operator Caribbean Connection (see p10)
Getting there: Car transfers from Norman Manley International Airport to Strawberry Hill (about 50 minutes) are US$40 one way for two passengers; helicopter transfers from the airport to Strawberry Hill are US$600 one way for up to four passengers
Accommodation: 12 Georgian-style cottages ranging from studio suites to three-bedroom suites
Amenities: High tea and Sunday brunch, new-Jamaican cuisine served all day in gourmet restaurant, bar, room service, freshwater negative-edge swimming pool, Aveda spa with plunge pool and sauna; fitness room featuring Nautilus equipment, travel desk, library/games room and gift shop
Dress code: No jackets required
Weddings: Beautiful sweeping lawns with awesome views are ideal for tailor-made weddings or functions for up to 200 people; contact Island Outpost for further information
Minimum stay: None
Rates: Rooms from US$325 to US$775; five-night honeymoon packages from US$2500
Credit cards: Most major
Taxes and service charge: Rates include taxes, but do not include 10% service charge

You know you are in for a treat as you approach Strawberry Hill – either by land cruiser or helicopter – climbing up through the Blue Mountains to one of the most magnificent natural settings on earth.

The dozen or so private Georgian-style cottages for guests are built entirely of Jamaican wood and furnished simply but elegantly with canopied four-poster beds and tiled baths. As part of Chris Blackwell's Island Outpost chain they are filled with the kind of tiny details which make his hotels so special, such as hand-carved island antiques and the solid colonial comfort of the mahogany four-poster.

Each villa has its own kitchen with coffee and tea maker and refrigerator stocked with wine, beer and sodas, CD players with a selection of CDs, TV and video, goosedown bedding with heated mattress pads (to provide warmth on cool mountain nights), bathrobes, beach towels and Aveda toiletries in the bathroom. They also have a parlour and, best of all, a private veranda so you can enjoy the breathtaking views across the mountains. Bird's Hill is the best choice for honeymooners as it comes with its very own garden and latticework gazebo that houses a private Jacuzzi – the ideal place from which to sip champagne at sunset and watch the lights go on in **Kingston Town**.

A dizzying view of Kingston over 3000 feet below can also be had from the negative-edge swimming pool, and the resort offers the Caribbean's only full-service Aveda Spa for some first-class pampering. Strawberry Hill offers some great tours of the island including a visit to the **Old Tavern Blue Mountain** coffee estate, as well as mountain hikes after which you are rewarded with cocktails at the wonderful **Gap Café**, and guided walks through **Spanish Town**, Jamaica's original capital. But perhaps best of all is the Kingston Night-life tour which stops off at all the dance hot-spots for a real taste of the legendary Jamaican night-life.

Should you want to get married at Strawberry Hill, the staff are incredibly helpful and will arrange almost anything you want.

Round Hill

Situated on a 100-acre plantation that once grew pineapples, allspice and coconuts, a cascade of pastel tropical flowers and stately palms now announces the elegant, glamorous island resort of Round Hill. With a private, reef-enclosed beach, its peaceful ambience makes it hard to believe that this was once the playground of Noel Coward and Clark Gable. 'Like a cashmere sweater,' say the owners, 'Round Hill is exquisite to experience but not the least bit showy'. This romantic hideaway still attracts the world's famous faces.

The graceful colonial-style hotel, just steps away from the freshwater swimming pool and private beach, houses just 36 superior and de luxe rooms with Ralph Lauren-designed interior. All have large louvered shutters folding back to give fabulous ocean views, private bathrooms with bath and

---

ROUND HILL
(☎ 876-952 5150, toll-free in the US ☎ 800-330-8272, 🖹 876-952 2505) PO Box 64, Montego Bay, Jamaica
Reservations: Direct or in the UK through Carrier (☎ 01625-547020)
Getting there: Transfers can be arranged from Montego Bay and Sangsters International Airport, 12 kilometres or 25 minutes' drive east
Accommodation: 36 superior and de luxe rooms in the Pineapple House, 27 private villas with 65 suites, 20 with private pool
Amenities: Terrace restaurant serving international and Jamaican cuisine; Ralph Lauren cocktail bar, private beach, freshwater swimming pool, five tennis courts (two floodlit), fitness centre, nearby golf course, boutique, wellness centre with aromatherapy treatments, massage, sailboats, paddleboats, water-skiing, snorkelling, PADI dive centre, yachts for charter
Dress code: Dress for dinner
Weddings: Wedding packages from US$750
Minimum stay: 3 nights
Rates: For three nights, superior oceanfront rooms cost from US$389; a two-bedroom villa, US$716, with pool, US$929; ask about the honeymoon package which includes lots of extras for US$110 more per person
Credit cards: Most major
Taxes and service charge: Included

shower, telephones, refrigerators, umbrellas (!), bathrobes, coffee machines and hairdryers; 20 have king-sized beds. If you want to wake up to the aroma of your private cook preparing Blue Mountain coffee and a traditional Jamaican breakfast, and laze around a private or shared pool all day, one of the 27 private villas that dot the lush hillside is the place to be pampered in style. With a staff of 220, there is someone to cater to your every whim. Indulge in a massage in your villa and then call up for a golf cart to take you the short distance to the beach.

Days are usually spent around the private beach where there's PADI diving and excellent snorkelling among the usual watersports on offer. Yachts are available for charter, and there are five tennis courts (two lit for evening play), nearby golf and a Wellness centre. Nights are casually elegant: pre-dinner drinks are taken in the Ralph Lauren Cocktail Bar and delicious dishes such as fresh lobster Jamaican-style are served on the terrace. Nightly entertainment includes dinner dances, beach bonfire picnics and folk music beneath the stars.

Other recommended hotels

Jamaica Inn (☎ 974 2514, 🖹 974 2449, US toll-free ☎ 877-470-6975, 🖳 www.jamaicainn.com, PO Box 1, Ocho Rios, St Ann) has long been one of the Caribbean's best loved hotels. This elegant hotel occupies a pretty private bay with a fabulous beach protected on either side by small headlands. If you're looking for refined colonial charm and a place to gracefully drift through the days, this is it. It's the sort of place where people really dress for dinner, some even wear black tie and there is nightly dancing to a small orchestra. Each of the 45 impeccable suites has its own colonnaded balcony looking out to sea. Double superior balcony suites start from US$300, premier veranda suites on the beach start from US$420 in low season; rates include breakfast, candlelit dinner, tax and service. The six-night wedding package costs US$1615 per person.

   Goldeneye (☎ 975 3354, 🖹 975 3620, 🖳 www.islandoutpost.com, Oracabessa, Jamaica) is a magical 17-acre retreat nestled among tropical forests and lush gardens on a high bluff overlooking the Caribbean Sea. This is the former home and hideaway of James Bond novelist Ian Fleming, who spent nearly 20 winters at this idyllic spot penning 14 of his famous 007 thrillers. It has been transformed as a Chris Blackwell resort and stamped with his informal style, providing simple luxury and casual comfort in an idyllic setting: Oracabessa is a small port on Jamaica's northern coast, approximately 15 minutes east of Ocho Rios. Doubles cost from US$600 including all meals, alcoholic beverages, 30-minute complimentary jet-ski ride, tax and service charge. Book through Island Outpost, UK (☎ 020-7440 4360); USA/Canada (toll-free ☎ 800-OUTPOST); 🖳 ukreservations@islandoutpost.com or through tour operators Abercrombie & Kent (see p10).

   For a wonderfully well-priced alternative spend a few days seeing 'real' Jamaica at **Jake's Place** (☎ 965 3145, 🖹 965 0552, Treasure Beach, Calabash PO, Saint Elizabeth). Part of the Chris Blackwell (founder of Island Records) Island Outpost chain, this wonderful little hotel has bags of character and if you are into Jamaican culture it has to be the perfect place to stay. The Blackwell signature colours are there, with bedrooms colour-washed in fantastic shades of cinnamon, cobalt and jade, and the kind of incredible attention to detail that makes his hotels so special, but at the same time everything has been kept very simple with corrugated roofs over huts that look more like Jamaican rum shacks than hotel rooms. Jake's is where celebrities such as Kate Moss choose to come and play at being nobodies, so you never know who may be sitting next to you at the evenings' entertainment. The most astonishing thing about Jake's is its price, with rooms costing only US$95 a night. Book direct or through Island Outpost: UK (☎ 020-7440 4360), USA/Canada (toll-free ☎ 800-OUTPOST) or 🖳 www.islandoutpost.com.

Cuba
(BEST TIME TO GO: DECEMBER TO APRIL)

Cuba has all the attractions of the Caribbean: beautiful beaches with plenty of water-sports, a relaxed culture, and rum – in the *mojito*, a cocktail invented by Hemingway – but it is still a bit different as a honeymoon destination. Don't expect wonderful hotels and fabulous food – five star may be adequate but doesn't mean beautiful or tasty. But the fascinating, unselfconscious culture preserved in a fifty-year time warp and the best music in the region played live on every street corner more than make up for it. And

The beaches in Cuba are as good as anywhere and there's Cuba's culture on your doorstep if you want it. What we found fascinating about a honeymoon in Cuba was stepping into a real time warp. There isn't any other place in the world you can do that.
Edward and Ariane Thompson

what's more, being slightly alternative Caribbean, Cuba is extremely good value as a honeymoon. The year 2000 saw the previously bureaucratic marriage laws relaxed – you can now get married with just a photocopy of your passport.

As a rule of thumb, opt for hotels owned by Habaguanex, whose boutique hotels in Havana are the most romantic in Cuba, and the Sol Melia Group which owns hotels throughout the rest of the island. Sol Melia (🖳 www.solmelia.es) offers special treatment to honeymooners such as fruit baskets, room upgrade, a romantic dinner etc.

Cuba is not a place to book direct – go with specialist tour operator Havanatour UK (☎ 01707-646 463), Belgium (☎ 627 4990); Germany (☎ 30-853 7041); Paris (☎ 1-44 51 50 884); Canada (☎ 1514-522-6868); Italy (☎ 02-669 82858); Australia (☎ 3-9614 7144); South Africa (☎ 11-770 7881); 🖳 sales@havanatour.co.uk – the largest, with its own ground handling company and legal firm for weddings, or UK specialist tour operators Captivating Cuba (☎ 01202-743 907, 🖳 www.worldwideholidays.co.uk) or the Cuba Experience (☎ 020-7431 0670, 🖳 www.theholidayplace.co.uk), who can all tailor make itineraries for you.

CUBA
Idyllic beaches, rum and fabulous music, with mountains and forests to explore and lashings of culture
When to go: December to April; January and April are sunniest, avoid the hurricane season from June to November
Average maximum temperatures °C

JAN	FEB	MAR	APR	MAY	JUN	JUL	AUG	SEP	OCT	NOV	DEC
22	22	23	25	26	27	28	28	27	26	24	23

Capital: Havana
Approximate flight times: to Havana from:
                London (see below): 10 hours
                Sydney/Melbourne: (via LA and Cancun) 26 hours
                LA (via Mexico): 4 hours
Note: From the UK it is best to opt for Air France (with a romantic night in Paris?) or Iberia via Madrid. Americans can go to Cuba, but cannot fly directly
Approximate exchange rates: Cuban peso is the official currency but US dollars are accepted/demanded everywhere. US$1 = 20 peso. American Express travellers' cheques are not accepted.
Time difference: GMT minus five hours
Voltage: 110V/220V in large hotels
Combine with: Other Caribbean destinations; South/Central America
Country dialling code: ☎ 53
Further information: Cuba Tourist Board: UK (☎ 020-7240 6655, 📄 020-7836 9265, 🖳 www.cubaweb.cu)

THINGS TO SEE AND DO IN CUBA

Most scheduled flights arrive in Cuba's crumbling but stunning capital, Havana, although charter flights go to certain resorts. From here, you can fly around the island or hire a 1950s car for around US$50 a day to drive around the island.

Flop on a beautiful island beach resort such as **Cayo Coco**, staying at the *Melia Cayo Coco* (☎ 3-30 1180) for a few days, doubles cost from US$145/£102 per couple all-inclusive, and then head south to soak up some culture in the historic city of **Trinidad**. A new and better hotel, the four-star *Brisas Trinidad* (☎ 4-19 6500), opened in mid-2001; doubles there cost from US$97/£68 all-inclusive.

For less tranquil beaches but with a more Cuban flavour, stay at the ornate *Melia Rio D'Oro* (☎ 2-43 0090), at Esmeralda Beach near **Holguin**, for US$139/£98 all-inclusive, where as well as indented bays you have rolling hills and woodland to explore in addition to the nearby **Sierra Maestra** mountain range and the music capital of **Santiago de Cuba**.

Three hours' drive west of Havana is the nature reserve of the **Pinar Del Rio** where the mist hovers over strange mogote rock formations – found in only two other places in the world.

For a hotel with a view, it's hard to beat the three-star, colonial-style *Los Jasmines* (☎ 8-93 6205) where doubles start from US$40/£28 with breakfast. En route stop at the secluded eco-tourism project of **Las Terrazas** in the forested hills of the Sierra del Rosario, and if you want to stay the pretty *Hotel La Moka* (☎ 8-52 2996) is very different from anything else you'll find in Cuba; doubles cost from US$68/£48 with breakfast. A tree grows through the middle of the hotel giving it the flavour of a safari lodge and rooms have a balcony garden outside the bathroom window. The pool is pristine and set among the forest where there is plenty of opportunity for hiking and horseriding. Food however, is a bit limited in variety.

Outside Havana most hotels are all-inclusives – you'll see why once you've eaten in a few restaurants.

Hotel Santa Isabel

Formerly the Count of Santovenia's palace, the five-star Hotel Santa Isabel is undoubtedly the most romantic hotel in Cuba. A typical three-storey Cuban Palace with pink stone walls, its entrance hidden behind a row of elegant arches, the Santa Isabel is stylish and exclusive. Tucked into the Plaza des Armas in Old Havana, you couldn't ask for a better location. From the terrace, where there is a bar and à la carte restaurant, you can see Old Havana's baroque buildings and the bay with its imposing fortresses. The streets, bars and restaurants in the squares around you are alive with music, and Obispo, the main shopping street, is right next door. The Plaza des Armas is quiet by day and is filled with a collection of ramshackle, bookstalls selling second-hand treaties of the revolution.

A hotel since 1867, it has seen many a ship fitter, merchant, artist and scientist walk through its heavy wooden, brass-fitted doors. Santa Isabel has kept its original elegance, comfort and splendour; staying within these walls is like taking a trip through Cuba's history, art, architecture and culture. The hotel is decorated with original art from some of Cuba's best artists, and although elegant, the wine-coloured sofas and heavy wooden furniture give it the atmosphere of a genteel home.

HOTEL SANTA ISABEL
(☎ 7-61 6423, 🖷 7-60 5628) Calle Baratillo No 9, Plaza de Armas, La Habana Vieja, Cuba
Reservations: UK specialist tour operators such as Havanatour (see p43)
Getting there: Tour companies can arrange private transfer from Havana airport, including being picked up in an American car.
Accommodation: 27 rooms: 17 rooms and 10 suites
Amenities: Three bars, a la carte terrace restaurant, tourism desk, boutique, laundry, pressing service, room service, parking, car rental
Dress code: Smart casual
Weddings: No
Minimum stay: None
Rates: Standard doubles from US$142/£100; Santovenia suite from US$199/£140 per couple, with breakfast.
Credit cards: Most major, none with American connections such as American Express
Taxes and service charge: Included

The Santa Isabel has just 27 rooms, ten of these suites with their own small living area, and you need to book early to stay here. The rooms are equipped with all mod cons: air conditioning, satellite TV, telephone, safe, minibar. The Santovenia suite is definitely the most romantic with its four-poster bed, beautiful antique furniture and balcony overlooking the Plaza des Armas. The hotel has a tourism desk and can arrange car rental, and after looking at the little there is to buy in Cuba, you may be pleased to know it has a boutique.

With a warm welcome on arrival, the Santa Isabel prides itself on its personalized service. 'The main purpose of the team is to earn the satisfaction of a smile from its clients'. It won't be difficult here.

Other recommended hotels

The four-star **Hotel Florida** (☎ 7-62 4127, ▤ 7-62 4117) is an 18th-century noble mansion that's also bang in the centre of Old Havana; with its majestic, palatial air and just 25 rooms, it is a good second choice if you can't get into the Hotel Santa Isabel. Doubles cost from US$85/£60 per couple including breakfast.

Hotel Nacional (☎ 7-33 3564), once owned by 'Lucky' Luciano of mafia fame, is Cuba's best-known hotel and its 1930s extravagance has to be seen to be believed. Imposing is the word that springs to mind. The Nacional is a bit out of the action in a modern part of town and is large, with 470 rooms. Set in spacious grounds and right on the coast, it has stupendous views over the Malecon and out to sea, as well as good facilities including two generously-proportioned swimming pools. Go for a cocktail at least, and soak up the atmosphere. Doubles cost from US$128/£90 per couple including breakfast.

The lavish **Parque Central** (☎ 7-66 6627) is the best choice if you want modern, international standards and good facilities, but also want to be in the centre of Old Havana. Owned by Golden Tulip, the hotel has a wonderful rooftop swimming pool, whirlpool and fitness centre, four bars and two restaurants and a snack bar to choose from. The 278 rooms have all the modern luxuries including separate bath and shower. Doubles cost from US$114/£80, suites up to US$213/£150 per couple including breakfast.

The Bahamas
(BEST TIME: DECEMBER TO JUNE)

Pink Sands

The very best thing about this hotel, as its name suggests, is the beach itself, which honestly does have a pink hue to it. Condé Nast *Traveller* was so impressed that it pronounced Pink Sands 'quite possibly the finest beach in the world'.

Pink Sands weds the traditions of the past with the most modern amenities and services. Part of rock promoter Chris Blackwell's Island Outpost chain, Pink Sands has

---

THE BAHAMAS
Offers the whole spectrum of honeymoon experience from the cosmopolitan to quiet and has approximately 700 islands, pristine beaches, casinos, historic landmarks, water sports and coral reefs
Average maximum temperatures °C

JAN	FEB	MAR	APR	MAY	JUN	JUL	AUG	SEP	OCT	NOV	DEC
25	25	26	27	29	30	31	31	31	29	27	25

Approximate exchange rate: Bahamas dollars (BS) – £1 = BS$1.42, US$1 = BS$1, A$1 = BS$0.52
Country dialling code: ☎ 1-242
Further information: ▭ www.bahamas.org has a honeymoon section

PINK SANDS
(☎ 333 2030, 🖷 333 2060, 💻 www.is landoutpost.com), Harbour Island, Bahamas
Reservations: UK Island Outpost (UK ☎ 020-7440 4360; USA/Canada toll-free ☎ 800-OUTPOST) or 💻 ukreservations@ islandoutpost.com; and specialist Caribbean tour operators (see p10)
Getting there: Fly from Miami to North Eleuthera where taxis can take you to the dock for a 5-minute ferry ride to Harbour Island and another taxi to the resort; transfer takes a total of 20 minutes and costs approximately US$20
Accommodation: 25 units: 21 one-bedrooms and 4 two-bedrooms
Amenities: Freshwater pool and a three-mile stretch of private pink-sand beach, beach restaurant and bar, three tennis courts (one floodlit), exercise studio, gift shop, library, videos for rental, library with state-of-the art audiovisual equipment; activities arranged include deep-sea fishing, snorkelling, scuba diving, jet skiing, sunset cruise, picnics to neighbouring islands
Dress code: No jacket required
Weddings: Tailor-made weddings and receptions for up to 60/65 people can be arranged, couples need to be resident for three days prior to their wedding; from July to September Pink Sands runs Wedding Packages
Minimum stay: Three nights
Rates: Doubles from US$500 including breakfast and 4-course dinner; honeymoon packages start at US$2688, five-night stay, champagne on arrival, one-day golf-cart rental, half board, Island Outpost CD, Bohemian basket, two Pink Sands T-shirts, and tax and service charges
Credit cards: Most major
Taxes and service charge: 20% government tax and service charge

long been a well-kept secret and has become a celebrity hideaway hosting such names as Keith Richards, Julia Roberts, Susan Sarandon, Tim Robbins and Robin Williams.

Situated on small, picture-perfect Harbour Island are 25 cottages set among tropical gardens, overlooking the spectacular 5km beach. This is the Bahamas at its most charming; **Dunmore Town** even has a preservation order on it, it's such a fine example of old Caribbean culture.

All meals are provided in the main alfresco garden dining area, where teak furniture and private candlelit corners create the perfect setting for an intimate dining experience; an à la carte lunch is also offered at the beach-side restaurant and bar. The restaurant, reception, library and pool table are all found in the main hotel building set around a small lily pond.

The décor is true Island Outpost style, with imaginative use of colour, exquisitely elegant and the bedrooms are really comfortable. This is the perfect place to do nothing in, or if you feel the urge to get active you can jump on one of the windsurfers or hobie cats.

Ocean Club

Resting between miles of exquisite white sand beach and Versailles-inspired gardens lush with brilliant hibiscus and fragrant bougainvillaea and scattered with elegant statues, Ocean Club is made for romance.

A legendary hideaway for royals and A-list celebrities – Cindy Crawford got married here – this is simply one of the most exclusive and gracious hotels in the Caribbean. Champagne greets you on arrival and delicious treats await you in your room each evening; room service is thrice daily and a personal butler takes care of you 24 hours a day, whether to prepare the Jacuzzi or to bring refreshments to the beach.

As sister hotel to the renowned Le Saint Géran in Mauritius, Sun International has carried out a spectacular US$100 million refurbishment and extension to restore Ocean Club to its former glory. Fifty spacious new beachside rooms and luxury suites have been added, all housed in the two-storey Crescent Wing. Each has a private terrace just steps from the pristine sand and magnificent ocean views. The original Hartford Wing and two-bedroom villas have been restored to their full grandeur.

Contemporary luxury define the rooms at the Ocean Club. They all reflect an elegant island décor with European antique reproduction furniture, rich fabrics and marble, with hand-painted stencils giving definition to the soft pastel colours. Superior garden view and de luxe ocean view rooms have a large patio or balcony, sitting area, ceiling fan and large marble bathroom. The luxury beachfront rooms are even bigger. The rooms have a king-size bed, some have a chaise longue, and all have mod cons: air conditioning, minibar, safe, telephone, satellite TV, video player, CD player and Internet access.

The à la carte **Dune Restaurant** has added a hip dimension to dining which is very much a focus here. It's difficult to not be enticed by the menu featuring a mélange of dishes from chef Jean-Georges Vongerichten's trendy New York restaurants, served from an open kitchen against a backdrop of sand and sea.

The Courtyard Terrace restaurant is gently romantic with tables set around a tranquil fountain and palm trees swaying in the breeze. Here, you can dine alfresco on Bahamian and classic French cuisine, and sample something from one of the most extensive wine lists in the Caribbean. For rustic charm, the Clubhouse and Beach Bar and Grill serve Mediterranean dishes. Breakfast can of course be served on your private balcony or patio.

Days are spent relaxing around the pool or on the beautiful beach. Watersports including windsurfing, aquacat sailing, scuba diving, kayaking and snorkelling are available from sunrise until sunset, with golf on a championship course nearby. After sampling the first-class tennis and fitness facilities too, you'll be ready to appreciate the great new spa. The Ocean Club is deservedly on the island named 'Paradise'.

OCEAN CLUB
(☎ 363 2501, 🖷 363 2424) PO Box N-4777, Paradise Island, New Providence (Nassau), Bahamas
Reservations: Direct or in the UK through Discover the Bahamas (see p10)
Getting there: 35-minute drive from Nassau International Airport; private car and limo transfers are available on request
Accommodation: 108 rooms: 89 rooms, 14 suites, 5 villas
Amenities: 3 restaurants, including the new beachfront à la carte Dune Restaurant and two bars, a beach bar, oceanside Tom Weiskopf-designed 18-hole championship golf course nearby, state-of-the-art health and beauty spa, nine floodlit tennis courts, fitness room, swimming pool, bicycles available, range of watersports (extra charge), library; guests also have full use of the facilities and casino at Atlantis Resort
Dress code: Casual during the day; smart in the evenings (no shorts or swimwear in formal restaurants)
Weddings: Ceremonies and receptions can be arranged, from the very simple to the elaborate, for any number of guests; the dramatic 14th-century French Cloisters overlooking Nassau Harbour is popular for ceremonies; private function rooms are available for receptions
Minimum stay: None – apart from Xmas and New Year
Rates: Doubles from US$415; suites from US$1130; seven nights for the price of six in de luxe and luxury rooms at certain times of the year
Taxes and service charge: Tax 12%, service charge 15%

Other recommended hotels

Hawks Nest Resort (☎ 342 7050, 🖷 342 7051) is a 400-acre paradise on the southern tip of Cat Island. Upmarket but low key, this is the place to kick off your shoes and be by yourselves. Fifty miles long and one mile wide, Cat Island is lush and green, with forests, rolling hills and mile upon mile of exquisite and peaceful deserted beaches edged with casuarina trees.

You can spend your days diving or snorkelling on the beautiful, shallow coral reefs, home to tropical fish, sea turtles and an occasional ray. There is also a new swimming pool, tennis courts, and complimentary use of kayaks, bicycles, snorkelling and golf carts to get around. There are even Pilates classes on offer. Nights are romantic; honeymooners are served a private, candlelit dinner under a gazebo on the beach.

Hawks Nest has ten ocean-front rooms decorated in soothing colours with fine linens, plush towels and elegant wicker furniture. It also has a fully-appointed house privately situated at the mouth of Hawks Nest creek. Hawks Nest Resort can be booked exclusively in the UK through Discover the Bahamas (☎ 01737-218 803, 🖳 www.discover-the-bahamas.co.uk). A 7-night holiday costs from US$1670/£1175 per person for an ocean-front double room, including flights with BA, overnight in Nassau (room only), return domestic flights to Cat Island, return transfers, all meals and non-alcoholic drinks.

Turks & Caicos
(BEST TIME: NOVEMBER TO EARLY JUNE)

Geographically part of the Bahamas, the Turks & Caicos are some of the last relatively unknown, quiet and unspoilt islands in the Caribbean. Nature lovers will adore these eight islands where iguanas roam and dolphins frolic in the surreal blue waters. While neither lush nor particularly tropical, their beauty lies in dazzling white sand beaches and the stunning blue of the ocean, and with 200 miles of reef, are rated among the world's top ten for divers. A trip here is easily combined with a week in the Bahamas, Florida and Jamaica, and direct flights with British Airways are now available from the UK. For general information, visit 💻 www.turksandcaicostourism.com.

Parrot Cay

Tucked away on its own 1000-acre island, the 60-room luxury resort of Parrot Cay is a peaceful, secluded sanctuary, and ideal for those looking to unwind in a blissfully natural Caribbean paradise. It opened in January 1999 as the creation of Christina Ong, owner of both the Metropolitan and the Halkin hotels in London, so understandably Parrot Cay is the ultimate in chic simplicity. This is a return to nature, with many hands quietly smoothing out the creases.

Keith Hobbs, who designed Nobu Restaurant and the Armani Store on Fifth Avenue, has taken elements of traditional colonial décor such as four-poster beds and brightened them with swathes of white fabric which makes them ooze exquisite comfort. Most rooms and suites are ocean-facing and from your wooden veranda you can smell the evening approaching – a blend of fresh cool salty air with wafts of simmering spices. One-bedroom beach-houses have plunge pools and all rooms are air conditioned with mod cons such as bath and shower, minibar, CD player, TV on request, phone, hairdryer, as well as a ceiling fan and tea/coffee maker.

As one of the rare unspoilt islands, Parrot Cay is an ideal place for nature walks and wildlife watching. The island's vegeta-

---

PARROT CAY
(☎ 649-946 7788, 📠 649-946 7789, 💻 www.parrot-cay.com), PO Box 164, Providenciales, Turks & Caicos Isles, British West Indies

Reservations: The Leading Hotels of the World reservation numbers worldwide (see p12), US toll-free (☎ 1-877-754-0726) or UK tour operators Elegant Resorts, Caribbean Connection (see p10)

Getting there: British Airways offer direct flights to Providenciales, alternatively there are two flights a day from Miami; staff pick you up in a luxury boat for the 30-minute ride to the resort

Accommodation: 60 rooms and suites

Amenities: Two restaurants (poolside and gourmet), in room dining; 5500 sq ft swimming pool, two floodlit tennis courts, Shambhala spa with juice and salad bar, gym, mountain bikes, nature trails, dive centre; excursions, hobie cats, windsurfing, snorkelling, canoes, water-skiing, golf (18-hole competition golf course on Providenciales); charter boats for various forms of fishing, island hopping and sightseeing; Calypso music, live steel band; laundry; gift shop

Dress code: Casual

Weddings: No

Minimum stay: None

Rates: De Luxe Garden Rooms from US$360; one-bedroom Ocean View Suites from US$850, Beach House with plunge pool from US$1200, all per couple with breakfast, transfers and use of non-motorized watersports; half board US$140 extra per couple

Credit cards: Most major

Taxes and service charge: 9% government tax and 10% service charge

---

(Opposite): Top: Pure white sand and blue waters: Antigua & Barbuda (see p32). **Bottom:** Ladera Resort, St Lucia (see p35).

tion of cactus groves, spreading mangroves and wetlands and its crystal waters make it a haven for kaleidoscopic marine life and birds including flamingos and ruby-throated hummingbirds. A library with large veranda is the place to read, rest and soak up the calming atmosphere in the afternoons.

As well as a good range of watersports on offer from the beach, Parrot Cay has a stunning infinity-edged pool, the largest in Turks & Caicos, overlooking the ocean. Other sports on offer include tennis, and activities such as scuba diving and fishing are easily arranged. For those who cannot resist 'going for the burn' there is a separate gym with state-of-the-art equipment.

The resort's restaurants offer delicious and nutritious dishes. In the day you can dine either alfresco on the beach, at the poolside grill or at the spa's juice and salad bar, and in the evening sample the delicacies of the gourmet restaurant.

A highlight of Parrot Cay is **Shambhala Spa**, where you can leave the world behind as you float into a blissful state on a Thai massage or a 'Caribbean Delight', and in pavilions so close to the water that you can hear nothing but the sand as it flows behind a retreating wave.

Hawaii
(BEST TIME: ALL YEAR ROUND)

Hawaii, the most isolated group of islands imaginable, is a string of eight islands located almost 3000 miles off the American coast. Because of its 'proximity' to California and Japan, most of Hawaii's visitors come from the sunshine state or elsewhere in North America and from Japan – fewer than 5% of visitors are from Europe – earning these naturally beautiful islands the reputation for being one big American (and now Japanese) holiday camp.

Over the years Hawaii has been a kingdom, a republic, a territory and it's now a state. These islands have wildly contrasting scenery from deserts and rainforests to snow and coral reefs: even the island's sandy beaches range from sugary white to red, green and even jet black.

HAWAII

America's most exotic state, Hawaii has a reputation for big glitzy resorts, but there are also some quiet hotels with long sandy beaches, as well as incredible rugged mountain interiors to explore

When to go: In general the islands have a warm balmy climate most of the year, but because temperatures vary from island to island check with your agent that you are going to the right place at the right time

Average maximum temperatures °C

JAN	FEB	MAR	APR	MAY	JUN	JUL	AUG	SEP	OCT	NOV	DEC
24	24	25	26	27	27	28	28	28	28	27	26

Capital: Honolulu on Oahu

Flight times: to Oahu from:
New York: 11 hours
LA: 5½ hours
London 16½ hours (via LA)
Sydney: 10 hours

Approximate exchange rates: US dollar (US$) – £1 = US$1.42, A$1 = US$0.52

Time difference: GMT minus 11 hours

Voltage: 110v AC, 60Hz – two-pin plugs

Combine with: Los Angeles or San Francisco; or go island hopping within Hawaii

Country dialling code: ☎ 1-808

Further information: www.hawaii.com

(Opposite) Top: Cocobay Resort, Antigua (see p33). **Bottom:** De luxe room, Curtain Bluff, Antigua (see p30).

Despite the increasing commercialization of the bigger islands, in particular **Oahu** and **Maui**, it is still possible to get away from it all and enjoy a dream honeymoon amongst magnificent scenery and incredible beaches, and stay in some impressive hotels.

FOUR SEASONS RESORT MAUI

(☎ 808-874-8000, 🖨 808-874-2222), 3900 Wailea Alanui, Wailea, Maui, HI 96753, Hawaii
Reservations: US (toll-free ☎ 1-800-332-3442); Canada (toll-free ☎ 1-800-268-6282); or through UK tour operator Elegant Resorts (UK ☎ 0870-909 5306)
Getting there: The hotel is 17 miles from Kahului Airport, airport transfers cost US$180 each way in the hotel's limousine
Accommodation: 380 guest rooms; 41 Four Seasons Executive Suites, 26 one-bedroom suites, four two-bedroom suites, the Ilima Suite, and the 5000 sq ft Maile Suite
Amenities: 24-hour room service, complimentary early arrival/late departure lounge, pool/beach attendants, Club Floor, beauty salon, use of Wailea Golf Club's three 18-hole championship courses, as well as nearby Makena and Silversword golf courses, use of Wailea Tennis Centre's 14 courts (three are floodlit), two floodlit tennis courts (on site), 40ft by 80ft formal pool with fountain and whirlpool spas, free-form pool with waterfall, snorkelling, scuba instruction available at the beach pavilion, putting green, volleyball, croquet lawn, complimentary use of on-site health club, power-walking, aquacise and aerobics classes, bicycles, sport-fishing, helicopter rides, horse-riding, one-day tours by boat or plane to other islands, running paths, complimentary transfer service between the hotel and the shops at Wailea and golf and tennis centres, Avis rental cars, several restaurants offering a wide range of dining options, shops
Dress code: Elegant casual
Weddings: Wedding ceremonies and receptions for up to 200 people can be held in an outdoor setting and up to 400 for an indoor wedding; wedding packages from US$3000 to US$14,000
Minimum stay: None
Rates: Doubles from US$310 to US$625; suites from US$585 to US$6200, ask about Romance for All Seasons (seven nights for US$4900 including lots of extras) and Romantic Interlude packages (three nights for US$1900 including some extras)
Credit cards: Most major
Taxes and service charge: 4.17% tax and 18% service charge

Getting to and around Hawaii

Both Aloha and Hawaiian Airlines offer frequent, daily jet services from island to island, with flights usually only taking a matter of 20 or 30 minutes.

On Oahu, Aloha's reservation number is ☎ 808-484-1111, while Hawaiian's is ☎ 808-838-1555. If you've always dreamed of having lunch on Lanai and Mai Tai cocktails on Maui, the Hawaiian Island Pass from Hawaiian Airlines is the thing for you. Passes provide unlimited travel for all Hawaiian islands (even the smaller ones that have traditionally been much harder to get to), and come in 5- to 14-day packages. Aloha offer a seven day island pass for US$321. From within the US, call Hawaiian Airlines on US toll-free ☎ 800-367-5320 or visit 🖳 www.hawaiianair.com, for Aloha call US toll-free ☎ 800-367-5250 or visit 🖳 www.alohaairlines.com.

Whichever island you are visiting, renting a car will provide you with the most freedom and mobility. All the major car rental firms operate in Hawaii and can be contacted through their respective toll-free central reservation numbers (see p14).

MAUI
Four Seasons Resort Maui

Four Seasons Maui is one of the world's most famous hotels. The very mention of it to anyone who has been there immediately seems to inspire a longing look. It's just that sort of place – once you've been there you'll dream about the ridiculous hedonism of the experience for years to come.

Where else are chilled face-cloths and Evian water sprays brought to you as you sunbathe; a computer-controlled fountain is even programmed to react to the strength of the trade winds so that the resort's precious guests don't ever get sprayed. This is one slick resort where only the best is available, and the clientele is wealthy enough not to worry about keeping an eye on the tab.

Situated on the largest and most beautiful of Wailea's white sand beaches and set in

THINGS TO SEE AND DO ON MAUI

Maui boasts 42 miles of beaches, ranging from little **Red Sand Beach** to the black sands of **Waianapanapa State Park**. With the beaches comes great snorkelling and diving, the best of which is to be found at **Honolua Bay** and the small islet of **Molokini**, a submerged crater. See 🖳 www.hawaii.com for a list of dive schools.

But there's more to Maui than golden sandy beaches. Known as the Magic Isle, Maui is a lush, mountainous island made up of deep valleys, forested mountains, grasslands, open plains and the world's largest dormant volcano, **Haleakala**. For viewing conditions telephone ☎ 808-871-5054.

The island is effectively split into two contrasting halves, one with the mountainous **Iao Valley** and the sheer **Iao Needle**, and the other dominated by the Haleakala Crater which rises a massive 10,023ft from sea level and over 16,000ft from the ocean floor.

You can drive from sea level to the summit in about an hour and a half, where you can look down on a lunar landscape 3000ft below and see **Science City**, an astronomical research centre where laser beams are bounced off the moon.

Designated a National Park, Haleakala is one of only two places in the world where the rare silversword plant grows, and there is a good network of trails for hiking or riding. There's no better time to see Mt Haleakala than at sunrise; arrange to take a breakfast picnic with you and wear some warm clothes. You may not relish the prospect of getting out of bed at around 3am in order to reach the summit in time, but you'll realize it was worth it when you get there.

On the other side of the island, in the **West Maui Mountains**, the towns and roads cling to the shoreline. This area is nice for hiking but the best way to see the spectacular waterfalls and the high walls of the volcano's often cloud-cloaked interior is by helicopter. For a helicopter tour call **Sunshine Helicopters** (☎ 808-871-0722). When you move to the dry, leeward side of the mountains you'll be rewarded with spectacular views over the islands of **Moloka'i**, **Lana'i**, **Kaho'olawe** and tiny crescent-shaped Molokini, sitting like droplets in the still blue ocean beyond. On a good day you can see the snow-capped tips of **Mauna Kea** and **Mauna Loa** on Big Island.

The channel between Maui and its neighbouring islands, where the water is calm and shallow, is the winter home of the humpback whales: they arrive every October from the Bering Sea to give birth to their young. The best way to see the whale close up is to join one of the whale-watching cruises running from **Maalaea** and **Lahaina** harbours.

The old whaling port of **Lahaina** is a living museum to Hawaiian history. Initially set-tled by Polynesians, Maui was an autonomous kingdom until Kamehameha I united all the Hawaiian islands and made Lahaina his capital, in 1802.

Missionaries and whaling men arrived soon afterwards and Maui was torn apart by these opposing forces. During the peak whaling year of 1846, more than 50 vessels at a time were anchored in the Lahaina roadstead.

Lahaina's tribute to whales is the **Hawaiian Islands Humpback Whale Sanctuary** (☎ 808-879-2818) at the Whalers Village Shopping Centre in **Kaanapali** (☎ 808-661-4567). By 1860, the civil war and the rise of the petroleum industry had brought the whaling era to an end. If you want to go whale watching, **Friendly Charters** (☎ 808-244-1979, 🖷 808-242-0890, US toll-free ☎ 1-888-983-8080) can take you.

Apart from the beautifully restored historic sites, Lahaina, with its richly coloured banyan wood architecture, features many great restaurants and lots of interesting curio shops.

In rural Maui, or Upcountry as the islanders call it, sugar cane and pineapple fields give way to cattle ranches, fields of flowers and picturesque farms. With its distinctly Old West ambience, charming shops, restaurants, bars and art galleries, **Makawao** lies in the heart of Upcountry. This is cowboy country: every year on 4 July cowboys and cowgirls from throughout the state gather for a two-day rodeo.

Hawaii may not be foremost in your mind as a wine-growing region, but it is worth popping along to the **Tedeschi Winery** on the 20,000-acre **Ulupalakua Ranch**. A tour of the ranch and tastings of the winery's champagne and unique pineapple wine are available from 9am to 5pm daily.

No trip to Maui would be complete without a visit to **Hana**. You can jet down there in no more than 15 minutes from Kahului Airport in a prop plane, but arguably more exhilarating is the 55-mile drive.

The road to Hana heads out of the north-shore town of **Paia**, curving past **Hookipa Beach Park** (known as the Aspen of wind surfing!), and then takes you along more than 600 hairpin bends eastward into East Maui's spectacular rainforests. The drive takes you past the most spectacular scenery: waterfalls plunge to create natural swimming pools; emerald green patchworks jut out into the sea below; the roads hang perilously to the cliff edge.

Hana itself is a place of sheer natural beauty: a huge round bay with black and red sand beaches, lush green pasture land and flowers in full bloom, and a totally unique atmosphere. Hana is definitely unmissable.

THINGS TO SEE AND DO ON HAWAII (BIG) ISLAND

Of all the Hawaiian islands, **Big Island** (as Hawaii Island is commonly known) boasts the most variety in terms of climate, terrain and scenery. It is an intriguing combination of mile upon mile of black lava and green meadows, cool misty rainforests and, of course, long golden sandy beaches. Twice the size of all the other Hawaiian islands combined, Big Island was formed 800,000 years ago by five volcanoes – Mauna Loa, Mauna Kea, Kilauea, Kohala and Hualalai. Today it spans over 4000 sq miles and is still growing.

The island is dominated by the peaks of two of these volcanoes, **Mauna Kea** and **Mauna Loa** which rise to nearly 14,000ft. Big Island's history is full of stories of Pele, the Fire Goddess whose home was in these mighty volcanoes. At the heart of **Hawaii Volcanoes National Park** (☎ 808-985-6000), is Kilauea where you can feel the rumbling energy of this vast mountain through your feet as you hike the many trails. Kilauea is the world's most active volcano, but is safe enough to be seen by over one million visitors annually. Even if you're not regular walkers, do go for a wander through the lacy tree fern forests, blooming ohia trees, barren craters and yellow sulphur banks; the scenery is mesmerizing. Just near the park headquarters is the **Volcanic Art Centre** filled with the works of local artists, craftsmen and photographers, which is worth a look.

Take **Saddle Road**, going west out of **Hilo**: the road bisects the interior of the island and leads to an access road that meanders skyward to the 13,796ft peak of Mauna Kea, though this is often shrouded in snow during the winter months.

North of Hilo, the **Hamakua Coast Highway** takes you through lush green valleys and the sleepy town of **Honokaa** to **Waipio**, nicknamed the Valley of the Kings, because it was a favourite retreat with Hawaiian royalty. If you want to explore the stunning Waipio Valley you'll either have to go in on foot, on horseback or rent a four-wheel drive.

On the island's west coast you'll find the seaside resort of **Kailua-Kona** where, along with the numerous shops, hotels and condos, acre upon acre of coffee plantations are found. Visitors are welcome at many of the farms, and are encouraged to take a self-guided tour and sample Kona's famous brew.

For old Hawaiian culture visit **Puu-honua o Honaunau**, a stone-enclosed sanctuary used as a safe haven for defeated warriors of victims of war years ago. Just down the road from Honaunau, Puuhonua o Honaunau, now administered as a National Park (☎ 808-328-2288), is a good place to see kapa pounding, lau hala weaving and traditional dance, and hear local music.

15 acres of gardens, the hotel is centred around an incredible array of swimming pools, fountains and Jacuzzis, and set amongst swaying palms. There are so many wonderful places to nestle down for the day that it's almost hard to choose between the grassy lawns, the loungers on the various pool sides, and, of course, the beach. There's also no shortage of guest activities: in usual Four Seasons' style, everything is here from a health spa, tennis courts and croquet, to snorkelling and diving instruction and the use of not one but three golf courses.

Covering a massive 600 sq ft each, the Four Season's 380 guest rooms are the largest in the Hawaiian Islands, all have large lanais (terraces) ideal for private sunbathing and alfresco meals, while 85% have ocean views. The large marble bathrooms have separate showers and lovely bathtubs, and all come with soft terry bathrobes and toiletries. You won't want for anything and if you do, it will quickly be arranged.

HAWAII ISLAND (BIG ISLAND)
Mauna Lani Bay Hotel and Bungalows

Mauna Lani Bay Hotel and Bungalows on Hawaii Island (also called Big Island) is another vast resort hotel which is always popular with honeymooners. Mauna Lani epitomises the best kind of self-contained resort, where its guests needn't leave its walls until they are refreshed enough to go home again. Its commitment to guests and the impeccable food and service are legendary among American resorts and it is Hawaii's only AAA Five Diamond Hotel.

Once the private estate of Frances I'i Brown, a descendant of Hawaiian royalty, this secluded coastal retreat was a refuge for King Kamehameha. Situated along 3$\frac{1}{2}$ miles of Big Island's rugged **Kohala** coastline, the setting is just magical. On one side there are prehistoric fish ponds, on the other the snow-capped peak of **Mauna Kea**.

The hotel offers a good variety of accommodation from garden view rooms to ocean-front suites, bungalows and villas. All are decked out in teak and cane with air conditioning, spacious lanais, king-size or double beds, remote TV/VCR, on-command movies, in-room safe, fridge, minibar, bathrobes and hairdryer, while the really decadent will head straight for the hotel's five bungalows.

The ultimate in luxury, the bungalows are on the ocean front and each is named after a Hawaiian flower. Discreetly screened away from other guests, they comprise 2700 sq ft of living space, with an additional 1300 sq ft of lanai where there is a private pool and a Jacuzzi. Each bungalow has two master bedrooms and bathrooms to match, with whirlpool baths and steam rooms overlooking private gardens. We're talking serious luxury at an initial cost of around US$2 million per bungalow, with a cool US$175,000 spent on the interior decorations alone!

Guests in the bungalows get their own 24-hour personal butler as well as a fully-equipped kitchen, though a private chef is also available so that you don't have to get your hands dirty. The list of goodies you can expect goes on and on: choice of cotton or satin linens, de luxe limo transfers, continental breakfast with fresh pastries and tropical fruits each day, full bar with cocktails, wines and sunset hors d'oeuvres. All of this with a million gallons of saltwater in lagoons full of tropical fish and the most staggering ocean views right on your door step – it doesn't come much better than that!

The two excellent golf courses, built on prehistoric lava flow, rank as some of the most challenging in the world. The **Mauna Lani Health Spa**, a swimming pool, 16 tennis courts, snorkelling and a variety of other amusements are available free to all guests as well as historic tours and special 'Hawaiian activities'. Sunset catamaran cruises can be arranged through the hotel. Morning coffee and newspapers are delivered to your room each day, along with breakfast if you wish – so that you can eat a long, lazy breakfast in the privacy of your lanai.

The Mauna Lani has always enjoyed a good reputation for its dining. The alfresco **Canoe House**, with its decked flooring and cane furniture, specializes in fresh local

---

MAUNA LANI BAY HOTEL AND BUNGALOWS
(☎ 808-885-6622, 🖷 808-885-1484, 🖳 reservations@maunalani.com), 68-1400 Mauna Lani Drive, Kohala Coast, HI 96743-9796, Island of Hawaii
Reservations: toll-free within the US (☎ 800-367-2323); Preferred Hotels & Resorts reservation numbers worldwide (see p12) or UK tour operator Elegant Resorts (☎ 0870-909 5306)
Getting there: Arrangements can be made at time of reservation for the 30-minute journey from the airport
Accommodation: 350 rooms, including 10 suites and five private bungalows
Amenities: Canoe House for casual, ocean-front dining with Pacific rim cuisine, Bay Terrace and the Beach Club for breakfast and dinner, Ocean Grill for casual poolside dining, Honu Bar, two championship golf courses, 16 tennis courts, garden, health spa, swimming pool, Jacuzzi, sauna, jogging trails, snorkelling, scuba diving, travel desk can arrange Catamaran cruises, shops, beauty salon, clinic, complimentary morning coffee and newspapers, Hawaiian activities, games and crafts, tropical flower arranging, historic tours
Dress code: Resort attire, jackets not required for dinner
Weddings: Ms Pinkie Crowe, the director of weddings and romance, is also a State Marriage License Agent and Notary Public and Wedding Consultant specializing in all wedding arrangements: packages from US$400 to US$1800 plus tax and gratuity, private dinners and receptions for two to 200 can be arranged
Minimum stay: None – but a minimum of three nights in the villas
Rates: Mountain view rooms from US$355; ocean view rooms from US$500; ocean-front suites start at around US$975; One-bedroom villas from US$550; bungalows from US$4400
Credit cards: Most major
Taxes and service charge: 11% tax

fish transformed into gourmet seafood dishes served on the ocean front by candlelight, while the serene and open-air **Bay Terrace** and the **Beach Club** both serve breakfasts and lunches. For a great alternative try the American cuisine with its distinctive Mediterranean twist at the **Gallery**, before heading to the **Honu Bar** for a little late night live music.

(French) Polynesia
(BEST TIME: MARCH TO NOVEMBER)

Some years ago my brother returned from months of sailing across the South Pacific declaring that he'd found the perfect place for his honeymoon – a stunning hotel in **Bora Bora** where the rooms were built on stilts hanging out over the turquoise waters. He showed me the photos and I was certainly convinced. He eventually chose Sark for his honeymoon and I went to Ireland, but we are both still firm believers that the thousands of islands in the South Pacific are indeed, paradise on earth.

French Polynesia comprises 130 islands divided into five archipelagos which constitute a French Overseas Territory. Of these the **Society Archipelago** is home to Tahiti, Moorea, Bora Bora and Huahine.

There is something quite magical about the Society Islands. They represent most people's blueprint for the perfect island, with an abundance of soft white sand, crystal clear waters in varying shades of brilliant blue, coral reefs and verdant interiors with majestic mountains. But they are quite different from other islands of the world such as the Seychelles, the Maldives and the Caribbean Islands: the difference lying essentially in their space – 130 islands spread out over a water mass the size of Western Europe – and their exotic inhabitants.

It was the people of French Polynesia who first captured the hearts of Robert Louis Stevenson, Somerset Maugham and Gaugin, all of whom managed to convey the native beauty and nobility in their work.

Bora Bora, with its immaculate powder-white sands and reef-protected lagoons, has received worldwide acclaim for the quality of its hotels. During July and August Bora Bora really comes alive for the **Heiva Festival**, an all-dancing, all-singing, all-drumming party that attracts people from all over South Polynesia.

But there is much more to French Polynesia than just Bora Bora and many visitors like to do a little island hopping, either by boat or plane as there are lots of inter-island flights. One general word of warning: because of high import tariffs French Polynesia is expensive and it is very difficult to have a really luxurious two-week honeymoon here for a great deal less than US$10,000 – probably another reason why these islands have stayed so magical!

FRENCH POLYNESIA

130 islands clustered in five archipelagos spread across an expanse of water the size of Western Europe

When to go: Avoid December, January and February

Average maximum temperatures °C

JAN	FEB	MAR	APR	MAY	JUN
32	32	32	32	31	30
JUL	AUG	SEP	OCT	NOV	DEC
30	30	30	31	31	31

Capital: Papeete on Tahiti

Flight times: to Papeete from:
New York: 16 hours
LA: 8¼ hours
London: 20 hours
Sydney: 9½ hours

Approximate exchange rates: Central Pacific Francs (CPF) – £1 = CPF189.75, US$1 = CPF133.33, A$1 = CPF69.19

Time difference: GMT minus 10 hours

Voltage: 110 or 220v AC, 50 Hz

Combine with: Perhaps combine one or two South Pacific Islands, or stop off en route in Sydney, Auckland, Hong Kong, Singapore or Los Angeles

Country dialling code: ☎ 689

Further information: 🖥 www.tahiti-tourisme.com

BORA BORA
Hotel Bora Bora

The 54 bungalows at Hotel Bora Bora boast the most exotic location of any hotel bedrooms anywhere in the world. Nestled on a palm-fringed promontory, with powder white beaches on either side spilling out into reef-protected lagoons, this incredible hotel is consistently rated among the world's finest. Owned by Amanresorts, a small chain of about a dozen incredible hotels, Hotel Bora Bora is just as amazing inside as the views are outside. When the Bora Bora Lagoon Resort first opened it gave Bora Bora's primary hotel a real run for its money, but a refurbishment has restored Hotel Bora Bora to its former glory and made it even more exclusive than it used to be.

The overwater bungalows, the first to be built on Bora Bora, provide a spacious bedroom, bathroom and split-level sun terraces shaded by a roof of hand-tied pandanus, with steps leading directly into the lagoon. The rooms are all decorated in trader-style. In the lovely white tiled and wood-panelled bathroom there is an elegant wood-trimmed Victorian tub, a separate shower, and a window with a wooden-slat blind looking onto the bedroom. The bedrooms are also wood-panelled, with large glass doors opening onto a balcony, so you can happily lie in bed gazing out at the lagoon beyond. The four-poster bed forms the focus of the bedroom, with its canopy of soft white muslin draped back at each corner, and soft glowing lamps either side of it.

HOTEL BORA BORA
(☎ 60 44 60, 📄 60 44 66, 💻 hotelborabora@amanresorts.com), Point Raititi, BP1, Bora Bora, French Polynesia
Reservations: Through Sterling Hotels and Resorts (see p12)
Getting there: Bora Bora Airport is 20 minutes away by complimentary private launch
Accommodation: 54 bungalows and farés (villas) including De Luxe Bungalows, Superior Bungalows, 15 Overwater Bungalows and eight farés with private pool, three farés with Jacuzzi and Premium farés
Amenities: Four restaurants and bars, lounge, boutique, floodlit tennis courts, watersports, snorkelling, sailing, jet skiing (extra charge), scuba diving, deep-sea fishing; yacht charters onboard catamaran, island tours in jeeps or on hired bikes, scooters or cars, helicopter tours, island picnics, parasailing, horse-riding, glass-bottom boat trips over the reef
Dress code: Smart casual
Weddings: Hotel Bora Bora offers couples a 'Marriage of Hearts', a non-binding, sentimental ceremony performed during a two-hour sunset catamaran cruise with canapés and French champagne to follow, for US$700
Minimum stay: None
Rates: Bungalows from around US$450; overwater bungalows from around US$725; pool faré from around US$725; ask about honeymoon packages
Credit cards: Most major
Taxes and service charge: All rates subject to 9% room tax and Government tax of US$1.50 per person per day

The hotel's 'farés', or villas named after the Tahitian term for home, are set either on the beach or in the lush tropical gardens and like the overwater bungalows they feature thatched pandanus roofs. Each faré has a separate living room with rattan and bamboo furniture and plump cream cushions, Tasmanian oak floors and red-cedar walls, a bedroom with en suite sitting room, bathroom with free standing bathtub and large sundeck. Eight farés have their own private swimming pool and three farés have a Jacuzzi set into a teak sundeck. Whichever room you choose they all come with bathrobes, complimentary toiletries, hairdryer, minibar, in-room safe, stereo cassette player, overhead fans and coffee and tea-making facilities.

Dining at Hotel Bora Bora is an event most guests look forward to all day: in the evening you can eat on the alfresco **Matira Terrace** staring out over the lagoon. During the day, lunch and refreshments are provided at the **Pofai Beach Bar** and there is a beach barbecue with dance show on Fridays.

The crystal clear waters of the lagoon form much of the focus for the day's activities with complimentary snorkelling and outrigger paddle canoes. The hotel also has a 50ft catamaran available for sport fishing, day sails, dinners on board, or cruising

BORA BORA LAGOON RESORT
(☎ 60 40 00, 🖹 60 40 01, 💻 bblr @mail.pf), Motu Toopua, BP 175, Vaitape, Bora Bora, French Polynesia
Reservations: Through Orient-Express Hotels (💻 www.orient-expresshotels. com), or Leading Hotels of the World reservation numbers worldwide (see p12)
Getting there: The resort provides a complimentary 15-minute boat ride from Bora Bora Airport
Accommodation: 50 overwater, 12 garden and 16 beach bungalows, 2 suites
Amenities: Café Fare, the Otemanu Restaurant, Hiro Lounge, Rotopa Bar, Tahitian feasts, limited room service, boutique, complimentary watersports, freshwater swimming pool, tennis courts, volleyball, fitness centre, Jacuzzi, games room, boat shuttle to Bora Bora, in-room videos, snorkelling, windsurfing and sailing; scuba diving, shark feeding and glass-bottom boating, jeep safaris can also be arranged at local rates
Dress code: Casual during the day; summer dresses for women, and trousers and short-sleeve shirts for men are usually worn in the evening
Weddings: The hotel does not have a wedding licence but does do 'romantic ceremonies' (not legally recognized) which include Tahitian dress for the couple and a Polynesian name (!), a waterfront ceremony with Polynesian music and dance, photos, sunset cruise and a intimate dinner in the Otemanu Restaurant for CPF110,000
Minimum stay: None
Rates: Double rooms from around US$500/CPF50,000 up to US$790/CPF79,000
Credit cards: Most major
Taxes and service charge: Tax 10%, plus government tax of US$1.50 per person per day, service included

through the Society Islands, as well as jeeps for safari excursions through the island's mountainous interior, horse-riding, bicycles and motor scooters for hire.

Bora Bora Lagoon Resort

Bora Bora Lagoon Resort is so good that some people even argue that it has usurped Hotel Bora Bora as the finest hotel in the South Pacific. When it first opened it was definitely better than its older rival but since the Hotel Bora Bora's refurbishment they're neck and neck.

A member of The Leading Hotels of the World and managed by Orient-Express, the Bora Bora Lagoon Resort, set on its own tiny motu (a coral islet) one and a half kilometres out from the island of Bora Bora itself, is the more private hotel. Due to its positioning it is also blessed with truly incredible views looking back over the waters of the lagoon to the mysterious mountain peaks of **Otemanu** on Bora Bora.

Once you arrive at Bora Bora Airport you are met by hotel staff who take you on a private cruiser across the brilliant blue lagoon to the jetty on Motu Toopua. Met with ice-cold coconut juice at the other end, you're already far away from mainstream tourism, on a private island paradise.

The 80 de luxe traditionally-styled overwater and beach bungalows are unashamedly modern inside. Although natural materials have been used there is nothing rustic about these bungalows with their oiled yucca wood floors featuring coconut shell inlay, timber venetian blinds covering the floor to ceiling louvred doors, mirrors framed in carved coconut husk and bright blue, yellow and orange cushions on the chairs, bedstead and chest at the foot of your king-sized bed. But it is the fantastic attention to detail that makes these rooms so wonderful, with incredibly imaginative touches such as the illuminated glass coffee table in the overwater bungalows which has sliding panels underneath so that you can sit at night watching the marine life rush about below you.

There are many lovely touches like this: the huge stone-carved figures gracing the jetties, the complimentary sun block provided in each room, the ice delivered daily, and the way your breakfast is brought out to your bungalow by a Tahitian couple in a traditional canoe. Everything about the resort is well-timed, cleverly thought out and perfectly executed. There's nothing like taking your time over breakfast on your overwater balcony, before heading off into the lagoon in a canoe of your own.

The fact that Bora Bora Lagoon Resort has a fabulously large freshwater swimming pool is a real plus point and is indicative of the quality of all the hotel's leisure

THINGS TO SEE AND DO ON BORA BORA

Located 264km north-west of Tahiti, Bora Bora is the most spectacularly beautiful island, with emerald green hills and crystal clear lagoons. Bora Bora is about 32km in circumference, so it is easy to travel around the whole island in just a few hours.

Bora Bora Jeep Safaris operate four-wheel drive round-island tours taking you through the interior and to all the remaining gun sites and radar stations left over from the Second World War.

If you want to go under your own steam, you can arrange car hire easily through your hotel or rental agencies. Alternatively, hop on a bike or scooter, both of which are available from most car-hire companies and from the big hotels.

If you'd prefer to see the island from the water, **Richard Postma**, a Californian who is now resident in French Polynesia, will take you out on his catamaran, based at Hotel Bora Bora. Whether you choose to go on a sunset cruise or overnight charter with dinner on board, make sure you do get out on to the water and venture outside the barrier reef as the views of Bora Bora on the horizon are wonderful. Ask at either hotel.

There is an International CMAS and PADI-certified dive centre at the Hotel Bora Bora.

Wherever you stay in Bora Bora, don't miss out on one of the shark feeds, run by most hotels, where you are taken by a guide out to a part of the lagoon that is roped off. Your guide then enters the restricted area throwing meat out to a cluster of black-tip reef sharks, while you stay outside the area watching the feeding frenzy at a safe distance.

If you fancy getting out of your hotel for a drink or maybe a bite to eat, head to the notorious *Bloody Mary's*, near Hotel Bora Bora, which is an island institution. A long-established celebrity hang-out, this sandy floored bar with its thatched roof and coconut tree stumps for chairs serves grilled fresh fish and some mean cocktails, often accompanied by local music – an obvious inspiration for the famous Cheeseburger in Paradise as Jimmy Buffet's name is even etched on the huge slab of wood that acts as the bar's celebrity list.

Further information at: 🖥 www.tahiti-tourisme.com

---

facilities. At the front of the motu is a superb white sand beach from which guests can snorkel, scuba dive, paddle away in outrigger canoes, windsurf, or go for a morning's catamaran cruise. The lagoon is very much the focus of the whole resort: it is there that you will spend your days, when you dine you'll marvel at the views it provides, and at night slide back that glass panel and enjoy your private slice of ocean.

MOOREA

Regarded as one of the world's most spectacular islands with its ragged cloud-topped peaks, deep valleys and emerald lagoons, Moorea is a really exotic place to explore.

Moorea Beachcomber Parkroyal

Moorea Beachcomber Parkroyal is a fabulous hotel perched right on the lagoon edge with a spectacular mountain range rising up behind it. The only real problem with the Moorea Beachcomber Parkroyal is that, being so close to Tahiti, it tends to get very busy at weekends. It is also worth noting that although the beach is lovely, it is man-made. However, for people who don't have thousands to fritter away, it gives you overwater accommodation for the price of a basic room at the Hotel Bora Bora, which is one very good reason why this hotel should be considered as a very romantic honeymoon destination.

The best rooms are the thatched roof beach bungalows set amongst the tropical gardens and looking out to the lagoon, or those actually set out over the water. Whichever room you choose it will be cool and comfortable with ample space provided by the separate sitting area, en suite bathroom and good-sized sundeck. Alternatively, there are standard rooms located in three-storey buildings but these have only small patios or balconies.

The hotel's sporting facilities are fabulous, whether you decide to launch your own outrigger or explore the lagoon on a glass-bottomed boat, play beach volleyball,

MOOREA BEACHCOMBER PARKROYAL

(☎ 55 19 19, 📠 55 19 55, 💻 www.tahiti-resorts.com), PO Box 1019, Papetoai, Moorea, French Polynesia

Reservations: USA and Canada (toll-free ☎ 800-835-7742); Australia (toll-free ☎ 0800 1 3229); UK (toll-free ☎ 0345-581 666) or 💻 reservations@sphc.com.au or through UK tour operators ITC Classics or Seasons in Style (see pp9-10)

Getting there: There are daily flights from Papeete to Moorea (10 minutes), followed by a 25-minute taxi ride to the hotel

Accommodation: 150 rooms, including overwater suite bungalows, beach and garden suite bungalows, and air conditioned lanai rooms

Amenities: Two restaurants, freshwater swimming pool, tennis, beach volleyball, PADI-certified scuba diving, outrigger canoes; glass-bottom boats, jet and water-skiing, parasailing through activities excursion desk; shop, spa; complimentary golf carts

Dress code: Informal

Weddings: Can be arranged; there is no church but you can get married on the beach or in the hotel grounds; the hotel's traditional wedding ceremony, where both wear Polynesian dress is popular

Minimum stay: None

Rates: Doubles from US$204; garden bungalows from US$260; beach bungalows from US$275; over-water bungalows cost US$445

Credit cards: Most major

Taxes and service charge: Included

tennis or practice your water-skiing. The scuba diving in Moorea is great and 'Bathy's Club' PADI dive centre is based at the hotel.

Reputed to have the best food on Moorea, there are two restaurants, the **Fare Hana** which offers day-time snacks in a very relaxed atmosphere and the open-air **Fare Nui** restaurant, where international dishes can be enjoyed as the sun sets over the sea.

COOK ISLANDS

Although officially part of Polynesia (not French Polynesia), the Cook Islands are included here because of their geographical affiliation: they are 1000km south-west of Tahiti and 3500km north-east of New Zealand, by which they are governed in 'free association'. Local currency is the NZ dollar, time difference GMT minus 10 hours.

Manuia Beach Boutique Hotel (☎ 682-22461, 📠 682-22464, 💻 www.manuia.co.ck, PO Box 700, Raratonga) is a small secluded hotel set on the sparkling blue lagoon of **Raratonga**. Accommodation is in 20 Polynesian-style thatched bungalows each of which has a king-sized bed, fridge, phone, a well-stocked minibar, tea- and coffee-making facilities and hairdryers, as well as a spacious veranda where dinner can be served. Guests are greeted on arrival with champagne and tropical fruit juice.

The best thing about the Manuia Beach is its wonderful beach bar where guests gather to watch the sun go down over the lagoon and for beach barbecues with live music. You can eat international as well as local dishes there, or you can arrange to have an intimate dinner in a quiet spot on the beach. The hotel's facilities are impressive with a swimming pool and spa, and there's an abundance of snorkelling, sailing and windsurfing excursions. This is a really romantic island hideaway, which specializes in island weddings (from NZ$550/US$231) and honeymoons, and where no children are allowed to spoil your peace. Doubles cost from around NZ$260/US$110 garden view, NZ$375/US$158 beachfront, both per night including tax and a tropical breakfast.

Fiji

(BEST TIME: MAY TO OCTOBER)

If your idea of paradise comprises desert island hideaways fringed with powder white sand and brilliant turquoise waters, where coral reefs are home to hundreds of different varieties of vividly coloured tropical fish, and where you can sit alone on a private jetty to dine by candlelight, then dream no more, and book your honeymoon in Fiji.

Significantly less commercialized than the Caribbean, the Independent Republic of Fiji consists of a group of more than 300 islands spread out over 1,295,000 sq km of ocean in the heart of the South Pacific. Here the enthusiasm of the local people, a mix of Fijians, Indians, Europeans, Chinese and other islanders, also form part of the magic. Many visitors have found the islanders' welcome most disarming as it is so overwhelming, and everyone who has ever been to Fiji will tell you that it is the islanders who make these pearl islands so unique.

The Fijian islands are rightly renowned for their diving. Reputed to be one of the top four dive sites in the world, the clear warm water around the many lagoons offers ideal conditions in which to explore the ocean world. In addition to diving there are lots of other beach and sea-related activities, as well as exploring the jungle either on foot or on horseback, but essentially the Fijian islands are a place to relax and truly unwind after the wedding and lose yourself to Fijian time. If you are looking for glamorous restaurants and evening entertainment, you'd better look elsewhere because being in Fiji is all about shedding your shoes, leaving your jacket and tie and jewellery at home, and walking barefoot along the beach to dinner on a moonlit shore.

> **FIJI**
> The perfect South Pacific hideaway for those looking for escapism, with little to do other than island hop, scuba dive and walk along empty white sand beaches
> **When to go**: May to October
> **Average maximum temperatures** °C
>
> | JAN | FEB | MAR | APR | MAY | JUN |
> |-----|-----|-----|-----|-----|-----|
> | 31 | 31 | 31 | 30 | 28 | 28 |
> | JUL | AUG | SEP | OCT | NOV | DEC |
> | 27 | 27 | 27 | 28 | 29 | 30 |
>
> **Capital**: Suva on Viti Levu
> **Flight times**: to Viti Levu from:
> New York: (via LA)
> LA: 11 hours (direct)
> London: 27 hours (via LA)
> Sydney: 4 hours (direct)
> **Approximate exchange rates**: Fiji dollar (FJ$) – £1 = FJ$3.25, US$1 = FJ$2.28, A$1 = FJ$1.18
> **Time difference**: GMT plus 12 hours
> **Voltage**: 240v AC, 50 Hz
> **Combine with**: Australia, Los Angeles, New Zealand
> **Country dialling code**: ☎ 679
> **Further information**: 🖳 www.fijifvt.gov.fj

I would suggest spending a few days on Fiji's largest island, **Viti Levu**, and then venturing out to one of the countless offshore emerald dots. A little island hopping is a wonderful way to get a feel for the size and beauty of the South Pacific.

If you are looking for total luxury in a private setting and have a sizeable amount of cash to burn, fly out to the **Yasawa Islands**, a chain of six principal islands and a string of smaller ones stretching out north-west from Viti Levu. These islands are home to some of the world's most exclusive island hideaways. Arriving by sea plane, you'll be met by saronged Fijians carrying hibiscus with which to welcome you and saying 'bula, bula', the multi-purpose greeting that means 'health' in Fijian.

You have to remove your shoes when you land because you step out of the plane into the turquoise shimmering water and you probably won't require them again until it's time to get back on the sea plane; the Yasawa islands are not known for their formalities. You can also put away your watch so that you can thoroughly immerse yourself in Fiji time, the locals' own self-deprecating version of Spain's *manana*.

THE YASAWA ISLANDS

The Yasawa Islands are home to a handful of extremely exclusive island resorts, aimed at couples who are seeking the perfect island hideaway and can afford to pay for it.

Yasawa Island Lodge

Arguably the best suited of the following four resorts for honeymooners is Yasawa Island Lodge as the clientele tends to be younger. It's also easy to arrange individual dining here.

Like the other Yasawa Island resorts, accommodation is in de luxe bures. There are only 16 one-bedroom bures, two two-bedroom bures, and one 'honeymoon hide-

YASAWA ISLAND LODGE
(☎ 66 33 64, 🖷 66 50 44, 💻 www.yasawa.com), Yasawa Island, PO Box 10128, Nadi Airport, Fiji
Reservations: Small Luxury Hotels of the World toll-free reservation numbers worldwide (see p12); or through UK tour operators Elegant Resorts or Sunset Travel (see pp9-10)
Getting there: 35-minute flight from Nadi International Airport in a light aircraft arranged by the hotel; standard charter US$310 round trip per person, a special charter US$1300 round-trip
Accommodation: 18 suites in luxury bures
Amenities: Restaurant, full room service, boutique, tennis court, four-wheel drive and walking tours, scuba diving, snorkelling, large horizon swimming pool; private beach picnics a speciality
Dress code: Smart casual for the evenings
Weddings: The lodge has a wedding licence and can host receptions for up to 32 guests
Minimum stay: None
Rates: Luxury bures from US$600 to US$840 inclusive of everything
Credit cards: Most major
Taxes and service charge: 10% tax will be added to your bill

VATULELE ISLAND RESORT
(☎ 2 9665 8700, 🖷 2 9665 7833), PO Box 9936, Nadi, Fiji Islands
Reservations: Through Small Luxury Hotels of the World (see p12); UK agent is Travel Portfolio (☎ 01284-700 444)
Getting there: Fly into Nadi and transfer to hotel via sea plane (about US$470 per couple return)
Accommodation: 18 luxurious bures
Amenities: Watersports, game fishing, PADI dive school, trekking, volleyball, tennis, nature walks, extensive library, restaurant
Dress code: No dress code
Weddings: Fijian wedding ceremonies can be arranged for guests staying a minimum of six nights, and feature a Fijian choir, minister and feast
Minimum stay: Four nights, but five are recommended, average stay is eight nights
Rates: From around US$1100 per couple per day all-inclusive
Credit cards: No credit cards but US$ cash and travellers' cheques accepted
Taxes and service charge: Included

away' called **Lomalagi** with just one bedroom. The bures are all on the beachfront and are really spacious, covering almost 90 sq metres on two levels, with a separate bedroom and living area, absolutely enormous timber sundecks and your own private mini-bure on the beach complete with a hammock.

Each bure has a traditional Fijian thatched roof and décor, a king-sized bed, air conditioning, ceiling fans, minibar, private bathroom with bathrobes and lots of toiletries including suntan lotion and coconut soap. There is also a fruit basket in your room which is replenished daily, tea- and 'real' coffee-making facilities, and full room service. The meeting area for guests is the octagonal, open-sided **Bure Levu** where the bar, dining room and relaxation area extend onto a split-level veranda overlooking the large horizon-style swimming pool. Dinner can either be taken in the restaurant overlooking the pool and ocean or on the beach by candlelight.

As well as the pool, guests can windsurf, snorkel, play tennis and croquet, scuba dive, sail catamarans and do some light game-fishing. The staff will also provide you with a champagne picnic and whisk you off to a secluded beach for the day, or guide you on local bush walks.

Vatulele Island Resort
Vatulele was created by Australian television producer, Henry Crawford, and means 'ringing rock' in Fijian. Apparently it took him two years to choose the perfect island and another two to realize his dream of creating the ultimate hideaway for stressed-out people. The resort was voted Small Luxury Hotel of the Year 1999/2000.

The island is shaped like a foot; both the eastern and northern coasts are protected by a 11km long and 5km wide barrier reef just over one and a half kilometres from the shore. Most of the island is densely jungled, and apart from the resort the only habitations are four villages with a total population of 900.

The very best thing about Vatulele is the peace, aided by the total lack of money, phones, newspapers, televisions, radios and children. (Children are only allowed on the island for two designated family weeks each year.) This is island living: no reception desk, no menus and no formal wine list.

Vatulele is an informal and spontaneous place which is more like a private house than a resort. The management try hard to strike a balance between a private house party where guests eat together each night, and allowing couples the chance to dine on their own. Meals can be arranged à deux in the privacy of your own terrace but you would probably feel pressured eventually into joining the other guests at dinner. If this doesn't appeal, choose somewhere else.

Located 32km south of Viti Levu, Fiji's largest island, there are 18 beautifully designed bures opening out onto the beach and nestled in tropical foliage, providing absolute privacy from other guests. Each bure has a king-size bed on a raised platform with a separate dressing area, a spacious sitting room and a large bathroom in a connecting wing. The furnishings are deliberately simple but extremely beautiful, with cane and canvas predominating, Italian white or terracotta floor tiles throughout, and cream stucco stone walls decorated with terracotta urns, heavy wooden bowls and primary coloured sofas and scatter cushions. The best thing about the rooms is that all areas open onto a spacious shaded terracotta terrace fronting the beach so, wherever you are, the views are amazing.

At Vatulele the emphasis is on food. Meals are taken on a terrace outside the large central pavilion, overlooking the lagoon, and by night tables are set out under the stars, lit by lanterns and candlelight. Much of the food is cooked outdoors in the large wood-fired pizza and tandoori ovens, the cuisine varying from Thai to Indian and Japanese: whatever you have you can be sure it will be superb enough to warrant the resort's Small Luxury Hotel of the World membership.

All the usual watersports are on offer but the diving on Vatulele is particularly spectacular, with PADI courses available.

Turtle Island Resort

Turtle Island Resort is another totally private island situated north-west of Fiji's largest island Viti Levu and shot to international fame as the location for Brooke Shield's 1980 island epic, *Blue Lagoon*. It has since attracted serious praise from visitors and the industry and has been described as 'romantic, intimate, comfortable and friendly almost beyond belief, Turtle Island is a world entirely beyond time and obligations'. If you are looking for your very own island paradise, and can afford it, this is it.

In 1972, Richard Evanson, an American businessman who was looking to escape the rat race of America's west coast, acquired Turtle Island to establish a private sanctuary. A few years, a hurricane and a major motion picture later, the tiny volcanic island is now the ultimate couples' hideaway with Richard still overseeing all the fun, like the host at a weekend house party.

One word of warning though: Turtle is very much run along the lines of a house party, so if you don't fancy joining in, don't go. Although you'll get plenty of opportunities to be on your own during the day, the emphasis is very much on socializing with other guests at the cocktail parties and the mountain-top barbecues: some guests have found the socializing a bit intrusive. Dining alone in a private bay by lantern light can be arranged but it is so popular that you're advised to request it when booking your holiday.

The landscape of the 200-hectare island is extraordinarily varied, the smooth white sands and calm waters on the lagoon side contrasting dramatically with the rugged black volcanic cliffs and rolling surf found on the windward side, while dense tropical forests give way to grassy highland interiors with breathtaking views.

Turtle's accommodation is restricted to couples who stay in one of the 14 thatched bures which are dotted along the island's main beach, but which are discreetly designed so that they do not overlook each other. On arrival you'll find your names carved on a sign on your door, and frangipani and hibiscus blooms scattered all over the place. You'll also find more than 100 Fijian staff to cater to your every whim.

TURTLE ISLAND RESORT
(☎ 3-96 18 11 00, ▤ 3-96 18 11 99),
Yasawa Islands, Fiji
Reservations: Through Small Luxury
Hotels of the World toll-free reservation
numbers worldwide (see p12), UK agents
Travel Portfolio (UK ☎ 01284-762 255,
▣ tpuk@globalnet.co.uk) or Turtle
Island Holidays, 411 Collins St,
Melbourne 3000, Australia
Getting there: Guests fly into Nadi and
are transferred to the island by sea plane
Accommodation: 14 beachfront bures
Amenities: Horse-riding, jungle walks,
scuba diving, snorkelling, sailing, wind-
surfing, canoeing, deep-sea fishing, 14
beaches, hammocks, private picnics on
desert islands, mountain biking, sunset
cruise, mountain-top dinner, island tour
Dress code: There isn't one
Weddings: The hotel can arrange both
Western and Fijian ceremonies
Minimum stay: Six nights
Rates: From around US$1308 per couple
per day, all-inclusive
Credit cards: Most major
Taxes and service charge: 10% government tax, and guests can contribute to the
staff's Christmas fund

Each bure is a spacious suite with two light, airy rooms, both looking out to sea. The bed-room has a queen-sized bed, there are rattan furnishings in the sitting room, immaculately tiled bathrooms and a fully-stocked bar and refrigerator. The bures also come equipped with mosquito repellent, plenty of books, and even baseball caps and sarongs for use while you are there. The turtle motif is everywhere: green terrapin-shaped soaps and little motifs on the bathrobes and towels. The vaulted ceilings are constructed in the traditional Fijian manner with hand-shaped and lashed native *noko noko* (wood) poles.

While there you can do as much or as lit-tle as you like: activities include horse-riding, mountain-biking, jungle walks, scuba diving, snorkelling, sailing, windsurfing, canoeing and deep-sea fishing. On lazier days you can explore the island's 14 powder sand beaches, such as **Honeymoon Beach**, a secluded cove where you can lounge around in the double hammock. Hotel staff are happy to take you out in the boat, dropping you off on a deserted beach with a picnic of lobster and champagne, or whatever else you chose that morning.

FIJI'S OUTER ISLANDS
The Wakaya Club

The Wakaya Club is situated among 80 hectares of emerald forest, pearly beaches and turquoise coral-ringed sea, at the north-west end of Wakaya Island. It's a slightly more formal resort than the other two: the staff will call you 'sir' or 'madam' and the aver-age age of the clientele at the Wakaya Club is about 45 years old.

You'll be met at Nadi International Airport and whisked away to this wonderful private island by Air Wakaya – the island's own twin-engined 1992 Britten Norman Islander plane.

The island itself spans 880 hectares of soaring cliffs, a dense forest interior where wild horses, goats and boars roam free, ringed by shell-strewn beaches and aquama-rine lagoons, protected by unspoilt coral reefs. Clichéd images, I know, but this is very definitely the real thing.

Natural materials were used to create nine sumptuous, 'cathedral ceiling', 140 sq metre guest accommodations discreetly placed along the beach. Each bure has its own living room with hand-plaited woven bamboo walls, a fully-stocked minibar and CD player, a four-poster king-size bamboo bed in the bedroom, and a separate bathroom with a private outdoor shower encased in a lava-rock wall, oversized bath tub and a bidet. Bloom toiletries, cotton bathrobes and hairdryers make each bathroom a place to wallow in. There is a selection of books on your dressing table but more books, games and CDs are also available at reception.

Wakaya also has an island estate called Vale O which has three pavilions housing up to three couples. Each pavilion contains a kitchen and couples also have the serv-ices of their own chef, laundry staff and an on-call driver.

The muffled beating of the 'Lali' drum summons guests to dinner in the **Palm Grove** dining pavilion, with its soaring 18m cathedral ceiling, while breakfast and lunch can be taken overlooking the lagoon.

The four resident chefs prepare all your meals using fresh seafood, locally-grown organic vegetables and fruit, accompanied by wines imported from France and Australia. All meals and drinks are included, so you don't have to worry what you choose, or how often you choose it! After dinner, guests can play pool, watch videos or DVD's, or just drink at the bar.

Along with the usual watersport activities, from glass-bottomed boats to diving on the reef beyond the lagoon, there is a freshwater grotto-like swimming pool, plus a nine-hole golf course, croquet and boules.

Other recommended retreats

Wadigi Island (☎/🖹 679-72 09 01, 🖳 wadigiisland@is.com.fj, www.wadigi.com, PO Box 10134, Nadi airport), discreetly tucked amid the picturesque **Mamanuca Islands**, is a very special three-acre island, which can be exclusively yours, if you can afford it. Accommodation is in two beautifully appointed guest rooms and a stunning Sunset Suite, all with breathtaking views of the ocean. The Sunset Suite is air conditioned, and has a large private deck cantilevered over the water, a romantic bath and outside shower.

Your two personal gourmet chefs will impress you with their extraordinary cuisine, and your personalized menu will be complemented with fine wines.

Wadigi is protected by a large coral reef which offers perfect snorkelling and diving in its clear, warm water. Your own personal boatman will take you to discover the numerous reefs and seahorses that live in the area. Deep-sea fishing or scuba diving is easily arranged. This unique Fijian Island charter is perfect for those seeking total privacy and a desert island experience without compromising on creature comforts.

Wadigi costs from US$339/FJ$775 per couple per day for private island charter including exclusive use, all meals and drinks (including alcohol) and all recreational activities. Booked exclusively in the UK through Tailormade Travel (☎ 01386-712000, 🖳 www.tailor-made.co.uk).

THE WAKAYA CLUB
(☎ 44 81 28, 🖹 44 04 06, 🖳 www.wakaya.com), PO Box 15424, Wakaya Island, Fiji

Reservations: Australia (toll-free ☎ 1-800 126 205); US and Canada (toll-free ☎ 1-800-828-3454); UK (toll-free ☎ 0800 968 986); New Zealand (toll-free ☎ 0-800 440 454); or through UK tour operators Elegant Resorts or ITC Classics (see p9)

Getting there: The hotel will arrange a twin-engine aircraft transfer from Nadi Airport in their own Air Wakaya (US$830 per couple plus 10% tax)

Accommodation: Nine elegant bures and Vale O 3-bedroom private villas

Amenities: Nine-hole golf course, tennis court, swimming pool, massage, deep-sea fishing, reef-casting, hand line fishing, glass bottom boat tours, snorkelling, boules, billiards and croquet, marina, scuba diving and archaeological tours

Dress code: Elegant casual; collared shirts with slacks for men in restaurant, collared shirts on tennis court and golf course

Weddings: Fijian or Western wedding packages can be arranged: Fijian ceremonies cost US$3500. Western from US$3000 which includes marriage licence, use of church or other site, a choir, bouquet and floral decorations, the ceremony and officiate, two flower girls in native dress, Wakaya village chief to escort the bride down the aisle, wedding-cake, champagne cocktail reception and dinner, and the island band

Minimum stay: Five nights; ten nights over Christmas and New Year

Rates: From around US$1475 to US$1875 double occupancy per day all-inclusive, including two scuba dives per day, but ask for promotional incentives; Vale O from US$3500

Credit cards: Most major

Taxes and service charge: 10% government tax, but service is included

The Philippines
(BEST TIME: NOVEMBER TO MARCH)

The 7000 islands comprising the Philippine archipelago, surrounded by the Pacific, Sulu, the Mindanao, and the South China seas, are some of the most underrated destinations in Asia. These emerald-green land masses with their lofty mountain ranges seem to have been scattered randomly in a sea of a dozen different shades of brilliant turquoise. The Philippines today are a huge contrast of cultures and lifestyles, an exotic paradise where East meets West. From the peasants in the paddy fields to the cities with their seedy reputation, the whole country is a conundrum of Chinese, Spanish, American and Malay influences.

A honeymoon in the Philippines has all the perfect ingredients – tropical islands ringed by white sand and clear azure water, spectacular coral reefs teeming with exotic aquatic life, and the stunning mountainous interior where volcanoes sit beside ancient rice terraces. For couples who have previously visited Asia and think of Thailand or Malaysia as 'tired' this is the ideal, totally unspoilt island retreat.

Amanpulo
Amanpulo has to be one of the most romantic hotels in the world. An Amanresort, on its own private island, Amanpulo epitomises everything that is perfect, and of course vehemently expensive, about the group. If you've got the money and want to do nothing in a stunningly elegant hotel surrounded by some of the world's most beautiful and remote scenery this is *the* place to do it. Throughout this book, whenever it comes to writing about an Amanresort hotel I am faced with the same conclusion. None of these hotels is cheap but if you can possibly afford even one or two nights in one, then go ahead – you won't regret it and definitely won't forget it in a hurry.

Amanpulo, meaning 'peaceful island', is on the island of Pamalican in the Cuyo group, at its widest point just 500 metres across. Surrounded by pure white sandy beaches, turquoise water and a coral reef just 50m off shore, Amanpulo boasts some of the best snorkelling and dive sites the world has to offer. You'll arrive via a one-hour private charter flight from Manila; from then on the only transport on the island is on open-sided carts, which make exploring a marvellously lazy exercise.

THE PHILIPPINES
A great place to really get away from it all among perfect unspoilt islands
When to go: November to March
Average maximum temperatures °C

JAN	FEB	MAR	APR	MAY	JUN	JUL	AUG	SEP	OCT	NOV	DEC
30	31	33	34	34	33	31	31	41	41	31	30

Capital: Manila
Flight times: to Manila from New York (via LA): 25½ hours
       LA: 17 hours
       London (via Bangkok): 17 hours
       Sydney: 8¼ hours
Approximate exchange rates: Pesos (P) – £1 = P72.65, US$1 = P49.10, A$1 = P27.28
Time difference: GMT plus eight hours
Voltage: 220v AC, 60 Hz, although most hotels have both 220v and 110v, two flat-pin plugs
Combine with: Hong Kong, Singapore, Sydney, Bangkok
Country dialling code: ☎ 63
Further information: 🖳 www.dotpcvc.gov.ph

(Opposite): Aboard the dhow; Kiwayu Safari Village, an island retreat 30 miles north of Lamu off the Kenyan coast. See p237.

Each of the 40 casitas (thatched huts), either down on the beachfront or nestled up on the hillside, is modelled on a Filipino *bahay kubo* (native hut) with polished timber floors. They are equipped with every luxury you could possibly want including king-size bed, CD player, phone, bathrobes and slippers, toiletries, minibar, satellite TV, hairdryer and the most incredible sunken bath in a spacious marble bathroom.

If you want complete seclusion Amanpulo really is the ultimate destination – you won't have to see anyone else, apart from the hordes of staff, from the day you arrive until the day you leave: even your meals can be taken in the privacy of your own outdoor terrace.

The hotel is of course well-equipped with a fabulous 30m swimming pool adjacent to the **Clubhouse**, and a good range of complimentary watersports including hobie cats, ocean kayaks, laser sails, windsurfers and traditional Filipino *banca* rowing boats. This kind of destination doesn't come cheap, but as the advert says, 'just do it'.

Other recommended hotels

El Nido Lagen Island (☎ 2-894-5644, 🖹 2-810-3260. 🖳 www.elnidoresorts.com, c/o Ten Knots Development Corporation, 2/F Builders Centre Building, 170 Salcedo Street, Legaspi Village, 1229 Makati City) is

AMANPULO
(☎ 2-759 4040, 🖹 2-532 4044, 🖳 amanpulo@amanresorts.com), Pamalican Island, Philippines
Reservations: Direct or through amanresorts (🖳 www.amanresorts.com) or in through tour operators Western & Oriental, Abercrombie & Kent, or Elegant Resorts (see pp11-12)
Getting there: One hour flight from Manila by private charter costing US$300 per person
Accommodation: 40 air-conditioned beachfront, treetop and hillside bungalows/casitas
Amenities: Air-conditioned panoramic restaurant, large swimming pool, clubhouse, beach pavilion and bar, 24-hour room service for private dining; snorkelling, scuba diving, sailing, rowing, fishing, two floodlit tennis courts, library, gallery, boutique, picnic grove, massage, telescopes
Dress code: Smart casual
Weddings: Non-binding ceremonies can be arranged at Amanpulo; but legal wedding ceremonies are too complex to arrange
Minimum stay: None
Rates: Treetop casitas from US$475; hillside and beachfront casitas from US$525
Credit cards: Most major
Taxes and service charge: 10% government tax and 10% service charge added

THINGS TO SEE AND DO AROUND PAMALICAN ISLAND

Amanpulo offers guided **eco-walks** for its guests twice weekly in the afternoon; the guide points out local flora and fauna and explains the island's history as you go.

Surrounding Pamalican Island, about 50m offshore, there are well preserved coral reefs and the most incredible array of tropical fish. With average water temperatures of 26°C and underwater visibility ranging between 15 and 30m, both snorkelling and diving are particularly good.

Amanpulo's **Dive Shop** offers courses for beginners and advanced divers. There can be few places as wonderful to start your diving as the stunning waters of Pamalican island because the sea water in front of the resort is calm and the drop-off very gentle.

For those with more experience there is plenty of exhilarating diving close by, and it is possible to rent one of the resort's boats and go off on your own to explore the many dive sites. Particularly impressive are **Fan Coral Wall** where turtles are quite common, **Windmill** where a resident 3m stingray has been sighted, and **South Point** where white-tip sharks, tuna, yahoo and mantra and eagle rays are common.

Back on top of the water, the island has a 5½km beach, two hills, and numerous paths to explore either on foot or on one of the hotel's mountain bikes available for guest use. Definitely worth a visit are the **giant clams**, some weigh up to 227kg, on the north-west side of the island.

Further information: 🖳 www.dotpcvc.gov.ph

(Opposite): **Top:** The Seychelles (see p81). **Middle and bottom:** Hotel Bora Bora (see p55), French Polynesia.

CALAMIAN CRUISES AND DIVING IN THE PHILIPPINES

Cruising in the Calamian Islands

At the northern tip of Palawan are a string of smaller, rarely visited islands. This group of satellite islands offers some of the most dramatic seascapes in Asia, prompting Jacques Cousteau to describe them as one of the most beautiful areas of the world.

A four-day, three-night cruise aboard the 24m catamaran M/V *Lagoon Explorer*, stops in tranquil coves so you can swim ashore for a picnic or explore the coral world below. The ten air-conditioned cabins all have private toilet and shower facilities, with hot and cold water.

This cruise can be booked through most tour operators specializing in the Philippines, or directly with **Cruise and Hotel Centre** (Manila ☎ 2-848-3920, 🖷: 2-848-3618; 🖳 bhtt_inc@mozcom.co). It costs around US$400 per person twin share and departs every Monday and Thursday, while the seven-day, six-night cruise leaves every Monday.

Diving in the Philippines

The Philippines offers some awesome diving on its 40,000 sq km of coral reefs that teem with a wide variety of marine life.

Here in one of the most productive marine ecosystems in the world, the tropical waters are enriched by currents coming from Japan, the South China Sea, the Indian Ocean, and the Celebes Sea. As a result, the country's waters are full of hundreds of different species of fish, shells and various marine invertebrates: there are no less than 800 species of corals.

There are dive sites of every description from perpendicular submarine cliffs covered with sponges, corals of varying shapes and sizes, gorgonians swarming with schools of pelagic fish, and dramatic drop-offs that reveal the vibrant marine world below.

The Philippines' dive sites are grouped into four major areas, **Batangas, Mindoro, Palawan** and the **Visayas**. If you are diving from Palawan, where Amanpulo and El Nido Lagen Island are located, you'll experience one of the last frontiers of the Philippines, where several endangered underwater species are found including manta rays, giant sea turtles, and the sea cow known locally as the dugong. At nearby **Cabilao Island** there are hammerhead sharks, tunas, dolphins and groupers.

---

located on the island of Lagen in El Nido, north-western Palawan. El Nido means 'birds nest' in Spanish and this extraordinarily beautiful hotel is set in a lush forest with a great view of the El Nido sunset.

Fifty-one luxury water cottages are built on stilts along its cove, and beachfront cottages lie just a few metres from the shore; forest rooms and suites nestle on the fringes of a tropical forest. All are air conditioned and built using indigenous materials, with antique wood floors. Each has a CD player, minibar, separate bath and toilet. Most have a private veranda.

The hotel has its own games room, library and boutique, as well as a swimming pool with poolside bar. A wide range of watersports are offered from windsurfing to scuba diving and nearby excursions include kayaking to bat caves, trekking under the giant trees and a mangrove safari.

Forest rooms cost from US$190, Forest suites US$245, water/beachfront Cottages US$230 per night. Weddings can be arranged. Book direct, or through tour operators such as British Airways Holidays or Hayes & Jarvis in the UK (see p9).

Indonesia
(BEST TIME: APRIL TO MID-NOVEMBER)

Indonesia is an incredible archipelago of over 17,000 islands, of which only 6000 are inhabited, covering over 80,000 sq km of coastline making it, somewhat amazingly, the fourth largest country in the world. The name Indonesia comes from two Greek words, 'Indos' (Indian) and 'nesos' (islands), but the unique character of these islands is derived from the fact that they are neither Asian nor Australian, despite their location between the Indian and Pacific Oceans.

AMAN-JUNKIES

One visit to any of the 11 Amanresorts will confirm that the word 'luxury' has indeed been redefined by the group. There's nothing flashy, but wherever you look sophisticated elegance is combined with such simplicity of design that you'll immediately wish your own home was designed and decorated in the same vein.

Indonesia, which has a big five of these resorts, is a paradise for 'Aman-junkies' – the growing number of people who having experienced one of these fantastic hotels, want nothing more than to visit the others, and for whom the group has now invented packages so that they can split their time between two or three different Amanresorts. Four of these are on Bali. In architecture and luxury each is very similar, but each has its special qualities.

Designed in traditional Balinese fashion combining local thatched roofs and stone with timber frames, terrazzo floors and mirrored glass, **Amankila** (363-41333, ▤ 363-41555, ▢ amankila@amanresorts.com) is built high on a hillside on the quieter eastern part of the island, commanding spectacular views of the **Lombok Straits** and the hotel's own palm-studded beach. This incredibly exclusive hotel attracts the likes of Jerry Hall, providing such celebrities with a polished haven of good style and taste. Amankila also offers guests opportunities to discover the Bali that still remains untrodden by tourist groups, with individual tours organized to see the incredible water palaces, temples and nearby villages.

Amandari (☎ 361-975 333, ▤ 361-975 335, ▢ amandari@amanresorts.com) is just outside Ubud, the inland centre of Balinese art, and set among rice paddies from where guests can enjoy walking in the **Monkey Forest**.

Amanwana (☎ 371-22233, ▤ 371-22288, ▢ amanwana@amanresorts.com), with 20 luxury tents on **Moyo Island**, a large nature reserve off which some of the world's most incredible dive sites are found, is a great place to go camping, Aman-style. Each tent has a teak floor, a library and a CD discman. Here you are guaranteed absolute tranquillity and remoteness, accompanied by the unmistakable quality of service and furnishings that has come to be expected from Amanresorts. In contrast, **Amanusa** (☎ 361-772333, ▤ 361-772335, ▢ amanusa@amanresorts.com) is really focussed around golf.

The new jewel in Aman's crown is **Amanjiwo** (☎ 293-788 333, ▤ 293-788 355, ▢ amanjiwo@amanresorts.com) on **Java**. Near Borobudur, the largest Buddhist sanctuary in the world, Amanjiwo means 'peaceful soul' and, listed in *Tatler*'s 101 best hotels 2001, is *the* place to stay on Java.

Rates for all four Amanresort properties are pretty much the same, starting at around US$525 a night, though Amanwana is slightly more expensive with jungle tents costing US$590 and US$725 for the best oceanfront tents – expensive, but absolutely worth it for the experience. Book directly (see above) or through Sterling Hotels & Resorts toll-free reservation numbers (see p12) or leading UK tour operators such as Western & Oriental (see p12).

The waters of Indonesia offer some of the world's most dramatic and unspoilt diving. Islands are continually being revealed or removed by the fractious volcanoes marking the edge of a tectonic plate running through Indonesia, lyrically dubbed the 'Ring of Fire'. Along the arc lie numerous rugged islands where tropical flora and cultivated rice paddies stand by areas of dense untouched tropical jungle. This sprawling chain of islands offers a staggering amount of contrasting beauty from the snow-capped mountain peaks of **Irian Jaya**, and the spectacular Buddhist monument of **Borobudur** on **Java**, to the volcanic craters of **Sumatra** and coral-fringed lagoons of **Bali**.

Over the last decade tourism has escalated so dramatically in Indonesia that the number of arrivals has increased by 350%. Most of the interest has focused on Bali and its beach resorts, with some parts now resembling an Australian suburb more than an idyllic hideaway: the beaches at **Kuta** and **Legian** in particular are now totally spoilt and full of backpacking Aussies and romantically named hangouts like the **Billabong Bar**. However, Bali is big enough for you to avoid the busy bits and does still have some truly wonderful hotels, beaches and stunning countryside, so don't let people tell you it's ruined.

BALI

The tiny volcanic island of Bali has lush green vegetation, coral seas and an intriguing Hindu-Balinese culture. The best way to see Bali is to split your time between one of

BALI

An exotic island of 20,000 temples, spectacular island scenery with unspoilt palm fringed beaches, stunning sunsets and creative, graceful people

When to go: During the dry season from April through to mid November, avoid Christmas and New Year when you can hardly move for tourists (most of them Australian)

Average maximum temperatures °C

JAN	FEB	MAR	APR	MAY	JUN
31	32	31	31	31	31
JUL	AUG	SEP	OCT	NOV	DEC
31	30	30	29	32	31

Capital: Jakarta (Java)

Flight times: To Denpasar (Bali) from:
New York: (via LA) 24 hours
LA: 18 hours
London: 22 hours
Sydney: 6½ hours

Approximate exchange rates: Indonesia Rupiah (R) – £1 = R16,666, US$1 = R11,111, A$1 = R5765

Time difference: GMT plus 8

Voltage: Usually 220v

Combine with: Australia, Singapore, or other Indonesian islands

Country dialling code: ☎ 62

Bali dialling code: ☎ 361

BEGAWAN GIRI ESTATE

(☎ 978 888, 🖹 978 889, 🖵 www.beg awan.com) PO Box 54, Ubud 80570, Bali
Reservations: Direct or toll-free from US/Canada (☎ 800-225-4255) in Japan (☎ 3 3216 0016) in the UK book through tour operator ITC Classics (see p11)

Getting there: The estate will arrange chauffered transfers for the 1½ hour drive from Denpasar Airport at no extra cost

Accommodation: 21 suites in 5 residences

Amenities: 24-hour butler service, serviced kitchen, 2 restaurants, bar and lounge, the Source spa offering massage and beauty treatments, library with CDs and videos, satellite and cable TV; natural spring pools and gardens, walks nearby

Dress code: Informal

Weddings: Can be arranged on request

Minimum stay: None but 3 days preferred

Rates: Suite US$475, Terrace Suite US$575, De Luxe Suite US$750, Master Suite US$950; entire residences can also be rented from US$2375

Credit cards: Most major

Taxes and service charge: 11% Government tax plus 10% service

---

the many five-star beach resorts overlooking gleaming white beaches, and the hill-side village of **Ubud** in order to enjoy the cooler mountain air and soak up a little culture. Two weeks in Bali will enable you to experience all that the island has to offer and maybe see one or two of the other Indonesian islands as well.

Begawan Giri Estate

A runner up for *Tatler*'s Hotel of the Year Award 2001, everyone's raving about Begawan Giri. A private estate that has emerged from the jungle near creative Ubud, it's so innovative and inspiring, and so unlike a hotel, this place has to be called awesome.

In lush private gardens, surrounded by rice paddies and mountains and fed by a holy spring that cascades into a waterfall, Begawan Giri's 21 sumptuous air-conditioned suites are housed in five fabulous residences. Each has its own butler and private pool, and its own special ambience. The suites all have king or queen-sized beds, and master suites have Jacuzzis on a private deck.

Features reflect the natural elements – earth, fire, air, wood and water – and are decorated with furnishings carefully chosen from all over Indonesia. In the rugged stone 'Sounds of fire' residence, a fire-pit is lit by the pool at night, and it is decorated in hues of indigo, dark red and brown, with raw black bamboo and tribal cloth furniture. From the meditative 'Clear water' residence built in antique Javanese teak, all that can be heard is the muted sounds of cascading water. It comes with a central floating pavilion and water gardens, and the master suite has a floating bathhouse.

Of sublime style, and really rather expensive, if there's a heaven on earth it must be at Begawan Giri. This is a place to bathe, walk and 'be' in nature and it has an exceptional spa. You can eat anywhere and anytime you like on the estate, if you don't want to go to the restaurants. New World cuisine is the order of the day with fresh ingredients from the garden and the estate's own poultry and prawn farms. When you want a change from the simple life, you can head to the colourful markets and vibrant streets of Ubud nearby.

As you share the living space in the residences, this isn't a place for complete priva-

---

THINGS TO SEE AND DO AROUND BALI

Nusa Dua, the location of the Four Seasons and Amanusa, is an upmarket tourist enclave on Bali's south coast. The area is so self contained with its hotels, shops and golf courses, that you wouldn't experience much of the real character of this country if you didn't stray out of the area.

A visit to **Ubud** is a must, even if you don't actually stay there. Ubud is the island's cultural centre, located inland amidst the rice terraces, where the book shops, museums and craft centres make great browsing.

There is so much shopping potential in Bali that it's difficult to know where to start but try to get a look at some of the following: antiques and stone carving in **Batubulan**, silver in **Celuk**, wood carving in **Mas**, woven cotton fabrics in **Sideman**, as well as textiles in Ubud. Just ten minutes from Amankila is **Tenganan**, a unique village dating back to pre-Hindu times, where the locals make the most exquisite double ikat fabrics and intricate basketry to be found in Bali.

If you want to incorporate some soft adventure in your honeymoon, local tour operators can sort you out with white-water rafting, sea kayaking, mountain cycling, bird walks and jungle trekking tours. Try sea kayaking to idyllic **Turtle Island**. For a gentler look at the coast, take a day or evening sunset dinner cruise aboard a sleek catamaran.

Little explored east Bali is today often referred to as 'the old Bali'. Free from tourists and development, this stunning area remains very much within the Hindu lifestyle of ages past. The region offers some of the finest trekking available on the island, ranging from beautiful and sedate walks through the forests and rice paddies to more strenuous hikes through the lofty mountains. Amankila has its own drivers and guides with an intimate knowledge of the region to help you find the best sights, or alternatively, you can hire a car and explore under your own steam.

The volcanic mountain, **Gunung Agung**, can be approached from the foothills of this region, while further east lies the ruined water palaces of **Tirta Gangga** and **Ujung**, from where much architectural inspiration was drawn by Amankila's architect.

Klungkung, just 20 minutes west of the hotel, is the former capital of Bali and home to the superbly painted ceilings of the **Halls of Justice**, as well as the starting point for tours to the artists' village of **Kamasan**, the **Mother Temple** at Besakih, **Sidemen's** fine weaving and terraced rice paddies and **Kintamani's** panoramic views of the volcanic **Lake Bratan**.

For further information see 🖥 www.touris mindonesia.com.

---

cy and seclusion. But with a staff to guest ratio of five to one, by the time you're through with being pummelled under a *bale* (an open-sided thatched roof hut) near the waterfall, and had a dip in the natural springs, you'll be so relaxed, you probably won't mind a couple of other people pottering about your very spacious home.

Four Seasons Jimbaran Bali

The best-known hotel in Indonesia is the Four Seasons Jimbaran Bali, which, since it opened in June 1993, has come to epitomise the utmost in hedonistic luxury, setting benchmarks by which other hotels continue to judge their progress. Despite being located on the southern tip of Bali, the most developed part of the island, Four Seasons Jimbaran is in a quiet village, and guests are so cocooned in luxury in the 14 hectares of tropical gardens that they'll forget the outside world exists anyway.

The luxuriously appointed villas are built into the gently terraced hill in groups of 20, clustered around seven village squares, each with its own designated village chief and group of 'service' family members. There are very few places in the world as romantic as the Four Seasons Jimbaran where, instead of rooms, guests are accommodated in Indonesian pavilions, each equipped with a private plunge pool. If you so wish, dedicated spa staff – one of the seven members of staff per guest – will pummel and swathe you to your heart's content in the privacy of your own villa.

The 139 one-bedroom villas are just perfect for couples and, with a minimum of 200 sq metres of outdoor and indoor living space, are really spacious. Three thatched-roof pavilions comprise an open-sided living and dining area, an air-conditioned sleeping pavilion with adjoining dressing area and closet, plus a luxurious bathing pavilion

FOUR SEASONS JIMBARAN

(☎ 701 010, 🖷 701 020), Jimbaran 80361, Bali, Indonesia

Reservations: Through Four Seasons' worldwide reservation numbers (see p13) and leading tour operators and travel agents worldwide (see pp11-12)

Getting there: Chauffeured Mercedes Benz or BMW limousine service available for transfers from Ngurah Rai International Airport

Accommodation: 147 units: 139 one-bedroom villas; six two-bedroom villas; two Royal Villas

Amenities: Pool Terrace Café, Taman Wantilan Restaurant, Terrace Bar and Lounge, PJs alfresco Mediterranean restaurant, Warung Mie noodle house; 24-hour villa service; 34m swimming pool with free-form soaking pool; award-winning spa; sauna and steam room, full selection of beauty services; fitness studio, complimentary windsurfing, sailing, snorkelling and instruction; two floodlit 'supergrass' tennis courts; comprehensive library; Ganesha art gallery; plus golf, scuba diving, white-water rafting, cycling and trekking tours arranged nearby

Dress code: Elegant casual

Weddings: Ceremonies can be arranged on the beach or within the hotel's wonderful tropical gardens – grounds fee from US$300; the hotel's own Bali-based agent will help with the necessary paperwork – registration handling fees from US$500; couples must reside in Bali seven working days prior to their wedding and couples must be of the same religion in order for the wedding to be lawful

Minimum stay: None

Rates: One-bedroom villa from US$550 two-bedroom villa US$1300, Royal villa US$2600; a five-night honeymoon package including private villa, transfers, champagne, flowers, full breakfast each morning, Bali by candlelight dinner in the villa, lunch at PJs and two Balinese massages costs around US$2800

Credit cards: Most major

Taxes and service charge: 21% tax and service charge will be added to your bill

with a large soaking tub, double vanity, separate shower, toilet and another shower outdoors in the adjacent secluded garden. But it is each pavilion's 15 sq metre private plunge pool nestled amongst beautifully landscaped gardens with two separate sun decks that has become the trademark extravagance of the Four Seasons Jimbaran.

Being a Four Seasons resort your pavilion, and the resort itself, is equipped with every kind of luxury amenity imaginable from slippers, robes, toiletries, CDs, minibars and 100% white cotton sheets, to full spa and beauty services.

There are also two floodlit 'supergrass' tennis courts, a 34m swimming pool which spills over into a seven-metre waterfall forming a free-form soaking pool below, and villa service around the clock so that you can enjoy all your meals in the privacy of your own dining area.

Kupu Kupu Barong

Kupu Kupu Barong is the perfect exotic mountain hideaway. Set high up among the rice terraces of Ubud, it is the most wonderfully relaxing and luxurious hotel and makes a superb place to spend the first few days of your honeymoon.

Guests stay in 19 beautiful Balinese-style bungalows which are spread out through the hotel's grounds so that you can't see any of the other bungalows from your balcony, just rolling green mountains with fantastic views over the **Ayung River**.

One of the best things about staying at Kupu Kupu is the all-pervading privacy: the chances are that when you use the pool you'll be on your own and the only non-jungle noises you are likely to hear from your bungalow are the occasional cries of white-water rafters as they are hurled down river.

The bungalows have a sitting area which has a minibar and tea- and coffee-making facilities and fabulous views through the huge window over the river. Beside the bed hangs a large mirror behind which is the bathroom. The bath, which is big enough for two, stands alone so that you can step in from both sides: there is also a separate shower. Some have an open-air shower. Batique-print robes are provided as well as a huge pile of properly fluffy white towels and another pile of striped swimming towels.

Kupu Kupu also has a luxurious two-storey Barong Suite, with its own private swimming pool, where Jerry Hall and Mick Jagger had their honeymoon. This spacious suite has a four-poster bed, bathroom with spa bath and a private swimming pool.

Kupu Kupu Barong is very near to paradise: stunning views, we had the run of the place and we had our own bungalow in the jungle. We went white-water rafting down the Ayung river and saw the resort from a different angle which was fun.

Bruce Walker

It was like being a very luxurious Tarzan and Jane only with air conditioning and room service; waking up with the jungle all around us and from our bed we could see straight out to the other side of the hills. Whenever we went to the swimming pool we always seemed to be alone and with the petals floating on the water it was like an enchanted garden.

Vanessa Walker

The bungalows are connected to the rest of the hotel via a labyrinth of pathways along which the scent of the flowers and exotic plants and abundance of butterflies is quite overwhelming. The open-air restaurant is in the hotel's main building and is very relaxed indeed with more wonderful views.

Kupu Kupu started life as a restaurant, famed for its views over the mountains, and the food is still renowned today. The best place to have lunch is by the bigger of the two swimming pools: the kind waitress does a very good job of keeping a low-profile while you're both swimming, but still manages to respond quickly should you feel like a pool-side snack of satay or a salad.

KUPU KUPU BARONG
(☎ 975 478, 🖷 975 079), PO Box 7, Kedewatan, Ubud Bali, Indonesia
Reservations: Direct or through tour operators Magic of the Orient, Abercrombie & Kent, Thomas Cook (see pp11-12)
Getting there: Transfer from Denpasar airport on request, approx US$20 per person one way, one-hour drive
Accommodation: 19 bungalows most with separate sitting rooms, spacious bedrooms and bathrooms; the Barong Suite has its own private pool
Amenities: Free use of mountain-bikes, restaurant, room-service, pool-side restaurant, two swimming pools, Hillside health spa; boutiques, art gallery, white-water rafting and golf can be arranged; courtesy shuttle to Ubud
Dress code: Relaxed casual
Weddings: Can be arranged, prices available upon request
Minimum stay: None
Rates: De Luxe Bungalow Doubles from US$335; Barong Suite US$699; honeymooners receive fruit and a bottle of sparkling wine on arrival
Credit cards: Most major
Taxes and service charge: 21% tax and service

There's lots to do around Kupu Kupu Barong, from mountain biking around the area to whitewater rafting on the river Ayung, but essentially it is a hotel for some serious relaxation spending the days lounging around the swimming pools.

OTHER INDONESIAN ISLANDS
Do try to see at least one of the other islands while you're in Indonesia, such as Sumatra, Kalimantan, Lombok, Sulawesi, Irian Jaya or Java. Each has differences in culture and landscape.

Lombok is constantly compared to Bali of ten years ago because of its unspoilt landscapes and unhurried pace of life. While Bali is lush and equatorial, Lombok is much drier and more rugged with some of the most spectacular geological features you'll ever see. Lombok is accessible from Bali by Pelini ferries departing several times daily, or by air with Garuda who fly to Mataram in Lombok almost hourly.

As well as pristine beaches, there is plenty to explore from ancient temples, palaces and local villages, to the stunning **Sindenggile** waterfall and the magnificent sunrise at the **Puri Mayura Royal Gardens**. The best beach is **Kuta** where unbroken white sand stretches all the way to **Tanjuna**. From Senggigi you can take the most incredible trip to **Gili Air**, **Gili Meno** and **Gili Trawangan**, three remote and unique islands which are only accessible by outrigger boats from **Bangsal Harbour**, which is an adventure in itself.

The Oberoi Lombok
If you need a reason to go to Lombok it has to be the wonderfully romantic Oberoi Lombok. On arrival you are greeted with a necklace of frangipani flowers. Looking out

THE OBEROI LOMBOK

(☎ 638 444, 🖷 632 496, 🖳 oberoi @indosat.net.id) Medana Beach, Tanjung, PO Box 1096, West Lombok 83001, NTB Indonesia

Reservations: The Leading Small Hotels of the World or Small Luxury Hotels of the World reservation numbers worldwide (see p12) or luxury tour operators such as Elegant Resorts in the UK (see pp11-12)

Getting there: Transfer provided for 28 km trip from Lombok Airport

Accommodation: 30 Terrace Pavilions and 20 Villas, 12 with private swimming pool

Amenities: Lumbung Restaurant for dinner and Sunbird Café for à la carte breakfast and lunch, Tokek bar; forty-metre eternity swimming pool, tennis court, gym, spa, PADI diving centre, snorkelling, water-skiing and windsurfing; mountain bikes, boat tours from beach club

Dress code: Smart casual

Weddings: Can be arranged

Minimum stay: None

Rates: Terrace Pavilions from US$240 Garden View, US$290 Ocean View; Villas from US$350; ask about romantic retreat or enchantment packages

Credit cards: Most major

Taxes and service charge: Tax 11% and service 10%

to sea the eternity pool is designed so that all you see is water ahead of you drifting into the ocean. There is water, water everywhere, and tranquil pools reflect an oasis of palm trees.

The extremely spacious and secluded cluster of Indonesian-style thatched roof, stone walled, luxury villas and terrace pavilions have private shaded balconies overlooking the lush gardens or the ocean. Villas have alfresco dining pavilions in the courtyard and most have their own swimming pools. The furniture is all made of local materials such as wood and bamboo and designer furnishings given a touch of the exotic with primitive art and artefacts. Lying in the sunken marble bath in the extravagant bathroom, you can gaze out over your own private garden and up at the sky as a tropically scented breeze wafts in through the window. Of course, the rooms are air conditioned and come with satellite TV, video and CD player and phone.

In the spa, which looks out over the lily pond, you can share a treatment room with your loved one and have a local Indonesian aromatic and volcanic clay body massage.

Cruises to secluded beaches for private picnics and to the enchanting Gili Islands, known for their fabulous coral and colourful fish, can be arranged, or you can hike to Mount Rinjani volcano. A PADI diving school offers courses, snorkelling and deep-sea diving and a new golf course has just opened up across the bay.

Before and after dinner you can relax with a cocktail in Tokek Bar to the sound of a classical guitarist. Lumbung Restaurant and the alfresco beachside Sunbird Café look out to the sea and up to the stars, both offer delicious continental and local dishes. Staying at the Oberoi offers the best of both worlds – unadulterated luxury in an unspoilt idyll.

Sri Lanka
(BEST TIME: AUGUST TO DECEMBER, FEBRUARY TO MAY)

Images of Sri Lanka range from the timeless plodding of water buffalo in paddy fields to raging waterfalls, lofty mountain peaks and colonial hill-stations. And of course, magical sandy beaches. The beauty of Sri Lanka as a honeymoon destination is that it has it all. In just a week, it is easy to see wildlife, explore the exotic scenery and rich culture and history. It also makes an ideal combination with a lazy week in the Maldives, or as a contrast to an Indian honeymoon.

SOUTH COAST

No honeymoon in Sri Lanka would be complete without starting or ending on a beautiful secluded stretch of Indian Ocean beach. The unspoilt south coast of Sri Lanka,

SRI LANKA
Lashings of culture, lush scenery and magical white beaches, in a small, relaxed ambience
Note: The fighting continues in the north and east of the country but the main tourist areas remain largely unaffected
When to go: August to December, February to May, avoiding the two monsoons
Average maximum temperatures °C (Colombo)

JAN	FEB	MAR	APR	MAY	JUN	JUL	AUG	SEP	OCT	NOV	DEC
30	31	31	31	31	28	28	28	28	28	28	28

Capital: Colombo
Flight times: To Colombo:
      New York:18 hours
      London: 11 hours
      Sydney: 10 hours
Approximate exchange rates: Sri Lankan rupee (SLR) – £1 = SLR123, US$1 = SLR75, A$1 = SLR46.83
Time difference: GMT plus 5½ hours
Country dialling code: ☎ 94
Voltage: 230/240v AC, 50 Hz
Combine with: Maldives, Indian Ocean destinations
Further information: Sri Lankan tourist board: 🖳 www.lanka.net/ctb

about three-hours' drive from Colombo, is where some of the best hotels and exclusive hideaways are found. You can choose from luxurious resort hotels on **Bentota** beach, a small, intimate hideaway nestled in the coconut palms near **Galle**, a charming, well-preserved 17th-century Dutch fort, or you can rent a villa or your own private island.

Saman Villas

Saman Villas, on a private, rugged headland jutting out into the Indian Ocean, is considered Sri Lanka's most luxurious and elegant retreat.

Situated in Aturuwella, a little fishing village just south of Bentota, it is about 66km from Colombo and a lovely peaceful spot for idyllic days and enchanting nights. Designed along the lines of ancient Ceylon, Saman villas has open-plan buildings, and is carefully arranged for glorious views from wherever you are.

An informal but indulgent hotel, it has just 27 spacious, open-plan suites offering breathtaking views along endless expanses of palm-fringed ocean from their large verandas. Each has a living room, sleeping deck, dressing room and a bathroom with a courtyard. Two suites are in a two-storey villa with a private garden. The rooms are opulently furnished and well-equipped with individual climate control, minibar, CD player, radio, satellite TV, telephone, safe and hairdryer.

From the main restaurant, serving Western, Eastern and spicy Sri Lankan dishes, there is a view of the large horizon swimming pool, which seems to merge with the

SAMAN VILLAS
(☎ 34 75435/70208, 🖷 34 75433, 🖳 samanvil@sri.lanka.net), Aturuwella, Bentota, Sri Lanka
Reservations: Direct, or in the UK through ITC Classics or Cox & Kings (see p11)
Getting there: Private car transfers can be arranged from Colombo International airport 66km (3 hours) away
Accommodation: 27 suites
Amenities: Two restaurants, two bars; outdoor swimming pool, sauna and steam bath; fitness centre, badminton, snooker, aromatherapy, massage; terraced gardens; library, jewellery shop; watersports, archery nearby, fishing and river cruises, excursions
Dress code: Informal/smart casual in evenings; gentlemen are expected to wear long trousers for evening meals
Weddings: Wedding packages start from US$800/£600 approx; room for receptions of up to 30 people
Minimum stay: None – weddings four days prior to the ceremony
Rates: Suites from US$150 to US$300
Credit cards: Most major
Taxes and service charge: Included

sea. At breakfast and barbecues in the Terrace Restaurant you can breathe in the delicate scents of the garden. There are two bars where you can go to just sit and absorb the view over a King Coconut cocktail.

There's plenty to do around here if you want to: excursions to Galle, fishing and river cruises, visits to a turtle hatchery, coral sanctuary or Buddhist temples nearby and a wide variety of watersports and entertainment in Bentota, including water-skiing on the river.

Other recommended hotels

Taj Exotica (☎ 34-75650, 🖹 34-75160, Bentota) is a modern, de luxe hotel set on a hillock overlooking the Indian Ocean. Although less intimate than Saman Villas with 162 rooms and suites, it offers perhaps the best facilities in Sri Lanka. There is a choice of restaurants serving both Sri Lankan and international food such as Thai and Chinese, and 24-hour room service. It has a beautiful swimming pool, health club and fitness centre, bicycles, tennis, watersports nearby, indoor games, excursions and entertainment such as live shows and a disco. Rooms are air conditioned with balconies offering views of golden beach stretching into the distance, and elegantly appointed with all the mod cons.

A standard double with sea view costs from US$155 per night, an executive suite from US$355, plus 10% tax and 12.5% service. The hotel offers a romantic package from US$445 per couple for three nights which includes bucks fizz on arrival, full board with breakfast in bed, transfers, a half-day sightseeing and a candlelit dinner on the beach. Book through UK tour operator Kuoni (see p11) and all main operators to Sri Lanka.

The **Sun House** (☎ 74-380275, 🖹 74-922624, 🖥 www.thesunhouse.com, 18 Upper Dickson Road, Galle) is a small luxury boutique-hotel with just six rooms. A tranquil oasis perched high above the town of Galle, the hotel has views across the harbour. Although within easy reach of Galle and breathtaking beaches, this previous home of a Scottish spice merchant is hidden behind high, creeper clad walls, it's whitewashed colonial pillars giving way to lush tropical gardens, a shady swimming pool and patio. The rooms at the Sun House are full of books, antiques and wonderful period furniture to give it the relaxed atmosphere of a stylish home, and the management are foodies which means you'll enjoy some of the best food to be found in Sri Lanka. There is no set menu, but the chef Ranavira can rustle up anything from Sri Lankan coconut curry to Thai chili-roasted Mahi Mahi fillet in lemon grass sauce and Cajun shark steaks with mango salsa.

At the Sun House you start the day with a hearty breakfast and linger over cocktails at sunset – a glorious place to completely unwind in elegant surroundings, with friendly but discreet, efficient service. The Cinnamon Suite costs US$180, De Luxe air-conditioned room US$130, standard rooms US$80. Also ask about the newly completed three additional suites at The Dutch House nearby. Book through UK tour operator Cox & Kings (see p11).

Renting a private villa

Two intimate, elegant villas along the south coast provide a tropical hideaway complete with housemaid, chef and security staff. Both are places to kick off your shoes and get back to nature in private. You may find it hard to choose between them.

The **Beach House** near Tangalle is a magical, beautiful spot on a private beach. A Dutch colonial plantation bungalow with colonnaded veranda, a few steps through the shady tropical garden, shaded by towering coconut palms, brings you to the stunning, deserted beach, which is excellent for boogie boarding, body or board surfing. The Beach House has plenty of space with three bedrooms (with ceiling fans) and lots of garden furniture to laze about on. From US$450 to US$650 per day, fully staffed.

Taprobane Island is a dreamy octagonal villa dominating a rocky islet just 200 metres from the shore, near Welligana. Built by Count de Mauny in the 1920s, it is totally private, with three tastefully decorated bedrooms and a sumptuous suite, a shady veranda wrapped around the villa and a swimming pool overlooking the ocean. This is a place for die-hard romantics. From US$550 to US$850 per day fully staffed. Book both properties through the Sun House (see p74) or through tour operators Abercrombie & Kent, or Western & Oriental (see pp11-12).

THE 'CULTURAL TRIANGLE'

As there is so much to see and do, you may want to base yourself here for a couple of days. Between the former Sinhalese capitals of Kandy, Anuradhapura and Polonnaruwa lie the ancient kingdoms of Sri Lanka, most now World Heritage sites.

Kandy, the last stronghold of the Sinhalese kings, is a lakeland paradise where visitors can escape the heat and spend tranquil afternoons relaxing in this wonderful village. Visit the Temple of the Tooth where Buddhists believe Buddha's tooth is housed, and explore the bustling bazaars. Drive from Kandy up to Nuwara Eliya and see its tea plantations and hill stations and across to hit bathtime at 3pm in the Pinnewala Elephant Orphanage, near Kegalle. Sigiriya Rock is where an international harem entertained an ancient banished king in the fifth century.

Recommended hotels

Hotel Kandalama (☎ 66 84100, 🖹 66 23482, 🖳 kandalama@aitkenspence.lk, PO Box 11, Kandalama, Dambulla), right in the heart of Sri Lanka's cultural triangle overlooking Sigirya, is a luxurious four-star eco-tourism hotel which relies on nature for its design. The tropical jungle grows literally across the roof made of terraces of wild grass, and flowering creepers hang like a curtain over the balconies and down the walls. Hotel Kandalama may be one of the most unusual hotels you're likely to stay in. Perched on the shores of an ancient reservoir, the forests surrounding Kandalama are teeming with wildlife such as deer, monkeys, porcupines and wild boar – best seen from the back of an elephant! The 162 rooms are simply furnished but airy, and all have balconies. Rooms are air conditioned with ceiling fan, bath or shower, TV and minibar.

There is plenty to do around here, from exploring the sights in the cultural triangle to elephant safaris, canoe rides or jungle trekking. Boating, swimming, windsurfing, horse-riding, badminton, tennis or indoor games are on offer as well as a welcome Ayurveda massage – perfect after a hard day's sightseeing and shopping.

The cuisine here is au naturel, with fruits, vegetables such as yam, curd, treacle and wild honey. You can eat either table d'hôte, lavish buffet or jungle barbecue while watching the sun set over nearby Sigiriya. Doubles cost from US$114/£80 per night including breakfast and government tax. A traditional Sri Lankan wedding package (arrival by elephant!) costs from US$796/£560. Book through UK tour operator Magic of the Orient (see p11).

The Maldives
(BEST TIME: MID-NOVEMBER TO APRIL)

The Maldives really are the ultimate islands – small lush green forested dots ringed by perfect white sandy beaches and coral reefs in a turquoise sea to the south-west of Sri Lanka. Some people love them and others wish they'd gone somewhere else, not because they were disappointed by the islands' beauty, which is indisputable, but because they felt claustrophobic staying on islands so small that you can walk round most of them in less than half an hour.

THE MALDIVES

Idyllic tiny islands ringed by white sand and coral, just perfect for beach lovers, very quiet in the evenings

When to go: The best time to visit is meant to be November to Easter (that's the theory – see p77); towards the end of May and into July/August the monsoons bring intermittent showers; at other times there may be occasional showers

Average maximum temperatures °C

JAN	FEB	MAR	APR	MAY	JUN	JUL	AUG	SEP	OCT	NOV	DEC
28	28	28	29	29	28	28	28	28	28	28	28

Capital: Malé

Flight times: To Malé from:

New York (via London): 18¾ hours

LA (via London): 25 hours

London: (via Dubai): 11 hours

Sydney: (via Singapore): 12½ hours

Approximate exchange rates: Rufiya (R) – £1 = R16.71, US$1 = R11.75, A$1 = R6.10

Time difference: GMT plus five hours

Voltage: 220/240v AC, 50Hz – all sorts of plug sockets are found in the Maldives

Combine with: Sri Lanka, Singapore, India, Dubai

Country dialling code: ☎ 960

Further information: 🖳 www.visitmaldives.com

The 1190 islands are scattered around 19 atolls spread over almost 800km of the Indian Ocean from north to south. Only 202 are inhabited, most of them home to Maldivian fishermen, but 70 have been transformed into tourist villages, each one occupying an entire island. These are found in the three central atolls: **Malé North**, **Malé South** and **Ari**.

If you are totally self-sufficient and don't need people around you or space to escape from other guests the Maldives will suit you – in fact you'll love them; likewise, if you are both enthusiastic divers and are keen to spend your days in the immense underwater playground that surrounds the islands. But be warned that if you are active people who like to sightsee, look elsewhere because you'll feel like prisoners on your own island in the Maldives.

You should also be warned that the food is not that exciting. While the fish is of course really fresh and the barbecues delicious, everything has to be flown into the island so don't expect extensive gourmet menus to be laid on each night. And even if a hotel does have lots of wonderful things on the menu you'll have to get used to the waiters saying that they've 'just' run out of that.

Assuming you do both like the sound of these charming little coral islands the next stage is to pick the right island for you. There are all kinds of resorts on offer in the Maldives from perfectly tranquil hideaways with only a dozen or so bungalows to a group of islands linked together so you can have peace and privacy on one and bars and restaurants on another, and there are even islands which are run as much bigger resorts with tennis courts, night-clubs and a range of different restaurants. Whoever you book your holiday through, make sure you state exactly what you expect from

CHARTERING A YACHT IN THE MALDIVES

Perhaps the best way to see these incredible islands without having to worry about being marooned on just one of them is to charter a yacht and sail from one to another.

A local Maldivian company called **Voyages** (🖹 325-336, 🖳 info@voyages.com.mv) runs dhoni charters which can be booked from the UK through **Andrew Brock Travel** (UK ☎ 01572-821 330): a 15-day package on-board one of Voyages' 15m dhonis costs from US$2904/£2042 per person which includes your flights, full board and a three- or four-man crew.

your island. Another good idea is to combine a week in the Maldives with some touring in Sri Lanka which is much bigger and more mountainous or, if you are coming from Europe, spend a few days acclimatizing in the worldly glamour of Dubai.

It is very difficult to say when is best to go to the Maldives. The weather pattern has changed so much over the years it is hard to tell when you should and shouldn't go. The optimum time is supposed to be between December and April during the north-east monsoon period because the weather is hot and dry and showers are only occasional – theoretically; having said that it always seems to rain at Christmas and New Year. February and Christmas are the busiest times, and weather charts show that June is wet but I've been there when it was wonderful. The best advice is to avoid August as the weather can be really mixed: otherwise take a chance and go – you may well get showers but they rush over the islands quickly because there are no mountains to trap the bad weather. Besides, you can always go to bed for the afternoon.

Soneva Fushi Resort

As you approach Soneva Fushi by air, you'll see why this hotel is a member of the Small Luxury Hotels of the World. Sand-fringed atolls in a turquoise sea, lagoons surrounded by coral reefs; opened in 1995, this incredible designer island is absolutely ideal for hedonistic escapists. Set on the otherwise uninhabited island of Kunfunadhoo, this haven of back-to-nature rustic chic was voted 'Top Hotel in the World 2000' by Condé Nast *Traveller* and is the only hotel in the Maldives to be listed in *Tatler*'s Best Hotels 2001.

All the rooms have bathrooms opening onto private walled gardens; each of the secluded duplex villas nestles in dense vegetation and has a patio with private garden, stunning views of the lagoon and its very own stretch of white sand beach just a few steps away. Rooms are decked out with simple but elegant, genuinely indigenous furniture made from bamboo, rattan and local woods; the lampshades are made from Mulberry bark. The rooms are mainly decorated in creams and whites but are set off with the merest dash of colour. And to pander to those seeking the Robinson Crusoe dream but nonetheless love their creature comforts, the hairdryer is hidden in the drawer of a coconut-wood desk; the minibar, safe, and quadraphonic hi-fi are concealed behind rattan, and the TV and VCR are delivered in a water hyacinth basket. Even fax messages are placed in natural bamboo canisters.

Honeymooners are given a bottle of champagne on arrival and a candlelit dinner – in your villa if you wish. And if you've had enough of seclusion, the General Manager, Alasdair Junor, holds a cocktail party every Tuesday, for guests to mingle. Soneva Fushi's cuisine matches every taste from simple barbecues to gourmet feasts accompanied by the best wines from around the world in the two alfresco restaurants. But it's the settings that are most memorable – a seaside moonlit barbecue, a desert island picnic,

SONEVA FUSHI RESORT
(☎ 230-304/5, 🖷 230-374, 💻 www.son evafushi.com), Kunfunadhoo Island, Baa Atoll, Maldives
Reservations: Small Luxury Hotels of the World toll-free numbers worldwide (see p12)
Getting there: 25 minutes by seaplane from Malé International Airport
Accommodation: 62 rooms and suites
Amenities: Kana Restaurant for creative Western cuisine, Me Dhuniye for an East-West fusion, Mihiree Mitha Sashimi lunch counter and Me Dhuniye bar; complimentary snorkelling, canoeing, windsurfing & hobiecat sailing, volleyball, badminton, tennis, cycling; table tennis, boules, games room, video and CD library; boutiques; PADI dive school, Six Senses Spa, fitness centre, speedboats, water-skiing, wakeboarding, cultural and diving excursions and picnics on deserted islands
Dress code: Casual
Weddings: No
Minimum stay: None
Rates: Rehendi rooms from US$150 to US$430, villas from US$230 to US$935; 30-minute complimentary massage if staying more than 4 days
Credit cards: Most major
Taxes and service charge: Included

a simple yet delicious lunch under a canopy of trees, or an intimate meal by lantern on a private beach. Soneva Fushi is where romantic fairytales turn into reality.

When you've done with cycling, nature walks, and sampled the wide variety of water sports including water-skiing, wakeboarding, snorkelling and world-class diving in the fully equipped PADI school, the masseurs in the heavenly Six Senses spa will help your soul catch up with your body.

Banyan Tree Maldives

The Banyan Tree resorts, of which there are only half a dozen worldwide, have got it pretty sussed. Here on Vabbinfaru, staying at the Banyan Tree means you can relax in the knowledge that you are on one of the most beautiful islands in the world, with accommodation to match.

Although the Maldives themselves are stunning islands, not all the resorts and hotels that have been built on them will live up to your expectations. At the Banyan Tree you can raise your expectations as high as you want and dream of elegant four-poster beds, delicious meals, impeccable room service and even relaxing spa treatments – you won't be disappointed.

Dotted around the island are 48 villas with conical thatched roofs and green louvered doors to allow you to make the most of the breezes coming in off the sea, and of course, the panoramic views.

The accommodation is really classy for the Maldives, with a solid king-sized four-poster shrouded in cream muslin, stone-tiled floors, wrought-iron candles and ornaments, and ornate carved wooden furniture. Each villa has a spacious terrace from where you can watch the sun dip below the horizon, and a private garden where room service will set up an alfresco meal for you. Some have a private outdoor Jacuzzi. Other amenities include ceiling fan, a phone, fully-stocked minibar, hairdryer, slippers and bathrobes, toiletries, coffee and tea-making facilities and an in-villa safe.

Honeymooners are offered a bottle of wine and fruit on arrival and a romantic dinner served on the terrace of your villa. The Banyan Tree will upgrade your room (subject to availability) and give you a lesson in how to massage your partner from a spa therapist – a good start to married life! The hotel's spa is a fabulous way to unwind after a long flight. Treatment options vary from ancient Eastern healing and relaxation to European rejuvenation therapies, using organic essences from aromatic plants and indigenous essential oils. And when you're invigorated, there are plenty of activities on offer from city excursions to snorkelling safaris.

> **BANYAN TREE MALDIVES**
> (☎ 443-147, 🖷 443-843), Vabbinfaru Island, North Malé Atoll, Republic of Maldives
> **Reservations**: Small Luxury Hotels of the World toll-free numbers (see p12)
> **Getting there**: 25 minutes on the hotel's speed-boat from Malé International Airport
> **Accommodation**: 48 private villas, most of which are sea-facing, with an open terrace and private garden
> **Amenities**: Spa facilities, badminton, volleyball, table tennis, pétanque, indoor games, video room and library, watersports including snorkelling, scuba diving, fishing, deep-sea fishing, water-skiing, windsurfing, sailing, sea plane trips, canoeing and glass-bottom boat trips; Ilaafathi Restaurant serving international cuisine and local Maldivian food, Sangu Garden Restaurant for barbecues, Naiboli Bar for cocktails and pastries with happy hour from 6.30 to 7.30pm; laundry, currency exchange
> **Dress code**: Casual or beachwear
> **Weddings**: The hotel does not cater for wedding ceremonies or receptions
> **Minimum stay**: None
> **Rates**: Suites from US$440 to US$940 full board
> **Credit cards**: Most major
> **Taxes and service charge**: All guests pay a US$6 bed tax per person per day

Four Seasons Resort Maldives at Kuda Huraa

Voted *Tatler*'s Hotel of the Year in 1999, Four Seasons Resort Maldives at Kuda Huraa epitomises elegant and fashionable escapism. But its beauty is more than skin deep –

with a Gold Palm-accredited diving centre, it also offers some of the most sensational diving in the world.

The living is easy in 106 beautifully-appointed, wooden, thatched-roof bungalows and suites. Water Bungalows and Navaranna Water Villas are set on stilts in the serene lagoon, from where you can simply walk down the steps into the azure water and swim amongst the neon-coloured fish (a freshwater shower conveniently awaits on the way back). Navaranna Water Villas are the most spacious. They have a lounge with wrap-round views of the sea and two bathrooms. In the Water Bungalows, the king-sized bed faces a glass-panelled window with a ceiling-to-floor view of the sea and the private veranda is perfect for secluded sunbathing. Beach Bungalows are situated on the fringe of the island fronting the sea, many with private plunge pools on the sand. All have private verandas and most have king-sized beds draped in mosquito netting.

The bungalows are all decorated in simple good taste with teak floors and wooden furniture. They all have mod cons such as air conditioning, ceiling fans, minibar, electronic safe, telephone, CD, video, satellite TV, full-length mirror, and brightly lit en suite bathrooms with thick absorbent towels, hairdryer, cotton robes and slippers, and Four Seasons luxury toiletries. Kuda Huraa is a reassuring place for comfort-loving Crusoes.

Swimming in the large, free-form, oval freshwater swimming pool lined with exotic blue tiles is a heady experience: extending to the edge of the lagoon, it seems to merge with the sea and sky. More earthly pleasures include a swim-up bar, an open-air Jacuzzi that overlooks the beach, and the Island Spa at Kuda Huraa which opened mid-2001 on a private island just minutes from the resort by *dhoni* (native Maldivian wooden boat) with innovative treatments from the Far East under its thatched pavilions. Being a Four Seasons resort, Kuda Huraa of course offers amazing service – if you want strawberries dipped in chocolate, you can have them. Honeymooners receive champagne on arrival, a daily fruit basket, honeymoon cake and a massage each.

A good range of watersports are on offer include snorkelling, canoeing, water-skiing, windsurfing and catamaran sailing, and the PADI dive centre runs courses and excursions (at local rates). There is also plenty to do when you feel like moving from your escapist paradise: photo trips by helicopter or seaplane, sunset fishing, shopping and sightseeing in Malé and, perhaps more romantically, being dropped off with a picnic lunch on your own private desert island.

FOUR SEASONS RESORT MALDIVES AT KUDA HURAA
(☎ 444-888, 🖹 441-188, 🖳 www.fourseasons.com), North Malé Atoll, Republic of Maldives

Reservations: Four Seasons reservation numbers worldwide (see p13) and luxury tour operators such as Elegant Resorts in the UK (see p10)

Getting there: 25 minutes by speedboat from Malé International Airport, US$78 per person roundtrip

Accommodation: 106 bungalows: 35 Beach Bungalows, 26 Beach Bungalows with pool, 6 Beach Bungalows with shower, 34 Water Bungalows, 4 Navaranna Water Villas, 1 Kuda Huraa Beach Villa

Amenities: Café Huraa signature restaurant serves à la carte Asian and Continental fare, Baraabaru restaurant for Maldivian fare, Reef Club, poolside terrace and bar, Nautilus Lounge; PADI dive centre, games room, huge freshwater swimming pool with swim-up bar, open-air Jacuzzi, private island spa with couple treatment pavilions; fitness centre; library and board games, activities include snorkelling, game fishing, sailing, island-hopping, excursions

Dress code: Casual; smart for dining

Weddings: Can be arranged; wedding package including frills (extra charge for musicians) costs US$1600 plus 10% service charge

Minimum stay: None apart from Christmas/New Year holiday period

Rates: Beach bungalow from US$325, beach bungalow with pool from US$500, Water Villa US$900, Beach Villa US$1200 all per couple including breakfast; honeymoon package includes champagne on arrival, fruit basket, honeymoon cake and massage for two

Credit cards: All major

Taxes and service charge: Government tax US$6 per person per night; 10% service charge

There is nightly entertainment in the Nautilius bar, which is open into the wee hours. The chef at Kuda Huraa took the trouble of bringing cooking pots from real Maldivian homes to be completely authentic. You can try freshly-caught fish Maldivian style at the Baraabaru Restaurant, tasty Mediterranean cuisine at the Reef Club, and at Café Huraa, the main restaurant, East-meets-West cuisine and buffet theme nights from around the globe are served under an open-sided thatched pavilion overlooking the lagoon. You may prefer an intimate dinner for two served in your own bungalow or on the beach. That, like most things you may desire here, is easily arranged.

Cheaper alternatives

If all the above sound ridiculously expensive a really good way of getting a great deal on a week or two in the Maldives is to call UK-based Kuoni (☎ 01306-747 000, 💻 www.kuoni.co.uk) two months before your wedding and ask them for their *Tropical Sun* brochure; this has a wide variety of good-value hotels and resorts. For example, two weeks in June at **Kurmathi Village** can be as little as US$1469/£1033 per person which includes absolutely everything: your flights, transfers, watersports, all meals and all drinks. UK-based Distant Dreams (☎ 0870-241 2400) offers seven nights all-inclusive on **Makunudu Island**, a small 2½-hectare island with 36 bungalows in North Malé Atoll from US$1605/£1129. Honeymooners receive fruit, flowers and a bottle of wine on arrival, champagne breakfast and candlelit dinner served on the beach.

The Seychelles
(BEST TIME: MAY TO NOVEMBER)

The Seychelles, an archipelago of over 100 islands in the Indian Ocean, is all about beaches. Known as 'the islands of love', if it's a romantic island setting you are after this place has all the right ingredients: palm trees, white sand beaches, brilliant aqua-marine seas and totally unspoilt coral reefs – sheer escapism for true romantics.

Holidays here aren't cheap, but for those searching for an idyllic beach paradise a long way from anywhere, and who don't mind bumping into other couples seeking the same, it is difficult to better the Seychelles.

THE SEYCHELLES

Lazy days spent on perfect island beaches, staying in beach bungalows, great watersports, and ideal for island hopping

When to go: May to September, when the south-east trade winds blow, is relatively dry; from October to April the north-west trade winds bring humid weather; the main rainy season is in December and January

Average maximum temperature °C

JAN	FEB	MAR	APR	MAY	JUN	JUL	AUG	SEP	OCT	NOV	DEC
30	30	31	31	30	29	28	28	29	29	30	30

Capital: Mahé

Flight times: to Mahé from:
New York: (via London) 24 hours
LA: (via Singapore) 26 hours
London: (via Nairobi or Europe)11½ hours
Sydney: (via Singapore) 14 hours

Approximate exchange rates: Seychelles rupee (Rs) – £1 = Rs8, US$1 = Rs5.5, A$1 = Rs3.02

Time difference: GMT plus four hours

Voltage: 240v, AC 50 Hz – 3-point square pin plugs

Combine with: Mauritius, Réunion, Kenya, South Africa, Dubai

Country dialling code: ☎ 248

Further information: 💻 www.aspureasitgets.com

THINGS TO SEE AND DO AROUND MAHE

Mahé is the largest of the islands in the Seychelles. Home to its international airport it is also the most lively of all the islands. Like many other islands here, Mahé is surrounded by a **coral reef** which protects the coastline and makes the crystal clear waters calm and ideal for snorkelling, diving and swimming.

Mahé has many beaches and coves of outstanding beauty: Beau Vallon is the largest and most sheltered beach and it offers an impressive variety of watersports (see box p83). And if you don't want to sit on an empty beach, you can hire a Mini Moke to drive around – it'll make you feel like Robinson Crusoe.

Mahé has two casinos and three nightclubs: the newest, *Jungle*, is run by Americans.

Arts and crafts in the Seychelles are some of the best in the Indian Ocean, with unique watercolour paintings, sketches and sculptures by local artists – not to mention the Creole music.

There are six walking trails marked out on Mahé, most of which are graded either as easy or medium and take only an hour or two at the most. From La Réserve suburb, a trail passes through a mahogany plantation, allowing you to compare the difference between a planted forest and a relatively undisturbed natural forest, and walk through one of the best areas of palm forest remaining on Mahé. Many people find it as spectacular as the **Vallée de Mai** on Praslin, in spite of the lack of coco-de-mer. You'll see five types of palm unique to the Seychelles, together with numerous other native plants and animals.

Another fantastic walk on Mahé takes you on the **Trois Frères** path through a section of **Morne Seychellois National Park** to the summit of the mountain overlooking **Victoria**. The National Park was created in 1979 and embraces a large part of the uplands of central Mahé. Alternatively take the steady climb up through Morne Seychellois National Park on to a huge expanse of granite rock (known locally as glacés) to **Copolia**, which at 500m above sea level has spectacular views of the east coast of Mahé.

Only a handful of these islands are visited by tourists. This part of the world may have been discovered a few centuries ago, but it was only when the international airport opened in 1971 that the Seychelles were put on the tourism map. Now over 100,000 visitors a year flock through the main island of Mahé.

Very few visitors remain on one island as it's so easy to take one of the many short boat or plane trips and go island hopping – over six islands are just ten to thirty minutes away. Nature lovers will marvel at the different islands' diverse and unusual bird life, while snorkellers and scuba divers can swim with the 150 species of tropical fish occupying the surrounding waters.

The Seychelles are not known for their nightlife, although there are bars dotted around Mahé – honeymooning here is all about being alone together on deserted stretches of beach and eating delicious alfresco meals.

Most island resorts and large hotels cater for weddings and the islands make a wonderful combination with a week on Mauritius. One word of warning though: because the Seychelles' beauty is natural rather than man made, spending your first week in the Seychelles lying on an empty beach will probably suit you both just fine; then go on to Mauritius, where there is more to do and the hotels' food, service, facilities and accommodation are generally superior.

MAHE
Le Meridien Fisherman's Cove

Le Meridien Fisherman's Cove has a very informal, club-like atmosphere which makes a few days here a very relaxing way to start your honeymoon. While it shouldn't be described as luxurious, Le Meridien Fisherman's Cove is without doubt the smartest hotel on Mahé.

Built in traditional Seychellois style, with its sweeping thatched roofs and rough-hewn local granite walls, this low-level resort blends in well with the stunning shore line at the western end of **Beau Vallon** beach. The tropical gardens are beautiful and

LE MERIDIEN FISHERMAN'S COVE
(☎ 247-247, 🖹 247-742, 🖳 www.lemeri
dien-fishcove.com), PO Box 35, Mahé,
Seychelles
Reservations: Through Forte-Meridien
Reservations (🖳 www.lemeridien.com);
or UK tour operators Elegant Resorts or
Sunset Travel (see p10)
Getting there: 30 minutes from Mahé
airport, the hotel can arrange transfers
Accommodation: 62 guest rooms: 19
standard rooms, 27 cottages, 12 junior
suites, 4 senior suites
Amenities: Two restaurants, one bar,
daily entertainment, 24-hour room service, boutique, excursions desk, car rental,
two tennis courts (floodlit), billiards,
table tennis, small freshwater pool;
water-skiing, windsurfing, deep-sea fishing and scuba diving at local rates, free
non-motorized watersports such as sailing, catamaran, windsurfing, canoeing,
kayaks, snorkelling
Dress code: Smart casual
Weddings: US$600 supplement per cou-
ple including all the trimmings
Minimum stay: None, apart from
Christmas and New Year when five nights
are required; stay five nights other times
of the year and receive champagne, flowers and fruit basket on arrival and either a
day's Mini Moke rental or a candle light
dinner for two
Rates: Superior doubles US$420,
Cottages US$550, junior suites US$680,
senior suites US$810, breakfast included
Credit cards: Most major
Taxes and service charge: 7% sales tax

full of colour and you could do worse than
start with the massage and aromatherapy centre to soothe any post-wedding tension away.

Each of the 19 standard rooms is housed
in a two-storey building. They all have air
conditioning, phone, satellite television and
video, radio, mini-fridge, tea and coffee
maker, private bath or shower, bathrobes and
personal toiletries, and furnished balconies
or terraces facing the ocean providing wonderful views.

There are also 27 terraced cottages at
Fisherman's Cove which open on to the gardens overlooking the sea. The décor is simple
with white tiled floors, wooden walls, white
cane furniture and colourful bed spreads and
curtains to brighten up the room. All rooms
have sea views and a balcony or terrace but
the best views of the water are undoubtedly
from the cottages which are closer to the
shore.

While the beach immediately in front of
the resort is swallowed up at high tide, the
adjacent beach, Beau Vallon, is only steps
away. This beautiful beach is superb for
swimming. Water-skiing, windsurfing, para
sailing, deep-sea fishing and diving are all
readily available on Beau Vallon beach at
local rates, while the resort's own complimentary facilities include three tennis courts
and a small freshwater pool where barbecued
food is served at lunchtime from **La
Carcassaille**, the poolside restaurant.

Free afternoon tea, coffee, cakes and
sandwiches are served daily in the **Blue Marlin Bar** overlooking the Indian Ocean. In
the evenings, guests can enjoy cocktails there (men are asked to wear long trousers).
Table d'hôte, à la carte and occasional theme night buffet dinners are served in the
Petit Pot restaurant. Red snapper and grouper are popular while meaty steaks of shark
and barracuda come grilled with tangy 'rougaille' sauce or are delicately transformed
into mouth-watering curries.

Other recommended hotels

Sunset Beach (☎ 261-111, 🖹 261-221, Glacis, PO Box 372, Mahé), perched on a bluff
on the island's west coast, is shining new throughout after a full renovation completed
in early 2001. It has retained its intimate, easygoing feel and secluded atmosphere and
the views over the hotel's perfect private beach and across the ocean to neighbouring
Silhouette Island are absolutely stunning, especially, of course, at sunset from the
new bar built on the rocks.

The hotel has only 18 de luxe rooms, six junior suites and one luxury villa, all of
which have private bath and toilet, air conditioning, a patio and sea views. In the rooms
are a minibar, hairdryer, safe and telephone. The hotel has a fabulous freshwater pool
and sundeck overlooking the ocean. Although snorkelling equipment is available for
use on the hotel's private beach, guests have to go to Beau Vallon beach for any other

SAILING AND DIVING IN THE SEYCHELLES

Sailing and yacht charters

If you're into sailing a few days' island hopping has to be one of the best ways of seeing these stunning islands.

UK-based **Sunsail** (☎ 02392-222 222, 💻 www.sunsail.com) offers flexible packages which allow you to plan your own route, although you need to go for a minimum of a week. They have a base at Port Victoria on Mahé, from where they take guests to La Digue in the north and to the unspoilt anchorages of Mahé's coastline in the south. From Victoria they will sail you east to the group of islands near **St Anne Marine National Park** where 150 different species of reef fish, crabs and sea urchins jostle in the crystal clear waters. They then sail south on a gentle cruise to **Anse Royale**, where silver sands stretch on endlessly. Prices per person for a week bareboat charter on a 35ft or 46ft yacht start at around US$1685/£1185.

Sunset Travel (UK ☎ 020-7498 9922, 💻 www.sunsetfaraway.com) offers flexible and luxurious catamaran cruises and honeymoon and wedding specials aboard the 42ft *Charming Lady*. Accommodation is in four double cabins with en suite facilities and an on board PADI diving instructor and equipment. Guests usually join the yacht at Praslin for a four- or five-day cruise around some of the Seychelles' most spectacular and remote islands. Fourteen nights including stay on Mahé and Praslin, international flights and transfers from US$2815/£1980 per person.

Diving

The warm waters and shallow inshore reefs attract a myriad of iridescent fish making the Seychelles the perfect spot for scuba diving, even if you haven't tried it before.

There are a number of dive centres where you can be trained by professionally qualified instructors who are members of the Association of Professional Divers. Most dive centres offer one-day introductory courses starting with a tutorial explaining safety precautions and the effects of diving and followed by a session in the swimming pool, familiarizing you with the equipment and techniques. Then, if you feel ready, you can experience the marvels of the Seychelles' reefs.

The centres also offer more intensive four-day PADI-certification courses encompassing tutorials, pool training sessions, and four open-water dives.

For more experienced divers holding a PADI or otherwise internationally-recognized certificate and log book, there are lots of exciting dive sites further offshore and on the outer islands. Manta rays, pelagic fish, ancient shipwrecks and even the wreck of the ill-fated naval tanker, *Ennerdale*, are there to be explored.

It is possible to dive in the Seychelles at any time of year, but the sea can be rough between June and September when the southeast trade winds blow, cutting visibility back to between 10 and 15m, while temperatures can fall as low as 24°C. From December to February the wind blows from the north-west making the Victoria side of Mahé sheltered. The very best months for diving are April/May and October/November when the seas are calm, visibility can reach over 30m on offshore sites and the water temperature is more likely to be around 29°C.

Most of the dives are from boats, on hard coral reefs (such as the Barrier Reef) and granite reefs encrusted with soft coral formations.

Dive centres

(* = PADI centre)

*Big Blue Divers (☎ 261-106, 💻 www.big bluedivers.net), Vacoa Village, Mare Anglaise, Mahé

*Bleu Marine (☎ 515-765), La Vanille Hotel, Anse La Blague, Praslin

*Island Ventures (☎ 247-845, 💻 www.island ventures.net), Berjaya Beau Vallon Beach resort, Mahé

Le Diable De Mers (☎ 247-104), Beau Vallon Beach, Mahé

*Underwater Centre (☎ 345-445, wwwdives eychelles.com.sc), Coral Strand Hotel, Beau Vallon Beach, Mahé

Denis Island Lodge (☎ 321-143, 💻 denis@seychelles.net) Denis Island

Pro-Diving (☎ 234-232, 💻 barbe@sey chelles.net), La Digue Lodge, La Digue

*Dive Centre (☎ 281-281, 💻 lemuria@sey chelles.net) Lemuria resort, Praslin

watersports. De luxe doubles start from US$260, Junior Suites, ideal for honeymooners, from US$340 including breakfast. In the UK, Sunset Travel (see p10) offers wedding packages from US$810 per couple. Honeymooners receive a tropical fruit basket and sparkling wine on arrival, a seafood dinner (excluding wine) and an upgrade to a Junior Suite subject to availability.

Xanadu (☎ 366-522, 🖹 366-344, 💻 www.xanaduresort.com, PO Box 3038 Anse Royale, Mahé) is a secret waiting to be discovered. Samuel Taylor Coleridge refers to the fabled city of Xanadu as a sunny pleasuredome – that is exactly what this modern-day resort is. It is Mahé's most southerly resort and is in a secluded spot far from the hustle and bustle of main roads, packed hotels and beaches. At Xanadu, yours may be the only footprints you find.

Designed to reflect a traditional fishing village, Xanadu comprises 8 spacious (100 sq metres), free-standing chalets. Sliding doors open onto a covered private patio with magnificent views – an ideal place to spend lazy days and evenings. Air-conditioned one- and two-bedroomed chalets have telephones, television and VCR, and a video library is available.

Comfort is the order of the day. Rooms are tastefully furnished with a huge lounge and a fully equipped kitchen that gives you the luxury of sleeping late. Xanadu restaurant is known for its superb Creole delicacies. The resort has a small freshwater swimming pool, breathtaking nature trails, an unspoiled, hidden private beach and snorkelling on the coral reef with over 800 species of exotic fish nearby. Enjoy at least one sundowner while watching the flying foxes from the patio with a 180° view of the endless ocean. One-bedroom chalets US$168/DM370 self catering, or US$235/DM517 half board. Book through UK Seychelles specialists Elite Vacations (see p10).

Keep a look out for the new **Banyan Tree**, a five-star hotel of 100 rooms and 36 pool villas (from around US$600 a night) at Anse Intendance on Mahé; it opened in December 2001.

PRASLIN
L'Archipel

L'Archipel on Praslin is without doubt one of the finest hotels in the Seychelles. Perched on the hillside, this charming little hotel has truly stunning views over the **Côte d'Or Bay**, and is the perfect place to escape for a few days.

Guests are accommodated in 30 hillside cottages built from local wood and granite, with Scandinavian-style interiors and green corrugated roofs. All the rooms measure 40 sq metres and have sea-facing verandas; they are either single or split-level with separate entrances to give you more privacy. Each comprises a double bed (some four-posters) covered with pretty muslin mosquito netting hanging down from the polished wood ceilings. The rooms also have simple pieces of beautifully-crafted furniture including a louvred wardrobe, cane chairs and table, and cool terracotta tiles on the floor.

They are well-equipped with minibar, in-room safe, phone, satellite TV, music, an overhead fan and tea/coffee-making facilities. A large bathroom comes complete with lovely freebie toiletries, lots of towels, two basins and a separate toilet. Most important of all there is a full-width balcony offering

L'ARCHIPEL
(☎ 232-242, 🖹 232-072, 🖳 www.lar chipel.com), Anse Gouvernement, PO Box 1346, Praslin, Seychelles
Reservations: Either direct or through Colours of the Indian Ocean or Sunset Travel in the UK and other Indian Ocean resort specialists (see p10)
Getting there: 20 minutes from Praslin airstrip, reached by a 15-minute flight from Mahé, the hotel can arrange for a taxi transfer
Accommodation: 23 hillside cottage rooms, three senior suites, four executive suites
Amenities: Cocktail lounge, two restaurants – gourmet dinners at La Feuilee d'Or, creole dishes at the Beach Restaurant; games room, gym and massage room, complimentary canoeing, snorkelling, windsurfing, and excursions to nearby coves by boat; scuba diving for qualified divers and deep-sea fishing can be arranged at local rates; car rental; beachcombing by helicopter
Dress code: Ties and jackets are not required but gentlemen are asked to wear trousers for dinner and women to dress up
Weddings: L'Archipel does wedding receptions for small groups of up to 20
Minimum stay: None
Rates: Standard doubles US$470; senior suite US$574; executive suites US$718, half board; basket of fruit and champagne for honeymooners on arrival, upgrade subject to availability and a day's car hire if staying five nights
Credit cards: Most major
Taxes and service charge: Included

THINGS TO SEE AND DO ON PRASLIN

Praslin is the second largest island in the Seychelles. Although quieter than Mahé, it still has three nightclubs and a casino.

Praslin is a good base from which to visit some of the other islands via inexpensive ferries. Approximately 40 km north-east of Mahé, it is reached by boat in two hours or in just 15 minutes by plane. There is enough to see and do on Praslin and its nearby islands to keep most couples entertained for a week, so it makes a good initial destination.

Once the haunt of Arab traders and treasure houses for pirates, Praslin is the perfect tropical island. Much of the interior is virtually virgin forest: the **Vallée de Mai** is an 18-hectare area of dense forested woodland off the road between **Grand Anse** and **Baie Sainte-Anne**. One of the Seychelles' most famous natural beauty spots the Vallée, now a World Heritage site, is home to hordes of different plant life: the

strangely-shaped coco-de-mer, an enormous indigenous coconut resembling the female pelvis, inspired General Gordon to dub the region the original Garden of Eden when he visited the island over a century ago. Such is the rarity and notoriety of the coco-de-mer, the fruit from an extraordinary palm tree found only in the Vallée and neighbouring **Curieuse Island**, its flesh has since become regarded as an aphrodisiac.

Make a point of eating out at **Les Roches**, Le Pointe one night, as the food and beach-side setting are truly excellent.

Ferries run from Praslin to neighbouring **Cousin Island**, a bird sanctuary, on Tuesdays, Thursdays and Fridays. This tiny island, spanning less than one kilometre, is home to just six people and quantities of exotic flora and fauna, including tortoises, turtle doves and turtles.

---

superb views of the bay below, while being discreetly secluded from your neighbours.

The four luxurious suites are quite magnificent: measuring around 100 sq metres they have a separate lounge and large wrap-around veranda where evening meals can be enjoyed, a walk-in wardrobe, bathroom with bath and shower, plus a second toilet and shower. Bathrobes and slippers are provided in the suites.

In the main building, high above the small private beach, is the reception area, cocktail lounge and a wooden open-fronted restaurant with wonderful views from the tables looking out over the ocean. **Le Feuille d'Or** serves gourmet dinners – some of the best food in the Seychelles – while creole specialities are served at the **Beach Restaurant**. Twice a week L'Archipel has live music in the evenings.

L'Archipel has a good reputation for service; staff are continually being trained and retrained in Mauritius or in the south of France. Owner/manager Louis d'Offray has done much for the reputation of this hotel and is usually on hand to ensure guests are comfortable and high standards are met.

Recent renovations have included a new gym, swimming pool and games room. Snorkelling, windsurfing, hobie-cat sailing and canoeing from the hotel's white sandy beach are available free of charge, as are the boat trips to visit nearby coves, while deep-sea fishing and scuba diving can be arranged at local rates. L'Archipel prides itself on being able to offer its guests almost any kind of excursion whether it be a boat cruise to visit a few nearby islands or beachcombing by helicopter.

LEMURIA

Named after a legendary lost continent where 'once ancient palm forests grew down the hillside to the beach; beaches that bore no imprint of human footsteps', no other hotel in the Seychelles can quite match up to the brand new Lemuria. This 88-suite hotel, the largest in the Seychelles, is a first. The first and only five-star de luxe hotel and the first and only to offer an 18-hole championship golf course in the whole of the Seychelles archipelago.

Cocooned in luxuriant vegetation, the main building hugs the hillside in a sheltered spot in the north-west of the island, just five minutes away from Praslin airstrip. Heavy double doors face you as you approach in a golf cart to check in. But parting, they reveal a stunning view of three swimming pools, set in natural granite boulders,

LEMURIA
(☎ 281-281, 🖨 281-000, 💻 www.lemuri
aresort.com) Anse Kerlan, Praslin,
Seychelles
Reservations: Either direct or in the UK
through Elite Vacations or other Indian
Ocean specialists (see p10)
Getting there: Five minutes from Praslin
airport
Accommodation: 88 suites: 80 junior
suites, 8 senior suites
Amenities: Three à la carte restaurants –
the Legend, serving international cuisine,
the Sea-Horse, serving Mediterranean,
and the Beach, with fresh seafood salads,
grills and 4 bars – three-level swimming
pool, 2 boutiques, library with videos and
CDs, hairdresser, beautician and spa with
massage available; complimentary sports
include fitness centre with sauna, Jacuzzi,
steam baths, plunge pool and gym, two
floodlit tennis courts, pedalos,
snorkelling, sailing, catamarans, kayaking, windsurfing; scuba diving with PADI
diving school, deep-sea fishing, watersports lessons and golf for an extra
charge; excursions and car rental
arranged
Dress code: Smart casual
Weddings: A wedding package with
marriage fees, fruit and flowers, polo
shirts and a bottle of sparkling wine on
arrival, one-tier wedding cake and bottle
of champagne costs US$288
Minimum stay: Seven nights
Rates: Junior suites from US$345, senior
suites from US$690 with breakfast; hon-
eymoon couples receive a bottle of champagne, fruit basket and t-shirts on arrival
Credit cards: Most major
Taxes and service charge: Included

cascading into one another, in front of a dazzling white beach. Greeted with a welcome
drink and cold towels as you arrive, you
immediately know you won't want to leave.
Lemuria achieves 'total tranquillity and
refined elegance' through its use of natural
wood and stone to create a harmony of architecture and nature and stylish simplicity.
Lemuria is for couples looking for privacy
and exclusiveness in an earthly paradise.

The suites nestled in the trees are a
fusion of natural wood, marble, stone and
pink granite with palm-leaf roofs, all set off
with cream fabrics and rich dark brown furniture with just a hint of colour in the scattered cushions and subtle pictures. Just 15
metres from the shore, all have fantastic
views of the Indian Ocean from their ter-
race/balcony and all have air conditioning,
ceiling fans, minibar, safe, TV, VCR and CD
and cassette player, telephone with answer
machine etc and an open-plan bathroom.

Among all this elegance, turtles still lay
their eggs in peace on Lemuria's three
secluded white sand beaches. Stepping outside you are in the midst of the beauty of
nature. Soak up the atmosphere on the wood-
en sun lounges or hammocks around the
three-level cascading swimming pool or follow it as it flows to the sea for complimentary watersports, snorkelling, sailing, catamarans, pedalos, kayaking or windsurfing. The
dive centre is PADI qualified and offers
courses for all levels and excursions, and of
course there's golf and tennis, and the spa
and fitness centre to explore.

After a complimentary glass of wine/champagne with 'amuse-gueule' in your
room, and a sundowner at the bar nestled among the trees, you have a choice of three
restaurants at Lemuria. But the Beach Restaurant overlooking the sea is the place to be
when the sky is clear and the moon is full.

Other recommended hotels

The **Village du Pecheur** (☎ 232-224, 🖨 232-273, 💻 village@seychelles.net, PO Box
372, Glacis, Mahé) is a very basic but informal and comfortable hotel in a wonderfully secluded location in the centre of Praslin's largest and most beautiful beach, Côte
d'Or.

For a slightly more authentic island experience book into one of the four superior
beach bungalows and you'll actually be living on the beach. Each of the 12 rooms and
one first-floor suite in Village du Pecheur is simply furnished, but they do have a king-
size bed, shower, toilet and bidet, phone, hairdryer, mini-fridge and air conditioning,
so they're not that spartan!

Life is very relaxed at the Village, so although men are meant to wear trousers
after 7pm, shoes are redundant from the moment you arrive. Guests enjoy the laid-

back 'house party' atmosphere of the buffet dinners, beach-side lunches, and hours spent lying back on the big cushioned chairs in the cosy bar.

Beach Standard from US$180, Beach Superior from US$250, Suite from US$325, all including breakfast.

LA DIGUE

La Digue Island Lodge

La Digue Island Lodge is the best known of the many lodges and guest houses stretching out along the west coast of La Digue. Here the lifestyle is simple, giving guests a real taste of Seychellois life.

Accommodation at the Lodge comes in all shapes and sizes: most of the 25 simply constructed 'A' frame chalets are right on the beach, and nine rondavels (thatched huts) are set among the palm trees and are ideal for couples. There are also eight rooms and nine suites in the pale Yellow House, a converted plantation house set on the other side of the road from the Lodge.

All rooms have been decked out with new teak furniture and are air conditioned with all the mod cons: minibar, TV with video and music channels, telephone, hairdryer, and tea/coffee-making facilities. Suites have spacious tiled bathrooms with bath, a separate shower, and bidet as well as a balcony looking out to Praslin. The A-frame chalets and rondavels are quite adequate for couples although the rondavels have showers only. The Yellow House rooms have luxurious bathrooms, but no terrace.

LA DIGUE ISLAND LODGE
(☎ 234-232, 📠 234-100, 🖥 www.la digue.sc), Anse Reunion, La Digue, Seychelles
Reservations: Either direct with the hotel or through UK tour operators Elegant Resorts, Elite Vacations and Sunset Travel (see p10)
Getting there: A short schooner journey from Praslin, once on the island you can arrange for an ox cart to transfer you from the jetty to the hotel, a return costs SR30 per person
Accommodation: 60 rooms: four first floor suites, five ground floor suites, 25 A-frame chalets and nine Rondavels, eight rooms in the Yellow House, plus seven annexe apartments
Amenities: Restaurant, poolside snack bar with swim-up seating, hotel bar, entertainment, barbecues, billiards, games room, reading room, TVs in the reading room and lounge, two boutiques, foreign exchange, complimentary daily boat excursions, dive centre nearby
Dress code: Casual elegance
Weddings: Ceremonies can either be carried out by local registrar on the beach or at a location of your choice or by a priest in the church; most people opt for the registrar as it involves less paper work; receptions can involve whatever you like and the hotel is well-equipped with a band, video, photographer etc all on hand
Minimum stay: Three nights
Rates: Garden villa from US$265/E300, beachfront chalet from US$350/E405 and from US$380/E440 for a suite, all half board per night
Credit cards: All major
Taxes and service charge: Included

Whichever room you opt for, the Lodge welcomes honeymooners with fruit and flowers in your room, and also decorates your bed.

The large open-air restaurant overlooks La Réunion beach, which lies to the front of the hotel and is ideal for long lazy days in the sun. Creole cuisine is taken very seriously at La Digue Lodge: the restaurant is simple but superbly built with a cool sandy floor and a lofty thatched and beamed roof. The swim-up bar enables you to spend long afternoons indulging in fabulous cocktails while keeping cool in the water. Snacks are also served here.

The Lodge is family-run; staff operate complimentary daily boat excursions to neighbouring islands and can organize fishing and scuba diving in association with **Marine Divers International**. Take a trip around La Digue, enjoy some fishing, snorkel off the beach, watch the birds at **Cousin**, **Aride** or **Fregate** islands, or venture further afield on one of the Lodge's yachts.

The beauty of staying on La Digue is that there's plenty to do if you choose to, or you can just as easily lie on the beach or on the teak sun loungers round the pool, doing absolutely nothing.

THINGS TO SEE AND DO ON LA DIGUE

Half an hour by boat from Praslin, La Digue is a place of tranquillity, where ox-carts and rusty old bikes are the only form of local transport, and time seems to stand still.

La Digue is known for two things: its superb beaches and its bizarrely-shaped granite rock formations, resembling vast Henry Moore sculptures. Most of the wide deserted beaches are just perfect for long walks, swimming and snorkelling, but particularly beautiful are the beaches on the west coast, between **Pointe Cap Barbi** and **Anse Pierrot**, while the most incredible rock formations are at **Pointe Source d'Argent** and **Pointe St Jacques**, three quarters of the way down the west coast.

The best way to see them is to find yourself a bicycle, grab a picnic and head off for a gentle pedal around the island, which, measuring only 3km by 5km, is very easy and enjoyable to cycle around. Look out for the rare Black Paradise

Flycatcher in the island's woodlands: although it was once judged to be near extinction recent estimates put the number at over 100 living on the island.

There is a lovely trail following the coast-line road south from the jetty at **La Passe**, which it is possible to do either on foot or by bicycle. You'll pass several old houses built in the architectural style of the French colonial era and continue inland across a broad plateau, through agricultural land and freshwater marsh-land. The path then takes you up a relatively gentle climb through woodland and orchards before descending through farmland and marsh and eventually coming to the remote white beach of **Grand Anse**. This is a lovely easy walk which will take a couple of hours on foot, or an hour by bike. Stop for a picnic at Grand Anse before returning the way you came.

DENIS ISLAND LODGE

(☎ 321-143, 🖷 321-010, 🖳 denis@sey chelles.net), PO Box 404, Victoria, Mahé, Seychelles

Reservations: Direct or through Indian Ocean resort specialists (see p10)

Getting there: 30-minute flight from the International Airport on Mahé (not daily), It costs around US$202 return; 'Bride travels free' special offered by some tour operators such as UK's Sunset Travel (see p10)

Accommodation: 24 cottages and one suite

Amenities: Breakfast room service, restaurant, lounge, bar and TV room, scuba diving, snorkelling, windsurfing, sailing, tennis, billiards, table tennis, visits to other islands, deep-sea fishing

Dress code: Casual attire, but men are asked to wear long trousers in the lodge after 7.30pm

Weddings: Denis specializes in weddings; a small chapel is available on the island and special requests are catered for

Minimum stay: Three nights

Rates: The cottages cost between US$440 and US$470 per couple per day full board; the suite costs an additional US$125

Credit cards: Visa, MasterCard, American Express

Taxes and service charge: Included

DENIS ISLAND
Denis Island Lodge

Denis Island is the place if you want to get right away from any signs of mainstream tourists and is a honeymoon favourite. The island lies on the Seychelles Bank where several record-breaking Dogtooth tuna and Bonito have been caught. A wonderfully relaxed French ambience pervades this 140-hectare coral island hideaway making it the sort of place where you kick off your shoes on arrival and don't bother finding them again until it's time to leave.

Guests stay in 24 pretty, thatched beach cottages laid out along this beautiful island's most sheltered beach with wonderful views over the ocean. The cottages are large and extremely comfortable, comprising a spacious en suite bathroom with a bath and shower, a separate toilet, a simply and traditionally furnished bedroom area and a large veranda at the front which is just perfect for escaping the sun. Although the beds aren't huge, they are comfortable and look very pretty shrouded in mosquito netting. Only one executive cottage and the lodge's only suite are fitted with a phone on request.

The caring attention of the staff is what makes people enjoy their stay at Denis so much. When you come back to your room at night, beds will be turned down, all the shutters will have been closed, and the floor is continually being swept. Denis's guests always remark upon how immaculately clean the rooms are kept: your sheets are changed every other day and both beach and bathroom towels are changed daily.

During the day guests either make the most of the incredible snorkelling or venture out to sea either for scuba diving or deep-sea fishing, which is reputed to be world class. There are also sailing boats, a tennis court and lots of inland walks through the jungle. A walk around the island is a lovely way to spend 45 minutes but do watch out for the tides, as you may end up swimming if you misjudge them.

Denis's food is just amazing. Unless you order breakfast in bed all meals are taken in the main lodge, a huge and very beautiful open-sided building where the lounge, bar and a TV room are also located. The house speciality is Creole curries: they are absolutely delicious and are accompanied by lots of salads, marinated tuna and other tasty raw fish dishes. Lunch is a buffet, while waiters serve gastronomic cuisine in the evening. The only thing to watch out for is the wine which is ridiculously expensive all over the Seychelles: a quite ordinary bottle will cost a good US$35!

Denis is a privately-owned island which, the owners state very clearly, they do not wish to turn into a hotel. As their brochure says: 'Our sole ambition is to enable you to accomplish a dream' – they seem to be doing this pretty well!

Other recommended hotels

Bird Island Lodge (☎ 323-322, 📄 323-335, reservations: ☎ 224-925, 📄 22407, 🖥 birdland@seychelles.net or bird@seychelles.net, PO Box 404, Victoria, Mahé) comprises 24 sea-facing bungalows on a tiny island where a million sooty terns mate between May and September, and other unique bird life can be seen year round. Also home to Esmerelda, the world's largest land tortoise, this private island offers peace and tranquillity to a maximum of 48 guests. Each bungalow has its own patio overlooking the gardens, with the sea just a few steps across the glorious pink sandy beach.

This is real *Blue Lagoon* stuff, with a few well-chosen luxuries such as the king-sized four-poster bed, ceiling fan, a lounge area and a large shower room in each of the simply designed, but cool, bungalows. The hotel has an informal bar and a more formal small restaurant serving Creole seafood, after which most guests choose to retire early.

There really isn't much to do on Bird, apart from wallow in the splendid isolation of it all, have an occasional rummage through the well-thumbed books in the library or wade out into the turquoise waters snorkel in hand. If you stay for just one night a double room costs from US$305 full board. Although tour operators in the UK such as Abercrombie & Kent (see p10) suggest combining just one night on Bird with another island, the rate goes down considerably the longer you stay.

If you really want to push the boat out you can honeymoon on or even hire **Frégate Island** (☎ 324-545, 📄 324-499, 🖥 fregate@seychelles.net, PO Box 330, Victoria, Mahé), a private, romantic tropical island just a 15-minute flight from Mahé. Sixteen impeccably designed air-conditioned villas are nestled in tropical trees and flowers overlooking the crystal clear water. All warm wood and thatched roofs, they are decked out in hand-carved furniture and antiques with a constant view of paradise through the glass wall/doors. Each spacious villa has a large private deck with hot tub and Jacuzzi, king-size sun beds and two large bathrooms.

Frégate offers the kind of service you would expect from the most exclusive resort in the Seychelles. With Elite Vacations (see p10) in the UK seven nights full board including international flights and transfers costs from US$5950/£4185 per person.

Mauritius
(BEST TIME: APRIL TO JUNE, SEPTEMBER TO NOVEMBER)

People go to Mauritius for the beaches and their palm trees, white sands and warm waters, but most of all they go for the unrivalled reputation of this island's upmarket hotels.

If you dream of a honeymoon filled with every conceivable luxury in an idyllic beach setting then this large tropical island, 1932km off the coast of Kenya, was made for you. It has to be the ultimate destination for people looking to drop their bags on the bedroom floor and head straight for the beach, cocktail in hand, safe in the knowledge that they won't have to leave the resort's gates for anything until it is time to go home.

With a coral reef almost completely surrounding the island, the waters of the lagoons are warm and tranquil, making them ideal for year-round watersports and allowing the island's devotees to refer to it as the 'world's largest swimming pool'. It certainly is the ultimate Indian ocean playground for beachcombers, swimmers, sightseers, fishermen, scuba divers, surfers and all escapists.

Unusually for idyllic islands Mauritius also enjoys an enviable reputation for fine cuisine, due largely to the ethnic variety of its people: dishes are touched with African, Indian, French and Creole influences.

The standard of service and the facilities of the hotels featured here are so impeccable that if you are going to combine a week in Mauritius with anywhere else in the world, such as a South African safari or a week in the Seychelles, you'd better leave Mauritius to last as no other hotel is likely to compare favourably afterwards. Mauritius's gourmet fare and its superior night-life, also mean that it is better to come here for your second week once you've had a chance to relax and are ready for a bit of sophistication. And make no mistake, Mauritius is all about style and sophistication: the kind of hotels you will encounter are summed up by one of the brochures to the island that advises visitors to 'take their best beach and casual wear' – these are not resorts for scruffy Bermudas!

MAURITIUS

An exotic Indian Ocean island which has become one of the world's ultimate honeymoon destinations largely due to its stylish, sophisticated resorts with their reputation for first-rate accommodation, service, facilities and best of all, food

When to go: The best weather is between April and June and September to November, although afternoon showers can occur at any time of year; avoid November and March because of cyclones

Average maximum temperatures °C

JAN	FEB	MAR	APR	MAY	JUN	JUL	AUG	SEP	OCT	NOV	DEC
28	27	27	26	25	23	23	23	24	25	27	28

Capital: Port Louis

Flight times: to Port Louis from:
New York: (via Paris) 19 hours
LA: (via NY and Paris) 27 hours
London: 12 hours
Sydney: (via Perth) 14 hours

Approximate exchange rates: Mauritian rupees (Rs) – £1 = Rs32; US$1 = Rs20, A$1 = R16.33

Time difference: GMT plus four hours

Voltage: 240v AC, 50 Hz; UK-type three-pin plugs

Combine with: The Seychelles, South Africa, Paris

Country dialling code: ☎ 230

Further information: 🖳 ww.mauritius.net

Le Saint Géran Hotel

Laid out among fragrant tropical gardens Le Saint Géran is Sun International's flagship property in Mauritius and a member of The Leading Hotels of the World. This famous, award-winning hotel has long been popular with honeymooners seeking sophistication and elegance in a superb beachfront location. From the moment you enter the magnificent gateway and spectacular hall with its superb curving arcades leading to the interior gardens, you know you are going to be cocooned in luxury, pomp and grandeur.

The hotel's facilities are just wonderful: a nine-hole golf course with its 4500 palm trees, extensive watersports, floodlit tennis courts and even a casino and a new tennis club and Givenchy spa. Refurbished and remodelled, it emerged in December 1999 even more glorious than before, and with the addition of 148 spacious and comfortable junior suites, 14 ocean suites and a sumptuous villa with its own swimming pool.

Already one of the best places to eat on the island, the new Spoon des Iles has been opened by Alain Ducasse, twice recipient of three Michelin stars, copying his restaurant of the same name in Paris. Thirty-five butlers, specially trained by Ivor Spencer, regular banquet organizer at Buckingham Palace, are now available 24 hours a day.

Decorated in pastel tones with pale, limed furniture, the rooms have a light, breezy feel and all have their own balcony or terrace. The huge beds are comfortable and are covered in flowers when you come back from dinner at night. All over the room there are pieces collected from every corner of the world: a wooden carved Thai head board, a Chinese painting on the TV cabinet and woven patent leather chairs that apparently come from the Philippines. The bathrooms are elegant and now spacious, full of pink marble, with all the expected trimmings including Molton Brown toiletries. The ground floor rooms are so close to the beach that you can be in the water within a minute of getting out of bed. Each room and suite has satellite TV and DVDs with a large choice of films.

The beach is wonderful, a huge long curve arching right around the hotel grounds and into the lagoon. The hawkers can be annoying, but that aside the beach is fabulous and the watersports facilities excellent. The hotel is also cleverly designed so that all motorized watersports take place in the lagoon, ensuring that they don't impinge on the peace of those relaxing by the poolside. Aside from the complimentary watersports

---

LE SAINT GERAN HOTEL
(☎ 401 1688, 📠 401 1668, 🖥 infostg @sunresort.com), Belle Mare, Mauritius
Reservations: Sun International offices worldwide (see p13), the Leading Hotels of the World toll-free numbers (see p12) and leading tour operators and travel agents worldwide
Getting there: The hotel can arrange transfers from the airport (1 hour)
Accommodation: 148 junior suites, 14 ocean suites and one villa
Amenities: 24-hour butler service; La Terrasse Restaurant main dining room, Paul & Virginie Alfresco Restaurant, Spoon des Iles, casino, Gary Player-designed nine-hole golf course, five tennis courts (floodlit); shuttle service to Le Touessrok; Givenchy Spa with sauna, massage, hairdressing and beauty salon, boutique, personalized excursions, gym with personal trainers, yoga and aqua gym, large swimming pool, full range of complimentary watersports including unlimited water-skiing, mainsails, hobie cats, laser sails, paddle boats, canoes, glass-bottom boats, snorkelling, windsurfing; scuba diving, catamaran sailing cruises, deep-sea fishing, para-sailing, horse-riding and cycling charged locally
Dress code: Although there is no formal dress code, Le Saint Géran is a smart hotel and guests usually dress up for dinner, especially in the à la carte restaurant
Weddings: The hotel operates a strict policy of only one wedding per day; you can get married three working days after your arrival (the legal formalities are carried out in Port Louis and the ceremony at your chosen location at the hotel), prices vary according to requirements but virtually anything can be arranged; there are no set limits for reception numbers
Minimum stay: None
Rates: De luxe doubles from US$700/Rs20,000, suites from US$3970/Rs113,335
Credit cards: Most major
Taxes and service charge: Taxes are included, service is discretionary

LE TOUESSROK & ILE AUX CERFS

(☎ 419 2451, 🖷 419 2025, 💻 www
.touessrok.com), Trou d'Eau Douce,
Mauritius; (note that Le Touessrok will
be closed for several months in 2002 for
complete refurbishment)
Reservations: Sun International offices
worldwide (see p13) and most leading
tour operators and travel agents
Getting there: The hotel can arrange
transfers from the airport (55 minutes)
Accommodation: 200 guest rooms: 80
standard rooms; 79 superior rooms; 37 junior suites; one Coral suite; one York suite;
one Princess suite and one Royal suite
Amenities: Four tennis courts (floodlit),
pétanque, volleyball, football, 1500 cubic
metres of pool surface and a smaller pool
on Ile aux Lièvres, free watersports on Ile
aux Cerfs including hobie cats, laser
sails, windsurfers, paddle boats, canoes,
water-skiing, snorkelling, glass-bottom
boat trips, five beaches with snack and
bar service, nightly entertainment, Le
Sega Bar, Les Paillotes Bar, La Passerelle
main dining room, Giannino Italian
restaurant, Les Paillotes à la carte restaurant (French cuisine) and Khazana
restaurant (Indian cuisine), 24-hour room
service, shops, sauna, beauty and massage salon, free shuttle bus to Le Saint
Géran; Ilot Mangénie private island with
restaurant and bar; Ile aux Cerfs with two
more restaurants, a bar and beach service;
deep-sea fishing, scuba diving, sailing
cruises, para-sailing, speedboat hire and
golf are all charged locally; nine-hole
golf course at sister hotel Le Saint Géran
– no green fees
Dress code: Although there is no formal
dress code Le Touessrok is a smart hotel
and guests usually dress up for dinner,
especially in Les Paillotes
Weddings: The hotel operates a strict policy of only one wedding per day; you can
get married three working days after your
arrival in Mauritius (the legal formalities
are carried out in Port Louis and the ceremony at your chosen location at the hotel)
although documents must be forwarded at
least 3 weeks in advance; prices vary
according to requirements, but virtually
anything can be arranged; there are no set
limits for reception numbers
Minimum stay: None
Rates: Double rooms cost around per
day with half board US$490/Rs12,670;
Junior Suites cost around US$665/
Rs17,200
Credit cards: Most major
Taxes and service charge: Taxes are
included, service is discretionary

there are five floodlit tennis courts and a
nine-hole golf course, and plenty of peaceful
corners for those who want to retire with a
book.

A honeymoon at Le Saint Géran is all
about enjoying an idyllic beach setting while
being totally enveloped in your own private
world of luxury. You name it and you've got
it at this hotel: oysters in the middle of the
night, a lagoon trip at dawn, a massage under
one of the palm trees, little nibbles served in
the morning, a chilled glass of champagne in
the privacy of your balcony as the sun sets.
Some might find the service and sheer abundance of facilities a little over the top – they
even present you with a rose when they bring
you breakfast in bed – but others will delight
in the knowledge that they are being pampered by 650 people in one of the world's
most luxurious hotels.

Le Touessrok & Ile aux Cerfs

Sister hotel to Le Saint Géran, Le Touessrok
is the more romantic of the two. As we go to
press, however, it has been announced that
Le Touessrok will be closed for several
months in 2002 for complete refurbishment.

Built on a small promontory on the eastern side of the island, Le Touessrok epitomises the kind of honeymoon hotels that we
all, at some stage in our life, have dreamt
about. Everywhere you look, impossibly
deep blue skies meet towering palm trees,
dark, thatched roofs and whitewashed
facades. Marble pathways span the shimmering waters of a swimming pool that circles
around the various parts of the hotel so that
wherever you look you can see turquoise
water. Clichéd yes, but absolutely perfect.

The architect's imaginative use of the
location is what makes Le Touessrok such an
incredible resort to stay in. Many of the
rooms occupy their own private islet, connected to the rest of the hotel via foot bridges
over the vast twisting swimming pool so that
it feels as if you're in some sort of mini
Venice; others are fanned out along the private beaches of the main island.

The standard of the rooms does vary
considerably: standard rooms have been
redecorated recently with small marble bathrooms and limed oak furniture; the décor in
the larger superior rooms is more dated, fea-

turing lots of dark wood and a wooden bath-room, but they are very spacious and are gen-erally cool and light due to the white walls, plus they have a sitting area. All the rooms have private balconies with a sea view, private bath and shower, satellite TVs with video channels, air conditioning and minibars. With twice-daily maid service you are assured of a constant stream of fresh towels and toiletries with the Sun International seashell logo.

We stayed at both Le Saint Géran and Le Touessrok, but Le Touessrok was definitely the more romantic of the two. It's spread out over a large area so it's easy to find peace and tranquillity. If you are looking for a beautiful setting with a mixture of luxury and privacy then go to the Touessrok. Le Saint Géran was very elegant and sophisticated, but the clien-tele was older and we felt it would be more suitable for silver weddings than honey-moons!' **Carolyn and Roger Reynolds**

Honeymooners are greeted with a bottle of sparking wine and a basket of fresh fruit on arrival, and are also given dinner in the romantic Italian restaurant **Giannino** or in the privacy of the room, and a sunset speedboat ride. Half-board guests eat in the main restaurant, **La Passerelle**, where typical meals are a mixture of buffet and à la carte service and a blend of different styles. The local Mauritian food is spicy and real-ly excellent, however there is a disappointing lack of seafood, though the fresh fish from the lagoon is good. In the evening the meals are either buffet-style, table d'hôte or a gala menu which can consist of as many as six or seven courses. Overall the serv-ice is faultless and breakfast, when served in the room, is always prompt and delicious.

Le Touessrok is a beach lover's paradise, with five superb beaches dotted around the hotel which never seem to be very busy and usually quieter than at Le Saint Géran. The hotel has two private islands: **Ilot Mangénie** which has amazing, uncluttered beaches and the **Ile aux Cerfs**, which is open to the public and offers a good selection of watersports.

Royal Palm

I have spoken to honeymooners who spent their first week at Le Saint Géran and then moved on to the Royal Palm and definitely preferred the latter.

A member of The Leading Hotels of the World chain, the Royal Palm is a truly first-class resort, continually laying claim to its reputation as the Indian Ocean's finest hotel. Obviously it depends on what you are look-ing for in a resort; some British couples said they found the Royal Palm a bit too 'Royal', rather smart, plush and almost too grown up; others loved it.

Situated on a perfect beach in the north-west of the island close to fashionable and more developed **Grand Baie**, the Royal Palm is a true 'resort' hotel. It is the sort of place where people come to be seen, armed with the hotel's own mobile phones designed to make ordering room service from the beach that bit easier, and where five out of the first seven sentences in the brochure end in an exclamation mark.

This stylish and sophisticated haven is a harmonious blend of stone, thatch and wood

ROYAL PALM
(☎ 209 8300, 🖹 263 8455, 💻 royal palm@intnet.mu), Grand Baie, Mauritius
Reservations: Beachcomber Hotels and Tours (UK ☎ 01483-533 008, 💻 b@bc tuk.demon.co.uk), or The Leading Hotels of the World reservation numbers world-wide (see p12)
Getting there: The hotel can arrange transfers from the airport
Accommodation: 84 guest rooms in total: 57 de luxe rooms, 26 suites and one Royal Suite
Amenities: Two à la carte restaurants, bar, 24-hour room service, swimming pool, water-skiing, windsurfing, sailing, deep-sea fishing, speed boats, three astroturf tennis courts, squash, golf practice, hair-dresser, sauna, massage, boutique, snook-er; plus use of all other Beachcomber hotels' facilities in Mauritius
Dress code: Smart casual
Weddings: Beachcomber has a policy that only one wedding a day can take place in each of its six resorts, giving the event much less of a packaged production line feel; they can arrange anything you want
Minimum stay: None, except Christmas and New Year
Rates: Double rooms from US$760/Rs 19,000, suites from US$1480/Rs 37,000, breakfast is included
Credit cards: Most major
Taxes and service charge: Included

and is located right on the edge of a lagoon. The hotel's 84 rooms are set in manicured gardens, all are sea-facing with their own balcony, private bathroom with separate shower and toilet, sitting area with radio, TV with in-house videos, minibar, in-room safe, hairdryer, and individually controlled air conditioning. The dark polished wood in the bedrooms provides a distinctly colonial atmosphere and all rooms have an ocean-front private terrace where the tasteful wooden furniture makes it the perfect place to sit out for breakfast.

The Royal Palm's two à la carte restaurants, **La Goelette** and **Le Surcouf**, offer truly fantastic cuisine which has earned them their place among the island's best. The evening entertainment is quiet and discreet, allowing you to enjoy your tranquil candlelit dinner in peace. In fact, this is a very quiet hotel in the evenings, but there are other restaurants and nightclubs not far away, or you could take a taxi to sister hotel **Trou aux Biches** only ten minutes away.

As part of the Beachcomber Hotels, guests of the Royal Palm are permitted to use facilities at the group's five other properties on the island, which is a real advantage as it's lovely to drive round the island stopping for lunch at another fantastic hotel.

Paradise Cove Hotel

Paradise Cove Hotel stands beside a secluded sandy cove at the north end of the island and is set in four hectares of landscaped gardens. It is a charming hotel and one of only two in Mauritius to be represented by the prestigious Relais & Chateaux.

Paradise Cove Hotel is the smallest of all the properties featured in this chapter with only 67 air-conditioned rooms, so you'll never find too many people on the beach and will always be able to find a lounger around the lovely swimming pool. Its secluded location and the limited number of residents mean Paradise Cove Hotel is a perfect place to get away from it all in unspoilt and unpretentious surroundings. The hotel-keeping is impeccable, guests are always greeted by name and are treated pretty much as though they own the place.

Guests are accommodated in one- and two-storey traditional Mauritian-style buildings clustered around the brilliant blue bay. All the buildings face the lagoon and have a terrace or a balcony and direct access to the beach. Each room has a TV with video/cable channels, minibar, music system, en suite bathroom with hairdryer and separate shower, and a separate lounge area with two chairs and a low table. In tune with the décor around the hotel, the bedrooms are furnished with an appealing mixture of bright sunny colours and peaceful cream walls and solid, comfortable furnishings.

PARADISE COVE HOTEL
(☎ 204 4000, 🖅 204 4040), Anse La Raie, Cap Malheureux, Mauritius
Reservations: Relais & Chateaux toll-free reservation numbers worldwide (see p12), plus most leading tour operators and travel agents worldwide
Getting there: Taxis from the airport take about 75 minutes and cost approximately US$73; helicopter transfers approximately US$174
Accommodation: 67 rooms: 47 de luxe rooms, 18 junior and 2 senior suites
Amenities: Outdoor swimming pool, free sports facilities include two floodlit tennis courts, volleyball, archery, mountain-biking tours, 'undersea' walk, water-skiing, windsurfing, kayaking, snorkelling, pedalos, hobie cats, glass-bottomed boat trip and catamaran cruise with picnic, submarine safari, aqua-gym classes and deep-sea fishing; submarine safari, para-sailing and scuba diving can be arranged at local prices, two restaurants, beach bar/restaurant, pool bar, cocktail bar
Dress code: Choice of informal or formal dining in the two restaurants
Weddings: Yes, approximately US$428 per couple
Minimum stay: Two nights
Rates: De luxe doubles from US$460 half board, Junior suites from US$560, Senior Suites from US$770; honeymoners receive complimentary sparkling wine on arrival, candlelit seafood dinner, free upgrade subject to availability and best of all, a 50% discount on the bride's accommodation
Credit cards: Most major
Taxes and service charge: Included

THINGS TO SEE AND DO ON MAURITIUS

Apart from lounging around under a palm tree and other beach-based activities, there isn't really that much to do in Mauritius; it really is a resort-based honeymoon. All the hotels featured here have an impressive range of leisure facilities including tennis, watersports, sailing, cruises, scuba diving, deep-sea fishing and golf, which should keep you occupied for most of your stay. When you fancy a change hire a car for a day and drive around the island, visiting nature reserves, extinct volcanoes and waterfalls.

White Sand Tours (☎ 212 3712) offer a good selection of excursions, such as the day-long **Romance of the South** and **Romance of the North** tours. The southern tour includes **Trou-aux-Cerfs**, an extinct volcano crater, **Curepipe**, the sacred Hindu lake in the **Grand Bassin**, and the waterfalls and seven-coloured earths of **Chamarel**. The **Pamplemousse Gardens**, which have a large collection of indigenous and exotic plants, form part of White Sand Tours' northern tour, along with a boat trip to Grand Baie for lunch.

Another great boat tour is a day on *Isla Mauritia*, a lovely old schooner built in 1852, which now takes guests out for day sails stopping off for a picnic lunch; you might find the music provided by the crew a bit tacky.

If you want to hire your own car, make sure you drive up to Chamarel as, apart from the beautiful scenery, there are some great restaurants up there. Try *Le Chamarel* (☎ 683 6421), a lovely airy French restaurant right up in the mountains with gorgeous views down to the sea, or *Le Domino* (☎ 683 6675) in **Le Monde** right up at the top of the mountain.

The best places to shop in Mauritius are at the market in **Port Louis**, the island's capital and main port, and at Curepipe, the main residential town; it has a good shopping area and is a fine place to escape the heat. Worthwhile buys include saris, silk shirts, basketwork, pottery, wood-carvings and locally made jewellery – look out for the intricate models of 18th- and 19th-century sailing vessels which are crafted at Curepipe. If you do buy textiles it is worth getting something made up while you are there as local dressmakers can easily rustle something up in 24 hours.

For enthusiastic photographers looking to capture an insight into island life it's worth getting up early and driving to one of the many salt farms near the island's main beaches: the local workers come to collect salt once the sea water has evaporated.

The hotel has three restaurants and two bars: the intimate thatched pavilions of **La Cocoteraie** on the shore line where delicious seafood is served in a casual environment, **Le Beach Bar** which provides light lunches and daytime snacks as well as being a bar, **La Belle Creole** restaurant which enjoys sweeping views over the lagoon and neighbouring islands. The cocktail bar and lounge is somewhat ridiculously named **Le Cosy Corner**! The watersports facilities are similarly extensive, and a catamaran makes day trips to nearby islands for snorkelling and picnics.

Only 8km away is fashionable Grand Baie, but you'll probably find days slip past very pleasantly at Paradise Cove Hotel without going anywhere else.

Other recommended hotels
The **Oberoi Mauritius** (☎/📠 204 3625, 🖳 reservations@oberoi.intnet.mu, Baie aux Tortues, Pointe aux Piments, Grand Baie) opened in 2000 and is a member of both The Leading Hotels of the World and Small Luxury Hotels of the World. With Thai-influenced architecture in lush subtropical gardens and an impressively long golden beachfront, the Oberoi Mauritius stands for unadulterated luxury, style and seclusion. Designed to reflect the mix of Mauritian cultures, spa treatments include massages using local Mauritian coconut oil, while the stone heads of deities around one of the magnificent pools give the place a mystical air.

Accommodation is in 76 thatched roof Villas and Terrace Pavilions, decorated in subtle colours with exotic and vibrant original artworks, teak furniture and marble bathrooms overlooking a walled garden. The Villas have a raised open-air dining pavilion where you can admire the impressive view of mountain ranges and turquoise sea over an alfresco breakfast, and most have private swimming pools in their courtyard. If you want a complete hideaway two Royal Villas have their own entrance and dining gazebo overlooking the large private swimming pool.

All watersports, golf and tennis are on offer during the day. And at night, while eating wonderful Creole food in the thatched roof open-air restaurant, you can hear the gentle tinkling of the pianist playing at the beautifully-lit bar converted from a ruined 18th-century inn, just 100 yards away. Terrace Pavilions from US$291/Rs8307, Villas from US$441/Rs12,600, with pool from US$530/Rs15,120, and Royal Villas from US$823/Rs23,500 including breakfast, tax and service. Book direct, or through The Leading Hotels of the World or Small Luxury Hotels of the World reservation numbers worldwide (see p12).

Then there's **Le Prince Maurice** (☎ 413 9100, 🖹 413 9129, 💻 www.princemaurice.com, Choisy Road, Poste de Placq). In June 2000, Relais & Chateaux gave Le Prince Maurice the honour of 'Palace' status, placing it amongst the 17 best hotels in the world. It's also the most expensive hotel on Mauritius. As you step inside, the vision from the vaulted lobby, leading to a stunning slate grey infinity pool that meanders through the restaurant and spills down to a pristine white sand beach, is simply awesome.

Located on the north-east of the island, about one hour by road from the airport or 15 minutes by helicopter, this 'new generation' hotel is distinctly luxurious. The design is one of understated elegance and cool sophistication, with suites scattered along the pristine beach, among luscious tropical gardens, or elevated on stilts over a natural fish reserve. Honeymooners will find the Senior Suites on the beach exceptional as they have their own infinity pool. They also have a private walled garden with a marble soaking bath and a dining terrace perfect for a silver service lunch of lobster and champagne.

An array of complimentary land and watersports are offered here, including golf at the nearby Belle Mare Plage 18-hole championship golf course. The ultimate in sublime pampering is offered by the Guerlain Imperial Beauty Centre, a holistic temple of aromatic courtyard gardens, lap pool and even a dual massage deck!

Evenings are spent dining at the à la carte L'Archipel restaurant or on delicious seafood fresh from the sea at Le Barachois, the unique floating restaurant accessed by a teak boardwalk meandering through the mangroves over the lagoon. Junior suites from US$232 to US$526, senior suites from US$464 to US$1052, Princely Suite from US$2417, including breakfast, tax and service. Flowers, a basket of fruit and a bottle of wine are offered to honeymooners on arrival and if you want to get married here, the bride is given a 50% discount in Junior and Senior Suites. Book through Hotels Constance UK (☎ 01233-770 067, 🖹 01233-770 069, 💻 AGA.Tourism@btinternet.com) or luxury tour operators to Mauritius (see p10).

La Pirogue (☎ 453 8441, 🖹 453 8449, 💻 www.lapirogue.com, Wolmar, Flic en Flac) is not as glamorous as its sister Sun International properties, and some people would say it's positively old-fashioned. But that, it seems, is its charm. It is a lot less pretentious than its sisters, yet with the same fantastic array of facilities and therefore ideal if you're looking for something not too formal. La Pirogue is popular with families, which means it has a convivial atmosphere, but is obviously not the place to go if the sight of children annoys you.

Spread out in tropical gardens along four kilometres of dazzling white beach are thatched, high-arched 'pirogue' bungalows housing 180 rooms. All the rooms are lovely, light and airy, with air conditioning, minibar, en suite bath and shower, in-house video, TV, radio and a terrace. The 40 superior rooms and two suites are the ones to go for, as they are much more spacious and right next to the beach.

At La Pirogue there is absolutely everything you could possibly dream of doing: easy-going glass-bottom boat trips and snorkelling; windsurfing, water-skiing, kayaking, laser sailing and para-sailing for the more active; land-based activities such as

(**Opposite**): Lemuria, The Seychelles (see p85).

pétanque, aerobics and tennis; and La Pirogue's big two, scuba diving and big-game fishing for which this island is so famous. All are complimentary apart from para-sailing, diving and big-game fishing. There is also a wide variety of dining options from barbecues and themed buffets to Chinese fare. Doubles in a superior room cost from US$154/Rs4400 to US$268/Rs765, Royal Suites from US$345/Rs9850 to US$438/Rs12,500 for half board including 14% taxes. Reservations through Sun International offices worldwide (see p13) and all leading tour operators and travel agents.

Finally we come to the **Residence** (☎ 401 8888, Coastal Road, Belle Mare). Some hotels make the headlines the day they open – the Residence is one of these. On the east coast of Mauritius, it opened in early 1998 and the same year was listed among the great names in luxury hotels. The dazzling white sand beach – one of the most beautiful beaches on the island – stretches out for over a kilometre and the hotel has recreated the charm and elegance of the colonial 1920s. The building resembles a traditional Mauritian manor house with dramatic vaulted ceilings, simple style and natural colours: subtle shades of beige and polished, honey-coloured hardwood highlighted by antiques collected throughout Asia (in contrast to the colourful interiors of many Mauritian hotels).

From the moment you arrive at the Residence – by helicopter if you like – you will receive the very best of Mauritian style, hospitality and service. Cold towels and iced tea welcome you as you register in your room and your bags are unpacked by your personal butler – whether in a room or suite. The gentle aroma of cinnamon and oriental spices wafts through the 151 well-appointed, spacious rooms, with their opulent marble bathrooms, vast dressing rooms and beige silk and white linen. From the fully-equipped boathouse you can go sailing, snorkelling, water-skiing and more. Scuba diving, catamaran cruising and fishing are available for an extra charge, or you can relax by the large pool or in the Sanctuary spa – the best on the island.

Dining is on top quality, authentic island cuisine at the Plantation, in a stunning ocean-front setting, and evening entertainment ranges from singers to jazz piano to the local sega dance groups. But it doesn't go until late so you can enjoy the quietness of evening strolls on the beach, floodlit tennis, or an exotic cocktail, fresh fruit or delectable ice-cream on your spacious balcony in the midst of the lush tropical gardens.

Ocean View Doubles cost from US$314/Rs8970, suites from US$393/Rs11,210 including breakfast and government tax. Ask about the special 7-night honeymoon packages. Book through UK tour operators Colours of the Indian Ocean, ITC Classics or Susie Freeman (see p10).

(Opposite): Rooms with idyllic watery views. **Top:** Lemuria, The Seychelles (see p85). **Bottom:** River Club, Victoria Falls, Zambia (see p249).

3

EUROPE

England
(BEST TIME: APRIL TO OCTOBER)

In 1804, William Blake wrote of England's green and pleasant land in a poem, *Jerusalem*, which has since been adopted as an English anthem, every bit as much as *Land of Hope and Glory*, or even *God Save the Queen*.

Although almost two centuries have passed since Blake was writing, much of the English countryside remains unchanged. The England of historic stately homes set in rolling green pastures, cream teas in quaint tea shops and roast beef served in front of roaring log fires on a Sunday is still very much in existence. If you are both lovers of old-world living, history and culture, then you'll enjoy exploring the ancient cities of **Oxford** and **Cambridge**, **Bath**, **Cheltenham** and **York**, and the countless picturesque 16th- and 17th-century villages, scattered throughout this 'green and pleasant land'.

A honeymoon in England can be romantic whether it's winter, spring, summer or autumn, with different, quintessentially English things to do during each of the seasons. England in the spring is a place where newborn lambs cavort on the Yorkshire Dales and wild yellow daffodils line the road side.

The summer really is all about clotted cream teas served on immaculately-mown lawns, with a game of croquet to follow; picnics washed down with jugs of cider in buttercup fields looking down on the Cornish coast; and the wonderful English summer sporting calendar including Ascot Races, rowing at Henley and, of course, tennis at Wimbledon.

ENGLAND
Rolling countryside peppered with ancient castles and historic houses, beautiful cities such as York and numerous small villages to explore
When to go: All year round: summer is from June to September, winter from December to the end of March; rain is possible in any season
Average maximum temperatures °C

	JAN	FEB	MAR	APR	MAY	JUN	JUL	AUG	SEP	OCT	NOV	DEC
London	4	4	6	8	11	14	16	16	14	11	7	5

Capital: London
Flight times: to Heathrow from:
    New York: 7½ hours
    LA: 11 hours
    Sydney: 21½ hours
Approximate exchange rates: Pound sterling (£) – US$1 = £0.70, A$1 = £0.36
Time difference: GMT (plus one hour from the last Sunday in March to the last Sunday in October)
Voltage: 240v AC, 50 Hz; three-pin plugs
Combine with: Ireland, the rest of Europe
Country dialling code: ☎ 44
Further information: Check websites 💻 www.travelengland.com or www.visitbritain.com

The Lake District is the place to be in the autumn; once the crowds have gone you'll be left virtually alone with the rolling hills and stunning lakeland scenery as the trees turn a thousand different hues of red and gold.

If you can cope with the cold, then winter is arguably the best season of all to experience the English countryside: enjoy long frosty walks in the New Forest until you stumble across a 16th-century pub for lunch and revel in the warm welcome inside as you settle down in front of a roaring log fire with a pint of beer and a steaming dish of steak and kidney pie. Bliss.

Most of the hotels I have included here were originally country houses and were built two or three centuries ago: thus they have great character and a charm all of their own. But one word of warning, don't go to the country houses of Yorkshire, Devonshire, or the New Forest expecting to find vast bedrooms. Almost without exception the rooms in these hotels are quite small, having been built so long ago, and it is strictly forbidden by English law to alter the features of these 'listed' buildings. So try to look upon the size of the rooms not as a fault of the hotel, but instead as part of its charm.

LONDON
Recommended hotels

Claridge's (☎ 020-7629 8860, 📄 020-7499 2210, Brook Street, Mayfair, London W1A 2QJ) is the place for the classic English experience, and in my mind the most romantic of the capital's leading hotels. For almost one hundred years it has been used as a pied à terre by foreign royalty, diplomats and some of England's most distinguished families. Despite its size, the hotel still manages to make guests feel as if they are part of a bygone age of elegance and refinement, and the art deco furnishings in the 141 rooms and 62 suites are authentic. Entering its glistening lobby with black and white chequered flooring and ornate mirrors you will feel more like you've arrived in a museum than a hotel. Liveried footmen come to take your drink orders, just as if you were staying in a private English country house in the 19th century.

One of the great thing about staying at Claridge's is all the rooms come with the sort of amenities that in many hotels are reserved for the best suites. And, it has the largest bedrooms and bathrooms of any London five-star de luxe hotel – the Egyptian suite is bigger than most flats in London. It is the thoughtful details that make Claridge's such a special hotel as well as its position near Bond Street, where London's most famous designers, auctioneers and jewellery shops are found, not to mention scores of first-class restaurants. Doubles cost from US$448/£315 to US$640/£450, suites from US$732/£515 to US$3548/£2495 and two Penthouse Suites from US$4977/£3500. Service is included but rates exclude 17.5% VAT.

Our suite was compact but elegant with a four-poster bed and adequate seating, small tables etc. The en suite bathroom had a beautiful claw feet bath plus TV. It was all very quiet and private and overall a pleasant stay although we were disappointed to discover that an English breakfast was extra to the room rate!

Andy and Rose

Reserve through Savoy Group (from the US toll-free ☎ 800-63-SAVOY; UK and other countries ☎ 020-7872 8080, 🖥 www.savoy-group.co.uk) or leading tour operators.

Over the last 30 years **The Portobello Hotel** (☎ 020-7727 2777, 📄 020-7792 9641, 🖥 www.portobello-hotel.co.uk, 22 Stanley Gardens, London W11 2NG), situated near Notting Hill's famous antique and bric-a-brac market on Portobello Road, has built up a reputation for its sumptuous, individually-decorated rooms, and has an enviably trendy address.

The hotel's 'special' rooms have unique features – No 46 is draped in kilims, Moroccan-style, while No 16 has a fabulous round bed and huge Victorian bathtub surrounded by mirrors. All are furnished with antiques and have separate showers and toilets in addition to the ornate baths. If you want big bustling lobbies full of uniformed bell boys and huge spacious suites you can strike the Portobello off your list immediately. But if you like small, quirky and infinitely friendly places, you cannot help but feel at home here. Double standard rooms cost from US$277/£195, special room No 46 from US$398/£280, and room No 16 from US$533/£375. Book through UK-based European Connection (🖳 www.europeanconnection.co.uk).

Blakes (☎ 020-7370 6701, 🖹 020-7373 0442, US toll-free ☎ 1-800-926-3173, 🖳 blakes-sales@easynet.co.uk, 33 Roland Gardens, South Kensington, London SW7 3PF) has long been regarded as one of London's most romantic hotels. Created and owned by fashion designer Anouska Hempel, Blakes was a seminal model for designer-inspired fashionable boutique hotels and is a member of Preferred Hotels and Resorts (see p12). The incredibly stylish furnishings incorporating rich colours and voluptuous fabrics, as well as Hempel's signature bows, make it the ultimate quiet retreat for hedonists who appreciate life's little luxuries and don't like sharing them with hordes of other people. Room rates range from US$341/£240 to US$462/£325 for

---

THINGS TO SEE AND DO IN LONDON

There's lots more to London than the obvious sightseeing attractions of **Buckingham Palace**, the **Crown Jewels** and **Big Ben**. Get along to Notting Hill's **Portobello Road** on a Saturday for its bustling antiques and bric-a-brac market, and stop off for brunch in the *First Floor Restaurant* (☎ 020-7243 0072), where you can sit and watch the locals over a cappuccino, while the market gets into swing beneath you. Julia Roberts and Hugh Grant might have moved on but The Travel Bookshop's still there.

London is full of wonderful restaurants. Try *Mezzo* (☎ 020-7314 4000), Sir Terence Conran's 700-seater on Wardour Street in the heart of **Soho**, the centre of London's café chic and also home to the theatres of the **West End**, and **Chinatown**. Both Soho and Chinatown are great places to wander around soaking in the atmosphere, and safe enough even at night: however, it's probably best to get a cab late at night. For a romantic evening meal you can't beat the *French House Dining-Room* (☎ 020-7437 2477) on nearby Dean Street. More expensive and more upmarket, but a fabulous place for celeb-spotting (if you can get in) is the *Ivy* (☎ 020-7836 4751), West Street.

If you're into books you can walk from Soho into nearby **Charing Cross Road** which has just about every kind of specialist book shop you could imagine, one of which was the inspiration behind the legendary love story, *84 Charing Cross Road.*

A real find of a restaurant, and right off the tourist track, is *Julie's* (☎ 020-7229 8331) in Holland Park – a west London institution which must be one of the city's most romantic restaurants, despite the food sometimes not being as good as it should be. Dinner at Julie's doesn't come cheap: a three-course dinner with wine will probably set you back about US$85/£60 each but it is the most beautiful location for a romantic supper. Around the same area, not far from Notting Hill underground station, is one of London's quintessential drinking experiences,

the *Windsor Castle* (☎ 020-7243 9551) on Camden Hill Road – not the royal residence but named because it was once possible to see it from the pub! This wonderful old pub is perfect for long winter evenings in front of a log fire or, in the summer, outside under the oak trees in the garden.

A great place to go any day but particularly on a Sunday is **Covent Garden**. Wander around the covered market in the Piazza, down Longacre, Floral Street and Neal Street (for clothes shopping) and stop for a drink or coffee at the *Opera Terrace*, or lunch at *Belgo's*, the new fangled Belgian beer-cellar on Neal Street, renowned for its bowls of 'moules' and chips. Or if you want a beer in one of London's oldest pubs head for the *Lamb and Flag* on Rose Street – it's a bit tricky to find but is a real English classic and worth the hunt.

If you're after more designer shopping go to **Bond Street** (just off Oxford Street) or **Knightsbridge** where the legendary Harvey Nichols and Harrods are found, as well as several individual designer shops, such as Joseph, DKNY and Nicole Fahri. If you get hungry or thirsty while you are there take the lift up to Harvey Nichols' restaurant – the perfect spot for a post-shopping livener.

At the other end of Sloane Street from Knightsbridge is **Sloane Square**, home to Peter Jones and the General Trading Company. **King's Road**, which was made famous in the 1970s as the heart of London's punk fashion scene, leads off from Sloane Square: it still has some great shops.

St James's and **Hyde Park** are lovely places for a walk in a park and you can't beat alfresco Shakespeare on a warm summer evening in **Regent's Park**, or opera in **Holland Park**. For tickets ask the concierge at your hotel.

For further information see 🖳 www. LondonTown.com.

a double to US$1130/£795 for the luxury suite, excluding tax. South Kensington is a great place to stay, just down the road from Harrods and within walking distance of Hyde Park.

The Halkin (☎ 020-7333 1000, 🖹 020-7333 1100, 🖳 res@halkin.co.uk, 5 Halkin Street, Belgravia, London SW1X 7DJ), a Leading Hotel of the World and a member of Design Hotels (see p12), is considered to be one of London's finest contemporary hotels. Italian in design with subtle oriental influences, its staff all wear Armani. Sister to the Metropolitan, The Halkin is ever so discreetly situated – in the heart of sophisticated London, between Knightsbridge and Mayfair.

The 41 individually decorated rooms and suites offer top comfort with all the mod cons including cable television, VCR, CD player and personal bar, and the all-marble bathrooms are stocked with Bulgari toiletries. Live harp music is played most evenings and the Halkin's award-winning Stefano Cavallini Italian restaurant is Michelin starred. Doubles are from US$405/£285 and suites range from US$604/£425 to US$889/£625, excluding tax.

Two new hot places to stay are One Aldwych and the Sanderson. **One Aldwych** (☎ 020-7300 1000, 🖹 020-7300 1001, 🖳 www.onealdwych.co.uk, 1 Aldwych, London WC2B 4RH), modern in design with clean, fresh lines and elegant décor, is old-fashioned in service. AA 'Hotel of the Year' 2001 and a Leading Hotel of the World, One Aldwych opened in July 1998 in a superb location in a building that once housed the communist *Morning Post* newspaper. Covent Garden, Trafalgar Square, St Paul's Cathedral and Westminster are on the doorstep and 15 of London's top theatres lie within ten minutes' walk.

In the 105 rooms, including 12 suites, you'll find the small touches that make this a special place. Fresh fruit and flowers arrive daily and the feather and down duvets with Italian linen sheets are to die for. Individually controlled air conditioning, mist-free mirrors and power showers in the bathroom all add to the luxury.

The hotel's restaurants, Axis and Indigo, have been hailed as two of London's most exciting, and the high-energy Cinnamon Bar, with its pebblestone floor tiles and glass-topped tables filled with cinnamon powder, is the place for an espresso. One Aldwych even has a private cinema with Italian leather chairs and you can listen to classical music playing underwater in the 18-metre lap pool. Doubles cost from US$355/£250, suites from US$540/£380. Book through Leading Hotels of the World reservation numbers worldwide (see p12).

The **Sanderson** (☎ 020-7300 1400, 🖹 020-7300 1401, 🖳 www.ianschragerho tels.com, 50 Berners Street, London W1T 3NG) is the cool new place to stay from the Schrager-Starck dream team. As you'd imagine, the interior is a wonderland of design: the buzzy Long Bar, the place to see and be seen, has eyes in the back of its seats and a galaxy-style lift carries guests to the sanctuary of the loft-style rooms. Inside there are paintings on the ceiling and a love letter in the carpet.

The Agua Spa, with its floor-to-ceiling drapes and enormous meditation beds, is the place to relax and be pampered after a long day's sightseeing followed by superb dining at Alain Ducasse's Spoon + restaurant with its open kitchen and mix and match menus. The Purple Bar, exclusive to guests, is where you can curl up together in a mysterious enclave after a long night out. Doubles cost from US$313/£220, suite from US$533/£375. Call toll-free from the UK (☎ 0800 634 1444).

BERKSHIRE

Berkshire is typical of England's south-eastern counties: it is full of rolling green fields and is a prime commuter residence because of its close proximity to London. If you are flying in or out of London's Heathrow Airport it is the perfect place to stop for a night or two before journeying on.

Cliveden

There can be few places in England as beautiful as Cliveden with its 376 acres of graceful parklands overlooking the River Thames – and it's just 40 minutes west of London. The hotel seems to have it all: location, beautiful surroundings, a Michelin star, and an extremely colourful history.

Designed by Charles Barry, who was also responsible for returning the Houses of Parliament in London to the Gothic style, it is a rare treat to stay in such a hotel and perfect for the first night of your honeymoon, or for your first couple of days in England, since it is only 20 minutes from Heathrow Airport.

England's history has over the centuries been fashioned at Cliveden by some of the richest men and most powerful women: the love affair of the scheming Duke of Buckingham and Anna Maria, Countess of Shrewsbury, resulted in a fatal duel on the house's side lawn; in their day Queen Victoria, Winston Churchill and Franklin D Roosevelt were regular visitors; Nancy Astor, whose husband Waldorf was given Cliveden on their marriage, gathered the influential Cliveden set around her in the 1930s – she became the first woman to sit in Parliament; and subsequently the house formed the meeting point for one of the British government's most notorious scandals when John Profumo met Christine Keeler around the Pavilion swimming pool.

As you wander through the glorious gardens on a sunny day, or sip pre-dinner cocktails in the magnificent oak-panelled Great Hall surrounded by fine works of art, ancient stone masonry and suits of armour, you cannot but wonder what these walls have witnessed before you. One of the most magical things about staying at Cliveden is this all pervading sense of history.

The great house's interior is every bit as stunning as the ornate gardens in which it is set. There are 38 luxurious guest rooms in all, including 15 suites. Everywhere you look in the rooms there are wonderfully personal touches all contributing to make your stay here that little bit more special and unbelievably comfortable. On the outside of each bedroom's large oak doors are brass plaques showing your name; the suites have music channelled into four different rooms, with individual volume controls in each one so that you can have your opera booming all around you as you stand under the drench shower without deafening your husband who's trying to read in the sitting room; there are even individually designed bed mats for honeymooners that have the dates of your stay embroidered on both sides, so that it says Saturday's date as you pass over it on your way into bed and Sunday's date as you get out of bed in the morning.

But without a doubt the best aspect of the rooms is their views. They have such a restful impact as you look down over the formal arrangement of box hedge encasing great bushes of swaying lavender, past the statue of Pluto at the end of the immense lawn and out to the shimmering River Thames. This view is what made my stay at Cliveden: we would return to the suite in the afternoon, place chairs in front of the two huge windows overlooking the lawn and sit and soak up the view that lay before us.

As well as the fabulous rooms, Cliveden has the spacious Spring Cottage (can sleep six), situated on the banks of the Cliveden Reach on the River Thames, a romantic hideaway popular with honeymoon couples. It comes equipped with its own butler and access to a vintage launch, the *Belmont*, for champagne cruises up the Thames.

I could go on and on about Cliveden but, suffice it to say, the cuisine in both restaurants is world class, the service not snooty, just friendly and attentive, the house elegant and welcoming (if a little overwhelming when you first come up the drive), and the facilities of the health spa, an indoor and an outdoor swimming pool, horse-riding, tennis, dreamy sunset river trips down the Thames on an old Royal Navy launch, and the endless beauty of the gardens littered with elegant statues and fountains, all make it the most incredible place to stay.

NORTH YORKSHIRE

A few days in the Yorkshire Dales and you'll know you've seen the England epitomised by the Brontë sisters and Turner. North Yorkshire is a wonderful blend of wild fells, pastoral valleys and rambling villages. The countryside is so scenic that a large part of it has been designated a national park in order to conserve the landscape. North Yorkshire is home to many of British racing's most famous yards, so for horse lovers there can be few finer experiences than getting out on the Dales on horseback.

The Devonshire Arms Country House Hotel

The Devonshire Arms is a splendid country house hotel which has been in the Devonshire family since 1753. Still owned by the present Duke and Duchess of Devonshire, this luxury hotel, occupying 12 acres of the Bolton Abbey Estate, has been filled with fine furniture, paintings and antiques borrowed from the Devonshire family's stately home, Chatsworth in Derbyshire.

There is something very charming about staying at the Devonshire; it may have something to do with the green wellies and cloth caps lined up in the entrance hall, the magical views from the bedroom windows, or the smell of log fires that permeates the sitting

---

THE DEVONSHIRE ARMS
(☎ 01756-710 441, 🖷 01756-710 564), Skipton, North Yorkshire BD23 6AJ, England
Reservations: Small Luxury Hotels of the World toll-free numbers worldwide (see p12)
Getting there: Taxis from York (35 minutes) or from Leeds (25 minutes) approximately US$34/£24; heli-pad; 23 miles from M62 and M1 (four and a half hours' drive from London)
Accommodation: 41 rooms: eight four-posters, one twin and one family in the Old Wing; one lady executive suite, 17 twins and 12 doubles in the Wharfdale Wing
Amenities: Health, beauty and fitness club with indoor heated swimming pool, spa bath, Turkish steam room, Scandinavian sauna, cold water plunge pool, high-powered sun bed, gym, beauty salon; all-weather outdoor tennis court, croquet lawn; one restaurant, cocktail bar and public bar; horse-riding, falconry, fly fishing, golf, clay-pigeon shooting can all be arranged nearby; 24-hour room service, laundry and pressing service and in-room safes
Dress code: Collar and tie in the dining room; elsewhere smart casual
Weddings: The hotel does have a wedding licence and is very popular for both wedding ceremonies and receptions; couples can choose between a church service, registry office or a civil ceremony at the hotel (rates available on request)
Minimum stay: None
Rates: Doubles with breakfast from US$220/£155 to US$277/£195; suites from US$355/£250
Credit cards: Most major
Taxes and service charge: Included

THINGS TO SEE AND DO IN NORTH YORKSHIRE

From the Devonshire Arms, follow the trails to **Pickles Beck** or the **Cavendish Pavilion** along the banks of the River Wharfe for a good introduction to the beauty of the surrounding countryside. Discover the nooks and crannies of the **Bolton Abbey Estate** which covers 75 miles of footpaths through spectacular riverside, woodland and open moorland scenery.

Wander around **Parcevall Hall Gardens**, which are open to the public daily from April to October and boast fabulous views of Simon's Seat and Wharfedale, or drive west over to **White Scar**, England's biggest cave.

If you happen to be in Yorkshire on a Sunday, hop on the **Embsay Steam Railway** for the two and a half mile trip from Skipton and back again or, for the more adventurous, join the **Leeds–Settle–Carlisle Railway**, which jour-

neys through lowland valleys and into the mountainous **Pennines** – some of England's most spectacular scenery.

Visit **Harrogate** with its wonderful healing baths and numerous tea rooms, the most famous of which is *Betty's*, or spend an afternoon in the historic town of **Richmond**, complete with its 11th-century castle. A day's visit to **York**, with its medieval buildings and stout city walls, is a must if you get to this part of the world. Make sure you take a look at the famous **York Minster** and the **Castle Museum**; plus you don't have to go far to get to places like **Castle Howard**, the fabulous stately home where Evelyn Waugh's *Brideshead Revisited* was filmed.

For further information contact Harrogate Tourist Information: (UK ☎ 01423-537 300) or visit 🖳 www.ytb.org.uk.

---

rooms, but I strongly suspect that it was the staff who made my stay there so enjoyable. I'm always reading about staff who anticipate your every need and have to say I think the phrase is utter twaddle, but I do love a place which provides unanticipated extras: when I asked for tea in the middle of the morning it came accompanied by freshly-baked biscuits – which I hadn't asked for. The staff here will leave you alone if that's what you want but they are happy to chat about the local countryside and the hotel if you are looking for information.

The 41 rooms are not huge but they are extremely comfortable, with every trimming that you'd expect from a member of the Small Luxury Hotels of the World chain. Decorated with striped Laura Ashley-style wallpaper and floral furnishings, eight of the rooms have four-poster beds. I'd strongly recommend that you request a room in the Old Wing, particularly the Crace Room, the Park Top and Chatsworth, because they all have four-posters.

Each bedroom has a colour TV, phone, radio, hairdryer, ironing board and iron, trouser press, tea and (fresh) coffee-making facilities and a selection of books and Christie's fine art catalogues, not to mention the most wonderful views of the Dales rising up all around you. The crisp white cotton sheets have 'The Devonshire' monogrammed in the corner, as do the white towelling robes in the bathroom. The bathrooms are well equipped – although the bath felt quite small when I was standing under the shower – and there are lots of white towels, Potter and Moore toiletries, and a vanity mirror.

Men are required to wear a jacket and tie in the hotel's award-winning **Burlington Restaurant**. Other facilities include a cocktail lounge for pre-dinner drinks or lunchtime snacks, the **Duke's Bar**, open to the public and run very much as a local Yorkshire pub, and a wonderfully luxurious beauty and fitness centre with indoor pool.

Middlethorpe Hall

Middlethorpe Hall, an extremely elegant Queen Anne country house hotel, is a great place to stay if you want to visit one of Britain's most historic cities, York.

Set in 20 acres of immaculately-kept gardens and parkland, and furnished throughout with antiques and objets d'art, the house was built in 1699. In 1980 Historic House Hotels 'rescued' it from an uncertain future and under their ownership it has been restored to its former glory. When I arrived at Middlethorpe the entire front façade was bathed in late afternoon sunlight, giving it a really magical and very

English air. The front door opens on to a flagged stone entrance hall, off which are the gloriously appointed drawing room, library and dining room.

Of the ten bedrooms in the main house, there are two beautiful four-poster rooms, with huge sash windows looking out over the grandest of cedar trees – one has a queen-size and the other a king-size bed. I'd definitely recommend one of these or the main house suite which has its own gas fire and where the trompe l'oeil window has a view of the racecourse. There are a further 17 bedrooms in the Classical Courtyard, a converted 18th-century stable block adjacent to the hotel, plus another cottage with two self-contained suites, both of which are doubles, and a garden suite.

In my mind the two four-poster rooms are perfect honeymoon material, with their wonderful window seats and views, an immensely comfortable and really solid four-poster bed, and the most invigorating drench shower in the bathroom. However, the junior suites and de luxe doubles in the courtyard are also very pretty and have spacious rooms, so don't rule them out if the four-posters aren't free.

As well as many fine antiques, rugs and paintings, all the rooms have a colour TV, radio, a bottle of mineral water, a collection of old books, a trouser press, and a well-lit vanity with hairdryer. In the bathroom there are big white fluffy towels and a robe as well as an ample supply of toiletries from Crabtree and Evelyn.

MIDDLETHORPE HALL
(☎ 01904-641 241, ▤ 01904-620 176, ▱ www.middlethorpe.com), Bishopthorpe Road, York YO2 1QB, England
Reservations: Relais & Chateaux toll-free numbers worldwide (see p12)
Getting there: Taxi from York station 1½ miles; transport from Manchester or Leeds airports can be arranged
Accommodation: In the main house: one suite, two four-posters, two de luxe doubles, three de luxe twins which can be zipped together and two single rooms; in the Classical Courtyard: two de luxe suites; a junior suite; six de luxe rooms; six standard rooms and two single rooms; plus two cottage suites along the lane; and a garden suite
Amenities: Formal dining room, croquet lawn, library, golf nearby, tennis, spa with 40ft indoor swimming pool, steam room, sauna, three beauty treatment rooms and small exercise room
Dress code: Jacket and tie in the dining room
Weddings: The hotel does not have a licence to perform weddings, but receptions for up to 50 guests can be catered for; room hire £500, including flowers, menus etc
Minimum stay: Two nights for the dinner, bed and breakfast package, but otherwise none
Rates: Doubles from US$240/£160; suites are US$345/£230; ask about the two-night dinner, bed and breakfast package which starts at around US$172/£115 per person per night
Credit cards: Most major (excluding Diners Club)
Taxes and service charge: Included

THE COTSWOLDS

Here in the 'heart of England', amidst a patchwork of rolling green fields, are some of England's best known and best loved hotels. The Cotswolds has long been a favourite destination for tourists, and as such can be unbearably busy in the middle of summer, but if you don't mind the crowds then this is when these idyllic English villages, with their century-old houses, immaculate stone walls and beautifully-kept gardens are at their best. Savour strawberries and cream on the lawn, or a glass of real lemonade after a game of tennis, and you'll immediately feel that you've been part of the English scene for ages.

The Lygon Arms

The Lygon Arms is situated right in the centre of Broadway, a mellow Cotswold village where stone houses surround a perfect village green. The hotel is a favourite with the Cheltenham Gold Cup racing brigade and has long been regarded as one of England's most celebrated country inns.

The inn, which has been here for almost 500 years, epitomises the fine English hostelry with a relaxed atmosphere produced by grandfather clocks, roaring log fires in

THE LYGON ARMS
(☎ 01386-852 255, 📠 01386-858 611, 🖥 www.the-lygon-arms.com), Broadway, Worcestershire WR12 7DU, England
Reservations: Reservations toll-free from the US (☎ 800-63-SAVOY); toll-free from Belgium, France, Germany, Ireland, Spain and Switzerland (☎ 00 800-7671-7671); toll-free from Japan (☎ 001-800 7671 7671) or through 🖥 www.savoygroup.com
Getting there: The hotel can arrange transfers to and from Evesham or Moreton-in-the-Marsh railway stations (£17.50), or from London Heathrow Airport (£180) and from Birmingham International Airport (£75)
Accommodation: 62 rooms (including seven four-poster rooms) and five suites
Amenities: The Great Hall dining room, Oliver's Brasserie, Patio restaurant, Goblets wine bar, Cotswold's Bar for cocktails, spa with pool, Jacuzzi, sauna, solarium, steam room, beauty salon, fitness room, billiards room, tennis; plus horse-riding, clay pigeon shooting, golf, hiking, squash and ballooning all nearby, cocktail bar, private dining rooms, 24-hour laundry, limo service
Dress code: Smart dress is requested
Weddings: Wedding ceremonies can be conducted in the Edinburgh Room (50 people) and the Torrington Room (80 people), receptions are usually held in the Great Hall (96 people) or the Russell Room (52 people)
Minimum stay: None
Rates: Doubles from US$228/£145 including breakfast; four-poster bedroom from US$302/£345; suites from US$345/£395 to US$473/£610
Credit cards: Most major
Taxes and service charge: Government tax 17.5%, service is discretionary

winter, and hearty food. Owned by the Savoy Group this world-class hotel is of course not quite like the old village inn it was for centuries but it is now famous for its first-class hospitality and fabulous modern-day luxuries.

Many historic figures and former kings and queens of England have slept in the 58 bedrooms and seven suites: Oliver Cromwell spent the night of 2 September 1651 in the suite that is now named after him, before the Battle of Worcester, the final and decisive battle of the Great Civil War. King Charles I stayed in the hotel the night after the same battle; he was in the first floor room that now bears his name. This room has a four-poster bed and many original features such as oak panelling, as well as a wide range of modern amenities including phone, remote control television with satellite channels, hairdryer, in-room safe, trouser press and sumptuous bathrobes. All rooms have 24-hour room service, satellite TV, and phones.

A new Orchard Cottage was added in 2000, a fairy-tale thatched residence in the beautiful English country grounds. Its four splendid rooms boast widescreen DVD TVs, four-poster beds and log-burning stoves.

The **Great Hall**, the hotel's splendid 17th-century dining room is resplendent with its original Minstrel's Gallery, stags' heads, heraldic friezes and barrel-vaulted ceiling. Dinner and lunch are served here, cooked by the Lygon Arms' award-winning chef.

If you fancy something less formal, there is **Oliver's Brasserie** and the **Cotswold Bar**, both of which serve light lunches. The patio is the perfect place for a late breakfast on a lovely summer's morning.

After all that eating it's reassuring to have impressive health, fitness and leisure facilities to hand (even if you don't use them!) in the Lygon Arms Spa. Guests have direct access via the hotel, which means you don't even have to go outside to get to it. The central feature of the building is the swimming pool and spa bath, down onto which sunshine is filtered by an electronically-operated skylight. There is a steam room, saunas, billiards, beauty treatment rooms offering exclusive treatments by Borghese and Versace, and a fully-equipped and newly enlarged gym, as well as a fitness consultant on hand to help you at all times.

THE NEW FOREST

For centuries, the New Forest was a popular hunting ground for English kings. This vast tract of countryside is now best known for the ponies who wander freely, and it is an idyllic place to enjoy long walks. 'Nova Foresta', as it was named by William the Conqueror, is still subject to the special laws that he created to protect the forest's red deer. Over 900 years later this nationally-protected forest and heath land is a reminder

THINGS TO SEE AND DO IN THE COTSWOLDS

The Cotswolds have pre-historic as well as Roman remains, with roads built as long ago as AD43-49. There are Roman remains throughout the area but the most famous are in **Bath**, a fine Georgian city in the Avon Valley.

Today the area performs a very important role in England's **social calendar**, hosting several world famous events including the Cheltenham Gold Cup in March, Badminton Horse Trials in April, polo matches throughout the summer at Cirencester Park, and Prescott motor-race hill climbs, a beautiful venue for a vintage meeting, in August.

The Lygon Arms is set in a great area for walking and cycling: the track to the right of the church in the town of Broadway leads into open countryside and out eventually to the **Cotswold Way**, a 100-mile walk though some of England's most idyllic countryside running from Chipping Campden to Bath. Contact Broadway Tourist Office (☎ 01386-852 937, 🖳 www.broadway-cotswolds.co.uk) for maps and things to see and do along the Cotswolds Way.

Places to visit nearby include: **Snowshill**, a mile away, where there is a large cottage garden;

Sezincote, near Moreton-in-Marsh, a grander garden with glorious Cotswold views; **Hidcote Manor**, near Chipping Campden, which was created at the turn of the 20th century by American, Lawrence Johnston, and which is now one of the UK's best-known gardens; and **Barnsley House Garden**, which was originally laid out in 1770 and is situated in Barnsley, a very attractive village with a Norman church.

You can visit **Stratford-upon-Avon**, where William Shakespeare lived and wrote in the 16th century. Wander around the houses where he lived, go punting down the beautiful river, stop for dinner in one of the many good restaurants before attending an evening performance by the resident **Royal Shakespeare Company.** If you fancy a pre-theatre dinner or post-theatre snack, try *Restaurant Margaux* (☎ 01789-269106) on Union St, which serves delicious food at reasonable prices (US$21/£15 average) in warm, bistro surroundings.

Look at 🖳 www.cotswoldsfinesthotels. com for plenty of ideas of other places to stay in this picture-perfect world. For tourist information, visit 🖳 www.glos-cotswolds.co.uk

of England's long-established hunting heritage. Within easy reach of Chewton Glen hotel in this section are **Salisbury** and **Winchester cathedrals**, **Stonehenge**, and **Beaulieu Abbey** with its Cistercian cloisters and ruins. **Romsey**, where you'll find Lord Mountbatten's **Broadlands** estate, and the gardens at Exbury and Spinners are also close by, as is **Lymington**, which has a wonderful bustling market on Saturdays.

Local pubs and restaurants to look out for include: the **Chequers** pub down **Maiden Lane** on the outskirts of Lymington which is usually full of yachties, and **Oysters**, overlooking the Isle of Wight in **Barton-on-Sea**, where the fish is particularly good. The **Trustee Servant** at **Minstead**, where Arthur Conan Doyle is buried in the Norman churchyard, is also worth a visit.

The forest offers a wealth of leisure activities: horse-riding, golf, sailing, fishing and of course, mile after mile of walking through some of England's most glorious countryside.

Chewton Glen

Chewton Glen is the New Forest's biggest and most luxurious resort-style hotel. Set in 130 acres of immaculate parklands, gardens, lawns and woodlands, Chewton Glen dates back to the early 1700s, and was remodelled in the Palladian style in the early 1890s. Since 1966 this prestigious hotel has been owned and run by the same private owners.

Chewton Glen tries to create the atmosphere of a large private house, and although it is just too big to truly carry this off, it is a first-class resort with tastefully decorated rooms, exquisite antiques and fine art, mixed in with an abundance of fresh flowers and many other little extras.

The bedrooms want for nothing. As the brochure proudly states: 'There is scarcely an amenity you can imagine that has not been included in your bedroom and bathroom'. Antique knick-knacks sit alongside a decanter of sherry, home-made biscuits, chocolates and fruit, as well as more practical items such as in-room safe, trouser

CHEWTON GLEN
(☎ 01425-275 341, 🖃 01425-272 310, 🖳
www.chewtonglen.com), New Milton,
Hampshire BH25 6QS, England
Reservations: Toll-free from USA ☎ 1-800
344-5087 or through Mason Rose 🖳
www.masonrose.com, or Relais & Chateaux
reservation numbers worldwide (see p12)
Getting there: The hotel can arrange
transfers from Heathrow Airport
(US$256/£180), Gatwick Airport
(US$256/£180), and Southampton
Airport (US$100/£70)
Accommodation: 43 rooms and 19 suites
Amenities: The Marryat Room
Restaurant, health club, beauty and spa
treatments, computerized gym, indoor
and outdoor pools, indoor and outdoor
tennis courts, golf course, croquet, billiards, hairdressing salon; fishing, horse-
riding, sailing and shooting nearby
Dress code: Informal during the day,
men are requested to wear jackets and
ties in the evening
Weddings: The hotel has a wedding
licence (ceremonies cost US$640/£450);
receptions can be arranged for up to 120
and cost US$100/£70 a head which
includes a three-course wedding breakfast, all wine, champagne with the cake,
floral decorations and room hire
Minimum stay: Usually none, but two
nights at certain times of the year
Rates: Doubles from US$355/£250;
suites from US$540/£380
Credit cards: Most major
Taxes and service charge: Included

press, so many huge towels you won't know what to do with them all, and towelling robes. All the bedrooms are very romantic and pretty in true country house fashion, with fine fabrics and private balconies or terraces looking out over the surrounding parklands.

The hotel's own health club provides a sanctuary where the body and mind can be refreshed and retuned. The centrepiece is a magnificent indoor swimming pool, surrounded by vast glass windows looking out onto the grounds, with an adjacent spa, steam room and saunas. Classically designed with trompe l'oeil frescoes, the pool uses the latest ozone treatment providing crystal clear water without condensation.

There's so much to do at Chewton Glen: indoor and outdoor tennis, gym, beauty treatments, croquet on the lawn, a nine-hole golf course, and the many walking and jogging trails to be explored close to the hotel. Riding, fishing, shooting and sailing can also be arranged at nearby locations.

The quality of the staff and facilities are the key attributes of Chewton Glen. The staff are as friendly as they are professional, and so attentive that they attempt to anticipate your every wish. Food is taken seriously and a wonderful mix of local seasonal produce, such as game, fish and wild mushrooms, are combined to create classic dishes.

DEVON AND CORNWALL

The ragged coastline of Devon and Cornwall is so pretty that it has always been a popular holiday destination with the British. Explore the traditional fishing villages with their countless fish restaurants (best known of which is Rick Stein's *Seafood Restaurant* in Padstow, Cornwall) and visit the charming pubs where you can sample scrumpy – a seemingly innocuous drink made from fermented apples. Devon and Cornwall are also great for walks; along the coastal paths or through woodland and open country.

Places to visit in Devon include villages such as **Salcombe**, and **Burgh Island** where an amphibious tractor takes you from the beach out to the island for a pint of cider at the *Pilchard Inn*, and in Cornwall, **Treen Beach** near Porthcurno, and **St Michael's Mount** which you can walk to across a sandbar when the tide is low, as well as the pretty villages of **Portloe**, **Veryan** and **Lerryn** to name but a few.

Recommended hotels

In the unspoilt village of St Mawes, **Hotel Tresanton** (☎ 01326-270 055, 🖹 01326-270 053, 🖳 www.tresanton.com, St Mawes, Truro, Cornwall TR2 5DR), by the sea, is *the* romantic place to stay in Cornwall. Bought by Olga Polizzi in 1997, it has been renovated as an eclectic mix of ancient and modern – work from contemporary local artists alongside antiques. Each of the 26 comfortable and elegant rooms, some with their own terraces and all with magnificent sea views past St Anthony's lighthouse, is decorated in a unique style. When you feel like a cuddly twosome, Tresanton has a cinema. It also has a 48-ft yacht, should you feel like heading out to sea. Fishing, riding, and golf can all be arranged nearby. You can get to Newquay by plane from Gatwick in an hour. Doubles cost from US$235/£165 per couple including breakfast and tax.

Renting a cottage in England

One of the best ways of getting an idea of life in rural England is to rent a cottage. The National Trust and the Landmark Trust have many wonderful properties and both were established to preserve Britain's countryside and the wealth of old buildings that were in danger of crumbling away.

Two National Trust properties on a beautiful stretch of the River Thames known as **Cliveden Reach** make wonderful honeymoon hideaways. **New Cottage** and **Ferry Cottage** cost around US$846/£595 for a week in the summer and considerably less at other times of the year. If you really want to get away from it all, the pentagonal 200-year-old **Birdcage** cottage in the fishing village of Port Isaac, Cornwall, is the place; US$566/£398 per week in summer. Contact the National Trust (☎ 0870-458 4422, 🖹 0870-458 4400, 🖥 www.nationaltrust.org.uk/cottages) for a copy of their handbook.

The Landmark Trust has a whole host of quirky buildings for rent including coastal castles, a clock tower, a gothic temple, the forebodingly named House of Correction (!), and even apartments in **Hampton Court Palace**. Prices start from around US$465/£300 for a week, depending on the kind of property and the time of year. Contact the Landmark Trust (☎ 01628-825 925, 🖹 01628-825 920, 🖥 www.land marktrust.co.uk) for a copy of their handbook.

Premier Cottages are a private company offering quality self-catering holiday cottages booked directly with the owners via their website (🖥 www.premiercot tages.co.uk). Take a look at the cosy **Stanley Ghyll Cottage** for two in the Lake District from US$384/£270 a week, or the award-winning **Combermere Abbey Cottages** on a privately-owned estate in Shropshire, from US$540/£380 a week. Designed by well-known designers such as Ralph Lauren, Combermere holds a wedding licence for the abbey if you want to get married there.

If you want to get married in style, and you can afford it, the exclusive **Samling** (☎ 015394-31922, 🖹 015394-30400, 🖥 www.thesamling.com, Ambleside Road, Windermere, Cumbria LA23 1LR) in the Lake District is breathtakingly beautiful. There are no whiffs of a 'bygone era' in Samling's style, it is emphatically a house in the country rather than a country house hotel. Samling means a gathering and as you have to rent the whole property, the name is suitable as the house is licensed for a small wedding party (there are ten suites and the restaurant seats twenty) and costs US$4266/£3000 for a 24-hour minimum period for six couples sharing which includes everything you may have dreamed of: spectacular views over the lake, the morning on a horse, a picnic on a hillside, a canoe to an island, sunset in an outdoor hot tub, a ten-course banquet and seclusion in some of the most beautiful surroundings you're likely to find in England.

Scotland
(BEST TIME TO VISIT: APRIL TO OCTOBER)

To me there is no more magical place than Scotland. There is nothing quite like standing with the wind blowing around you, surrounded by wild terrain and some of the most spectacular scenery anywhere in the world.

If you're planning on going to Scotland though, you'd better be prepared to put concerns about the weather right out of your head, as there is absolutely no way you

---

SCOTLAND

The attractive and lively cities of Edinburgh and Glasgow plus the staggering beauty of the west coast of Scotland and the wild grandeur of the Highlands

When to go: All year round in the south but snow makes travel difficult in the Highlands in winter; summer is from June to September, winter from December to the end of March

Capital: Edinburgh

Flight times: to Glasgow: USA: 8/9 hours (direct)

Approximate exchange rates: Pound sterling (£) – US$1 = £0.70, A$1 = £0.36

Time difference: GMT (plus one hour from the last Sunday in March to the last Sunday in October)

Voltage: 240v AC, 50Hz; three-pin plugs

Combine with: England, Wales, Ireland, the rest of Europe

Country dialling code: ☎ 44

Further information: 🖳 www.holidaysscotland.net or www.visitscotland.com

---

should go there if mixed weather will ruin your honeymoon. It's not that it rains any more than it does in England or Ireland, it's just that big weather is really what it's all about in Scotland – to pick this wonderful country for your honeymoon you've got to be the kind of incurable romantic that loves hilltop walks in the rain and huddling up together in front of a log fire with the wind whistling round the house. However, I have had weeks on the west coast when we might as well have been in Greece it was so hot. In fact, the uncertainty of the weather adds to the mysticism of Scotland.

The hotels listed here epitomise for me everything that is great in Scotland. They are, by and large, not the sort of hotels that have 24-hour room service or TVs in the rooms (apart from Gleneagles and the Scotsman of course!). Instead they have excellent home-cooked and often home-grown food, large comfortable beds, fantastically friendly and professional service, and are set in historic buildings surrounded by endless views of this beautiful country. They are, in short, the kind of hotels where you could easily wind up taking the proprietor's dogs with you on your walk, or sit up supping whisky with the owners and other guests into the early hours of the morning. And of course, since Madonna got married in one, castles are becoming fashionable places to stay (see box p117).

If you've not been to Scotland it may be an idea to pick two or three of these hotels and do a mini-tour starting in Edinburgh, so that you get a feel for the country and its vast open, unspoilt, spaces. Scotland is now one of the few parts of Europe where there is any real wilderness.

EDINBURGH
The Scotsman

The Scotsman opened its doors in April 2001 in an old, baronial building and is the most stunning and stylish hotel in Edinburgh. The former home of the *The Scotsman* newspaper for nearly 100 years, this value for money hotel is bang in the centre of town, just a minute's stroll from both Princes Street and the Royal Mile.

THE SCOTSMAN

(☎ 0131-556 5565, 🖷 0131-652 3652, 🖳 www.thescotsmanhotel.co.uk), North Bridge, Edinburgh, Scotland

Reservations: Direct with the hotel

Getting there: Waverley Railway Station is one minute's walk away; the hotel can arrange taxis from Edinburgh airport for US$21/£15 one way, limousine US$64/£45 plus VAT for four people

Accommodation: 56 bedrooms and 12 Suites: 12 Study Rooms, 32 De luxe Rooms, 12 Editors Rooms, 8 Publishers Suites, 3 Director Suites, 1 Baron Suite, 1 Penthouse Suite

Amenities: Two restaurants, bar, health club and spa with 16-metre stainless steel pool, sauna, steam room, fully-equipped gym, beauty treatments

Dress code: Smart casual; jacket and tie in Fine Dining restaurant

Weddings: Can arrange weddings and receptions for up to 180 people; private dining rooms are also available

Minimum stay: None

Rates: Doubles from US$212/£149 to US$277/£195, suites from US$427/£300 to US$1138/£800; ask about special packages. Honeymooners get complimentary champagne in their room on arrival.

Credit cards: Most major

Taxes and service charge: Included

THINGS TO SEE AND DO IN EDINBURGH

A week's touring around Scotland will give you a really good taster of this incredibly beautiful country. If you're coming from London the train is a great way to arrive as the journey up through the east side of England, particularly the last hundred miles along the coast, is really enjoyable: apart from which the views of Edinburgh as you come out of the station are breathtaking and fully warrant the city's appellation, 'the Athens of the North'.

The main tourist sights are: the **11th-century castle** which looms down over the city and where the original chapel, built around 1130 by King Malcolm's son, David, in memory of his mother, Margaret, still stands and is almost certainly the oldest building in the city; the **Royal Mile**, the cobbled street connecting the castle with Holyrood Palace; **Victoria Street** which winds downhill to the **Grassmarket** where you'll find all sorts of interesting shops selling lace, antiques and candles; the **National Gallery of Scotland**, just off Prince's Street, full of fantastic works by some of Europe's great masters; and **Calton Hill** and **Arthur's Seat**, from where the views back over the city are fabulous.

The best way to experience this elegant city is to walk. A good place to begin is **New Town**, which is actually 200 years old and quite stunning with its huge Georgian buildings and cobbled streets. Start on **Dundas Street** and turn right when you get to the top of the hill on **George Street**, before turning left down **Castle Street**: this brings you out directly opposite the castle. Pop into the National Gallery and then catch a bus up the **Mound** to save your legs and get off on the Royal Mile, where you can either go right to the castle, or left down to **Holyrood Palace** (the latter is too far to walk!). Victoria Street (see above) is also in the vicinity. When

you're done with the **Old Town** go back over **North Bridge** so you can admire the fantastic views of the castle on one side, the sea and Salisbury Crags on the other.

The city really comes alive during the **Edinburgh Festival** (arts and drama) in August and at **Hogmanay** for Europe's biggest New Year's Eve party: if your honeymoon coincides with either of these periods you can't possibly miss a couple of nights in Edinburgh (but book well ahead).

The city is also known for its many great restaurants, bars and cafés. There are so many it's hard to pick just a few but try some of the following: while you're on the Royal Mile stop for lunch at *Le Sept* down the steeply cobbled Old Fishmarket Close; for steaks there's no better place than the *Witchery*, a wonderfully atmospheric restaurant just below the castle at the top of the Royal Mile (the theatre supper is good value); *Rick's*, which opened in 2000 on Frederick Street close to Hanover Street is an award-winning bistro, a cosmopolitan place to see and be seen and to have breakfast or a snack (they also have rooms should you want to stay in the middle of the action).

For seafood and fish head down to the gentrified parts of **Leith Docks** where *Skipper's*, the *Shore*, *Vintners* and the ever-popular *Waterfront* all have a great atmosphere and delicious fish; pop into the *Café Royal* on West Register Street, or to the *Abbertsford* close by on Rose Street for a pint of 'heavy' (bitter) in one of Edinburgh's oldest pubs, and last but not least, don't miss *Bar Kohl* on George IV Bridge which has over 50 different flavours of vodka and some wicked cocktail combinations.

Call Edinburgh Tourist Board for more information (☎ 0131-473 3000) or visit 💻 www.edinburgh.org.

Although the Scotsman looks 21st century in design, with a focus on comfort and all the mod cons, what makes this hotel so interesting is its publishing history, reflected in features throughout – no two bedrooms are the same and a few have been named after former editors. The 56 spacious bedrooms and 12 suites offer different advantages depending on what you want: a magnificent view over the city, enhanced space or self-sufficiency in a suite with a kitchen, library and sauna. In some rooms, roll-topped baths sit in turret spaces with great views over the city and, if you can afford it, there is a wonderful penthouse with a sauna, and a balcony with a barbecue and, of course, fabulous views across Edinburgh.

Tweeds from Scottish estates have been given a contemporary style to create special furnishings and every room has state of the art technology such as DVD and CD player, widescreen TV, as well as telephone, trouser press, iron and ironing board, minibar, coffee machine, privacy hatch and luxurious toiletries in the bathrooms.

The oak-floored drawing room with its fireplace, stylish bar and lavish seating, is an ideal place to relax after seeing the city sights, and there's a state of the art health club and spa complete with a unique six-lane stainless-steel swimming pool, fresh juices and light snacks. Dining in the evening is in the gallery of the **Classic Brasserie** on local Scottish cuisine or in the modern **Fine Dining Restaurant** which boasts the most attentive and discreet service in the city. You can then enjoy one or several of the 399 Scottish malt whiskies in the bar in the dramatic old entrance hall or head to the hotel's exclusive nightclub for some live entertainment.

The Scotsman is ideally placed for visiting all of Edinburgh's delights: museums, galleries, theatres, the Edinburgh Festival in August and superb shopping arcades. A short drive will take you into the beauty of the Scottish Highlands, lochs and historic houses and gardens.

PERTHSHIRE
The Gleneagles Hotel

Set in the heart of Scotland on an 850-acre estate in Perthshire, Gleneagles is Scotland's most complete resort offering luxury accommodation and endless leisure facilities against a matchless scenic backdrop.

The hotel has 13 suites, all of which have their own individual colour schemes and are located at each corner of the hotel, thus offering the best views over the surrounding countryside. Each suite comprises a bedroom, bathroom and lounge area with a dining table for those intimate room-service breakfasts and dinners. There are Gleneagles branded toiletries in the bathrooms, a television, minibar, hairdryer, and bathrobes. Two of the suites also have four-poster beds.

To most people Gleneagles means golf but the resort also boasts a wide range of other leisure facilities. The list of pursuits with which to fill your days is staggering: there are, of course, the three 18-hole championship golf courses (the King's, Queen's and the PGA Centenary), as well as a pitch-and-putt course and the Wee, a nine-hole course; but there is also a beautiful Club and Spa with a lagoon-shaped indoor swimming pool; the Gleneagles Equestrian Centre – one of the best equipped centres in the world with fantastic riding to be had all around the estate; the Gleneagles Jackie Stewart Shooting and Fishing School; the British School of Falconry at Gleneagles; lochs for brown and rainbow trout fishing; off-road driving; four all-weather and one grass tennis courts, and a croquet lawn.

A quick read through the above list will confirm for you that this is no ordinary hotel. Gleneagles is a totally self-contained luxury

THE GLENEAGLES HOTEL
(☎ 01764-662 231, 🖳 01764-662 134, 🖳 www.gleneagles.com), Auchterarder, Perthshire PH3 1NF, Scotland
Reservations: The Leading Hotels of the World toll-free reservation numbers worldwide (see p12)
Getting there: The hotel can arrange chauffeur-driven transfers from Edinburgh or Glasgow airports, £84 each way
Accommodation: 216 bedrooms including 13 suites
Amenities: Four restaurants and the Bar, Ballroom, private function rooms, shopping mall and additional fashion, sports and gift shops at all the leisure locations, three 18-hole championship golf courses, a nine-hole course, the Club and Spa, the Gleneagles Equestrian Centre, the Gleneagles Jackie Stewart Shooting and Fishing School, the British School of Falconry at Gleneagles, four all-weather tennis courts, one grass court, lochs for brown and rainbow trout fishing, off-road driving, croquet, putting, pitch-and-put, jogging trails
Dress code: There is no special dress code at Gleneagles
Weddings: Civil and religious marriages can be held either in the hotel or the grounds, and receptions for up to 300 people can be catered for; menus start at £48.50 a head; the hotel will cater for virtually anything you require from hairstyling to a Highland piper
Minimum stay: None
Rates: Doubles from US$412/£290 and suites from US$967/£680 per night, both including full Scottish breakfast; honeymoon packages can be tailor made, perhaps with flowers and/or a champagne breakfast in your room, a carriage drive around the estate, a chauffeur-driven transfer to any airport in Scotland, as well as a first anniversary dinner at the hotel's Strathearn Restaurant
Credit cards: Most major
Taxes and service charge: Included

(Opposite): Luttrellstown Castle (see p117). The bathing facilities are very grand in some of the rooms.

resort the like of which you won't very often come across in Britain, or even in the rest of Europe. You can choose between four restaurants and the bar, there are private function rooms which are perfect for weddings, and a complete shopping mall with branches of Harvey Nichols and Alfred Dunhill.

A ratio of more than one staff member per guest ensures you'll be utterly pampered, and this really is one of those hotels where no wish seems too much for the friendly, enthusiastic staff and management. Don't miss afternoon tea which comes with the most fabulous assortment of sandwiches, savouries, scones and cream cakes.

THE ISLE OF SKYE
Kinloch Lodge

Kinloch Lodge, Isle of Skye, is owned by Lord and Lady Macdonald, and has been in the Macdonald family for over three hundred years. The hotel's gourmet food is now so celebrated that Claire Macdonald has written many books dedicated to Scottish food and drink.

Situated at the head of the loch (Kinloch means head of the loch) and at the foot of a hill at the southern end of Skye, this large white manor house with its slate-grey roof is more a house than a hotel. The Macdonalds are very careful to preserve this atmosphere, wishing to lure their guests on the promise of delicious food, fine wine, friendly company and truly comfortable surroundings rather than with the promise of extensive facilities and bedroom amenities. If you derive great pleasure from your food and drink, and enjoy being in relaxed and informal rural surroundings you'd be hard pressed to beat this lovely lodge.

You start to get an impression of the lodge's remoteness as you travel down the mile long, rough-hewn track off the main (tiny single track!) road. The countryside of

KINLOCH LODGE
(☎ 01471-833 333, 🖷 01471-833 277, 🖳 www.kinloch-lodge.co.uk), Sleat, Isle of Skye IV43 8QY, Scotland
Reservations: Direct with the hotel
Getting there: The hotel can arrange for a taxi to collect you from either Mallaig or Kyle of Lochalsh
Accommodation: Nine bedrooms in the lodge, five rooms in the new house
Amenities: Two lounges, bar, dining room, limited room service, fantastic walking nearby, TV (for occasional use)
Dress code: Whatever is comfortable
Weddings: No
Minimum stay: None
Rates: Doubles from US$108/£76 to US$165/£116 bed and breakfast
Credit cards: Most major
Taxes and service charge: Included

the Isle of Skye is rugged and wild and therein lies its beauty – walking in the nearby mountains and along the edges of the lochs is fabulous, and is the very best way of working up an appetite.

Guests are encouraged to treat the place very much as their own and will find utter tranquillity and relaxation among the calming apricot walls of the drawing room, while the strong green of the dining room walls sets a richer tone for the sumptuous dinners produced in Claire's kitchen. The downstairs rooms are filled with elegant antiques, family portraits in gilt frames, photographs and piles of books, and from every window there are restful views. Upstairs are nine bedrooms, three of which are reasonably large but the rest fairly small, although prettily and individually furnished. In June 1998, a beautiful new house, Kinloch, was completed, barely fifty metres from the lodge. It has five fully-appointed bedrooms with a great view, a sumptuous sitting room and a special kitchen for Claire's cookery demonstrations.

If you must have a huge bedroom or need to be constantly entertained this isn't the place for you, but if you're happy with a good book, a comfy sofa, walks among fantastic scenery and delicious meals, it will suit you both down to the ground.

(Opposite) Top: Château de la Chèvre d'Or, Côte d'Azur, France (see p138). **Bottom:** Villa San Michele, Fiesole, Italy (see p152), designed by Michelangelo.

Renting in a cottage in Scotland

Cottages both simple and splendid – either by the water or in the isolated highlands – are a romantic choice for your honeymoon. **Ecosse Unique** (☎ 01835-870 779, 📄 01835-870 417, 🖥 www.uniquescotland.com, Thorncroft, Lilliesleaf, Melrose, TD6 9JD) offers a whole range of wonderful holiday cottages throughout Scotland. Among those worth considering is the **Eilean Shona** on its own tiny islet between the islands of Mull and Skye. Talk to Jill Bristow who is more than happy to sort out something suitable from her careful selection. Or contact **Country Cottages in Scotland** (☎ 0870 -444 1133, 🖥 www.countrycottagesinscotland.co.uk) for other choices.

On a much grander scale you could consider **Stucan-T-Iobairt** (☎ 0141-339 2774, 🖥 www.colemanscottage.co.uk) a tranquil retreat right on the edge of **Loch Lomond** where a 370-year-old detached stone cottage has been converted to offer a richly decorated hideaway. Inside, the house really is luxuriously furnished with flowing tartan drapes, old wooden beams, marble worktops in the kitchen and a glowing log fire. Surrounded by mature woodland, there is a babbling burn and fantastic views over Loch Lomond to the mountains beyond. The cottage stands in the shadow of a thousand-year-old yew tree where Robert the Bruce is reputed to have assembled his troops. A week's rental at Stucan-T-Iobairt costs US$870/£600 throughout the year.

Wales
(BEST TIME: APRIL TO OCTOBER)

Wales (see 🖥 www.visitwales.com) is the perfect place to take life slowly and really unwind in beautiful mountainous scenery, and there are few more magnificent places than **Snowdonia** in North Wales. Days can be spent driving along secluded lanes and narrow mountain roads, but you should leave the car in order to explore the many bridleways and footpaths which lead you to some of the wildest scenery in Europe. Wales is not a place for fair-weather travellers as the mountains in the north often bring rain and drizzle, but if you are looking for views, privacy and peace it's hard to beat.

Bodysgallen Hall

Standing in 200 acres of its own parkland, you'd be hard pressed to find a more wonderful and relaxing place to spend a few days than beautiful Bodysgallen Hall. It is set in some of Wales's most scenic countryside, just south of Llandudno, and looks down on **Conwy Castle** and towards the spectacular mountains of Snowdonia to the south.

From the moment you unbolt the huge front door of this grand old stone manor and enter the oak-panelled hall where an open fire burns in the hearth, you'll feel the tiredness of the journey subside.

The Hall has been carefully restored by the Historic House Hotels group, which own a handful of similar properties in Britain and is well known for their first-rate housekeeping, service and dining. The backing of this group has enabled the Hall to be refurbished exactly as it should be, using antique-style paints, original prints and fabrics, which sit well alongside the many antiques and fine paintings spread about the rooms. It has been winning awards since it opened its doors in 1982.

With only 19 bedrooms the Hall is an intimate place, making you feel that bit more special as a guest, but for utter privacy choose one of the 16 cottages situated in the grounds, all of which come with their own gardens and evocative names such as Dove Cottage or Gingerbread House. All the rooms are furnished with mod cons, including en suite bathroom, electric trouser press, TV, toiletries and bathrobes. Wherever you stay there's plenty of space to find a quiet corner to snuggle up with a book, or enjoy afternoon tea in front of the fire in the beautiful first-floor drawing room.

Much of the Hall was built in the 17th century; the ancient look-out tower dates back to the 13th century. The views from the top of the tower are breathtaking and make the long climb up the winding stone staircase worthwhile.

Despite being steeped in history, Bodysgallen Hall also features just about every modern amenity that you would want on your honeymoon including a great health spa. Approached by a short walk through the garden, the spa occupies the original stone buildings of Bodysgallen Farm, but now houses a Club Room, a terrace, a good-sized indoor swimming pool, a whirlpool spa bath, as well as a steam room, sauna, three beauty salons and a gym.

Other recommended hotels

Hotel Portmeirion (☎ 01766-770 000, 🖹 01766-771 331, 🖳 www.portmeirion-village.com). Hotel Portmeirion is at the heart of the unique and unusual fantasy village of Portmeirion, on its own private peninsula looking out to sea. The village is an enchanting jumble of different architectural styles: Indian, oriental and Italian, and the hotel's 40 rooms are correspondingly eclectic, based on different themes. The Mirror Room has floor to ceiling gilt-framed mirrors, and some of the antiques dotted around the place are from as far away as China. The hotel's dining room, serving classical cuisine and with an impressive wine list, looks out over an estuary and at high tide gives the impression that it's floating. The beauty of this hotel is that

BODYSGALLEN HALL
(☎ 01492-584 466, 🖹 01492-582 519, 🖳 www.bodysgallen.com), Llandudno, Gwynedd LL30 IRS, Wales
Reservations: From the US toll-free (☎ 800-260-8338); through Relais & Chateaux toll-free reservation numbers worldwide (see p12)
Getting there: The hotel can arrange transfers from Llandudno Junction railway station but many guests arrive by car
Accommodation: 19 rooms in the main Hall and 16 cottages
Amenities: The Bodysgallen Spa with swimming pool, sauna, steam room, whirlpool bath and beauty salons, historic gardens including a rare 17th-century parterre of box hedges, two dining rooms, bar, library, tennis, croquet, sailing in Conwy Harbour, sea and river fishing, horse-riding and golf nearby
Dress code: Jacket and tie are requested for dinner
Weddings: The Hall's former stable block, the Wynn Rooms, has been converted and can be used for weddings
Minimum stay: None, apart from two nights for the Historic House Summer Breaks (see below)
Rates: Doubles from US$199/£140, four-poster bedrooms from US$291/£205, cottage suites from US$235/£165 room only; ask about their Historic House Summer Breaks which cost from US$156/£110 per person and include two nights' accommodation, early morning tea, cooked breakfast, table d'hôte dinner, and free entry into the historic property of your choice
Credit cards: Most major
Taxes and service charge: Included

the village closes to visitors at sunset, leaving the village in peace. Nearby are the mountains of Snowdonia, and the wildly beautiful coastline of the Llyn Peninsula. Doubles cost from US$192/£135 to US$284/£200, suite from US$235/£165 to US$355/£250 (some have four-posters).

Not far away from here lies **Plas Bodegroes** (☎ 01758-612 363, 🖹 01758-701 247, 🖳 www.bodegroes.co.uk, Pwllheli LL53 5TH, Wales). It has accommodation in 11 rooms in an elegantly decorated Georgian manor house (some four-posters), but what attracts people to Plas Bodegroes is its food – some of the best Wales has to offer. If you're foodies, this is the place to come. Contact **Welsh Rarebits** (☎ 01686-668 030, US toll-free ☎ 800-873-7140, 🖳 www.welsh.rarebits.co.uk) for a comprehensive list of distinctive hotels in Wales.

Renting a cottage in Wales

English Country Cottages (☎ 0870-585 1122, 🖹 0870-585 1150, 🖳 www.english-country-cottages.co.uk), despite its misleading name, has some fabulous cottages ideally suited to honeymoons spread all over Wales. Choose from 500-year-old, thick, whitewashed wall cottages such as **Cwmmegan** which was originally a shepherd's cottage, or the cosy little **Retreat** in **Aberglaslyn** which is tucked away behind trees and shrubs with its own little garden near to Snowdonia National Park. The cottages come well-equipped with mod cons such as microwave ovens and barbecues for the summer, and offer a unique insight into living in Wales.

Ireland
(BEST TIME: APRIL TO OCTOBER)

Ireland is the perfect place for a honeymoon if you dream of walking round rugged coastlines hand in hand, riding across untouched sandy beaches and emerald green fields and lingering in local pubs for long lunches over pints of Guinness and a chat with the locals. It's also a place for fine dining on hearty gourmet fare, where everything from the lobster to the beef will be of local origin.

For some reason the Emerald Isles cannot fail to conjure up romantic images of a charmed existence now lost to most of the developed world, where the Irish charm and wit still presides and holds a magnetic attraction for people from all corners of the world. Ireland is indeed a place of great history and romance, where the hospitality and local 'craic' – the Irish colloquialism for good times – will remain lodged in your heart forever.

We had our honeymoon in Ireland, touring about from place to place. We were drawn by the idea of staying in historic country house hotels, from which we could stride out to explore the surrounding countryside after a good hearty breakfast. We would return in time to take tea before a roaring peat fire, where we'd nestle for hours until it was time to change for our gourmet five-course dinner.

For us a honeymoon in Ireland was all about eating and drinking – and what wonderful food we had! Perhaps our judgement was swayed by being on our honeymoon but I always swear I've never experienced better food than at **Ballymaloe** or **Ballylickey**. All the hotels I have listed offer such high standards in cuisine, accommodation and service that they'd be quite at home among the very best hotels in the world, but they have somehow managed to remain some of Europe's best-kept secrets.

You might like to make Ireland just a three-day stopover in a longer European tour, in which case just pick one or two hotels close to each other. But the best way to see Ireland is by car, staying in three or four hotels dotted around the country. Driving

---

THE REPUBLIC OF IRELAND
Country house hotels set in rugged scenery, delicious gourmet food washed down by pints of Guinness in a pub with fiddle-strumming locals
Capital: Dublin
When to go: May to October but you could go anytime as long as you don't mind the winter weather
Average maximum temperatures °C

JAN	FEB	MAR	APR	MAY	JUN	JUL	AUG	SEP	OCT	NOV	DEC
5	5	6	8	11	14	15	15	13	11	7	6

Flight times: to Dublin from:
      New York: (via London) 8 hours
      LA: 12 hours
      London: 50 minutes
      Sydney: 25 hours
Approximate exchange rates: Euro (€) – £1 = €1.59, US$1 = €1.11, A$1 = €0.57
Time difference: GMT (plus one hour from the last Sunday in March to the last Saturday in October)
Voltage: 230v AC, 50 Hz, three-pin flat or two-pin round wall sockets
Combine with: Britain and Europe
Country dialling code: ☎ 353
Further information: Irish Tourist Board at 🖳 www.ireland.travel.ie

STAYING IN CASTLES IN SCOTLAND AND IRELAND

As Madonna has shown, castles are a great place for a wedding. They are also a romantic choice for a honeymoon and range from the tiny to the tremendous. Although there are castles all over the UK, the best-known are in Scotland and Ireland.

Scotland

If you can't get into **Skibo Castle** (☎ 01862-894 600, Dornach, Inverness), where Madonna was married, but want a castle for your wedding party, try **Myres Castle** (☎ 01337-828 350, 🖷 01337-827 531, 🖳 www.myres.co.uk, Auchtermuchty, Fife, KY14 7EW). It dates from the 16th century and once hosted Mary, Queen of Scots. The rooms are decorated to a high standard in understated Scottish style, all have fantastic bathrooms and Tom's Room has a four-poster bed. Myres Castle can accommodate up to nine couples and costs US$3347/£3000 per night (US$374/£335 per couple plus VAT) which includes all meals and non-alcoholic drinks.

Dundas Castle (☎ 0131-319 2039, 🖷 0131-319 2068, 🖳 www.dundascastle.co.uk), South Queensferry, Edinburgh, EH30 9SP, just 8 miles from Edinburgh, is a stunning castle offering really friendly hospitality in magnificent surroundings. Built in 1818 and now the home of Sir Jack and Lady Stewart-Clark, the castle has been beautifully restored over the last few years. As well as a 15th-century keep, available for wedding ceremonies, there's a stag chamber, armoury and Great Hall. Up to 60 guests can be catered for in the Georgian dining room, or there's the Pavilion Marquee which can host receptions for up to 200. Wedding packages start from £3750.

Ireland

Dromoland Castle (☎ 061-368 144, 🖷 061-363 355, Newmarket-On-Fergus, Co Clare) is one of the best-known castles in Ireland. Standing proud among almost 160 hectares of private estate, Dromoland must be incorporated into your stay if you've ever dreamt of sleeping within castle walls. Some honeymooners might be put off by the size and opulence – with 100 rooms, state rooms and suites the castle is not exactly intimate. Dromoland is all about

impressive chandeliers, suits of armour, crystal glassware and taking tea in the kind of drawing room where the Queen Mother wouldn't look out of place. Dining is taken seriously at Dromoland: the restaurant has been awarded a Michelin and an Egon Ronay Star. There are plenty of distractions to help burn off the calories during the day, from the Golf and Country Club with the castle's own 18-hole championship course, indoor swimming pool, sauna etc to tennis, trout fishing, riding and shooting. Doubles from US$295/€336, but most standard rooms get snapped up early so expect to pay US$366/€416; suites from US$948/ €1080. Book through Preferred Hotels and Resorts reservation numbers worldwide (see p12) or UK tour operator Seasons in Style (see p14).

Ballyhannon Castle (☎ 065-682 5640, 🖳 markevans@eircom.net, County Clare) is a 15th-century Irish keep or tower house with great views over the River Shannon – and just 15 minutes from Shannon Airport. Its oak ceiling beams, flagstone floors and medieval arches transport you back to Ireland's past. There is a splendid minstrel's gallery and inglenook fireplace in the living room and beautiful antiques throughout. A winding spiral stone staircase takes you up a further four floors and into rooms with all the mod cons: TV, stereo, telephone/fax and underfloor heating, and two of the three rooms have four-poster beds. Ballyhannon comes with maid service and a cook if you wish. Fishing, hunting, riding, golf and the coast are all nearby. Ballyhannon costs from US$2789/ €3175 (low season) to US$3570/ €4064 the rest of year per week to rent (booked direct). It can also be booked through UK tour operator Elegant Resorts (see p14).

If you'd like to get married in Ireland, **Luttrellstown Castle** (☎ 01-808 9900, 🖷 01-808 9901, 🖳 www.luttrellstown.ie, Castle-knock, Dublin 15), just 20 minutes from Dublin airport, is a magnificent 15th-century building, completely refurbished in 2000. With just 14 bedrooms, five of which have four-poster beds, and furnished with fine 18th-century Irish antiques, fully staffed it costs for US$5020/ €5714 for the night or US$2231/€2540 for the day/evening.

is easy in Ireland although the lack of major roads tends to mean journeys take a little longer, so give yourself a few days in each hotel to truly savour the slow pace of life.

COUNTY CORK

Cork, down in the south-west, is the republic's largest county. The town itself is the sailing capital of Ireland and in the summer months it's a really bustling place.

Ballymaloe House

If you fly into Cork, Ballymaloe House is a good place to start your honeymoon as it's only an hour's drive north-east from Cork airport: it is easy to hire a car at the airport.

THINGS TO SEE AND DO AROUND CORK

Nearby **Kinsale** is considered to be Ireland's gourmet capital and is a super place to visit for a taster of old Ireland. Among its 13 restaurants, the *Cottage Loft* (☎ 021-477 2803) and the *Vintage* (☎ 021-477 2502) are particularly good and if you're there in early October you'll catch the city's annual Gourmet Festival. You can get details of the festival from Peter Barry (☎ 021-477 4026). If you just fancy a couple of pints of Murphy's, head for the *Spaniard* out at Scilly which is much more cosy and a really lovely pub.

On the road to **Clonakilty** pop into the **Timoleague Castle Gardens** if you're at all into horticulture and take a detour via quaint **Courtmacsherry**. Clonakilty is a great town which was founded in the 17th century by the first Earl of Cork and is now both very Irish and very Catholic.

Another rare treat is *Heir Island Restaurant* (☎ 028-38102, 🖳 www.islandcottage.com) situated on Heir Island in **Roaringwater Bay**. You have to catch a ferry across to the small restaurant: the ferry from Cunnamore drops you off as the sun sets (leaving at 7.55pm) and returns just before midnight to take you home again. In between you'll have had one of the best set meals of your life and the whole evening will seem like some kind of magical dream. Do book early as the restaurant is very popular: it seats 24 people on three tables so you need to be prepared to share a table if

necessary – it's definitely worth it. (Closed Monday and Tuesday). Also note that the restaurant doesn't accept credit cards.

A drive down the **Mizzen Head Peninsula** is worthwhile for the beautiful scenery around **Mount Gabrielle**, the views of **Fastnet Rock** which is the turning point for the sailing race of that name that marks the end of Cowes Week each year, and the lovely sailing village of **School**, at the foot of Mount Gabrielle. Drive on to **Crook Haven** and stop for a pint there. The views all around here are amazing.

Make sure you also make a detour to kiss the Blarney Stone in **Blarney Castle** (open from 9am to 7pm or sundown Monday to Saturday and Sunday 9.30am to 5.30pm or sundown), although it's painfully touristy it just has to be done: the theory goes that if you kiss the stone you'll never be at a loss for words.

Other touristy places worth visiting are beautiful **Bantry House** (open daily from 9am to 6pm, and to 8pm in the summer) and the town of Bantry itself, the **Jameson Heritage Centre** in **Midleton** where whiskey has been distilled since the early 19th century, and catch the ferry across to Cape Clear and the **Skerkin Islands** for their lovely sandy beaches and a great pub, the *Jolly Rodger* which serves food.

For further information contact Cork Tourist Board on Ireland ☎ 021-427 3251, or West Cork's Office, Skibbereen (☎ 028 21766) or visit 🖳 www.cork-kerry.travel.ie.

BALLYMALOE HOUSE
(☎ 021-652 531, 🖹 021-652 021), Shanagarry, Co Cork, Republic of Ireland
Reservations: Direct
Getting there: 40 minutes' drive from Cork Airport
Accommodation: 13 rooms in the main house; 10 in the old coachyard; eight larger rooms opening out over the lawns; plus one room in the Gatehouse
Amenities: Heated outdoor pool, tennis court, craft shop on site; horse-riding, fishing, and championship golf all nearby
Dress code: Smart casual
Weddings: No
Minimum stay: None
Rates: Double rooms from US$190/€216 to US$212/€242 between May and the end of September; ask about special offers because they often do a three-day dinner, bed and breakfast package
Credit cards: Access, Visa
Taxes and service charge: Taxes are included, service charge is optional

A lovely Georgian manor turned hotel, Ballymaloe House has long been famous for its exceptionally fine food. Owner and chef Myrtle Allen, who has won awards from critics and been praised by food lovers throughout the world, has overseen a resurgence in the popularity of traditional Irish dishes and now runs a cookery school close to the hotel. The kitchens at Ballymaloe produce food from a bygone era, when summertime was all about freshly squeezed lemonade and when people had time for full breakfasts. Still a working farm, everything is prepared for you on site that day – from the white triangles of toast baked that morning to the hand-churned butter, with fish having only arrived in the kitchen minutes before it arrives at your table.

This small luxurious hotel has an incomparable homely feel with flowers fresh from the garden in the 32 bedrooms, wonderfully pressed white cotton sheets on king-sized beds, huge towels in the en suite bathrooms, and no television, radio, or even locks on the door to bring you back to the present day. Thirteen of the bedrooms are in the main house while five new larger rooms open on to the lawn and a stream on the north side of the building. Further bedrooms are housed in the old coach yard – if you get offered these because the main house is full don't turn them down as they are lovely spacious rooms and the food in the restaurant is just the same!

Days at Ballymaloe are spent walking, riding or touring the countryside by car. This part of Cork has rolling fertile farmland and a mixture of sandy beaches, deserted headlands and rocky inlets along the coastline. The family's 160-hectare farm also has its own outdoor swimming pool, tennis court, a small golf course and excellent craft shop. Sea and river fishing as well as a championship golf course are available close by. Whatever you do, try to get back to the hotel for tea by the fireside: you can easily while away the time before getting ready for the main event of the day – dinner.

Other recommended hotels

Ballylickey Manor House (☎ 027-50071, 🖹 027-50124, 🖳 ballymh@eircom.net, Ballylickey, Bantry Bay, Co Cork) is a wonderful hotel overlooking **Bantry Bay**, in the very south of County Cork. Built 300 years ago, the Manor House was originally used by Lord Kenmare as a shooting lodge.

Over the last 50 years the current owners of this lovely white house have extended it so that guests can choose between the elegant and spacious sunny suites in the main house or more rustic bedrooms and suites in the garden cottages.

The immaculately-kept gardens are the perfect place for a mid-afternoon potter, a game of croquet on the lawn, or just a sumptuous tea while looking out to sea. As well as being close to the sea which provides great fishing and walking, the hotel has its own outdoor swimming pool and there is golf nearby and a really good riding school where you can hire horses for a hack if experienced. The house is filled with antiques and fine art, a cosy log fire, and an intimate dining room with exceptional cuisine – I had the most fantastic lobster soufflé at Ballylickey that I've ever tasted anywhere. Doubles cost from US$145/€166, suites from US$201/€229 with breakfast, but excluding 10% service charge. The hotel is closed from November to the end of March. Book through Relais & Chateaux reservation numbers worldwide (see p12).

COUNTY KERRY
Park Hotel Kenmare

Park Hotel Kenmare is without doubt one of Ireland's most popular hotels.

Built on the estate of the Marquis of Lansdowne, a descendant of the Cromwellian landlord Sir William Petty who designed the local town, the building was later turned into a resting place for travellers on the Great Southern and Western Railway. It stands amidst four hectares of parkland with spectacular views over Kenmare Bay and is perfectly positioned for the Ring of Kerry.

PARK HOTEL KENMARE
(☎ 064-41200, 🖹 064-41402, 🖳 info@parkkenmare.com), Kenmare, Co Kerry, Republic of Ireland
Reservations: Small Luxury Hotels of the World toll-free reservations numbers worldwide (see p12)
Getting there: 1½ hours from Cork Airport; one hour from Kerry Airport; the hotel can arrange transfers for about US$61/€70 from Kerry and US$117/€134 from Cork
Accommodation: 41 rooms, nine suites
Amenities: 18-hole golf course, tennis court, fitness centre, croquet; horse-riding and fishing nearby, restaurant with Michelin star, 24-hour room service
Dress code: Neat dress after 6pm
Weddings: The hotel can have wedding ceremonies for up to 65 people, and hosts receptions for up to 120 people, prices start at €70 a head for dinner
Minimum stay: None
Rates: Double rooms from US$223/€254 to US$335/€381, suites from US$404/€460 to US$475/€541
Credit cards: Most major
Taxes and service charge: Included

THINGS TO SEE AND DO AROUND COUNTY KERRY

The stunning **Ring of Kerry** is one of the most scenic parts of Ireland. The 177km stretch from Kenmare to Killorglin and back via the MacGillycuddy Reeks that comprises the Ring of Kerry, has to be seen. It is easy to do the circuit, by car, in a day or two but don't try in the middle of summer unless you are known for your patience with caravans and tour buses on single track roads. If you are there in the height of the season the best option is to go clockwise: the opposite direction to most of the other tourists who will be doing it the 'right' way.

I'm not a fan of Kenmare, the so-called 'jewel of the Ring of Kerry', with its pastel-painted shops and houses, or indeed Sneem, mainly because they are both so popular with tourists, but there is lots to do in the surrounding area.

Contact the regional tourist board (☎ 064-31633, ▤ 064-34506) for details on **cycling** routes and where to hire bicycles, **pony trekking** over the mountains and along the beaches, **salmon and trout fishing** and even deep-sea fishing, and of course for information on how to play at the two championship courses in **Killarney** or the one in **Waterville**.

Kerry is also brilliant **walking country** with routes and paths to suit all kinds of fitness and abilities. To the north lie the MacGillycuddy Reeks, Ireland's highest peak **Carrantuohill** (over 1000m) as well as several other munros (peaks that are smaller than mountains) and 40 peaks over 600m. To the south of Kenmare are the gentle **Cahas** which are usually covered with a rich layer of blanket bog (peat) and which stretch from Gougane Barra to the Atlantic Ocean. Or you can walk the **Kerry Way**, Ireland's longest footpath with a marked trail which starts and finishes in Killarney – just don't expect to be the only ones doing so in the summer time!

Other great driving routes in the area are the 21km scenic route over the twisting **Moll's Gap** road to Killarney and the 130km tour of the **Dingle Peninsula**, which is a great deal less touristy and just as beautiful.

For a classic Irish night out try *Nick's* (☎ 066-976 1219), Lower Bridge Street, Killorglin, where good hearty food such as a rack of lamb will no doubt be washed down by several pints and a sing-song around the piano, and for a delicious night out in Kenmare you can't beat *Packie's* (☎ 064-41508), Henry Street, where Maura Foley serves simple but delicious dishes in lively bistro surroundings.

For further information see ▯ www.cork-kerry.travel.ie.

The hotel's public rooms, full of exquisite antiques, grand interior furnishings and roaring fires, welcome you with the kind of atmosphere aimed to make you feel you have just stepped back in time to a Victorian country home. Somehow, owner Francis Brennan's hotel seems to epitomise all that should be expected of a truly great hotel.

Although there are only 50 bedrooms, don't expect a small, quaint hotel as the Park Hotel Kenmare is an imposing grey stone building which resembles a rather austere château. The bedrooms and suites are all spacious with rich, dark wooden furniture enhanced by pretty pale fabrics and en suite marble bathrooms. All the standard rooms have lovely views over the surrounding mountains, while spectacular sea views can be enjoyed from all the superior rooms and suites. They are all equipped with bathrobes, Floris toiletries, TV and hairdryer.

A member of Small Luxury Hotels of the World, the hotel restaurant serves a mix of classic and progressive Irish cuisine, and has received numerous international awards, including one Michelin star. Because of the culinary expertise and extensive wine list most guests dine at the hotel. The lounge, bar, alfresco drinks terrace and dining room boast stunning views over the gardens and the estuary.

During the day there are a whole host of activities on offer including the hotel's own fitness suite, croquet on the lawn, an 18-hole golf course and a tennis court. Fishing, horse-riding and some watersports can easily be arranged nearby.

COUNTY GALWAY

A few days on Ireland's west coast and you'll soon really understand why the place has always been known as the Emerald Isle. The west coast of Ireland is, in my mind, its most beautiful, and Connemara boasts some of the most splendid scenery on earth.

Cashel House

Cashel House is a small, mid-19th-century country home standing at the head of Cashel Bay in 20 hectares of award-winning gardens. Owned and run by Dermot and Kay McEvilly who offer guests a warm Irish welcome, this lovely white Georgian manor house is the perfect environment in which to unwind and take in the many pleasures of the surrounding Connemara countryside.

The house is full of inviting public rooms where leather and floral-patterned sofas give guests lots of opportunity for private relaxation in front of well-laid peat fires. Ornately-framed oil paintings adorn the walls, which are painted in warm cinnamon and deep red tones. Throughout the house there are lots of oak antiques and wonderful fresh flower arrangements from the garden.

The bedrooms are also very comfortable and all individual, with TVs, en suite bathrooms and vivid floral prints. Avoid the standard rooms as they are all very small but the garden suites are extremely spacious with their separate living and sleeping areas.

CASHEL HOUSE
(☎ 095-31001, 🖅 095-31077), Cashel, Co Galway, Republic of Ireland
Closed: Mid to end January
Reservations: Relais & Châteaux reservation numbers worldwide (see p12)
Getting there: 67km from Galway Airport; 2¹/₂ hours from Shannon Airport and 280km from Dublin via the N59
Accommodation: 32 rooms including 13 garden suites
Amenities: On-site equestrian centre offering guided treks, lessons, jumping; tennis; golf at nearby Ballyconneely, salmon and sea fishing also nearby; conservatory restaurant
Dress code: Most guests do wear a jacket and tie in the evening, but there is no official requirement to do so
Weddings: Not catered for
Minimum stay: None
Rates: Doubles from US$140/€150, Garden Suites from US$188/€201
Credit cards: Most major
Taxes and service charge: Taxes are included, but there is a 12.5% service charge on the room and food bills

THINGS TO SEE AND DO IN COUNTY GALWAY

Connemara is all about long, leisurely strolls, island hopping from one emerald dot in the shimmering blue sea to another, and of course oysters, for which the area is famous.

Make sure your stay here incorporates a visit to the **Aran Islands**, **Dunguaire** and **Portumna** castles and as many of the **idyllic beaches** – Ballyconneely, Gurteen and Dog's are particularly beautiful – as you can.

There is a regular boat service from Galway to the Aran Islands: the journey takes around an hour and a half, or alternatively go from Rossaveal, which takes only 30 minutes. A round-trip fare from Galway city docks (☎ 091-567 676) costs €18 and €20 from Rossaveal; for further details call ☎ 091-561767.

There are lots of wonderful restaurants in the area. Even if you don't stay there, do go along to **Rosleague Manor** (see p122; ☎ 095-41101, 🖅 095-41168), Letterfrack, Connemara, for afternoon tea or dinner. The food is delicious and the beautiful wooden dining room very elegant.

Clifden, the capital of Connemara, is a curious place, a strange mix of tourist seaside resort and working fishing village, but it is very nice and is blessed with two great restaurants.

We went for a light snack one evening, having eaten delicious meals for days on end, but I got so over-excited about the menu at **O'Grady's Seafood Restaurant** (☎ 095-21450) that I ended up ordering the dressed lobster. O'Grady's is a bit like that, something about the menu (not the surroundings!) and the smells from the kitchen tells you to expect some seriously good seafood and you end up ordering accordingly.

Just outside Clifden is the area's other most famous restaurant, **High Moors Restaurant** (☎ 095-21342), Dooneen, Clifden. Located in the somewhat unlikely setting of a room in the owners' (Eileen and Hugh) bungalow, High Moors, which is only open for dinner (closed Monday and Tuesday) has a great atmosphere and even better food, especially the Connemara lamb.

If you feel you need to work off the seafood, it is possible to hire bicycles from **Mannions** (☎ 095-21160), or just head on foot for the hills in the **Connemara National Park**, just outside Letterfrack. The park's visitors' centre (☎ 095-41054) usually has small local exhibitions and maps for all grades of walks. If you do make it to the top of one of the famous **Twelve Bens** the sea views are incredible.

Contact Galway Tourist office (Ireland ☎ 091-563 081), Clifden Tourist Office (Ireland ☎ 095-21163) or see 🖥 www.westireland. travel.ie.

The service, accommodation and food at Cashel House are good enough to have earned it membership of the prestigious Relais & Châteaux group – largely due, no doubt, to the hotel's excellent location on **Cashel Bay** which ensures that the lobster, scallops, salmon and mussels are all really fresh. In the summer meals are served outside in the garden or in the pretty conservatory where guests dine by candlelight on lobster, oysters au gratin, Connemara lamb and fine Irish cheeses.

Days at Cashel House are spent either out on the hotel's fine horses, walking in the nearby Connemara hills or along the many deserted beaches taking in the scenery along the nearby and aptly-named Sky Road, or enjoying the 25-minute sail out to the nearby **Aran Islands**.

Tennis, golf, salmon and sea fishing are also close to hand and can easily be arranged for you by the hotel. Rowing boats are available for residents and are ideal for exploring the coastline – make a day of it by taking a picnic. There are also a number of paths through the woods and up the summit of nearby **Cashel Hill**.

Other recommended hotels

Rosleague Manor (☎ 095-41101, 🖹 095-41168, 🖳 roseleaguemanor@ireland.com, Letterfrack, Connemara, Co Galway) is a lovely Regency manor house that looks down on **Ballynakill Harbour**. It is not as luxurious as some of the hotels in this chapter but it will really suit you if you are looking for something a little more understated. It is comfortable but the bedrooms are ever so slightly austere with their dark wood furnishings, though the ones at the front of the house have the most dreamy views over **Diamond Hill**, **Speckled Hill** and **Letter Hill**. We loved Rosleague Manor for its tranquil, laid-back atmosphere. The food is delicious and the gardens were inundated with that ubiquitous Irish rhododendron. Doubles from US$68/€76 per person, suites from US$80/€89 including breakfast; three-night half-board package from €331/US$295.

COUNTY KILKENNY

County Kilkenny is one of those traditional hunting, shooting and fishing counties where the beautiful surrounding countryside provides the perfect playground. Try to visit the 12th-century Cistercian Abbey at **Jerpoint**, just south of **Thomastown**. Shopping in Kilkenny itself is also really good – a great place to buy presents to take back home and especially for your own home.

Mount Juliet Estate

Mount Juliet Estate is one of the most famous country house hotels in Ireland. There is so much for guests to do in the 640 hectares of woodland and gardens that there probably won't be much time to see anything of the rest of the county.

This beautiful grey building with its ivy-clad stone walls stands majestic, but welcoming. Most guests opt for one of the lovely rooms in the Georgian manor house itself where antique furnishings, lifted by pastel fabrics, take you back to the house's former

---

MOUNT JULIET ESTATE
(☎ 056-73000, 🖹 056-73019, 🖳 info@mountjuliet.ie), Thomastown, Co Kilkenny, Republic of Ireland
Reservations: Small Luxury Hotels of the World toll-free reservation numbers worldwide (see p12)
Getting there: Two hours from Dublin airport; the hotel can arrange taxi transfers at a cost of US$307/€350 one way or from Cork, approximately US$117/€134
Accommodation: 32 bedrooms: 11 in Mount Juliet House, 13 rooms in Hunters Yard, eight two-bedroom Rose Garden Cottages
Amenities: 18-hole par championship golf course, three-hole golf academy, driving range, David Ledbetter Golf Academy, tennis, indoor swimming pool, sauna, steam room, leisure centre and beauty therapist, gym, horse-riding, croquet, fishing, clay pigeon shooting, archery, two restaurants, three bars and room service
Weddings: No
Minimum stay: None
Rates: Doubles from US$178/€204 to US$335/€381, suites from US$268/€305 to US$591/€673
Credit cards: Most major
Taxes and service: Included

age of glory. Many have sweeping views over the surrounding countryside. Around the stable, and not far from the main building, Hunter's Yard offers less formal Club Rooms with old timber beams, stone walls and wooden ceilings, producing a rustic, sporting atmosphere. Rose Garden Lodges are the most spacious. Hunter's Yard has its own **Kendals Restaurant**, which offers more casual dining than the main house's elegantly appointed pale blue **Lady Helen Dining Room**. **Spike Bar** serves snacks all day.

Mount Juliet offers its guests a broad range of facilities: two restaurants, three bars, an impressive leisure centre with a swimming pool, gym, steam room, tennis, croquet, clay shooting and archery, an 18-hole Jack Nicklaus designed golf course, its own equestrian centre with riding trails, and a stretch of river for fishing.

You'll want for nothing at Mount Juliet: the fresh fruit and flowers in your room are changed daily, there is a fine wine list and distinguished Irish cuisine and impeccable service pervades every aspect of your stay.

DUBLIN

It would be a shame to miss out on Ireland's capital, Dublin, a cosmopolitan city buzzing with energy. There's plenty to see and do here, from strolling along the banks of the River Liffey and visiting the designer shops on Grafton Street to nights out in the vibrant Temple Bar area pulsing with art, theatre and music, or in the lively pubs and restaurants around St Stephen's Green.

Some fabulous hotels have sprung up in Dublin in the last five years, making it a comfortable, lively start or finish to an Irish honeymoon (see box p124).

The Merrion

Dublin is renowned for its Georgian architecture and the award-winning Merrion, opposite the home of the Irish Government, is a living example of this bygone era.

A five-star luxurious hotel, which opened in 1997, The Merrion was created from four carefully-restored Georgian townhouses, with the addition of a contemporary Garden Wing, set around two sheltered 18th-century landscaped gardens. These townhouses were once the home of Irish nobility – the duke of Wellington is said to have been born in Mornington House.

Walking into The Merrion you'll be transported back to the 18th century but without the gloom. Decorated in period colours, Irish fabrics and antique furniture with magnificent Roccoco plasterwork ceilings with carved flowers, fruit and birds, it feels like a nicely-run private home and has a welcome to match.

This hotel is a must for art lovers, as hanging from its walls is the most important collection of 18th and 19th century art in Ireland, featuring artists such as Martin Mooney, Paul Henry and William Leech.

THE MERRION
(☎ 01-603 0600, 🗎 01- 603 0700, 🖳 www.merrionhotel.com), Upper Merrion Street, Dublin 2, Ireland
Reservations: Through Leading Hotels of the World reservation numbers worldwide (see p12) or UK tour operators Elegant Resorts, Seasons in Style (see p14)
Getting there: Dublin International Airport
Accommodation: 125 rooms and 20 suites
Amenities: Two restaurants: Morningtons and Restaurant Patrick Guilbaud; two bars: the Cellar Bar in the 18th-century vault and No 23 for an intimate cocktail; Tethra spa with 18m pool, E'SPA treatments, steam room and gym, 18th-century landscaped gardens, 24-hour room and valet service, shoe shine service, complimentary private car park, laundry, dry cleaning and pressing service
Dress code: Smart casual
Weddings: Up to 50 people dining for receptions
Minimum stay: None
Rates: Main House de luxe doubles from US$346/€394, junior suites from US$502/€572; Garden Wing superior doubles from US$268/€305, one-bedroom suites from US$614/€699, room only. 'The Honeymoon Hideaway' package includes champagne on arrival, a gift on departure, and one night in a luxurious double room with full Irish breakfast for US$313/€280 per couple
Credit cards: Most major
Taxes and service charge: Tax included, no service charge

DESIGNER HOTELS IN DUBLIN

The last five years has seen the birth of some exciting hotels in the heart of Dublin combining convivial Irish style with contemporary sophistication.

The Morrison (☎ 01-887 240, 🗎 01-878 3185, 🖳 www.morrisonhotel.ie, Ormond Quay, Dublin) was designed by Irish fashion designer John Rocha. Its rooms, decorated in refined clean lines with a blend of natural materials, have all the mod cons. The *Halo Restaurant*, deemed 'one of the 60 great new restaurants worldwide' by Condé Nast *Traveller*, serves modern, fusion-style food. From the Morrison Bar you can watch the sun go down over the River Liffey, or hang out in the late-night oriental supper bar, *Lobo*. Doubles cost from US$195/€223, Georgian room US$279/€318, suites from US$390/€445, penthouse US$1394/€1588 per couple including tax. Book through European Connection (🖳 www.europeanconnection.co.uk) or UK tour operators Elegant Resorts (see p14).

The Morgan (☎ 01-672 7752, 🗎 01-672 7753, 10 Fleet Street, Temple Bar, Dublin), one of the most stylish hotels in the city, is all about comfort and luxury through minimalism.

Dublin's only member of Design Hotels, bright beige and cream generate a light interior, and classic furniture is by designers Le Corbusier and Eileen Gray. It has one art deco-style Morgan Suite, and as well as the usual mod-cons, the rooms have beechwood furniture creating an uncluttered elegance. Entertainment ranges from relaxing massage and aromatherapy treatments to clubbing at 'XS'. Doubles cost from US$145/€166; Morgan Suite US$418/€477 including tax and service. Book direct toll-free UK (☎ 0800-912 0021) or toll-free USA (☎ 1800-869-4330) or through Design Hotels (see p12).

The Clarence (☎ 01-407 0800, 🗎 01-407 0820, 🖳 www.theclarence.ie, 6-8 Wellington Quay, Dublin 2), overlooking the River Liffey is my favourite of the city's new hotels. Built in 1852 it was bought by U2's Bono and The Edge in 1992 and transformed into their perfect hotel. Contemporary design is fused with traditional structure using wonderful materials such as American white oak, Portland stone and Italian limestone. Doubles cost from €285, book through Leading Hotels of the World reservation numbers worldwide (see p12).

In the contemporary Garden Wing, gracious Georgian-style light and airy bedrooms with crisp Frette linen and other luxurious fabrics overlook the box hedges, water features, pathways, statues and obelisks of the period garden whilst the suites in the Main House capture the full grandeur of the Georgian era. Some are vaulted with delicate Roccoco ceilings; others have magnificent original marble fireplaces.

The Merrion boasts the most spectacular bathrooms in Dublin. Dripping with opulent Italian marble, they have contemporary chrome fittings, separate power showers and baths, divine fluffy bathrobes and slippers and Kenneth Turner toiletries. All the rooms are air-conditioned and fitted with satellite and cable TV, in-house movie channel, mini-bar, in-room safe, hairdryer, trouser press, three telephones(!), mobile phones and CD player on request. Traditional Irish hospitality is on call 24 hours a day.

The Merrion sits in the heart of Georgian Dublin, where at weekends, horse-drawn carriages clip-clop past railings hung with the work of local exhibiting artists. A leisurely stroll brings you to the 'golden mile' of lively pubs, shops and restaurants. Not that you'll need anywhere else to dine; the Merrion's **Restaurant Patrick Guilbaud** is the only 2-star Michelin restaurant in Ireland. In summer, guests can eat and drink outside on the terrace overlooking the distinctive and unusual gardens.

France
(BEST TIME: APRIL TO OCTOBER)

France and romance have always been synonymous. Much is due to the language itself which, like Italian, sounds so innately sensuous. But I also suspect that this long-established reputation has been passed on in the minds of individuals who believe that there are very few things more romantic than sharing a three-course lunch washed down with a good bottle of wine. And nobody lunches better than the French.

FRANCE
A honeymoon for gastronomes with hundreds of châteaux to stay in and beautiful countryside to explore
When to go: All year round: summer is from June to September, winter from December to the end of March
Average maximum temperatures °C

	JAN	FEB	MAR	APR	MAY	JUN	JUL	AUG	SEP	OCT	NOV	DEC
Paris	8	8	10	15	16	22	24	24	20	16	12	8
Lyons	8	7	11	15	17	24	26	26	22	16	11	8
Nice	12	12	14	18	20	25	27	27	24	21	16	14

Capital: Paris
Flight times: Paris Charles de Gaulle from:
New York: 8 hours
LA: 15 hours
London: 1 hour 10 minutes
Sydney: 25 hours
Approximate exchange rates: Euro (€) – £1 = €1.59, US$1 = €1.11, A$1 = €0.57
Time difference: GMT plus one hour (GMT plus two hours from the last Sunday in March to the last Sunday in October)
Voltage: 220v AC, 50 Hz- plugs with two round pins
Combine with: Britain, Ireland and the rest of mainland Europe
Country dialling code: ☎ 33
Further information: www.franceguide.com

Think for a minute about your images of France and you'll soon realize that they all revolve around food and drink: cycling up to the village in the morning to pick up freshly-baked croissants, and coming home to sit on the terrace, dunking them in great bowls of steaming coffee; wizened old men huddled around small tables in a café, the air thick with the blue smoky haze from their Gitanne, their gnarled hands raising small shots of Pernod to their lips; sitting outside bustling Parisian cafés enjoying a mid-morning espresso; the historic châteaux and rivers of the Dordogne where the set gastronomic menu will guide you through six or seven hearty courses; or just long sunny evenings sipping kir or Provençal rosé. Whatever your favourite thoughts of France are, they are bound to include food and drink. The strength of this association has ensured that France has long been a popular honeymoon destination but its attraction also lies in the large number of romantic châteaux spread throughout the countryside and the many amazingly unaltered medieval villages.

There are literally thousands of suitable destinations and combinations for a French honeymoon: skiing in the **Alps**, the glitzy, glamorous beaches of **St Tropez** or the elegant chic of **Cap-Ferrat**, the châteaux of the **Dordogne**, the vineyards of the **Loire** and, of course, **Paris**, long regarded as the world's most romantic city – so romantic that they have somehow succeeded in convincing us that even a rainy day in Paris is the stuff that dreams are made of.

My idea of the perfect French honeymoon would be to find an open-top sports car, pick out three hotels and enjoy leisurely driving along the lanes of the French countryside. If you stay off the autoroutes and stick to these local lanes you will see how little rural France has changed over the last century. You'll find the most memorable views doing it this way while also discovering wonderful village cafés to stop for lunch: you'll sit alongside builders and bankers as the nation halts at 12 noon to enjoy a three-course lunch and carafe of house red.

PARIS
It may sound a little clichéd but there are very few things more romantic in life than walking along the banks of the **River Seine** hand in hand, stopping for a mid-morning espresso at a pavement café, or dining at the **Jules Verne** restaurant in the **Eiffel Tower**

looking down over Paris as the city lights up beneath you. Paris is dreamy, and there is something unmistakably chic about going there on your honeymoon.

Paris also has a good range of hotels to suit every budget, from the grand hotels around the **Champs Elysées** to smaller, more intimate hideaways in the **Marais** quarter. Eurostar now also makes it easier and much more enjoyable to get between London and Paris. It is, however, very definitely worth avoiding Paris at Easter and in August when the city is so inundated with tourists and many of the restaurants close.

The Lancaster

Comfortable and intimate, the Lancaster is a secluded five-star retreat in the heart of romantic Paris. Just steps away from the Champs Elysées, the lived-in atmosphere of this 19th-century Parisian town house has made it the home away from home for kings, princes and duchesses as well as legendary artistes Noel Coward, Marlene Dietrich, Greta Garbo and Clark Gable.

Previous owner Emile Wolf liked to say, 'I've never had any customers, only friends' and new owner Grace Leo Andrieu has made it her motto. It has an exceptional collection of antiques such as Baccarat, tapestries, fine furnishings and ancient paintings which makes it a monument to French good taste. Combining the modern with the classic, the Lancaster manages to be elegant and refined without being ostentatious.

A 24-hour room service and concierge will cater to your every whim – the Lancaster prides itself on efficient yet unobtrusive service. Privacy is assured in the elegant Café-Bar restaurant which serves contemporary French cuisine for hotel guests only. Opening onto the courtyard garden filled with flowers in summer, it's perfect for romantic dining.

The de luxe guest rooms and suites offer views into the tranquil, Zen-like courtyard garden with its gentle soothing murmur of the wall fountain, or onto the street. Perhaps the most interesting is suite 45, where Marlene Dietrich established her Parisian home. Predominately decorated in lilac, her favourite colour, it has mauve and pale green curtains and swathes of ivory silk.

For the ultimate in romance and secluded intimacy, request an upgrade to the sumptuous penthouse suite No 80, and become sole occupants of the hotel's top floor. Opening the door of this honeymoon suite unveils a stylish but sensual boudoir. Walls are covered in crimson-red silk from floor to ceiling and the two private terraces have sweeping views of the Eiffel Tower and the Sacré Coeur. The bedroom is reminiscent of a French château and in the sleek marble bathroom you can pamper yourself with Grace Leo-Andrieu's specially designed Contemporel range.

THE LANCASTER
(☎ 01-40 76 40 76, 🖷 01-40 76 40 00, 🖳 www.hotel-lancaster.fr) 7, rue de Berri, Champs Elysées, 75008 Paris

Reservations: The Leading Hotels of the World toll-free numbers worldwide (see p12) or tour operators Abercrombie & Kent (see p14)

Getting there: Situated just off the Champs-Elysées, the Lancaster is a two-minute walk from either George V or Franklin Roosevelt metro stations. A taxi from the Gare du Nord (Eurostar) will take 15 minutes, or from Orly and Charles de Gaulle airports 30-45 minutes. Transfers can be arranged for a fee

Accommodation: 46 bedrooms and 10 suites all with private bathrooms, cable television & video, and minibar. Suite 45 is where Marlene Dietrich made her home, and honeymoon suite 80 is secluded on the top floor

Amenities: Le Café-Bar restaurant serves contemporary French cuisine, fitness centre, 24-hour concierge service, laundry, dry cleaning and pressing service, garden patio, private underground car park and limousine service

Dress code: Smart casual

Weddings: Ceremonies cannot be performed at the Lancaster. A small reception room, the Salon Fontenoy, holds up to 16 people

Minimum stay: None

Rates: Doubles from US$343/€390, one-bedroom suites from US$659/€751; breakfast US$22/€25, Suite 80 US$884/€925. Honeymoon package approx US$632/€720 per night

Credit cards: Most major

Taxes and service charge: Included

THINGS TO SEE AND DO IN PARIS

When you've seen the **Eiffel Tower**, **Notre Dame**, **Montmartre** and **Place Vendôme** and taken a trip on the Seine, it's time to explore some of the lesser known parts of the city.

Head up to **Villiers** in the 17th arrondissement and stroll round **Parc Monceau**, with its beautiful gold-studded gates, ornamental rocks and statues and perfectly-clipped lawns. You'll pass nannies walking their charges in one of the city's most elegant neighbourhoods.

Nearby **rue Levis** is an altogether different scene, where the all-day market is open seven days a week and you're more likely to bump into locals hurrying home with their baguettes than into other tourists. The stalls and shops, piled high with fresh fruit and vegetables, fish, meat, cheese and bread, are a wonderful sight.

One area you shouldn't miss is the **Marais**, over in the 4th arrondissement: it is full of interesting art shops and boutiques at much more affordable prices than the rue Faubourg St Honoré. Walk along **rue Temple** and you're sure to find at least one little café suitable for morning coffee. The lovely **Musée Picasso**, tucked away at 5 rue de Thorigny, provides a splendid setting for some 200 of Picasso's paintings as well as sculptures, ceramics and drawings, and is well worth a visit. Less well-known but just as impressive in architectural style is the Musée Cognac-Jay at 8 rue Elzevir. The Marais is studded with little bars, cafés and restaurants.

Don't miss the **Musée Auguste Rodin**, at 77 rue de Varenne in the 7th arrondissement, for not only is the inside of the lovely 18th-century **Hôtel Biron** home to his works, but you can also wander round the picturesque gardens and stand face to face with some of his finest sculptures.

If you fancy a French film there's no better

place than **La Pagode**, 57 bis rue de Babylone also in the 7th; unquestionably the most unusual and also the loveliest cinema in Paris.

Rue Vignon is a good place for lunch, especially if you're shopping in Fauchon, near Place de la Madeleine. Rue Vignon is just around the corner and home to the most incredible cheese shop, *La Ferme Saint-Hubert*, with its 180 different varieties of cheese.

The series of little arcades, where the 2nd arrondissement meets the 9th, is one of those often undiscovered gems of Paris. Start in **Passage des Panoramas**, at 11 boulevard Montmartre, and then head into **Passage Jouffroy**, at 10-12 boulevard Montmartre and 6 rue de la Grange-Batelière. You'll see the **Hôtel Chopin**, with its charming little dolls' house entrance, at the end of the first arcade, and plenty of antiquarian book shops and artisan gift shops. Then find **Passage Verdeau**, at 6 rue de la Grange-Batelière and 31 bis rue du Faubourg-Montmartre. This is the most elaborate of the arcades and it is full of shops with old books, postcards and posters. The Galerie Vivienne, at 4 rue des Petits-Champs, has a luxurious feel about it.

A ramble through the wonderful shops under the arches at **Place des Vosges** is a must: this lovely tree-lined square has to be one of the most romantic places in Paris. It was originally built to house the king's state apartments on one side and the queen's on the other. There are now lots of intriguing shops to wander in and some lovely cafés and restaurants too. Alternatively take a book and sit in the park in the middle of the square and watch the Parisians as they come and go.

For further information visit 🖳 www.paris-touristoffice.com.

The Lancaster can arrange small, personalized wedding receptions and offers a honeymoon package which includes a guaranteed upgrade to a suite, champagne in your room on arrival, a gift of Lancaster bathrobes and late check out.

The understated luxury and standards of the Lancaster will appeal to those who appreciate quality over ostentation, and elegance over fashion.

Other recommended hotels

Hôtel de Vigny (☎ 01-42 99 80 80, 🖹 01-42 99 80 40, 9-11 rue Balzac, 75008) is very much in vogue with the travelling cognoscenti. If you've got the money and really fancy pushing the boat out, this discreet, modern boutique hotel is hard to beat. It has the kind of unobtrusive service and peaceful atmosphere that makes it feel as if you are staying in a private residence.

The Hôtel de Vigny is located right in the heart of Paris, two minutes' walk from the Champs Elysées. The hotel's 26 rooms and 11 suites are all individually decorated and have air conditioning, minibars, TVs and marble bathrooms with hairdryers. Doubles cost from US$335/€382 to US$402/€458, suites from US$402/€458 to US$670/€763. Book direct or through Relais & Chateau (see p12), or Abercrombie & Kent (see p13).

Relais Christine (☎ 01 40 51 60 80, 🗎 01 40 51 60 81, 3 rue Christine, 75006) is a pretty, converted 13th-century abbey in the heart of the Latin Quarter. With its lovely flower-filled garden and cobbled courtyard the Relais Christine is a peaceful haven. All the 51 rooms are air conditioned and most look out over the courtyard or into the garden. Double rooms from €351/US$313, suites from €496/US$442 to €679/US$605. Book direct or through Small Luxury Hotels of the World (see p12).

THE LOIRE VALLEY
Domaine des Hauts de Loire
Domaine des Hauts de Loire is one of the best run and best known of all the French châteaux: it may not be cheap but it is fabulous. There can be no more luxurious base for touring the wineries of the Loire Valley than this.

Built as a hunting lodge in 1860 by publisher Panckouche, the Domaine des Hauts de Loire is the very model of a classic French château. Facing a beautiful lake, its white shuttered windows poke through rambling ivy below a grey slate roof.

This very grand château is full of Louis XIV furniture and ormolu-decorated antiques, oriental rugs, polished parquet flooring and rich organdie curtains, so you may find the grand salon a little over the top but the pretty dining room has the most wonderful, serene atmosphere. As it's a member of Relais & Châteaux you can expect the food to be delicious, accompanied of course by the very best local vintages.

A spiral staircase leads up to the hotel's bedrooms and suites decorated in traditional French style with fine antique armoires, thick cream carpet and heavy cream curtains with apricot piping matching the warmth of the apricot walls.

The bathrooms are just as stunning with either oak panels or pretty honey-coloured marble and the odd oak beam running through the middle. There are several rooms in the adjacent timbered wing which are also tastefully furnished and decorated.

There's lots to do at the Domaine apart from visiting this region's numerous other châteaux and their wineries. The hotel has its own tennis court and outdoor swimming pool; you can borrow bicycles and explore the forest paths running throughout the hotel's 70-hectare private park, go horseriding or mountain-biking or even look down on the glorious countryside from a hot-air balloon.

> **DOMAINE DES HAUTS DE LOIRE**
> (☎ 02-54 20 72 57, 🗎 02-54 20 77 32),
> Route de Herbault, 41150 Onzain, Loire-et-Cher, France
> **Closed**: Dec 1st to Feb 15th
> **Reservations**: Relais & Châteaux worldwide reservation numbers (see p12)
> **Getting there**: Most guests tour the Loire by car: from Tours follow the River Loire (N152) towards Blois, in Chaumont-sur-Loire go to Onzain, then follow signs to Mesland and Herbault for 3km to the hotel; 200km from Paris Orly Airport
> **Accommodation**: 25 rooms, 10 suites
> **Amenities**: Swimming pool, tennis court, restaurant, walking in the park, mountain-biking, fishing; golf nearby, horse-riding, hot-air ballooning, hunting
> **Dress code**: Jacket and tie in the restaurant
> **Weddings**: No
> **Minimum stay**: None
> **Rates**: Doubles from US$94/€107 to US$228/€260; suites from US$268/€305 to US$402/€436
> **Credit cards**: Visa, Eurocard, American Express, Diners Club
> **Taxes and service charge**: Included

BURGUNDY
Château de Gilly
Château de Gilly at Vougeot is a simply amazing château set deep in the heart of the famous Burgundy vineyards, half way between Dijon and Beaune.

The palatial, moated abbey was built in the 14th century by Cistercian monks and has since been transformed into a 48-bedroom hotel with the most wonderful atmosphere. The owners were careful to retain the abbey's ancient charm and authenticity,

THINGS TO SEE AND DO IN THE LOIRE VALLEY

A stay in the Loire usually revolves around seeing the region's many wonderful **châteaux**. There are over a thousand fabulous castles strung out along the Loire River valley of which around a hundred are open to the public. If you possibly can, try to avoid July and August when the European school holidays mean the roads, not just the châteaux themselves, become unbearably crowded – hardly a honeymoon scenario!

From the Domaine des Hauts de Loire the most worthy are **Chenonceaux**, which spans the River Cher and is one of the most beautiful of all the châteaux; **Amboise**, which was visited by Leonardo da Vinci and was at one time home to Francis II and his wife Mary, Queen of Scots; and the fabulous **Cheverny** where many of the original 17th-century decorations and furnishings can still be seen. From Chenonceaux you can take to the skies in a **hot-air balloon**, which is the most superbly relaxing way to view the stunning countryside; call France-Montgolfière (☎ 01 47 00 66 44).

Aside from the famous **Valois** château, the Loire Valley is also known for its wines, in particular for the great estates of Vouvray (☎ 02-47 52 75 03) and Chinon (☎ 02-47 93 20 75), both of which can be visited and offer wine tastings. The charming old town of **Beaugency** is also definitely worth a visit with its majestic arched bridge and intriguing narrow medieval streets.

For further information see ⌨ www.loire valleytourism.com.

---

and with such success that this really is one of those properties in France that people rave about.

The lounges are grand enough to make the Château feel more like a former palace than an abbey while all the bedrooms are individually decorated and very comfortable. There is a honeymoon suite set apart from the main building, located in the grounds of the park close to the river, with its own 'salon', a balcony and a king-sized bed.

The Château operates a variety of honeymoon packages offering guests either a de luxe room or the honeymoon suite, a welcome aperitif, a gourmet dinner served in **Le Clos Prieur**, tours of the local vineyards and ancient castles by horse-drawn carriage, and lunch at Bernard Loiseau's celebrated restaurant, **La Côte d'Or**, nearby. The prices vary depending on which package you go for: although they are all pretty expensive they do make a really good way of seeing the surrounding countryside.

French cuisine at its best and local vintage Burgundies are served in the impressive 14th-century vaulted dining room which was formerly the palace's cellar. Fresh produce from the Château's own grounds are used to prepare such delights as filet de boeuf de Charolias à la lie de vin, while breakfast is served in the **Pierre de Nivelle** room, with its lovely adjoining loggia.

The hotel has its own tennis court, an outdoor heated swimming pool, a bowling green and bicycles for guests' use, not to mention the 'Jardins à la Française' which are lovely for a pre-dinner stroll. It is also very well placed for discovering the surrounding Burgundy countryside and its celebrated vineyards, either by hot-air balloon, horse-

---

CHATEAU DE GILLY
(☎ 03-80 62 89 98, ▤ 03-80 62 82 34, ⌨ www.chateau-gilly.com), Gilly-les Citeaux, 21640 Vougeot, Côte d'Or, France
Closed: From end January to early March
Reservations: Small Luxury Hotels of the World worldwide reservation numbers (see p12)
Getting there: Gilly les Cîteaux is 5km off the Nuits Saint Georges exit from A31
Accommodation: 39 rooms and eight suites
Amenities: Tennis court, heated outdoor swimming pool, table tennis, bowling green, bicycles; room service until midnight; a local beautician and hairdresser can visit the hotel if requested
Dress code: Informal but elegant dress
Weddings: Buffet receptions can be arranged for up to 150 people, and sit-down dinners for up to 140 guests; the hotel is not licensed to perform wedding ceremonies
Minimum stay: None
Rates: Double rooms from US$80/€92; suites from US$188/€214; honeymoon package from €686 for two people including dinner, drinks and breakfast and a night in the honeymoon suite
Credit cards: Most major
Taxes and service charge: Included

THINGS TO SEE AND DO IN THE COTE D'OR

The Côte d'Or, an abbreviation of Côte d'Orient or 'eastern slope', is home to some of France's finest vineyards. The Côte d'Or is divided into the **Côte de Beaune** to the south, where legendary names such as Volnay, Meursault and Pommard are found, and the smaller **Côte de Nuits**, named after Nuits St Georges in the north from where Burgundy's best-known and long-lasting reds derive.

Make a start at **Beaune**, the former home of the dukes of Burgundy and the area's capital. Beaune has obviously prospered from the wine trade: there are many lovely houses rich in architecture, delightful cobbled streets and squares. Some local vineyards have a shop in

Beaune where you can happily while away the hours in tastings, but the best way to get to grips with the vineyards is by doing one of the tours. Alternatively, do a tour under your own steam by joining the Route des Grands Crus in **Gevrey Chambertin**: the route takes you right through the most important wine-growing villages.

A bit further afield, but definitely worth the drive, is one of France's best restaurants, *La Côte d'Or* (☎ 03-80 90 53 53, 🖹 03-80 64 08 92, 🖳 www.bernardloiseau.com), where the celebrated chef Bernard Loiseau holds court. Book well in advance.

For further information visit 🖳 www.burgundy-tourism.com.

---

drawn carriage, or even bicycle. Make sure you visit the **Clos de Vougeot**, the **Abbaye de Cîteaux**, and the **Hospices de Beaune** and **Dijon**, the former capital of the Burgundy dukes.

BEAUJOLAIS
Château de Bagnols
Château de Bagnols is without doubt one of the most gracious, luxurious and spectacularly romantic places to stay in the whole of Europe, let alone France.

Located right in the heart of Beaujolais country this enchanted castle encircled by lavender stands alone in terms of service and beauty. The region is constantly likened to Italy's Tuscany because of the rolling hills with their historic hilltop villages, châteaux and ancient churches. There are wonderful authentic markets to visit where you can pick up local cheeses and woven basketwear, while the abundance of vineyards makes this one of the best areas of France to tour around.

Owned by English publisher, Paul Hamlyn and his wife, the Château de Bagnols is a Grade 1 Listed Building which has been artistically renovated. It has been decorated so perfectly that you could easily convince yourself you've travelled back centuries into the lands of medieval knights.

THINGS TO SEE AND DO AROUND BEAUJOLAIS

The ravishing countryside around the Château de Bagnols is the perfect place for a leisurely stroll. A really good **walk** leaves Bagnols eastward towards Frontenas and past the 'pigeonnier', which was once a local status symbol as only the Lord of the Manor was allowed to keep pigeons. Otherwise take the walk westwards towards Légny, which is also really scenic.

There are lots of wonderful **villages** to be explored by car, in particular Frontenas and Theizé, Le Bois d'Oingt, St Vérand and Ternand, Chessy, Bully and Le Breuil.

Wine enthusiasts will also enjoy following the **wine trail** around the many 'caves' in the Beaujolais region which are open to visitors. Start at Beaujeu, where the huge, multi-roomed

cellar has an effigy of Anne de Beaujeu, daughter of Charles XI and once ruler of the area. If you are planning to visit the caves during the week it's probably a good idea to ask the Château to make appointments for you.

If you fancy an evening out, you can choose from over 20 **gourmet restaurants** all within a 40-minute drive of the Château, the majority of which have Michelin stars.

Few of the local châteaux are open to the public but **Lyon** has an abundance of historic buildings, two dozen museums celebrating the city's 2000-year-old history and a maze of fascinating back streets in the old town to explore.

See 🖳 www.tourisme-gironde-cg33.fr for more information.

Described by *Tatler* magazine as the grandest small hotel in the world – 'so luxurious as to be almost sensual' – the Château is, of course, expensive. But even if you can only stay there one night, do so, because you'll quite simply never find another hotel like it, anywhere.

Four hundred craftsmen and US$43 million were required to turn this 700-year-old castle with its golden stone walls into a 21st-century luxury hideaway. Millions more have been spent in recent renovations which have resulted in the addition of a lavish swimming pool in the Roman ruins. Everywhere you look there are fine antiques, most of them priceless, collected by Mme Hamlyn from all over Europe: there is the Renaissance fireplace in the Grand Salon, the Napoleonic bath in the Suite aux Bouquets, 17th-century sofas, and many original wall paintings, some 15th century. All this combined with latter-day comforts such as heated floors, complimentary toiletries, bathrobes, hairdryers, TVs and pristine Swiss linen, makes for a pretty hedonistic experience.

There are 20 double rooms which include eight apartments – two in the Residence adjacent to the main building; all are en suite. Each has been individually decorated with exceptional attention to detail: the soft velvets extravagantly inlaid with gold ribbons and the shimmering draped silks will surely take your breath away as you enter your room.

In the summer, guests can eat outside on the south-facing terrace under the 100-year-old lime trees, looking out over the surrounding fields. The Château's restaurant has a much sought-after Michelin star and offers guests typical Machon fare of spit-roasted meats and game and inspired new dishes in the **Salles des Gardes**.

On summer evenings, the Château holds baroque music concerts, followed by drinks in the garden and a full gourmet banquet. There can be few more romantic ways to spend an evening than listening to Beethoven in the magnificent surroundings of the Château Bagnols, so do make sure you ask before you book your stay which nights the concerts will be held and book well in advance.

Tennis, pétanque, croquet, badminton and mountain biking are just some of the activities on offer. However, one of the most enjoyable things to do from the hotel is a horse carriage ride taking you through the country lanes and stopping off for a sumptuous picnic prepared at your request by the hotel. Although not cheap, this gourmet picnic is just heavenly. Similarly wonderful are hot-air balloon trips organized by the hotel, taking off either first thing in the morning or for a couple of hours in the early evening before dinner.

CHATEAU DE BAGNOLS
(☎ 04-74 71 40 00, 🖹 04-74 71 40 49, 🖳 www.bagnols.com), 69620 Bagnols en Beaujolais, Rhone, France
Closed: January to March
Reservations: Relais & Chateaux worldwide toll-free numbers (see p12); or through tour operators, Abercrombie & Kent, Western & Oriental, Seasons in Style (see pp9-10)
Getting there: 45 minutes from Lyon Satolas Airport; the hotel can arrange transfers
Accommodation: 20 rooms including 8 'apartments'
Amenities: Restaurant, bar, library, swimming pool, tennis, pétanque, croquet, boutique, badminton, mountain bikes; golf nearby; the hotel can also arrange vineyard tours, walking tours, cycling, ballooning, horse-riding, horse carriage rides, gourmet picnics
Dress code: Smart casual
Weddings: Ceremonies and receptions can be arranged at the Château
Minimum stay: None
Rates: Double rooms from US$400/€427; to 'Lady Hamlyn apartment' US$930/€991, breakfast not included
Credit cards: Most major
Taxes and service charge: Included

SOUTH-WESTERN FRANCE
Château de la Treyne
Château de la Treyne is a wonderfully isolated château set deep in the heart of the Lot Valley and spectacularly situated on the banks of the river Dordogne.

This lovely hotel really is a classically romantic Dordogne château, set on a lofty clifftop with golden stone walls, turrets and mullioned windows. The earliest of the surviving structures date from the first half of the 14th century when the Vicomte de Turenne authorized the local lords of the manor to erect a fort at a place called Treyne. After being burnt down during the Wars of Religion, the Château was rebuilt by the de Cluzels family under Louis XIII.

Inside, the Château has been restored tastefully with traditional furnishings and a particularly beautiful painted ceiling in the Louis XIII formal drawing room. A member of the prestigious Relais & Chateaux, you'll breakfast beneath the 100-year-old cedars and enjoy excellent hearty dinners in true Dordogne fashion, either outside on the terrace overlooking the river or inside, on colder nights, with silver candlesticks in front of a roaring fire.

The 14 bedrooms and two suites are decorated just as you'd imagine a castle should be: walls covered in deep red damasks, polished floors with intricate rugs, solid four-poster beds with hand-carved posts, and lovely large sash windows with views over the river. Honeymooners are welcomed with flowers in their room, a slice of cake and a glass of champagne.

Among the 120 hectares of gardens and woodland there is a classic formal French garden as well as a 300-acre forest with several ancient trees including two magnificent cedars of Lebanon, and a Romanesque chapel which is used for piano recitals in the summer and for weddings. There is a swimming pool, a tennis court and plenty of

CHATEAU DE LA TREYNE

(☎ 05-65 27 60 60, 🖷 05-65 27 60 70, 🖳 treyne@relaischateaux.com),Lacave 46200, Lot, France
Closed: Mid-November to Easter
Reservations: Relais & Châteaux reservation numbers worldwide (see p12)
Getting there: 180km from Toulouse-Blagnac Airport, 40km from Brive, 200km from Bordeaux; RN20 south of Souillac, D43 towards Lacave (6km)
Accommodation: 14 rooms and two suites
Amenities: Billiards, piano playing, tennis, heated swimming pool, kayaking, fishing on the Dordogne river, hunting in season; horse-riding and golf nearby
Dress code: Casual elegance
Weddings: Wedding ceremonies in the Château's chapel which seats 60 people, otherwise an outdoor wedding in a marquee with a reception can be organized for a maximum of 150 people
Minimum stay: Guests are asked to stay two nights in low season
Rates: Double rooms from US$100/€115; suites from US$261/€298
Credit cards: Most major
Taxes and service charge: Included

THINGS TO SEE AND DO IN SOUTH-WESTERN FRANCE

The south-west of France, deep in the gulf of Gascony, is all about truffles, dwarf oaks, vineyards and orchards. This is my favourite area of France: the countryside is undulating and sometimes surprisingly cliffy, the scenic villages are overshadowed by small charming castles, and every moment of the day evolves around gastronomy.

Brantôme, in the north of the Dordogne, is a lovely village on the banks of the river Dronne. Walk across the unusual elbow bridge to the abbey or just linger in the village's characterful cafés.

Most visitors to this area visit the **Lascaux Caves** lured by their incredible 15,000-year-old paintings: but the fact that they are so popular, attracting 2000 visitors a day in the height of the summer, combined with the fact that you are no longer allowed to see the originals but are taken round a 1960s copy, cunningly named Lascaux II, is reason enough to avoid them altogether.

Much further down the Dordogne valley is **Beynac**, a small hamlet nestled beneath a cliff upon which sits a 12th-century fortress. The castle is open between March and October and is well worth a visit, mainly for the views. Equally picturesque are **La Roque Gageac** which clings to the cliff edge and, just upstream, Domme which is a wonderful medieval walled village.

A good day-trip from Château de la Treyne is to **Rocamadour** where the castle, chapel, houses and streets are all built right on the edge of the steep cliff-face.

For further information see 🖳 www.cr-aquitaine.fr/tourisme.

opportunity for touring the beautiful surrounding countryside by kayak, horseback or on foot. The Château de la Treyne would make a great base for a few days' relaxation and for touring the Dordogne.

Auberge des Ecureuils

The Auberge des Ecureuils nestles in a hamlet at the head of a small valley high up in the Mediterranean Pyrenees. Just a few miles from the Spanish border, its tranquil setting makes this an ideal choice if you want to escape the crowds.

The highlight here is the food – the charming host, Etienne Lafitte, runs a wonderful restaurant which combines classic and regional dishes. The desserts are superb and Monsieur Lafitte has an excellent wine cellar.

The hotel's spacious bedrooms are beautifully appointed with fine oak fittings and stylish, well-equipped bathrooms. They're all equipped with TV and phone and as you would expect in such a setting, the majority offer wonderful views and no noise other than the occasional dog barking to disturb your stay. For true romantics, it is worth paying a little extra for room 'S', furnished with a king-size four-poster bed.

Auberge des Ecureuils is a great base for exploring a little-visited corner of the Pyrenees. Days can be spent touring the

> **AUBERGE DES ECUREUILS**
> (☎ 04-68 04 52 03, 🖹 04-68 04 52 34), Valcebollère, Cerdagne, France
> **Closed:** First three weeks of May
> **Reservations:** Direct or through UK tour operator, Inntravel (UK ☎ 01653-629 000)
> **Getting there:** Most guests hire a car from from Perpignan airport (98km) or Toulouse airport (172km)
> **Accommodation:** 15 rooms
> **Amenities:** Fitness room, sauna, piano bar with wood-burning fire, lounge, restaurant, free ski equipment hire for winter stays
> **Dress code:** Informal
> **Weddings:** No, but they can arrange receptions
> **Minimum stay:** None, but three nights if you book through Inntravel
> **Rates:** Inntravel's 7-night fly-drive holiday including flights to Perpignan, car hire and half-board costs from US$823/£579 per person
> **Credit cards:** Most major; but not American Express
> **Taxes and service charge:** Included

mountains or walking along smugglers' trails, and in winter the hamlet of Valcebollère offers excellent cross-country skiing and snow-shoe walking.

Other recommended hotels

Le Moulin de L'Abbaye (☎ 05-53 05 80 22, 🖹 05-53 05 75 27, 1 route de Bourdeilles 24310, Brantôme-en-Perigord, Dordogne) is one of the most romantic hotels in France. This is the place for you if you like small, personal hotels set deep in the heart of the countryside where you can eat delicious food.

Any stay in the Dordogne must include **Brantôme**, the 'Venice of Perigord' where a Benedictine abbey is tucked into the cliffs, and **Le Moulin** restaurant which is situated right on the edge of the beautiful river **Dronne**. Guests stay in one of the hotel's three residences: the ivy-covered 15th-century mill, the miller's home set against a cliff, or the home of Pierre de Bourdeilles, the abbot of Brantôme. There are only 16 bedrooms and three suites so make sure you book early. Doubles cost from US$127/€145 to US$147/€168; suites from US$181/€206 to US$201/€229. A member of Relais & Chateaux, book through their worldwide reservation numbers (see p12).

SOUTH-EASTERN FRANCE

There is such a mixture of landscapes in south-eastern France that it is easy to spend time both at glamorous coastal resorts and also in the numerous unspoilt medieval hillside towns. **Nice** is the focal point of the south-east, and probably your arrival point: the famously chic seaside resorts of **Cannes**, **St Tropez** and **Monte Carlo** are within an hour and a half's drive. At the coastal resorts there is no getting away from the feeling that you are right in the very midst of the fashionable élite.

AUBERGE DE LA VIGNETTE HAUTE
(☎ 04-93 42 20 01, 📠 04-93 42 31 16), 370 Route du Village, 06810 Auribeau sur Siagne, near Cannes, Provence, France
Closed: Restaurant closed in November, the hotel is open year round
Reservations: Small Luxury Hotels of the World toll-free numbers worldwide (see p12)
Getting there: The hotel is situated on the D509 just off the D109 between Cannes and Grasse through Mandelieu; it is 40km or 45 minutes from Nice Airport
Accommodation: 12 guest rooms
Amenities: Outdoor swimming pool, terrace, garden, river fishing, hiking, restaurant and bar, room service; tennis, golf, and fishing nearby
Dress code: Informal
Weddings: Weddings for up to 150 people at a cost of US$74-80/€84-92 per person for menus that include wine and an aperitif
Minimum stay: None
Rates: Doubles from US$118/€135, suites from US$208/€237
Credit cards: Most major
Taxes and service charge: Included

HOTEL LE CALALOU
(☎ 04-94 70 17 91, 📠 04-94 70 50 11), 83630 Moissac-Bellevue, Provence, France
Reservations: Direct or through UK tour operator Inntravel (UK ☎ 01653-629 000)
Getting there: Most guests hire a car from Marseille Airport (46km)
Accommodation: 35 bedrooms, including two suites
Amenities: Restaurant, bar, reading and video room, tennis court, heated outdoor swimming pool, private parking
Dress code: Informal
Weddings: The hotel can cater for receptions for up to 160 people
Minimum stay: Three nights
Rates: Inntravel's 7 nights' fly-drive package including scheduled British Airways flights to Marseilles, seven days' Avis car hire and half board costs US$931/£655 per person
Credit cards: Most major
Taxes and service charge: Included

Auberge de la Vignette Haute

Set deep in the heart of Provence, the Auberge de la Vignette Haute is the perfect little hotel for escaping the summer crowds and experiencing this wonderful region of France at its very best.

Nestled halfway between **Grasse**, the capital of perfumes, and glamorous Cannes, this charming 17th-century inn seems a world away from the bustling coast. It has been lovingly restored by its owners and offers 12 guest rooms, each of which is individually decorated. There are wonderful views of the undulating countryside from the rooms' tiny balconies. All the rooms are well equipped with colour TV, minibar, in-room safe, air conditioning, toiletries, hairdryer, make-up mirror, trouser press, bathrobes and slippers, and some come with Jacuzzi-bath.

The terrace is the perfect place to sit either during the day under one of the large umbrellas or, at night, to look down over the swimming pool.

All around the inn, the rolling hills of **Auribeau sur Siagne** are covered with fields of lavender and huge wild sunflowers, punctuated only by the odd stone house. If you've never been to Provence you'll be amazed at the vivacity and vastness of this rolling carpet of purple, green and yellow.

Eating in the restaurant is very romantic: the flames from the oil lamps flicker on the rough stone walls, you sit at solid oak tables, pour your wine from pewter jugs and drink from goblets. The local cuisine is hearty Provençal in style and absolutely delicious.

Hôtel Le Calalou

The lovely Hôtel Le Calalou nestles below the picturesque hilltop village of **Moissac**, amongst some of Provence's most breathtaking scenery. The impressive Provençal manor house has been built in the typical long low style with a wonderfully cool interior which is simply but elegantly decorated.

The hotel's 35 bedrooms are comfortable and beautifully appointed. There are two mini suites which have a small sitting area, while all rooms are en suite with TV, phone, minibar and hairdryers. If you can, try to get room No 18; it is decorated in white and blue and has a small sitting area and a magnificent view of the surrounding countryside.

There is a bar, a restaurant which draws much inspiration from the local region and specializes in dishes from the Antilles, and a reading and video room. There are spacious gardens of cork-oak and ancient olive trees, and a shady terrace which is a perfect place to sip the local rosé and dine.

From the lovely swimming pool you can stare out to the south across field after field of purple lavender swaying in the breeze. This is Provence at its best, a land of lavender, cork-oaks and chirping cicadas. The hotel is close to **Moustiers-Ste-Marie**, a village famed for its beautiful ceramics and the start of the dramatic **Gorges du Verdon**. The sheer scale of the gorge is breathtaking, for at points the cliffs are 900m high with dizzying views down to the turbulent river below.

Other recommended hotels
Le Bastide de Marie (☎ 04-90 72 30 20, 🖹 04-90 72 54 20, 🖳 www.labastide de marie.com, Route de Bonnieux, Quartier de la Verrerie, 84560 Ménerbes, Provence) is a glamorous hotel created in an 18th-century farmhouse in scenery straight out of a Cezanne or Van Gogh painting, just an hour from Marseilles. The great thing about Le Bastide de Marie is that apart from lunch, everything is included, so it is truly a home away from home, but with nothing wanting.

Set in a 15-hectare private estate, Le Bastide de Marie has two swimming pools and its own vineyard. With just 12 rooms and suites, decorated with traditional furniture and antiques and painted in the colours that reflect their names such as Rose, Vanilla and the more elaborate Miel d'Oranger. Herbs from the garden are used in the traditional Provencal cooking and Chateau Marie wine from the vineyard accompanies your meal in the discreetly lit, intimate restaurant.

A great base for exploring, you can walk or go on horseback to the ancient hillside village of **Menerbes**, the dramatic castle of **Lacoste**, and Gordes and Bonnieux if you're tempted a little further. Doubles cost from US$308/€351 (low season) to a maximum of US$536/€610 (high season). Abercrombie & Kent (see p13) offer three nights half board including flights, transfers and car hire from US$1031/£725 per person.

ON AND AROUND THE COAST
Le Saint-Paul
Le Saint-Paul is definitely one of the most romantic small hotels in France. Located in the heart of **Saint-Paul-de-Vence**, a superb medieval village, the hotel is a great place to spend three or four days savouring the exclusivity of remaining here long after the crowds have departed each night.

Because it is so lovely with its winding cobbled streets, medieval ramparts, profusion of tiny dwellings housing exclusive shops and bustling restaurants, Saint-Paul-de-Vence is the second most visited village in all France, so don't come here expecting to find an undiscovered hideaway. If you like your hotels small, intimate and old, and are also passionate about wining and dining then you'd be hard pressed to beat this lovable 16th-century bourgeois house.

The hotel's 15 rooms and four suites are all individually furnished with warm Provençal-style fabrics producing a light and elegant atmosphere in contrast to the rustic

---

LE SAINT-PAUL
(☎ 04-93 32 65 25, 🖹 04-93 32 52 94, 🖳 stpaul@relaischateaux.com), 86 rue Grande, 06570 Saint-Paul-de-Vence, Alpes-Maritimes, France
Reservations: Relais & Châteaux worldwide reservation numbers (see p12); or through Abercrombie & Kent (see p13)
Getting there: 20 mins to Nice Airport
Accommodation: 15 rooms and 4 suites
Amenities: Lounge/bar, restaurant and terrace, golf nearby
Dress code: Elegant casual
Weddings: No
Minimum stay: None
Rates: Double rooms from US$127/ €170 to US$241/€220; suites from US$214/€250 to US$469/€320
Credit cards: Most major
Taxes and service charge: Included

stone walls of the lounge/bar area. The rooms are air conditioned and have a TV, mini-bar and en suite tiled bathroom, but they are small and you shouldn't expect the facilities of a big hotel. While some rooms overlook the village the best views are out over the valley. If you really want to splash out, there is a wonderful honeymoon suite and another suite with a beautiful flower-filled terrace.

The first-class cuisine and service found here can be credited to Olivier Borloo, the former managing director of Relais & Châteaux. Since taking over Le Saint-Paul, Borloo has had it completely refurbished so that its Provençal-style rooms are now immaculate. While all is elegant and pristine inside, the outer walls of this ancient hotel are ancient sandstone so eating outside under the stars on the flower-decked dining terrace leaves you in no doubt that you are in the very heart of rustic Provence. Book your place in this restaurant when you book your room as it is small and very popular.

Hôtel de la Cité

Hôtel de la Cité is a truly excellent hotel in the most unbelievable setting. Situated in a delightfully sheltered position behind the ramparts of the incredible medieval city of Carcassonne, this luxury hotel is built on the site of the former episcopal palace.

Inside the hotel is just as exciting as outside. There are magnificent tapestries, original wood panelling, a superb library which is the oldest part of the hotel and the most wonderful place to sit and read the paper or a good book over afternoon tea. The best bedrooms overlook the ramparts from where the views are breathtaking. Owned by Orient-Express, Hôtel de la Cité has undergone recent renovations and expansion which has put it firmly on the map for the world's travelling élite; it is also a member of Leading Hotels of the World.

The restaurant **La Barbacane** has mock Gothic windows and miniature golden fleurs-de-lys shield and lion motifs on the deep green walls, and it ranks among the world's best-known restaurants. During the summer months, **Le Jardin de L'Eveque** is open for alfresco dining and for a more casual alternative there is the brasserie **Chez Saskia**.

Set in beautiful gardens and with the only swimming pool in town, the hotel overlooks the city and the surrounding **Languedoc** countryside with its vineyards and Cathar castles. I can think of few places more unusual to be on your honeymoon – this really is a fairytale place where, crossing that heavily fortified drawbridge, you step back into a completely different world.

HOTEL DE LA CITE
(☎ 04-68 71 98 71, 🖷 04-68 71 50 15, 💻 www.hoteldelacite.com), Place de l'Eglise, 1100 Carcassonne, France
Reservations: Leading Hotels of the World toll-free reservations numbers worldwide (see p12) and luxury tour operators to Europe (see pp13-14)
Getting there: Carcassonne Airport is the nearest; you can also take a train to Carcassonne station. The hotel's minibus will pick you up from either
Accommodation: 49 rooms, 12 suites
Amenities: Outdoor heated swimming pool, tennis, hiking, cycling, horse-riding, golf nearby
Dress code: Casual, even in La Barbacane
Weddings: The hotel cannot perform wedding ceremonies but does host receptions for up to 250 people on the garden terrace
Minimum stay: None
Rates: Doubles from US$201/€240 to US$321/€380; suites from US$335/€400 to US$469/€600
Credit cards: Most major
Taxes and service charge: Included, government tax €1 per person per night

---

Other recommended hotels

If you want a grand hotel in France, don't look further than the two grandes dames that battle it out on the coast: the Grand Hôtel du Cap-Ferrat and La Réserve.

The **Grand Hôtel du Cap-Ferrat** (☎ 04-93 76 50 50, 🖷 04-93 76 04 52, 💻 www.grand-hotel-cap-ferrat, Boulevard du Général de Gaulle, 06230 Saint-Jean-Cap-

Ferrat, Alpes-Maritime) is a living legend long known as one of the world's most luxurious hotels. Blessed by a wonderfully private location right on the tip of the exclusive Cap-Ferrat peninsula, the views are quite unbeatable and the magnificent white façade of the hotel speaks of unmistakable chic and grace.

The facilities are all first rate: from the seawater from the Olympic-sized pool that glides seamlessly over its invisible edge to the beach club, the Club Dauphin. Jean-Claude Guillon's wonderful cuisine has attracted a Michelin star, and the restaurant, **Le Cap**, is the epitome of opulence with its original marble floors, murals on the walls and mosaic dolphins.

The 44 bedrooms and nine suites at the Grand Hôtel du Cap-Ferrat have been entirely renovated and are furnished in soothing pastel colours and 'princely materials', with huge French windows. They all boast air conditioning, TV, minibar, and views of either the sea or the pine woods behind the hotel. The marble bathrooms have everything you would expect.

The best thing about staying at the Grand Hôtel is that you can have it all: either relax with a kir royal at the **Piano Bar** before enjoying a sophisticated night in with an alfresco dinner, or don your glad rags and hit the roulette tables in nearby Monte Carlo.

Doubles cost from US$195/€214 to US$964/€1098, suites from US$670/€763 to US$2210/€2516. If you intend to stay here during July or August make sure you book well in advance. A member of Small Luxury Hotels of the World (see p12), this hotel is also offered by all luxury tour operators (see pp13-14).

La Réserve (☎ 04-93 01 00 01, 🖹 04-93 01 28 99, 5 Bd General Leclerc, Beaulieu-Sur-Mer, 06310), a 19th-century Florentine-style palace overlooking the Mediterranean, can be counted amongst the very greatest hotels in the world and its prices are very reasonable.

Just 20 minutes from Nice, La Réserve has been operating as a hotel since 1894. The hotel has a Mediterranean character along with its famous apricot hue. Throughout the interior, pastel shades predominate blending with soft coloured fabrics and Bottichino marble. La Réserve is an intimate hotel with 23 rooms and one suite, all spacious and tastefully decorated with views over the bay through their bay windows. Many of the bedrooms are shades of cream, with fine antique furniture and elegant light fittings and all the mod cons. The Michelin-rated restaurant offers truly gastronomic dishes, while there is also a lovely alfresco dining terrace. Service at La Réserve is impeccable.

La Réserve is an extremely refined hotel, with an exceptionally elegant, not to mention famous, clientele. The hotel has its own heated saltwater pool, with wonderfully comfy pink and white striped loungers and parasols lining its edge and an adjacent restaurant, as well as boat trips and watersports, and use of the beach at the nearby Royal Riviera hotel. Monte Carlo and Cannes are just 20 minutes away. Doubles cost from US$74/€84 to US$194/€222, suite from US$261/€298. Book through Relais & Chateaux toll-free reservations numbers worldwide (see p12).

There is a continual debate between the travelling cognoscenti as to the relative merits of the two world-renowned **cliff-edge hotels** in tiny **Eze Village**. The village is just incredible, with its narrow cobbled streets, medieval château, steep panorama of the Mediterranean and hundreds of tiny houses with terracotta-tiled roofs occupying every inch of space. It can only be reached on foot and is therefore not for the faint-hearted – donkeys are even used to carry guests' luggage up to the hotels. Both hotels are indisputably romantic, both have breathtaking views looking down on Cap Ferrat and both have small, well-decorated bedrooms in medieval châteaux.

Château Eza (☎ 04-93 41 12 24, 🖹 04-93 41 16 64, 06360 Eze Village, Côte d'Azur; closed November to April), perched right on the cliff-edge is a former residence of a Swedish prince. With only ten bedrooms the problem with Château Eza is managing to get a room in the first place. Everything about the hotel is stunning: the views, the half-timbered bedrooms some of which have four-posters and many of which have terraces or balconies, and the Michelin-star Provençal restaurant.

Double rooms cost from US$268/€305; suites from US$469/€534 including tax and service. Book through Small Luxury Hotels of the World toll-free reservations (see p12).

Château de la Chèvre d'Or (☎ 04-92 10 66 66 , 📄 04-93 41 06 72, Moyenne corniche, rue du Barri, 06360 Eze Village, Côte d'Azur; closed end November to 1st March) has some truly wonderful air-conditioned rooms and the views from the dining room, the bar or the terrace pool are simply dazzling. The addition of two swimming pools is one factor in the Chèvre d'Or's favour, and the lovely suites perched right on the cliff-edge in detached cottages make the perfect room with a view.

Double rooms cost from US$241/€275; suites from US$469/€534, but do ask about their honeymoon package which offers two nights' accommodation in a standard room, breakfast each morning, dinner at the Chèvre d'Or on one night and one lunch at the Grill du Château, and includes tax for US$756/€861 during the week off season and US$876/€998 during the week in peak season.

THE ALPS
Recommended hotels

Le Melezin (☎ 04-79 08 01 33, 📄 04-79 08 08 96, 🖥 www.amanresorts.com, rue de Bellecote, 73120 Courchevel 1850), overlooking the French Alps in **Courchevel**, has to be the ultimate honeymoon destination for winter sports enthusiasts, and as it's owned by Amanresorts, a haven for 'Aman-junkies'. In one of Europe's premier ski resorts, it is difficult to imagine a more superior ski chalet and with a prime location in the heart of Courchevel you can ski in and out of the front door. Le Melezin is terribly expensive but worth it. It is not only the hotel's location that is so amazing: so is its incredibly sophisticated and elegant decorations, every possible amenity and the awesome standards of hotel-keeping – recognized hallmarks of Amanresorts. Where else in the Alps are your boots warmed for you before you leave each morning, where else can you lie back in your huge foam-filled bath looking straight out across the surrounding snow-capped peaks, and where else is afternoon tea provided outside on tables hewn out of local logs? Like all Amanresorts this place is just magical. Doubles cost from €366/US$326 to €1190/US$1060.

Les Fermes de Marie (☎ 04-50 93 03 10, 📄 04-50 93 09 84, 🖥 www.fermesdemarie.com, Megeve) is a small 200-year-old chalet with 69 fabulously romantic rooms including a Honeymoon Suite.

The traditional vaulted beams and log fires, stone flagstones, and warmth of seasoned wood make it feel like home. The lovely tartan and check fabrics, and detail such as baskets of fruit and rickety candelabras, give it rustic charm. Jocelyne and Jean-Louis Sibuet have created a charming, comfortable haven in this cluster of eight weathered farm-houses in the Alps, with delicious, regional food and plenty of modern comforts. A year-round destination, it is the perfect winter ski resort. You can gather around the fire in the library for tea on wintry nights, and enjoy pre-drinks in the intimate piano bar. A spa using mountain plants will make you feel as good as new after a day on the slopes, and wonderful alpine walks and picnics means Les Fermes de Marie is equally enchanting in summer.

Doubles cost from US$273/€312 per couple per day half board; the Honeymoon Suite is US$568/€647. Seven nights with UK tour operator Elegant Resorts (see p14) costs from US$1078/£758 per person, including BA flights to Geneva, transfers and breakfast.

Spain
(BEST TIME: MARCH TO OCTOBER)

While travel snobs may wince to hear that you are heading off to Tuscany or the Dordogne on your honeymoon (despite being heavenly both areas are 'just too clichéd') it is currently quite acceptable to have fallen in love with Spain. Not the southern coast of course, that was effectively ruined over a decade ago, but the interior where places like **Catalonia**, **Andalucia** and **Salamanca** are reassuringly undiscovered and you can find your own pace of life in traditional rural communities.

A week or two touring in Andalucia or Catalonia is a great way to see this amazing country. Pick one hotel to stay in for a week and maybe another one or two for just a few days each: this will enable you to relax, see the lovely countryside and explore its countless historic Moorish towns and cities, the vast mountains, parched plains, verdant forests, mass of olive groves and the many remote hilltop villages. And, with the hordes heading further afield, **Majorca** is now a hip place to be.

CATALONIA

Many people underestimate Catalonia: close to its capital **Barcelona**, it is the country's undisputed gastronomic centre. People are forever telling me that they couldn't believe the quality of the cuisine: I hear many 'I've never eaten so well in my life' kind of comments. For shopaholics, duty-free Andorra is close by, and all around are charming medieval villages and wonderful Pyreneean scenery.

Recommended hotels

If fine food and wine are likely to play a pretty important part in your honeymoon I can strongly recommend a stay at **Hotel El Castell** (☎ 973-350704, 🖹 973-3515 74, 🖳 elcastell@relaischateaux.com, Route N-260km 229, Apto. 53, E-25700, La Seu d'Urgell), which stands on a hill beneath the ruins of an old castle and is surrounded by the lovely mountain scenery of the high Pyrenees. Built in local rustic style, it has

---

SPAIN

A dignified land with a rich heritage of castles, culture and gastronomy where rural life still continues as it has for centuries

When to go: All year round, but March to June and September and October are the best months for warm sunshine and fewer crowds

Average maximum temperatures °C

	JAN	FEB	MAR	APR	MAY	JUN	JUL	AUG	SEP	OCT	NOV	DEC
Madrid	10	11	15	18	20	26	29	28	24	18	13	10
Costa del Sol	17	17	19	20	22	26	27	28	27	22	19	17
Majorca	14	15	17	19	21	25	27	27	26	22	18	16

Capital: Madrid
Flight times: to Madrid from:
  New York: 7$\frac{1}{2}$ hours
  LA: 13 hours
  London: 2 hours
  Sydney: 29 hours
Approximate exchange rates: Euro (€) – £1 = €1.59, US$1 = €1.11, A$1 = €0.57
Time difference: GMT plus one hour (two hours from the last Sunday in March to the last Sunday in October)
Voltage: 220v AC, with two-pin plugs
Combine with: Anywhere else in Europe
Country dialling code: ☎ 34 (omit the first digit 9 when calling from outside Spain)
Further information: 🖳 www.tourspain.es

a really relaxed atmosphere, with sufficient luxury and impeccable service to remind you that you're staying somewhere very special. Nothing is too much for its owner managers, Jaume and Katia Tapies.

The hotel's renowned cuisine which has earned it membership of Relais & Chateaux is matched by its wine cellars, reputed to be the second largest in Spain. The 37 comfortable rooms and suites are all elegantly furnished with en suite bathroom, toiletries, TV and minibar. Some have incredible sunset views from their balconies and terraces. There's lots to see and do in the surrounding mountainous countryside, be it a balloon flight over the **Cadi-Moixero National Park** or one of the hotel's terrific jeep tours into the local forests, with the most incredible picnic lunch laid out for you on the forest floor and waiters in black tie standing ready to pass you a glass of champagne and quails' eggs. Heaven. There's also a sauna and fitness centre. Doubles cost from US$124/€142, suites from US$187/€214 including breakfast, excluding 7% tax.

Mas de Torrent (☎ 972-303292, 🖹 972-303293, 🖳 mastorrent@relais chateaux.com, E-17123 Torrent, Girona) is a simply gorgeous hotel in absolutely beautiful, tranquil countryside surroundings. The main part of the hotel, including the gourmet restaurant decorated in paintings in homage to Picasso, is a converted 18th-century farmhouse reminiscent of Provence's golden stone buildings. Some of the 25 rooms and 12 suites, named after flowers such as Iris and Geranium, are scattered amongst the hotel's lovely gardens, close to the swimming pool. All have good amenities, most of those in the main building have a balcony and individual bungalows all have private gardens rich with the smell of lavender, agapanthus and green cypress trees.

Located just 10km from the beaches of the **Costa Brava**, the Mas de Torrent makes a relaxing base for touring the most picturesque parts of this coastline, such as **Palafrugell** and **Begur**. With comfortable, spacious rooms and delicious food to return home to each evening, you can join the long list of people who rave about this hotel. Doubles cost from US$174/€199, suites from US$411/€245, plus 7% tax.

The perfect Catalonian honeymoon would be to combine four or five days in El Castell or Mas de Torrent with the much simpler, but equally gastronomic, **Can Boix**, (☎ 973-470266, 🖹 973-470281) just 45 minutes away in the lower Pyrenees. The lovely Can Boix has 35 bedrooms, but do make sure you request a superior suite as it's not much more expensive and it is certainly worth the extra cost. You can reserve all these

---

THINGS TO SEE AND DO IN CATALONIA

Catalonia is an autonomous region with a totally distinct culture, language and history. It is one of Spain's most prosperous areas and is as rich in its cultural heritage, thanks to Dalí and Picasso, as it is in its gastronomy. The region is particularly noted for the way its kitchens combine meat and seafood in one dish, known locally as Mar y Montana, producing meals such as 'pollo con langosta' (chicken with langoustines).

There is much to experience in Catalonia, quite apart from **Barcelona**. The rugged coastline of the **Costa Brava** is full of undiscovered retreats and the national parks, and peaks and valleys of the Pyrenees are magnificent in their beauty.

Whether or not you are staying at Hotel El Castell (see p139), the hotel can arrange a whole host of visits and activities, such as balloon flights over **Cadi-Moixero National Park**, cross-country skiing, mountain biking, and duty-free shopping in **Old Andorra**. One thing you mustn't miss are the jeep tours through the surrounding forests which culminate in a sumptuous picnic.

From the Mas de Torrent there are many wonderful **small villages** to explore, including nearby Pals and Peratallada, as well as Monells, Ullastret, Vulpellac and Fonteta, all of which are within a 14km drive of the hotel and have many historical monuments and churches of interest. La Bisbal is also worth a visit to wander round the numerous ceramic shops which have gained this city international recognition.

The **Dalí Museum** in **Figueres**, the second most visited museum in Spain, is a definite must for art lovers and is only 40km from Torrent.

See 🖳 www.gencat.es for more information.

hotels direct, or through Relais & Châteaux reservation numbers worldwide (see p12), or UK tour operator Magic of Spain (see p14).

ANDALUCIA
Finca Buen Vino

About 100km from **Seville** and near **Aracena**, Finca Buen Vino, which is owned by Sam and Jeannie Chesterton, is a perfect private hotel. With only six rooms, guests are guaranteed a feeling of warm hospitality in very special, homely surroundings.

The Finca (a farm) is set amidst 60 hectares of woodland, which makes it a wonderful place for walking and horse-riding. It's a romantic hotel and is ideal for those who like peace and quiet and prefer not to be surrounded by lots of other guests. Upstairs there are two charming bedrooms, each with its own bathroom – one has a queen-size bed, the other a twin – while the downstairs bedrooms have adjoining bathrooms. In summer the bedroom in the pool house is available and has en suite bathroom. All the cooking is done by Jeannie, who is Cordon-Bleu trained and who enjoys using ingredients from the surrounding area, giving her creations a distinctly Mediterranean flavour.

The villa has been tastefully decorated using English and Spanish country furniture and fabrics, producing a wonderfully welcoming and lived-in feel. The view from the large sitting room overlooks the surrounding hilly countryside. Further up the hill from the house is a lovely pool. Drinks are taken by the pool or in the conservatory – you just help yourself, fill in the bar-book and are billed at the end of your stay.

If you are looking for peace and quiet in a rural setting and are not into large pampering hotels then Finca Buen Vino is the place. The tranquillity is absolute. Also hidden away on the estate, along country tracks, are two idyllic self-catering cottages each designed to sleep four to five people, with private pool, which can be rented by the week.

> **FINCA BUEN VINO**
> (☎ 959-124034, 🖹 959-501029, 💻 www.buenvino.com), Los Marines, 21293 Huelva, Spain
> **Reservations**: Either direct or through CV Travel (UK ☎ 020-7591 2810, 💻 www.cvtravel.net)
> **Getting there**: The Chestertons recommend a charter flight to Seville from where they can organize a taxi; or fly to Faro and hire a car (a 2¼-hour drive)
> **Accommodation**: Five/six rooms and two self-catering cottages
> **Amenities**: Pool, fabulous natural surroundings for horse-riding and walking
> **Dress code**: Informal
> **Weddings**: None
> **Minimum stay**: Minimum stay is three days at the main house and one week in the cottages (rental from Friday to Friday, but you can stay an extra night in the main house)
> **Rates**: Doubles from US$148/€169 to US$180/€205 half board; cottages from US$427/€483 to US$924/£650 per week
> **Credit cards**: Visa and MasterCard
> **Taxes and service charge**: Included

Casa de Carmona

Staying at Casa de Carmona is just like being a guest in a private house, and a very beautiful one at that.

This 16th-century conversion of the former Lasso de la Vega Palace retains many beautifully preserved original features and is furnished throughout with lovely antiques and stunning fabrics. The 33 individually decorated bedrooms are all provided with central heating and air conditioning, bathrobes, toiletries, minibar, TV, videos and a stereo in the de luxe suites. Although it is lovely to have such luxuries, it is the exceptional décor and architecture of the rooms that make people so enthusiastic about the Casa de Carmona. The rooms couldn't be more romantic with their draped fabrics hanging over four-poster beds, and strong imaginative use of colour on the arched walls.

THINGS TO SEE AND DO IN ANDALUCIA

The **Alhambra** in Granada, the **Mezquita** of Cordoba, and the **Alcazar** in Seville, are among the most awesome, sensual and romantic monuments to be found anywhere in Europe. These legacies of the Moorish kings of Granada have to be seen to be believed: walk around the old Santa Cruz quarter of Seville and the maze-like narrow streets surrounding the Mezquita, and the amazing water world of the 14th-century Alhambra.

To see the undulating Andalucian countryside from another perspective arrange a hot-air balloon flight with Graham Elson (☎ 95-287 7249, 🖳 www.andalucia.com/balloons), whose trips around the town of Rhonda are a wonderfully serene way of experiencing the dramatic Andalucian countryside. You leave first thing in the morning from the National Park at Ronda for a 60- to 90-minute flight with a champagne breakfast on landing. Both trips can be booked directly through Graham and cost £100.

Most of the hotels listed here either have their own horses or an arrangement with the local riding school. **Riding** in Andalucia is wonderful and in most places you will be given a horse and left to explore the surrounding countryside on your own, so it's probably more suited to those with some experience.

Ronda is a charming town, reached by a bridge across a steep gorge. Home to the oldest bullring in Spain, the village is packed with Spanish heritage and history. Avoid it in July and August when it gets crowded and much too hot, but during the rest of the year it is a lovely place to walk around.

Further south takes you to the coast which, to be honest, has been largely ruined by mass-tourism, but it can be fun to head down to **Puerto Banus** for a night on the marina-front watching the holiday-makers go by.

Further information from 🖳 www.andalucia.org.

The most wonderfully relaxed atmosphere really does make you feel as if you are in a private home, a sentiment enhanced by welcoming touches such as the free bar in the library: guests help themselves to drinks. The hotel's restaurant is open from 1.30 to 4.30pm for lunch and from 8.30 to 11.30pm for dinner, which gives you plenty of time to explore in the mornings, eat a long, lazy, late lunch, followed by an even longer and lazier siesta and then dine at a typically late Spanish hour.

Carmona is ideally situated for exploring the famous cities of **Jerez**, **Granada** and Seville, and lesser-known towns like **Cordoba**. Carmona itself is a beautifully preserved hilltop town, with some of the buildings dating back to Roman times. The Roman walls and necropolis are well worth visiting and hotel staff are more than happy to arrange local excursions as well as horse-riding, tennis, and tickets for local events such as a flamenco show.

CASA DE CARMONA
(☎ 95-4143300, 🖷 95-4190189), Plaza de Lasso 1, 41410 Carmona, Seville, Spain
Reservations: Either direct or through tour operators such as Magic of Spain, Abercrombie & Kent (see pp13-14)
Getting there: The hotel can offer transfers from the nearest train station and airport for US$26/€31
Accommodation: 33 guest rooms, including 13 standard rooms, 17 de luxe suites and one Grand Suite
Amenities: Outdoor swimming pool, sauna, small gym, free parking area, 24-hour room service, restaurant, free bar; golf, horse-riding, tennis; flamenco shows can be arranged
Dress code: No jacket or tie required
Weddings: The hotel can host weddings and receptions, prices depend on your requirements
Minimum stay: None
Rates: Standard doubles from US$116/€133, de luxe suites from US$137/€157
Credit cards: Visa, American Express, Diners Club, Master Card
Taxes and service charge: 7% tax, service is included

Hotel La Bobadilla
If you are driving up from Malaga it's quite likely you will be utterly convinced you are in the depths of nowhere, and you will be about to reach for the map, when up looms the Hotel La Bobadilla, one of the most amazing purpose-built hotels imaginable. King Juan Carlos of Spain and Tom Cruise are among the countless celebrities who have been drawn to this remote spot by tales of its privacy and tranquillity.

Built a couple of decades ago by a German engineer, the hotel was designed to echo the fabulous Moorish architecture that originally made this region famous. While the Alhambra Palace in Seville and the Mezquita in nearby Cordoba may have been built many centuries ago, this new addition is just as sensual and ridiculously extravagant in its grandeur.

Set in the middle of a vast area of olive and vine groves in the rolling Andalucian countryside, La Bobadilla is more like a Moorish village than a hotel – it even has its own church.

The sprawling white buildings with their rustic tiled roofs, pillars and arches are interconnected via a labyrinth of stone walkways, flower-covered overhangs, pretty courtyards and soaring marble colonnades.

Inside, the rambling hotel is equally impressive; tucked away off pebbled plazas are some of the most incredible hotel suites ever built. Each of the 62 rooms and suites is architecturally different and individually decorated. They have lots of ethnic furnishings, kilim rugs and cushions, and beds so high that steps are provided as well as a sumptuous bathroom with a huge sunken Jacuzzi. They are also well-equipped with air conditioning, minibar, colour satellite TV, hairdryer, in-room safe, and bathrobes and there is 24-hour room service.

Apart from being a heavenly place in which to do next to nothing, La Bobadilla makes a perfect base from which to explore Andalucia. You can either jump in the car and head off to nearby Seville and Granada, or hop on a horse, bike or just don your walking shoes and explore the estate. Most of the facilities are complimentary; there are two swimming pools, a beauty parlour with masseur, a fitness club and lots of unusual sports on hand, such as clay pigeon shooting and archery.

HOTEL LA BOBADILLA
(☎ 958-321861, 🖷 958-321810, 🖳 info@la-bobadilla.com), Finca La Bobadilla, PO Box 144, 18300 Loja, Granada, Spain
Reservations: The Leading Hotels of the World toll-free reservation numbers worldwide (see p12) or through UK tour operator Magic of Spain (UK ☎ 08700 270400)
Getting there: Most guests hire a car from Malaga and drive the 70km to Loja; transfers from the airport cost US$68/€79, plus 7% tax
Accommodation: 62 rooms, including 23 doubles, 28 junior suites, 9 suites
Amenities: The award winning La Finca specializes in international haute cuisine, El Cortijo serves traditional Spanish fare, poolside barbecues in summer, two terraces, reading lounge, 24-hr room service, a 1500m outdoor heated pool, heated indoor pool and Jacuzzi, four saunas, two Turkish steam baths, two Finnish saunas, beauty parlour, massage, hairdresser; hiking tracks, horse-riding, archery, small game hunting, clay pigeon shooting, cycling, pétanque, fitness club, boutique, organ concerts and lessons, piano, two artificial grass tennis courts; golf on the Costa del Sol (60km from the hotel)
Dress code: Jackets and ties are recommended at dinner time but not required
Weddings: Ceremonies and receptions are available, the cost depends on what you want; use of the chapel is free
Minimum stay: None
Rates: Doubles from US$195/€222 to US$287/€327 including breakfast; suites from US$331/€377 to US$645/€734
Credit cards: Most major
Taxes and service charge: 7% tax added to your bill, service charge is included

Molino de Santo
Molino de Santo is a family-run converted watermill situated just 15 minutes outside Ronda. Set in lovely gardens beside a mountain stream and waterfall, the 2-star Molino del Santo is arguably one of the best hotels that you will find in Andalucia. It is one of those hotels which makes you want to laze around, so the perfect place to relax for a week or even longer, as there's plenty to do around historic Ronda.

The Molino has 14 airy whitewashed bungalow-style cottages, including a junior suite, set amongst its lovely tree-filled gardens, 12 of which have terraces overlooking the pool. All the rooms are en suite, mostly with showers but some do have baths. They are simply but very comfortably furnished in local style with white walls, terracotta

MOLINO DE SANTO
(☎ 952-167151, 🖹 952-167327, 💻 moli
no@logiccontrol.es), Bda Estación s/n,
29370 Benaoján, Málaga, Spain
Reservations: Either direct or through
tour operators Magic of Spain (UK ☎
020-8748 4220) or Inntravel (UK ☎
01653-629 000)
Getting there: Most guests hire a car and
drive from Gibraltar Airport, 91km away;
alternatively the hotel can arrange for a
local taxi to pick you up if you fly into
Malaga for US$63/€73 one way
Accommodation: 14 double rooms;
standard, superior and three junior suites
Amenities: Swimming pool heated with
solar panels, gardens, residents' lounge
with games, car park, mountain bikes for
hire, well-stocked library, information
service on excursions and maps for
walks, air-conditioned bar and dining
room, terraces by the river
Dress code: None
Weddings: The hotel cannot do ceremonies, but can do receptions for up to 50
people
Minimum stay: None
Rates: Standard doubles US$30/€35 to
US$50/€57, superior doubles
US$34/€40 to US$54/€62, US$41/€47
to US$61/€69 all per person per night
breakfast/half board
Credit cards: Most major
Taxes and service charge: Included

tiles and pine furniture. Each has a phone, tea and coffee-making facilities, heating and electric fans. Hairdryers are available at reception.

In the summer, meals are served outdoors on the terrace shaded by willow and fig trees, and traditional English tea and cakes are served every afternoon. The homely cooking is superb and has made the hotel famous within the region, and the service both from its English owners and Spanish staff is friendly and helpful.

The hotel is in a splendid location just below the village of Benaojan and there is lots to see in the area if you can tear yourselves away from the pool. Hop on the quirky local train down to **Ronda** or drive along the beautiful stretches of coastline or to the unspoiled **Grazalema Natural Park**. You can also hire mountain bikes which are great fun for a day.

Other recommended hotels
Hacienda Benazuza (☎ 95-5703344, 🖹 95-5703410, 💻 hbenazuza@arrakis.es, Sanlucar la Major, Seville) is a charmingly intimate 10th-century hotel set in an ancient hilltop estate with a fascinating and chequered history dating back to the Moors.

The tranquillity of its verdant gardens and the tinkling fountains beyond its colonnades and whitewashed walls today make it hard to believe that just over a century ago it was owned by a family that bred the fiercest fighting bulls in Spain.

Hacienda Benazuza can only be described as lavish. Space is the obvious luxury in the 26 rooms and 18 magnificent suites. Each room is individually decorated with antique furniture and terracotta tiles, and has every modern comfort – many even have a private Jacuzzi.

Days here are spent lounging around the geometrically-shaped outdoor swimming pool where you only need to raise your head to get a drink or tapas from the poolside La Alberca (there is a formal restaurant for evening dining). Tennis, horse-riding and golf are just minutes away.

The Hacienda is a great base for exploring the region – Seville is 15 minutes away and Cordoba nearby and if you want to head for the great outdoors, **Donana National Park** is just 40 minutes drive. Flamenco performances and visits to stud farms are arranged free of charge, and massage on request. Being a first-class hotel, the Hacienda can arrange everything for you and offers 24-hour room service. It even has its own heliport, so if you want, you can arrive in style. But one of the best experiences you can have here has to be a balloon ride over the beautiful countryside.

Doubles cost from US$211/€241 to US$312/€355, suites from US$285/€325 to US$924/€1052, plus 7% tax. Book through Leading Hotels of the World toll-free numbers worldwide (see p12) or tour operators Mediterranean Experience or Abercrombie & Kent (see p13).

Casa No 7 (☎ 95-4221581, 🖹 95-4214527, 🖳 www.casanumero7.com, Calle Virgines 7, Seville) is a simple but incredibly stylish hotel that was nominated Best Small Hotel 2001 by *Tatler*. Tucked away in a narrow street behind a high wrought iron gate in the heart of the city, Casa No 7 is a peaceful, intimate place with only four, gracious, guest rooms. Arranged around a small courtyard in typical Andalusian style, the Casa is decorated with impeccable taste, with antiques and paintings from the owner's private collection. Double from US$128/€146. Book direct or through UK tour operator Abercrombie & Kent (☎ 0845-070 0612).

There are lots of other wonderfully personal fincas and country houses throughout Andalucia, many of which make perfect rural locations for honeymoons. Talk to UK specialist tour operator CV Travel (UK ☎ 020-7591 2810) about **Cortijo El Puerto del Negro** and **Eleonora**, and Elegant Resorts (UK ☎ 0870-333 3350) or the Magic of Spain (UK ☎ 08700-270 400) about **Hacienda de San Rafael** in Seville, or Spain at Heart (UK ☎ 01373-814 222) who have a whole brochure full of properties in Andalucia .

MAJORCA
If Majorca immediately conjures up images of British lager louts eating egg and chips and packed night-clubs in built-up holiday villages, then think again. **Magaluf** aside, which is definitely worth avoiding if you want to get away from the crowds, Majorca is one of the most beautiful, tranquil and unspoilt islands in the Mediterranean. If you are looking for two weeks of absolute peace and quiet after your wedding you'd be hard pressed to beat it. Unless you are looking for some hectic night-life, the best time to go is from March to June, and between September and November, when you should get lots of sunny days, and the temperatures and the crowds won't be unbearable.

Recommended hotels
La Residencia (☎ 971-639011, 🖹 971-639370, Deia, Majorca), while now not the only good hotel in Majorca, is justly regarded as one of the finest hotels in the Mediterranean. Richard Branson's stylish and beautiful hotel, created from two 16th-century Majorcan manor houses, owes much to its glorious location being set in the middle of one of the island's most idyllic rural villages, **Deia**.

While the hotel is immaculate throughout, you still get a feeling of the heritage of the building, enhanced by the beautiful antiques in each classic Mediterranean-designed room. Some of the 18 suites have private pools, four-poster beds and balconies with fantastic views over the mountains and sea.

Days at La Residencia are extremely tranquil: although there is a floodlit tennis court and new health and beauty spa, most guests choose to lie on one of the loungers by the 32m pool, or find a quiet spot in the beautifully terraced gardens amongst the fruit trees. Dining here is wonderful: La Residencia's El Olivo restaurant is set in the old olive press and the scores of candles on huge wrought-iron stands, terracotta floor and wicker chairs make the perfect contrast to the formal crisp white linen and crystal glassware on the tables. Doubles cost from US$129/€147 to US$314/€358, suites from US$221/€252 to US$665/€758. Book through Relais & Chateaux reservation numbers worldwide (see p12) and leading tour operators to Spain (see pp13-14).

Gran Hotel Son Net (☎ 971-147000, 971-147001, 🖳 www.sonnet.es, E-07194, Puigpunyent, Majorca), one of the most stylish hotels on Majorca, lies on a secluded hilltop above a quaint mountain village, just 15 minutes' drive from Palma. Within the traditional Moorish arches of this 17th-century finca is the modern glamour you'd expect from a Relais & Chateaux member and one listed in *Tatler*'s Best Hotels of 2001. White tented cabanas surround the 100-ft pool near a rose garden and the Sa Tafona restaurant, headed by chef Thierry Buffeteau, formerly of the Paris Ritz, lies within the old olive press.

THINGS TO SEE AND DO IN MAJORCA

Palma

As you'll fly in and out of Palma, Majorca's capital, it's a good idea to spend a couple of days either at the beginning or at the end of your honeymoon exploring this beautiful city, except in July or August when it's best avoided because of the holiday crowds.

Palma's magnificent Gothic **cathedral** dominates the city and is definitely worth a visit. Below the cathedral, the intricate labyrinth of narrow winding streets stretching outwards from the city's main square, **Plaza Major**, is a great place to explore. You'll find all sorts of wonderful ceramics painted in bright Mediterranean colours and beautiful coloured glassware at much more reasonable prices than you'd get at home.

Stop for lunch at *Parlament Restaurant* (☎ 971-726 026), which is essentially a local hang-out so it's a good place to escape the tourists. We stumbled across this restaurant quite by chance and were inspired to go in by the hordes of Majorcans flocking up the steps one Friday lunchtime. And what a find it was. Order the paella – the speciality of the house – and wash it down with a bottle of Rioja.

Spend at least a day in Palma, hopping from bar to bar for tapas and into pavement cafés for coffee and the delicious local pastries, called emsaimadas. Try *Bon Lloc* (☎ 971-718 617), on San Felio 7 for lunch: dishes are all vegetarian and healthy and you'll be with the locals. It's advisable to book ahead. But best of all, make sure you leave time for cocktails at *Abaco*. Hidden away behind imposing wooden doors just off La Llonga, Abaco has to be one of the world's most romantic bars. Inside, the stone floor of the immense courtyard is crowded with great piles of oranges and lemons, small green box shrubs protrude from every corner, and the most ornate flower arrangements and Mediterranean statues, fountains and wrought-iron work, all make you feel that you've somehow stepped back into the land of the gods: stirring classical music completes the picture. Drinks are of course expensive here, but no more so than in most major cities, and infinitely more wonderful for the decadence of the surroundings.

After drinks, dine at *Caballito del Mar* (☎ 971-721 074) one of the best restaurants in Palma, on one side of La Llonga, the palm-fringed square next to the cathedral and over-looking the port. This restaurant was closed for renovations in summer 2001, so check that it's open before turning up!

Around the island

The north of the island and the west coast are the best areas if you are looking for unspoilt areas. Good places to visit include **Inca** where you can pick up good quality leather jackets, shoes and handbags at bargain prices. Sunday morning in **Pollensa** is market day, an event which throws this normally sleepy town into chaos with mounds of olives and giant piles of tomatoes and lettuces strewn across the streets.

If you want to pack a picnic and get out and discover your own sites, the **west coast** is a great place to do it. There are lots of craggy paths leading down to deserted sandy beaches, and others that will take you through pungent pine woods and remote villages where old men in berets really do sit outside cafés all day long. Walk up **Puig da Maria**, 'puig' meaning peak, to the monastery at the top, from where you can look back over the 365 cypress-lined steps that lead up to Pollensa's **El Calvari** and the 700-year-old statue of the Virgin.

Visit **Porto Petro** where the quay is lined with palm trees, and white Majorcan fishing boats are tied up along the water's edge.

If you like your walks to have a hearty reward at the end of them, drive to **Alaro** and ask anyone there to point you in the direction of the ancient **Castillo d'Alaro**. The drive takes you halfway up the mountain on a very steep rubble path (just made for hire cars!). Park your car and continue on foot. The views from the castle are breathtaking.

For further information see 🖳 www.caib.es.

The 17 rooms and seven suites in the Gran Hotel Son Net have flagstone floors and ancient wooden beams, but sophisticated décor with paintings by Chagall, Hockney and Warhol, and luxurious modern marble bathrooms. The hotel has a clay tennis court, spa and fitness centre, mountain bikes and Francese, a private tour guide, for hire. Watersports, hiking, and golf can all be arranged nearby. Doubles cost from US$179/€211 to US$282/€331, suites from US$538/€632 to US$640/€752, plus 7% tax. Book through Relais & Chateaux worldwide reservation numbers or UK tour operators such as Mediterranean Experience (☎ 020-8445 6000).

Petit Hotel Son Foguero (☎ 971-525343, 🗎 971-525676, 🖳 www.sonfogue ro.com, Maria de la Sud, Majorca) is a luxurious and special all-suite hideaway, ideal for honeymooners. Set in beautiful countryside in the centre of the island, the owner, a well-known interior designer, has converted this old finca with exquisite style. The four junior suites and suite, some set under Moorish arches, are as fine as you'd find anywhere in the world; each has a double bed, satellite TV, minibar, CD player and large terrace.

Guests can relax on the wooden loungers by the cute swimming pool, set in delightful shady gardens, taking a few drinks from the honesty bar, or go horse-riding or play tennis nearby. A set menu dinner, made from fresh local produce, is served in an intimate, attractive restaurant in the evening. Junior suites from US$164/€193 per couple including breakfast. Honeymooners receive a bottle of Cava, fruit and flowers on arrival when booking with UK specialist tour operator Magic Of Spain (☎ 0870-027 0400).

Hotel La Moreja (☎ 971-718071, 🖹 971-533418, 🖳 hotel@lamoreja.net, Cala San Vincente, Majorca) is a beautifully-furnished former private mansion, with excellent service, just 5 minutes' walk from the town and beaches of pretty Cala San Vincente. The 17 bedrooms in an adjacent newer building, have period furniture and antiques, and their spacious terraces face towards the pine-clad mountains and gardens. They all have air conditioning, ceiling fan, satellite TV, minibar, and a small lounge area. Hotel La Moreja has two swimming pools, a restaurant and snack bar and doesn't take children aged under 14. Rates are US$1136/£799 per person for a week with transfers and breakfast, with UK specialist tour operator Magic Of Spain (☎ 0870-027 0400).

Renting a villa in Spain

The best way to experience Spanish life is to rent a villa. There are hordes of tour operators offering non-descript villas in Europe, but for something really special talk to **CV Travel** (UK ☎ 0870-606 0013), **Meon Villas** (UK ☎ 0173-026 8411), **Spanish Affair** (UK ☎ 020-7385 8127) or **Magic of Spain** (UK ☎ 0870-027 0400). Many of these companies' villas are high up in the mountains in the middle of nowhere so you can busy yourself with little more than staring out across the olive groves or just lying in the pool, with a glass of wine close at hand. If you want to relax on your own, free from the tyranny of hotel meal regimes and other guests, this is the way to do it.

Ask CV Travel about **Casa Muneca**, Andalucia. Situated high on a south-facing ridge, surrounded by open countryside, the views from Casa Muneca to the coast are spectacular. Furnished with antiques, rugs, books and paintings the house is beautifully rustic and cosy. Alternatively, **Hacienda el Alamo**, Andalucia, hidden in a forested valley, is sensational. The main courtyard, with lovely traditional tiles and central fountain, leads to the rooms, featuring beamed ceilings and terracotta tiled floors. The master bedroom has a wonderful spa bath and a Jacuzzi on its terrace. The large swimming pool is set amidst lawns and fruit orchards with lovely views of 'the valley of the springs'. Seven nights at Casa Muneca will cost you from US$1507/£1060 and US$2247/£1580 at the Hacienda el Alamo both include maid service. Further up into the hills near Gaucin, El Puerto del Negro (also in Andalucia) comprises four comfortable and elegantly-designed cottages hidden away on a private mountainside estate, with spectacular views.

Italy
(BEST TIME: APRIL TO OCTOBER)

Italy has to be the ultimate destination for any romantic holiday. Nowhere else in the world does the past combine with beautiful scenery in such a stylish and evocative way. This amazing country stretches thousand of kilometres from the snow-capped Alps to balmy southern climes. Wherever you go, the grandeur of the architecture will transport you back to the many different ages of antiquity as images of the Etruscans, the mighty Roman empire and Renaissance artists capture your imagination.

While you will no doubt be drawn by the reminders of Italy's incomparable past, today's Italy is just as romantic: imagine tucking into bowls of perfectly-cooked fresh pasta, sipping local wine in the cool shade of cypress trees, and looking out over the endless olive groves.

Whether you dream of the cocooned luxury of the Venice-Simplon Orient Express, exploring the waterways of **Venice**, the languid elegance of the Italian lakes, the Renaissance palaces and museums of **Florence**, the rolling countryside and terraces of **Tuscany** and **Umbria**, or an exotic hideaway retreat perched 90m up on **Positano**'s cliff edge, it is difficult to go wrong with a honeymoon in Italy.

There is so much to see and do that a book entirely devoted to Italy as a honeymoon destination could still barely do justice to the country and its multitude of treasures. I have therefore picked out the most romantic of the country's hotels, and arranged them in three sections – cities, rural and coast – on the assumption that you'll want to incorporate a bit of each into your stay.

VENICE   [see also The Veneto, p157]
Hotel Cipriani
The most celebrated hotel in Venice is the Hotel Cipriani. Guests can enjoy the best views of Venice from a magical hideaway: as one travel writer wrote: 'The Cipriani is irresistibly there, like Everest'. Of course, this kind of élitism and luxury doesn't come

---

ITALY

A stunning coastline, 3000 years of classical history, delicious food and even better wine enjoyed overlooking the rolling fields filled with olive groves and vines – there is nowhere as magical as Italy

When to go: April to the end of October (avoiding August because it is so busy and hot)

Average maximum temperatures °C

	JAN	FEB	MAR	APR	MAY	JUN	JUL	AUG	SEP	OCT	NOV	DEC
Florence	6	6	10	13	17	21	24	23	20	15	12	7
Positano	9	9	12	14	17	21	23	24	21	17	13	10
Rome	8	8	12	14	18	22	24	24	21	17	13	9
Venice	5	5	9	13	17	20	22	22	20	15	11	6

Capital: Rome

Flight times: to Rome from:
  New York: 9³/₄ hours
  LA: 15¹/₂ hours
  London: 2¹/₂ hours
  Sydney: 24³/₄ hours

Approximate exchange rates: Euro (€) – £1 = €1.59, US$1 = €1.11, A$1 = €0.57

Time difference: GMT plus 1 hour (2 hours from the last Sunday in March to the last Sunday in Oct)

Voltage: 220v, mostly three round pins

Combine with: Anywhere else in Europe

Country dialling code: ☎ 39

Further information: 🖥 www.enit.it

cheap and, as they say, if you need to be looking at the bill you shouldn't be staying there. It's not just expensive, it's exorbitant, but if you have got the money and enjoy rubbing shoulders with the world's élite, this is *the* place to stay in Venice.

In Venice yet not in Venice because the hotel was built across the lagoon on the island of Giudecca, you can see the Campanile of **San Giorgio Maggiore**, the rooftops of **Dorsoduro** and the **Zattere**, the floating pink square of the **Doge's Palace**, and the domes of the Basilica of **St Mark's** from the hotel.

Dining outside on the terrace among fragrant flowers and looking out over this view is one of the most truly romantic experiences imaginable. Now an Orient-Express hotel the Cipriani really does incorporate the very best in luxurious accommodation, attentive service and fine cuisine, in an all-pervading atmosphere of tranquillity and seclusion.

Completed in 1958 by restaurateur extraordinaire, Guiseppe Cipriani, the hotel is set around its own formal gardens and Olympic-sized swimming pool. Each room is different and elegant in its simplicity: the rooms to the south look onto the lagoon; to the east and north, the San Giorgio Maggiore church.

It is partly the fabulous pool which accounts for the cost of staying at the

---

HOTEL CIPRIANI
(☎ 041-520-7744, 🖷 041-520-3930, 💻 info@hotelcipriani.it), Giudecca, 10, 30133 Venice, Italy
Closed: November to March
Reservations: Through Orient-Express Hotels (💻 www.orient-expresshotels.com), or Leading Hotels of the World (see p12)
Getting there: The hotel's private launch crosses the lagoon from Piazza San Marco in just four minutes; 30 minutes from Marco Polo Airport, 15 minutes from the station
Accommodation: 55 rooms and 51 suites
Amenities: 24-hour room service, hairdresser, boutique, swimming pool, sauna, massage, hydro-system, tennis court, private yachting marina, 24-hour motorboat service to St Mark's Square, de luxe motorboat available for outings in the lagoon; golf can be arranged at the Lido, 40 minutes away by boat
Dress code: Elegant casual
Weddings: Weddings and receptions can be arranged, prices on request
Minimum stay: None
Rates: Doubles from US$585/€672; suites from US$1575/€1808; ask about honeymoon, spring and autumn packages which give a much better deal
Credit cards: Most major
Taxes and service charge: Included

Cipriani as it's the only hotel in Venice to have one (and it is for residents only); so if you're going to splurge out all that money insist on at least having a poolside room – and get it in writing so that they can't shove you in a back room at the last minute when some celebrity turns up.

Alternatively, you can stay in the all-suite **Palazzo Vendramin**, or at the adjacent newly opened **Palazzo Nani Barbaro**, composed of all junior suites, both part of the Cipriani. Regulars in Venice argue they have better views and more elegant accommodation than the main body of the Cipriani, although they are even more expensive. Linked to the Hotel Cipriani by an ancient courtyard and flowered loggia, only part of the 15th-century Palazzo Vendramin is open to guests. Seven de luxe suites with full butler service and easy access to all the adjacent hotel's facilities make it one of the city's most exclusive destinations. All three hotels are incredibly expensive, but you are paying for the very best and the most prestigious Venice has to offer.

Hotel Danieli

Hotel Danieli is a great alternative to the Cipriani if you haven't got a small fortune to fritter away and don't want to sacrifice the sense of history. Besides, the only real difference between the Danieli and the Cipriani is the latter's swimming pool: so if you can suffer without a pool for a few days and if you book through one of the UK tour operators shown below you can stay for half the price in equally elegant surroundings – in fact some would argue that the Danieli has a greater feeling of history than its rival, and that a complimentary launch to a private beach at Venice Lido more than compensates for not being able to recline at a poolside.

HOTEL DANIELI
(☎ 041-522-6480, 🖹 041-520-0208, 🖳 www.starwood.com), Castello 4196, 30122 Venice, Italy
Reservations: Either direct, through Starwood Hotels (🖳 www.starwood. com), or through tour operators Abercrombie & Kent or Elegant Resorts (see pp13-14)
Getting there: A shuttle service operates from Marco Polo Airport 10 kms away, at extra cost
Accommodation: 231 rooms: 178 are doubles, 44 single, three junior suites, and six suites
Amenities: Terrazza Danieli rooftop restaurant, piano bar, bar Dandolo and in the summer a terrace bar and complimentary shuttle to beach
Dress code: Generally casual, but the hotel does prefer jackets for dinner
Weddings: Are available and costs vary depending on what is requested
Minimum stay: None
Rates: Double room with lagoon view US$612/€680, junior suite US$896/€995 and Royal Suite US$2489/€2763
Credit cards: Most major
Taxes and service charge: Included

Set in a 15th-century Doge's palace, the Danieli was first converted into a hotel in the early part of the 19th century and, although the atmosphere is still very much part of a bygone era, it has all the modern amenities that you'd expect from a hotel that is one of ITT Sheraton's chain of luxury hotels.

Inside there are many grand and elegant rooms including the most impressive galleried entrance hall with its glass chandelier and marble arches. Although the guest rooms vary a great deal in style and character, all are en suite and very luxurious featuring air conditioning, hairdryers, bathrobes, toiletries, slippers, minibar, TV and phone. Some have unforgettable lagoon views.

The Danieli enjoys one of the most superb positions in Venice, situated on the edge of the lagoon only a few steps away from St Mark's and the entrance to the Grand Canal. The views from the rooftop restaurant are quite magical, especially in the early morning light.

Other recommended hotels

At around half the price of the Cipriani, **Hotel Flora** (☎ 041-520-5844, 🖹 041-522-8217, San Marco 2283/A, Via XXII Marzo, Venice) is a dreamy and tranquil small hotel situated down a little alleyway, just off St Mark's Square. There are no canal views, but three sides of the hotel frame a pretty walled garden with wrought-iron tables, rampant greenery and the soothing sound of a fountain in the middle, making it the ideal place to escape the city heat. The 44 air-conditioned rooms vary consider-

THINGS TO SEE AND DO IN VENICE

For the first-time visitor there is so much to see in this staggeringly beautiful city that it's difficult to know where to start.

The 'must see' tourist sights are **Palazzo Ducale** (Doge's Palace), **St Mark's Square** and **Basilica**, **Bridge of Sighs** and **Rialto Bridge**. The best way to explore is on foot – with the occasional *vaporetto* or water bus – so that you can really take in all there is to see. Go into the various churches as you stumble upon them to see works of great masters such as **Tintoretto**, **Titian**, **Bellini** and **Canaletto**. Wherever you go in Venice the churches are full of Byzantine mosaics, St Mark's Basilica being perhaps the most beautiful and exotic of all Europe's cathedrals. Take a good map; you'll no doubt get lost along the way but that is all part of the fun and often leads to real finds.

One of the most incredible sights in Venice is the **Rialto**, Venice's biggest market where

barges are stacked high with produce.

Another good day out is to visit the islands in the lagoon – **Murano**, **Burano** and **Torcello** – famous respectively for their Venetian glassblowing, lace-making and the 7th-century cathedral.

There are of course numerous fantastic restaurants in Venice. Here are just a few worthy of note: *Harry's Bar* (☎ 041-528 5777), Calle Valaresso, is legendary and no trip to Venice would be complete without a visit to this famous restaurant; right next door is the *Grand Canal Restaurant* (☎ 041-520 0211), Hotel Monaco e Grand Canal, Calle Vallaresso, which is one of the stalwarts of Venice.

Hotel Cipriani's supremely elegant *Cipriani Restaurant* is undoubtedly one of the best and most romantic restaurants in Venice.

For further information see 🖳 www.comune.venezia.it.

THE VENICE-SIMPLON ORIENT EXPRESS

Undoubtedly the most romantic way to enter Italy is on the legendary Orient Express from London to Venice. Since 1883 this train service has embodied luxury and refinement.

The cream and umber British Pullman leaves London's **Victoria Station** at 11am on Thursdays and Sundays between mid-March and mid-November. The journey starts with a champagne lunch on the way to the coastal town of Folkestone in Kent, before the short crossing to France by **SeaCat** (high-speed catamaran).

By 5pm you'll be ensconced aboard the magnificent blue and gold train, swept up in a world of absolute luxury and fine dining on your way to Venice. By about 9pm the train draws briefly into Paris and then continues its journey while you enjoy dinner in one of the train's three restaurant cars.

As you start your ascent up into the spectacular Alps and Dolomites the next morning, full-breakfast is served. Lunch is served as you descend towards Verona, followed by tea and pastries just before you draw into **Santa Lucia Station** on Venice's Grand Canal. The one-way trip from London to Venice costs US$1990/ £1165 for a double cabin.

For reservations contact Orient-Express (💻 www.orient-express.com).

ably but all have traditional antique furnishings: the price hasn't changed in years and it's very popular so book early. Doubles cost from US$126/€145.

Pensione Accademia – Villa Maravege (☎ 041-521-0188, 🖹 041-523-9152, Dorsoduro 1058, Fondamenta Bollani, Venice) is just off the **San Trovaso Canal**. This wonderful rambling 17th-century villa also has the advantage of being in one of the prettiest and least touristy parts of Venice, on a small piece of land almost completely surrounded by canals. Unusually for Venice it has two gardens, one of which overlooks the San Trovaso canal and the other which surrounds a Palladian-style villa: rooms have views over the garden and canal. There are all sorts of styles and sizes of rooms: some are in the wisteria-covered palazzo and others in a neighbouring building. They are all stylishly done, with marble floors and air conditioning, satellite TV, phone and hairdryer. In summer, breakfast is served in the garden. With doubles from a very reasonable US$90/€103, you need to book as early as possible.

FLORENCE
[see also Tuscany and Umbria, p159]

Torre di Bellosguardo

The Torre di Bellosguardo is a fabulous 13th-century villa perched on a hill overlooking Florence. It was built by a nobleman friend of Dante's, confident that he'd found the perfect location for his home. The view, very definitely one of the finest vantage points over the city, is just fantastic – you can just about see the façade of every church in Florence.

From the moment you step into the frescoed ballroom, where guests are welcomed on arrival, you'll know this is no ordinary place. No two rooms are alike. Each one holds a surprise: warm wooden beams or a 16th-century rosette-studded ceiling, a gilded four-poster bed in which to dream or small 15th-century drawers to hold your belongings. Bellosguardo means beautiful view, and the view from each, whether over the city or towards the surrounding country-

TORRE DI BELLOSGUARDO
(☎ 055-229-8145, 🖹 055-229-008), via Roti Michelozzi 2, 50124, Florence, Italy
Reservations: Direct
Getting there: Taxis from the station cost approximately US$9/€11
Accommodation: 16 guest rooms: eight doubles, seven suites, one single room
Amenities: Small bar open 24 hours, outdoor swimming pool, indoor sports centre, with pool, sauna and Jacuzzi
Dress code: Casual
Weddings: The hotel is able to organize wedding ceremonies between December and February when it is less busy
Minimum stay: None
Rates: Double rooms US$221/€254; suites US$266/€305 year-round; breakfast costs extra
Credit cards: Most major
Taxes and service charge: Included

side, is different. Cypress trees frame sculptures in the gardens; at night, the flower garden shimmers with hosts of fireflies and releases waves of aromatic perfume after the day's heat.

Don't come here expecting to find all sorts of modern facilities in your room: there's no minibar, few rooms have air conditioning, largely because few need it, and if you want a hairdryer you have to borrow one from reception. But this is part of the authentic old world charm of this lovely romantic villa: it bears no resemblance to a modern resort hotel with its many restaurants, tennis courts and tour desks, but there is a sports centre with an indoor pool, sauna and Jacuzzi and a small house bar is open 24 hours a day. The views and immense character of the place make up for anything the hotel lacks.

People return time and again to the Torre di Bellosguardo, having fallen in love with the serene atmosphere of its homely rooms and the immaculate gardens with their unsurpassed views. In summer, guests eat lunch around the outdoor swimming pool, but when it comes to dinner you have to go down the hill to Florence as there is no restaurant in the hotel. But, before you go, get yourself a long, cool drink from the bar and settle down on the terrace to watch the setting sun turn the whole city a magical pinky hue beneath you.

Villa San Michele

Villa San Michele, perched high on the wooded hillside in Fiesole with the most magnificent views over Florence, is perhaps even more exclusive and luxurious than its sister Orient-Express Hotel, the Cipriani in Venice. A runner-up for *Tatler*'s Hotel of the Year 2001, it's a classic.

The façade of this 15th-century Franciscan monastery was built by Michelangelo, thus its beauty should probably not come as a surprise. With its traditional terracotta tiled roof, ancient masonry, classical loggia, original frescoes and graceful pillars it is one of those few places in the world that is quite overwhelmingly graceful and elegant.

THINGS TO SEE AND DO IN FLORENCE

Home of the court of Lorenzo the Magnificent, power-house of art and thought in the Renaissance period and today famous for its fashion and antiques, this city has to be part of any honeymoon in Italy.

Florence, built predominantly on the patronage of the church and the Medicis, is a complete work of art unto itself. The wealth of artistic achievement within its ancient walls is, at times, totally overwhelming.

The basic sights are: the **Uffizi**, though try to leave it until late in the afternoon when it is quieter; the Michelangelos at the **Accademia**, Donatello at the **Museo dell'Opera del Duomo**, Titian, Raphael and Veronese at the **Palazzo Pitti**, Renaissance sculpture at the **Bargello** and Fra Angelico at the **Museo di San Marco**; the Brunelleschi cathedral domes and church interiors of **San Lorenzo** and **Santo Spirito**; and finally a climb to the top of the **Duomo** is well worth it for the views. Do your touring on foot as most of the sights are within a very small area.

If you're not staying at the Villa San Michele, it is worth driving out to **Fiesole**, the

aristocratic hilltop suburb where Florentines go to escape the heat and enjoy the summer plays and concerts at the well-preserved amphitheatre. For a totally authentic Tuscan experience spend a few hours looking round **Sant' Ambrogio** market.

When you've had enough of sightseeing it's time to relax in some of Florence's wonderful restaurants and bars. *Canietta Antinori* (☎ 055-292-234), Palazzo Antinori, serving Antinori wines by the glass is a great place for a drink or light bar snack in very stylish surroundings. It also has a full restaurant menu.

For something cheap and cheerful for lunch or dinner try *Il Cantinone del Gallo Nero* (☎ 055-218-898), Via S. Spirito, which serves authentic and hearty Tuscan food. For something much smarter try *Enoteca Pinchiorri* (☎ 055-242-777), Via Ghibellina, one of Florence's most famous restaurants which although very expensive is perfect if you feel like spoiling yourself.

See 🖳 www.firenze.tourismo.toscana.it for further information.

Guests dine either in the elegant **Cenacolo Restaurant** overlooking the gardens, where the bar boasts the most magnificent fresco of *The Last Supper* and many other original oil paintings, or less formally in the **Loggia**. Dining outside on the Loggia's terrace, which stretches the full length of the building, on a balmy summer's evening, has to be one of the most romantic experiences imaginable; as you look down through the cypress trees at the lights coming on over Florence you can observe the most incredible transformation from daylight through dusk to a light-studded cityscape.

The Orient-Express Hotel group has furnished the villa with a perfectly minimalist Italian sense of design; as a result the modern furnishings sit effortlessly beside the classical features of the building. While the hotel's public areas are full of antiques, oriental rugs and glistening candelabra arranged in a very traditional fashion, some of the 22 bedrooms and 16 suites have more modern overtones.

The only problem with the hotel is that unless you go for one of the superior rooms or the suites the bedrooms are actually incredibly poky, which for this kind of money isn't great, especially as the very high windows mean there are no views from some of the bedrooms.

VILLA SAN MICHELE
(☎ 055-567-8200, 🖹 055-567-8250, 🖳 reservations@villasanmichelle.net), Via di Doccia, 50014, Florence, Italy
Reservations: Through Orient-Express Hotels (🖳 www.orient-expresshotels. com), or the Leading Hotels of the World (see p12); or through tour operators, Elegant Resorts, or Abercrombie & Kent (see pp13-14)
Getting there: The hotel operates a courtesy shuttle bus to/from Florence
Accommodation: 22 rooms, 16 suites
Amenities: Open-air Loggia restaurant, intimate dining in the Cloister and Cenacolo Restaurant, piano bar; outdoor heated swimming pool, Italian terraced garden, gym, horse-riding, golf and tennis nearby, chauffeur service, courtesy shuttle bus
Dress code: Jacket and tie are requested in the Cenacolo Restaurant
Weddings: The hotel is very small and more suitable for honeymoons than wedding ceremonies and receptions
Minimum stay: None
Rates: Per person half board from US$708/€813 to US$895/€1028; suites from US$1485/€1705; ask about honeymoon spring and autumn programmes which give a much better deal
Credit cards: Most major
Taxes and service charge: Included

The suites, however, are of course fantastic. The Limonia has an unmistakably contemporary theme to its décor – a sort of Mulberry meets Conran image – combining honey-coloured walls, large terracotta floor tiles and cream-covered sofas, with the dark tones of fine antique chests and wrought-iron furnishings.

All the rooms are equipped with air conditioning, minibars, phone and spacious bathrooms, while the junior suites have four-poster beds and many have Jacuzzis.

The hotel's swimming pool and adjacent bar also enjoy stunning views over Florence and have the wonderful feel of a private garden, making it a lovely place to relax if you feel like escaping the bustle of the city for the day. Or you can wander through the immaculate landscaped gardens past cypresses and olive trees to

The Villa San Michele is stunning and so grand, but it was really expensive, especially the food with a tomato and mozzarella salad at lunch costing around £15. But you are paying for the absolute exclusivity of the house, the huge amount of space and privacy and the surroundings, not the bedrooms. We felt really it was more of a long weekend place, as it's too expensive to relax in unless you have an awful lot of money.
Nick and Vanessa McDonald Buchanan

two small chapels, a reminder of this incredible villa's impressive heritage. Despite the hotel's seclusion it is only minutes from Florence and is within easy reach of **Bologna** and **Pisa**, making it an ideal base for touring this glorious area, providing you can afford its staggering room prices!

Other recommended hotels
Helvetia & Bristol (☎ 055-287-814, 🖹 055-288-353, Via dei Pescioni 2) is arguably central Florence's finest retreat. Just one minute from Piazza della Republica but

immaculate and charming, this 52-roomed hotel manages to maintain the ambience of a tranquil country house.

Lovingly restored to the full glamour of Florentine aristocratic style, the hotel is exclusive, but not stuffy. The salon has a welcoming fireplace and velvet sofas and armchairs along with lavish wall hangings and priceless antiques. Breakfast and lunch are served in the delightful Giardino d'Inverno, with its wicker furniture and potted plants, once a meeting place for artists and intellectuals such as Stravinsky and Bertrand Russell. Mouthwatering traditional Tuscan delicacies are served in the evocative Bristol Restaurant.

Bedrooms at the Helvetia & Bristol are sumptuous with swathes of ornate fabrics everywhere. Many have a private Jacuzzi in their superb Carrara marble bathroom. Doubles cost from US$198/€228, suites from US$329/€378. Book direct, or through tour operators Abercrombie & Kent or Magic of Italy (see pp13-14).

Brunelleschi (☎ 055-290-311, 🗎 055-219-653, Piazza Santa Elisabetta, 50122 Florence) offers exceptionally good value for money in the middle of the city. Built around an unusual 6th-century Byzantine tower and the medieval church of San Michele in Palchetto right behind the Duomo, the 96-roomed Brunelleschi with its distinctive façade is a superior hotel with antique walls and ceilings but no shortage of modern comforts. Doubles cost from US$257/€295 including breakfast and taxes during the low season. Book through UK specialist Magic of Italy (☎ 0870-027 0500).

ROME   [see also The Coast, p162]

So much is said about Florence and Venice that I was totally unprepared for the outstanding beauty and magnificence of Rome. Unlike other European capital cities where new-fangled creations stand alongside historic monuments, you can walk for ages in the centre of Rome and never see a modern building. And there is something in the chaotic nature of the Romans – the way young and old charge round the city on scooters without helmets – that gives the whole place a wonderfully spirited atmosphere that I've never come across anywhere else.

Hotel de Russie

Hotel de Russie's fabulous location between the Spanish Steps and Piazza Del Popolo is just one reason why this hotel was a magnet for Europe's élite as they passed through Italy on a cultural tour in the 19th century. In the 20th century, lavishly restored and updated by Rocco Forte, the Hotel de Russie reopened its doors. And with Rome's delights on its doorstep and nothing but style inside, it is again the place to be, and accordingly, one of the most expensive.

The Russie is a great place to spend the first few nights of your honeymoon before heading to the Umbrian countryside. A peaceful sanctuary to retreat to when sightseeing and shopping on fashionable Via Condotti gets too much, the 127 big bedrooms and 27 suites are elegant with calming traditional furniture yet with all the mod cons such as air conditioning and interactive tele-

HOTEL DE RUSSIE
(☎ 06-32-8881, 🗎 06-32-888-888, 🖵 reservations@hotelderussie.it, www.rf hotels.com), Via del Babuino 9, Rome, Italy
Reservations: Through Preferred Hotels and Resorts worldwide reservation numbers (see p12), through RF Hotels (☎ 020-7321 2626, 🖵 www.rfhotels.com) or through UK tour operator Mediterranean Experience (see p14)
Getting there: 30 minutes from the airport
Accommodation: 129 rooms including 27 suites
Amenities: Extensive, terraced gardens; health club and spa with hydropool, Jacuzzi, sauna, Turkish steam bath, beauty treatments and gym
Dress code: None
Weddings: Indoor and outdoor receptions catered for up to 100 people
Minimum stay: None
Rates: Doubles from US$428/€491; suites range from US$765/€878 to US$1620/€1860 for the Picasso Suite
Credit cards: Most major
Taxes and service charge: Government tax at 10%

vision. The Picasso suite – yes he really did stay here – is the most luxurious, designed by Olga Politza, Rocco Forte's sister; dulcet tones and 'greige' covered footstools and chairs are scattered throughout.

But the Russie's most stunning feature is its extensive, terraced gardens. Here, you can dine alfresco – the restaurant's head chef is from the Relais le Jardin in Rome – or enjoy an open-air reception if you decided to get married in one of the world's most romantic locations and the best hotel Rome has to offer.

THE DOLOMITES
Berghotel Zirmerhof

This delightful mountain hotel is a real find. Set in a superb location above the **Val di Fiemme**, the Zirmerhof, originally a working farm, dates from around 1600 and has been run by the Perwanger family for over a century.

Peacefully situated just outside the tiny hamlet of **Radein**, the hotel has magnificent views of the valley below and the surrounding mountains, including the **Weisshorn** and **Schwarzhorn**.

It is currently run by Sepp Perwanger and his family: they offer warm and genuine hospitality giving the Zirmerhof a really special feel. Traditional, regional cuisine is served in the restaurant using recipes created by Sepp's grandmother, Hanna, whose imaginative and delicious creations have been published locally. The superb restaurant has a fresco, painted by Ignaz Stolz, covering two of the walls and splendid views out over the countryside.

The hotel has the feel of a traditional farmhouse; it has old hand-crafted wooden furniture, timbered ceilings and wonderful creaky wooden floorboards. Rooms No 6, No 14, No 15 and the suite, No 11, are the best because they are the largest and they have a balcony or loggia with panoramic views over the valley. The bathrooms are marble but only four of the hotel's 31 rooms have baths, the rest have en suite showers.

BERGHOTEL ZIRMERHOF
(☎ 0471-887-215, 📠 0471-887-225, 🖥 www.zirmerhof.com), Radein, I-39040, Italy
Reservations: Either direct or through UK tour operator Inntravel (UK ☎ 01653-629 000)
Getting there: The hotel is 241km from Verona Airport; most guests hire a car but the hotel can arrange transfers from Ora railway station
Accommodation: 31 rooms and one suite, all en suite
Amenities: Restaurant, bar, library, lounge, terrace area with outside seating, private parking
Dress code: Informal
Weddings: The hotel can host receptions for up to 80 people
Minimum stay: Three nights
Rates: Superior doubles from US$63/€72 to US$70/€81, suites US$69/€80 to US$81/€93 for four nights or more half board; Inntravel's seven-night package including BA flights to Verona, seven days' Avis car hire and seven nights' half board in a superior room costs around US$1062/£747 per person in June
Credit cards: Credit cards are not accepted, bills must be settled by Eurocheque or cash
Taxes and service charge: Included

Few places can rival this delightful little hotel if you are looking for somewhere cosy in a stunning mountain setting and where you can be guaranteed delicious meals. There's lots to do in the area apart from walking: you can go swimming, mountain biking or horse-riding and play tennis.

THE LAKES
Villa D'Este

Villa D'Este has a huge crowd of devotees who will tell you that it is the best hotel in the whole of Italy. Those who go there come back raving about it, which is all very well providing you can afford it: even if you think you can, do watch out for the extras bill which has a nasty habit of getting way out of control.

VILLA D'ESTE

(☎ 031-3481, 📠 031-348-844, 🖥
www.villadeste.it), Via Regina 40, Lake
Como, 22012 Cernobbio, Italy

Closed: December to February

Reservations: The Leading Hotels of the
World toll-free reservations numbers
worldwide (see p12); or through tour
operators, Elegant Resorts or
Abercrombie & Kent (see pp13-14)

Getting there: The hotel can arrange
transfers from Milan Airport on request

Accommodation: 108 rooms, 45 junior
suites, 11 suites

Amenities: Three restaurants, four-
hectare private park, night club, disco,
piano bar, beach bar, Sports Club with
three swimming pools, eight tennis
courts, squash court, gym, putting green,
windsurfing, canoeing, water-skiing,
hang gliding, excursions on the lake,
sauna and Turkish bath, massage rooms,
spa treatments, boutiques and beauty
salon; seven 18-hole golf courses nearby

Dress code: Jacket and tie are required
for dining in the Veranda Restaurant

Weddings: Weddings and receptions
can be arranged for a maximum of 200
people

Minimum stay: None

Rates: Three night romantic package in
de luxe accommodation, half board from
US$635/€729 per person, includes
spumante and flowers on arrival, taxes,
massage and free use of sports facilities

Credit cards: Most major

Taxes and service charge: Included

There is a long, romantic tradition behind the Villa D'Este. The first photos of Edward VIII with Mrs Simpson following his abdication were taken at the villa and the couple returned many times as the Duke and Duchess of Windsor. Rita Hayworth stayed there with Orson Welles, and other guests include Ava Gardner and Frank Sinatra. Recent guests such as Billy Joel and Whitney Houston give you some idea of the current clientele.

Located on the far side of Lake Como in **Cernobbio**, this fabulous 16th-century villa used to belong to Cardinal Tolomeo Gallio, before being transformed into a grand hotel in 1873. As its management are fond of telling you, the Villa d'Este is 'more than just a hotel, it is an idea born in the minds of a group of people dedicated to anticipating every wish of their guest' – an encouraging start.

The legendary service will indeed make a big difference to your stay, but what really makes this villa so incredible is its awesome lakeside position in four hectares of spectacular gardens. Some parts of the gardens are so beautiful they inspire the same kind of veneration as the gardens of the English stately home, Cliveden. The formal design, perfect box hedges and elegant statuary make you want to stay there forever.

The villa is extravagantly furnished: ceremonial staircases sweep down to marble floors, gleaming chandeliers hang from lofty ceilings supported by mighty pillars, and dainty French ormolu-decorated chairs are arranged throughout the public rooms – this isn't really the place to snuggle down with a good book or put your feet up! The bedrooms are equally ornate being decorated with rich colours and great swags of heavy fabrics and furnished with fine antiques. They're also not short of modern amenities: they all come with satellite TV, radio, in-room safe, minibar and telephone. The marble bathrooms have a Jacuzzi, hairdryer, bathrobes and slippers and the best toiletries of course.

If you like your hotels to be self-contained resorts with every kind of facility and hundreds of formal staff at hand, you'll love the Villa d'Este. Somewhat unusually for Europe, it is the kind of big resort hotel that has everything: there are two restaurants serving Italian haute cuisine, a disco and nightclub, piano bar, beach bar, three swimming pools including a fantastic outdoor pool floating on the lake, eight tennis courts, a squash court, a gym, sauna and Turkish baths, massage and spa treatments, seven golf courses nearby and a whole range of watersports and shops. You could stay here for two weeks without leaving the grounds and want for nothing.

Obviously this is not the place to come for a quiet intimate stay, but if you love the glamour of big hotels and can drag out the odd Hermès scarf and Prada beach bag, this is about as chic and slick as it gets.

Other recommended hotels

Hidden on a rocky outcrop, just off the main body of **Lake Garda**, is the ancient domain of **San Vigilio**. Here at the end of a tree-lined pathway and narrow cobbled street, the **Locanda San Vigilio** (☎ 045-725-6688, 🖹 045-725-6551, 🖳 www.locanda sanvigilio.it, 37016 San Vigilio, Lake Garda) is the perfect romantic hideaway. It is set in lush gardens of cypress and olive trees, and lemon and orange groves. With just three suites and four bedrooms, a small restaurant with some of the tables right on the edge of the lake and a private harbour and beach, the Locanda has been receiving guests for five centuries.

Although the Locanda is expensive, it's a good deal more reasonable than staying at any of the really flash hotels further along the lake. This hotel will really suit you if you are looking for a tranquil place to be alone together and like to avoid the kind of hotels where you feel you have to speak in hushed tones. Double rooms cost around US$203/€233, suites from US$311/€357 including breakfast and taxes.

THE VENETO

The Veneto, just a short drive from Venice (see p148), is home to some of Italy's most beautiful countryside and the former residences of the Venetian nobility. The following hotels are all within a couple of hours' drive of Venice.

Villa Cipriani

The Villa Cipriani is one of those honeymoon classics. If you are planning a surprise honeymoon and you take her to the Villa Cipriani she'll love you forever. I would! Just an hour from Venice, at the foot of the Dolomites, the villa is found in the small, walled hill town of **Asolo**, a haven since the 15th century for artists, musicians and writers from Titian to Robert Browning. One of Italy's most famous hotels, the Villa Cipriani,

which no longer has anything to do with the celebrated Venetian hotel of the same name, truly is a place favoured by the gods.

Today's hotel offers the unique and unchanging charms of a patrician 15th-century residence with honey-coloured stone and dark green shutters; it is ever so slightly dilapidated with rough patches and cracks showing in the exterior walls but, to the kind of people suited to this hotel, the slightly shabby feel only augments its charm. It seems to assert an almost mystical attraction on its guests, causing many to pledge to return again.

The 26 superior rooms and five exclusive de luxe rooms are all en suite and air conditioned, and enjoy fabulous views over the surrounding countryside and the English-style garden, while cool corridors of polished stone lead to the excellent restaurant where you'll discover Italian cuisine that brings out the finest provincial and Mediterranean flavours.

Although there is no pool at the hotel, guests can use one nearby, and tennis and golf can also be arranged. But somehow these activities don't quite fit in with life in

VILLA CIPRIANI
(☎ 0423-523-411, 🖹 0423-952-095, 🖳 www.sheraton.com), Via Canova 298, 1-31011, Asolo, Treviso, Italy
Reservations: Relais & Châteaux toll-free reservation numbers worldwide (see p12) or through the Sheraton website (see above).
Getting there: From Venice take the A27 towards Treviso north and then the SS248 towards Bassano del Grappa, or take a taxi from Treviso Airport (20km)
Accommodation: 31 rooms including 24 superior and five exclusive de luxe doubles
Amenities: Lounge, bar, restaurant divided into two rooms, Veranda and Contarini, room service from 6am to midnight, English garden; golf, tennis, swimming all nearby
Dress code: Casual, but formal for dinner
Weddings: The hotel does cater for wedding ceremonies and receptions
Minimum stay: None
Rates: Doubles from US$270/€311 to US$410/€471 for valley view rooms breakfast included; dinner (wine not included) US$70/€80
Credit cards: Visa, Eurocard, American Express, Diners Club
Taxes and service charge: Included

WINE ROUTES OF THE VENETO

One-third of Italy's classified wines (recognized under the DOC and DOCG labels) come from **Veneto**, **Trentino-Alto Adige** and **Friuli-Venezia Giulia**, and the countryside that produces them is absolutely stunning. Whether you are on your way up to the Lakes, staying close to Verona itself or even based in the heart of Valpolicella country at La Foresteria Serego Aligieri, it would be a crime to miss out on seeing some of this glorious wine country. Long sunny days spent meandering along picturesque rural lanes and popping into the odd estate for a tasting is sheer bliss.

From the Lakes the nearest wines of note are produced in **Bardolino**, close to Lake Garda, where there is a clearly marked wine route, *strada del vino*, to follow. Even if you don't follow the prescribed route make sure you take in **Lazise**, **Cisano**, **Calmasino** and **Affi**.

You'll find some of the most splendid vintages in the Classico hills of **Valpolicella**. Close to the Alighieri estate is the well-known **Masi Winery**, but you can continue exploring in both directions. To the west is **San Giorgio**, with its beautiful 18th-century church, and to the east lies the high wine country of towns such as **Fumane** and **Marano**, linked by classically rugged Valpolicella terrain. Further east still will take you into the **Negrar Valley** until you reach Negrar, where Giuseppe Quintarelli's wines are legendary, and the tiny hamlet of **Mazzano**.

Asolo, where a gentle stroll around the gardens or a leisurely root around the shops is much more appropriate.

La Foresteria Serego Alighieri

La Foresteria Serego Alighieri, an absolutely stunning private villa, is without doubt one of the most heavenly places to stay in northern Italy. Set in the heart of the beautiful Valpolicella wine region, La Foresteria forms part of a vast wine and olive oil producing estate which has been run by the same family for six centuries and twenty generations, and all of them are direct descendants of the poet Dante Alighieri.

The present Count Alighieri, who lives on the estate with his family, has carefully transformed the stables and farm buildings into eight immaculately furnished apartments in super-chic Milano style. Each apartment combines parquet floors, rustic beams and brass rods supporting muslin drapes, with pristine grey kitchens.

LA FORESTERIA SEREGO ALIGHIERI
(☎ 045-770-3622, 🖷 045-770-3523, 🖳 www.seregoalighieri.it), Via Stazione 2, 37020 Gargagnago di Valpolicella, Italy
Reservations: Direct
Getting there: La Foresteria is 18km north-west of Verona and 20km east of Lake Garda
Accommodation: Eight apartments with kitchens
Amenities: Kitchens and dining areas, vineyard and cellar tours, small estate shop, light continental breakfasts served
Dress code: There isn't one
Weddings: No
Minimum stay: None
Rates: Double apartments with breakfast from US$104/€119 per night in the low season going up to US$140/€161 during the high season; from the fifth night it is cheaper, costing from US$86/€99 per night (low) and US$126/€145 (high); Oseleta costs US$104/€119 (low) and US$140/€161 (high)
Credit cards: Most major
Taxes and service charge: Included

Best of all the apartments is No 8, Oseleta, the dove tower, which covers three floors and can only be reached through a trapdoor staircase. Just made for honeymooners, the bedroom is tucked away up in the eaves where light streams in through the original dove holes. The bed virtually runs from one wall to the other, and there are the most fabulous views of the countryside.

You can buy wine, balsamic vinegar, olive oil and jams from the estate shop, tour the vineyards and even help with the harvest in October. Don't be put off by the thought of self-catering as there are lots of superb restaurants in other country house hotels nearby and breakfasts can be provided. **Verona**, with its famous opera, is only 16km away. The opera season at the **Arena Di Verona** runs from the beginning of July until September.

TUSCANY AND UMBRIA

Once you've had your fill of Florence (see p151), hire a car and drive south through magical Tuscany and adjacent Umbria, where the rolling hills are filled with green cypresses and an ocean of olive and vine groves. Follow the **Chianti Route** through hundreds of vineyards perched on steep hillsides. Don't miss **San Gimigniano**, Italy's best preserved medieval town, with its 15 towers dominating the landscape. Between Florence and Siena, in the rolling Tuscan countryside lie some of Italy's most classic hotels.

La Suvera

Staying at La Suvera, a gorgeous 12th-century villa about 30 minutes west of Siena, is rather like living in your own private medieval castle. Set right in the very heart of Tuscany, La Suvera is surrounded by olive groves and green fields, making it a perfectly secluded and tranquil retreat.

Created around a medieval castle, La Suvera later became the papal villa of Pope Julius II and is now the home of the Ricci family who live in one part of the castle. The entrance to the villa is dominated by a large square with several different buildings along one side including a tiny, beautiful ancient church. Guests are accommodated in 16 rooms and 19 suites either in the papal villa itself or in the former stables, farmhouse or the old olive-pressing mill.

Each room is decorated in a highly individual theme; for instance one has a butterfly collection, and they are all full of antiques and artefacts picked up from all over the world by the Ricci family's ancestors. All are air conditioned with full en suite facilities, TV and minibar. There are several lounges, a library and a music room and all are adorned

LA SUVERA
(☎ 0577-960-300, 🖷 0577-960-220, 🖥 www.lasuvera.it), 53030 Pievescola di Casole d'Elsa, Val d'Elsa, Italy
Reservations: Direct or through tour operators Magic of Italy, Abercrombie & Kent, Elegant Resorts (see pp13-14)
Getting there: Most guests hire a car, approx 2½ hours' drive from Pisa Airport, and one hour from Florence Airport; the hotel can arrange transfers
Accommodation: 16 rooms and 19 suites
Amenities: Room service, swimming pool, tennis court, mountain bikes, restaurant, several lounges, library, bar, poolside restaurant and bar, music room, horse-riding is available nearby, massage on request
Dress code: Jackets for men and dresses for women are requested at dinner
Weddings: The hotel is happy to host ceremonies and receptions: its lovely little church can take up to 40 people
Minimum stay: Two nights
Rates: Double rooms from US$203/€233 to US$225/€259; suites from US$450/€517 to US$540/€620
Credit cards: Most major
Taxes and service charge: Included

with fine oil paintings and magnificent antiques, making it more like staying in some sort of medieval artefacts' exhibition than being in a hotel.

The **Oliviera**, across the road, houses the hotel's restaurant where organic produce from the farm is incorporated into delicious and typically Tuscan cuisine accompanied by estate wines. The terraced gardens are equally amazing: the beautiful heated swimming pool is surrounded by ancient statues and rambling ivy, swans glide across the lake, and more statues peep out from the topiary.

Tenuta di Ricavo

In the heart of the fabulous Chianti countryside this lovely little residence is a real slice of heaven. If you are searching for a remote and tranquil base to explore Tuscany among very private surroundings then look no further, as Tenuta di Ricavo is truly out of this world. The hamlet of **Ricavo**, whose medieval origins date back to the year 994, was transformed into a comfortable country residence back in the 1950s using traditional Tuscan architectural techniques to maintain the historic ambience.

Eight of the 23 rooms are located in the main house, while the other 14 are in the former hamlet's cottages, so staying here is hardly like being in a hotel but much more

TENUTA DI RICAVO
(☎ 0577-740-221, 🖷 0577-741-014, 🖳 www.ricavo.com), 1-53011 Castellina in Chianti, Italy
Closed: Mid November to March
Reservations: Direct or Internet booking 🖳 www.thatromantikhotel.com or through US agents JDB toll-free (☎ 800-346-5358, 🖷 703-548-5825)
Getting there: It is essential for guests to hire a car as there is no public transport to and from the hotel; the nearest airport is Florence (taxi costs €104), the nearest station is Siena or Florence (NOT Castellina Scalo!)
Accommodation: 22 guest rooms: five suites (three double), 8 double rooms, 8 twin rooms, one single room
Amenities: Walking trails, two outdoor swimming pools, gym, library, chess, cards, TV room with satellite, à la carte restaurant La Pecora Nera (closed Tues – restricted hours of opening), bar, limited room service
Dress code: The hotel requests that guests be well dressed, even if casually, when dining in the restaurant, but ties are not required
Weddings: The hotel cannot cater for wedding parties
Minimum stay: Five to seven nights in high or mid season, although they will accept you for just one night if you call at the last minute and they have a vacancy
Rates: Double rooms from US$132/€152 with breakfast
Credit cards: Visa, Master Card
Taxes and service charge: Included

like renting a cottage in a small private village. All rooms have satellite televisions, but this is a quiet hotel and the views over the idyllic wooded-hills are much better than any television programme. About half the rooms have a balcony.

The rooms are rustically furnished with solid antique furniture, wrought-iron beds and lovely Persian or Tuscan carpets. Lots of them have exposed original wooden beams and 14th-century tiles and are all equipped with a hairdryer, fridge and in-room safe.

When you make your booking ask for room No 5, which is particularly beautiful and really spacious. It boasts a wooden renaissance double bed, marble floor, antique paintings and furniture and even prayer stools. It also has a marble bathroom (although it doesn't have a balcony).

Charming gardens surround the cottages and the main building so you can easily find a private place to sit with a good book, or take a walk further afield on one of the many marked trails through the estate's 160 hectares of idyllic countryside. These often take you along old dirt roads, so bring some good walking shoes. Meals are taken outside in the summer months, and often well into October if the weather lasts, in Ricavo's main square. Local Tuscan cuisine created by chef Alessandro Lobrano is accompanied by the delicious wines of Chianti.

We had eight days here and drove out each morning for an adventure. Siena, Florence, San Gimigniano are all within easy driving distance so that we were usually home by 4pm in time for a swim and relaxing in the sun. The only thing to break the perfect silence at this lovely small hotel are the pigeons cooing, the swallows nesting and the cuckoo calling, it really is quite dreamy. **Biddy and Morgan Fahey**

Recommended hotels
Hotel Le Tre Vaselle (☎ 075-988-0447, 🖷 075-988-0214, 🖳 www.trevaselle.it, Via Giuseppe Garibaldi 48, 06089 Torgiano, Perugia), set in the centre of the old fortress town of **Torgiano**, is a charmingly rustic 17th-century hotel owned by the Lungarotti family, producers of Umbria's finest wines.

This is the place if you are looking for an unpretentious and friendly village inn from where you can explore the Umbrian countryside, safe in the knowledge that you've got a charming room and a delicious meal to return to each night.

This lovely hotel has thick stone walls the colour of sand, wooden beams, terra-cotta roof and floor tiles and impressive stone fireplaces. The interior decoration is also traditional, featuring hand-woven fabrics from central Italy, oil paintings, embroidery, antique etchings of viticultural scenes, and the three 17th-century monastic jugs displayed in the lobby from which the hotel derives its name. Dishes are pure and wholesome in time-honoured Umbrian fashion, based on ingredients supplied by the hotel's own farms.

THINGS TO SEE AND DO IN TUSCANY AND UMBRIA

Tuscany has long been synonymous with romance, while Umbria is less well known and is very much like Tuscany was 30 years ago. Despite rumours that Chianti is about to be renamed Chiantishire (making it another British county!) the countryside is still just as beautiful now as it has always been. All that has changed is the ownership and while it is true that more of the hillside villas are holiday homes than permanent residences, the magic of the place still exists. And if you do feel strongly about going somewhere authentic, not packed with fellow tourists, visit Umbria.

A stay in Tuscany and Umbria is all about long relaxing days spent either lying by the pool gazing at the smooth rolling hills; wandering the medieval streets of hilltop towns such as **Assisi**, **Orvieto**, **San Gimigniano**, and splendid **Siena**; or exploring the vineyards of **Chianti**, **Monetepulciano** and **Montalcino**. If you want to drive the wine route through Italy's most famous vineyards, symbolized by the black rooster symbol of Chianti Classico, follow the *strada del vino* between Florence and Siena, and give yourselves time for plenty of enjoyable diversions en route.

One of the most romantic ways to see this beautiful countryside is in a **hot-air balloon**. Seek out a company who will take you up on a journey over the Chianti hills where you'll watch the early morning mist rise up off Siena, culminating in a hearty breakfast an hour later.

But whatever you do the days will no doubt revolve around eating, just as it has always been for the region's locals. The following restaurants should give you a taste of the area. On the main road between Florence and Siena, the SS22 (not the autostrada), about a kilometre north of Castelini en Chianti, is the fabulous bar/restaurant *Pietrafitta* (☎ 0577-741-123), set on a hilltop with panoramic views over the surrounding vineyards. Guests dine outside on the large terrace beneath parasols from where they can see glorious sunsets (try to get there before 8pm to witness this stunning sight). Italian-owned, the delicious food is produced by Alberto Giordano.

The dishes here are essentially Tuscan and all their meat comes from the famous Dario Cecchini in Panzano (well worth a visit). Typical dishes are braised beef in red wine, grilled lamb meatballs with a really spicy mustard sauce, and fresh pasta with seasonal sauces. The scrumptious desserts, including homemade ice cream, are made by Marie, an Australian. At about €310 per person excluding wine from what is an exceptional wine list, the Pietrafitta is well worth a visit.

In Greve in Chianti, *Cantinetta di Rignana* (☎ 055-852-601), Via Rignana, specializes in steak, and these are some of the finest you are ever likely to eat, in a farmhouse restaurant.

Radda in Chianti has several lovely restaurants. In particular, try *Ristorante Le Vigne* (☎ 0577-738-640), Podere Le Vigne, which is a charming old farmhouse restaurant surrounded by vineyards offering exceptionally good value.

If you find yourselves in San Gimigniano around lunchtime pop into *Ristorante Dorandò* (☎ 0577-941-862), Vicolo dell'Oro just off the Piazza Duomo, where medieval dishes are rustled up in cool 14th-century surroundings. Lots of the items on the amazingly descriptive menu are strange combinations but there is also pasta if you're not feeling adventurous.

Further information from: 🖳 www.umbrie2000.it and www.turismo.toscana.it.

All the hotel's 61 rooms and junior suites are decorated with antique furnishings, and have separate bath and shower. They are air conditioned and have good modern amenities and the hotel has an outdoor swimming pool. Double rooms from US$158/€181, executive doubles with Jacuzzis from US$171/€197, junior suite US$203/€233 all including breakfast. Book directly or through UK tour operator Magic Of Italy (UK ☎ 0870-027 0500).

You could very easily pass through Assisi without ever knowing about the wonderful little **Hotel le Silve di Armenzano** (☎ 075-801 9000, 🗎 075-801 9005, 🖳 www.lesilve.it, 06081 Localita Armenzano, Assisi), perched high up above the town on the peaceful hillside. But once you have found your way up the 13km of steep winding road to Armenzano, you'll find the most perfect seclusion where you can unwind among awe-inspiring views and the hotel's ancient stone buildings.

The hotel has 20 rooms: all of them are individually decorated in a rustic fashion and incorporate vital honeymoon amenities such as minibar, hairdryer, safe, TV, bath and shower with bathrobes and wonderful toiletries.

Most guests spend their days either exploring the hotel's 200-hectare estate on horseback, lazing around the outdoor pool, or visiting Assisi or Spello, two of

Umbria's most splendid hilltop villages. There is also tennis, mini-golf, table tennis and a sauna if you want it. Meals are taken on the terrace of the separate restaurant building, where the ambience is extremely laid back and there are lots of local dishes to set your mouth watering. Bed and breakfast from €83 per person per day, half board from €109 per person per day. Book direct or through UK tour operator Cita Italia (☎ 020-8686 5533).

Renting a place in Tuscany and Umbria

Renato's Tower is one of the most unusual little country hideaways. This 1000-year-old tower has one room on each of its four floors, starting with a kitchen/dining room on the first floor, then leading up to a second floor sitting area, a double bedroom with a shower room on the third, another sitting room on the fourth, and last, but not least, a delightfully bizarre battlement rooftop terrace complete with reclining chairs, sun umbrella and a small swimming pool. You don't have to worry about hours of clearing up as a maid comes for two hours a day three days per week, and you can eat out in nearby **Calzolaro** on the other nights! This delightfully quirky tower can be booked through UK agents **CV Travel** (UK ☎ 020-7591 2811), for around US$1841/£1295 per week in high season (June to mid-September), US$1083/£760 per week in low season for seven nights' villa rental only. Make sure you book Renato's Tower as soon as you can as it is very popular.

If Renato's Tower is booked up ask about alternatives such as **Casa Piccola**, near Cortona in Umbria, a pretty and romantic house for two surrounded by lovely gardens, with private use of a swimming pool – seven nights from US$1095/£770 to US$1472/£1035. For great views of the Cararra hills and proximity to the Cinque Terre, the ideal honeymoon hideaway is **Ca' di Carlino**, near Aulla in Tuscany. Tastefully restored with a private pool, seven nights here costs from US$1884/£1325 to US$2630/£1850.

Italian self-catering holiday specialist **Cottages to Castles** (☎ 01622-726 883, ⌨ www.cottagestocastles.com) offers numerous hand-picked properties throughout this region and can also arrange flights and car hire. Ask about **Apartment San Giovenale**, perched above the medieval city of Orvieto, or the unusual **La Torre Giordano**, a medieval tower for two in Asciano from US$768/£540 per week.

THE COAST

Hotel Splendido

The Splendido is another one of those hotels that has etched its way into people's minds so firmly that it has become an institution in its own right. Get any serious traveller to name the ten most luxurious hotels in the world, and the Splendido would be one of them.

The greatest thing about the Splendido is its marvellous location providing some of the most stunning views in the whole Mediterranean. You'll never tire of the picture postcard view of the pretty pink and yel-

---

HOTEL SPLENDIDO
(☎ 0185-267-801, 🖹 0185-267-806, ⌨ reservations@splendido.net), Viale Baratta, 16, 16034 Portofino, Italy
Reservations: Through the Leading Hotels of the World (see p12); or through tour operators Elegant Resorts, Abercrombie & Kent (see pp13-14)
Getting there: The Splendido can arrange transfers from Genoa and Milan airports and the local railway stations, but most guests arrive by car
Accommodation: 69 guest rooms: 44 bedrooms, 17 junior suites and eight suites
Amenities: Outdoor salt-water swimming pool, all-weather tennis courts, water-skiing, private speedboat charter with chauffeur, sauna, solarium, small gym, two restaurants, lounge and bar; golf nearby
Dress code: Elegant casual (European chic)
Weddings: Can be arranged
Minimum stay: None
Rates: Half board from US$347/€398; suites from US$529/€607 to US$740/€850, but ask about spring and autumn breaks which give a much better deal
Credit cards: Most major
Taxes and service charge: Included

low houses crowding the edge of the harbour, or studying the comings and goings on the yachts bobbing around in the waters below.

But there is also more to this hotel than impressive vistas: much of the hotel's character is derived from the clientele itself where elegant guests sit in their finely coutured Italian blazers and Gucci loafers, beside Versace sunglasses and Hermès scarves. You could never be in any doubt that a stay at the Splendido puts you in the epicentre of the sophisticated social life of this chicest of resorts. You probably won't realize quite what an art there is to lying on a sun-lounger until you've seen the elegant Italian women gently lower themselves in practised fashion – the whole place is just one long pose, nobody speaks to anyone and at times the place is so hushed that it's almost like being in a church!

The hotel is a former monastery, which is somewhat hard to relate to the amazing luxury and opulence that the same building houses now. The trompes l'oeil in the bedroom are exquisite, the Jacuzzi is an enjoyable extra, the saltwater pool terraced into the hillside is wonderful. Lunches washed down by chilled white wine on the Terrazza with the lattice of vines above and views of the port below are infinitely romantic.

Wander down the hill into the village for a drink, play tennis on the all-weather courts or else charter the hotel's private speedboat for chauffeur-driven trips to nearby villages and waterskiing.

Il Pellicano

Porto Ercole has long been the holiday destination of well-to-do Italian families, many of whom have their summer villas here, making it a very swish kind of place. But the best thing about Porto Ercole is the lovely Il Pellicano.

Much is made at Il Pellicano of the extraordinary love and bond that existed between Patsy Daszel and Michael Graham, the Anglo-American couple who built it, but quite why the fact they were so in love should make it such a romantic place slightly mystifies me. It is, however, indisputably romantic, mainly because of its location – it is built into a recess of the rocky peninsula, snugly enclosed by pines and cypresses hanging out over the dark, blue sea of this beautiful stretch of coastline.

Romantic, too, are the perfectly decorated bedrooms which manage to be smart as well as elegant with their bold reds and ochres juxtaposed against cool white walls and dark wooden beams. There are also individual touches such as the huge basket of Bulgari toiletries and knuckle-jointed towel rails in the bathroom.

But it is the staff who really make Il Pellicano so special. Everyone is helpful, courteous and takes time to get things right. Unlike most hotels, for instance, where your

IL PELLICANO
(☎ 0564-858-111, 🗎 0564-833-418, 🖳 www.pellicanohotel.com), Cala dei Santi, 1-58018 Porto Ercole, Grosseto, Italy
Closed: End Oct to end March
Reservations: Relais & Châteaux worldwide reservation numbers (see p12); or through tour operators Abercrombie & Kent or Seasons in Style (see pp13-14)
Getting there: The hotel can arrange transfers from Orbetello (14km), otherwise guests get a taxi or rent a car from Rome (150km), Florence (193km) and Siena (125km); from Rome, take the A12 towards Civitavecchia, exit at Orbetello towards Porto Ercole
Accommodation: 31 rooms, ten junior suites and nine de luxe suites
Amenities: Piano bar, candlelight barbecues, occasional dinner and dancing, sightseeing to Roman and Etruscan ruins, saltwater-heated swimming pool, private rocky beach, all-weather tennis court, waterskiing, sailing, snorkelling and fishing, spa with beauty centre and gym; horse-riding nearby and golf an hour's drive away
Dress code: Informal
Weddings: Wedding receptions for up to 120 people are catered for off season, but the hotel is not licensed to perform wedding ceremonies
Minimum stay: None
Rates: Double rooms from US$239/€274; junior suites from US$371/€427, suites from US$599/€672 with breakfast (half board compulsory in high season)
Credit cards: Visa, American Express, Diners Club
Taxes and service charge: included

breakfast is plonked down on a tray, at Il Pellicano they make the effort to lay the whole ensemble out on the balcony for you, complete with starched tablecloth, English jams, croissants, pain au chocolat, brioche, rye bread and even French toast, just to ensure they've catered for every taste.

Apart from choosing a superb location, the loving couple also did well to create such a classically Italian villa, so that despite being merely decades, as opposed to centuries, old the rambling rust-coloured villa with its heavy cloak of ivy and terracotta roof tiles looks as if it has been around forever.

We went to too many hotels in two and a half weeks, but it was at Il Pellicano that we unwound the most. When we arrived we had a late lunch for a few hours and by the end of it we felt we'd been there for weeks. It's the most wonderful, friendly hotel and completely unsnobby – you don't have to tip them to be nice to you. The interiors are very tasteful, in fresh English style, but it's the location that really makes it. **Nick and Vanessa McDonald Buchanan**

The management claims that this is not a glamorous hotel and indeed it does have a very discreet atmosphere, rather like a private club, but for these very reasons Il Pellicano has for years attracted all sorts of celebrities from Charlie Chaplin to Leonard Bernstein, so it's hardly a rustic retreat.

Dining at Il Pellicano is a rare treat, especially by candlelight out under the trees, with food delicious enough to merit Relais & Châteaux membership for the past 20-odd years and regular favourites such as riz aux langoustines al dente and the fabulous spaghetti Il Pellicano. It is pretty expensive but well worth it, though the barbecues seem overpriced at around €68 a head.

During the day, guests make the most of the hotel's lovely cliff-edge swimming pool which is surrounded by deck chairs and tasteful cream parasols. The views from the pool over the sea to the neighbouring islands of **Giglio** and **Giannutri** are truly dreamy, especially in the early morning light and again as the sun sets. Alternatively you can go down the steps to the water's edge and the rocky beach where several comfortable loungers are lined up on small individual terraces. From here you can dive straight out into the deep waters of the sea.

La Posta Vecchia

La Posta Vecchia is without doubt one of Italy's most exclusive hotels. Built right on the edge of the Mediterranean this grand palace was the former residence of John Paul Getty and, as such, boasts incomparable architecture and facilities.

When the brochure describes La Posta Vecchia as a place that 'speaks of harmony and beauty – luxury, peace and pleasure' it doesn't exaggerate. The villa is so elegant, with such a timeless air of refined beauty and splendour, that you really will be able to imagine yourselves as house guests of the big JP himself.

Because of the sheer size of the place and the fact that it has only ten rooms and

---

LA POSTA VECCHIA
(☎ 06-994 9501, 🖷 06-994 9507, 🖳 posta@relaischateaux.com), Palo Laziale, 1-00055 Ladispoli, Rome, Italy
Closed: November to March
Reservations: Relais & Châteaux worldwide reservation numbers (see p12) or through leading travel agents and tour operators to Italy (see p14)
Getting there: By car, 30 minutes from Rome Airport, 45 minutes from Rome city centre; from Rome take the SS1 towards Ladispoli, then follow signs to Paol Laziale
Accommodation: Ten double rooms and eight suites
Amenities: Restaurant, and large ocean-terrace for dining in the summer, 24-hour bar and room service, horse-riding and tennis nearby, golf courses 20 and 40 minutes away, excursions, indoor swimming pool, private beach, gardens, Roman antiquities museum, library, helipad, gym and beauty centre with spa and sauna
Dress code: Jacket and tie are required in the evenings
Weddings: Wedding receptions for up to 80 people are catered for in-house, but up to 250 can be accommodated if outside catering is used; La Posta Vecchia is not licensed to perform wedding ceremonies
Minimum stay: None
Rates: Double rooms from US$270/ €310, suites start from US$720/€827
Credit cards: Most major
Taxes and service charge: Not included

eight suites there seems to be endless space wherever you look. Originally a Roman post house and built as early as 1600, La Posta Vecchia is filled with priceless artefacts: Roman antiquities, exposed Roman mosaics, Venetian lamps, elegant marble busts, hand-woven French tapestries and original fine art adorn the walls. A series of salons occupies the ground floor, each one appointed with objets d'art gathered from all over the world.

Despite the existence of the beautiful terrace, just a few easy steps away from the sea, John Paul was encouraged by one of his mistresses to build an indoor swimming pool hewn out of solid granite. The pool is surrounded by huge arched windows through which the sunlight pours on to the shimmering pool below.

Each of the suites is decorated differently and is furnished with wonderful antiques from the 16th and 17th centuries, but modern comforts such as air conditioning, CD players, satellite TV, hairdryers and phones are not forgotten. The Medici, with its pink marble tub, is the suite to go for.

Fine Italian cuisine, worthy of its Relais & Châteaux membership, is served formally in the dining room each evening on beautiful marble tables set with sparkling crystal and silverware. During the day, guests spend their time around the pool, down at the villa's private beach or exploring the adjacent parklands. Horse-riding, tennis and golf can also be easily arranged, while **Cerveteri**, **Tarquinia** and Rome are not far away.

Hotel San Pietro

Perched high up above picturesque **Positano**, the jewel of the Amalfi coast, clinging to 100m of craggy rock face, it is certainly difficult to imagine a more spectacular location for a hotel. The panoramic views are incredible and the San Pietro is one of those hotels that could have been designed for honeymooners. With its terraces and balconies projecting over the sea, shaped according to the contours of the cliff edge, exterior staircases and sloping gardens full of massed bougainvillaea, you'd be hard pressed to find anywhere more romantic.

Each of the 61 bedrooms has its own balcony, every one offering breathtaking views across the **Tyrrhenian Sea**. Neapolitan ceramics, in yellow, blue, green and white hues, adorn the benches on the immense terrace, the floors of the rooms and the pink marble bathrooms. Everywhere you look there are views, facilitated by the clever use of glass panels.

Guests can either enjoy the hotel's small pool, or take the lift from the reception hall down an 88m shaft excavated into the cliffedge to the hotel's private dark-sand beach where there are watersports, a tennis court and a sundeck and bar nestled between the rocks and the sea.

Dinner is taken by candlelight outside on one of the hotel's terraces looking out over the bay. The cuisine pays tribute to the aromas and flavours of the south, with such favourites as langoustines sautés and risotto

HOTEL SAN PIETRO
(☎ 089-875-455, 🖷 089-811-449, 🖳 sanpietro@relaischateaux.com), Via Larito 2, I-84017 Positano, Italy
Closed: 1st November to 1st April
Reservations: Relais & Châteaux worldwide reservation numbers (see p12); or through tour operators Elegant Resorts, Abercrombie & Kent or Harlequin (see pp13-14)
Getting there: From the north take the A2 Napoli, A3 towards Salerno, exit Castellanmare di Stabia; 17km south of Sorrento, 60km south of Naples
Accommodation: 61 standard, superior and special rooms
Amenities: Tennis court, swimming pool, restaurant, bar, terraces, private beach with sundeck and bar, waterskiing, Jacuzzi, fishing, 24-hour shuttle to Positano, complimentary boat excursions
Dress code: Gentlemen are requested to wear long trousers in the restaurant, and although jackets and tie are not needed people usually dress up for dinner
Weddings: No
Minimum stay: None, but most guests stay for four or five days
Rates: Doubles from US$306/€352; suites from US$428/€491, breakfast included
Credit cards: Visa, American Express, Diners Club
Taxes and service charge: Included

aux langoustines, and is good enough to have earned the hotel Relais & Châteaux status long ago. It is difficult to fault this gracious hotel with its antique ambience; indeed, the only problem you are likely to encounter is managing to get a room in the first place.

Hotel Santa Caterina

Hotel Santa Caterina on the Amalfi coast is one of the world's top honeymoon hotels and a member of the Leading Small Hotels of the World. Sitting majestically on a clifftop surrounded by lemon groves and terraces, this charming villa boasts uninterrupted views out to sea and along the superb coastline.

The lounge and bar are linked by huge floor-to-ceiling windows which look onto a spectacular terrace where bougainvillaea grows on a pergola-style frame, making it the perfect spot from which to soak up the view. The gardens lead down to the sea and, just above sea level, to the hotel's beautiful pool and sun terrace. The pool can be reached by a lift or a flight of stairs. The only problem with the pool is that it loses the sun by about 3.30pm, prompting guests to make an early start with their sunbathing and producing competition for the best spots. Otherwise you can't fault this hotel.

Built during the early 1900s, it became a favourite venue for artistic, political and cultural figures of the time. The original interiors are beautiful and all the bedrooms are tastefully decorated in understated style.

The Santa Caterina has always been popular as a romantic destination due to its lovely gardens, immaculate service and incredible location, but the addition of its two garden cottages make it one of the most sought-after destinations in Europe.

What makes the two cottages, La Follia Amalfitana and Casa degli Sposi 'Giulietta & Romeo', so special is their superb layout maximizing the Santa Caterina's prime asset, the views. You can lie back in the huge white sunken Jacuzzi, with only a plate glass window separating you from the cliff edge and the views beyond. The two detached suites are totally isolated and are reached via a pathway through the lemon grove. Each one has a lounge with TV and minibar, a mini Jacuzzi in the bathroom, and a private terrace situated right above the sea. Giulietta & Romeo is laid out on two floors, with two bathrooms and a large terrace.

> **HOTEL SANTA CATERINA**
> (☎ 089-871-012, 📠 089-871-351, 💻 www.hotelsantacaterina.it), SS Amalfitana, 9, 84011 Amalfi (SA), Italy
> **Reservations**: The Leading Hotels of the World reservation numbers worldwide (see p12)
> **Getting there**: The hotel can arrange transfers in its air-conditioned Mercedes from either Naples Airport (US$81/€93) or Rome Airport (US$306/€352)
> **Accommodation**: 53 rooms, 14 suites
> **Amenities**: Panoramic restaurant, open-air restaurant above swimming pool, piano bar, swimming pool, private beach, fitness centre, massage room, lift from hotel to pool and beach
> **Dress code**: Casual
> **Weddings**: Wedding receptions for between 50 and 300 people can be catered for
> **Minimum stay**: None
> **Rates**: Doubles from US$200/€207 to US$400/€414; suites from US$400/€414; the cottages cost from US$475/€491 all include breakfast
> **Credit cards**: American Express, Eurocard, MasterCard, Visa
> **Taxes and service charge**: Included

The Santa Caterina is a really lovely, very private hotel with an old world elegance about it. The food was wonderful, the swimming off the rocky beach was nice and our bedroom was quite large and very comfortable and it had a private balcony overlooking the sea. Surrounded by interwoven lemon groves built into the cliffs it was so tranquil, and we enjoyed walking into Amalfi each afternoon to explore the town.

Diana and Peter Pásint Magyar

Other recommended hotels

People keeping telling me that their favourite hotel on the coast is **La Sirenuse** (☎ 89-875066, 📠 89-811798, 💻 info@sirenuse.it, Via Colombo 30, 84017 Positano). It was described to me by one recently returned honeymooner as 'spectacular, it might be my favourite hotel ever'. A member of Leading Hotels of the World (see p12 for reservation numbers) La Sirenuse has long been regarded as one of Italy's loveliest hotels and, apart from its dramatic cliff-top location overlooking the beach, is celebrated for its perfect taste, quiet elegance and intimate European charm. There are 60 bedrooms and two suites: superior and de luxe bedrooms and junior suites have balconies overlooking the sea, and there are an abundance of charming details such as the Acca Kappa toiletries and Jacuzzis in the bathroom. The hotel has a new Aveda Concept Spa, which is another plus point. Doubles cost from US$207/€238, suites from US$369/€424 including breakfast and taxes.

Greece
(BEST TIME: APRIL TO OCTOBER)

Greece is known for its incredible coastline of heavily indented shores and sandy beaches. Inland, however, are the vast mountains, such as the Pindus range which forms the country's backbone and Mt Olympus, which was immortalized in Greek mythology, as well as hundreds of villages where the pace of life has been little altered by modern society.

Greece, consisting of mainland Greece and the islands of the Aegean and Ionian seas, forms Europe's southernmost tip. The Aegean Sea, with its crystal clear waters, dolphins, and wonderful fresh fish is host to some of the most idyllic islands in the Mediterranean.

Crete is the largest island in Greece and forms the border between the Aegean and the Libyan seas and between Europe and Africa. This mountainous island comprises rocky coasts, vast sandy beaches, pebbled shores and over 3000 large and small caves, with impressive stalactite and stalagmite formations. Dotted throughout the countryside are dry-stone farm buildings, villages perched on high plateaux, monasteries, isolated castles and chapels. Home to Europe's very first civilization, the Minoan (2800-1150BC), today's Crete is the product of a succession of invading nations, each having left its influence over the years. Apart from its beaches, Crete is a fabulous place to hang out in the hundreds of cafés sipping a sweet coffee, or a glass of raki while playing backgammon.

GREECE
Sparkling seas, soaring mountains, magic skies, and that perfect little taverna on the waterfront – so good that even the gods chose it as their heaven on earth
When to go: April to October (except July and August which are too hot and busy)
Average maximum temperature °C

	JAN	FEB	MAR	APR	MAY	JUN	JUL	AUG	SEP	OCT	NOV	DEC
Athens	12	12	14	17	20	24	26	26	23	20	17	14

Capital: Athens
Flight times: to Athens from:
New York: 10¼ hours
LA: 18½ hours
London: 3¼ hours
Sydney: 22 hours
Approximate exchange rates: Euro (€) – £1 = €1.59, US$1 = €1.11, A$1 = €0.57
Time difference: GMT plus two hours (plus three hours from the last Sunday in March to the last Sunday in September)
Voltage: 220v AC, 50 Hz, round two-pin plugs
Combine with: Other parts of Europe
Country dialling code: ☎ 30
Further information: 🖥 www.gnto.gr

CRETE

Recommended hotels

Elounda Beach Hotel & Villas (☎ 0841-41412/3, 🖹 0841-41373, 💻 elohotel@eloun dabeach.gr, Elounda, near Aghios Nikolaos, Crete, GR-72 053; open March to November) is widely acknowledged as an outstanding hotel. If you want the full-blown luxury resort hotel and have money to burn go for one of Elounda Beach's waterfront bungalow suites.

Built in traditional Cretan-style with white plastered and stone walls, the bungalows have fantastic balconies with steps down to private platforms and the shimmering blue water below. Both the sea-view bungalows and the waterfront bungalows have luxury marble bathrooms with Jacuzzi tubs, TV in the bathroom and CD players. The bungalow suites have a private freshwater heated pool. Inside, the rooms are whitewashed with traditional furnishings, rattan sofas, and refreshing blue and white striped cotton fabrics on the beds.

As a member of the Leading Hotels of the World and Small Luxury Hotels of the World, the hotel's facilities are superb, but in my mind the best feature is the **Veghera Bar**, located at the end of a jetty with 360° sea views. This kind of luxury doesn't come cheap however; sea-view bungalows cost from US$450/€500, while the waterfront suites with pool start from US$1500/€1665 including breakfast, tax and service charges. Book through the Leading Hotels of the World or Small Luxury Hotels of the World reservation numbers worldwide (see p12), or UK tour operators Elegant Resorts or CV Travel.

Hotel Elounda Mare (☎ 0841-41102/03, 🖹 0841-41307, near Aghios Nikolaos, Crete, GR-720 53; open March to November) is also in the village of Elounda, but has the advantage of having 45 bungalows with their own private, or shared, swimming pool. From an aerial view this Relais & Châteaux hotel looks just incredible – a sprawling confusion of pristine white bungalows nestled along the contours of the Aegean, with scores of turquoise swimming pools separated from the similarly coloured sea by a lush band of fertile gardens.

The 44 rooms in the main body of the hotel start at US$108/€124, while the 45 bungalows cost from US$137/€156 including service charges. Book through Relais & Châteaux reservation numbers worldwide (see p12) or UK specialist Simply Travel (see p14).

THINGS TO SEE AND DO AROUND CRETE

The best way to get a feel for Crete is to hire a car. Don't miss the **Samarias Gorge** at the western end of the island. It is the largest and most imposing gorge in Europe and it is only possible to go through it in the summer months.

The route is not difficult but it will take around four to five hours and you'll need good footwear. Its width ranges from just three metres at its 'doors' to 150m in places, while the steep, vertical walls towering up to 500m high are absolutely staggering. The gorge makes a lovely walk with wild vegetation, a huge variety of grasses and the constant smell of wild herbs. In the middle of the gorge is **Samarias village**, where the church of Osia Maria has some beautiful wall paintings. At the other end of the gorge stop off at **Aghia Roumeli**, an isolated fishing village built on top of ancient Tarras, where you can revive yourselves with a dip in the crystal clear waters.

Further back down the coast lies **Hora Sfakion**, a beautiful, historic community with old houses and churches, from where it is possible to take a boat out to the island of **Gavdos**, or to the picturesque seaside communities of **Loutro** and **Aghia Roumeli**.

For further information visit 💻 www.crete.tourner.gr.

SANTORINI

The Tsitouras Collection

The Tsitouras Collection (TC as it is modestly referred to!), in exclusively upmarket Santorini, must be one of the most romantic places to stay in the Mediterranean. Perched on the top of a 300m cliff, this traditional-style villa has the most spectacular views.

The brochure, itself worthy of coffee-table status, describes the Tsitouras Collection as 'a work of sculptural art in that it is ravishingly beautiful from every possible angle, its spaces, its volumes, its ornamentation, its colours are all flawless'. The ridiculous thing is that this is not just a load of over-exuberant narrative – the place does actually do the brochure justice! It seems inaccurate to call the TC a hotel, because it is more like a work of art and a gallery than a private villa, let alone a hotel.

The TC comprises five suites each of which is designed, decorated and furnished in accordance with their names. The **House of the Sea** has fabulously framed English,

---

THE TSITOURAS COLLECTION
(☎ 0286-23747, 🖷 0286-23918), Fira, Firostefani, 847 00 Thira, Santorini, Greece
Reservations: Head office in Athens (☎ 01-362 2326, 🖷 01-363 6738) or through tour operators such as Mediterranean Experience or the Greek Islands Club (see p14)
Getting there: Fly to Santorini or take the ferry from Piraeus (Athens); TC will collect you for no extra charge
Accommodation: Five one and two bedroom guest houses
Amenities: There is no swimming pool or restaurant, although meals can be taken out on the terrace; air-conditioned rooms have hairdryer, minibar, CD player (but bring your own CDs), bathrobes, telephones
Dress code: Smart casual
Weddings: Yes
Minimum stay: Three nights
Rates: From US$410/€455 to US$610/€677 per couple with breakfast
Credit cards: Most major
Taxes and service charge: Included

Italian and German sea charts from the 16th to the 19th centuries adorning its walls, while a ceramic dish by Pablo Picasso sits in a glass case on top of an antique chest; the **House of the Winds** has high, vaulted ceilings in an airy light blue and a piano below; the **House of Portraits** has beautifully framed portraits gracing its walls, a 19th-century wooden baptismal font makes a novel coffee table, while the bedroom ceiling is covered in a fresco with cherubs at each corner; the **House of Porcelain** derives its name from the valuable white and blue 19th-century Minton and Royal Copenhagen porcelain plates that it contains; and the lilac-tinted **House of Nureyev** is the most romantic of them all, perched above the others and named after the collection of sketches depicting the late Rudolf Nureyev. This last house is the only one with its own veranda overlooking the caldera.

Elegant, decadent, serenely beautiful, the TC is all about aesthetics. It is the most stunning collection of rooms imaginable and if you can possibly afford to spend a few days there you'll never forget them.

Renting a villa in Greece

The luxurious **Terrace House**, in Nissaki, **Corfu**, is a true honeymoon hideaway and one of the most elegant and stylish places to stay in Corfu, particularly for a couple who want to be alone. The whitewashed interior with its bright Mediterranean colours and lovely framed prints perfectly complement the simple outdoor living on the spacious terrace overlooking a seemingly endless ocean.

The Terrace House is just one of a range of villas represented by UK tour operator, **CV Villas** (UK ☎ 0870-606 0013, 🖳 cv.travel@dial.pipex.com) – ask them in particular about the **Cottage**, the **Bijou Studio**, **Villas Eleni** and **Margarita**. As a rough guide a week's holiday in the Terrace House would cost around US$1223/£860 (peak season) and US$867/£610 (low season) per person including maid service, while a week at the Bijou would cost about US$697/£490 (peak) and US$511/£330 (low).

The **Greek Island Club** (UK ☎ 020-8232 9780) has a sumptuous house set in private grounds on a hilltop in the most beautiful and unspoilt part of Skopelos. Views from the house are spectacular, with most rooms having sea-facing terraces. Two weeks at **Villa Petaloutha** start from US$1049/£738 per person (based on two sharing) which includes return flights, transfers, car hire and maid service. Other recommended villas on the Greek Island Club's books are **Potami House** and **Kastani House** on the east and west coast respectively.

Six kilometres from Crete's north-west coast at Kalives, tucked away on a hillside in a secluded rural hamlet, is the beautifully-restored terrace of **Maheri Village Houses**. Here you can relax on your private terrace or beside a shared pool or hide away in a treehouse set among fig and olive trees before adjourning to the tiny kafenion opposite for a glass of wine. From US$799/£562 for two people sharing with **Simply Crete** (☎ 020-8541 2201, 💻 www.simply-travel.com).

If you want to be beside the sea, ask about **Tamarisk Cottages**, simple converted fisherman's cottages right on the edge of the sea near Agriolivado, perhaps the best – and quietest – sandy beach on the island of Patmos. Spend your time on the terrace dangling your toes in the sea, reading under the shade of the tamarisk trees, or stretched out on a sunlounger. Prices start from US$785/£552, based on two people sharing with **Simply Travel's Greece** (☎ 020-8541 2203, 💻 www.simply-travel.com).

Cyprus
(BEST TIME: APRIL TO OCTOBER)

Gently rolling hills, ancient vineyards and slumbering villages, wild and dramatic craggy clifftops and mountains, Cyprus is the island where Aphrodite, the Goddess of Love is said to have sprung from the sea. It is also the third largest island in the Mediterranean. If you need a better reason to come here, it has to be Anassa. Completed in 1998, Anassa in Polis, the ancient capital of Cyprus, is the most elegant, prestigious and luxurious five-star de luxe resort in the Mediterranean.

Anassa
Anassa, the classical Greek for 'Queen', is certainly fit for one. Sitting majestically on a headland perched above a magnificent sweeping beach, Anassa is surrounded by pine-covered mountains and olive groves.

A discreet and trendy hotel, its blue louvred shutters, terracotta tiled roofs and whitewashed walls resemble a traditional Cypriot village. In spring and summer, when the ground is carpeted with wildflowers and the air thick with the scent of lemon blossom, Anassa's palatial acres of cool marble are definitely the place to be cool. Once

---

CYPRUS
Sunshine and beaches, timeless and varied island scenery, and the best resort hotel in the Med
When to go: April to October but very hot in July and August
Average maximum temperatures °C

JAN	FEB	MAR	APR	MAY	JUN	JUL	AUG	SEP	OCT	NOV	DEC
14	17	19	25	28	29	30	32	31	29	22	17

Capital: Nicosia
Approximate exchange rates: Cyprus pound (C£) – £1 = C£0.94, US$1 = C£0.66, A$1 = C£0.34
Time difference: GMT plus two hours
Voltage: 240 AC
Combine with: Anywhere else in Europe
Country dialling code: ☎ 357
Further information: 💻 www.cyprustourism.org

you're there, this is the perfect soothing place to drop, flop and surrender. And if you want to get married surrounded by this Mediterranean scenery, the romantic and intimate Byzantine chapel in the recreated village square is the perfect place.

Exclusive, private and romantic, the path to the beach winds down through shaded gardens of olive, eucalyptus and carob trees. The spacious rooms are decorated in restful shades of pastel and neutral colours with cream marble floors to provide a warm ambience. All have air conditioning, a minibar, hairdryers, TV and a private balcony where you can have a romantic dinner for two.

The spacious suites have spectacular views over the shimmering Mediterranean and the gardens have their own pathways. Eleven have their own private plunge pool and the Adonis/Aphrodite one-bedroom Presidential Suite has an outdoor whirlpool where you can dream your days away. All have vast a marble bathroom with de luxe toiletries and bathrobes as you'd expect.

If you want the ultimate in privacy and luxury, rising above the three Presidential suites is the Alexandros Residence, a stunning private villa, complete with full-size swimming pool and personal chef.

Anassa is the place for lovers of elegant luxury; the odd classical bust, fine Greek antiques, and a Roman mosaic or two warm the monastic purity and nature looms large with views of sand, sea and sky through the

ANASSA
(☎ 06-888000, 🖷 06-322900, ⌨ anassa@thanos-hotels.com.cy), Anassa, PO Box 66006, CV-8840 Polis, Cyprus
Reservations: Through Preferred Hotels & Resorts Worldwide (see p12) or in the UK through Mediterranean Experience (see p14)
Getting there: Anassa is a 45-minute taxi ride from Paphos Airport 60km away
Accommodation: 186 rooms and suites
Amenities: Three outdoor pools and one heated indoor pool; watersports include scuba diving, sailing, waterskiing, paragliding and snorkelling; private yacht for charter, tennis, gym, table tennis and pool table; spa offering Thalassotherapy, sauna, massage, whirlpool spa, beauty treatments and hairdressing; boutique; four restaurants and two bar/cafés; five music, folkloric shows, barbecues and theme nights
Dress code: Smart casual
Weddings: Marriages in Byzantine chapel in the recreated village square; wedding package includes room upgrade, champagne, fruit and flowers on arrival, bridal bouquet and wedding cake, a candleit romantic dinner for two and a honeymoon breakfast in your room for US$592/C£390
Minimum stay: None; three days with wedding package
Rates: Suites from US$501/C£330, Adonis/Aphrodite Presidential Suite with outdoor whirlpool US$1671/C£1100; Alexandros Residence US$2241/C£1475
Credit cards: Most major
Taxes and service charge: Included

huge windows, between fluted columns and from balconies. Anassa's décor is dramatic but not cold, and as it is family-run you should feel immediately at home.

In between the jasmine and lavender-bordered pathways and rampant scarlet bougainvillea lie three outdoor pools: with cascading sculpted waterfalls, one a magnificent horizon pool and one with a mosiac that looks as if it's encrusted with jewels. Tennis and squash courts are also available, and inside lies a heated pool flooded with natural daylight, a gym and magnificent Roman-style spa offering the widest range of Thalassotherapy treatments in the Mediterranean. The restorative and rejuvenating properties of the sea may be just what you need after the wedding.

Four restaurants offer everything from poolside to gourmet dining and are supplied with fresh produce from Anassa's own farm and local fishermen. Entering the intimate Basilico, the gourmet restaurant with its vaulted ceiling is like walking into a monastery. Candlelit, this is the place for an intimate dinner – a fusion of Mediterranean herbs and oriental spices. The other two restaurants are light and airy so you feel as if you're dining 'alfresco' beside the sea. For a rustic change of scene, Latchi, the romantic fishing village nearby, has a great little fish restaurant. The wide range of watersports on offer includes waterskiing, paragliding, snorkelling, sailing, and scuba diving – PADI five palm. And, if you feel like going further afield, you can charter the hotel's private yacht and sail off into the sunset.

4 NORTH AMERICA

Canada
(BEST TIME: ALL YEAR ROUND)

There can be few parts of Canada as breathtaking as the province of Alberta, where the soaring mountains, blue-green lakes and glaciers are majestic both in summer and in winter. Despite the undeniable lure of Quebec City and Montreal, the Rockies are the epitome of Canada, the country of the great outdoors.

THE CANADIAN ROCKIES

The Canadian Rockies really reveal their awesome beauty from the slopes, as you look down on thousands of acres of tree-covered wilderness. Between them, Jasper, Banff and Lake Louise cover Canada's second largest ski area. But the Rockies are just as impressive in the summer when you can canoe on the lakes, whitewater raft down the rivers or just enjoy the stunning mountain scenery on leisurely walks.

Lake Louise is the archetypal winter wonderland: you can take a horse-drawn sleigh-ride on a moonlit night with only the dark shadows of the vast craggy mountains all around you, or be pulled on a sled by pure-bred huskies through the trees and snow-covered creeks.

Jasper National Park is Canada's largest and oldest Rocky Mountain park and it boasts some of the most magical lake and mountain wildernesses you are likely to encounter anywhere in the world. The park spans 4200 sq miles of rushing rivers, sparking lakes, virgin forest and

---

CANADA
Skiing and hiking in the Rockies and scenic journeys by luxury train
When to go: All year round
Average maximum temperatures °C

	JAN	FEB	MAR	APR	MAY	JUN	JUL	AUG	SEP	OCT	NOV	DEC
Toronto	-2	0	2	12	19	24	26	24	20	12	5	1
Calgary	-3	-2	2	10	10	18	23	21	17	12	4	0

Capital: Ottawa
Flight times: to Vancouver from:
  New York: 8 hours
  LA: 3 hours 10 minutes
  London: 10 hours
  Sydney: 18¾ hours
Approximate exchange rates: Canadian dollar (C$) – £1 = C$2.20, US$1 = C$1.53, A$1 = C$.81
Time difference:
  Toronto: GMT minus 5 hours
  Vancouver: GMT minus 7 hours
Voltage: 110v AC, 60 Hz, two-pin plugs
Combine with: USA, Central America, the Caribbean as a stopover, Australia, New Zealand, South Pacific
Country dialling code: ☎ 1
Further information: 🖳 www.travelcanada.ca

THE ROCKY MOUNTAINEER

The Rocky Mountaineer is a luxury train that makes two-day excursions through the Canadian Rockies.

The 'most spectacular train trip in the world', as the company quite rightly calls it, takes you through vast landscapes where you could see mighty bears swiping at salmon in the river one minute, an eagle soaring overhead the next, as well as numerous elk, deer, moose and osprey.

This fabulous blue and white train has to be the most romantic way to see this untamed landscape – up close but cocooned in luxury – with every last detail of the train and the journey carefully planned so as to maximize viewing potential and comfort.

You can choose from several different routes, between Vancouver and Jasper, or between Vancouver and Banff and on to Calgary.

If you can afford it do opt for the super-luxurious **Gold Leaf Service** (US$713 compared to US$353 Red Leaf Service). Not only does this give you better seats travelling on

an upper deck in a dome car with all-glass sides, but there is a fabulous observation platform below which is great for taking pictures and videos, and a proper art deco-style restaurant car complete with silver cutlery, white linen and china where you can enjoy gourmet meals.

Whichever route you take, the train stops overnight in **Kamloops**. The next morning the train departs early for Jasper (perfect for Jasper Park Lodge) or on to Banff, for Banff Springs Hotel.

The Rocky Mountaineer can be booked from the US and Canada (US and Canada toll-free ☎ 800-665-7245); other countries check the international directory at ⌨ www.rkymtnrail.com. Alternatively book through tour operators such as Thomas Cook or Connections Worldwide (see p11).

Melissa Graham's *Trans-Canada Rail Guide* (Trailblazer, see p 318) is a useful guidebook that gives full details about what to see along the way on this fascinating rail

majestic snow-clad mountains. The best thing about Jasper is its relative quietness, especially compared to Banff which is much more touristy.

Jasper is surrounded by emerald lakes, the most incredible of which is **Maligne Lake**, the second largest glacier-fed lake in the world. There is a spectacular walk from the very top of **Maligne Canyon** right down to the canyon floor. If you are looking for a thrill, Maligne River is the scene for whitewater rafting – you can book at Jasper Park Lodge. Jasper, Banff and Lake Louise are within easy driving time of each other, so you can easily leave Jasper after lunch and arrive in Lake Louise before dinner.

The respected Canadian Pacific/Fairmont Hotels and Resorts offer three exceptional places to stay in the Rockies. The stunning cream-coloured **Château Lake Louise** (☎ 403-522-3511, 🖹 403-522-3834, Lake Louise, Alberta, TOL 1EO) enjoys an incredible picture-postcard setting with nothing but mountains and pine trees around it and the vast Lake Louise stretching out in front. From Bavarian curling on the frozen lake to dog-sled and horse-drawn sleigh rides, bonfires and hot chocolate on a cold winter evening, this 'Diamond in the Wilderness' really has got it sussed. Although voted the most romantic hotel in North America, don't expect a small intimate chalet. With 489 well-equipped alpine guest rooms including 81 suites, Château Lake Louise is pretty vast, but with scenery and space like this you're hardly going to feel claustrophobic. The leisure facilities are superb with four restaurants, two bars, a deli and a night-club, indoor pool and whirlpool, steam room and gym, as well as massage. In summer you can choose from canoeing, hiking, mountain biking, horse-riding, whitewater rafting, rock-climbing, tennis and fishing, while the opportunities for winter sports are endless. The three ski mountains around Banff and Lake Louise jointly form Canada's second largest ski area and the runs suit everyone from beginners to intermediate with an average of 30ft of snow guaranteed. The 'Height of Romance' package offers three nights in a de luxe lakeside room, breakfast in bed each morning, a gourmet picnic basket, and his and hers massages, a fondue for two and a moonlit horse-drawn sleigh ride from C$1578/US$1052.

Not far away is **Jasper Park Lodge** (☎ 403-852-3301, 🖹 403-852-5107, PO Box 40, Jasper, Alberta), set in 1000 acres of the big scenery of Jasper National Park. This is a proper lodge where moose heads stare down at you from the walls, glass chandeliers are replaced by light fittings made from antlers, real log fires roar in stone hearths, and deep cushioned sofas are covered in plaids in warm country colours. You can see why this was the setting for Hollywood films and celebrities such as Marilyn Monroe have signed the register. The lodge has 446 rooms all in authentic log cabins or cedar chalets spread along the lake shore – room service is by bicycle! The facilities are awesome. You can choose between skiing, hiking and fishing, horse-riding, canoeing, mountain biking or the 18-hole championship golf course. There are four restaurants, two lounges featuring regional Canadian cuisine, a café, a pub, and of course a health club. Look out for packages such as the 'Romantic Getaway' which includes two nights in a suite with fireplace, wine and cheese on arrival, breakfast in bed one morning, and a gourmet dinner for C$349/US$239 per person.

If a choice of 17 restaurants and a world-class spa with cascading waterfalls and natural hot springs sounds more your thing, **Banff Springs Hotel** (☎ 403-762-2211, 📄 403-762-6055, PO Box 960, Banff, Alberta TOL 0C0), built to resemble a Scottish baronial castle, might be worth considering; 'Romance in the Rockies' costs from C$244/US$170 per couple per night.

Reservations for all properties through Fairmont Hotels and Resorts (🖥 www.fairmont.ca), toll-free from US/Canada (☎ 800-441-1414); in the UK through tour operator Connections Worldwide (☎ 01494-473173, 🖥 www.connectionsworldwide.net).

USA
(BEST TIME: ALL YEAR ROUND)

The USA has so much to offer from the sunny Californian coast and the awesome scenery of the **Grand Canyon**, to the snowy slopes of **Colorado**, as well as the glittering cities of **New York**, **San Francisco** and **New Orleans**, and the famous art

---

USA

Everything from cruising the Californian coast to skiing in Colorado and some of the most exciting cities in the world

When to go: All year round

Average maximum temperatures °C

	JAN	FEB	MAR	APR	MAY	JUN	JUL	AUG	SEP	OCT	NOV	DEC
Los Angeles	18	18	18	19	20	21	23	24	24	22	20	18
San Francisco	12	15	16	17	19	20	21	21	22	20	17	14
Phoenix	17	19	23	27	32	36	38	36	34	29	22	18
Denver	6	8	10	15	20	26	29	29	25	19	11	8
New York	5	5	9	15	20	24	27	26	23	18	12	6
Tampa	21	22	23	26	29	30	30	30	30	27	24	22

Capital: Washington DC

Flight times: to LA from:
New York: 5½ hours
London: 11 hours
Sydney: 11 hours
to New York from:
London: 7½ hours
Sydney: 20½ hours

Approximate exchange rates: US dollar (US$) – £1 = US$1.42, A$1 = US$0.53

Time difference: West coast: GMT minus 8 hours
East coast: GMT minus 5 hours

Voltage: 110v AC, 60 Hz, two-pin plugs

Combine with: Canada, Mexico and Central America, the Caribbean, Australia, New Zealand, South Pacific as a stopover

Country dialling code: ☎ 1

deco hotels of fashionable **Miami Beach** and the islands of the **Florida Keys**. The options are endless, so I've picked some of the United States' most famously romantic hotels and some destinations to give you a taster of the country's enormous honeymoon potential.

LOS ANGELES

Until I went there I have to admit that I wasn't too convinced about California as a honeymoon destination but one look at the sun-drenched coastline, lined with its characteristic petticoat palms, and I was won over.

The really classic thing to do is to fly into either **LA** or **San Francisco**, hire a car – perhaps some kind of racy red convertible or a sleek Cadillac – and drive the 400-mile coastline along the famous Highway One between these two fantastic cities. It is truly stunning and the hotels en route couldn't be more romantic.

Los Angeles, the city of beautiful people and, when they are past their prime, facelifts, is a fun place to start or finish your honeymoon. Wander down **Sunset Boulevard**, shop on **Rodeo Drive**, or take a tour around the affluent streets of **Hollywood** and **Beverly Hills**. For a hassle-free honeymoon I'd avoid downtown LA, and stick to the beaches such as **Venice** and **Malibu** for your entertainment. LA is also ideally placed for visiting **Disneyland** or **Universal Studios**.

The Regent Beverly Wilshire

The Regent Beverly Wilshire, which overlooks Tiffany & Co, Saks and Valentino, on Beverly Hills' **Rodeo Drive**, cannot fail to give a romantic start to your holiday. This hotel has been at the centre of culture and glamour for over 73 years. And as the hotel featured in *Pretty Woman*, the Regent has now gone down in the annals of history as one of those places that epitomises romance: as you stroll through the lobby you cannot forget the images of Julia Roberts strutting along in her thigh-length boots and Richard Gere's long raincoat.

Having undergone a US$35 million renovation, completed in 1999, the Regent has 395 rooms in all, and the city's largest number of suites at 120. It can now also boast two presidential suites – one a penthouse. Prices have gone up accordingly. It has also cleverly achieved two distinct hotels in one, with the Wilshire Wing remaining classic and traditional and the Beverly Wing a more contemporary look and feel. But the Regent has not lost its romantic feel. There's something magical about it, some kind of feeling that you truly have arrived – which makes your walk just that little bit more swanky as you stride out onto Rodeo Drive.

All the rooms have air conditioning, colour televisions in the bedroom and some in the bathroom and wonderfully comfortable beds. The bathrooms are marble and divided from the bedroom by a spacious walk-in closet. There is an abundance of white fluffy towels, large bottles of toiletries,

THE REGENT BEVERLY WILSHIRE
(☎ 310-275-5200, US toll-free ☎ 800-427-4354, 🖷 310-274-2851), 9500 Wilshire Boulevard, Beverly Hills, CA 90212-2405, USA
Reservations: The Leading Hotels of the World or Regent Hotels toll-free reservation numbers worldwide (see pp12-13)
Getting there: 30 minutes by taxi ($25) from LA's international airport; the hotel can arrange transfers at an approximate cost of US$94 one way
Accommodation: 395 rooms including 120 guest suites
Amenities: 24-hour personal room attendant, two phone lines in each room, voicemail, dataports for Internet access, in-room safes; video and Internet, DVD players, complimentary newspaper and shoeshine
Dress code: Elegant casual; jackets are not required in the dining room, but recommended
Weddings: The hotel caters for wedding receptions in rooms which hold from 10-1000 guests
Minimum stay: None
Rates: US$405 to US$590; suites from US$600; Presidential Suites US$5500-7500
Credit cards: Most major
Taxes and service charge: 15.68% tax

a separate shower, white bathrobes and, best of all, a perfectly positioned TV in some so you can lie back among the foaming bubbles and watch classic movies. Perhaps the most romantic is the Veranda Suite, where Warren Beatty lived for nearly ten years. A studio loft on a private floor, it includes a canopied bed, high French windows, a large pink marble bathroom and a private roof-top garden.

The hotel's facilities include an outdoor Mediterranean-style swimming pool, a state-of-the-art fitness centre, spa with steamroom, sauna and two Jacuzzis. From award-winning dining ranging from casual to sophisticated, and trendy cocktails in the bar, the Regent Beverly Wilshire hotel has a reputation for some of the best places to eat or drink in the city and serves one of the most authentic afternoon teas outside of London.

Hotel Bel-Air

Hotel Bel-Air has long been recognized as one of the world's most incredible hotels and wins awards every year. As travel journalists are fond of saying: 'it's not so much a hotel, as a way of life'. The only problem is it can be difficult getting a room if you are a mere nobody!

Located in the prestigious Bel-Air district, just a mile down the road from **Beverly Hills**, this low-rise hotel is the prettiest in LA. Its 94 rooms, including 42 suites, are all beautifully ulphostered, furnished with exquisite Italian linen and decorated with antiques and art. These are all built in one- and two-storey red-tiled Mediterranean villas set amongst 11 acres of beautifully maintained gardens, giving the hotel a tranquil atmosphere in this frenetic city.

The best suite is No 160, the Grace Kelly suite, which has a sitting room with wood-burning fireplace and a bedroom opening on to its own private terrace with Jacuzzi and a whiff of jasmine, while the best room is No 240, which also has a private terrace and its own tangerine tree.

All the rooms have air conditioning with individual controls, cable TV and VCR, stereo and CD, minibar, plus all the toiletries and bathroom goodies you could possibly imagine, right down to bathroom scales and nail files.

> **HOTEL BEL-AIR**
> (☎ 310-472-1211, 📄 310-476-5890, 🖥 www.hotelbelair.com), 701 Stone Canyon Boulevard, Los Angeles, CA 90077 USA
> **Reservations**: The Leading Hotels of the World's toll-free reservations numbers worldwide (see p12); in the US toll-free ☎ 1-800-648-4097, or through Mason Rose (🖥 www.Masonrose.com)
> **Getting there**: 13 miles from LA's international airport
> **Accommodation**: 52 rooms, 42 suites
> **Amenities**: 24-hour fitness centre; beauty salon; 24-hour room service including in-room massage; video library; on-site limo and car rental; multilingual concierge; boutique; outdoor heated oval swimming pool; tennis, golf and other sporting facilities available nearby
> **Dress code**: Jacket in dining room after 6pm
> **Weddings**: Can arrange weddings and receptions
> **Minimum stay**: Two nights
> **Rates**: Doubles cost from around US$375/£270; suites from US$625/£430
> **Credit cards**: Most major
> **Taxes and service charge**: 14% tax,

Recommended hotels

The Peninsula, Beverly Hills (☎ 310-551-2888, 📄 310-788-2319, 🖥 pbh@peninsula.com, 9882 South Santa Monica Boulevard, Beverly Hills, CA 90212), equally popular with locals and visitors, is a discreet three-storey spacious hotel in the heart of Beverly Hills where you can mingle with locals – and the locals around here happen to be the likes of Julia Roberts, Catherine Zeta Jones and Michael Douglas.

Looking more like a villa than a hotel and spread in beautiful gardens, the hotel's Club Bar is the rendezvous for the Hollywood crowd and makes a glamorous start to a honeymoon. The Peninsula, Beverly Hills, has a fabulous rooftop swimming pool where you can hire your own cabana – like a mini marquee – to have a massage, pedicure or manicure around the pool. A courtesy Rolls Royce waits to take you shopping on nearby Rodeo Drive, and the beautiful beaches of Santa Monica are also nearby. You can also rent villa apartments in the hotel grounds if you want more privacy.

Superior doubles cost from US$375, suites from US$500, villa US$2500. Book direct in the US/Canada toll-free (☎ 800-462-7899) or through Leading Hotels of the World reservation numbers worldwide (see p12) or UK specialist tour operator, North America Travel Service (see p11).

CALIFORNIAN COASTAL ROUTE

Four Seasons Biltmore (Santa Barbara)

Nestled on **Butterfly Beach** at the foot of the **Santa Ynez Mountains**, the Four Seasons Biltmore with its splendid Moorish architecture, turreted rooms and individual cottages spread throughout blossoming gardens is, not surprisingly, popular as a wedding location.

The Four Seasons Biltmore has the feel of a really lavish, grand hotel with 217 rooms spread out over 20 acres of tropical landscaped grounds. It is obviously a resort for those looking for the ultimate in everything – from the Olympic-size beach-side swimming pool, to the health centre, the two large dining rooms, the croquet lawns and tennis courts. Like its sister Regent properties throughout the world, the Biltmore is run impeccably offering guests every kind of facility and luxury imaginable in very slick surroundings.

The bedrooms are certainly full of all mod cons, with twice-daily maid service, terry-cloth bathrobes, marble bathrooms, complimentary newspapers delivered each morning, a fully-stocked private bar, TV and VCR, radio, in-room safes and hairdryers. Some rooms also have fireplaces which are wonderful on spring evenings when there's a chill in the air.

The views out to sea, looking across to the **Channel Islands**, are what really make the Biltmore. With its beautiful, long sandy beach: you can even walk the whole way round the bay into town. One of the most magical experiences is to sit out on the front terrace at dawn watching groups of whales as they swim across the bay.

> **FOUR SEASONS BILTMORE (SANTA BARBARA)**
> (☎ 805-969-2261, 🖷 805-565-8323), 1260 Channel Drive, Santa Barbara, CA 93108, USA
> **Reservations**: Four Seasons reservation numbers worldwide (see p13)
> **Getting there**: 20 minutes from Santa Barbara Municipal Airport
> **Accommodation**: 217 rooms and suites, including 12 cottages
> **Amenities**: Bar, three restaurants featuring contemporary California cuisine and ocean views; casino, two health clubs, massage and spa treatments, three flood-lit tennis courts, croquet and shuffle-board, putting green, bicycles, two swimming pools; nearby golf, horse-riding, sailing, hiking, wineries and quaint shops
> **Dress code**: Smart casual
> **Weddings**: The Biltmore is a very popular venue for wedding ceremonies and receptions, from small private gatherings in the gardens to a reception for 500 people in Le Pacific Ballroom
> **Minimum stay**: None
> **Rates**: Superior Doubles cost from US$435, suites from US$895
> **Credit cards**: Most major
> **Taxes and service charge**: 10% tax, service charge discretionary

The Biltmore offers great Romance Packages during the week, with one night's accommodation, a bottle of champagne on arrival and a candle-lit dinner in **La Marina** restaurant where you can gaze out across the Pacific Ocean, for US$610 each.

San Ysidro Ranch

For a more intimate hotel with a more personal feel go for the San Ysidro Ranch, up in the foothills of **Montecito**, the other side of Highway 101. With 38 bedrooms/suites housed in 20 separate cottages, the San Ysidro is the perfect place to get away from it all.

SAN YSIDRO RANCH
(☎ 805-969-5046, US toll-free ☎ 800-368-6788, 📠 805-565-1995, 💻 www.sanysidroranch.com) 900 San Ysidro Lane, Montecito, California 93108, USA
Reservations: Direct
Getting there: 85 miles north of Los Angeles, 20 minutes from Santa Barbara Municipal Airport
Accommodation: 38 bedrooms/suites in 20 cottages
Amenities: Stonehouse Restaurant featuring American regional cooking, outdoor poolside dining and 24-hour room service, the Plow & Angel Pub built in 1893, 49ft heated swimming pool, health club facility with cardiovascular equipment and free weights, two tennis courts, tennis professional, hiking trails, golf nearby
Dress code: Elegant casual
Weddings: Popular for weddings and receptions
Minimum stay: None
Rates: Double Rooms from US$375; de luxe cottages from US$695
Credit cards: Most major
Taxes and service charge: 10% tax will be added to your bill, service charge discretionary

The emphasis is on simple, exquisite furnishings in elegant colours, with oak floors, exposed beams and French windows – nothing is over-chintzed here making it the definite choice if you don't like your furnishings too over-the-top. Don't think I mean by this that it's not luxurious – it's romantic enough to have been chosen by Jackie and John F Kennedy as their honeymoon destination, while Lawrence Olivier married Vivien Leigh on the lawn.

Each cottage has its own private deck, many with spa pools, and inside there are real log fireplaces which are lit on winter evenings. They have all the usual amenities such as VCR, king-size beds, goose down comforters and newspapers delivered to your room each morning. The cottages have been cleverly designed so that once you've walked up your own private pathway you feel totally secluded; it's rather like having your own summer home in the countryside.

The nearby hills are great for walking, whether it's just for a short amble or a more challenging day-long hike with a picnic provided by the hotel. The hotel can arrange a whole host of activities in the area from hang-gliding to Channel Island cruises, polo, winery tours and ocean or lake fishing. There's also a 49ft heated swimming pool, tennis courts, exercise facilities, and a full array of body and beauty treatments are available in the privacy of your own cottage.

I loved the San Ysidro. To me it was the perfect combination of comfort, luxury and privacy in very informal, relaxed surroundings. This ranch will provide you with the type of service you won't forget in a hurry. The staff, dressed casually in denim shirts, floral ties and chinos, always seem to be walking smartly off towards a cottage armed with champagne in an ice bucket, a plate of strawberries and a friendly smile. Stylish and efficient but casual, which just about sums up the hotel itself.

Post Ranch Inn

Post Ranch Inn has long been recognized as one of the world's most incredible hotels. This is where the likes of the Hollywood jetset come to get away from it all.

The Post Ranch is particularly famous for its architecture, which is a combination of post-modern and environmentally friendly steel, concrete and redwood huts. The architects were so careful to protect the surrounding environment that only one tree was moved during building. The result is the most awesome hotel protruding from and nestled into the cliff edge, with the particularly stunning **Sierra Mar** restaurant where huge sheets of glass, held together by steel tubing, stand between you and the Pacific.

Some of the 30 lavish rooms are virtually submerged in the earth and surrounded by wild flowers, others are amid the trees looking out over the giant redwood forest towards the mountains. But the most famous rooms are the ten coast houses which hang right out from the cliff edge some 1200ft above the Pacific, so that all you can see through the large glass windows is the seemingly endless ocean.

Each room comes complete with the kind of luxuries that are standard in this quality of hotel, such as king-sized beds, stereo systems, minibar and hairdryers. But what makes this hotel quite so incredible is all the not-so-standard extras: each room has its own massage table – inspired by Barbara Streisand – its own spa baths, a selection of walking sticks, a roaring open fire for when you come in from your walks, and a private deck so that you can gaze out over the magical Big Sur wilderness day and night. There are even star-gazing lectures to help you make the most of the area's incredible night skies.

Highlands Inn, Park Hyatt Carmel

Highlands Inn, just as the brochure says, is 'a visual masterpiece'. The awesome surroundings can certainly take much of the credit for making this hotel so incredible, but credit must also go to the architects and interior designers who have made this such a magical place. Located on the **Monterey Peninsula**, only four miles south of pretty Carmel and just up the road from Big Sur, the hotel occupies a remote stretch of cliff-side pine forest overlooking **Point Lobos** with fabulous views of the big, blue Pacific stretching out beneath you. Wherever you are in the hotel the views seem to dominate.

Outside, the hotel is built along the contours of the hillside with weather-boarded cottages clustered in small groups and arranged to provide the best views from the rooms. The lovely suites all feature spa baths, separate living areas, wood-burning stoves, decks with fantastic views, plus their own fully-stocked kitchens. The bedrooms are modern in style and have good amenities such as bathrobes and great aromatherapy toiletries in the bathrooms, king-sized beds, TV and VCR, minibar, iron and board, hairdryers, and binoculars to maximize the views.

Below the cottages is the hotel's lovely kidney-shaped swimming pool, surrounded by comfortable loungers and café-like tables and chairs.

While the outside décor is essentially rustic, inside the Highlands Inn is a masterpiece of design made up of glass walls, skylights, precisely angled beams and

---

POST RANCH INN
(☎ 831-667-2200, 📠 831-667-2824), Highway 1, Big Sur, Monterey County, CA 93920, USA
Reservations: Small Luxury Hotels of the World toll-free reservation numbers worldwide (see p12)
Getting there: 35 miles from Monterey Peninsula Airport; the hotel does not arrange transfers as guests really need their own car to drive around the area
Accommodation: 30 rooms
Amenities: Outdoor heated swimming pool, basking pool, spa, exercise room, health and beauty facilities, nearby beaches and horse-riding, Sierra Mar restaurant serving Californian cuisine, limited room service, gift shop; activities include hiking, yoga and star-gazing lectures
Dress code: None
Weddings: The hotel can host weddings and receptions for up to 50 people
Minimum stay: None
Rates: Double rooms from US$455 to US$835
Credit cards: American Express, Visa, MasterCard
Taxes and service charge: Not included

HIGHLANDS INN, PARK HYATT CARMEL
(☎ 831-620-1234, 📠 831-626-8105), 120 Highlands Drive, Carmel, CA 93923, USA
Reservations: Hyatt Hotels and Resorts reservation numbers worldwide (see p13)
Getting there: The hotel is 10 miles from Monterey Peninsula Airport and 90 miles from San Francisco Airport, transfers not included
Accommodation: 142 rooms including 105 suites
Amenities: Restaurants, lounge, concierge, fine dining, swimming pools, health club, plus tennis, golf, horse-riding and whale-watching nearby
Dress code: None
Weddings: Ceremonies and receptions for up to 115 seated or 165 standing are catered for and specialized full service wedding coordinators available
Minimum stay: Guests staying at the weekend must stay for two nights
Rates: Doubles from US$285 to US$460; suites from US$435 to US$765
Credit cards: Most major
Taxes and service charge: Not included

THINGS TO SEE AND DO ON THE CALIFORNIAN COASTAL ROUTE

Just an hour and a half's drive up the coast from LA is **Santa Barbara**, a relatively small city renowned for its year-long sunshine, sheltered coastal location and stunning backdrop of the Santa Ynez mountains. The architecture of the town and the surrounding area as well as street names such as Castillo Drive give the place a Spanish feel. Santa Barbara is a heady mixture of celebrity estates, sun-drenched golden beaches, rugged mountains and terraced vineyards.

The actual town is very beautiful and a really lovely place to wander around and browse through the shops. There are shops devoted to olive oils and nuts, antiques, children's clothes, shoes and lots of home interior and houseware stores. Stop for coffee and a Danish at the *Santa Barbara Coffee Roasting Company*, just off State St, or for the most wonderful pizzas and a bottle of cold Budweiser at the *California Pizza Kitchen*.

Moving up the coast, it's a good idea to take **Highway 154** from just outside Santa Barbara. This road will take you high up into the spectacular Santa Ynez mountains, past **Lake Cachuma** which is great for boating, fishing or even just picnics, and on to the towns of Solvang and Santa Ynez.

Solvang itself is certainly worth a look, for its remarkable Danish architecture. The whole town was only built around 40 years ago, and resembles something out of a Hans Christian Andersen fairy tale: there is a museum commemorating the writer and many of the streets have Danish names.

The advantage in staying in Solvang is that it is a great base from which to see the dozen or so surrounding **wineries**, for which this region is famous. All the local vineyards are open daily for tastings and tours, but perhaps the best and most original way of touring the area is by bicycle. Ask at the visitor centre in Solvang about cycling winery tours – you can always get a taxi home and pick up your bikes the next day should you get carried away sipping chilled glasses of Sauvignon Blanc overlooking the vineyards.

Another possibility is taking to the skies in a glider. For around US$135 you can take the 35-minute Mile High flight from Santa Ynez Airport and see this truly spectacular landscape from above, not to mention looking out for red-tailed hawks and the occasional golden eagle, and even taking a hand at the controls. For further details contact **Windhaven Glider Rides** (☎ 805-688-2517).

The stretch of road along Highway One between **Hearst Castle** and **Monterey** is breathtaking, mainly for its views but quite often due to the 1000ft cliff drops and numerous narrow bridges – it's an experience! Make sure you stop off at **Big Sur** where the Santa Lucia mountains meet the Pacific Ocean – the views from the rugged clifftop are fantastic. North of Big Sur, perched on a rocky cliff 100ft above the pounding surf, is a lovely place for lunch – *Rocky Point Restaurant* (☎ 408-624-2933). If you stop off in Big Sur for a few days make sure you visit *Ventana Inn* (US toll-free ☎ 800-628-6500) and sample its famous gourmet food.

Go to **Carmel** to shop but only stay if you don't mind the mass of tourists in the summer and if you have an abundance of cash as it is wildly expensive. Sunday lunch at *Blums* in downtown Carmel is legendary.

Monterey Peninsula is a good place to base yourselves for a few days as there's loads to do both inland and of course, out on the water. If you want to get out on the water why not try sea-kayaking with **Cannery Row's Adventures by the Sea (ABTS)**. Apart from kayaking trips to see the sea otters, ABTS has mountain bikes and roller blades for hire as well as guided bike tours to Big Sur, Carmel and 17-Mile Drive. A great roller-blading trail runs from the easterly end of Monterey to **Lovers' Point** in Pacific Grove out to Seaside. There are hordes of fantastic **restaurants** in Monterey - make sure you try at least one of them.

For further information see ▱ www.visit california.com.

beautifully lacquered wooden floors and pillars, the whole effect set off by cleverly placed low-voltage spotlights.

The Highlands Inn has long been popular for weddings – the hotel's gazebo looking out over the Pacific Ocean makes the perfect place to take your vows. The cliff-hanging restaurant, the **Pacific's Edge**, with its dramatic ocean views, features world-class, award-winning cuisine, and at the **California Market** guests can dine inside or alfresco on a deck overlooking the spectacular coastline.

Other recommended hotels

Simpson House Inn (☎ 805-963-7067, US toll-free ☎ 800-676-1280, ▤ 805-564-4811, ▱ www.simpsonhouseinn.com, 121 East Arrellaga St, Santa Barbara, CA 93101) is a beautiful Victorian inn right in the middle of town, offering more moderately priced bed-and-gourmet-breakfast in 14 beautifully decorated bedrooms, suites and garden cottages. Sandstone walls and tall hedges screen the inn and expansive lawns are dotted with oaks and magnolias.

The rooms in the main house are the most reasonably priced but if you can afford it go for one of the weather-boarded cottages or suites in the converted barn. Each has its own stone fireplace, king-sized bed, or in the cottages, antique canopied queen featherbeds, a 'loveseat' and an in-room Jacuzzi with concealed TV and VCR and small fridge. With many original features including stained-glass windows, high-beamed ceilings, a wood-burning fireplace and teak, pine or solid oak floors, the inn is the perfect place to relax in tranquil and unpretentious surroundings.

You can take your breakfast tray full of freshly-squeezed fruit juices, home-made granola and house specialties such as fresh strawberry crêpes and apple French toast out into the lovely English gardens, or sit on your own patio admiring the foliage, plants and beautiful topiary. Local Santa Barbara wines and hors d'oeuvres are served each afternoon. There is a spa in the Inn and access to a nearby health club with pool if you need pampering, otherwise you can try a spot of croquet!

Bed and breakfast costs from US$215 to US$435 in the main house, and from US$525 to US$550 for the Old Barn or cottages.

SAN FRANCISCO
Recommended hotels

Hotel Triton (☎ 415-394-0500, US toll-free ☎ 800-433-6611 📄 415-394-0555, 💻 www.hoteltritonsf.com, 342 Grant Avenue, San Francisco, CA 94108), right across the road from one of the huge gates in **Chinatown**, gives its guests a real flavour of this fantastic city with cutting edge décor from local designers in the very good value rooms: where else would you get Nintendo and environmentally-friendly bedrooms?

As soon as you enter the lobby it is obvious the Triton is a hotel devoted to style. It has plush red sofas and towering Egyptian-style gold columns, beautifully designed lamps and tables, and murals painted on the walls.

There's no wishy-washy patterned carpet or dreadfully unassuming standard-issue prints on the walls here. Each of the 140 guest rooms is decorated with real flair and minute attention to detail: there are hand-painted wall finishes, art deco sun mirrors and mock-Zebra skin sofas and armchairs.

Each room also comes with all mod cons, and complimentary morning coffee and newspapers. Try one of the four designer suites where top-notch design gurus such as Joe Boxer and Suzan Briganti have been allowed to run riot, or one of the 24 environmentally-sensitive eco-rooms. A member of Design Hotels (see p12 for reservation numbers worldwide), doubles at the Triton cost from US$220 per night.

Hotel Monaco (☎ 415-292-0100, US toll-free ☎ 800-214-4220, 📄 415-292-0111, 💻 www.hotelmonaco.com, 501 Geary St, San Francisco, CA 94102) is a mixture of classic style and Bohemian flare, and the place to be for the savvy. In the middle of the theatre district, people stay at the Hotel Monaco because it is 'fun, warm, and stimulating'. You'll know this is no ordinary hotel as soon as you lay eyes on the corridors, wrapped in Chinese red lacquer coverings, with a coin-patterned carpet. Newly restored, the Monaco's French-inspired architecture is set off by a sensually rich décor which speaks of seduction and pampering.

The Monaco's 201 rooms have the 'dreamiest' canopy beds, some with romantic drapes while most of the 34 suites have whirlpool tubs for two. Room furnishings are warm and eclectic: Chinese-inspired armoires and bamboo writing desks are juxtaposed with round, buttoned ottomans and high-backed upholstered chairs.

Like the Triton, the Monaco has Nintendo, but it goes one step further. A tarot reader is on hand at the evening wine and cheese reception and there's a limo to take

THINGS TO SEE AND DO IN SAN FRANCISCO

San Francisco is one of the most user-friendly cities in the world as it is relatively compact and has a very easy transport system, which is just as well as it's too hilly to cover on foot. The best areas to explore are **Haight Ashbury**, where flower power flourished so radically in the 1960s, and the restaurant and club-filled **SOMA** (South of Market), **Chinatown**, **North Beach** and **Hayes Valley**, the bohemian centre of today's San Francisco.

The food in San Francisco is particularly good: if you go to *Kate's Kitchen* (471 Haight/Filmore) for breakfast on the weekend, the *Pork Store* (Haight Street) or *Dotti's True Blue Café* (Union Square) for lunch and on to *Stars* (150 Redwood Alley/Van Ness) for dinner, you can live safe in the knowledge that you've been to some of the right places. For a more intimate, romantic dinner atmosphere it's hard to beat *Masas* – but it is very expensive. Hayes Valley is great for shopping if you want to see goods by young designers and artisans, but stay between blocks 300 and 500 for safety and don't turn up until after lunch when the shops open. **North Beach**, San Francisco's Italian district, is good for breakfast. It's also

worth visiting the church where Marilyn Munroe married the baseball player Joe DaMaggio.

Take a ferry boat from Fisherman's Wharf to **Sausalito**, a pretty fishing village and an expensive suburb on other side of the bay, passing Alcatraz on the way. Stop for lunch at one of the many little restaurants and bars. Afterwards hire bikes and cycle up to the **Marin Headlands**. If you've got a car, it's worth crossing the Golden Gate Bridge, stopping off in Sausalito and then driving up to the Marin Headlands. There's nothing quite like standing with a panoramic view of the city before you as the fog rolls in off the ocean like a cotton wool quilt, leaving the bridge suspended above it.

Also worth a visit is the **San Francisco Museum of Modern Art**, and take a stroll around **Yerba Buena Gardens**, which are a great place to people watch. For views, you can't beat the top of **Telegraph Hill**: it is easily recognizable because of its landmark, the **Coit Tower**.

San Francisco is big on acid jazz – visit ⌨ www.sfvisitor.org to find the hottest place to go and for further information about the city.

you the short distance to the shops. There's plenty of pampering available in the spa, even for pets, and in the Grand Café, original murals and an ornate vaulted ceiling set an artistic, whimsical tone in happy contrast to the impeccable service. Doubles cost from US$259, suites from US$329.

Other recommended hotels

Auberge du Soleil (☎ 707-963-1211, 🖹 707-963-8764, 180 Rutherford Hill Road, PO Drawer B, Rutherford, CA 94573) is outside San Francisco in **Napa Valley** wine country. The Auberge's 31 rooms and 19 suites have a really Mediterranean feel and the cuisine is superb enough to warrant membership of the Relais & Châteaux group. Set among olive trees and grapevines, the rustic colours and tranquil ambience make this a delightful haven to spend a few days of unadulterated luxury. Each of the rooms has a fireplace and private terrace and is housed in a country cottage. There is a two-night minimum stay at weekends but it would be almost sinful to spend only one night in the Auberge! Guests very rarely stray out of the hotel at night, attracted by the delicious cuisine of Claude Rouas' restaurant, accompanied by one of 500 of California's best wines. But during the day there's lots to do aside from lying by the pool – cycling, horse-riding, or even browsing for antiques nearby. Doubles cost from US$450, suites from US$850 room only. Book through UK tour operator Carrier (see p11).

NEVADA

If you like to play, you can't beat larger than life **Las Vegas** for a honeymoon. Here you can have entertainment in excess in sparkling surrounds without ever going near a casino. Bars with 'the biggest and best show in the world' call from every street corner and the dining is good modern American – in innovative surroundings.

The centrepiece at *Aureole* (☎ 632-7401, Mandalay Bay, 3950 Las Vegas Boulevard South) is a four-storey glass tower where the wine is kept, and hanging in

Bellagio's (see below) *Picasso* restaurant is an original by the artist himself. The night-life options are of course, endless and all you may imagine – including the caged dancers. The hot spot of the moment is Studio 54 at the MGM Grand, the hotel with over 5000 rooms, at 3799 Las Vegas Boulevard South.

After thrill-seeking rides, the best – or worst – of which has to be the scary Big Shot at the **Stratosphere Hotel** (2000 Las Vegas Boulevard South, 💻 www.stratlv.com), you can shop until you drop at **Belz** (7400 Las Vegas Boulevard South) which with 155 stores may live up to its claim to be the largest factory outlet in the world.

On your doorstep are the **mountains** and **deserts** of Nevada – some of America's most untamed countryside. A scenic flight will give you a feel for this vast wild expanse and you can go trekking, camping and whitewater rafting in Monument Valley and Bryce Canyon with Scenic Tours (☎ 638-3300, 💻 www.scenictours.com).

Vegas is also known for its quickie and elaborate fantasy **weddings**. As well as the famous drive-in chapels symbolizing all that's irreverent and kitsch, you can get married in a hot air balloon, get hitched in the desert or bungee jump your way to wedded bliss.

Recommended hotels

The hotels in Las Vegas are all fiercely competitive and try to lure you off the strip with the promise of some spectacle: prices here are not fixed so you could just get lucky. **Bellagio** (☎ 702-693-7111, 📄 702-693-8585, bellagiolasvegas.com, 3600 Las Vegas Boulevard South), being luxurious, entertaining (with Cirque du Soleil's O show – the best in town) and efficient, is truly wonderful and a runner up in *Tatler*'s Hotel of the Year 2001. A thousand fountains spurt to music and the garden is a fantasy of lights. The villa suites have an Italian garden, pool, gym, sauna massage room, an excess of rooms and bathrooms, a kitchen and even a hairdressing salon! Picasso's son Claude runs the wonderful Picasso restaurant. Doubles cost from US$213, suite from US$355.

If you want to escape from the mad chaos of the strip to something a little more enduring and refined, and with a view of the mountains and desert beyond, one of the sparkling suites at **Four Seasons Hotel Las Vegas** (☎ 702-632-5000, 💻 www.foursea sons.com/lasvegas, 3960 Las Vegas Boulevard South) may be just the ticket; with 434 rooms and suites, it's small by Vegas standards. Doubles with king-size bed cost from US$175, suites from US$350 room only.

You won't miss **Luxor** (☎ 702-262-4000, 💻 www.luxor.com, 3900 Las Vegas Boulevard South) at night because a light beam projects straight into the sky from the top of its life-size pyramid shape. It has tower or pyramid rooms and Jacuzzi suites to choose from as well as five swimming pools. You can get doubles from as little as US$71. **Le Mirage** (☎ 702-791-7111, 💻 www.themirage.com, 3400 Las Vegas Boulevard South) attempts to outdo it with a fire-spitting volcano. Doubles cost from US$79 excluding tax.

Adventure resort, **Treasure Island** (☎ 702-894-7111, 💻 www.treasureisland.com, 3300 Las Vegas Boulevard South) stages a sea battle with pirates. It has attracted a AAA Four-Diamond Award and has a sumptuous Bucaneer Suite for honeymooners with floor to ceiling windows facing the Pirate battle; costs from US$139 excluding tax.

Talk to UK tour operators Virgin Holidays, Carrier, North America Travel Service (see p11), or for further information check the following websites: 💻 www.vegas.com or 💻 www.lasvegastourism.com; 💻 www.lasvegas24hours.com.

COLORADO

Names like **Vail**, **Aspen** and **Steamboat Springs** cannot fail to conjure up romantic images of crisp sunny days spent out in the snow followed by long cosy evenings – just the two of you snuggled up in front of a roaring log fire with the snow falling silently outside. Going to a ski resort can make a wonderfully romantic honeymoon, but only if you are both around the same standard as you don't really want to spend your days apart or with one of you always miserably trying to catch up. And remember, you don't have to ski like lunatics for 10 hours a day, nor do you have to be expert skiers to enjoy this kind of winter wonderland. This is your honeymoon so don't feel guilty about getting up late, skiing to a mountain restaurant and tucking into the wine and chips at lunch time!

Vail is the ideal resort for a two-centre holiday and can easily be teamed up with **Jackson Hole** (for a completely different style of holiday), nearby **Aspen**, or even **Whistler** in Canada. The ski season runs from December to the middle of April.

The Little Nell

The Little Nell is one of the world's best mountain resort hotels and probably America's most chic ski hotel. Ringed by 14,000ft peaks, alpine meadows and snow-fed streams, the Little Nell is a snug base at the foot of the Aspen Mountains.

The hotel's management set out to blend the finest attributes of an intimate country inn with the personalized service and amenities of a grand hotel, and they do it rather well. It is a very special little hotel, a far cry from normal ski resort accommodation. Guests are surrounded by fine antiques and the kind of old-world, understated furnishings that you dream of having in your own home.

No two rooms are alike and all feature the quintessential assets of any mountain holiday – a fireplace and a breathtaking view. Soothing tones of cream, ochre and chocolate brown make the bedroom a cosy place to return to for a pre-dinner snooze in front of the fire. Down-filled sofas and lounge chairs are just the thing for tired limbs, and if you don't have the energy to leave the room there's 24-hour room service, an in-room minibar and a remote control TV with VCR.

The king-sized beds have down comforters and there is a Belgian wool carpet to add to that feeling of cocooned luxury. The en suite marble bathrooms are well-equipped and fitted with deep baths and more fluffy white towels and toiletries than anyone could possibly need.

The living rooms are filled with leather armchairs, comfortable sofas, and fine paintings hanging on dark rust- and deep ochre-coloured walls. You can warm up with a steaming bowl of soup and watch skiers swooshing down the Little Nell slope from the award-winning restaurant and courtyard café. If you're there in winter you can relax in the Jacuzzi after a hard day on the slopes before heading to listen to live jazz music in the the bar.

Located right in the heart of the town, the Little Nell is only steps away from the many shops, restaurants and galleries that

---

THE LITTLE NELL

(☎ 970-920-4600, 🖷 970-920-4670), 675 East Durant St, Aspen, Colorado 81611, USA

Reservations: US (toll-free ☎ 888-843-6355); Relais & Châteaux toll-free numbers worldwide (see p12); from the UK book through Seasons in Style (☎ 0151-342 0505)

Getting there: 186 miles from Denver, take the 1-70 towards Glenwood Springs, then Highway 82 to Aspen; 4 miles from Aspen-Sardy Field Airport from where the hotel can arrange complimentary transfers

Accommodation: 77 rooms and 15 suites

Amenities: The Bar, the Grand Salon, the Restaurant and Courtyard Café, several adjoining private dining rooms, swimming pool, ski concierge, Jacuzzi, spa and thalassotherapy, dry cleaning and laundry, 24-hour room service, plus hiking, fishing, tennis, golf and concerts in the summer

Dress code: Casual

Weddings: Can be arranged in the private dining rooms, such as the oak-panelled library

Minimum stay: Three nights over a weekend in summer and four nights over a weekend in winter

Rates: Doubles cost from US$350 in summer to US$550 in winter; suites from around US$900 in summer and US$1100 in winter

Credit cards: Most major

Taxes and service charge: Tax 8.2%, service is discretionary

have made Aspen famous, and which in summer are full of music and cultural activities, but is also ideally situated beside the Silver Queen gondola (the resort's main ski-lift). Of course, this kind of location and elegant living doesn't come cheap, but this is Aspen and if you can afford it, the Little Nell is just about the best place to stay.

The Sonnenalp Resort of Vail

The Sonnenalp Resort of Vail is right in the centre of Vail and strives to be the most European hotel in America. Known for its world-class skiing, Vail boasts the largest single ski mountain in the whole world, stretching seven miles across with 4000 skiable acres serviced by 25 lifts – pretty impressive stuff.

The best thing about Sonnenalp is that it has reinvented all that is romantic about skiing in the Alps and transported it to America. Deservedly one of Vail's most prestigious hotels, the Sonnenalp Resort of Vail is certainly the most luxurious. With 88 suites, two restaurants, a piano bar, library and a vast area given over to every kind of spa treatments, it's hard to beat as a mountain retreat.

You are bound to fall in love with the Sonnenalp Resort of Vail as soon as you see it: the attractive white building with its red and white striped shutters, little wooden balconies protruding from French windows, its stone arches at ground level. Inside, the hotel is designed like any chalet in Europe with hand-crafted woodwork and traditional stonework.

Everything is done in European style from the comforter on your king-sized bed to the European breakfast buffet in the morning, and the traditional Austrian-style uniforms of the staff. The bedrooms are the best place to unwind when you come in from the slopes, and they are all furnished with a gas fireplace, a TV and VCR and a fully-stocked minibar. The marble floors in the bathrooms are heated, there are double basins, a large soaking bath with separate shower, robes, iron and ironing board and hairdryers.

The best suites are the Bald Mountain Suite overlooking the Gore Creek, the Blue Spruce Suite and the two-bedroom Vail Mountain.

The resort helps you plan your day by providing the latest snow and trail conditions with your breakfast, but Vail also has a lot to offer if you fancy a day away from the slopes. The hotel arranges the most incredible hot-air balloon rides taking you peacefully over the majestic mountains, or go for a moonlit sleigh ride or even dog-sledding.

THE SONNENALP RESORT OF VAIL
(☎ 970-476-5656, 🖷 970-476-1639, 💻 www.sonnenalp.com), 20 Vail Road, Vail, Colorado 81657, USA
Reservations: US (toll-free ☎ 1-800-654-8312); from the UK book through Ski Independence (☎ 020-7713 5337)
Getting there: 100 miles away from Denver International Airport, take the I-70 to exit 176 in Vail; Eagle County Airport is 35 miles away
Accommodation: 88 suites
Amenities: Ludwig's Restaurant serves breakfast and dinner, Bully Ranch Restaurant serves south-western and western cuisine at lunch and dinner, King's Club has fireside piano music nightly, the Spa-Steam rooms offer sauna, indoor and outdoor Jacuzzis, light spa menu and an extensive range of spa treatments, indoor/outdoor heated pool, juice bar, full bar
Dress code: Casual
Weddings: The hotel does cater for weddings and receptions
Minimum stay: 7 nights in winter
Rates: Doubles including full breakfast from US$220; $2000 for a suite in winter
Credit cards: Most major
Taxes and service charge: 9.8% tax added to bill, service is discretionary

Other recommended hotels

Wyndham Peaks Resort & Golden Door Spa (☎ 970-728-6800, US toll-free ☎ 1-800-996-3426, 🖷 970-728-6175, 💻 www.wyndham.com, 136 Country Club Drive, Telluride, Colorado 81435) is one of North America's best-kept secrets.

This lovely hotel is perfectly placed to take advantage of the powder snow this region is renowned for, and also pretty good for those who don't ski, with a vast

42,000 sq ft given over to the most incredible spa, offering an impressive 44 different programmes. Surrounded by some of the most awesome scenery, but off the beaten path on the far slopes of the Colorado Rockies, the hotel is as good in summer as it is in winter. The 172 lavish cabins and penthouses have sweeping views of Mt Wilson and the 14,000ft **San Juan Mountains** as well as all mod cons. Ask about the Romance package which includes five nights' accommodation with breakfast, champagne and gift on arrival, a spa treatment each and a dinner for two in Appaloosa restaurant (without drinks) for around US$2665 in peak season and as low as US$1415 in low season.

The Gant (☎ 970-925-5000, US toll-free ☎ 800-345-1471, 🖺 970-925-6891, 🖳 www.gantaspen.com, 610 West End St, Aspen, CO 81611) has a wide selection of privately owned condos for anything from US$155 a day in low season to US$565 a day in peak holiday season.

Each condo in the Swiss-style wooden chalet is individually owned and has a private patio or balcony, wood-burning fireplaces and fully-equipped kitchens. Be warned there are only about eight or nine one-bedroom condos so you'll have to book early. Morning newspapers are delivered to your door and there is a daily maid service (even your washing up will be done for you). All guests have use of the Gant's two heated outdoor swimming pools, three outdoor hot tubs and dry saunas. One of the best aspects of staying at the Gant is the services of the 'Gantman' who, equipped with a van and complete knowledge of the area, will meet you at the airport, collect you after dinner or a concert, deliver your firewood and generally make sure every aspect of your stay is comfortable and convenient.

VERMONT
Twin Farms

TWIN FARMS
(☎ 802-234-9999, 🖺 802-234-9990, 🖳 www.twinfarms.com), Barnard, Vermont 05031, USA
Reservations: Either direct with the hotel or through Carrier in the UK (see p11)
Getting there: Twin Farms can arrange transfers from West Lebanon Airport in New Hampshire (40 minutes)
Accommodation: 14 guest rooms: four suites in the main house, 2 rooms in the lodge and 8 cottages; no children under 18 allowed; non-smoking property
Amenities: 24-hour room service, pub, lounges, health and beauty club and fitness centre, Japanese tubs; seasonal activities include lake swimming, croquet, skiing, biking, tennis, fishing, canoeing, ice-skating and golf nearby
Dress code: Casual
Weddings: Both ceremonies and receptions are catered for; prices on request; entire package costs US$16,000 per night
Minimum stay: Two nights at weekends, three on public holidays
Rates: Suites in the main house from US$900, cottages from US$1050 per couple includes all meals, drinks and sporting facilities
Credit cards: Most major
Taxes and service charge: 8% tax and 15% service charge

Twin Farms must be one of the most luxurious country retreats ever constructed. So exclusive is Twin Farms that it even has its own ski slopes, and so romantic are its Japanese soaking tubs known as *furos*, set in the vast surrounding forest, that you can't help but dream about the place long after you've left.

The main house where the four suites are found has been decorated with a total disregard for expense. The Washington Suite is the most plush. But if you really want to go the whole hog, book into one of the 10 cottages in the forest – however expensive, you won't regret it. Choose from the most exclusive Treehouse, and the Studio, or one of the themed cottages. Each cottage is unique and set apart from the others in Twin Farm's 300 acres of grounds. The spectacular interior designs were the work of Jed Johnson, one of America's most celebrated interior designers who died tragically, in July 1996, in the TWA disaster. Twin Farms remains a show case for Johnson's work. Described as 'special, stylish and sensual', it was *Tatler*'s Best Hideaway 2000.

The bedrooms are absolutely perfect for a winter honeymoon: you sleep in a magnificent four-poster bed and can snuggle up together in front of a roaring log fire in the privacy of your own cottage. The cottages and suites are all undeniably romantic and were specifically designed to accommodate one couple each.

There is no menu at Twin Farms, but mouthwatering meals, prepared by a world-class chef, reflect the changing seasons, and fresh organic vegetables and herbs from Twin Farms' gardens are used.

Widely regarded as the most exclusive hotel in America and understandably popular for celebrity weddings since privacy is guaranteed, Twin Farms could also be the most expensive place to stay. But then, nothing is too much trouble here, and, as its manager is quick to remind you, a night at Twin Farms is actually particularly good value considering the monumental costs of running such an establishment. Luckily the extortionate price of the rooms includes everything: skiing on a private slope, canoeing, massages, breakfast, lunch, dinner, room, endless wine and anything else you'd care to order.

NEW YORK
The Mark

The Mark, recently taken over by the Mandarin Oriental Hotel Group, is regarded as one of the best hotels in New York. This Upper East Side hangout even attracts local New Yorkers, so you can be sure you'll feel you're in the right place. It is also perfectly situated for shopping on Upper Madison Avenue, where some of New York's most exclusive art and antique galleries are located, as well as numerous fashion boutiques and great restaurants.

The bedrooms are equipped with king-sized beds, overstuffed chairs, and prints reflecting the hotel's style which lies somewhere between new-classic and English-Italian. Throughout the hotel, dark green and red velvets sit beside heavy custom-designed curtains and bedspreads, while Biedermeier furniture stands on marble floors.

Most guest rooms have wonderful black pantries equipped with refrigerator, sink and stove. All rooms have two phone lines and in-room fax capability, while the very largest suites have everything you could ever dream of including a foyer, library, stereo system with CD player, wet bar and the most incredible large landscaped terraces with views over **Central Park**.

There is marble everywhere in the bathrooms, lovely large soak tubs, hairdryers and scales (not that you should be looking at them on your honeymoon!).

The best way to stay at The Mark is on their US$525 Honeymoon Package which gives you a night in a junior suite or US$625 for an executive suite, half a bottle of

THE MARK
(☎ 212-744-4300, 🖨 212-744-2749, 🖂 reservations@themarknyc.com), Madison Avenue at East 77th St, New York, NY 10021, USA
Reservations: Small Luxury Hotels of the World or the Leading Hotels of the World toll-free reservation numbers worldwide (see p12)
Getting there: 45 minutes from JFK International Airport, 25 minutes from La Guardia Airport, transfers are available
Accommodation: 120 guest rooms; 60 suites; there are various categories of luxury rooms and suites: superior and de luxe rooms, junior suites, one-bedroom suites, two-bedroom suites, the Tower and the Presidential suites
Amenities: Clefs d'Or concierge; 24-hour room service; limousines; Marks Bar; Sunday brunch; afternoon tea; cocktails and after-theatre drinks and desserts; banquet facilities; shuttle to the theatre district on Friday and Saturday nights; Wellness suite with sauna, steam shower and massage available
Dress code: Jacket and tie required for dining
Weddings: Ceremonies and receptions catered for up to 300 people, the cost of which varies depending on your requests
Minimum stay: None
Rates: Doubles from US$520; suites from US$700
Credit cards: Most major
Taxes and service charge: Not included

champagne, cocktails for two, a dozen red roses, and continental breakfast in your room. Considering a junior suite usually costs US$700 and an executive from US$750 this is a relatively good deal.

The cosy **Mark's Bar** has a club-like atmosphere which is perfect for pre-dinner cocktails or post-theatre snacks: more substantial meals, a great Sunday Brunch, and afternoon tea are all served in **Mark's Restaurant**.

The Royalton

The Royalton is a must for design-gurus. Without doubt one of the funkiest hotels in New York, the Royalton is also home to one of the city's greatest bars.

From the outside the hotel is unassuming with two big stone columns and a plain mahogany door to distinguish it. However, open the door and you enter a purple haze of exquisite design full of beautiful New Yorkers sipping cocktails, people-watching and listening to ambient music.

The hotel lobby and bar area are very subtly lit, with seats covered in rich tones of greens and purples and a lot of white and velvet-covered chairs; the concierge and porters are dressed in black jackets and a Parisian barman operates a cosy, hidden Vodka bar. Fresh flowers have been replaced by Japanese fighting fish swimming around in bowls. However, the most legendary aspect of this wonderful bar is the gents' toilet where, instead of using conventional urinals, men urinate against a fountain of water cascading down from the ceiling to the floor. Somehow this says it all about the Royalton, the hotel created by former Studio 54 disco kings, Ian Schrager and the late Steve Rubell.

If you are at all interested in design you'll love this hotel. It was the first of Schrager's projects to employ design guru Philippe Starck, and the result proved so successful that the partnership is still producing new hotels today. The hotel rooms lead off from long, weaving corridors which are dark and sexy, enticing you to enter your bedroom. The bedrooms are painted a dark matt grey and furnished minimally with just a comfortable low-level mattress bed covered by a mahogany hood with white cotton sheets and big square pillows. Without doubt the most impressive thing about staying at the Royalton is the bathrooms – all slate, chrome and glass – with the best showers in **Manhattan** taking up half the entire bathroom space and encased by a floor to ceiling glass wall with a door cut into it.

THE ROYALTON
(☎ 212-869-4400, 🖷 212-869-8965), 44 West 44th St, New York, NY10036, USA
Reservations: Either direct with the hotel on the above number or within the US toll-free (☎ 1-800-635-9013)
Getting there: The hotel can arrange all sorts of transfers to/from the airports, a limo will cost from US$90 to US$130, plus 20% for tax and tips
Accommodation: 168 rooms and 20 suites
Amenities: A fitness room, plus an arrangement allowing guests to use the New York Sports Club
Dress code: Dressy casual
Weddings: Small wedding parties can be arranged in the penthouse – prices are subject to negotiation
Minimum stay: None
Rates: Doubles from US$295 (reduced to US$245 at the weekend); suites US$390 to US$500 (reduced to US$325 at the weekend)
Credit cards: Most major
Taxes and service charge: 13.25% sales and local tax plus US$2 per room

The standard rooms are very small which could be cosy, but if you need your space go for a superior, de luxe or suite. Make sure you ask for a room overlooking the street, as they are definitely the best, with great views of the Big Apple.

The Royalton is very trendy, and a little bit mysterious because of the way it sits so discreetly on W44th St. The rooms were luxurious without being opulent and were very cool. It wasn't just a place to stay, it felt like we were at the centre of trendy New York life.
Lizzie and Nigel Walley

THINGS TO SEE AND DO IN NEW YORK

The best way to see **Manhattan** is to get up into the air: Liberty Helicopters and Helicopter Flight Services both operate **helicopter rides** from heliports around 12th Avenue and 34th St, whisking you over the Hudson River and hovering by the Statue of Liberty within a matter of minutes. The views are stunning, not just of Lady Liberty but also of the vast Manhattan skyline. Make sure your helicopter tour takes you over the Downtown area and that it flies along 5th Avenue passing the Empire State Building and the Rockefeller Centre on your way to Central Park. Within 15 minutes you'll have seen most of New York's landmarks.

Ten blocks from the heliport is **Times Square** where you can book tickets for a **Broadway show**: the best place to go is the TXTS ticket outlet in the middle of the square.

No visit to New York would be complete without a wander down **5th Avenue**: in winter you can ice skate at Rockefeller Plaza and in summer just sit in the café which replaces the ice rink; Saks, the famous spires of St Patrick's Cathedral and the pink marble Trump Tower are all worth a look.

Central Park in many ways epitomises New York: immense and diverse, it is the very heart of the city. Approximately 850 acres in all, the park contains a zoo, the Woolman Ice Rink, an open-air theatre, an observatory, numerous lakes and walkways and a six-mile loop around which New Yorkers jog, roller blade and cycle. Serene and peaceful in winter when the lakes are frozen over and snow lies everywhere, the park also offers an escape from the heat in summer when you can lie and watch kids dancing and roller-skating. A great place to watch some of the best in New York is outside the *Tavern on the Green*: groups congregate here and try to out-do each other.

Close to the Park, and still on 5th, is the **Metropolitan Art Museum**, housing impressive collections of 18th-, 19th- and 20th-century art, an armoury and musical instrument section, many wonderful statues and vast sections recreating the palaces of pre-Revolutionary France. Also definitely worth a look is the **Guggenheim**, close to the Met, which houses an incredible modern collection in a wonderfully groovy building.

Once you've done all your culture bashing it's time to relax in **SoHo**, so-called because of its location south of Houston St. A hip and trendy area to hang out and be seen in, SoHo is home to many of New York's contemporary artists. The main drag, **West Broadway**, and the surrounding area are full of galleries, chic coffee bars and restaurants. Both the upstairs and downstairs bars at the *Mercer Hotel* (see below) are very chic and romantic and great for star spotting. *Pravda*, on Lafayette between Houston and Prince, is an underground Russian Vodka bar and is reputed to be a sexy place to hang out.

Lots of small designers have shops in the area selling individually designed jewellery, clothing and art. The best way to experience SoHo is to just wander around for a few hours: the hordes of converted warehouses with their external fire escapes will make you feel you've seen the real New York.

Little Italy is another great place to wander around, especially in the evening when it is usually bustling largely due to the number of popular restaurants there. Walking down Mulberry St you are greeted by the strong aromas of espresso and parmesan, and incredible displays of cakes and pastries. Everywhere you look in Little Italy there are stretch limos – a hint that this formerly notorious area's past is not so distant!

And then there's **Harlem**. You'd be wise to take a cab there, but there's nowhere like *Sylvia's Restaurant*, 328 Lenox Avenue (in between 126th St and 127th St) for soul food and cool jazz music on a Sunday morning. Right in the heart of Harlem, Sylvia's is the original soul food restaurant, frequented by the likes of Jesse Jackson and Woody Allen.

You haven't really seen New York until you've seen it at night. Take the **Staten Island Ferry** – for free – from the tip of **Battery Park** to **Staten Island**. The ferry passes the Statue of Liberty and provides fantastic views of the financial district. Then round off your evening by going to the **Empire State Building**, open from 9.30am to midnight, seven days a week. Ascend to the viewing platform so that you can get a different perspective on the places you've been to.

Other recommended hotels – New York City

The Mercer (☎ 212-966-6060, 🖹 212-965-3838, 147 Mercer Street, New York) is SoHo's first luxury hotel, and one of a new wave of loft-style hotels. In a Romanesque revival building its interiors were completely redesigned by French designer Christian Liaigre and its pervading feeling is of calm. Long entrance hallways lead into the 75 rooms, all elegantly appointed with exclusively designed furniture made from African woods, wenge and ipe. The high ceilings with fans, arched windows and oversized bathrooms, some with king-size tubs, add to its gracious atmosphere.

All the important little details are there – black out drapes in the rooms, a masseuse, 24-hour butler and unpacking service when you arrive. The Mercer has a vintage library in the intimate lobby to make you feel at home and a 24-hour restaurant 'The Kitchen' with communal tables so you can eat whenever you like. Doubles cost from US$375 to US$2250. It is a member of Design Hotels so book through them in the US toll-free (☎ 888-563-4464), or through Sterling Hotels and Resorts reservation numbers worldwide (see p12).

Other recommended hotels – New York State

The Point (☎ 518-891-5674, 🖷 518-891-1152, HCR1, PO Box 65, Saranac Lake, New York 12983), nestled in the **Adirondack** wilderness, has the most amazing setting, right on the edge of a peninsula overlooking the pristine Saranac Lake, and is consistently ranked as the number one resort hotel in North America. The A-lined log cabins sit amongst the tall pine trees, and when you walk inside it's difficult not to warm to the homely atmosphere created by the wood-panelled rooms with sumptuous beds, and filled with hunting trophies, oriental carpets and antique furniture.

The Point is superb in all seasons: summer days are filled with sailing, fishing or taking a speedboat ride around the lake; autumn is the time for horse-riding, canoeing, waterskiing or hiking or even a gentle stroll around the lake edge, while **Saranac** golf course is a few minutes away; and in winter months you can snuggle up in front of the log fire or brave the outdoors with some cross-country skis, snowshoes or even try out the ice skating. Everything is included at the Point: breakfast, lunch and dinner and unlimited wine. The food, cooked by one of the world's most renowned chefs, is really quite extraordinary. Rates for the 11 rooms start from US$1000 to US$1900 for two people but don't include NY State taxes (7%) or service charges (18%). Book through Relais & Châteaux reservation numbers worldwide (see p12).

FLORIDA

The last decade has seen a wave of hotel gentrification and new hotels springing up around Miami, making the area the perfect destination for honeymooners in search of chic design-conscious hotels.

The art deco hotels in particular, many owned by Chris Blackwell, promoter of U2 and owner of the Island Outpost chain, have regained their former popularity and funk status. What's more, many of the Hollywood stars that used to visit including Madonna, Lenny Kravitz and Robert De Niro, liked it so much they bought houses, clubs, or restaurants here.

The Delano

The Delano on Miami Beach is recognized as one of America's coolest hotels and symbolizes elegant but simple chic. Owned by Ian Schrager and designed by Philippe Starck, it was conceived as the next generation urban resort – the hub of social activity and at the same time a sophisticated,

---

THE DELANO
(☎ 305-672-2000, 🖷 305-673-0954), 1685 Collins Avenue, Miami Beach, Florida 33139, USA
Reservations: Either direct or US toll-free (☎ 800-555-5001) or through UK travel agency Earth Travel (UK ☎ 020-7793 9993)
Getting there: The hotel can arrange limo transfers
Accommodation: 208 guest rooms, lofts, suites and duplex poolside bungalows
Amenities: Water Salon, private beach area for Delano guests, watersports, poolside private cabanas, state of the art 24-hour gym, rooftop women's bathhouse and solarium with health bar, gift and magazine shop, entertainment centre, 24-hour room service, portable phones and computers available, video on demand
Dress code: Informal (white!)
Weddings: Can be arranged in the ballroom
Minimum stay: Three nights over weekend in high season (November to May), two nights during weekend in low season (June to October)
Rates: Doubles from US$245; suites up to US$2600
Credit cards: Most major
Taxes and service charge: 12.5% tax, service is discretionary

serene retreat. Everything is whiter than white at the Delano, from the remote control for the TV and the stereo in your bedroom to the abundance of white orchids. It was designed to be soothing and tranquil and the large blocks of white colour were used as a direct response to the era of 'over design'.

Located on Collins Avenue, directly on the beach, the core of this 15-storey hotel is its lobby area spanning both in and outside, where rigid functional spaces such as reception desks and waiting chairs have been replaced by a more fluid series of areas given over to an **Eat-in Kitchen**, the fully upholstered **Rose Bar** with roving service, and various other indoor and outdoor eating and drinking areas in which to mill about.

The Delano also boasts the most incredible collection of art and furniture from all over the world, including pieces by Man Ray, Salvador Dali and Antonio Gaudi. Instead of a swimming pool, Starck designed a Water Salon, modelled on ancient Roman baths and comprising several different areas of floating, meditating, sleeping, underwater classical music and furniture not around but in the pool.

There is nothing conventional about the Delano, even in the orchard and garden there is a huge chess board designed by Starck, as well as a bed. Throughout the hotel the emphasis is on natural materials. The 208 bedrooms, which all come with the full range of amenities, feature poured-in-place art gallery floors, furniture and lamps designed specifically for the hotel by Starck, and many examples of his design cheek, such as angels hovering over the bed and ceiling-to-floor mirrors.

The Marlin

This incredible little hotel combines art deco with Jamaican funk in a way that only Blackwell could make work. It is where the fashion and music world flock for their holidays, the latter inspired by the world-renowned recording studio on site, the former drawn by the buzz of **South Beach** and the Elite modelling agency on the 2nd floor. As a result the Marlin is *the* place for people-watching. The desire for a glimpse of the stars means the hotel bar gets painfully crowded at night, but to the right clientele this can only be considered an advantage, not a drawback!

Each of the 11 suites has the feeling of a spacious, contemporary loft, with earth tones of red, ochre, brown and beige, custom-designed furnishings, hardwood floors and brushed stainless steel accents on counter tops, bathroom fixtures and doors. Each suite features an unusual design aspect: suite No 205 with its circular bed and Moroccan inspired décor is perfect for honeymooners.

The rooms are well kitted-out, with their own kitchenette with fully-stocked refrigerator, coffee-maker and microwave, hairdryer and in-room safe.

As you'd expect there are batik robes in the place of impersonal white hotel bathrobes, and state-of-the-art communications equipment with a great video and CD library to raid for your own use.

THE MARLIN
(☎ 305-604-5000, 🖷 305-673-9609, 🖳 www.islandoutpost.com), 1200 Collins Ave, Miami Beach, Florida 33139, USA
Reservations: Through Island Outpost, UK (☎ 020-7440 4360); USA/Canada toll-free (☎ 800-OUTPOST) or 🖳 ukreservations@islandoutpost.com
Getting there: 15 minutes from Miami International Airport, taxi costs US$20
Accommodation: 11 suites
Amenities: Roof-top deck with Jamaican-inspired bar, nightly turn-down service, room service available from the Tides hotel menu, laundry service, reduced rates at Crunch Fitness, and VIP access to local clubs
Dress code: Casual
Weddings: The Marlin allows guests to make their own arrangements for a licensed minister or Justice of the Peace to conduct the ceremony; the hotel can cater for anything upward from a tented wedding on the beach with musicians
Minimum stay: Two-nights on Fridays and Saturdays (Oct to May)
Rates: From US$195 to US$325 (June to Sept); US$325 to US$450 (Oct to May)
Credit cards: Most major
Taxes and service charge: 12.5% city and state taxes; service charge is at your discretion

WHERE TO STAY AND WHAT TO DO ON SOUTH BEACH

The white sandy beaches of Miami have long attracted tourists to South Beach, but what is much newer and just as exciting is the art deco renewal that keeps on growing. There are more **art deco buildings** concentrated in South Beach than anywhere else in the world.

The rows of small hotels built here in the 1930s have undergone some serious face-lifts and the result is the creation of one of America's hippest, most happening places. The strip that is known as South Beach, the bottom third of Miami Beach, is fringed on one side with deep blue ocean and on the other with a veritable rainbow of art deco condos and hotels, scores of brilliant shining convertibles and a few thousand palm trees. Home to Robert De Niro, Meg Ryan and Whitney Houston and with clubs and restaurants owned by top celebs, the place is just one long party and has to be seen to be believed.

Although it's hard to choose where to stay among the plethora of fab hotels, a few stand out for honeymooners. **The Hotel** (☎ 305-531-5796, US/Canada toll-free ☎ 877-The-Hotel; 🖷 305-531-972, 🖳 www.thehotelofsouthbeach. com) recently restored by Todd Oldham using a Persian motif and colours of the sea for inspiration, is a sexy art deco gem a block from the legendary **Ocean Drive**. The rooftop pool and terrace offers an incredible view, and soft lighting, mirrors opposite the beds and black-out curtains deck the rooms. The colourful and hip 'Wish' vegetarian restaurant serves mouthwatering morsels such as parsnip ravioli and Indian-scented carrots made by Robins, one of the country's most promising young chefs. Surrounded by a lush, leafy patio, its ceiling is covered with 100 handblown glass lanterns. Doubles cost from US$275 per room.

The **Cavalier** (☎ 305-604-5000, 🖷 305-531 5543, US/Canada (toll-free ☎ 800-OUTPOST); UK (☎ 020-7440 4360); 🖳 www.islandoutpost.com) is a less expensive Chris Blackwell property right on Ocean Drive. A beautifully-restored art deco hotel, the Cavalier is a fun place to be. Its rooms are brilliantly executed with excellent amenities, and with rates from US$130 a night (June to Sept) it also offers extremely good value. Another wild and wacky choice is the **Pelican**

(☎ 305-673-3373, US toll-free ☎ 800-7-Pelican, 🖷 305-673-3255, 🖳 www.pelicanhotel.com). Facing 15 miles of beach on Ocean Drive, its theme rooms have original art deco furnishings and it has two 'James Bond' penthouses. Rooms from US$125-US$2000.

To see South Beach, all you have to do is rent a convertible, lace up your roller blades or simply stroll the streets and join in. Check out *News Café* on Ocean Drive, the *Van Dyke Café* on Lincoln Road, and if you fancy something smart and quite delicious try *Pacific Time*, also on Lincoln Road. For celebrity dining you're spoilt for choice. Try the *South Beach Brasserie* owned by Michael Caine, or Cameron Diaz' new restaurant, *Bambu*, both of which are on Lincoln road. For a bit of star-studded dancing late at night slip into *Bash* (owned by Sean Penn and Mick Hucknell), 320, Level (take a peek at 🖳 www.levelnightclub.com), Lenny Kravitz' *Crobar* on Washington Avenue or Ricky Martin's *Casa Salsa* on Ocean Drive.

The shops are also quite incredible. You can pick up anything from zany wigs to funky clothes and tasteful house and garden goodies. There are late night book stores such as the famous **Books & Books** on Lincoln Road, along which you'll also find a thriving gay scene and galleries, roller-bladers and African drummers, and even the Miami City Ballet.

Somewhere more traditional to stay is the opulent and romantic old world **Biltmore Hotel** (☎ 800-727-1926, 🖷 305-445-1926, 🖳 www.biltmorehotel.com) in Coral Gables – Miami's most exclusive neighbourhood. Deluxe doubles cost from US$299. And for the relaxed but luxurious ambience of a private beachfront home, try the **Beach House Bal Harbor** (☎ 305-535-8600, US toll-free ☎ 877-RUBELLS, 🖷 305-535-8601). Designed by Polo Ralph Lauren, it is steps away from Bal Harbor shops, considered 'the rodeo drive' of Miami. Doubles cost from US$215, Ocean-front Suite with balcony US$750.

For more ideas check out the tourist board's website: 🖳 www.TropicoolMiami.com

FLORIDA KEYS

The other big honeymoon thing to do in Florida is to hire a car in Miami and head down to the Florida Keys, the 42 islands arranged in an arc around the southernmost tip of Florida. The 110-mile drive down the **Overseas Highway** from **Key Largo**, just 40 miles south-west of Miami, to Key West, will take you past some spectacular scenery and great hotels.

Key West is unlike any other part of America, having evolved a culture of its own. Once a haven for contrabandistas, this tiny island – only two miles by four – now plays host to poets, pirates, artists and tourists alike. This unlikely combination makes Key

West a bizarrely sophisticated small town, one of the wealthiest in America, and a great place to visit with a good selection of bars, restaurants and shops.

Other recommended hotels

Little Palm Island (☎ 305-872-2524, 🖹 305-872-4843, 🖳 www.littlepalmisland.com, 28500 Overseas Highway, Little Torch Key, Florida 33042) is situated on a fabulous, three-mile long little island, and is the perfect southern seas' island hideaway, only on Florida's doorstep.

A favourite retreat of US presidents, the island is now a luxury hotel that attracts the likes of Robert Wagner and Ivana Trump, and is impressive enough to warrant membership of the exclusive Relais & Châteaux group (see p12 for toll-free reservation numbers worldwide).

The hotel was certainly created with escapism in mind: in place of TVs, radios, phones and computers, there are hammocks, outdoor showers, sauna and massage rooms, in-room whirlpools and a poolside tropical bar. There are only 30 suites in 14 rustic looking but very luxurious thatched cottages scattered discreetly among flaming bougainvillaea, oleander, hibiscus and palm, lined up along the water's edge. You can be assured of privacy here, and no screaming kids – none are allowed on the island.

Unusually for the Keys, the island is blessed with a lovely white sandy beach which is just great for sunbathing, kayaking and windsurfing, both of which are complimentary. The hotel also has a lovely freshwater swimming pool and lots of other activities to keep you occupied during the day; scuba diving to **Looe Key National Marine Sanctuary**, sunset sails, seaplane and Key West excursions, nature tours and fishing charters.

Fantastic also means expensive. Doubles cost from US$550 in the summer plus 11.5% tax and 10% service charge and a five-night honeymoon package from around US$4899 per couple full board with snorkelling trip, a body massage each, and complimentary watersports. Little Palm Island also has a selection of wedding packages – ask about the Sunset Sail Wedding which costs US$1750 or Tropical Breezes costing US$850.

The Gardens Hotel (☎ 305-294-2661, 🖹 305-292-1007) 526 Angela St, Key West, Florida 33040, in the heart of the historic district of **Key West**, captures all the colonial charm and elegance of a Caribbean homestead, with its white pillars and balconies peeking through lush green gardens overflowing with huge palm fronds. A 17-bedroom hideaway tucked within the island's best-known tropical botanical gardens, the hotel provides calm and tranquillity in marked contrast to the bustling wining, dining and shopping centre just a few blocks away.

The hotel's rooms are decorated with European-style floral chintz and stripes, with subtle lighting to set off the many American antiques and impressionist paintings. All the rooms have hardwood oak floors, king-size beds with antique headboards, pristine white marble bathrooms with Jacuzzi baths, white cotton robes, Nina Ricci toiletries, TV, phone, make-up mirrors and a fully-stocked minibar with imported beers. The best rooms are the two 'historic' bedrooms on the second floor of the main house: Eyebrow Cottage tucked away in a corner of the estate, which has the most incredible cathedral ceiling and a huge Jacuzzi bath and shower; and the Master Suite which has a separate sitting room overlooking the courtyard, pool and garden from its cloistered terrace, and a sauna, steam shower and Jacuzzi.

Doubles cost from US$175 to US$355; the two suites from US$385 to US$685, Eyebrow Cottage from US$295 to US$465 including continental breakfast, but excluding tax. Book through Small Luxury Hotels of the World reservation numbers worldwide (see p12).

Mexico
(BEST TIME: NOVEMBER TO MAY)

Mexico's tourist industry is the best developed of all the countries in Latin America, which doesn't mean that Mexico itself is developed, although some parts of it undoubtedly are: rather that it has the widest choice of the kind of hotels that you want for a honeymoon. The best thing about Mexico is that it is easy to combine a wonderfully relaxing beach holiday – lots of great watersports – with a few days experiencing some of this country's amazing 3000 years of history. Mexico is the ideal destination if you fancy something a little adventurous but don't want to rough it.

There are some truly fantastic beaches in Mexico. Some like **Cancún** and **Acapulco** have become very touristy: rows of sky-scraping international hotels now line the water's edge, while others can be found in small villages where local fishermen still cast their nets each morning. But with over 9600km of coastline covering four distinct bodies of water, you should be able to find something to suit your taste and budget.

With Mexico's regular and efficient system of internal flights it is easy to visit two or three different places in a two-week holiday (ask your travel agent about the Mexipass, a domestic airline pass). I've organized this chapter in two sections to help you plan a honeymoon that combines the best beach hotels with a few days' sightseeing: the first section deals with the Pacific and Caribbean coasts, while the second suggests different places to visit for cultural insight or archaeological interest. Having said that, the proliferation of wonderfully romantic, first-class hotels makes Mexico the best country in Latin America if you just want to stay in one place for your entire holiday.

ACAPULCO
Stretching out along the Pacific coast, Acapulco was the birthplace of the Mexican tourist industry. Today the town that was responsible for giving the world cliff-diving, tequila slammers and swim-up bars is one large, glittering, glamorous resort with a slightly has-been feel to it. It is an extremely popular destination for American cruise ships so, if it's small, intimate, romantic hideaway beaches you are looking for, avoid

---

MEXICO
A great combination of palm-fringed beaches and ancient Mayan culture
Capital: Mexico City
When to go: The temperate dry season is November to May (avoid Christmas and Easter because the Mexicans crowd the beaches and everything is booked up)
Average maximum temperatures °C (Mexico City)

JAN	FEB	MAR	APR	MAY	JUN	JUL	AUG	SEP	OCT	NOV	DEC
19	21	24	25	26	24	23	23	23	21	20	19

Flight times: to Mexico City from:
New York: 5 hours
LA: 5½ hours
London: 10 hours
Sydney: 19 hours
Approximate exchange rate: Peso (P) – £1 = P13.03, US$1 = P9.17, A$1 = P4.76
Time difference: GMT minus six hours
Voltage: 110v AC, 60 Hz, US-style two-pin (flat) plugs
Combine with: Belize, Costa Rica, Los Angeles
Country dialling code: ☎ 52
Further information: 🖳 www.merida.gob.mx or www.mexico-travel.com

Acapulco. There's no doubt that Acapulco Bay, the U-shaped, mountain-framed, natural harbour, is one of the most stunning in the world but you have to be a fan of really big resorts, and all that comes with them, to decide upon Acapulco.

Las Brisas

Las Brisas continues to be the one good reason to choose Acapulco as your honeymoon destination. Famed for years as one of the world's most romantic hotels, the pink and white *casitas* (thatched huts) of Las Brisas span the hillside, each with a private patio and either a private or a shared swimming pool.

The 263 casitas, including 32 suites of Las Brisas, offer guests a relaxed kind of elegance amidst 44 hectares of beautiful gardens filled with bougainvillaea, fuchsias, and the hotel's trademark, hibiscus blooms, plus endless, stunning views of the vast Acapulco Bay. It's definitely worth asking for one of the higher casitas where the views are better.

Each room has glass sliding doors opening onto stone terraces and contains all the extras that you'd expect of a luxury hotel: fresh flowers, air conditioning, in-room safe, phone, minibar, colour satellite TV, lots of toiletries beside the marble bath, a separate vanity unit, hairdryer and bathrobes. However, the rooms themselves are rather simply decorated.

The multi-levelled suites have their bedrooms on the upper level, which also has a terrace and a Jacuzzi, while the lower level features a separate dining area, sitting room, patio and pool, so it feels as if you've got your own private house.

Each morning your breakfast will be delivered through a small cupboard built into the bedroom wall which can be opened from either side, so room service can leave your order in it allowing you to enjoy a relaxing breakfast alone without any form of interruption.

There are three restaurants to choose from: **Bellavista**, serving gourmet international cuisine, another offering local dishes, and seafood and a bar at **La Concha**, the hotel's own private beach club. Guests can either eat outside on the terrace looking out over the bay, or get room service delivered through the magic box.

One of the best features of Las Brisas is La Concha, the hotel's fabulous leisure club a short drive away. Guests are driven to the club in one of the hotel's signature pink and white jeeps. An attendant meets each jeep and helps guests select sun loungers beside the pools, lays their towels out for them and keeps them served with refreshments from the bar. Two saltwater lagoons carved into the rock means you meet face to face with tropical fish, and the large freshwater pool

---

LAS BRISAS
(☎ 7-469-6900, 🖷 7-446-5328, 🖳 www.brisas.com.mx), Carretera Escenica 5255, PO Box 281, Acapulco, Mexico, 39868
Reservations: The Leading Hotels of the World worldwide toll-free reservation numbers (see p12); in USA/Canada ☎ 1-888-559-4329
Getting there: 15 minutes from Acapulco International Airport; guests staying in suites are met at the airport
Accommodation: 263 casitas including 32 suites: including Share Pool Casitas (2 or 3 rooms), Private Pool Casitas (private pool), Brisas Beach Club (private pool and terrace), Junior Suites (private pool and terrace), Master Suites (1- and 2-bedroom; private pool and large terrace)
Amenities: The Bellavista for international gourmet dining, seafood at La Concha, private beach club; five floodlit tennis courts, La Concha offers 2 saltwater lagoons and one freshwater swimming pool with swim-up bar; health club with massage and beauty parlour; golf nearby; shopping arcade and delicatessen, automatic jeeps for rental and safari, and of course, the 210 swimming pools!
Dress code: Casually elegant; jackets optional for men
Weddings: Can be arranged in the Chapel of Peace on the top of the hill
Minimum stay: None
Rates: Doubles with share pool with Continental breakfast from US$240, private pool from US$360; Junior suites from US$520
Credit cards: Most major
Taxes and service charge: 17% government tax, service charge US$20 daily per person

has a swim-up bar. The club has a good range of facilities including waterskiing, sailing, deep-sea fishing, scuba diving, parachute sailing and speedboats. There's also tennis at the hotel, golf nearby, a shopping arcade and delicatessen and the jeeps are always available for touring the scenic grounds, transporting you to your casita, or for getting into town for some night-life.

ZIHUATANEJO

Ixtapa is another large coastal resort teeming with modern hotels, much like Acapulco and Cancún. But just down the coast from Ixtapa is Zihuatanejo, a small fishing village with some of Mexico's most intimate and romantic hotels scattered around the edge of its beautiful bay. If you want to get away from the big international hotel chains and are searching for the charm of a classic Mexican pueblo, this is the place to come.

Hotel Villa del Sol

> **HOTEL VILLA DEL SOL**
> (☎ 755-42239, 📠 755-42758, 💻 www.hotelvilladelsol.net), PO Box 84, Playa la Ropa, 40880 Zihuatanejo, Guerrero, Mexico
> **Reservations**: US/Canada toll-free ☎ 888-389-2645 or through Small Luxury Hotels of the World reservation numbers worldwide (see p12) or UK tour operator Exsus (see p11)
> **Getting there**: 15 minutes from Ixtapa-Zihuatanejo International Airport
> **Accommodation**: 56 rooms/suites: 4 standard rooms, 19 superior mini-suites, 11 de luxe minisuites, 6 Lagoon suites, 4 Garden suites, 11 Beach Suites and the Presidential Suite
> **Amenities**: Beauty parlour, fitness rooms, laundry and valet service, four swimming pools, 18-hole golf course, fishing and horse-riding nearby, two tennis courts, private beach with hobie cats, waterskiing, snorkelling
> **Dress code**: Casual
> **Weddings**: Ceremonies and receptions can be arranged for up to 150 people
> **Minimum stay**: None
> **Rates**: Mini standard suites from US$220 to US$450; suites from US$400 to US$800; in winter mandatory half board US$60 per person added
> **Credit cards**: Most major
> **Taxes and service charge**: 15% tax and 10% service

The Hotel Villa del Sol has long been regarded among the cognoscenti as one of Latin America's best retreats. As a member of Small Luxury Hotels of the World, guests can be assured of finding luxurious accommodation, delicious food and stylish surroundings in this wonderfully romantic beachfront hideaway. No children are allowed in the hotel during the high season so you are guaranteed complete and utter peace.

Set on one of Mexico's loveliest beaches, the Playa la Ropa, among palm trees, lush gardens and cascading fountains, the Villa del Sol has four standard rooms and 52 split-level thatched bungalow suites, all appointed with traditional furnishings and colourful native art works. Each bungalow has a king-sized canopied bed, ceiling fan, air conditioning, a spacious bathroom and a separate sitting area: some even have plunge pools.

The bungalows also have their own private terrace, so guests can either relax there in their hammock or wander down to the beach where all the usual watersports are on offer. Other facilities include a beauty parlour, Orlando's beach bar, two floodlit tennis courts, an 18-hole golf course and four swimming pools. The award-winning alfresco restaurant serves both Mexican and Continental dishes and on Fridays offers a buffet to a background of live Mexican folk music.

La Casa Que Canta

Also overlooking Zihuatanejo, with staggering views of the bay, is La Casa Que Canta, described by many travellers to Mexico as the country's prettiest hotel. The 'house that sings' has been so beautifully built among terraces set on the edge of a steep cliff, and its terracotta architecture has been blended so well into its surroundings, that you'd never know the hotel was built only a few years ago. Everywhere there are terracotta pots sprouting lush green foliage, huge palm fronds rising up from the balcony below, and thatched roofs sitting atop rust-coloured adobe suites.

I've only heard good things of La Casa. It is a truly wonderful hotel, adorned throughout with traditional Mexican artefacts and furnishings. The hotel has a very personal but relaxing feeling: as the brochure says 'we invite you to share our lifestyle at our home and yours', which just about sums up the atmosphere of this luxurious but unpretentious hotel.

The individual décor of the 24 rooms and suites has been inspired by Mexican folk art, using wonderfully cool shades of palest blue and cream, with red-tiled cool floors, brightly-coloured fabrics draped effectively over the wooden king-size bed frames and hand-painted furniture everywhere. All the suites have magnificent views of the dazzling bay from the bedroom balcony and the living room terrace, as well as air conditioning, fans, minibars, in-room safes, marble bathrooms with double sinks, bidets, walk-in showers, and enormous towels.

> **LA CASA QUE CANTA**
> (☎ 7-55-57030, 🖥 7-55-47900), Camino Escenico La Playa la Ropa, Zihuatanejo, Guerrero 40880, Mexico
> **Reservations**: Small Luxury Hotels of the World toll-free reservations numbers worldwide (see p12) or UK tour operator Cazenove & Loyd Expediciones (☎ 020-7384 2332, 🖥 www.caz-loyd.com)
> **Getting there**: 20 minutes from Ixtapa-Zihuatanejo International Airport, 40-minute flight from Mexico City; the hotel will provide transfers by arrangement
> **Accommodation**: 24 rooms
> **Amenities**: Fitness centre, boutique, fresh and saltwater swimming pools, saltwater Jacuzzi, boutique and restaurant; plus 18-hole golf, deep-sea fishing, horse-riding, all watersports, scuba diving and tennis nearby
> **Dress code**: Casual
> **Weddings**: Can be arranged for up to 34 people
> **Rates**: Suites from US$270 to US$415; Master Suites with pool from US$485 to US$680
> **Credit cards**: Most major
> **Taxes and service charge**: 15% government tax, plus 10% service charge recommended

The architecture of La Casa enhances your privacy: you can walk through your suite's wooden louvred doors onto your patio, which is partially thatched for seclusion. It would be easy to spend all day there on the two comfy loungers, eating from the brightly painted wrought-iron garden furniture, or just lounging in your hammocks enjoying the view.

Meal times at La Casa are very informal with delicious salads and grilled snacks offered at both poolsides during the day, while candlelit dinners on the terrace overlooking the bay in the evening are extremely romantic.

The ten master suites have their own private pool, but one of the best aspects of La Casa is its saltwater Jacuzzi and its two stunning swimming pools available to all guests. One of the pools is a freshwater horizon pool – the water seems to flow endlessly straight out into the Pacific way down below – while the saltwater pool is set amongst boulders and towering palm trees at the bottom of the cliff. As well as the pools, the hotel has its own private beach club on **La Ropa**, a five-minute walk away, with bed chairs and refreshments.

Other recommended hotels

You'll be spoilt for choice for hotels along the Pacific Coast. This is where some of the most seriously exclusive, expensive properties lie as well as some of the most stunning Mexico has to offer. I've chosen four different alternative destinations: two small and truly exclusive hotels, with a price tag to match; another newer and larger hotel with international service and standards; and the fourth, one of a new generation of eco-hotels which combines luxury with a love for the environment.

Las Alamandas (☎ 328-55500, 🖥 328-55027) is one of the world's most exclusive and ultimate resorts, set halfway between **Puerto Vallarta** and **Manzanillo**. Owned, designed and decorated by Isabel Goldsmith, Las Alamandas has long been popular with celebrity guests. Most people fly directly into the resort's private airstrip on private charter flights from either Puerto Vallarta or Manzanillo airports, costing around US$750 per couple each way. It costs US$200 for road transfer. A maximum of 22 guests are accommodated in four villas of varying size. Each room is large with high vaulted ceilings and is beautifully decorated in bright Mexican fabrics and warm colour-washed walls with stunning hand-carved wooden furniture. They all have a Mexican-tiled bathroom, equipped with bathrobes and toiletries, a private terrace, a full-sized living room and a dining room, so that you can eat alone if you want.

A junior suite starts at US$699 per couple full board, excluding drinks, tax and service. The Presidential Suite costs US$1200. While the hotel is exceptionally pricey, you get what you pay for – a really exclusive hotel where you are made to feel like guests instead of customers: there is no check-in desk, no formalities and the excellent service is never intrusive. Book through UK representatives Cathy Matos Mexican Tours (☎ 020-8492 0000).

Mahakua – Hacienda de San Antonio (☎ 331-34411, 📄 331-43727, 🖥 www.mahakua.com, Municipio de Comala, CP 28450 Colima, near Guadalajara) is the first of a new generation of 'Maha resorts' from Adrian Zecha, the gifted creator of Amanresorts. Opened in October 2000, this hotel will excite Amanjunkies the world over. Set within the 5000-acre working ranch and coffee plantation of the late Sir James Goldsmith, with an active volcano as a backdrop, Zecha has transformed a 19th-century hacienda into a magnificent suite-only sanctuary for a maximum of 52 guests.

The 26 suites, more like private residences, have been beautifully refurbished and artistically decorated using mirrors, paintings, tapestries, ceramic lamps, hand-woven carpets and yards of silk. Each has a terrace or balcony overlooking courtyards and gardens inspired by Spain's Alhambra Palace, and all have fireplaces and spacious bathrooms. The dining room has a beautiful barrel-vaulted brick ceiling and a fireplace made of volcanic rock.

You can spend your days here swimming in the 115-ft pool, playing tennis on a floodlit court, mountain biking, horse-riding or going on guided nature walks in the forest, where you can see finches, woodpeckers, wild turkeys, and flycatchers. Excursions to nearby towns and volcanoes can also be arranged but, alas, there's no beach for miles. Seriously expensive, a suite will set you back US$800 a night and the fabulous Volcano Suite US$1450, but after you've dipped into your pocket once you won't have to worry about anything else as almost everything is included. Book direct or through UK tour operator Western & Oriental (☎ 020-7313 6600).

Four Seasons Resort Punta Mita (☎ 329-16000, 📄 329-16060, Bahia de Banderas, Nayarit), which opened its doors in 1999, is an exclusive property situated on the 'Mexican Riviera' just a 30-minute drive from Puerto Vallarta. It has 113 guest rooms and 27 suites housed in 13 quaint, clay-tile-roofed casitas all of which have inspiring full ocean views from their private terraces or balconies. Most suites have private plunge pools.

During the day you can float dreamily in the large free-form pool and whirlpool, laze on the chaise longues on the pristine white sandy beaches or do a bit of snorkelling on the coral reef. If you need more there is a fitness centre and spa, four tennis courts illuminated at night and a private, Jack Nicklaus-designed championship golf course with eight holes right next to the ocean. Being a Four Seasons Resort, this hotel has tremendous amenities and facilities – you'll want for nothing.

Standard doubles start from US$560 to US$790 in peak season – January to May and October to Mid-December – but are US$360 to US$590 the rest of the year. Book through Four Seasons reservation numbers worldwide (see p13) or through tour operator Abercrombie & Kent (☎ 0845-0700 614).

Hotelito Desconocido (☎ 322-22526, 📄 322-30293, 🖥 www.hotelito.com, Jalisco) is an eco-tourism resort nestled on a wetland estuary between the Sierra Madre Mountains and the Pacific Ocean, 60 miles south of Puerto Vallarta (complimentary airport transfers included). On one of the most important sea turtle and bird reserves in Mexico, the Hotelito is built in the style of an old Mexican fishing village with 30 *palafitos* (thatch-roof bungalows) with solar-powered ceiling fans, built on stilts, each overlooking either the estuary or on the 40 miles of unspoilt beach beyond. The interiors are unmistakably Mexican with wooden floors, handpainted murals and antiques, and the oversized bathrooms come with open-air solar-heated bamboo showers. Go for one of the ten individual palafitos for maximum privacy.

Breakfast is delivered to your dock by canoe at the raise of a flag, and at night the Hotelito is enchantingly lit by hundreds of candles as you enjoy the fresh catch of the day at the thatch-roof **El Cantarito** restaurant overlooking the estuary.

There is plenty to do here, including a saltwater pool, sailing, kayaking, windsurfing or horse rides at sunset on the beach or biking through the palm groves. In June, sea turtles make their way onto Hotelito's beach to lay their eggs. Massage alfresco is also available at the hotel, and after that you'll probably feel like lying in a hammock to gaze at the breathtaking view and soak up the dreamy, romantic atmosphere. Doubles cost from US$215, suites from US$260 inclusive except for additional 17% tax; transfer free with a minimum stay of three nights. In the US call toll-free (☎ 877-486 3372) or book through UK operator Cathy Matos Mexican Tours (see p11).

CANCUN AND THE YUCATAN PENINSULA

If you like big, buzzing resorts, you'll love Cancún where international high-rise hotels, discos, and sports facilities abound.

Recommended hotels

You need not spend a fortune on accommodation in Cancún. The best deals are to be found through British tour operators such as Kuoni and BA Holidays (see p11), who offer fantastic packages to Cancún in really top-class hotels, many of them on an all-inclusive basis. For example, Kuoni offers seven nights at the **Moon Palace** – the most popular destination for honeymooners – for around £1089 per person in

---

THINGS TO SEE AND DO AROUND CANCUN AND THE YUCATAN PENINSULA

Just off Cancún, **Isla Mujeres** is a great place to visit with a really rustic atmosphere. The island is a birdwatchers' paradise but it is also great for diving and snorkelling and, because it is so small, it is easy to cycle from one end to the other. The beaches at the north end of the island are the best while the coast at the south end is rocky. Isla Mujeres is easily accessible for a day trip: a ferry goes 16 times a day from Puerto Juarez, north of Cancún.

Cozumel is Mexico's largest island and it has the same friendly, laid-back attitude as any Caribbean island as well as excellent beaches and diving. Only 56km away from Cancún, Cozumel is perfect for those who are seeking to get away from it all, in hotels that are unpretentious and which have lots of Mexican charm. Cozumel is reached by a 50-minute flight from **Merida**, a ferry from Playa del Carmen, or a 20-minute flight from Cancún with Aerocaribe.

If you want to dive, the best dives are at Palancar, Santa Rosa and Colombia. There are plenty of certified **dive schools** on the island to choose from.

It is easy to fly from Cancún or Cozumel inland to **Chichen Itza**, or you can explore this from Hacienda San Jose (see p200). Originally a Mayan city, Chichen Itza became the capital of the Toltec Empire in the 12th century, before the Mayans reclaimed it a century later. To see these incredible ruins from the air is an awesome experience. Equally worthwhile is a visit to the Mayan site of **Tulum**, where the white city walls are set against a backdrop of cliffs and coastline. Approximately 125km south of Cancún, the ruins were dedicated to the worship of the setting sun and have to be seen to be believed. If you take your swimming gear you can scramble down the rocks to the sea and dive on the reef.

Playa del Carmen, a very Mexican port which is especially colourful on Sundays, is also worth visiting for its relatively peaceful beach and slow pace. The best white sandy beaches are north of the town but the sandflies can be annoying.

For further information visit 🖳 www.gocancun.com or www.mayayucatan.com.

STAYING IN A HACIENDA IN THE YUCATAN

Not only does the Yucatan hold the key to the mysteries of Mayan life in its archaeological sites, but it also offers the chance to stay in some magnificent, opulent haciendas. These sprawling properties combine Spanish colonial elegance with the legacy of ancient Mayan tradition. You can combine staying in several and they make the best base from which to explore the region's wonders.

Hacienda Katanchel (99-234 020, ▤ 99-234 000, ▯ www.hacienda-katanchel.com, Km 26, Highway, 180 Merida-Cancun, Yucatan 97470), built in the 17th century on the grounds of an ancient Mayan settlement, is the most luxurious hacienda in the Yucatan and its only member of Small Luxury Hotels of the World.

Hacienda Katanchel's 39 separate pavilion suites are set in 740 acres of lush gardens and luxuriant tropical jungle. They each have invigorating mineral water plunge pools, and a wonderful veranda front and back where you can dream on a hammock overlooking the Maya-style garden in the utmost privacy. The honeymoon suite has a king-size bed and an indoor plunge pool, and all suites are decorated in an opulent and unique colonial style dotted with curious Mayan symbols such as little flags flying from the top of the beds.

After a sundowner at the elegant Grand Salon, guests dine on exquisite organic, Mayan-inspired delights in the gourmet *Casa de Maquinas* restaurant, ranked among Mexico's top five. When you've had enough of swimming in your own pool or lounging on the deck around the semi-Olympic-sized hotel pool, there are even your very own Mayan ruins to explore in the hacienda's grounds and nature walks. Colonial towns and convents, wildlife reserves, natural swimming pools, golf and beaches are all within an easy drive. There is a small chapel in the grounds if you want to get married here. Pavilions cost from US$250, Honeymoon Suite US$350, plus 17% tax and 10% service. Book through Small Luxury Hotels of the World reservation numbers worldwide (see p12) or UK operator Cathy Matos Mexican Tours (☎ 020-8492 0000).

As **Hacienda San Jose** (☎/▤ 99-501 272/73, Km 30 Tixkokob, Tekanto Highway, Tixkokob, Yucatan) appears through the trees, what strikes you are the bright blue arches of the veranda with its orange back walls. The 15 light and airy rooms and suites of this exclusive luxury ex-plantation house are beautifully painted in strong, lively Mexican colours, but are restful at the same time. The San Jose is located in a great spot near the Yucatan coast and close to the ruins of the famous Chichen Itza.

Hacienda Temozon (☎/▤ 99-501 271/74, Km 182 Merida, Uxmal Highway, Temozon Sur, Yucatan), with its grand dark red exterior with long cloisters of columns and arches, spacious gardens and spectacular neo-classical swimming pool, recreates the atmosphere of the Belle Epoque of south-eastern Mexico. The 26 rooms and suites with traditional tiled floor, rich wooden louvred shutters and lace-trimmed bedspreads are all in the original hacienda building and many have their own tiny plunge pool. There is a 17th-century chapel if you want to get married here, and the jewel of Mayan architecture, Uxmal, nearby.

Hacienda Santa Rosa (☎ 99-282 042, ▤ 99-104 362, Km 129 Merida, Campeche Highway, Santa Rosa, Yucatan) is the closest of the haciendas to the gulf of Mexico and a good base for visiting the wildlife sanctuary at Celestun. There are just 11 uncluttered rooms in the original 17th-century building, so it feels very much like a private home. This is the place to sling up your hammock and gaze into the gardens or sit with a cool drink around the reflective pool.

The three haciendas above are owned and managed by Starwood hotels and can be booked direct through them (▯ www.starwood.com). UK's Journey Latin America (☎ 020-8747 8315) offers a 'Hacienda Experience' for £728 per person which includes two nights bed and breakfast in the San Jose and the Santa Rosa or Temozon, two day-trips in a private car with an English-speaking guide – one to Chichen Itza and Valladolid, the other to Uxmal and nearby Puuc ruins – transfers, taxes, tips and one candlelit dinner with Mexican wine.

November/December all-inclusive with flights and transfers from their Worldwide brochure. The Moon Palace, 20 minutes' drive from Cancún Airport, is set in the midst of 55 acres of gardens just steps from a white sand beach with plenty of watersports. It has a large free-form swimming pool, a lively night-life with restaurants, bars and a disco, and a double Jacuzzi in the spacious rooms for when you want to just chill out together.

Maroma Resort & Spa (☎ 987-28200, ▤ 987-28220, ▯ www.maroma.net) is a secluded luxurious hideaway on the Riveria Maya, nestled between Tulum's Mayan temples and Cancun's glittering night-life, offering handmade hospitality in a beachfront location. The beautiful setting is echoed in the simple stylish architecture of whitewashed buildings in gardens populated with iguanas and exotic birds; some of the rooms have thatched balconies with a fabulous view of the swaying coconut palms on the beach just steps away. The 36 rooms and suites glow with mahogany and bamboo-filtered light while a rainbow hammock beckons from the balcony. Each is individually decorated with hand-painted tiles, soft wool rugs, original art, a king-size bed and a sunken tub. This is a stylish, beautiful place where you can be pampered with a range of spa treatments, music, hearty Mexican breakfasts and fresh seafood from the reef, and where they promise 'more honey and all of the moon' to honeymooners!

Ocean view rooms cost from US$324 with breakfast, transfers and snorkelling trip, but excluding 10% service and 12% tax. Maroma's three-night honeymoon package includes transfers, an ocean view room with breakfast, champagne and flowers on arrival, romantic dinner for two with wine, snorkelling trip, Mayan-style steam bath, sunset cruise and handcrafted gift from US$1556. Book through UK tour operator Cathy Matos Mexican Tours (see p11).

OAXACA

Founded in 1529 this historic and quite magical city is the place to come if you want to discover the real charm of this amazing country. Oaxaca has to be one of the most romantic colonial cities in Mexico; it is very easy to fall in love with it because of its exquisite baroque architecture and charming cobbled winding streets.

The city sits on an arid plateau, high up in the **Sierra Madre del Sur** mountains, giving it a wonderfully fresh spring-like climate all year round. Try to be there on a Saturday as the Indian market is one of the best in Mexico for hand-embroidered clothing and jewellery. Even a short stay in Oaxaca will give you ample opportunity to visit some of the area's extraordinary archaeological sites, created by the Zapotec and Mixtec Indians long before the Spanish conquest. The three best sites, **Monte Albán**, **Mitla** and **Yagul**, all lie within 40km of the city. With a direct flight from Acapulco to Oaxaca it is very easy to combine these two destinations.

Camino Real

Camino Real, built within the hallowed walls of the 16th-century convent of Santa Catalina, is the best place to stay in Oaxaca. The hotel boasts 400-year-old frescoes overlooking flagstone walkways set amidst cooling fountains and scenic gardens. The fres-coes and the treasured canvases line the passageways, giving the hotel a very old world air.

The hotel has 91 air-conditioned rooms and suites which are all decorated in authentic Mexican style, using brightly coloured rugs and Mexican artefacts. Whitewashed walls set off dark wooden furniture, terracotta tiled floors and wooden beamed ceilings. Facilities in the bedroom include satellite TV, phone, minibar and hairdryer and many of the rooms come with two double beds.

Guests can dine on regional specialties in El Refectorio, decorated with an attractive

---

CAMINO REAL
(☎ 951-60611, 🖷 951-60732, 🖳 oax@caminoreal.com), Calle 5 de Mayo 300, 68000 Oaxaca
Reservations: Either direct with the Mexico City office (☎ 5-227-7200), from the US and Canada (toll-free ☎ 1-800-7-CAMINO or 1-800-722-6466), from the UK (☎ 08705-300 200), from Belgium (toll-free ☎ 0800-71 053) and from Germany (☎ 01805-521 2645)
Getting there: Taxis from Oaxaca International Airport (15 minutes)
Accommodation: 91 rooms and suites
Amenities: Swimming pool, restaurant, two bars, phones, laundry, concierge, room service, tour desk
Dress code: Casual
Weddings: Wedding ceremonies and receptions can be arranged either in the hotel grounds or in the private chapel
Minimum stay: None
Rates: Doubles from US$195 room only; suites from US$265 with continental breakfast
Credit cards: Most major
Taxes and service charge: 17% tax, service included

wall of embedded pitchers, and drinking in either the **Bugambilias** bar or **Las Novicias**. At night the gardens around the pool are illuminated, and there is a courtyard with a fountain where you can sit and gaze at the stars.

At weekends the chapel hosts traditional folk art displays called Guelaguetza, an ancient Oaxacan ritual stemming from the tribe's belief in giving without expecting anything in return. The festivals involve handicrafts, dances in colourful costumes, and a lavish buffet.

There's plenty to do from and at the Camino Real: I'd recommend a three or four-day stay so that you can see some of this country's culture. This, combined with a week or so at a beach resort, would be a great honeymoon.

CENTRAL MEXICO

If you want to see some of Mexico's colonial heritage, then a visit to the beautiful central highland region of **Bajio** is a great way to experience the impact of the country's 300 years under European rule. Wonderfully unspoilt colonial cities, such as **Querataro**, **San Miguel de Allende** and **Morelia**, are within a day's drive of Mexico City. These cities have plenty of old-world charm, fine-art and handicrafts shops, museums, and hundreds of colonial buildings, many of which have hardly changed for centuries.

La Casa de la Marquesa

La Casa de la Marquesa in Querataro, 217km north of Mexico City, is one of the most beautiful and romantic hotels you'll ever see. As a member of the Small Luxury Hotels of the World group, this architectural jewel makes a wonderfully luxurious base from which to explore the picturesque nearby towns of San Miguel de Allende and Morelia.

The palace is located in the heart of the historic downtown and is one of the oldest and most impressive mansions in the city of Queratero. A baroque building dating back to 1756, the ornate, pale yellow sandstone exterior and the lavish, but totally in keeping, interior decorations have to be seen to be believed. The carved stonework, intricate design and Moorish details, the living room and the chapel, are overwhelmingly beautiful.

> **LA CASA DE LA MARQUESA**
> (☎ 42-120 092, 📠 42-120 098), Madero No 41, Centro Querataro, QRO 76000
> **Reservations**: Small Luxury Hotels of the World toll-free reservations numbers worldwide (see p12)
> **Getting there**: Five minutes by taxi from Querataro
> **Accommodation**: 25 suites
> **Amenities**: Restaurant, bar, 24-hour room service; golf, horse-riding and a swimming pool are all available nearby
> **Dress code**: Elegant casual
> **Weddings**: The hotel can host weddings and receptions for up to 120 people
> **Minimum stay**: None
> **Rates**: Suites from US$150 to US$300 including continental breakfast
> **Credit cards**: Most major
> **Taxes and service charge**: Not included

The hotel has 25 air-conditioned suites, all of which have original décor, either double or king-size beds, cable TV and phones, as well as homely touches such as fresh flowers.

The menu in La Casa de la Marquesa's dining room reflects traditional flavours and aromas, while the **Don Porfirio** bar is a great place to relax.

This hotel is the perfect contrast to a beach hotel, giving you another, much more authentic, insight into Mexico.

MEXICO CITY

If you need or want to stay in Mexico City, the new, futuristic **Habita** (☎ 5-282 3100, 📠 5-282 3101), a member of Small Luxury Hotels of the World (see p12 for reservation numbers worldwide), is a good choice. It floats in frosted glass above a leafy boulevard in the middle of Mexico City's chic district. From the sun-loungers on the redwood deck around the pool you feel far away from the bustle of the city, with a view of tranquil clean lines and geometric designs. Habita offers the comfort and tradition of Mexican hospitality with all that is modern. Doubles cost from US$225, suites from US$275.

THE COPPER CANYON

The spectacular train ride from **Los Mochis** into the Copper Canyon at **Chihauhua** is a great four-night, five-day tour into the heart of northern Mexico. The Copper Canyon is without doubt one of the most stunning sights in the world. Deeper and four times larger than the Grand Canyon, the 644km railway line links the wild beauty of the **Tamahumara Range** with the Pacific coast.

Fly from Mexico City to Los Mochis (US$150 per person using a Mexipass) and stay the night at the **Plaza Inn** (☎ 6818-1042, ▤ 6818-1590), ready for the train's early departure the next day. The five-hour train journey takes you through a diversity of scenery from tropical forests, peach and apple orchards and semi-arid plains to snow-covered mountain peaks and upland lakes. The best hotels are at **Divisidero**: they also have the best views of the canyon. Stay at **Hotel Divisidero Barrancas** (☎ 1-415-1199, ▤ 1-4156-575) for at least two nights as there is lots of see and do in the area, all of which can be arranged by tour companies based in the town. Although this pretty pink hotel is not luxurious, it is simply and comfortably furnished and has one of the most wonderfully romantic locations, set right on the edge of the canyon at a height of 7000 feet. Each of the 50 rooms in the two-storey building has a private terrace with staggering views.

Two trains run daily in each direction so, if you stop another night in Los Mochis on your way out, the whole trip will take you five days. You can book a four-night package through UK tour operators **Cathy Matos Mexican Tours** (☎ 020-8492-0000) for US$550 per person, or **Journey Latin America** (☎ 020-8747 8315) which includes accommodation (four nights), first-class train tickets both ways and transfers for US$900 per person.

BAJA CALIFORNIA

The long thin peninsula of Baja California is a place where 'the deep blue Pacific seas meet azure skies and painted sands race toward purpled mountains' and whales frolic nearby. But the main reason to come here has to be **Las Ventanas al Paraiso** (☎ 52-114-40300, ▤ 52-114-40301, 💻 www.lasventanas.com, Los Cabos, Baja California Sur), a secluded, opulent paradise, reminiscent of the gracious haciendas of old, just 15 minutes' drive from San Jose del Cabo International Airport. Part of the Rosewood Group, Las Ventanas is a member of the Leading Hotels of the World.

Furnishings are luxurious and elegant throughout but traditional paintings, carvings and artefacts give it a distinctly Mexican atmosphere. The 61 all-suite accommodation with garden or ocean views includes 28 fabulous rooftop terrace suites. Some have splash pools, fireplaces and telescopes for whale watching. All are fitted with traditional tiled floors and marble bathrooms, air conditioning, satellite TV, CD players, video library and an in-room Tequila setup.

The resort has a horizon pool, watersports and world-class golf and a European spa which offers couples massages. This is a place for desert excursions on horseback, walks on sunlit beaches, cooling off in the shade of tropical gardens and starlit dinners on your private terrace.

Ocean view junior suite costs US$675 not including tax, service and transfers; a package for two including seven nights with most meals, transfers and champagne, massage, and five activities from US$5100. The outdoor plaza can hold 200 guests for a wedding reception. Reservations through the Leading Hotels of the World reservation numbers worldwide (see p12).

Belize
(BEST TIME: OCTOBER TO MAY)

Although not exactly what you'd call a classic honeymoon destination, the tropical rainforests, coral reefs, mountains, stunning offshore islands and Mayan culture of Belize cannot fail to fascinate visitors.

Belize is best suited to people looking for somewhere far off the tourist track who are keen to visit the jungle and who don't mind sleeping in stylish yet simple accommodation. Some of the lodges are very comfortable and there is luxury to be had in **Chaa Creek**, **Blancaneaux** and especially in the new luxurious Cayo Espanto (see p00), voted one of 101 Best Hotels 2001 by *Tatler*. All properties here can be booked through UK booking agents, Reef and Rainforest Tours (☎ 01803-866 965, 🖹 01803-865 916, 🖳 www.reefrainforest.co.uk)) who are happy to put together complicated honeymoon itineraries!

It would help your enjoyment here if you were avid scuba divers, as one of the best things about Belize is the spectacular diving, or snorkelling, on the world's second largest barrier reef, but particularly on the three coral atolls, one of which contains the famous blue hole of Jacques Costeau fame. But there is more to Belize than diving. It has jungle and Mayan ruins to see, and is within easy reach of Tikal in Guatemala, one of the best ruins.

BEACH AND ISLANDS

The **Cayes** (pronounced 'keys') has some good hotels with beachfront casitas but don't expect the kind of luxury accommodation or service that you'd find in the nearby West Indies. Between the months of June and September (low season) the sand-flies can be so dreadful that they'd ruin your honeymoon – you have been warned!

The best marine places to stay are on **Ambergris Caye**, the biggest of the Cayes and home to many dive schools. However, don't go to Ambergris Caye expecting to find the true Belize as much of the island is owned and operated by North Americans. Regular ferry services operate to the island from **Belize City**: services depart from the pier in front of **Bellevue Hotel**, Monday to Friday 4pm, Saturday 1pm, no service Sunday. There are also frequent, daily flights from Belize City (the best way to get there), plus direct flights from **Corozal** in the north of Belize if you're coming from Mexico.

Recommended hotels

Victoria House (☎ 026-2067, 🖹 026-2429, 🖳 www.victoria-house.com, PO Box 22, San Pedro, Ambergris Caye) has the best reputation for maintaining standards of all the island's hotels. This very elegant and comfortable beach-side hotel was where

---

BELIZE
Tropical rainforest, coral reefs, mountains, beautiful offshore islands and Mayan culture
Average maximum temperatures °C

JAN	FEB	MAR	APR	MAY	JUN	JUL	AUG	SEP	OCT	NOV	DEC
27	28	29	30	31	31	31	31	31	30	28	27

Approximate exchange rates: Belize dollar (BZ$) – £1 = BZ$2.80, US$1 = BZ$1.97, A$1 = BZ$1.02
Time difference: GMT minus six hours
Voltage: 110v/220v AC, 60 Hz
Country dialling code: ☎ 501
Further information: Belize Tourism Board: 🖳 www.travelbelize.org

Harrison Ford chose to stay when he filmed *Mosquito Coast*. The beach cabanas are air conditioned and look onto the beach where there is a good selection of watersports, and the hotel has a swimming pool. As one of the island's best hotels it tends to get booked up way in advance, so make your reservations early. Beach bungalows cost from US$254/BZ$500, plus 17% tax.

Cayo Espanto (☎ 021-3001, ▣ www.aprivateisland.com, PO Box 49, San Pedro, Ambergris Caye), a large private islet for 14 guests situated just off the mainland, is the first design sensation to hit Belize. The most expensive and exclusive property in Belize, (wealthy honeymooners can rent it for exclusive use), it is visually impressive. Guests stay in five small houses, and enjoy intense service with five staff, including a personal butler, to every guest. You can dine anywhere as the restaurant comes to you, and with plunge pools (but no beaches), in-room massage and plenty to read, you may not want to venture far from here. If you do, however, bear in mind it will cost you US$20 every time you want to get to the mainland. Doubles cost from US$356/BZ$700.

JUNGLE AND CULTURE
The best surviving examples of ancient Mayan culture are at **Lamanai** and **Caracol**, deep in the jungle: exotic wildlife, like the native black howler monkey, is also common here. Most of the accommodation in the jungle is in simple lodges, three more luxurious than the others.

Recommended hotels
Chan Chich Lodge (☎/▤ 02-34419, US toll-free ☎ 800-343-8009, ▣ www.chanchich.com, 1 King Street, PO Box 37, Gallon Jug) is reached by a 30-minute charter flight from Belize City. This extraordinary hotel is set amidst the ruins of an ancient Mayan city in the **Rio Bravo Conservation Area**, located within 50,000 hectares of untouched rainforest. The owners had to get the government's permission to be allowed to build within the plaza of these classic protected ruins. This is paradise for nature lovers: you can see monkeys, all manner of exotic birds and other wildlife from your balcony; some guests have even been lucky enough to see a jaguar. The lodge has 12 thatched cottages made from local wood and tastefully decorated, each with its own en suite shower, two queen-sized beds, private porch and two hammocks. The hotel will organize wonderful archaeological tours as well as fabulous rides in the surrounding reserve, canoeing and river swimming. Doubles cost from US$147/BZ$290 plus 17% tax.

The best place to stay in the mountain pine ridge near San Ignacio is **Blancaneaux Lodge**, (☎ 092-3878, ▤ 092-3919, PO Box B, Central Farm, Mountain Pine Ridge, Cayo District), owned by Francis Ford Coppola. Although the lodge is very isolated and a pain to get to, the views over the river and waterfalls are stunning, the food is good and the accommodation pretty luxurious for Belize. Double cabanas from US$183/BZ$360 including breakfast, plus 15% tax.

The **Lodge at Chaa Creek** (▣ www.chaacreek.com) is Belize's original forest lodge and, surrounded by tropical butterflies and birds such as parrots and toucans, a great place for a romantic jungle experience. Chaa Creek has high standard cabanas, luxury Jacuzzi suites and a Complete Luxury Garden Suite. From here you can take excursions to the Pine Ridge, to Tikal and Caracol, or ride horses or mountain bike through its private woodlands or be pampered in its new state-of-the-art spa housed in a modern architect-designed building and enjoy the stunning views. The lodge will also arrange dive trips. Doubles cost from US$135, Complete Luxury Garden Suite from US$295 plus government tax and 10% service. Its honeymoon package includes suite accommodation and a float by canoe down the Makal River with a picnic lunch for US$200 per person.

Costa Rica
(BEST TIME: DECEMBER TO APRIL)

After Mexico, Costa Rica is the Central American country most suited to honeymoons. You'd both have to have a thirst for adventure, but there are some truly idyllic beach resorts and plenty of opportunity to see some of the wonders of the jungle and its abundant wildlife.

Costa Rica was a fabulous place. Don't go expecting the beaches to be the kind that you find in resorts – all manicured and perfect with lots of comfy bed chairs – because they are all natural, windswept and misty from the jungle, which we loved. Make sure you hire a car as half the excitement was driving around on our own.
Victoria and Piers Hankinson

A honeymoon in Costa Rica is all about beautiful scenery and eco-tourism. There's no real Indian culture, no markets and no impressive colonial buildings to speak of but the landscape is so dramatic that you'll be truly swept away. The natural beauty of Costa Rica is world renowned; you'll see it all here, cloud forest, rainforest, iguanas, sloths, extraordinary birds and hundreds of brilliant and rare butterflies.

Rich it indeed is, but not in the way it was originally anticipated. The country got its name from Columbus, who, when he landed in 1502, believed the area was full of gold and named it Costa Rica, meaning rich coast. Now a haven of peace and tranquillity in the middle of Central America, sandwiched between volatile Nicaragua to the north and equally chaotic Panama to the south, Costa Rica has somehow managed to escape the political and social unrest of its neighbours.

Although it is very possible to combine Costa Rica with other Central American countries, such as Mexico, there is so much to see and do here and travelling around is so easy, that I'd recommend spending two weeks in just this country alone.

SAN JOSE
There's little point in staying in San José as the city is a bit of a dump but only 15 minutes away is one of Costa Rica's most perfect romantic hideaways, Finca Rosa Blanca.

Finca Rosa Blanca
Finca Rosa Blanca is a real treat. Without doubt one of the most individual hotels in Central America, it makes a wonderful place to unwind and relax at the start or end of

---

COSTA RICA
Perfect for adventurous couples who are keen on wildlife, the jungle and idyllic beach resorts and who also like being far away from other honeymooners
When to go: December to April
Average maximum temperatures °C

JAN	FEB	MAR	APR	MAY	JUN	JUL	AUG	SEP	OCT	NOV	DEC
24	24	26	27	27	27	26	26	27	26	25	24

Capital: San José
Flight times: to Juan San José from:
    New York: (via Miami) 6 hours
    LA (via Miami): 7¹/₄ hours
    London: (via Miami) 9¹/₂ hours
    Sydney: (via LA) 20 hours
Approximate exchange rates: Colón (C) – £1 = C461, US$1 = C325, A$1 = C168
Time difference: GMT minus six hours
Voltage: 110v AC
Combine with: It's best to concentrate on Costa Rica alone
Country dialling code: ☎ 506
Further information: 🖳 www.tourism.costarica.com

your holiday. The Finca is as extraordinary from the outside as it is within. Looking up at the turreted white building from below it looks a pretty strange shape – an intriguing combination of traditional Hispanic ranch house with white walls and something not unlike a lighthouse tower in the middle. This is a pretty odd description but it's hard to put this unique building into words, and if I've made it sound ugly I've done it a vast injustice.

Because of its unusual architectural design the Finca looks incredible inside with irregularly-shaped glass windows letting light in on every side. In the middle of the house you come into a central foyer with a circular seat and lots of lush green foliage and various interesting artefacts displayed about you. This is used as the hotel lounge and there is an honesty bar for guests.

Each of the seven guest rooms and suites in this small, family owned inn is furnished differently or, as the owners like to put it, 'each has its own name and personality'. The **Rosa Blanca Suite**, in particular, is out of this world with a huge sunken bath painted turquoise, surrounded by stone flagging and ornate murals of jungle scenes on the walls and light streaming in from an adjacent window looking out onto the gardens. There's even a separate shower painted in bright tones of aqua, turquoise and royal blue. It's not only the sunken bath that has helped this room to work its way into the pages of glossy magazines all over the world: up an amazing spiral

FINCA ROSA BLANCA
(☎ 269-9392, 🖷 269-9555, 🖳 www.finca-rblanca.co.cr), Apdo 41-3009, Santa Barbara de Heredia, Costa Rica
Reservations: Through UK tour operator Worldwide Journeys and Expeditions (☎ 020-7386 4646)
Getting there: The hotel can arrange transfers
Accommodation: Seven rooms, standard to suite and two villas
Amenities: Restaurant serving Costa Rican and international fare, swimming pool with cascades, large Jacuzzi, open-air game room/lounge, library, horses, three hectare fruit orchard
Dress code: Casual
Weddings: Can be arranged, with a maximum of 30 guests
Minimum stay: None
Rates: Doubles from US$155, Rosa Blanca Suite from US$240 with breakfast; four-course dinner US$30 per person plus tax
Credit cards: American Express, Visa, MasterCard
Taxes and service charge: 16.4% government taxes on lodging and food

*At **Finca Rosa Blanca** our only complaint was with the food which we felt was a bit of a rip off, although it was good – sort of middle of the road French with local bits and pieces like the gallo pinto, a traditional dish of black beans, rice and onion, which we had for breakfast. Otherwise it was a very quiet, very relaxed and a very friendly hotel and was quite unusually decorated.*
Moyra and Alastair Murdoch

staircase is the bedroom where lace covers the bed and windows open out onto balconies on all sides. The entire room is incredible. The Finca also has two spacious villas for hire.

Meals are expensive but good: they are taken with the Finca's other guests around a large central wooden table which seats about 20 people. Guests spend their days either by the lovely oval swimming pool which appears to flow seamlessly into the coffee plantation below, or out on day tours to the **Braulio Carillo National Park Cloud Forest**, **Barva**, **Poás** and **Irazú** volcanoes, coffee plantations and butterfly farms. If you are thinking about Costa Rica do make a point of fitting in a couple of days at the Finca Rosa Blanca either at the beginning or the end of your trip as it's a wonderfully friendly little hotel and the bedrooms are quite divine.

Lapa Rios

Lapa Rios is the best jungle lodge in Costa Rica and it offers first-rate accommodation, service and dining, among primary and advanced secondary forest 90m above sea level. Wherever you stand at Lapa Rios the views of the **Golfo Dulce Forest Reserve** are absolutely magnificent. This 400-hectare property was the brainchild of John and Karen Lewis from Minnesota; they decided to build the luxury lodge to help finance rainforest conservation.

LAPA RIOS
(☎ 735-5130, 🖷 735-5179, 🖥 www.laparios.com), PO Box 100, Puerto Jimenez, Peninsula de Osa, Costa Rica
Reservations: Either direct or through UK tour operators Worldwide Journeys and Expeditions (☎ 020-7386 4646) and Cox & Kings (see p11)
Getting there: Via charter flight or the domestic airline, Travel Air, to Puerto Jimenez, from where Lapa Rios is a 40-minute journey in the owners' four-wheel drive
Accommodation: 14 thatched bungalows
Amenities: Restaurant and bar; uncrowded jungle trails accompanied by naturalist guides; riding; kayaking; game fishing; surfing; boat tours of Golfo Dulce; swimming pool and poolside bar service
Dress code: Informal
Weddings: Weddings and receptions can be held here but they require a minimum of 20 and a maximum of 78 guests
Minimum stay: None
Rates: Bungalows for two cost from US$160 to US$238, full board
Credit cards: American Express, Visa and MasterCard
Taxes and service charge: Included

Included in *Tatler*'s 101 Best Hotels 2001, the first-class facilities have been built in total harmony with their natural habitat, incorporating local woods, bamboo and thatch roofing over zinc and white concrete to create typical palenque-style cottages.

The Lewises have kept the buildings as open as possible, so although the cottages have bamboo roll-down shades, the 'walls' are actually just screens, and the aspect has been designed carefully so that the cottages are completely private. You do get insects in your room but that's the price you pay for this kind of jungle experience and there are mosquito nets for protection.

In the main lodge there are bamboo settees with pillows in vivid jungle prints, and bamboo and smoked glass tables in the dining room, where the food is quite good. The focal point of the dining room is the somewhat adventurous addition of a spiral wooden staircase which winds up three storeys and out on to a roof-top walkway affording a breathtaking 360° view above the forest canopy and out to the ocean beyond. After dinner everyone goes straight to their rooms, so don't come here expecting any kind of evening entertainment or late night drinking. The 14 thatched cottages at Lapa Rios are really comfortable and airy, with two queen-sized beds in each, covered in lovely white- and green-striped cotton sheets and prettily draped mosquito nets. Particularly nice touches are the screened windows in the en suite solar-heated shower room, giving the illusion of bathing outdoors with the most incredible views of the gulf, and the second shower outside in your private garden where there really is nothing between you and the view! The bedrooms have ample towels, white blankets in case it gets chilly at night, electric ceiling fans, kerosene lamps for power cuts, and heavy tropical vanity units, closets, bamboo easy chairs and a writing desk. Each bungalow has an ocean view, private deck and patio garden.

Lapa Rios, part of the **Golfo Dolce Forest Reserve**, has many private, uncrowded trails for guests to explore. You can go with guides who are trained to point out the remarkable wildlife – make sure you do the walk to the large waterfalls. The hotel also offers horse-riding, kayaking, game fishing and a huge sandy beach to stroll along, but do watch out as their activities can be a bit pricey.

PACIFIC COAST

At one point the Pacific and the Atlantic coasts are only 113km apart, but they couldn't be more different. The Pacific coast consists of long deserted beaches, while the Atlantic side is wind-lashed with roaring surf, so head south if it's beaches you are after. The province of **Guanacaste** boasts some of the most exotic and idyllic beaches in Central America. Although this coastline is more heavily developed there are still some long stretches of unspoilt sandy beaches with a few really great hotels which are perfect for recharging your batteries before you do some serious touring.

(Opposite): The ruins of the lost city of Machu Picchu, Peru. The only hotel in this dramatic location is the luxurious Machu Picchu Sanctuary Lodge (see p216).

Hotel Villa Caletas

Hotel Villa Caletas is located up in the hills, 457m above sea level with magnificent views over the **Gulf of Nicoya**. One of the most romantic hotels in Costa Rica, the Villa Caletas is an unusual combination of coastal, mountain and tropical resort. As you lie beside the wonderful swimming pool which appears to be spilling out over the horizon you can detect the sea breezes mingling with the mountain air.

Set in six hectares of land near **Jacó**, high above the Pacific Ocean, the hotel is just 68km from Santamaria International Airport in Costa Rica's capital, San José. The 360° panoramic views look out on the **Nicoya Peninsula**, the gulf islands, the crescent beaches of Jacó, **Herradura** and **Punta Leona** as well as the mountains.

The hotel's design was influenced by French colonial architecture and the Victorian homes still found in San José. The eight guest rooms and thirteen villas are painted in bright colours – yellows, oranges and greens – and most come with a private terrace or balcony with ocean views. The double rooms have either queen-sized or twin beds, air conditioning and ceiling fans and a private bathroom with hot and cold water, while the villas also have a good-sized living room and queen-sized beds (one has a king-sized bed), minibars and coffee maker. Suites, added recently, have private plunge pools.

HOTEL VILLA CALETAS
(c/o ☎ 257-3653, 🖹 222-2059, 🖳 info@hotelvillacaletas.com), PO Box 12358-1000, San Jose, Costa Rica
Reservations: Through tour operator Sunvil (see p11)
Getting there: The hotel can arrange transfers from San José Airport
Accommodation: Eight double rooms, 15 villas, four junior suites and one master suite
Amenities: 74 sq m swimming pool, bar-terrace, lounge, two restaurants, cellular phones, security deposit boxes, laundry, towels for the swimming pool, tour desk, transfers to Caletas beach, plus horse-riding, scooter and bicycle hire, seadoos, waterskiing, boating, fishing, island hopping, scuba diving, snorkelling all and golf arranged nearby
Dress code: Casual
Weddings: Can be arranged, Greek-style amphitheatre spectacular spot for ceremonies
Minimum stay: None
Rates: Double rooms from US$116; villas from US$136; suites from US$163; three-night Honeymoon package in a villa from US$708; luxury suite with private plunge pool from US$899 per couple; includes sunset cocktails, candlelit dinner with champagne, American breakfast and taxes
Credit cards: Visa, MasterCard, American Express
Taxes and service charge: Tax 16.39%

The airy restaurant and bar where French cuisine is served also have incredible views. The hotel staff are more than happy to arrange transportation to any of the nearby beaches for you, as well as trips to volcanoes, Tortuga Island, Carara National Park or activities such as horse-riding and sailing.

Other recommended hotels

Hotel Capitan Suizo (☎ 653-0075, 🖹 653-0292, 🖳 www.tamarindo.com/capitan) at Playa Tamarindo is regarded as one of the best of Costa Rica's beach hotels. This very friendly, informal hotel in the Province of Guanacaste enjoys a prime beach location, a great area with lots to do: swimming, surfing, horse-riding, scuba diving, sport-fishing or kayaking. The hotel has eight bungalows and 22 rooms (11 air conditioned), all of which have been carefully decorated by its Swiss owners. Every room has an ocean view, a terrace or a balcony, and a white tiled en suite bathroom.

This isn't a really luxurious beach resort, so don't come here expecting Four Seasons pampering or facilities, but it was good enough to be listed as one of *Tatler's* 101 Best Hotels 2001, and if you are looking for a small hotel with a relaxed atmosphere and simple but comfortable accommodation this will suit you well. The

(**Opposite**) **Top:** Château Lake Louise (see p173), superbly located in the Canadian Rockies.
Middle: Hotel Salto Chico enjoys the most spectacular location amongst the Patagonian wilderness of Torres del Paine, Argentina (see p221). **Bottom:** Hayman Island Resort (see p299), Great Barrier Reef, Australia.

THINGS TO SEE AND DO IN COSTA RICA

The **Tortuguero National Park** in the north of Costa Rica, on its Caribbean coast, is particularly spectacular and worth visiting for its animal life. Flat bottom boats will skim you along the twisting labyrinth of canals and creeks, where the dense jungle hangs down over the water's edge and your guide will slow down to point out small alligators, birds, monkeys and huge butterflies in the trees.

Tortuguero is known for its enormous turtles and is the place to see them dragging themselves laboriously up the beach to dig pits in which to lay their eggs, before covering them up and returning to the sea again, exhausted.

Another wonderfully romantic place to visit in Costa Rica is **Arenal**, home to both **Lake Arenal** and **Volcano Arenal**. The live volcano last erupted in 1968 and it still rumbles and billows smoke today, though the proliferation of bubbling geysers and mud pools in the vicinity mean it is unlikely to blast ever again.

At night, the views of the volcano are mesmerizing, as small bursts of fiery red lava erupt, pushing incandescent material down the sides of the volcano. A visit to the nearby hot mineral springs at **Tabacon** is highly recommended, allowing you to lie back in the pool's warm waters at night and watch the spitting volcano.

En route for the Pacific coast from Arenal, you'll pass through **Monteverde**, one of the world's best-known cloud forests, with its own micro-climate. A biological reserve since a US conservationist saved it from logging in the 1970s, Monteverde is now Costa Rica's top tourist spot. Despite the abundance of gringos, it is still definitely worth seeing for the jungle experience, the views and the wildlife. Trails lead through dense forest where trees covered in orchids fight for space against a multitude of tropical plants. Sloths hang from branches and monkeys leap from tree to tree high above your head.

large free-form swimming pool is a great place to spend quiet days engrossed in good books, punctuated by walks along the beach and a cold beer with lunch at the poolside restaurant and bar. Although there are some other wonderful hotels in Costa Rica, most are perched up on the headland looking down over the sea, so if you want to be actually on the beach this is the best option. The hotel will also arrange to collect you from Tamarindo Airport. Doubles cost from US$95 without air conditioning, US$110 with air conditioning and US$130 for the bungalows (which don't have air conditioning). All rates include breakfast but do not include 16.39% tax.

Venezuela
(BEST TIME: ALL YEAR ROUND)

Venezuela, quite simply, has everything: a beautiful and unspoilt Caribbean coastline; the power of the **Angel Falls**; the timeless majesty of the snow-capped **Andes**; the wide open spaces of the **Llanos**; and vast areas of dense Amazonian rainforest.

Although undeniably spectacular, a honeymoon in Venezuela won't suit everyone, but it will lure those who have had enough of lying on beaches and want to start married life by experiencing something new and exciting together.

My only real tip if you do choose Venezuela is not to do too much. Spend a good four days on the coast either at the start or end of your holiday so that you can unwind, go to **Canaima** to see the Falls and choose just one other destination, especially if you've only got two weeks – there's nothing worse than trying to fit too much in and just getting more and more tired, especially as you are likely to start off pretty exhausted in the first place. If you love it that much you can always come back another time.

With this in mind I have picked **Villa Mangrovia** on the coast as it is absolutely heavenly, and **Villa Majugual**, which is near a collection of untouched islands, and also given you information on what to expect from Canaima and **Merida**. In Canaima the only accommodation is at **Hoturvensa Camp** which, luckily, is fine. The best way to find somewhere good to stay in Merida is to ask your travel agent or the Venezuelan Tourist Board at the time of booking, particularly as the quality of

---

VENEZUELA

An excellent starting point to explore the grandeur and beauty of South America as it has just about everything: jungle, stunning coast, Andean mountains and the world's highest waterfall

When to go: The climate is fairly constant throughout the year, although it varies with altitude; to see the Falls at their best you have to go between July and September

Average maximum temperatures °C (Caracas)

JAN	FEB	MAR	APR	MAY	JUN	JUL	AUG	SEP	OCT	NOV	DEC
26	26	28	28	28	27	26	27	27	25	27	26

Capital: Caracas

Flight times: to Caracas from:

New York: (via Miami) 5 hours

LA: 9 hours

London: 12 hours

Sydney: (via LA and Miami) 22 hours

Approximate exchange rates: Bolivar (B) – £1 = B1020, US$1 = B714, A$1 = B370

Time difference: GMT minus four hours

Voltage: 110v, 60 cycles AC is used all over the country, US-type flat two-pin plugs

Combine with: Miami, Trinidad/Tobago, but there's so much to see in Venezuela that you'll probably want to concentrate your time there

Country dialling code: ☎ 58

Further information: 🖳 fondotourismo@cantv.net

VILLA MANGROVIA
(☎ 1494-15176) Parque Nacional
Morrocoy, Estado Falcon, Venezuela
Reservations: As contact with the villa is
only by local radio you have to book
through UK tour operator Last Frontiers
(☎ 01296-658650, 🗎 01296-658651, 💻
www.lastfrontiers.co.uk)
Getting there: Four hours from Caracas
by car, about US$200 by private transfer
Accommodation: Three double rooms:
two with twin beds, one with a double
bed
Amenities: All meals provided on the
villa's veranda, trips to neighbouring
islands and beaches and to the river
Yaracuy; scuba diving can be arranged
Dress code: Informal
Weddings: No
Minimum stay: None
Rates: Approx US$95/£67 per person
per night; US$510/£359 per person for a
four-day/three-night package through
Last Frontiers including transfers, all
meals and boat trips to islands
Credit cards: Most major
Taxes and service charge: Included

---

accommodation changes so rapidly. If you want to stay on a working Venezuelan ranch, **Hato Pinero**, high in the Llanos, is fabulous, especially if you're into birds.

THE CARIBBEAN COAST
Villa Mangrovia
Villa Mangrovia is the perfect place to get away from it all. The villa is located in the **Morrocoy National Park** high up above the mangrove trees. The park is a collection of sand-fringed islands and mangrove swamps about four hours' drive west of Caracas.

The villa is the home of Irina Jackson who, because she takes only six guests in at any one time, will make you feel more like house guests than hotel visitors. This is a really magical place to spend a few days: the white sand, palm trees and turquoise water provide the ideal environment for utter relaxation. If you want to spend some time on the coast during your trip to Venezuela this is the place to do it, not at **Margarita** which is full of high-rise hotels. The best cabin to request is the one set on its own in the villa's garden: it is the only one out of the three with a double bed. The two double rooms in the villa have twin beds.

Don't expect luxurious accommodation or even air conditioning or hot water. Villa Mangrovia doesn't have any of these things and in my mind is better for it: the rooms are simple but comfortably furnished, you won't need hot water, the ceiling fans are quite adequate and the excellent food and really personal service are far more important than a minibar, gold taps and marble bathrooms. Villa Mangrovia is unique in Venezuela and is the perfect place to start or finish your honeymoon.

All six guests have their breakfast on the veranda of Irina's elegant whitewashed house. Then each couple is taken by the boatman to one of the beautiful nearby islands with their Caribbean-style beaches. Guests are provided with a delicious picnic, a hammock and snorkelling equipment. This is the key to Villa Mangrovia and what makes it such a special place to stay. While **Margarita Island** attracts people looking for big resort hotels, Villa Mangrovia is the perfect alternative for couples who long to be alone on their own private Caribbean retreat.

Everything is included in the price at Villa Mangrovia, from the beers with your lunch-time picnic to all your meals and drinks at the Villa, and the island trips. Irina can also arrange, at extra cost, excursions to local sites of interest such as the river **Yaracuy** and local farms for bird-watching, or scuba diving at the **Tucacas NAUI-approved Centre** where the dives on the coral reef are marvellous.

Other recommended hotels
Villa Majugal (☎ 93-332120) is situated on a private peninsula in the **Mochima National Park** near some of the best beaches in Venezuela. Many of these untouched islands with their crystal clear waters are accessible only by boat. Twenty-eight guests are housed in twelve well-appointed cabanas but as it is quiet, you may find yourselves the only ones there! Rooms all have private bathrooms, hot water, ceiling fans and individual verandas where you can sip morning coffee with a view of the national park and the islands. You can be dropped off with a packed lunch on an island where you're unlikely to see anyone,

THINGS TO SEE AND DO IN VENEZUELA

Due to international flight schedules, most people need to spend their first night in Venezuela in **Caracas**. Many hotels out by the coast were damaged or destroyed by the floods of 1999, so it is currently best to stay near the city. A lovely hotel in the suburbs is **Hotel Avila** (☎ 2-515 128, 🖹 2-523 021, Av Washington, San Bernadino, Caracas 1011); doubles cost from US$80 per night. Caracas is the kind of hot, smelly, bustling city that epitomises South America and although it has an intriguing mix of Latin and American influences with some amazing cathedrals, plazas, museums and botanical gardens, it is not worth spending much time there if you only have a couple of weeks.

From Caracas you can fly straight into the jungle at **Canaima**, close to the **Angel Falls**, the world's highest waterfall dropping a staggering 979m. The only comfortable accommodation is at **Hoturvensa Camp** in individual grass-thatched cabins built on white sand overlooking the lagoon. The falls can be seen year-round, but are most spectacular during the wet season, between June and October. The hotel's location is outstanding, overlooking the lagoon as the Carrao river plunges over a series of falls right in front of you. The only access to Canaima is by air and Avensa, one of Venezuela's national airlines, has the most direct flights. The airline also owns the hotel so prices tend to be pretty high. If you are booking from the UK, specialist Venezuelan tour operator **Last Frontiers** (see below) offers three-day, two-night packages including all meals, internal flights, a fly past of the Angel Falls in an ageing Douglas DC3 and short trips around the lagoon for around US$725 per person. Canaima is also a great place to explore the rainforest with local guides who will take you on short walks through the dense jungle to rivers full of natural swimming holes. Alternatively do one of the day-long canoe trips. The local tours can be arranged when you get there through tour companies operating out of Canaima.

Sierra Nevada de Mérida, 1600m up in the snow-clad Andes, is one of Venezuela's most popular destinations. The best way to explore the region is to fly in from Caracas and then hire a car. Due to the altitude, Mérida is a welcome cool retreat from the heat of the jungle or the coast and is a fabulous place if you enjoy walking. The mountain scenery is just fantastic: look out for the frailejon, an indigenous flower, as you walk through the dense pine forests to dark lagoons. One of the key attractions of Mérida is the famous **Teleférico**, the world's highest and longest cable car which spans 12km and climbs 4765m, taking you rapidly from banana trees to snow-capped mountain peaks.

You can **fish** in the deep blue lakes or discover the more remote and interesting villages high up in the mountains, accessible only by mule. If you fancy **trekking**, talk to Rowena Hill or Andreas Fajardo at Torcaza Trails (☎/🖹 74-445 694) who are based in Mérida and can organize all kinds of tours. One trip takes you across a spectacular river gorge up to the high páramo with its hardy shrubs and brightly coloured flowers, and down a long ride through the cloud forest to the plains near Barinas. The best places to stay in Mérida are the local guest houses offering bed and breakfast for around US$40. However, the standards change rapidly so it's best to check which one is currently in favour with a local tour operator once you arrive in Venezuela. On the winding road down to the east stay at **Hotel Los Frailes** (Santo Domingo, Estado Mérida), built in the style of a 17th-century monastery which for US$100 per room is a mere snip for one of the most beautiful locations in the Andes. The hotel's service can be a little patchy, so don't go expecting Four Seasons' treatment, but it is a wonderful place to stay. There is no telephone or fax but bookings can be made through Last Frontiers (see below).

Enter **Los Llanos** and you will find a completely different landscape and an abundance of wildlife. This open, flat savannah land is a perfect haven for ornithologists with over 340 different bird species and frequent sightings of big white and grey herons, pink spoonbill ibis and fire red scarlet ibis, as well as a great number of wild horses, cattle and deer.

The best known and best loved of the Venezuelan ranches is **Hato Pinero** (☎ 2-916965, 🖹 2-916776, El Baúl, Estado Cojedes), a fabulous estate in the 'high' Llanos, particularly of interest to bird lovers. Rates start at US$240 per room plus 16.5% tax which includes all meals, an open bar, twice-daily guided excursions and land transfers from Caracas. Last Frontiers also does four-day/three-night packages to Hato Pinero costing US$624 per person in the low season and US$741 in the high season, including transfers from Caracas (five hours).

All properties can be booked through Last Frontiers (UK ☎ 01296-658 650, 🖳 www.lastfrontiers.co.uk).

and picked up later, so if you're beach people this is a great place to be. A bit more luxurious and secluded than Villa Mangrovia, the Villa Majugal is a special hotel and its personal service is ideal for honeymooners. The food, cooked by the Belgian chef, is as good as in any French restaurant back home; its only drawback is the lack of English spoken. Doubles start from US$134/£94 per person; three nights/four days with UK tour operator Last Frontiers costs US$437/£307 per person and includes transfers from Barcelona, meals and national drinks.

Ecuador
(BEST TIME: ALL YEAR ROUND)

A visit to Ecuador isn't complete without a cruise round the **Galapagos Islands**, famous for their incredible wildlife, or a stay in some of Ecuador's beautiful haciendas (privately-owned homes). An easy itinerary for a fabulous two-week honeymoon would be to spend one week on a boat in the Galapagos and another relaxing in Ecuador's beautiful Andean countryside visiting the various local markets.

Escapists should try **Kapawi Lodge** (🖳 www.kapawi.com), run by the Achuar tribespeople; it is in a pristine remote spot in the Amazon Basin, close to the Peruvian border. With the closest town ten days' walk away, you can only get there by a two-hour private plane ride from Quito, followed by an hour's ride in a dugout canoe. The lodge has 20 beautiful and comfortable individual log cabins on stilts, constructed without using a single nail and powered entirely by solar energy. All are en suite and have large private balconies where you may see parrots and toucans around Kapawi Lagoon from your hammock, and can listen to the frog chorus at night. Dining is on Ecuadorian and International cuisine and there's a bar, shop and library at Kapawi.

Despite its isolated position, there is plenty to do at Kapawi day and night: canoeing, visits to local communities, night camping. The wildlife is spectacular with over 500 bird species and river turtles, tortoises, monkeys, giant otters and freshwater dolphins. Three nights (minimum stay) costs US$985 per person, all-inclusive.

UK tour operator Destination South America's (☎ 01285-885 333) 17-day Classic Ecuador trip with three days at Kapawi, two days in Quito, one day in Otavalo and five days cruising in the Galapagos costs US$4977/£3500 per person including flights, transfers, transport, accommodation, excursions and most meals.

THE GALAPAGOS ISLANDS
Although discovered by the Spanish bishop of Panama in 1535 while on an exploratory mission for the king of Spain, the Galapagos Islands were only really brought to the world's attention three centuries later when, in 1859, Charles Darwin published his famous tome, *Origin of Species*, following a five-week exploration of these fascinating islands on *HMS Beagle*. Today, the islands are still worth discovering and remain very much a living laboratory of evolution where birds and animals live without fear of man. Anyone remotely interested in animals, ecology or natural history will be impressed by these graceful islands where blue and red-footed boobies, flightless cormorants, playful sealions, land and sea iguanas and giant tortoises roam freely.

The best way to experience the 13 major islands and the dozens of smaller islets is by boat. The boats travel at night in order to maximize the area covered. December

---

ECUADOR
Incredible wildlife in the Galapagos and haciendas in the spectacular Andes
Average maximum temperatures °C (Galapagos Islands)

JAN	FEB	MAR	APR	MAY	JUN	JUL	AUG	SEP	OCT	NOV	DEC
31	32	32	32	30	29	27	26	26	27	28	29

Approximate exchange rates: Sucre (S) – £1 = S33,330, US$1 = S25,000, A$1 = S12,970
Time difference: GMT minus five hours
Voltage: 110v/220v AC
Country dialling code: ☎ 593
Further information: 🖳 www.tourismo.gov.ec and www.vivecuador.com

to April is the best time to go because the water is pleasantly warm and the sea is at its calmest. The only problem is that you miss the celebrated albatrosses, who usually arrive in the islands in April and can be seen at their best, during courtship, in June. **Quasar Náutica** (Ecuador ☎ 02-441-550, 🖹 02-436-625); UK (☎ 01962-779 317, 🖹 01962-779 458) and US (☎ 305-599-9008, 🖹 305-592-7060; 🖳 www.quasarnauti ca.com) have a fleet of six boats (yachts and motor cruisers) ranging from 17m to 38m in length. Two boats, *Mistral* and *Lammer Law*, have diving equipment. Seven nights in a cabin with en suite facilities on the *Lammer Law*, a 28m motorsailer trimaran, will cost US$2605 in high season (November to May) per person and US$2350 in low season, including all meals. Small sail boat *Diamante* costs US$2335 high season, US$2174 in low season and the larger *Eclipse*, with 47 passengers and perhaps more privacy, costs US$3084 for suite cabins, US$2777 in low season. Other costs are flights from Quito (US$386 in high season), the National Park entry fee (US$100) payable in cash on arrival, and tips for the staff on your boat which can be as high as US$100. These islands don't come cheap but they really are a holiday of a lifetime.

Alternatively there are a number of UK-based tour operators who offer packages to the Galapagos. **Worldwide Journeys and Expeditions** does an 11-day trip on *Beagle III*, a lovely boat with really good, sheltered outside seating (which is absolutely crucial) but without en suite facilities, for US$3263/£2295 per person including all flights, stopovers in Quito, transfers, accommodation and meals on *Beagle III*. Tour operators **Abercrombie & Kent**, **Cox & Kings**, **Last Frontiers**, **Roxton Bailey Robinson**, **Sunvil** and **Destination South America** also operate in the Galapagos (see pp9-11).

Although some companies offer three- or four-day cruises I've never met anyone who regretted going for the whole week. It is also possible to go on a two-week cruise, allowing you to cruise between **Isabela** and **Fernandina** which are grander and much more beautiful than the comparatively austere islands you visit in the first week: the only problem is that you may not want to spend two weeks of your honeymoon cooped up on a boat with strangers!

STAYING IN HACIENDAS

Some haciendas continue to operate as farms or mills while others have abandoned their original purpose in order to focus on tourism. You can either book the haciendas direct, through Last Frontiers (see below), or through **Metropolitan Touring** in Quito (Ecuador ☎ 02-464-780, 🖹 02-464-702, 🖳 info@ecuadorable.com). If you choose the latter I suggest you fax or email them your dates of arrival and needs and ask them for a brochure and some sample prices. They can suggest combinations of properties to enable you to experience different types of hacienda in different areas of Ecuador.

One of the loveliest of these country retreats is **Hacienda Cusin** (☎ 0691-8013, 🖹 0691-8003, San Pablo del Lago, Imbabura, Ecuador). It was originally built in the 1600s but was carefully renovated in 1990 to retain the old charm. Guests are accommodated in 25 rooms, either in the main building, the owner's suite, cabañas in the lovely gardens or in the newer Monasterio building, five minutes' walk from the old house through the gardens. All the rooms have private bathrooms (some with baths), lovely garden or mountain views, and are furnished with antiques, local art and artefacts. In addition, many have open fireplaces. They are not big on in-room facilities, but this is part of the feel of staying in a hacienda. There is loads to do including 15 spectacular valley walks, hill and mountain climbs for which you can take a guide (or a picnic!), horses for guest use, mountain bikes, a four-wheel drive vehicle for local touring and several hundred books. Guests are required to stay a minimum of two nights. Double/Garden cottage/suite US$98/120/200 for room with breakfast; US$98/220/300 per person inclusive with horseback or mountain-bike riding, plus 10% tax and 10% service. Contact UK representatives **Last Frontiers** (☎ 01296-658 650, 🖹 01296-658 651) who do a three night package for £410 with transfers; or the hotel toll-free in the US (☎ 800-683-8148). If you want to be off the beaten track, it may be worth considering **Hacienda San Agustin de Callo** (☎ 371-9160, 🖹 226-9884) in Lasso, nestled in the foothills of snowcapped and dramatic Cotapaxi, the highest active volcano in the world. This beautiful and little known colonial farmhouse offers fabulous, personalized service and as a working farmhouse gives a great glimpse into Ecuador's colourful past. Built into the site of an important Inca palace, it has five rooms with private bathrooms, a sitting room and chapel and you dine in a room built by the Incas. Hacienda San Agustin provides the perfect setting to enjoy this unique countryside by horse, mountain bike or foot.

Peru
(BEST TIME: JUNE TO SEPTEMBER)

Along with the Pyramids and the Taj Mahal, Machu Picchu is one of those magical places that many people long to visit once in their life. Somehow the very name Machu Picchu, and indeed Peru itself, is synonymous with mystery and romance.

CUZCO AND MACHU PICCHU

This lost Inca citadel was discovered only in 1911 by the American explorer, Hiram Bingham, and is undoubtedly the most incredible archaeological site on the continent. Very little is known about the origins of Machu Picchu, but from the buildings' scale and ornamentation it is clear that it held some very significant ceremonial value.

There are few more dramatic locations from where to experience sunrise and sunset than the **Machu Picchu Sanctuary Lodge** (☎ 84-21-1039/38, 🖹 84-21-1053, 🖥 www.orient-expresshotels.com), the only hotel at the site of the ruins. Recently completely refurbished following its takeover by Orient-Express and re-opened in May 2001, the hotel's 31 rooms and one suite are now improved and service is good, although the prices remain high. Doubles with a view of the ruins US$285, suite US$335 including breakfast but not tax and service.

You may want to consider staying at **Machu Picchu Pueblo** (☎ 51-84-211-032, 🖹 51-84-211-124, 🖥 www.inkaterra.com.pe) a prettier and better value hotel in a valley on the edge of Aguas Calientes, a 25-minute bus ride from the ruins. Guests stay in two- to three-roomed tile-roof cabins, with elegant décor and comfortable extra-long beds, scattered in the cloud forest gardens with over 180 species of orchid. Doubles cost from US$169, one of the nine suites from US$188 including taxes. For direct booking from the US, call toll-free (☎ 1-800-228-0088).

You can start and end your stay at **Hotel Monasterio** (☎ 51-84-24-1777, 🖹 51-84-23-7111, 🖥 www.monasterio.orient-express.com), a converted 16th-century monastery built on the remains of a pre-Columbian royal palace. One of the most splendid colonial hotels in South America, the highly individual rooms are all set around a beautiful courtyard, just steps from the main square. Doubles cost from US$250 and suites from US$330. Ask for one of the newly oxygenated (to help with altitude sickness) rooms, refurbished recently in lighter warmer tones. Book through Leading Hotels of the World reservation numbers worldwide (see p12).

All tour operators to Peru operate packages to Machu Picchu. Talk to UK tour operators such as **Trips Worldwide** (☎ 0117-311 4400), **Last Frontiers** (☎ 01296-658 650), **Roxton Bailey Robinson** (☎ 01488-689 700), **Reef and Rainforest Tours** (☎ 01803-866 965) **Sunvil** (☎ 020-8758 4774) or **Destination South America** (☎ 01285-885 333). It is also possible to see it under your own steam: trekking the **Inca Trail** to the ruins takes three full days and offers awesome views of snow-capped mountains and the cloud forest en route, though it is now compulsory to travel with a guide. For further information see *The Inca Trail* by Richard Danbury (Trailblazer, see p317) and check out the tourist board website ▣ www.peru.org.ge.

Brazil
(BEST TIME: ALL YEAR ROUND)

It is the wide variety contained within one country that draws people to Brazil: in just a couple of weeks you can move from city to jungle to waterfalls to beach and explore historic civilizations and colonial ruins. Many of these sights are in a marked contrast to the latter-day extravagance of **Brazilia**, the nation's capital city that was purpose-built only four decades ago. Names such as **Rio**, **Salvador**, **Ipanema** and the **Amazon** cannot fail to evoke powerful images of this awesome country that occupies a vast chunk of the entire South American continent. This chapter does not try to guide you around this huge country but instead suggests some hotels that you might try to work into your itinerary as each, in its own way, expresses Brazil's multifarious character.

Designed like an aeroplane, Brazilia was the first capital in the world purpose-built in an attempt to open up the country's interior. For architecture and design enthusiasts the city is totally mind-blowing with its incredible modern architecture rising out of the Central Plateau like some kind of sci-fi film.

In total contrast is Salvador, one of the great cities of South America, where lavish churches boast breathtaking baroque gold interiors and numerous impressive colonial buildings stand as reminders of former settlements. Salvador is the capital of **Bahia**, an area which is a melting pot of Africans, Latin Americans and Europeans and which has a totally distinct culture with unique food, lots of rhythmic music with heavy drum beats and even a little black magic.

Most visitors to Brazil try to visit the mighty **Iguazú Waterfalls** on the border with Argentina and Paraguay, and **Pantanal**, the flood plains on the border with Bolivia and Paraguay – a wilderness region full of cowboy characters and colourful wildlife; and spend a few days at an Amazon lodge.

If you have time **Angra**, a little coastal town on the **Costa Verde** about three hours' drive west of Rio, has lovely beaches, lots of islands and secluded bays to

---

BRAZIL

An incredible concoction of vibrant cities, beautiful beaches, elegant colonial cities and the Amazonian jungle

When to go: All year round

Average maximum temperatures °C

	JAN	FEB	MAR	APR	MAY	JUN	JUL	AUG	SEP	OCT	NOV	DEC
Rio	29	29	29	27	25	24	24	24	24	25	26	28
Salvador	29	29	29	29	28	27	26	26	27	28	28	29
Manaus	30	30	30	30	31	31	32	33	33	33	32	31

Capital: Brazilia

Flight times: to Rio de Janeiro from:
    New York: 10 hours
    LA: 14 hours
    London: 11 hours
    Sydney: 20 hours

Approximate exchange rates: Cruzeiro (C) – £1 = C3.32, US$1 = C2.33, A$1 = C2.91

Time difference: GMT minus three hours (Rio de Janeiro)

Voltage: 110v and 220v, most hotels have adapters

Combine with: Concentrate on Brazil, there is so much to see

Country dialling code: ☎ 55

Further information: ▣ www.brazil.org.vu

COPACABANA PALACE
(☎ 021-548-7070, ▤ 021-235-7330), Av Atlantica 1702, CEP 22021-001 Rio de Janeiro, Brazil
Reservations: Through Orient-Express Hotels (▢ www.orient-expresshotels.com)
Getting there: The hotel can arrange transfers from the airport about 35km away, or you can get a taxi costing around US$45
Accommodation: 226 rooms
Amenities: Outdoor swimming pool, florist, bookstore, hairdresser, car rental, laundry service, 24-hour room service
Dress code: Elegant casual, people do dress up for dinner
Weddings: Can be arranged
Minimum stay: None
Rates: Doubles from US$385; suites from US$580; ask about their four-night honeymoon package which includes a suite, breakfast in bed, dinner including wine, flowers and champagne, two bathrobes as a gift, and limo transfers
Credit cards: Most major
Taxes and service charge: 15% service tax will be added to your bill

discover. **Paraty**, a small fishing village close by, is particularly pretty and well worth a visit. And then there's **Rio**, with its fantastic beaches and Carnival. Rio is always an unbelievable and exhilarating place to be, even if it's not Carnival season. Don't be put off by Brazil's 'dangerous' reputation, both Rio and Salvador have put in a big effort to clean up their act and now have a really good tourist police. However, it's always wise to leave your valuables in the hotel safe and not to walk along empty beaches and be discreet when carrying a camera.

RIO DE JANEIRO
The Copacabana Palace
The Copacabana Palace is Brazil's best-known hotel, which also means that it is one of the country's most expensive. But at least you get the kind of luxury that will make you smile deep inside your pampered soul time and time again.

The rooms are equipped with the furnishings and facilities that you'd expect from a hotel owned by the elegant and lavish Orient-Express Group. Just about everything you could possibly need, as well as a comforting amount of things you probably won't, is there – frigobar, in-room safe, satellite TV and air conditioning are just a few of the goodies.

The Copacabana Palace was one of the first buildings in Rio over two storeys high and today it is one of the few original buildings still standing on the beachfront. Of course it is really quite ritzy and particularly grand, but I can think of nowhere finer to start or end your honeymoon in Brazil.

THINGS TO SEE AND DO IN RIO

Known familiarly as the Cidade Maravilhosa, or the Marvellous City, Rio will always be known as the **Carnival City**, and even if your visit doesn't coincide with the extravagant festivities that occur between the Friday and Tuesday preceding Lent (usually in February), you can't help falling for the infectious atmosphere.

The safest way to get to **Sugar Loaf Mountain** is by taxi to the bottom of the cable car, so that you can take your camera and not be worried about thieves. Do, however, be wary if you get vertigo as the second cable car really does dangle a long way up. There are bars, knick-knack shops and snack restaurants at the top as well as fantastic views. The best time to go is in the early evening: the queues shouldn't be too long and you can see the sunset. To see the **Corcovado**, the 40m-high statue of Christ, get a taxi to the funicular railway station or right to the top. The Corcovado is surrounded by rainforest and, being really high, the views

overlooking the city, the coast and its islands are just amazing, whether it's day or night.

Maracana Stadium, the biggest football stadium in the world, may not automatically find its way on to your list of honeymoon activities but the atmosphere at a football match on a Sunday afternoon is unbeatable and totally mad: it will give you a better insight into life in Brazil than any mainstream tourist attraction.

Copacabana and **Ipanema** (the next beach round) are still the best beaches. They are both quite mind blowing with thousands of people everywhere, and huge volleyball tournaments, concerts and festivals going on all year round. It's just a really groovy place to wander around. All along the beach there are bars and restaurants serving massive barbecue grills – not exactly a haven for vegetarians.

Visit ▢ www.rio.rj.gov.br/riotour for further information.

Apart from its legendary status, the hotel has a number of features which put it head and shoulders above its neighbours, including a much bigger swimming pool than the tiny roof-top efforts that are so common here.

The food in the restaurant is very good and you can enjoy light lunches overlooking the beach and retreat to the English tea room in the late afternoon.

My only word of warning is that you make sure you get a proper sea view when you're booking as you don't want to end up looking out at the next door hotel: the extra price of the beachfront rooms is definitely worth it.

OURO PRETO

Ouro Preto, founded in 1711 and the former capital of the state of **Minas Gerais**, with its unspoilt churches, colonial architecture and winding cobbled streets, is a superb place to wander around. Ouro Preto developed as a mining town and the wealth of gold and other minerals in the area funded the wonderful array of buildings which are still immaculately preserved.

Built on rocky ground 1000m above sea level, the city was declared a national monument in 1933. Gleaming mansions, fountains, churches and gardens all combine to give the town a delightful 18th-century feel. Of particular interest in many of the churches and museums are the baroque carvings, in wood and soapstone, by the sculptor Aleijadinho: many of them were created with tools strapped to his feet after his hands were crippled by illness.

Places worth visiting outside the town include **Mariana** and **Congonhas do Campo**, two colonial towns with beautiful churches, as well as the deserted gold mines.

Solar da Ponte (☎ 32-335-51201, 🗎 32-335-51201, Tridentes, Ouro Preto), sitting beside the stone bridge that leads to the tree-lined village square of this old gold-mining town, is one of the best hotels of its kind in Brazil.

Within this architectural gem that reflects the style of the area are 12 comfortable apartments each with its own veranda, lovingly decorated by Englishman John Parsons and his Brazilian wife.

With a beautiful garden, good-sized swimming pool, sauna and local restaurants to try, the *pousada,* or country inn, of Solar da Ponte is a good value and comfortable base from which to explore this remote area of unusual beauty. Doubles start from US$142/£100. Book through UK tour operators Cazenove & Loyd Expediciones (☎ 020-7384 2332, 🖵 www.caz-loyd.com) or Last Frontiers (☎ 01296-658650).

ILHEUS

Recommended hotels

Hotel Transamerica, Comandatuba Island (☎ 73-686-1122, 🗎 73-686-1457, 🖵 hotel@transamerica.com.br) is reputed to be the best resort on Brazil's north-eastern coast and is great for those honeymooners who like it big. The island is absolutely stunning: wherever you look there are coconut trees, coconut trees, and more coconut trees, and of course a fabulous beach from which you can watch the sun slowly slip past the horizon or indulge in a variety of watersports.

The hotel is beautifully decorated in light colours with ocean themes (shells and fish) running through a number of the rooms which have private balconies and all the mod cons. One of the best features of the Transamerica is its astonishing sculpted freshwater swimming pools, canals and waterways – five pools in all. You could sail off for a day in the hotel's private schooner around scenic Comandatuba Island, or try some deep-sea fishing in one of the hotel's private fleet of motor boats. Book through the Leading Hotels of the World reservation numbers worldwide (see p12).

Pousada do Corsario (☎ 21-522-0262) at Paraty, on the banks of the Parereque river, is a haven of colonial squares, courtyards and tiled roofs, just steps from the historical centre of Paraty. Guests stay in 30 comfortable rooms in separate cabins scattered around the garden, each with its own veranda with views across the river from their hammocks. The Pousada also has a swimming pool and its own schooner for trips around the bay. Doubles cost from US$50 per person with breakfast. You can book this pretty place through UK tour operator Destination South America (☎ 01285 885333).

Hotel Manary Praia (☎ 84-219-2900, 🖳 www.manary.com.br) in Natal is a small hotel with 25 rooms, some overlooking the city beach, but what sets it apart is its helpful archaeologist owner, Eduardo Bagnolio. He'll take you to see cave paintings, dinosaur footprints and some of the best beaches in Brazil. A three-night package with UK tour operator Last Frontiers (☎ 01296-658 650) in a de luxe room with airport transfers costs US$308.

Argentina and Chile
(BEST TIME: NOVEMBER TO MARCH)

Argentina and Chile are quite unlike any other part of the South American continent: they are a great deal more European and have a smaller population of indigenous Indians. They're also a lot safer and are easier to travel around. Because these two countries sit side by side along the length of the southern half of this astonishing continent, most travellers visit both in one trip. Once you are in the **Lake District** (in the lower half of both countries) or even further south still in the mountainous wilderness of **Patagonia**, it's very difficult not to find yourself wandering across the border between the two.

The hotels I have chosen here are pretty much the best that Argentina and Chile have to offer. They are by no means cheap, but they are really first class and each one is individual. Although you are unlikely to go to all of them these are special places to relax in after or before your adventures in Patagonia or on a cattle drive, a soothing reminder that you are on your honeymoon and not an expedition.

Check out 🖳 www.visitchile.org and www.tourismo.gov.ar for more information.

THE LAKE DISTRICT
No trip to Argentina or Chile would be complete without a visit to the Lake District. When I first toured the region I thought it the most beautiful place I'd ever seen and vowed to go back and live there someday. Whitewater rivers flood into scores of vast blue lakes surrounded by dense pine forest, above which snow-capped volcanoes tower into the sky.

You can be as active or inactive as you want, simply enjoying a gentle stroll around the lakes or hiring a bike from one of the many rental places, trekking up volcano sides, windsurfing on the lakes, whitewater rafting on the rivers and even snow-skiing on the sides of the volcanoes.

The region's towns have that wonderful feel of anticipation and exhilaration akin to a ski-resort. There are also lots of good bars to retire to at the end of the day where you can talk about your adventures over addictive pisco sours – the Chilean national drink similar to a margarita only better!

On the Argentinian side, people flock to **Bariloche** in the winter (June to September) to ski and also in the summer to spend the Christmas holidays in their summer houses.

Not far from Bariloche is **Lago Nahuel Huapi**, a glacial relic over 100km long which is surrounded by beautiful alpine scenery and great blankets of flowers in summer-time. There is a particularly good hotel in Bariloche, the Relais & Châteaux member **Hosteria Las Balsas** (☎/📠 54-2944-494-308, Villa la Angostura, 8407 Neuquen), a luxurious rambling manor house on the edge of Nahuel Huapi. This pretty, blue wooden house is a place where you can relax or go walking, riding or biking during the day before returning to gastronomic meals in the evening. Doubles start from US$280.

Take the **Cerro Campanario** chair lift there which affords panoramic views of the lake, and the chair lifts and cable car up **Cerro Catedral**, a ski centre 20km west of Bariloche, which also has incredible views and several good walking trails. Note many hotels around here close between June and September.

PATAGONIA

Bordering on Patagonia, in a stunning position near the blue glaze of Perito Moreno Glacier, lies **Estancia Alta Vista** (☎ 02902-491-247, 📠 02902-491-247, 💻 altavista@ relaischateaux.com). This 1920s-style *estancia* (ranch), with a frontier atmosphere, only has six rooms and one suite. This 'must have' honeymoon suite (the only one with a double bed!) was once the most expensive room in Argentina. The service is fantastic here and the price, although expensive, includes all meals and activities such as riding, mountain-biking and hiking on the glacier. Honeymoon suite from US$634. Book through tour operators Cazenove & Loyd Expediciones (☎ 020-7384 2332, 💻 www.caz-loyd.com), or Abercrombie & Kent, Exsus or Last Frontiers (see pp9-11).

Deeper into Argentinian Patagonia the ultimate destination for riding and big country enthusiasts is **Estancia Huechahue** (☎ 54-2973-491303, 8371 Junin de los Andes, Provincia del Neuguen). This incredible estancia has opened its doors to just a handful of paying guests. It is a good base from which to ride out each day into the foothills of the Andes or into areas only accessible on horseback on a few days trail-riding into the land of the gauchos. An experience like this doesn't come cheap and you'll be looking at around US$213/£150 per person each day inclusive, but imagine a few days' riding out alone, just the two of you with your guide, into one of the least populated areas of the world, and camping under the Southern Hemisphere stars at night. Book through UK tour operator Last Frontiers (see p11).

If you don't ride (although you don't have to be experienced riders to go to Heuchahue) there is another way of experiencing the incredible landscapes of Patagonia by crossing the border and heading down to **Torres del Paine National Park**, north of Puerto Natales in Chile.

Here, in the middle of what is universally recognized as South America's finest national park, is the extraordinary **Hotel Salto Chico, Explora** (☎ 56-02-699-2922, 📠 56-02-699-0137, Parque Nacional Torres del Paine s/n, Patagonia). If you are readers of the travel pages of glossy magazines you may have seen pictures of this incredible hotel. Voted into *Tatler*'s 101 Best Hotels 2001, it is set amongst Patagonia's wildest granite peaks, emerald lakes, raging waterfalls, sprawling glaciers and dense forests. At first glance it looks like some modern Antarctic research station but on closer inspection is one of the world's most design-conscious hotels.

For anyone interested in architecture and modern design, and enthusiastic enough to explore this unbelievable land, the Salto Chico has to be seen. The hotel's brilliantly polished interior, made from local wood, is quite magnificent. There are roaring fires, huge deep baths with windows looking out over the mountains, a stunning swimming pool totally surrounded by polished pine, bed linen brought from Barcelona, tapestries from New York and wicker furniture from Chimbarongo. There's even an outside Jacuzzi where you can lie back and drink champagne with the snow falling all around you.

The hotel is beautifully run, and each day the Explora team take you off on 'explorations', by boat, on foot, on horseback, mountain bikes, or in four-wheel drive vehicles. Now that you're convinced, here's the painful part: the minimum hotel package of three nights and four days per person will set you back from US$1040 to US$1773 for a suite, which includes all meals and house wine, transfers to/from Punta Arenas Airport, and all Explora excursions with an English-speaking guide which, of course, are the highlights of the trip. To book direct fax toll-free from the USA (☎ 800-858 0855), Canada (☎ 800-275-1129) or Germany (☎ 013-082 2353).

If this is just your scene, you may want to check out its sister hotel, the **Explora Atacama** (☎ 56-55-851-110, ▤ 56-55-851-115) set in the rugged landscape of Andean peaks, volcanoes, salt flats, geysers and hot springs of North Chile. Talk to UK tour operators Cox & Kings (☎ 020-7873 5000), Roxton Bailey Robinson (☎ 01488-689 700) or Exsus (☎ 020-7292 5050) about both these hotels.

Morocco
(BEST TIME: OCTOBER TO JUNE)

If you are coming from Europe, Morocco makes a particularly good honeymoon destination as it is a truly exotic country with a fascinating panoply of cultural styles and landscapes, and best of all you don't have to endure a long-haul journey to get there.

Most travel agents' brochures tend to paint a very different picture of Morocco to the one described here; instead of concentrating on the overcrowded beaches of **Agadir** there's a much more enchanting side to Morocco, a land rich in history, colour and mystery where not much has changed since the coming of Islam. Morocco's contrasting landscapes, the bustling imperial cities of **Fes** and **Marrakech**, the fertile agricultural lands of the north, the vast craggy wilderness of the **Atlas mountains** with their Berber kasbahs and the endless dry emptiness of the **Sahara**, mean that this is a honeymoon with a difference.

From the moment you land you'll be in no doubt at all that you have entered another world: a world where the smells, wails and colours of a way of life virtually untouched by the modern world will continue to surprise and even shock you at every turn. But the great thing about going to Morocco is that you don't have to compromise on hotels: two of the world's most extravagantly luxurious hotels, **La Mamounia** and **La Gazelle d'Or** are found in Morocco. Excluding these hotels, dress is casual, and if you're looking for somewhere intimate to stay, **riads** and **maison d'hôtes** (small guest houses) are scattered throughout; very romantic and

---

MOROCCO

Step back in time to an intriguing world of mosques, minarets and palaces, the bustling and colourful labyrinth of souks and the timeless majesty of the Atlas Mountains

When to go: October to June are the best months to visit Morocco but southern Morocco is really a year-round destination

Average maximum temperatures °C

	JAN	FEB	MAR	APR	MAY	JUN	JUL	AUG	SEP	OCT	NOV	DEC
Marrakech	20	21	22	25	27	28	31	34	29	26	23	20
Taroudant	21	22	25	26	28	30	34	34	33	30	24	21

Capital: Rabat

Flight times: to Casablanca from:
    New York: 6½ hours
    LA: 13 hours
    London: 3 hours
    Sydney: 23 hours

Approximate exchange rates: Dirham (D) – £1 = D16.52, US$1 = D11.62, A$1 = D6.03

Time difference: GMT

Voltage: 110v/220v AC, 50 Hz is also common, two-pin round plugs

Combine with: It's best to devote your time purely to this fascinating country

Country dialling code: ☎ 212

Further information: 🖥 www.tourism-in-morocco.com

the 'in' places to stay. Be warned, however, that the food in some can be limited in choice and sometimes alcohol is not even on the menu.

My only word of warning is that you avoid the inland sights, including Marrakech and the Atlas mountain ranges, during the summer months (June, July and August), as the heat and volume of tourists rise to quite unbearable levels – not at all romantic. These months aside, Morocco is pretty much a year-round destination.

LA MAMOUNIA HOTEL
(☎ 04-44 44 09, 🖷 04-44 49 40, 🖳 man agement@mamounia.com), Avenue Bab Jdid, Marrakech

Reservations: The Leading Hotels of the World toll-free reservation numbers worldwide (see p12) and most travel agents and tour operators specializing in Morocco (see p12-13)

Getting there: The hotel operates a courtesy shuttle bus to and from Marrakech Menara Airport 4km away; two and a half hours by road from Casablanca and three hours from the seaside resort of Agadir

Accommodation: 171 rooms: 110 garden or pool view rooms; 45 rooms on the Koutoubia mosque side of the hotel; 16 overlooking the courtyard; 57 suites and 3 villas

Amenities: The Marrakech L'Imperiale, L'Orangerie, L'Italien and the poolside Les Trois Palmiers restaurant; four bars, a nightclub and casino; a range of boutiques, Jacuzzi, hair and beauty salon, massage, sauna and hammam (Turkish bath); heated outdoor swimming pool, clay tennis and squash courts, gym, boules games area, table tennis, 18-hole golf course near the hotel, snow-skiing within 72km

Dress code: Jacket and tie required for dining

Weddings: Wedding ceremonies and receptions are catered for, depending on time of year and availability – ballroom holds 400 people

Minimum stay: None

Rates: Double rooms cost from US$172/D2000 to US$413/D4800, suites from US$258/D3000 to US$1549/ D18,000; the hotel offers a three-night honeymoon package which includes a buffet breakfast each day, a bottle of champagne, flower and fruit in your room, one dinner and a horse-drawn carriage ride; the package costs from US$1686/D19,590 for a room overlooking the gardens and from US$3150/ D36,590 for the Honeymoon Suite

Credit cards: Most major

Taxes and service charge: US$3/D40 city tax per person per night, service charge is included

---

MARRAKECH

A visit to Marrakech, the city of madness, magic and miracles, gives one an awesome insight into a life that most of us assume is all but forgotten. It is one of the world's enchanted cities where time seems to have stood still, and through the open doors of its souks and temples today's visitor can catch a glimpse of another world.

La Mamounia Hotel

La Mamounia Hotel is legendary. A member of the Leading Hotels of the World, it is unbelievably ornate. From the moment you are greeted by the porter, dressed all in white with a sword at his side, you'll know you've arrived somewhere quite out of the ordinary.

Having first opened its doors in 1925, La Mamounia was totally remodelled in 1986 to produce interior décor that is a staggering combination of art deco with Moorish influences, and the south-facing rooms – towards the Atlas Mountains – were completely renovated in 2000. Set in seven hectares of fruit and flower-filled gardens within the massive ochre ramparts of Marrakech, the hotel has some kind of magical essence, imbuing its guests with that strangely thrilling feeling that only comes from staying in a really special hotel.

La Mamounia has 171 guest rooms and 57 themed suites all decorated with coordinating fabrics, architecture, furnishings and colours. All 110 garden- and pool-view rooms have large balconies with table and chairs making this the perfect spot for breakfast. There are a further 45 rooms on the Koutoubia mosque side of the hotel and 16 overlooking the courtyard. The hotel also has three private villas. Whichever room you opt for, it will have one of those snappy little control panels by which you can control the TV, radio, central heating and air conditioning and even call room service or house porters without so much as having to move a muscle.

(Opposite) Top: La Mamounia, Morocco. **Bottom**: Keeping the lawn well mown; Loldia House, on the shores of Lake Naivasha, Kenya (see p232).

THINGS TO SEE AND DO IN MARRAKECH

The only way to discover Marrakech is to grasp each other firmly by the hand and launch yourselves upon the mad frenetic world of the city's **souks**. Amidst all the confusion, calls and colour you'll find hand-made Moroccan carpets, rugs, leather goods and silverware, all of which are good buys, especially if you enter into the haggling spirit. If you don't fancy getting lost you can always arrange to be shown round by an official English-speaking government guide (just ask your hotel concierge). The guide will also be able to steer you towards the best quality shops and help if the French-Moroccan haggling gets too much for you.

The best way to see the **Djemaa el Fna**, the city's main square, during the day is to head for the Café de France's roof terrace: you can gaze down on the bustling market while enjoying a relaxing meal of couscous, washed down with the ubiquitous cup of sweet mint tea. At dusk the square really starts to come alive with a cacophony of snake charmers, preachers, tum-blers, singers, sorcerers and herbalists all vying for your attention. Try a few spicy nibbles from the stalls surrounding the square or head to *Yacout* (☎ 38 29 29) which is straight out of Arabian Nights. Metal filigree chandeliers dance a speckled light on the blue mosaic and starched linen tablecloths are strewn with rose petals. Book well in advance for dinner or go for a cocktail. Arguably, the best Moroccan cuisine in the Medina is to be found at *Dar Moha Almadina* (☎ 38 64 00) – mountains of couscous under a starry sky.

Other points of interest are **Koutoubia Minaret**, the **Ben Youssef Mosque**, **Medina** (the old city), and the **Saadian Tombs**, or just wander around Yves St Laurent's cacti-filled garden, the **Jardins de Majorelle**.

Among the best day-trips from Marrakech is a trip to see the spectacular waterfalls, the **Cascades d'Ouzoud**, or the drive into the Atlas Mountains to the top of the **Tichka Pass** at a breathtaking elevation of 2255m.

The suites at La Mamounia are of course outrageous – huge, lavish and really rather expensive. The Orient Express suite is furnished with original pieces from the celebrated train; if you can, opt for the amazing Honeymoon Suite.

The food in the five restaurants is universally impressive: dress for dinner for L'Imperiale where delicacies are served in elegant surroundings. From there you can retire to the famous Churchill's Piano Bar for a nightcap.

Although La Mamounia is a large hotel you can be alone there as the rooms are very private, but it's really a place to see and be seen. Anybody who is anybody has stayed at La Mamounia – Mick Jagger was even thrown out – so, if you haven't been it's worth going once. It is the ultimate hotel for the first two or three nights of your honeymoon if you can afford it, providing you with the kind of glitz, glamour and hedonistic spring board that will become your benchmark for hotels for years to come.

Other recommended hotels

Les Deux Tours (☎ 044-31 20 71, 🖷 044-31 20 57, Douar Abiad BP513, Marrakech), in the heart of the exclusive Palmeraie, is probably the most seductive hotel in Morocco. Its six luxury villas each have their own small pool (not heated) and walled garden and it was designed by Morocco's best – Charles Boccara, who also designed the Tichka Hotel. Mosaic floors, ceilings decorated with Oleander wood and the 15 rooms and 10 suites, all individually styled, display an exquisite taste and charm. Many of the rooms have fireplaces which reflect the earthen colours and some of the bathrooms have spectacular brick domes.

A swimming pool with a view of the High Atlas mountains, hammam (steam bath) and massage room provide pampering and relaxation and guests can select their own private dining spot on a secluded terrace or among the enchanting gardens with their gurgling fountains. Doubles cost from US$200.

La Roseraie Hotel (☎ 04-43 91 28, 🖷 04-43 91 30, Vallée Ouirgane BP 769, Marrakech) is a haven of tranquillity high in the Atlas mountains standing at 914m. Just an hour's drive from Marrakech, the hotel is set in 20 hectares of flower-filled gar-

(Opposite) Top: Relaxing in the shadow of Mt Kilimanjaro after a day's game viewing, Tortilis Camp, Amboseli, Kenya (see p234). **Bottom**: Houseboat on Lake Kariba, Matusadona Water Wilderness, Zimbabwe (see p247).

STAYING IN RIADS AND MAISON D'HOTES

Hidden behind plain façades in the cobbled back streets of Marrakech Medina, riads and maison d'hôtes appear like small oases in this desert city. Traditional Moroccan houses converted into guesthouses, they combine luxurious Moroccan sensual style and colour with Western management. Rooms are individually decorated, and in these beautiful mosaic-lined environments, bougainvillea drips from wrap-around balconies surrounding an inner courtyard with fountain, and ripe oranges may hang from trees reaching up towards the roof terrace. Riads or maison d'hôtes allow you to absorb the atmosphere of Morocco in intimacy, peace and privacy. You can also find riads in Essouria and Fes. UK tour operator, the Best of Morocco (☎ 01380-828 533, 🖹 01380-828 630, 🖳 www.morocco-travel.com) has the best selection and you can book all the following through them.

Superbly decorated in traditional style, **Villa des Orangers** (☎ 044-38 46 38, 🖹 044-38 51 23, 6 rue Sidi Mimoune, Marrakech Medina), only opened in February 2000, but has fast become a favourite and is a member of the prestigious Relais & Chateaux. The 16 air-conditioned rooms are decorated in rich, warm hues, half of which have private terraces. Informal and relaxed, you can leave the buzz of the square – just three minutes' walk from here – to cuddle up in one of the cosy nooks in its lounge, or to take a cool dip in the rooftop swimming pool while savouring views of the High Atlas Mountains. Doubles cost from US$215/D2500, suites from US$301/D3500 including breakfast. With only three rooms and three suites, each lavishly furnished and named

after the characters in *A Thousand and One Nights,* **Dar Zina** (☎ 044-346 645, 🖹 044-304 252) 4 Jnane Brika, Targa, 6km from Marrakech) is the most intimate of the maison d'hôtes. The tranquil, fairytale gardens with palm, olive trees, bougainvillea and a swimming pool are lit by candle light and lanterns at night. Doubles cost from US$145.

The charming and discreet **Riad Kaiss** (☎/🖹 044-44 01 041) in the heart of the Medina is an undiscovered secret. It has eight rooms, each with private bathroom, and authentic Moroccan-style features. The two courtyards with gurgling fountains, roof terrace and comfortable salons with open fireplaces provide plenty of scope for peace and relaxation. Probably the most stylish of all the smaller riads in Marrakech, it was lovingly and tastefully created by the French Architect Christian Ferre. Double room with breakfast cost from US$125/£88. Norbert Furnon-Roberts, the owner of **Riad Noga** (☎ 044-37 76 70, 38 52 46/47, 🖹 044-38 90 46, 🖳 riadnoga@iam.net.ma, 78 Derb Jdid, Douar Graoua) is so friendly that he can keep you talking to lunchtime. Of the seven individually decorated rooms, the sumptuous Red Room is made for honeymooners and costs from US$192 to US$230 per night including breakfast.

For something unique, new, and very ethno-chic, try the **Caravanserai** (☎ 044-43 69 82, 🖳 caravanserai@iam.net.ma) a tasteful haven within a mud village on the doorstep of the city. Although it only opened in Feb 2001, Caravanserai is already looking to steal the scene from more traditional choices. Doubles cost from US$200.

dens in the heart of Berber countryside. La Roseraie has 40 rooms and suites all with en suite bathrooms and a patio leading into the gardens; some of the junior suites have an open fireplace. This is the place to come if you fancy a few days of real adventure such as horse-riding through the incredible mountain villages and even staying in remote Berber houses en route. It's also a great place for walkers and those who like wildlife, wild flowers, or even just lying by a pool and being pampered. Regular rooms cost around US$83 while junior suites are US$112 per person for half board including tax.

TAROUDANT

A three-hour drive from Marrakech brings you to Taroudant, a majestic ochre-walled city famous for its rambling souks, ruddy clay houses and stark Atlas mountain backdrop. After a few frenetic days in Marrakech you'll welcome the change of pace.

From Taroudant you can make easy day excursions into the Ante-Atlas (the western end of the Atlas range) by car, or even head off on horseback or mountain bikes for a couple of days exploring the countryside and its Berber villages.

La Gazelle d'Or

La Gazelle d'Or is a place where people come to celebrate an anniversary, a wedding or some other landmark in their lives. It's just that kind of place: special beyond your dreams and where self-indulgence is de rigueur. The hotel's guest book is unbelievable: it's crammed full with celebrity names. Set amongst ten hectares of mature gardens, the hotel is cocooned by orange groves with the majestic Atlas mountains providing a time-honoured backdrop. The hotel originally started life as a retreat for a French aristocrat but fell into neglect until it was reincarnated as a hotel. Days at La Gazelle d'Or are all about hours spent relaxing by the palm-fringed pool with a good book, punctuated only by gourmet meals or perhaps a visit to the steam baths and some aromatherapy, or a stroll around the nearby souks.

The hotel's decorations give it an incredibly opulent feel with polished marble floors, tented ceilings, the Berber-motif lounges and white robed staff, but the atmosphere is more of a country club. The hotel provides a rare combination of Moorish architecture and metropolitan chic, where guests are encouraged to feel that they are part of a house party rather than staying in a hotel.

Huge buffet lunches are served by the pool with views over the snow-capped mountains, while gastronomic seven-course dinners comprising international and Moroccan cuisine are served in the tented Moorish-style dining room and are the high point of each day.

> **LA GAZELLE D'OR**
> (☎ 048-85 20 39, 🖷 048-85 27 37, 🖳
> http://membres.tripod.fr/gazelleor.htm),
> BP 260, Taroudant, Morocco
> **Closed**: Mid-July to early September
> **Reservations**: Direct with the hotel or through leading tour operators and travel agents specializing in Morocco (see p12-13)
> **Getting there**: The hotel's cars and drivers are available for transfers to/from Agadir Airport (about one hour), costing D600 each way
> **Accommodation**: 30 double rooms, including one suite and one junior suite
> **Amenities**: Large outdoor swimming pool (heated in winter), two clay tennis courts, golf practice, croquet, horse-riding, steam bath, massage/aromatherapy and beauty treatments, guided excursions and walking/trekking in the surrounding countryside and up in the Atlas Mountains, room service from early morning to late evening
> **Dress code**: Men should wear a jacket and tie for dinner
> **Weddings**: No
> **Minimum stay**: None
> **Rates**: Double rooms from US$432/D5020, junior suite US$525/D6100, suite US$864/D10,040 full board
> **Credit cards**: Most major
> **Taxes and service charge**: Included

Accommodation is in 30 creeper-covered non air-conditioned bungalows curving away from each side of the hotel's central pavilion. All the rooms are beautifully appointed with exquisite furnishings, mosaics, ornate décor, hand-woven rugs, log fireplaces and private terraces for long, drawn-out breakfasts.

Within the hotel there are tennis courts and horses available for desert rides, although most guests get their recreation by taking advantage of the hotel's close proximity to the walled town of Taroudant, a five-minute walk away. Give yourself at least three days here and up to a week if you can afford to and are feeling especially self-indulgent.

ESSAOUIRA

Originally planned by a French hostage in 1760, this delightful white walled town is becoming more popular as a honeymoon destination.

Located on a sandy bay with shallow, clean water, the mood at Essaouira is more akin to that of a Greek island than that of Agadir, a comforting 160km down the coast. Get grilled sardines and a can of Coke from down by the harbour and just relax in the sun. It is, however, known as the windy city for good reason, and this is an important factor to consider.

Villa Maroc

If you want to get away from the star-studded pampering havens described above and are looking for somewhere more individual, Villa Maroc in Essaouira is a great place right off the tourist route. At Villa Maroc you'll see the real Morocco without having to feel you've got to dress for dinner each night.

VILLA MAROC
(☎ 044-47 31 47, 🖷 044-47 28 06), 10, Rue Abdellah Ben Yassin, Essaouira 44 000, Morocco
Reservations: Direct, or through leading tour operators and travel agents specializing in Morocco (see pp12-13)
Getting there: The hotel can arrange a taxi to collect guests from Marrakech Airport (D600), Agadir Airport (D600), or Casablanca Airport (D1100)
Accommodation: 12 double rooms, five mini suites, three suites and an apartment
Amenities: Private residents' bar, private dining rooms for all guests
Dress code: Casual
Weddings: No
Minimum stay: None
Rates: Doubles from US$86/D1000, mini suite from US$102/D1180, suite from US$122/D1420, apartment from US$164/D1900 all half board
Credit cards: Most major
Taxes and service charge: D6 per person per night accommodation tax, service is not included

The villa has the intimate feel of a private house, rooms are filled with antiques and Moroccan wall hangings, candlelit dinners are served in private rooms off the central courtyard and there is cobalt blue woodwork everywhere. A wonderful end to a Moroccan honeymoon and we resolved to return.
Vanessa and Bruce Jones

Located within the historic ramparts of Essaouira, Villa Maroc was formed by joining together two extraordinarily beautiful 18th-century houses built in Spanish-Moroccan style. With only 12 double rooms, eight suites and an apartment, staying at the Villa is more like being a guest in a private house than a hotel resident.

Whitewashed walls and cobalt blue railings and other trimmings adorn the villa's exterior while the inside is an interior designer's dream. Rooms are gathered around a central courtyard, three or four to each floor. The whitewashed walls are hung with Moroccan tapestries, old traditional costumes displayed on poles and paintings by local artists. The bedrooms feature carved beds and wooden floors while the bathrooms are individually designed and just fantastic; some have mosaic-tiled baths and others have shower cubicles made from coloured glass. The rooms don't come with TV, in-room safe or minibar because the villa's ethos is to stick to Moroccan style and keep the structure of the rooms as simple as possible. If you feel you need to use a safe ask in the office.

Owned by a Swiss woman and her Moroccan husband, one of the highlights of staying at Villa Maroc is the evening meal, which is prepared only on request. Dinners are served in lounges dotted around the hotel courtyard so that each couple or party of guests gets their own dining space. There is also a private bar for use by hotel guests only. I have had recent reports of grouchy staff – it seems the villa's success is making for some complacency, but the couple I spoke to still agreed that the villa itself and the food made it a lovely place to stay.

There is no swimming pool, nightclub or tennis court at the villa – as the management are keen to remind you, this is meant to be a place of relaxation and charm, not some kind of holiday resort. Besides you'll find plenty of entertainment just wandering around the souks and bazaars of Essaouira, or you could nip down to the beach which is only minutes away.

Egypt
(BEST TIME: OCTOBER TO APRIL)

The land of the Pharaohs cannot help but conjure up exotic images of former civilizations and, with 5000 years of noble heritage, Egypt is certainly an exotic honeymoon destination for those looking for something out of the ordinary.

No trip to Egypt would be complete without a visit to one of the famous Seven Wonders of the World, the **Great Pyramids** at **Giza**, towering out of the desert sands; **Cairo** itself is an extremely aggravating place to visit, so it may be best to limit your stay there to a couple of days. It pays to be patient if you are planning to visit Egypt

EGYPT
Ancient tombs and monuments, luxury cruising on the Nile, and diving in the Red Sea
Average maximum temperatures °C

JAN	FEB	MAR	APR	MAY	JUN	JUL	AUG	SEP	OCT	NOV	DEC
19	21	24	28	33	35	35	35	32	30	26	21

Approximate exchange rates: Egyptian pound (E£) – UK£1 = E£5.53, US$1 = E£3.89, A$1 = E£2.02
Time difference: GMT plus two hours (plus three hours from May to September)
Voltage: 220v AC, 50 Hz
Country dialling code: ☎ 20
Further information: 🖳 www.touregypt.net

for your honeymoon: everything takes about three times as long as you'd normally anticipate so think seriously about doing an organized trip which will instantly cut down on the hassle-factor.

There are hotels to suit all budgets in Egypt from five-star luxury to basic bed and breakfasts. If you want to set aside a few days to relax in colonial splendour it's hard to beat the legendary **Old Cataract Hotel** (☎ 97-316 000, 📄 97-316 011, 🖳 www.accorhotels.com, Abtal El Tahrir Street, Aswan) which inspired Agatha Christie's *Death on the Nile*. Doubles start from US$132 per couple per night (plus 19.6% tax).

The **Red Sea**, with its crystal waters, white sand beach and underwater treasures is now more tempting with the opening of the Oberoi's **Sahl Hasheesh** in Hurghada (☎ 65-440 777, 📄 65-440 788, 🖳 toshres@oberoi.com.eg). The first all-suite luxury resort on the coast, the Arabic-style domes, arches and columns on 48 acres of hillside lead down to a private beach. All ground level suites have an enclosed private court-yard and Royal and Grand suites have their own swimming pool. Bathrooms overlook a peaceful landscaped garden. De luxe suites cost from US$250 to US$325, Grand suites from US$400 to US$500 and one of the six Royal Suites US$900 to US$1150. Wedding receptions are catered for; special honeymoon packages with a desert safari or sea trip cost between US$1800 and US$4330. Book through the Leading Hotels of the World reservation numbers worldwide (see p12).

NILE CRUISES

From Aswan you are ideally placed for one of the world's most romantic journeys, a cruise down the Nile, northwards to **Luxor** and the **Valley of the Kings**. If you prefer to start your holiday in Cairo this trip can just as easily be done from Luxor going upriver to Aswan. The best way to see the many ancient temples and observe life is on the river.

If you can afford it, it's well worth spending a little extra on your cruise, thereby guaranteeing you better (and safer) food and a nicer cabin. From the UK and the US, cruises can be booked through Abercrombie & Kent, or Cox & Kings (see p12). Both companies offer truly luxurious cruises in full Edwardian splendour aboard ships equipped with swimming pool, sundecks, and en suite cabins, some of which even have their own private balconies. You'll be welcomed on board with afternoon tea, and have just enough time to relax and get your bearings before dressing for the cocktail reception which is, of course, followed by dinner – all guaranteed to get you into the swing for this kind of sophisticated, elegant travel. A ten-day tour of Egypt, including four nights on the *Oberoi Philae*, built in the style of an old paddle-steamer but only completed in 1995 and beautifully decorated with European antiques, oriental carpets and hardwood floors, costs around US$1784/£1395 to US$2481/£1745 per person with Cox & Kings (see p12). Nights are spent in the lovely **Oberoi Mena House** (☎ 2-38 33 222, 📄 2-38 37 777, 🖳 www.oberoihotels.com) set in 40 acres of ornamental gardens at the foot of the Pyramids in Cairo – make sure you request a room in the old part of the hotel – and the Old Cataract in Aswan (see above).

Kenya
(BEST TIME: JULY TO END OF MARCH)

Kenya has become one of the most popular tourist destinations on the African continent, largely because it offers an impressive and easily accessible range of safaris and beaches at prices that are often a good deal cheaper than many of its neighbours. Situated on the east coast of Africa, close to the equator, there can be no doubt that Kenya makes a perfect honeymoon destination.

Kenya is difficult to beat if you've never been to Africa before and like the idea of going on safari but don't want to spend too much time in the bush. Home to the legendary game reserves of the **Masai Mara** and **Tsavo**, Kenya offers plenty of opportunities to see the big five – lion, leopard, elephant, rhinoceros and buffalo – in some of Africa's greatest game parks while staying in safe, comfortable lodges.

The Kenyan coast also offers a good selection of watersports, particularly scuba diving on the immense coral barrier reef that fringes the coast, great snorkelling not far from the shore and world renowned big-game fishing.

Safaris

When booking your safari make sure you let the tour operator know exactly what kind of safari experience you want. If you have been to Africa before you may be looking for a much wilder safari experience, perhaps sleeping out at night and tracking on foot with your own personal guide, well away from the buzz of other Land Rovers. But if you haven't been before, a first-timer safari where you'll be driven around one of the bigger parks in closed Land Rovers might suit you better and will still give you a really good feel for this vast country and its inhabitants. Many British tour operators, such as Tropical Places (UK ☎ 0870-727 7077) and British Airways Holidays (UK ☎ 0870-242 4245) offer one- to three-day safaris in minibuses straight from your hotel in Mombasa.

If you want to visit the more exclusive and less commercialized parts of Kenya, head for **Ol Donyo Wuas** or the private lodges on the **Rift Valley** lakes, but understand

---

KENYA

The famous Masai Mara with its incredible game viewing and the warm Indian Ocean coastal waters with their golden sandy beaches and great diving opportunities

When to go: The coast rarely dips below 20°C so Kenya is a year-round destination, but avoid April to June when the rains come

Average maximum temperatures °C

	JAN	FEB	MAR	APR	MAY	JUN	JUL	AUG	SEP	OCT	NOV	DEC
Nairobi	25	26	26	24	23	22	21	22	24	25	23	23
Mombasa	32	32	33	31	29	29	28	28	29	30	31	32

Capital: Nairobi

Flight times: to Nairobi from:
New York: 16½ hours
LA: 21½ hours
London: 7½ hours
Sydney: (via Johannesburg) 20 hours

Approximate exchange rates: Shilling (S) – £1 = S11.61, US$1 = S78.49, A$1 = S40.73

Time difference: GMT plus three hours

Voltage: 220v/240v AC, 50 Hz, although some hotels are equipped with 110v wall sockets for American plugs

Combine with: The Seychelles, Tanzania and Zanzibar

Country dialling code: ☎ 254

Further information: 🖥 www.magicalkenya.com

that these are specialist safaris with prices to match so they are probably best suited to those who have been out in the bush before.

SAMBURU

Wilderness Trails at Lewa Downs

One of Kenya's longest established and most popular hosted homestays, Lewa Downs is the perfect base for walking and riding out in the African bush amongst really beautiful scenery.

Your hosts, the Craig family, have owned the ranch since 1924 when the grandparents of today's owners, William and Emma Craig, arrived from England and began raising cattle. Now, William and Emma welcome just a few privileged guests to their private 24,000-hectare game ranch on the northern slopes of **Mt Kenya**, an hour's drive north-east of **Nanyuki**.

Guests stay in one of five stone and thatch cottages, three of which have two double rooms, and two with one double room. Each cottage has a central rondavel-style living room with an open fireplace and easy chairs, plus a large veranda with lovely comfortable seats, which are just ideal for napping, and queen-size beds. Days at Lewa Downs are spent either in four-wheel drive vehicles on game drives or out in the bush on foot, tracking game with an experienced and incredibly knowledgeable guide. Elephant, lion, leopard, cheetah, black and white rhino and two types of zebra reside on the ranch, as well as countless other game such as giraffe, warthog, impala, gazelle and buffalo.

Horses, and even camels, are available for rides through the local countryside. The ranch's horses are very well trained and will enable even the most novice rider to get much closer to the game than on foot – sometimes it's almost possible to touch a giraffe. In the afternoon, guests can cool off with a refreshing dip in the lovely pool and enjoy tea on the lawn for a restful hour or so before dinner or go on a night-drive with a spotlight to look for nocturnal wildlife.

WILDERNESS TRAILS AT LEWA DOWNS
(c/o ☎ 2-571 661, 🖷 2-571 665), PO Box 56923, Nairobi, Kenya
Closed: April, May and November
Reservations: Most leading specialist African tour operators and travel agents or direct through Bush Homes of East Africa (see above number for Lewa Downs)
Getting there: Guests can take the daily Air Kenya scheduled flight from Nairobi to Lewa Downs (depart 9.15am and arrive 10.15am), take a private charter flight, or drive from Nairobi which takes about 4 hours
Accommodation: Eight double rooms en suite in five cottages
Amenities: Small swimming pool, dining room, safaris on foot, in four-wheel drive, on horseback or by camel, day and night drives
Dress code: Informal
Weddings: Yes
Minimum stay: Three or four nights are recommended
Rates: US$330 per person per night full board including all game drives, horse-riding, bush walks and camel treks, excludes mini bar in the rooms
Credit cards: Visa or American Express for any extras; guests prebook their stay through one of the above companies who will accept all major credit cards
Taxes and service charge: Included, but tips welcomed

Other recommended camps

Borana Camp (☎ 2-331 871, 🖷 2-726 427, 🖳 www.governorscamp.com, c/o Musiara Ltd, PO Box 48217, Nairobi) is perfect honeymoon material. This luxury camp has six individual cottages built from local materials and decorated using attractive fabrics sourced locally and in South Africa. The cottages are huge compared to most bush camps, have two queen-size beds and are exquisitely decorated with local wood incorporated into their design. Guests can go horse-riding, walking, on game drives in open-

Absolutely wonderful, wonderful time, loved every minute. We've had the most amazing three weeks and have now decided we want to be posted out here. Borana was fantastic and so unlike a hotel, we were very, very sad to be leaving.
Kathryn and James Redfern

top vehicles or on a helicopter ride over the bush. There is also a rhino sanctuary near-by. Borana has been carefully conceived and executed with impressive results – this has to be the most luxurious, non chichi bush accommodation in Kenya.

Rates are US$370 full board per person per night including all beverages apart from spirits, plus US$30 ranch fee. Borana can also be booked through Theobald Barber in the UK (☎ 020-7723 5858, 📠 020-7723 5417).

Private lodges and bush homes

One of the best ways to start a holiday in Kenya is to avoid Nairobi altogether: instead fly straight to **Lake Navaisha**, only one and a half hours by plane from the capital. The lake is a beautiful and tranquil place to start your holiday: you can spend long lazy days watching the pink flamingos and spotting the myriad of birdlife around, take a boat out on the freshwater lake, or explore the surrounding bush on horseback.

Loldia House, on the shores of Lake Naivasha, is a pretty red-brick private house set amongst well-tended lawns and acacia and fig trees. The family-run farm offers luxury accommodation to 14 privileged guests, either in the main house or in cottages within the grounds: all the rooms have private facilities and magnificent views across the lake over to **Mount Longonot**. While dinner is served in the dining room, day-time meals are taken under the shade of Loldia's beautiful giant fig tree. The lodge's staff will take you to visit lakes **Nakuru**, **Elementait** and **Bogoria**, the hot-springs at **Hell's Gate**, as well as boat trips on Lake Naivasha to see the amazing birdlife or to fish. Just opposite **Hippo Point** is **Elsamere**, the former home of Joy Adamson and her lions, made so famous by the book and film *Born Free*. Doubles cost from US$275 per person including all meals, laundry and the activities above. Loldia can be booked through the Governor's Camps (☎ 2-331 871/2, 📠 2-726 427, 💻 govscamp@africaon-line.co.ke, PO Box 48217).

Alternatively, **Bush Homes of East Africa** (☎ 2-571 661, 📠 2-571 665, 💻 www.bush-homes.co.ke, PO Box 56923, Nairobi) have a number of small, owner-run wilderness properties worth looking at, including Rekero and **Lewa Downs** (see p231), both of which can be booked in the UK through Cazenove & Loyd Safaris (☎ 020-7384 2332; 💻 www.caz-loyd.com), or through US representative Uncharted Outposts International (☎ 404-888-0909), or Australian representative the Classic Safari Company (☎ 2-9327 0666).

THE MASAI MARA

To the south-west the Masai Mara, which adjoins Tanzania's Serengeti, is practically the only place where you can see game in the kind of abundance that was common in colonial times.

A 50-minute flight from Nairobi will take you to the open rolling savannah grassland that is home to the proud Masai tribes, who continue to live alongside their cattle and the hordes of big game roaming the plains. You are likely to see zebra, wildebeest, lion, leopard, cheetah, elephant, antelope and giraffe. Take a hot-air balloon trip at sunrise: soaring high above the African plains is a magical experience and certainly worth getting out of bed for – especially as you are rewarded with an alfresco champagne breakfast once you touch down.

Little Governor's Camp

Extremely upmarket, exclusive, and unspoilt, each of the Governor's Camps offers four-wheel drive safaris and lots of bush walking, picnicking and sundowners in wonderful vantage points. Set among immaculately-kept grounds and lit at night by paraffin lamps, these are the most romantic safari camps.

Little Governor's Camp is the smallest of the three main Governor's Camps. Approached by boat, crossing over the Mara River, the small site has 17 de luxe, en suite tents arranged close to a popular watering hole. It is a great place to catch sight of large herds of migrating wildebeest between July and October.

Each day there are three game drives in four-wheel drive Land Rovers, half-day morning walks with bush breakfast outside the Reserve, and incredible hot-air ballooning trips – with a champagne breakfast when you land. The camp staff will also arrange a picnic for you and take you to the **Oloololo** escarpment where the last scene of *Out of Africa* was filmed. Breakfast and lunch are served outside under the shade of the trees, while dinner is in the dining tent after drinks at the bar. There is also a swimming pool.

For those seeking a truly romantic, private experience, Il Moran, their new luxury camp comprising just ten tents hidden in the shadow of ancient trees on the banks of the Mara River is just made for honeymooners. Opt for this if you can afford the extra US$170 per night.

LITTLE GOVERNOR'S CAMP
(☎ 2-331 871, 🖹 2-726 427, 🖳 www.governorscamp.com), PO Box 48217, Nairobi, Kenya
Reservations: Leading tour operators and travel agents specializing in Africa worldwide (see pp12-13); in the UK Hartley's Safaris (☎ 016-738 61600)
Getting there: Air Kenya flight to Governor's Camp approx US$230 per person return
Accommodation: 17 tents – en suite bathrooms with hot running water and bidets
Amenities: Game viewing; variety of bird-life, walking safaris daily; hot-air ballooning daily for one hour, after landing a champagne and traditional English breakfast served (US$385 per person)
Dress code: Casual
Weddings: Can be arranged, prices on request
Minimum stay: None
Rates: US$250 per person full board including game drives, but not park fees or beverages
Credit cards: Most major
Taxes and service charge: Included

AMBOSELI NATIONAL PARK
This park is situated south of Nairobi near the majestic snow-capped **Mt Kilimanjaro**: you are likely to see some of the largest elephants in Africa, giraffe, buffalo, wildebeest and zebra.

Ol Donyo Wuas
Ol Donyo Wuas, meaning 'spotted hills' in Masai, is an exclusive hideaway among the open plains and rolling **Chyulu hills**, looking over to the snow-capped peak of Mt Kilimanjaro. Here is Africa as it used to be: abundant game and the Masai herdsmen continuing to live side by side in an unspoilt corner of Kenya.

OL DONYO WUAS
(☎ 2-884 475/882 521, 🖹 2-882 728, 🖳 www.richardbonhamsafaris.com), PO Box 24133, Nairobi, Kenya
Reservations: Either direct or through UK reps Roxton Bailey Robinson (☎ 01488-689 702, 🖹 01488-682 977) or Theobald Barber (☎ 020-7723 5858, 🖹 020-7723 5417)
Getting there: Access is by charter aircraft, usually from Nairobi (50 minutes) to a private airstrip near the lodge, from where guests are transferred to the lodge; a charter aircraft costs US$450 and takes three people
Accommodation: Seven large secluded thatched cottages
Amenities: Main dining room, game viewing by four-wheel drive, on foot and on horses, and fly camping, bush dinners, cultural visits to Masai villages
Dress code: Informal
Weddings: Have been arranged
Minimum stay: Although there is no minimum stay, two to six days are recommended
Rates: From US$370 per person per night, including transfers, meals and game viewing, not including drinks or fly camping (US$460 per person per night)
Credit cards: The camp itself will not accept credit cards so any extras must be paid for in cash (preferably US$); most people book their stay through one of the above companies who will accept credit cards
Taxes and service charge: Included, although tips are welcome

This private home-stay, owned by Richard Bonham one of Africa's best-known guides, accommodates guests in seven individual thatched cottages. The open front of the cottages and the main building give stunning views over the surrounding Masai land to Mt Kilimanjaro. Each cottage has an en suite bathroom, electric lighting, an open fireplace and a veranda. The beds are covered in mosquito netting and there is a cupboard with hanging space, as well as bedside lights and locally-made decorations. The whole experience is fabulous – very exclusive and of course, very expensive.

Bonham set his heart on building his home in this spot after scouring the land in his light aircraft. Once he started building the ranch, in 1986, he also assumed honorary game manager status for 10,000 hectares of Masai land.

Game viewing usually starts soon after dawn. Having been woken with a cup of tea, guests head out either on horseback or on foot, or in one of the camp's specifically converted open-top Land Rovers. Among common sightings are antelope, zebra, eland, cheetah, lion, giraffe and wildebeest. The camp staff then catch up with you around 9am armed with breakfast which they lay out under the shade of an acacia tree. Viewing continues until lunch-time which is usually back at camp.

After a good lunch of cold meats, salad and cheese most guests take the opportunity for a siesta in the heat of the day. At around 4pm there is tea to refresh you before returning to the bush for a few more hours tracking the game. Bonham and his crew are always careful to find you a wonderful spot in which to enjoy the magical sunsets with a chilled sundowner, before heading back to camp for a well-earned wash up and dinner as darkness and the noises of the jungle close in around you.

Other recommended camps
Tortilis Camp (☎ 2-604 053, 🖨 2-604 050) is nestled in an unspoilt corner of **Amboseli**, far away from the busy lodges, close to the Tanzanian border. Tortilis offers its 34 guests four-wheel drive safaris and lots of bush walking, picnicking, and a lovely sitting/dining area on a small hill looking down on the camp and over to fabulous views of Mt Kilimanjaro. Ten of the thatched cottages at Tortilis have king-size beds and there's a swimming pool, with bar, on site. It is reached by a 45-minute flight from Nairobi. It costs from around US$310 per person per night, but you'll have to pay extra for things like bush dinners.

TSAVO NATIONAL PARK
Exceptional birdlife and elephant viewing, the distant views of Mt Kilimanjaro, and the vast sense of space are what make Kenya's largest wildlife stronghold, Tsavo, so incredible.

Galdessa
Galdessa, part of a huge rhino release project, is *the* place to go if you want to get totally away from it all and experience the wild, pure Africa where nature remains untouched by time.

Right in the heart of Tsavo East National Park, overlooking the Galana river, Galdessa Camp comprises eight semi-tented thatched roof bandas (bungalows) providing spacious luxury accommodation in the finest safari tradition.

The canvas tents each have lovely, fresh, white cotton sheets on the seven-foot square beds, and stone tables. The en suite spacious bathrooms have running water but the owner, Pierre Mourgue d'Algue, decided to preserve the romance of the safari canvas shower. The most remote honeymoon banda has its own sitting room, viewing platform and water wallow.

The tents have their own mosquito netting, so, after an evening of alfresco dining, you can retire to your tent and listen to the noises of the bush just beyond the canvas walls, safe in the knowledge that they will stay that way.

Thirty friendly people are at your service in the camp and nothing in your tent is left to chance so there's no reason to feel unsure about your safety or the camp's cleanliness: your laundry is washed and ironed each day, and the rooms are kept perfect.

The guides at Galdessa are all highly experienced. Whether you travel on foot, on horseback, by jeep, or in a hot-air balloon, they are sure to provide you with moments of sheer magic, as you encounter game in a way that few even dream of.

THE COAST

Kenya's coastline stretches for more than 322km and it offers seemingly endless pristine white sandy beaches, fringed by palm or casuarina trees, and lapped by turquoise waters where diving, deep-sea fishing and snorkelling are all fantastic.

To the north are the unspoilt beach hideaways of **Lamu** and **Manda** islands, perfect for true escapists, an exotic combination of African and Arabian cultures.

Hemingways

Hemingways is recognized as one of the best beach hotels on the Kenya Coast. Twenty-nine kilometres south of **Malindi**, perched on quiet **Watamu Beach** (featured in the *Sunday Times* Top Ten Beaches of the World), Hemingways has the most wonderfully relaxed atmosphere. In front of you lie the waters of the Indian Ocean while behind is the mighty African bush.

Relaxed it may be, but the service and cuisine at Hemingways are pretty well faultless and all the bedrooms have air conditioning and other essential extras – as well as plenty of unessential but very welcome ones too, such as the roses that are left on your pillow nightly.

GALDESSA
(☎ mobile +254-72 744 614, ▭ www.galdessa.com), PO Box 714, Village Market, Nairobi, Kenya
Reservations: By email through Nairobi office or website or through tour operator Africa Archipelago (UK ☎ 020-8780 5838)
Getting there: Guests can be flown in from Nairobi for around US$150 per person or road transfer from the coast for approx US$400 per vehicle
Accommodation: Eight luxury semi-tented bandas (four twin and four double), of which one is a honeymoon banda
Amenities: Game drives in four-wheel drive vehicles, walking safaris, fishing, sundowners, bush breakfasts and night drives (all included in the price)
Dress code: Casual
Weddings: Can be organized, costs depend on what you want
Minimum stay: None
Rates: From US$244 to US$325 per person per night on an all-inclusive basis except for alcohol
Credit cards: The camp will accept Visa and MasterCard for extras; but the stay must be paid for in advance by bank transfer, cash, or through an agent
Taxes and service charge: Included, but tips and park entrance fees of US$23 a day are not included

---

HEMINGWAYS
(☎ 122-32624, ▤ 122-32356, ▭ hemingways@swiftmalindi.com), PO Box 267, Watamu, Kenya
Reservations: Through the UK office (toll-free ☎ 0800-0328 8885, or ☎/▤ 01442-236 789) or Small Luxury Hotels reservation numbers worldwide (see p12)
Getting there: The hotel can arrange free transfers free from Malindi Airport, or for US$120 from Mombasa Airport
Accommodation: 72 de luxe guest rooms and six junior suites
Amenities: Main restaurant, two outdoor swimming pools with bar, hotel bar and terrace, fully-equipped gym, snorkelling, tennis, deep-sea and creek fishing, glass-bottom boats, windsurfing, diving and dhow cruises; squash and horse-riding are available nearby
Dress code: Jackets and ties are not required but men are requested to wear long trousers or smart tailored shorts for dinner
Weddings: Yes
Minimum stay: None (except over Christmas and New Year)
Rates: Double rooms from US$170 per room per night includes breakfast, afternoon tea and dinner
Credit cards: Visa, MasterCard, American Express
Taxes and service charge: Taxes included, service is discretionary

The *makuti* (traditional thatched) roofs of Hemingways contain the reception, the main bar and restaurant. The large round sit-up bar, with its relics of old fishing battles and lovely carved wooden chairs, opens out on to the ocean terrace. Guests can choose between eating here alfresco or, if a wind picks up, in the sunken main restaurant with its high-vaulted thatched roof. The terrace is the best place to watch the outstanding sunsets.

Of the resort's 78 rooms only the 26 standard ones are in the hotel's original block, while the superior and de luxe rooms and six junior suites are all in the new wing – superior rooms occupy the second and third floors and de luxe are on the ground floor. All rooms have en suite bathroom with showers, mosquito nets, phone, in-room safes, kimonos, and a terrace or patio, while the de luxe have a bath and a shower. Double beds are available on request in five of the de luxe rooms.

Hemingways is renowned for its leisure facilities, in particular deep-sea fishing and scuba diving. When you're tired of lazing about on the beach there's water-skiing, windsurfing, snorkelling and dhow excursions, as well as two fabulous swimming pools: one fresh and one with saltwater. You can swim in the safe, warm waters inside the reef, snorkel out to the coral gardens, or take a small boat to watch the local dolphins frolic beside the boat and even slip in beside them.

Hemingways' success lies in its ability to combine informality with punctuality. While you'll never feel pressured by pompous staff, they'll also never fail to deliver on a promise. The seafood is wonderful, the accommodation comfortable and the beach just perfect – although be careful to avoid the end of April through to October when the changing winds tend to cover the beach with seaweed.

The Funzi Keys

THE FUNZI KEYS
(satellite ☎ 00-873-762 203 955, satellite 📠 00-873-762 203956, 🖳 www.thefunzikeys.com), PO Box 92062, Mombasa, Kenya
Closed: Easter to Mid July
Reservations: Either direct or through Worldwide Journeys & Expeditions or Carrier (see pp12-13)
Getting there: The hotel has its own landing strip only 15 minutes' flying time from Mombasa, or you can get there by road, or hotel launch across the sea
Accommodation: Six thatched cottages with private Jacuzzi
Amenities: Large free-form pool, Snorkelling, sailing, canoeing, windsurfing, dhow and boat trips in the bay and to the Ramisi River, and sundowner dhow cruises
Dress code: Informal
Weddings: Can be arranged
Minimum stay: None apart from at Christmas and New Year
Rates: Doubles from US$500 per person per night which includes all meals, laundry, all watersports apart from diving and deep-sea fishing, and drinks other than champagne
Credit cards: Visa, MasterCard, JSB
Taxes and service charge: Included but not service which is discretionary

The Funzi Keys, on a remote island south of Mombasa, opened its doors in 2000 and is the hot new place to go in Kenya. It's also the most expensive, but people come back raving about the heaven on earth, barefoot luxury of this place.

The main building reflects the influence of coastal Omani architecture, with Lamu ceilings made from coral blocks amid mangrove poles, and intricate plaster carvings on the walls. The six spacious thatch-roof cottages built of stone are set along the beach, and have large windows where the netting blows in the sea breeze and dramatic views of the African sunset can be had.

The airy rooms are decorated in carefully thought-out, ultra-rustic style and imaginatively furnished with locally carved wood and artefacts. In addition to a large four-poster bed, each room has a Jacuzzi under a striped silk awning with a spectacular sea view. As well as having fully-stocked coolboxes, rooms are equipped with thoughtful extras such as sun creams, insect repellents, straw hats, kikois, flip-flops and beach bags.

A campfire is lit in the private sitting area in front of your cottage each night where you can watch the sunset while having a sundowner. Dinner of wonderful local seafood and fresh fruit and vegetables is served every evening on the deck of a dhow anchored off the beach.

The Funzi Keys is the kind of place where you can spend the week without shoes, or dress up if you feel like it. You also won't have to dip into your pocket much once you are there. Activities included in the price are snorkelling, sailing, canoeing, windsurfing, dhow and boat trips to see the dolphins which regularly visit Funzi Creek and to see the brilliantly-coloured kingfishers and crocodiles on the Ramisi River. Deepsea fishing and scuba diving can be arranged locally with advance notice, at extra cost.

When you're not out exploring you can unwind on the wooden deck which surrounds the large free-form pool, with the only sound the haunting cry of the fish eagle echoing across the water. A sunset dhow cruise or a beach barbecue makes a wonderfully romantic end to a gloriously relaxed day.

Recommended hotels in Lamu

Kiwayu Safari Village (c/o ☎ 2-503 030, 🖹 2-503 149, 🖥 www.kiwayu.com, PO Box 56923, Nairobi), an island retreat 30 miles north of Lamu off the Kenyan coast, is a great honeymoon getaway. A true Robinson Crusoe-style island combined with perfectly understated luxury, faultless service and excellent dining.

The beach is idyllic white sand, the central mess tent really wonderful with lots of comfortable cushions for lounging around on and doing nothing, and the seafood is delicious. I've never heard a bad word spoken about Kiwayu, and as long as you're not the sort of person who can't live without a hairdryer you'll fall in love with the place; if you do need a hairdryer go to Hemingways (see p235)!

There are 20 rooms in individual 'bandas', reed matting and thatched cottages. They are well spread out among the sand dunes and each one has a private shower and a wonderful large veranda with colourful scatter cushions and hammocks. If you want total privacy, the Baobabs of Kitangani, three kilometres away, is the perfect setting. The living room perches graciously under an enormous baobab, leading to a dazzling bedroom with en suite facilities. Staff and boatmen are at your beck and call and over a kilometre of beach is exclusively yours. Rates which include full board, transfers and many activities are approximately US$290 per person per night at Kiwayu, US$1000 per person per night at Baobabs of Kitangani. Book through tour operator Roxton Bailey Robinson (UK ☎ 01488-689 702, 🖥 www.roxtons.com).

Kipungani Bay (c/o Nairobi ☎/🖹 254-121-33432, PO Box 74888, Nairobi) is a romantic and affordable hotel comprising 14 spacious, secluded 'bandas' (chalets) above the soft white 14km deserted sands of Kipungani Bay, on the south-western tip of Lamu. Constructed from natural materials with grass floors and *makuti* thatch roofs, the rustic but fantastically stylish bandas have giant king-size beds with mosquito netting, furniture made from local mangrove and palm woods, beautiful verandas with local *funzi* sofas and chairs piled high with colourful cushions. Each spacious banda has its own en suite shower, basin and flush toilet. There is no hot water, but the temperature makes this completely unnecessary. All the huts have a view of the sea – those at the back are on stilts.

Dining is whenever you want, as staff are on hand to serve you fresh prawns, crab or lobster 24 hours a day; one member of staff is assigned to your banda. There are plenty of activities at Kipangani, including windsurfing, sailing, fishing trips in motorized dhows and safari walks to see the wild buffaloes.

Kipangani means the 'place of fresh air' in Swahili. There are no windows in the bandas – but a pleasant breeze. And with just the odd fallen coconut between you and the sea, this is a place to relax in nature.

Book direct through Nairobi office (🖹 2-716 457, 🖥 www.heritagehotels.co.ke); seven nights in a standard room full board with UK tour operator Tropical Places (☎

01342-330 700, UK toll-free ☎ 0800-093 9499, 💻 www.tropical.co.uk) costs US$1847/£1299 per person including international return flight and transfers.

Peponi Inn (☎ 121-33421/2/3, 📄 121-33029, 💻 www.peponi-lamu.com, PO Box 24, Lamu), although not a classic honeymoon beach hotel (the beautiful beach here disappears at high tide), it is an old time favourite. John Hemingway's quotes in the Peponi brochure sum up this unique 24-roomed hotel. He says: 'There are too many luxury hotels around the world and they offer the same: a chocolate on the pillow, canned romance and a cuisine called haute because it's spelled in French. Peponi stands apart from them all ... yes, you come here to be pampered, but at Peponi, luxury is the engine not the destination.'

People who have been to Peponi all come back saying the same thing: that it is simply dreamy, unlike anywhere else in the world they've seen. Having changed little over the years, Peponi epitomises the laid-back atmosphere of Lamu Island. Double rooms are a maximum of US$330 full board. Book through tour operator Worldwide Journeys and Expeditions (UK ☎ 020-7386 4646).

Tanzania
(BEST TIME: JUNE TO MARCH)

If you are looking for the authentic safari experience and for deserted beaches and islands, look no further than Tanzania. In this land of magnificent and diverse beauty you will find unparalleled game viewing, in much less touristy surroundings than in neighbouring Kenya.

From the vast and seemingly never-ending **Serengeti Plains**, to the rugged mountains and stunning soda lakes of the **Rift Valley**, and the awesome **Ngorongoro Crater** – a giant Noah's Ark crowded with black rhino, buffalo, elephant and lion – Tanzania offers an experience for real safari enthusiasts. Between November and July the plains are home to droves of wildebeest, stalking lions, hyenas, jackals and eagles. All of this with the added attraction of the idyllic Indian Ocean beaches to look forward to after a week in the bush.

Only 20 minutes off the coast of Tanzania by plane from the capital Dar Es Salaam is the famous spice island of **Zanzibar**. This intriguing Muslim island had

---

TANZANIA
Incredible wildlife in the Serengeti, and a stunning tropical coastline
When to go: Avoid April to the end of May when the rains are bad, expect intermittent rain around November and December
Average maximum temperatures °C

JAN	FEB	MAR	APR	MAY	JUN	JUL	AUG	SEP	OCT	NOV	DEC
30	31	31	30	30	29	28	29	29	29	30	30

Capital: Dar Es Salaam
Flight times: to Dar es Salaam from:
      New York (via Europe) 16½ hours
      LA: (via New York and Europe) 22 hours
      London: 12¼ hours
      Sydney: (via Johannesburg) 22 hours
Approximate exchange rates: Tanzanian shilling (S) – £1 = S1266, US$1 = S893, A$1 = S463
Time difference: GMT plus three hours
Voltage: 240v AC, 50 Hz, although some hotels are equipped with 110v wall sockets for American plugs
Combine with: Kenya, Zanzibar and its islands
Country dialling code: ☎ 255
Further information: 💻 www/tamzamoa-web.com/home2.htm

until recently waned in popularity as news of its growing commercialization spread, but I have found some new properties which are truly excellent and some exclusive private island resorts off the coast, which are far from being over-commercialized or scruffy.

Safaris in Tanzania

The Serengeti is the best-known game reserve in Africa and no trip to Tanzania would be complete without a visit. In just a couple of days in the Serengeti you'll see an awesome variety of game; nowhere else is there such an abundance of lion, leopard and cheetah – you may even see a kill or two.

The best place to stay is either **Klein's Camp** or **Grumeti River Lodge** (call both at Conservation Corporation Africa on South Africa ☎ 11 809 4300, 🖹 11 809 4514, 🖳 www.ccafrica.com); book direct or through UK tour operator, Tanzania Odyssey (☎ 020-7471 8780). Kleins is just outside the park in the north-eastern Serengeti and Grumeti is in the Western Corridor of the Serengeti. Both Kleins and Grumeti are fantastic small lodges in beautiful settings and cost around US$600 per person per night full board.

Make sure you do one of the early morning hot-air balloon safaris: you take off before sunrise, drift gracefully above the majestic plains for an hour or so and then land for champagne and a full English breakfast cooked on the balloon's burner. You could even get married in a hot-air balloon! Balloon safaris can be arranged through either of these camps once you are out there or by talking to Mike Toogood at **Serengeti Balloon Safaris** (UK ☎ 020-8455 0065).

Apart from visiting the **Serengeti**, a day or two at the **Ngorongoro Crater**, a World Heritage site, really should be part of any Tanzanian itinerary. There can be few who have not heard of, or seen on TV documentaries, this staggering 20km-wide volcanic crater with its 600m walls packed with just about every type of African wildlife. Apart from the staggering views from the rim, it will also allow you to see rhino, which you won't have seen in the Serengeti. And, the superb **Ngorongoro Crater Lodge** (contact Conservation Corporation, South Africa ☎ 11 809 4300, 🖹 11 809 4514, 🖳 www.ccafrica.com), which perches on the rim, is probably one of the most romantic hotels in the whole of Africa. Inspired by ancient African architecture, the lodge is arranged in three small villages each with ten cottages made from primeval earth. There is nothing primitive about the luxury baroque interiors however, or the level of service. Staying here costs US$600 per person per night. Book direct or through Small Luxury Hotels of the World reservation numbers worldwide (see p12).

A week of unrivalled game viewing in Tanzania is likely to put you back around US$5000 per person if you stay in the camps featured above. However, cheaper alternatives exist for about US$350 per person per night (see below). For even cheaper safari holidays my advice is to look at Kenya where the greater presence of tour companies has brought the price down. Game viewing, however, may be marred by the large number of tourists.

SELOUS GAME RESERVE

A vast wilderness in Southern Tanzania covering 54,000 sq km, the Selous has the largest elephant population in the world and is truly one of the wildest most untouched areas left to discover. This is a safari for the enthusiast, where walking with extremely knowledgeable guides will reveal the hidden Africa, but it's definitely not for the faint-hearted.

Selous Safari Camp

Selous Safari Camp is located in the north-east sector of the Selous. This sector is the most densely populated game area in the whole reserve and is one of the few places in

SELOUS SAFARI CAMP

(☎ 22-213 4802), PO Box 1192, Dar es Salaam, Tanzania

Closed: Mid April to the end of May

Reservations: Either direct or with Tours and Trade International (UK ☎ 01367-253 810); or alternatively through most leading African specialist tour operators and travel agents worldwide (see pp12-13)

Getting there: Selous Safari Camp can arrange your transfer from Dar es Salaam Airport by light aircraft or charter flight to the camp (scheduled flights cost around US$120 per person one-way but will be included in your final bill)

Accommodation: 12 luxury tents

Amenities: Open top four-wheel drive game drives, aluminium boats, game scouts for treks, swimming pool, three meals a day and open bar, laundry service, and transfer service

Dress code: Casual, but most guests wear long trousers to avoid mosquitoes

Weddings: Can be arranged if given notice well in advance

Minimum stay: None

Rates: US$320 per person per day for full board

Credit cards: American Express, Visa, MasterCard

Taxes and service charge: Included

the world where game can be viewed without the disturbance of hordes of other tourists.

The camp is situated on the banks of a lagoon which is part of the **Rufiji River**: you can sit on your tent's veranda and watch the game coming down to the lagoon to drink – a mesmerizing sight.

The camp's 12 green tents, five doubles and seven twins, convertible to doubles, are mounted on wooden platforms which face towards **Lake Nzerekera**, and which are carefully placed in order to provide maximum privacy. Each one is 3.4m wide and 7m long, well-ventilated and luxuriously appointed with an en suite flushing toilet and basin, with attached shower cubicle, plus solar-powered lighting.

The bar is exceedingly well stocked and is open for as long as you want – they just keep on serving until the last guests have gone to bed. Dining is a pretty spectacular event, especially in the evening when you are served three courses with silver service. The day gets off to a good start with a hearty breakfast comprising fruit, freshly baked breads and eggs to order. Lunch is buffet style with a selection of salads.

Between all this eating and drinking guests get on with the game drives that attracted them to Selous. There is so much to see and do that you won't know whether to go for one of the three-hour safaris in the open-top, four-wheel drive vehicles (each of which is fitted with VHF mobile radios to keep them in touch with the other vehicles and camp), an afternoon boat trip, or a walk into the surrounding bush accompanied by one of the experienced game scouts. And when you've had enough of all that activity, there's a swimming pool to come home to.

The best time to visit is between June and October because it is the dry season and it is not too hot. Between November and December it is pleasantly hot but you can expect some short rain showers, and from January through to April it just gets hotter and hotter before the rains come. Selous is closed during the rainy season from the middle of April to the end of May.

Selous Safari Camp is the perfect solution if you want to experience what it's like to sleep under canvas in the middle of the African bush but don't really want to sacrifice your comforts on your honeymoon.

Sand Rivers Selous

Sand Rivers Selous consists of just eight thatched cottages set amidst over 50,000km of land that is home to impala, elephant, hippos and crocodiles. Come here if you want to see game in its natural habitat and if you don't want to be surrounded by hordes of other tourists. There's no point in going to Sand Rivers if you're scared of the bush or need to blow-dry your hair every evening, but if you really want to get back to nature you'll love Sand Rivers. Set in the shade of a baobab tree on the banks of the river Rufiji, the lodge was established by Richard Bonham, who has long been known as one of the finest guides in East Africa.

The eight thatched cottages have no fronts and are on stilts overlooking the river, so you can lie in bed and look straight out over your private wooden balcony to the bush. The cottages are all built in rustic style, offering complete comfort and sophistication but using local materials. Each has an en suite bathroom with power shower and a four-poster bed with mosquito netting, a fan and a cupboard with hanging space, so you won't exactly be roughing it!

The lodge also features a large open bar and dining area with an open fire, sofas and armchairs. A swimming pool has been built into the rocks by the river in the shade of the baobab tree. There is a changing room with a shower and toilet, and lots of chairs around the pool.

Activities here include boat trips on the river and game drives in Richard Bonham's open-top Land Rover, but the highlight of Sand Rivers is heading off into the bush on one of his 'fly camping' treks in search of the big five – Bonham is armed only with a mobile phone and a gun. You camp under the stars with only a mosquito net between you and the African sky.

The types of game you are likely to see at Sand Rivers include elephant, hippo, crocodile, lion, wild dog, giraffe, antelope, buffalo and the most superb birdlife.

> **SAND RIVERS SELOUS**
> (☎ c/o Kenya ☎ 2-884 475, 🖹 2-882 728, 🖳 lizzy@srs.simba.glcom.com), Selous Game Reserve, Tanzania
> **Closed**: April and May
> **Reservations**: Direct or through UK representatives Roxton Bailey Robinson (☎ 01488-689 702, 🖹 01488-682 977) or Theobald Barber (☎ 020-7723 5858, 🖹 020-7723 5417)
> **Getting there**: Guests are met at Dar es Salaam Airport and are then flown to the lodge's airstrip (45 minutes), from where it's a 10-minute drive to the lodge; scheduled flights from Dar es Salaam to Sand Rivers cost around US$120 per person
> **Accommodation**: 8 thatched cottages
> **Amenities**: Dining area, sitting area, open bar (payable on departure), swimming pool with changing room; game viewing by four-wheel drive, on foot and by boat, plus fly camping trips
> **Dress code**: Informal
> **Weddings**: The camp's management say that the prospect cannot be discounted!
> **Minimum stay**: Three nights recommended
> **Rates**: From US$365 to US$425 per person per night, including transfers, meals and game viewing, excludes drinks and fly camping
> **Credit cards**: Are not accepted so extras will have to be paid for in cash (preferably US$); your travel agent/tour operator will accept credit cards for the actual holiday bill
> **Taxes and service charge**: Taxes are included, but tips are appreciated

THE TANZANIAN COAST

Ras Kutani Beach Resort

Ras Kutani Beach Resort is *the* place to relax after a southern Tanzania safari. Rustic and relaxed, the hotel is built on the side of a wooded hill, overlooking the golden beach and beside a freshwater lagoon.

Like its sister property, Selous Safari Camp, the Ras Kutani was built using natural materials so, while it may be luxurious, from the air it looks just like a tribal village. You'll stay in one of the 12 large cottages which have either double or twin beds, a flush toilet, shower and basin, and cover around 70 sq metres.

The cottages were built from bamboo and thatch and inside bold, coloured fabrics are used to brighten up the natural fibres of the floor, walls and ceiling. Some of the cottages are up on the hill, others line the side of the lagoon while the best are on the seashore.

In front of each cottage is a fabulous veranda with a brightly-coloured hammock perfectly strung to make the best of the view, as well as a sofa, table and chairs, and a wonderful Swahili day bed. In the middle of your bedroom lies the bed, shrouded in white mosquito netting suspended by a canopy hanging down from the ceiling. All the furniture is locally made and beautifully carved.

Staying at the Ras Kutani is all about chilling out big time. Watersports are available but nothing motorized is allowed to interrupt the tranquillity of the area: most peo-

RAS KUTANI BEACH RESORT
(☎ 22-213 4802), PO Box 1192, Dar es Salaam, Tanzania
Reservations: Either direct or through Tours and Trade International (UK ☎ 01367-253 810); most leading African specialist tour operators and travel agents worldwide (see pp12-13)
Getting there: The lodge can arrange your transfer from Dar es Salaam Airport, taking you by scheduled or charter flight to the resort (about 15 minutes) or a road transfer which takes about 45 minutes
Accommodation: 12 large cottages, twin, double or single
Amenities: Bar, restaurant serving European food with African touches and an emphasis on fresh seafood; snorkelling, windsurfing, sailing, boogie boarding, fishing on nearby reefs, island trips, nature walks, laundry
Dress code: Casual
Weddings: Can be arranged if given good advance notice
Minimum stay: None
Rates: US$200 per person per day all-inclusive
Credit cards: American Express, Visa, MasterCard
Taxes and service charge: Included

ple spend their days lounging around in hammocks reading or taking the occasional dip.

If you do fancy getting up and doing something the hotel will pack you off horse-riding or trekking, or with a lunch and snorkel to explore the reefs, or you could take out one of their boogie boards and surf the breakers.

ZANZIBAR AND OTHER ISLANDS
The spice island of Zanzibar off the coast of Tanzania has miles of white sandy palm-fringed beaches and coves with excellent reefs for snorkelling and diving, fantastic deep-sea fishing, watersports and, of course, delicious fresh fish. In **Stonetown** you can wander among ancient Islamic ruins and noble Arabic houses or follow your nose to visit the spice plantations (cloves, cinnamon, nutmeg, vanilla, cardamom and others).

Zanzibar's west coast has some lovely hotels but very little to boast about in the way of beaches. The east coast has great beaches and is lovely but full of backpackers and Italians, while the north of the island has the most incredible beaches and is much less tidal. Further information about Zanzibar from 🖳 www.zanzibartourism.net.

Ras Nungwi
Ras Nungwi has the finest beaches in the whole of Zanzibar and the best setting of all the island's hotels. It is still relatively undiscovered which makes it an even better find. You get a wonderfully remote feeling staying there, as there are no other hotels in the area: you can walk for ages along beautiful soft sandy beaches without seeing another soul. The food is also surprisingly good, though I wouldn't recommend a visit to Zanzibar if you don't like fish!

RAS NUNGWI
(☎ 24-223 2512) A Lala Salama Resort, PO Box 1784, Zanzibar, Tanzania
Reservations: Through UK tour operator World Archipelago (☎ 020-8780 5838)
Getting there: Taxi from Stonetown costs around US$30 per person
Accommodation: 35 beach chalets
Amenities: Dive centre, deep-sea fishing, watersports and dhow trip, swimming pool
Dress code: None, but smart in the evening
Weddings: Can arrange both ceremonies and receptions
Minimum stay: None
Rates: From US$125 to US$165 per person full board
Credit cards: Visa, American Express
Taxes and service charge: Included, but tips welcome

The 30 beach bandas, or chalets, all have a patio, a double four-poster bed and are very well furnished. They would have been even nicer had they tiled the en suite bathrooms and given them a slightly more substantial door but, this gripe aside, the bedrooms are extremely comfortable.

The central sitting area is full of scatter cushions which are just perfect for lazing around on at any time of the day. Separate to the sitting area is the restaurant and bar, both of which are open plan: in the evening the tables are smartly laid for dinner and the meal is served by professional waiting staff – somewhat unusual in this part of the world.

Breakfast is much less formal, comprising an assortment of pastries baked freshly at the hotel, fresh ground coffee or, better still, their home-made hot chocolate which is an absolute must. You can also have your breakfast brought to your room.

Ras Nungwi is the sort of place where there is absolutely nothing to do apart from laze around on the beach all day, or around the wonderful swimming pool overlooking the Indian Ocean, and maybe nip off for a bit of snorkelling or diving. The dive school is great and all the usual water-sport facilities such as windsurfers and dinghies are there. They are a bit short on loungers but somehow it's not that sort of hotel, it's much more of a get-the-sand-between-your-toes-and-lie-on-the-beach kind of place. Very relaxed, very remote and very, very beautiful.

Other recommended hotels on Zanzibar

Mbweni Ruins (☎ 24-223 1832, 🖺 24-223 0536, PO Box 2542, Zanzibar) is great for a night or two, particularly if you want to be close to Stonetown but don't want to be woken by the chant of the muezzins from the mosques at 4am. The beach, however, isn't so good. Doubles cost from US$120 bed and breakfast.

Emerson & Green Hotel (☎ 24-223 0171, 🖺 24-223 1038, 🖳 www.zanzibar.org/emegre, PO Box 3417, 236 Hurumzi Street, Zanzibar) is a funky alternative for honeymooners in Stonetown. The former home of one of the richest men in the Swahili empire, it is the second tallest building in town. The experience of sitting shoeless on the Persian carpets in the open-sided rooftop restaurant is heightened by the fabulous views over the mosque minarets, Hindu temples and church spires of Stonetown, and of the Indian Ocean.

Original Zanzibari antiques of varied origins and styles make the ten spacious rooms unique, and all except one have large stone bathtubs. The stunning sultan-sized rooms on the first and second floors have 20-ft ceilings, carved doors, original stucco décor and hand-painted glass lamps and window panes. All rooms have large Zanzibari beds with mosquito nets, air conditioning and ceiling fans. As a romantic touch, fresh jasmine flowers appear on the pillows at bedtime.

Doubles cost from US$150 per room with bed and breakfast. Book direct or through UK tour operators Nomadic Thoughts (☎ 020-7604 4408) who specialize in tailor-made honeymoons or Worldwide Journeys and Expeditions (☎ 020-7386 4646).

Mnemba Island Lodge

Created by Italian hotelier Bruno Brighetti and managed by Conservation Corporation Africa since 1993, Mnemba Island Lodge is the ultimate all-inclusive island getaway, for those who can afford it: Bill Gates is rumoured to have stayed here for the Millennium.

Situated between two coral reefs 2km off the north-east coast of Zanzibar, the lodge was constructed with minimal impact on the environment, using local materials and powered by a solar-power unit.

MNEMBA ISLAND LODGE
Mnemba Island, Zanzibar, Tanzania
Closed: April and May
Reservations: Through Conservation Corporation Africa (South Africa ☎ 11 809 4300, 🖺 11 809 4514, 🖳 www.ccafrica.com), UK tour operator Tanzania Odyssey (☎ 020-7471 8780), or tour operators specializing in East Africa (see pp12-13)
Getting there: Mnemba Island Lodge provides transfers to the island from Zanzibar Airport at additional cost; the road transfer takes approximately one hour followed by a boat transfer of 20 minutes; transport from Arusha, Nairobi or Dar es Salaam by private air-charter is available on request at extra cost
Accommodation: 10 cottages
Amenities: Bar/lounge cottage, open-plan dining cottage, library cottage
Dress code: Very casual
Weddings: Can be arranged, but the whole island must be taken by the wedding group – maximum of 20
Minimum stay: None
Rates: From around US$650 per person per night inclusive; excludes PADI diving instruction, deep-sea fishing, cognac, champagne and cigars
Credit cards: American Express, Visa, MasterCard
Taxes and service charge: Included

This beautiful, uninhabited island epitomises the concept of barefoot comfort. The ten timber and makuti (thatch) bandas have coconut-matting floors, and are decorated in a wonderfully simplistic but relentlessly design-conscious fashion – varnished director's chairs covered in cream canvas and billowing mosquito nets enclosing enormous beds sit side by side with handcrafted Zanzibari furniture and island artefacts such as driftwood and shells. Hot water is available all day.

Mnemba is a place to relax. Instead of a television your cottage has a large veranda with the most awe-inspiring view over the Indian Ocean. If you want to be active the snorkelling and diving on the island's own 16km of unspoilt coral reef is captivating, and in the evening there's first-rate seafood and a cold beer or cocktail to look forward to.

If you can possibly afford it this is undoubtedly a contender for the most remote, luxurious, private and exclusive destination in Africa.

Kinasi Camp

Kinasi Camp, on Mafia Island, is one of the most beautiful places in the world. This highly exclusive lodge is one of only two hotels on Mafia Island: the island is about the size of nearby Zanzibar where there are as many as 50 hotels.

Kinasi's main lodge is set up on a hillside looking down over the sea, with a beautiful neo-classical swimming pool and large sundeck adjacent to it. The pool is elegantly tiled and looks more like something found in Greece than a Tanzanian construction.

Spread out over the grounds are 13 luxury chalets. They are built from local materials but are much more solid than some rustic bandas. Each chalet has a lovely big four-poster bed and a separate, properly tiled bathroom with shower and toilet. At the front of the chalet is a veranda which is equipped with hammocks, royal blue director's chairs and a table. The hotel staff are quite happy to bring any meal up to your veranda so that you can enjoy it in privacy.

In the main lodge there is a huge open-plan drawing room and bar, where you can flop into one of the all-enveloping lily-pad chairs and slowly drift off with a book, or if you're feeling mentally active play chess or Trivial Pursuit. The hotel's dining room is quite smart, even slightly austere in these surroundings, with its mock Queen Anne furniture.

Every day is different at Kinasi. In the morning, most guests head off somewhere: scuba diving, snorkelling, or for a picnic on the sand bar. The hotel's dive school is really well run and the area offers some fantastic diving. If you're not into snorkelling and diving and all you want to do is slob on the beach there are better places to do it than Kinasi.

KINASI CAMP
(☎ 811-325 820), PO Box 26, Mafia Island, Tanzania
Reservations: Either direct with the Dar es Salaam number above or through tour operator Africa Archipelago (UK ☎ 020-8780 5838)
Getting there: Scheduled flights from Zanzibar or Dar es Salaam to Mafia Island cost US$120, the hotel will meet you from the plane
Accommodation: 13 luxury chalets
Amenities: Swimming pool, diving, watersports, bird-watching, picnic boat trips
Dress code: None, but smart in the evening
Weddings: Can arrange both ceremonies and receptions
Minimum stay: No, but three nights recommended
Rates: From US$160 per person all inclusive
Credit cards: Most major
Taxes and service charge: Included, but tips are welcome

Zimbabwe
(BEST TIME: APRIL TO OCTOBER)

If you don't mind early morning wake-up calls, communal dining, or sleeping it rough for a few nights, and if you both share a thirst for adventure and excitement, Zimbabwe could be the perfect destination for you. The great thing about a holiday in Zimbabwe is that you are virtually guaranteed good weather, there's lots to do from whitewater rafting to big-game trekking, and also some wonderfully luxurious hotels where you can indulge yourselves.

This captivating country is home to the magnificent **Victoria Falls**, the mighty **Zambezi River** as well as an abundance of wildlife. All sorts of waterborne activities are available on the river if you are seeking adventure. It is definitely worth noting that limited places are available on the canoeing safaris so do make sure you book as early as possible.

Excellent light aircraft services make it very easy to travel around within Zimbabwe and also make it an easy destination to combine with other countries in **Southern Africa**. For example there are flights direct from **Kariba** to nearby **Botswana**. Just check the political and security situations before you go.

LAKE KARIBA

The beautiful man-made **Lake Kariba** is the starting point for many of the canoeing trips down the Zambezi river. It is also a great place for watching wildlife or for relaxing on a houseboat. If you sit quietly in your boat for long enough, your patience is likely to be rewarded with the sight of buffalo, zebra, elephant and impalas which all come down to the water's edge to drink. From Kariba you can hop in a boat and head off to the less known **Matusadona National Park**, where there are fewer tourists than at most of Africa's game parks.

Sanyati Lodge

Sanyati Lodge is situated at the mouth of **Sanyati Gorge** across the lake from Kariba town. Sanyati underwent a massive refurbishment programme in 2000, which trans-

---

ZIMBABWE
Fantastic wildlife, canoeing and whitewater rafting on the Zambezi and the awesome Victoria Falls
When to go: April to October to avoid the rains, but make sure you take socks and a warm jumper for early mornings and evenings
Average maximum temperatures °C

JAN	FEB	MAR	APR	MAY	JUN	JUL	AUG	SEP	OCT	NOV	DEC
26	26	26	25	23	21	21	23	27	29	27	26

Capital: Harare
Flight times: to Harare from:
New York: (via Europe) $17\frac{1}{4}$ hours
LA: (via New York and Europe) 23 hours
London: $9\frac{3}{4}$ hours
Sydney: (via Johannesburg) $19\frac{3}{4}$ hours
Approximate exchange rates: Zimbabwe dollar (Z$) – £1 = Z$78, US$1 = Z$55, A$1 = Z$29
Time difference: GMT plus two hours
Voltage: 220v AC, US appliances will require an adapter, plugs are usually 13 amp square pins
Combine with: Botswana, Zambia, South Africa, Mauritius
Country dialling code: ☎ 263
Further information: 🖥 www.tourismzimbabwe.co.zw

SANYATI LODGE

(☎ 4-701 732/706 408, 🖷 4-701 737, 🖳 scottres@mweb.co.zw), c/o Scottlee Resorts Limited, 124 Josiah Chinamano Avenue, PO Box CY 3371, Causeway, Harare, Zimbabwe

Reservations: Either direct or through leading African-specialist tour operators and travel agents worldwide (see pp12-13)

Getting there: Transfers from Kariba Airport to the harbour and then from the harbour by boat to the lodge cost US$80 per person one way; self boat hire is available but expensive and not recommended

Accommodation: Nine thatched units and two suites

Amenities: Swimming pool, game safaris (walking, by boat, by vehicle), fishing, sunset cruises, library, room service, open bar, gym

Dress code: Jackets and ties required for evening meal

Weddings: The lodge does not perform wedding ceremonies unless the entire lodge is booked by the wedding party, costs depend on the time of year and requirements

Minimum stay: None

Rates: Standard room from US$290 per person per night; Matusadona Suite from US$345, includes all meals, morning and afternoon tea, laundry and activities

Credit cards: Most major

Taxes and service charge: 2% government levy, service included, an additional 15% sales tax charge added to your bill if you pay in Zimbabwean dollars

formed the lodge into the most exclusive retreat on Lake Kariba and added a new health spa. The cluster of luxuriously furnished chalets looks out over the lake but is camouflaged by the surrounding wooded hills.

The lodge offers game viewing on the lake by speedboat, as well as walking and driving safaris in Matusadona National Park with professional guides where you can expect to see black rhino, elephant, lion, buffalo and cheetah.

Each of the nine thatched chalets has double beds with an en suite bathroom and outdoor state of the art shower, and a covered thatched sun deck looking over the lake.

The lodge has two suites, one of which, the Matusadona Suite, is ideal for honeymooners. It has a lovely setting high up overlooking the lodge and its own private sun deck and swimming pool. The bedroom has a double bed and spacious bathroom with twin basins, a large bath overlooking the lake and an open-air shower.

For absolute privacy in extremely lavish surroundings, you could opt for the exquisitely-appointed Royal Tonga Suite, which offers a breathtaking view and even has its own wine cellar.

All the chalets are made out of stone and have thatched roofs with ethnic décor and overhead fans, minibar and telephone; shampoo and conditioner, soap, insect repellent and suntan lotion are all provided. Each chalet is totally private but these hideaways are open-sided so don't be surprised if you see monkeys staring at you in the mornings.

The accommodation is very comfortable here and the food served in the central dining room excellent. There is also a bar, and tea and coffee are available first thing in the morning, at mid-day and in the afternoon. The lodge has always prided itself on its personalized service and is a truly beautiful and tranquil bush haven.

Luxury houseboats

Renting a houseboat is one of the best ways to experience Lake Kariba. The lake is usually calm as there are few strong winds and your relative quietness on the water enables you to get much closer to the animals: you'll find you can drift right up to the shore line where the elephants are bathing. Apart from observing the wildlife, being on the water also gives you the freedom to explore the various islands.

For the best guiding experience, it is recommended to take boats from the lodges, but if you want to organize it yourself two Zimbabwean-based companies offer a variety of boat rentals. **Run Wild** (☎ 795841, 🖺 795845/6) offers houseboats and yacht charters on Lake Kariba, while **Rhino Rendezvous** (☎ 745642, 🖳 rhino@pci.co.zw) has a range of boats to suit all budgets. A pontoon comes with a skipper but no guide;

CANOEING SAFARIS

If you prefer to view game without the continual hum of Land Rover engines, a canoeing safari down the **Zambezi** is a wonderful way of seeing hippos, giraffe, elephants, fantastic bird life and even crocodiles. You'll spend days gliding effortlessly through the tranquil waters, viewing the game that have come down to the water to drink, and at night you camp under the stars around a fire.

The great thing about canoeing trips in Zimbabwe is that you can either go for a day, three days or even six days. You can also choose to stay on the more popular strip between **Kariba** and **Chirundu** or go into the more remote waters around **Mana Pools** and down to the **Mozambique** border, or wait until you get up to Victoria Falls and canoe the reaches of the **upper Zambezi**.

A whole host of tour companies run trips on the lower Zambezi between Kariba and Chirundu: the best known is **Shearwater** (☎ 061-2459) which has gradually taken over many of its competitors, but you might also try talking to Anthony Elton at **River Horse Safaris** (061-2422) and **Nature Ways** (☎ Harare 86176 or book through **Safcon** ☎ 425 2262).

For canoeing trips departing from Victoria Falls try **Kandahar Safaris** (☎ 013-2279, 🖥 013-2014), owned by Kerry and Clive Bradford. The Bradford's small, family-run company is well suited to honeymooners because they give much more individual attention than the bigger companies and generally they are great people to go with. Their canoeing safaris start at US$220 per person for a one-day trip. If you don't have time for a full day, opt for the ultimate sundowner cruise: gin and tonic in hand and nibbles at your side as you are paddled downstream watching the sunset.

---

although the skipper may sound as if he knows about the local wildlife, it's worth paying for a professional guide for the best experience. You can also ask them for catering or do your own.

The other option is to stay at **Matusadona Water Wilderness**, a small custom-made colony of houseboats in a really quiet part of the lake, which can be booked through most leading African-specialist tour operators (see pp12-13). The four houseboats at Matusadona Water Wilderness don't actually move, but you can spend your time paddling around on your own Canadian canoe that comes with the houseboat or tracking on foot with one of the camp's experienced trackers. Book through UK operators Wild Africa Safaris (☎ 01483-579 991, 🖥 was@bctuk.demon.co.uk) or other African specialists (see pp12-13).

VICTORIA FALLS

No visit to Zimbabwe would ever be complete without a visit to the mighty Victoria Falls. The volume of water cascading over this huge 90m precipice is so huge that the spray can be seen from 30km away.

On my first visit to the Falls I noticed that people returning from them were soaked to the skin: I assumed this meant it was raining ahead. However, it wasn't long before I started to get wet and then I realized that the 'rain' was coming from the Falls rather than the sky. Nothing can prepare you for the immensity of the sight, or the clouds of water rising high above your head and soaking you through – earning the Falls the local name of 'the smoke that thunders'.

The Victoria Falls Hotel

For true romantics the only place to stay in Victoria Falls is, of course, the Victoria Falls Hotel. This famous five-star colonial hotel is perched close to the edge of the vast gorge and is a wonderful place to relax. The Edwardian architecture and old world charm cannot fail to woo you.

Set in lovely well-kept gardens, the Vic Falls (as it is known locally) has the most splendid views of the bridge spanning the **Batoka Gorge**, while the thundering noise of cascading water acts as a constant reminder of your prime location.

THE VICTORIA FALLS HOTEL
(☎ 113-4751/61, 🖷 113-2354/4762, 💻 vicfallshotel@tvfh.zimsun.co.zw), PO Box 10, Victoria Falls, Zimbabwe
Reservations: Through Leading Hotels of the World (see p12) or most leading specialist-African tour operators and travel agents worldwide (see pp12-13)
Getting there: The hotel does not offer transfers but you can take a taxi which costs US$20 one way
Accommodation: Capacity 349 guests in a range of accommodation including six Executive Suites and one Royal Presidential Suite
Amenities: Swimming pool, room service, gift shops, hair salon, two tennis courts; Livingstone Restaurant, Stanleys, Jungle Junction, and the swimming pool bar
Dress code: Smart casual
Weddings: Wedding ceremonies can be arranged at the hotel either on the Terrace, Jungle Junction or in the chapel and will be performed by the local magistrate or the Catholic minister
Minimum stay: None, unless you are getting married in which case you must stay for two nights
Rates: Doubles from US$372; suites from US$700
Credit cards: Most major
Taxes and service charge: Taxes are included, there is no service charge

---

All the bedrooms are en suite and air conditioned and feature colonial architecture and traditional furnishings. They are well fitted-out with modern amenities including in-room safe, hairdryer, bathrobes, toiletries, radio, phone; the suites also have a minibar.

Facilities include two tennis courts, a swimming pool with pool-side bars as well as several other restaurants and bars. Don't miss the legendary braes (barbecues) at the Jungle Junction.

Tongabezi

Tongabezi, named after a combination of the local Tonga tribe, and *bezi,* meaning river, is on the other side of the Falls and thus is actually in **Zambia**. It is one of Africa's most exciting hotels and the perfect honeymooner retreat. It is also extremely popular for weddings.

If you are flying into Victoria Falls Airport on your way to Tongabezi, do take advantage of the lodge's rather unusual transfer arrangements. Instead of being picked up by road they can arrange a Flight of the Angels for you, before landing at the hotel: swooping down over the Victoria Falls in a light aircraft is really the only way to get an idea of the scale and immense grandeur of this rushing torrent of water.

Tongabezi Lodge is situated in a tranquil grove of ebony trees on a sweeping bend of the Zambezi River, facing west into the setting sun, 20km upstream from the Victoria Falls. Guests stay either in five cottages, four of which have oversized beds, or in one of the four 'houses', which are open to the wild and couldn't be more perfect. Both the cottages and houses are built using natural materials and all have their own private river frontage.

Each of the four houses (bird, tree, dog and honeymoon) has a four-poster bed with a large, airy mosquito canopy, private bathroom with a bath big enough for two,

---

THINGS TO SEE AND DO AROUND VICTORIA FALLS

There's lots to do from Victoria Falls. Many people find the river cruises and the curio (craft) villages disappointingly touristy, but there's lots of less tame entertainment to be had if that's your want.

Go for the Flight of the Angels, a 15-minute trip in a twin-engined light aircraft flying low over the Falls: it's particularly thrilling at sunset. Better still, grab a paddle and head down one of the world's most exciting whitewater rapids on a raft. The 5m inflatable rafts buck

and leap down the wild rapids, guided by experienced oarsmen.

There are hordes of companies offering whitewater rafting and other thrills from Victoria Falls, for about the same price. Whichever company you pick, make sure your day starts at Rapid No 1, the so-called **Boiling Pot** at the base of the Falls: you get spectacular views and four extra rapids before you even get to the point where most companies start their day!

flush toilets with the most incredible views, and hot and cold running water. Each also has a different style and décor: Honeymoon House has a wonderful sunken bath and is elevated above the river and Dog House is decorated in vivid colours and has a bath at the water's edge.

One of the best aspects of staying in Tongabezi, and something that everyone comments on, is the privacy. While guides and management are on hand at all times, they do their best to be unobtrusive and, because of the careful positioning of the houses and cottages, you won't find anyone wandering around in front of your patch. The fact that there are no walls can at times be almost comical when room service arrives and instead of knocking the waiter is obliged to say out loud: 'knock, knock, Missy, room service is here'; but don't worry you are kept totally insect-proof.

Just 3km downstream by private motorized banana boat takes you to Sindabezi where eight guests at a time are treated to a safari experience unlike any other. Sindabezi is the only island lodge in the Falls area. As such it is unique: you may get elephants in your room, hippos on your doorstep and you will undoubtedly be woken by a vociferous dawn chorus. Try to work a couple of nights on the island into your itinerary if you can.

Dining here is an indulgent experience. Champagne brunches can be arranged at the edge of Victoria Falls. Candlelit dinners in camp are accompanied by live African music and a sampan dinner for two can be organized in the middle of the Zambezi, with each course delivered by canoe.

Other recommended hotels

Close to Tongabezi, in an equally beautiful spot, is Wilderness Camps' **River Club** (🖳 www.wilderness-safaris.com), a newer property comprising of ten luxury, thatched chalets set in lush riverine vegetation, with a distinctly Victorian flavour. The River Club offers daily trips to the Falls, boating to the Zambezi River's islands, and fishing and sundowner trips. Lion calls can often be heard coming from Zambezi National Park at night and hippo are regularly sighted along the river's edge. Doubles cost from US$245 per person full board. Book through UK Africa specialists The Art of Travel (☎ 020-7738 2038, 🖳 www.artoftravel.co.uk) or Wild African Safaris (☎ 01483-453 731, 🖳 was@bctuk.demon.co.uk).

TONGABEZI
(Zambia ☎ 3-323 235/96, 🖹 3-323 224, 🖳 www.tongabezi.com) Private Bag 31, Livingstone, Zambia
Reservations: Specialist African tour operators (see pp12-13) such as Carrier (☎ 01625-547 010) in the UK
Getting there: Road transfers from Livingstone Airport or the Zambian/Zimbabwe border (25 minutes) or from Victoria Falls Airport or Victoria Falls Hotel (75 minutes) cost US$15 and US$30 respectively; alternatively an air transfer on the Flight of the Angels costs US$130 from Victoria Falls Airport (20 minutes) and US$170 from Kasane Airport (40 minutes)
Accommodation: Cottages: 4 double and 1 twin; houses: 4 double; 2 twin and 2 double in thatched cottage on Sindabezi Island
Amenities: Lounge, dining room, Swimming pool, two grass tennis courts, croquet, bird-watching, fishing, boating, canoeing, walks, room service, private dinners, laundry
Dress code: Casual
Weddings: Tongabezi is incredibly popular for weddings and really helpful but do book early; a four-day wedding package costs around US$1678/£1180 per person through a UK tour operator including your accommodation in a house and all arrangements
Minimum stay: None
Rates: Doubles in cottage from US$300 per person, in house US$375, both include accommodation, meals, drink (not premium imports), laundry service, park fees, sunset/sunrise boat trips, fishing, bird walks, gorge walks, afternoon canoeing, excursions and game drives; four night honeymoon package from US$1560 per person; US$200 per person on Sindabezi Island which includes accommodation, meals and all river activities
Credit cards: Most major
Taxes and service charge: Included

Botswana
(BEST TIME: MAY TO OCTOBER)

Because of their close proximity, Botswana and Zimbabwe can easily be combined on a two-week holiday, giving you the best of both worlds, especially if it's game you're after. You could also easily combine Botswana with South Africa, or Mauritius if you're after a beach.

Botswana is technically a desert, which makes the wetlands of the **Okavango's** 15,000 sq km delta, produced every spring as the Okavango river floods into the **Kalahari** sands, all the more remarkable. This is home to countless numbers of hippo, crocodiles, elephant and buffalo as well as diverse birdlife which can best be experienced from a mokoro (a traditional dug-out canoe made from the ebony or sausage tree) or in the drier areas by riding, elephant back, four-wheel drive and walking safaris. The 10,000 sq km **Chobe National Park** is known for its elephants in the dry season, and giraffe, lion, leopard and the endangered white rhinoceros also roam the plains. While open-top game drives through the grasslands of the **Moremi Wildlife Reserve** will reveal kudu, impala, buffalo, elephant, leopard, lion and wild dog, in the quiet unexplored region of the **Makgadikgadi Pans** quad-bikes can be used in the dry season to explore the unique white salt pans that stretch as far as the eye can see.

Operating a policy of quality not quantity (most of the best camps here are owned by Wilderness Safaris), Botswana is home to some of the best run and unspoilt, game reserves in Africa. It is now more popular than Zimbabwe for safaris, but be warned, it tends to be expensive.

MOREMI WILDLIFE RESERVE

Mombo Camp

Mombo Camp and Little Mombo are situated on scenic Mombo Island, within the Moremi Game Reserve. The camp offers true exclusivity and privacy in the central Okavango, and arguably the best game viewing in Botswana – National Geographic and the BBC are among those who have filmed here. Mombo is ranked as one of the best lodges in Southern Africa according to the July 2000 issue of *Harpers & Queen,* it was also listed as one of *Tatler's* 101 Best Hotels 2001.

Mombo has a concentration of plains game and all the predators – including the big cats, so leopard sightings are particularly good here. Completely rebuilt and re-opened in June 2000, Mombo lies under huge shady trees and overlooks a floodplain that teems with game.

BOTSWANA

Five-star lodges and game viewing on off the beaten track safaris in the Okavango Delta and one of the world's greatest deserts, as well as among perhaps the most exclusive wilderness in Africa

Average maximum temperatures °C

JAN	FEB	MAR	APR	MAY	JUN	JUL	AUG	SEP	OCT	NOV	DEC
31	30	29	27	25	22	22	25	28	30	31	31

Approximate exchange rates: Pula (P) – £1 = P7.98, US$1 = P5.61, A$1 = P2.91

Time difference: GMT plus two hours

Voltage: 220v AC

Combine with: Zimbabwe, South Africa, Mauritius

Country dialling code: ☎ 267

Further information: www.botswanatourism.org

The guests' rooms and walkways that connect them to the living areas are raised off the ground, allowing game to wander freely through the camp – but at the same time keeping guests well out of harm's way. Mombo and Little Mombo accommodate a total of 24 guests in large, superbly furnished luxury tents (nine tents at Mombo and three at Little Mombo). The twin beds in each tent have custom-made linen, so can be converted into a king-sized bed on request, and there are fans to keep you cool. All rooms have en suite facilities under canvas and an additional outdoor shower for those who want to shower alfresco. Soaps, shampoos and insect repellents are all supplied. Mombo Camp has a lounge, library, and pub and a boma for outdoor dining under the stars.

Guests could see lion, leopard, large herds of buffalo, cheetah, wild dog, elephant, hyena, giraffe, wildebeest and zebra on open-top game drives; birdlife, particularly waders, is prolific here. Both camps have a plunge pool in which to relax in the heat of the day, and safari walks are organized for the brave among the giant umbrella thorns and ilala palms at siesta time.

Sandibe Safari Lodge

Nestled between permanent water and grass-swept plains and bordering Moremi Game Reserve, no trees were sacrificed in the building of this solar-powered lodge. Opened in 1998, *Tatler* listed this lodge as one of the 101 Best Hotels of 2001.

Sandibe Lodge comprises eight de luxe African-inspired thatched cottages decorated in a rich fusion of ochre, silk and leather, with woven mats, copper and rough-

---

MOMBO CAMP
c/o Botswana office, Private Bag 14, Maun, Botswana
Open: Year round
Reservations: Through leading specialist African tour operators such as Gane & Marshall (UK ☎ 020-8441 9592)
Getting there: Access into the area is only by aircraft, Mombo airstrip located 15 minutes' drive from camp; flying from Maun 30 minutes or from Kasane 80 minutes (included in the package price below)
Accommodation: Nine luxury tents at Mombo and three at Little Mombo
Amenities: Dining room, pub, lounge, plunge pool, library, curio shop, game drives in 4x4 Land Rovers, safari walks
Dress code: Relaxed during the day – smart casual in the evening
Weddings: No
Minimum stay: None
Rates: From US$660 per person including accommodation, all meals, all activities, park fees and all drinks (except premium imports), package US$1580 per person includes two nights' accommodation with the above and transfers to and from Maun
Credit cards: Visa or MasterCard
Taxes and service charge: Taxes are included, suggested service charge guides US$5, camp staff US$3 per person per day

---

SANDIBE SAFARI LODGE
(☎ Conservation Corporation, South Africa ☎ 11 809 4300, 🖹 11 809 4514, 🖥 www.ccafrica.com)
Open: All year
Reservations: Through Conservation Corporation Africa (see above), UK tour operators Thomas Cook Holidays (☎ 01733-418 650) and most leading specialist African tour operators (see pp12-13)
Getting there: 20 mins by light aircraft from Maun
Accommodation: Eight twin-bedded/double rooms
Amenities: Boma, swimming pool, curio shop, viewing deck, guided day and night game drives in open vehicles, mokoro adventures, picnics, interpretative walks, birding, fishing
Dress code: No code; comfortable bush wear
Weddings: Able to arrange weddings with up to 16 people with private bush breakfasts or dinners, fantastic wedding cakes; priest and photographer can be flown in at extra cost
Minimum stay: None
Rates: US$355 to US$430 in high season per person full board including most drinks, safari activities, local transfers (not from Maun), park fees and laundry service
Credit cards: All major
Taxes and service charge: Tax included, but not service; US$10 each per day recommended for your guide and butler

hewn wood. The spacious cottages have en suite bathrooms, open showers and private elevated game-viewing decks overlooking the Santantebi River.

After an elegant bush breakfast, Sandibe offers guided day and night game drives in open Land Rovers, guided bush walks with a san (bushman), river cruises, mokoro (dugout canoe) trips, bush dinners under the stars and bird-watching. At Sandibe you can expect to see kudu, impala, giraffe, lion, hippo, crocodile, wild dog, sitatunga (antelope), 89 fish species, over 500 bird species and roaming herds of elephant and buffalo.

When not on safari, guests can laze in hammocks on the shaded decks and cool off in the swimming pool. Pan-African cuisine such as fire-roasted Botswana beef with caramelized onions and chilli served with sweet potatoes rubbed in cumin is served in a half boma by candlelight under a soaring canopy of trees facing the sunset, with a charcoal-cooled wine cellar nearby. A more intimate dinner can be served on your veranda.

A medicine man worked his magic to protect Sandibe from bad spirits, sickness and fire, and it has a special atmosphere.

Other recommended camps

To the west of Mombo lies **Jao Camp** (🖥 www.wilderness-safaris.com) with eight stunningly beautiful rooms with full facilities, connected by walkways. Jao offers a diversity of both land and water activities on the Okavango. From US$340 per person including meals and activities, park fees and all drinks (except premium imports). Book through UK tour operator Art of Travel (☎ 020-7738 2038, 🖥 www.artoftravel.co.uk).

Xigera Camp (🖥 www.wilderness-safaris.com) lies on an island by a permanently flowing river, so you can simply glide off in a mokoro from the camp. Its eight comfortable tents have en suite facilities. Doubles cost US$340 per person including meals and activities, park fees and all drinks (except premium imports). Book through UK tour operators Art of Travel (☎ 020-7738 2038, 🖥 www.artoftravel.co.uk) or ITC Classics (☎ 0870-751 9503, 🖥 cc@itc uk.com).

MAKGADIKGADI PANS

Jack's Camp

Jack's Camp, one of only two permanent tented camps in the grasslands at the edge of the Makgadikgadi Pans, is just amazing.

One of Botswana's longest established camps, the spacious and luxurious green bedouin-style tents overlooking the rolling desert and grasslands hold only 16 guests at a time, so you're guaranteed a highly personal service.

Perhaps the most atmospheric of Africa's luxury tented camps, the style is 1940s safari with Persian carpets, bonehandled silver cutlery and polished copper water jugs, canvas basins and chambray sheets. There is no electricity here, no running water

---

JACK'S CAMP
(☎ 267-21 2277, 🖷 267-21 3458) PO Box 173, Francistown, Botswana
Closed: December to February
Reservations: Through leading UK based African tour operators such as Gane & Marshall (☎ 020-8441 9592) or Africa Archipelago (☎ 020-8780 5838)
Getting there: Transfer by light aircraft from Maun, from US$133 per person each way, can be booked through Jack's
Accommodation: Eight luxury tents
Amenities: Quad-bikes, bushman trackers, exploring local area
Dress code: Safari wear
Weddings: Can arrange both ceremonies and receptions if whole camp taken over, prices on request
Minimum stay: None, suggested stay three nights
Rates: From US$445 per person per night inclusive of everything except transfers: meals, activities, drinks, laundry, park fees, government levies etc
Credit cards: No, but can prepay accommodation by credit card with tour operator, bank draft if want to book direct
Taxes and service charge: Included, guide tips discretionary

(which means bucket showers) and no ringing phones, but Jack's rustic atmosphere is curiously romantic.

San Camp, Jack's sister camp nearby, is possibly even more romantic with its white billowing tents, but it doesn't have flush loos and is open less of the year (May to November only).

Makgadikgadi Pans is the largest salt pan in the world; in the wet season it attracts flocks of flamingo. In the dry season, guests can venture onto the pans on four-wheel-drive quad bikes looking for stone age tools and fossils of extinct giant zebra or hippo, and search for the rare brown hyena. At a certain time of year, you can witness the migration of tens of thousands of wildebeest and zebra – the last true migration in Africa. After a day spent in the harsh but mesmerizing Kalahari, coming back to the excellent food served under a blanket of stars and the soft feather-bedding at Jack's Camp, feels like discovering an oasis in the desert.

Chobe National Park

Kings Pool Camp (🖥 www.wilderness-safaris.com) is located in Linyanti Wildlife Reserve, on the western boundary of Chobe National Park. The camp overlooks the oxbow-shaped Kings Pool Lagoon and the Linyanti River, an area known for its enormous elephant population – especially dense during the winter months. Big game such as lion, leopard, cheetah, wild dog and hyena are regularly sighted, and impala, lechwe, kudu, zebra, giraffe, sable, waterbuck, buffalo, bushbuck and the smaller plains antelope can also be viewed here. The reed and papyrus swamps attract numerous and diverse species of birds and are a magnet for game in the dry season.

Guests stay in ten comfortably appointed, twin-bedded, tented rooms overlooking the hippo-filled lagoon in front of the camp, with swanky en suite tiled bathroom facilities under thatch. Each bathroom has a shower, hand basin and flush toilet and an outdoor shower, too, for those who prefer to be closer to nature. The main lounge, pub and dining room are under a thatched roof, and there is a swimming pool built into the deck. Activities at Kings Pool include game drives in open Land Rovers, night drives, boat safaris (water levels permitting) and guided walks.

Kings Pool costs from US$340 per person including full-board accommodation, all activities, park fees and all drinks (except premium imports). Book through UK African specialist Okavango Tours & Safaris (☎ 020-8343 3283, 🖥 info@okavango.com).

South Africa
(BEST TIME: OCTOBER TO MAY)

South Africa is such a perfect holiday destination it's worth setting your wedding date between October and May just so that you can have your honeymoon there. However, like New Zealand, Australia and South America, South Africa is not the sort of destination where you are likely to fly to one resort and stay there for two weeks.

So much of the country is worth seeing, it makes the selection process painful: as the national tourist board is known to boast 'it's a world in one country'. With its spectacular landscapes of deserts, mountains, beaches and cliffs, fertile farmlands and modern cities, South Africa has all the ingredients for a wonderful honeymoon and the holiday of a lifetime.

The main elements of any holiday in South Africa should be a trip to **Cape Province**, where the Atlantic and Indian Ocean's meet; **Cape Town** and the vineyards of **Stellenbosch**; a drive up the spectacular coastline between Cape Town and **Port Elizabeth**, known as the **Garden Route**; a few days' safari in **Kruger National Park**;

SOUTH AFRICA
Mountains, coasts, wine lands and safari all interspersed with truly luxurious hotels for gastronomes
When to go: October to May; mid-December to mid-January is holiday time in South Africa and as such the country's key destinations are a great deal busier and more expensive; the east coast is always warm(ish) and Durban really humid; unless you're up in the mountains the winters are rarely very cold
Average maximum temperatures °C (Cape Town)

JAN	FEB	MAR	APR	MAY	JUN	JUL	AUG	SEP	OCT	NOV	DEC
26	26	25	22	19	18	17	18	19	21	23	25

Capital: Johannesburg
Flight times: to Johannesburg from:
    New York: 14$^{1}/_{4}$ hours
    LA: (via New York and Europe) 21 hours
    London: 10$^{3}/_{4}$ hours
    Sydney: 18 hours
Approximate exchange rates: Rand (R) – £1 = R11.36, US$1 = R8, A$1 = R4.15
Time difference: GMT plus two hours
Voltage: 220v/230v, AC 50 Hz, plugs have three round pins
Combine with: Zimbabwe, Botswana, Mauritius but there's plenty to keep you occupied in South Africa alone
Country dialling code: ☎ 27
Further information: 🖥 www.south-african-tourism.org and www.southafrica.net

and perhaps an overnight journey on the **Blue Train** or **Rovos Rail** – South Africa's sumptuous answers to the Orient Express. I would avoid Johannesburg, as it is little more than a large, modern, inland city.

Although South Africa's tourist industry is only just emerging from the ravages inflicted by apartheid, the country is full of first-class hotels and restaurants, originally created to satisfy the demands of an incredibly discerning local population.

I first went to South Africa fifteen years ago and, however backward it was politically then, it was an unforgettable culinary experience. From the brais (barbecues) on the beach to the freshest crayfish brought in by local fishermen, and some seriously elaborate six-course marathons; this is definitely a destination for gastronomes, with hotels to match.

If you like the idea of combining walks along empty beaches pounded by deafening surf, sundowners on top of the magnificent **Table Mountain**, wine tasting and dining in some of the world's greatest wineries, and donning your khakis for a few days of 'real' Africa, then this is the honeymoon for you. All the above can easily be achieved in a fortnight, with plenty of time to relax and really enjoy the surrounding countryside.

CAPE TOWN
Built on a peninsula where the Indian and Atlantic Ocean meet, Cape Town is, without doubt, one of the most naturally blessed cities in this world. With the most dramatic of backdrops supplied by the omnipresent Table Mountain and the craggy Apostles, plus a beautiful harbour, numerous surfstrewn beaches, and the wonderfully cool south-westerly breezes, it is difficult to imagine a more perfect summer city.

The Mount Nelson
The most gracious and the best-known hotel in Cape Town is the Mount Nelson, known to its friends as the 'Nellie'. This elegant pink hotel celebrated its centenary in 1999 and is part of the revered Orient-Express Hotels group.

The Nellie's dreamy setting at the foot of Table Mountain helps make it a wonderfully romantic hotel. It is within an easy stroll of the city centre, although you'd never know it because you're surrounded by three hectares of beautifully landscaped gardens. This hotel has everything you could possibly want, from the swimming pool to the beauty centre, as well as casual and formal dining. But one of the highlights about staying in the Nellie is undoubtedly its high teas, voted best in the world by Elegant Resorts in 2000, and served either in the lounge or on the veranda: you may well spot visiting dignitaries. Sipping tea in such elegant surroundings with the chink of bone-china, it is difficult to imagine that you are in Africa and you'll immediately feel as if you've been transported back to the 1920s. The Nellie claims to be the only hotel to offer steak tartare on the breakfast menu – one of the most extensive you'll find anywhere – apparently a relic from Lord Kitchener's days.

The 168 bedrooms and 58 suites also personify the hotel's old world grandeur and have lovely views over the gardens, the city or towards Table Mountain, and from the gardens you can see **Lion's Head** and **Devil's Peak**. Many of the rooms have been redecorated in the last few years by renowned South African interior designer, Graham Viney. He has worked hard to restore the feel of the colonial days and has produced bedrooms with a very light and airy feel, full of English chintz and luxurious bathrooms. A favourite with honeymooners is Room No 507 which has its own small conservatory for breakfast.

The Penthouse Suite in the Green Park wing has a wrap-around balcony with the

THE MOUNT NELSON
(☎ 21 483 1000, ◫ 21 424 7472, ☐ reservations@mountnelson.co.za), 76 Orange Street, Cape Town 8001, South Africa
Reservations: Through Orient-Express Hotels (☐ www.orient-expresshotels.com), or the Leading Hotels of the World reservation numbers worldwide (see p12)
Getting there: The hotel can arrange transfers from the airport
Accommodation: 168 bedrooms and 58 suites
Amenities: 24-hour room service, curio and gift shop, hairdresser and beauty salon, free parking, Cape Colony restaurant, the Oasis Restaurant overlooking the pool, the Lounge and Veranda for coffee and afternoon tea, the Lord Nelson bar, several function rooms, two heated swimming pools, two all-weather tennis courts (floodlit), gym, full range of watersports available at nearby beaches including surfing, windsurfing and scuba diving; hill walking, climbing and a wide choice of golf courses nearby
Dress code: Smart casual
Weddings: Ceremonies and receptions can be arranged in the beautiful landscaped gardens
Minimum stay: None
Rates: Double rooms cost from US$380/R2640; honeymoon packages include free upgrade to suites subject to availability
Credit cards: All major
Taxes and service charge: Tax 1%; Service charge included

best view of Table Mountain and 18 stunning suites with private kitchens have been created in the newly purchased Helmsley Building, previously a Jewish Synagogue. You might also try one of the eight Garden Cottage suites, which are surrounded by their own individual garden and have wrought-iron furnishings and a private swimming pool.

The Cellars-Hohenort Hotel

The Cellars-Hohenort Hotel enjoys a prime location, only 15 minutes from Cape Town but right in the heart of one of the Cape's best wine-growing regions, **Constantia**. The lush valley of Constantia running between Cape Town and the Cape of Good Hope has been famous for its superb wines for centuries, while back in the 18th-century Cellars was the Cape governor's wine cellar.

This beautiful country house, set in exquisitely landscaped gardens with orchards and vineyards all around, offers wonderful accommodation and exceptional food, making it the perfect place to wind down after a long flight and the emotional highs of a wedding. It's really easy to get into town and to the many great beaches around Cape Town but even nicer to return to serene Constantia at the end of the day.

The 38 rooms and 15 suites are individually decorated to reflect the gracious elegance of a historic Cape country house. They are decorated in chintz fabrics, period furniture and local artwork. All have stunning views over the mountains. Rooms No 2

THE CELLARS-HOHENORT HOTEL

(☎ 21-794 2137, 🖷 21-794 2149, 💻 info@cellars-hohenort.co.za), 15 Hohenort Avenue, Constantia 7800, Cape Town, South Africa

Reservations: Relais & Châteaux worldwide reservation numbers (see p12)

Getting there: The hotel can help with transfers on request, Cape Town airport is 20km away

Accommodation: 38 rooms and 15 suites

Amenities: Two restaurants, private dining room, swimming pool, tennis, golf, 24-hour room service

Dress code: Jacket and tie is required in the restaurants

Weddings: During May, June and July wedding receptions are catered for in the Cellars Restaurant (maximum 60) and in the private dining room, the Jade and Gold Room (maximum 40), although the hotel is not licensed to perform wedding ceremonies there are some beautiful old stone churches nearby, ask the hotel for advice

Minimum stay: None

Rates: Double rooms cost from US$192/R880; suites from US$216/R990 to US$331/R1520

Credit cards: Most major

Taxes and service charge: Included

ELLERMAN HOUSE

(☎ (021)-439 9182, 🖷 021-434 7257, 💻 www.ellerman.co.za), 180 Kloof Road, Bantry Bay, 8001 Cape Town, South Africa

Reservations: Relais & Châteaux reservation numbers worldwide or their website (see p12)

Getting there: The hotel will arrange airport transfers, the price of which is included in your room bill

Accommodation: 9 rooms and 2 suites

Amenities: Outdoor swimming pool; tennis; golf nearby; sauna and private fitness centre; private dining room

Dress code: Smart/casual in the restaurant

Weddings: The hotel can do weddings as long as the entire house is taken over in which case you'll pay the usual prices for accommodation, plus whatever food you want for the reception

Minimum stay: None

Rates: Doubles from US$300/R2400 to US$488/R3900; suites from US$676/R5400; breakfast included

Credit cards: Most major

Taxes and service charge: Included

and No 41 are particularly beautiful: room No 2 is one of the oldest rooms in the house and the most romantic with its wooden ceilings, large brass bed and its cream and blue furnishings; room No 41, a junior suite, has spectacular views of the Constantia Valley and **False Bay** in the distance, it is decorated in pale yellow and light green giving it a really fresh appearance.

As a member of Relais & Châteaux you'd expect the food at Cellars to be good. And it is. There are two restaurants to choose from, the famous **Cellars Restaurant** where you can expect dishes such as Cape Rock lobster and Karoo lamb, washed down with fine Cape wines, and the **Malay Kitchen**. Jacket and tie are expected in both – this is Cape Town and people like to take their food seriously!

Guests can play tennis or golf or just relax by the lovely pool, set amidst landscaped gardens, soaking up the sunshine and the total tranquillity of Constantia. But you should also make a point of exploring the wonderful residences in the area and the beautiful **Kirstenbosch** botanical gardens.

Ellerman House

Also just outside Cape Town, and equally welcoming and tranquil, is Ellerman House, named after Sir John Ellerman, a wealthy ship owner who bought it at the turn of the 20th century.

Today, Ellerman House is a beautiful haven situated in **Bantry Bay**, a charming part of Cape Town, with terraced gardens and palm trees facing the Atlantic. This wonderful hotel, extremely highly rated within South Africa, is run very much like a private house – helped by the fact that with only nine rooms and two suites, there are never more than 22 guests.

The restaurant is for residents only and, instead of having a set menu to choose from, you are asked after breakfast each day if you'll be in for lunch and dinner and, if so, what you might like. Local seafood is a speciality. With such a generous policy the chef has been known to prepare totally different meals for every guest. To make matters even better this small hotel operates 24-hour room service so it's no problem if you fancy eating on your balcony, or if you prefer they will recommend and book a local restaurant.

THINGS TO SEE AND DO AROUND CAPE TOWN

At the end of the 17th century, the largely Mediterranean climate lured the French Huguenot refugees to the Cape where they planted the original seeds of what are now world-class **wineries**. These glorious wine estates with their Cape Dutch colonial-style architecture are still well preserved. Paarl, Stellenbosch and Franschhoek have developed **wine routes**. Hire a car and spend a few days touring the wine lands: you won't need to do much driving as they are all within easy reach of Cape Town, and many offer wonderful accommodation and restaurants so you can relax in style and don't need to worry about driving home.

One of my favourites is *Lanzerac* (☎ 21-887 1132, ▤ 21-887 2310), PO Box 4, Stellenbosch 7599, Western Cape, a 300-year-old manor house on the outskirts of Stellenbosch where 40 individually furnished rooms and suites all have access to the hotel's beautiful gardens. There are few better ways to spend an afternoon than lying on the beautifully-mown lawns of a winery, with a bottle of Cape Blush (rosé) to share and only the prospect of a sumptuous dinner and bed ahead of you. Double rooms start at US$78/R620 per person for bed and breakfast in a Classic room and go up to US$149/R1185 per person for a junior suite, but there is also the most fabulous Royal Pool Suite in deep rich copper and gold hues, which has a double bedroom, two bathrooms, a separate living room and a beautiful small rectangular swimming pool set in a pretty courtyard, costing from US$222/R1765 per person, bed and breakfast. Take a wander around the winery, choose a few bottles and retire to the pool for an afternoon of decadent heaven. You can book this delightful place through most leading tour operators to South Africa.

Hiring a car will also enable you to drive down to the tip of the Cape peninsula, Cape Point, taking you through the **Cape of Good Hope Nature Reserve**. The road along Chapman's Peak Drive is one of the most beautiful stretches of **coastal highway** you are ever likely to see. The best way to drive it is to do a clockwise loop around the peninsula, starting at Kirstenbosch Botanical Gardens, and then going through Muizenberg. If you leave in the morning you'll have plenty of time to find your own perfect beach en route to the Cape, see the magnificent views where the two oceans meet, and get back to Chapman's Peak in time to enjoy the most wonderful moules and other seafood at **Hout Bay**. This really is paradise for seafood and wine lovers, and all with a backdrop of relentlessly crashing surf. Try *Chapman's Peak Restaurant* in the hotel (☎ 21-790 1036) and the *Mariner's Wharf Grill* (☎ 21-790 1100), which although a bit touristy is a good open-air bistro serving fantastic fish.

A trip to the top of **Table Mountain** is a must for visitors. Pick a day when there is no cloud (affectionately referred to by the locals as its table cloth because of the way it hugs the mountain top and drapes down the side) and either take the **cable car** (☎ 21-424-5148) or, if you're feeling very energetic, walk. If you do go by cable car, make sure you avoid the long queues by getting there first thing or towards late afternoon, giving you time to get up there for a sundowner – traditionally you take up your own 'cold tinnies'. It is possible to book the cable car at the Waterfront Information Centre in town (☎ 21-408 7600). You can drive up far enough to get a pretty good view but it is worth getting to the top if you can.

You haven't really been to Cape Town until you've sampled its **beaches** – as the locals are fond of saying, 'life's a beach', and nowhere is that quite so true as in Cape Town. The city's most popular beaches are at **Clifton**: they are numbered 'First', 'Second', 'Third' and 'Fourth', and the little one at the end is called Moses (it disappears with the tide). This is where the beautiful people flock at the weekends and on holiday: to surf, to pose, to gossip and to bronze themselves. Other fantastic beaches are at **Camps Bay**, although it is normally pretty windy, **Llandudno** where the surf is great and the clientele a bit less posey (watch out for the undertow), and across the other side north of the city at **Bloubergstrand** where you get that distant picture-postcard view of Table Mountain that we always see in photographs and paintings.

For more information visit: ⌨ www.cape-town.org

Tucked away on the slopes of Cape Town's famous **Lion's Head**, there can be few better views in the city. All nine rooms are en suite and are decorated in Edwardian style, with English period furniture and lovely antiques. The Ellerman Suite, on the top floor, is the house's grandest room: it has a totally separate, fully furnished lounge and a bathroom with sunken bath. Along with the East Wing Suite it has incredible views over the ocean. Alternatively, go for mini suites Nos 1, 2 and 4, which have great views and balconies.

The reception rooms offer intimate relaxation surrounded by typically Cape furnishings, such as plush leather armchairs, fine wood panelling and warm colours. A

THE ROVOS RAIL AND THE BLUE TRAIN

South Africa is blessed with two sumptuous trains, the Rovos Rail and the Blue Train, offering the kind of luxury epitomised by the famous Orient Express.

The Rovos Rail
The Rovos Rail, a beautifully restored train pulled by four **vintage locomotives**, makes several wonderful trips any of which is just perfect for honeymooners who can afford it.

The bi-monthly 55-hour **Safari** between Pretoria and Durban includes game drives in Kruger National Park, Mkhaya Game Reserve, in Swaziland, and Hluhluwe Reserve, in Zululand. You could otherwise opt for the monthly 48-hour journey from Pretoria to Cape Town (R6695 per person sharing a de luxe suite).

You can also board the Rovos Rail for a one-day trip up the **Garden Route** from Cape Town to George with a wine-tasting excursion (US$537/R4295 per person sharing a de luxe suite), or take the train from Pretoria through historic villages and then fly from Pietersburg to **Victoria Falls** in Zimbabwe for a night at the *Victoria Falls Hotel*.

All these trips, as you can imagine, are very popular so check availability before you set your heart on one. If they are in your budget any of them would certainly be the experience of a life-time, as the train has been fastidiously restored and is truly luxurious with thick carpets, a huge double bed, en suite bathroom with black and white chequerboard floor tiles, and varnished mahogany and chrome furnishings. The train can accommodate a maximum of 72 people in either a de luxe or royal suite (a little bigger with bath and shower).

For details of these and other routes call the Rovos Rail reservations (South Africa ☎ 12-323 6052, 🖷 12-315 8242) representatives in the UK

Three Cities (☎ 020-7225 0164, 🖷 020-7823 7701) or in the US, Henry Kartagner (☎ 0631-858-1270, 🖷 0631-858-1279).

The Blue Train
The Blue Train is a similar operation. The train's proud and noble history is said to have begun at the turn of the 20th century when a Train de Luxe first travelled between Cape Town and Bulawayo. The service was upgraded just before the outbreak of WWII when South African Railways took delivery of the Blue Train – the most luxurious rail carriage the continent had ever seen.

The Blue train travels on four return routes: Cape Town to Pretoria (1 night), Pretoria to Victoria Falls (2 nights), Pretoria to Hoedspruit (1 night) and Cape Town to Port Elizabeth on the Garden Route (2 nights).

Everything about the trains is luxurious so that you can guarantee you'll have a comfortable and entertaining journey. Prices per room for a luxury suite compartment in the Blue Train with a private bathroom and toilet are US$1051/R8400, while a de luxe compartment with a private shower and toilet costs US$951/R7600 including everything but French champagne.

The Blue Train travels most frequently between Pretoria and Cape Town leaving in the morning and arriving the following lunch-time, and makes the return journey to Pretoria on the same day. It travels from Pretoria to Victoria Falls every Thursday and to Hoedspruit on Fridays. The train leaves Cape Town for Port Elizabeth on Sundays, arriving on Tuesday morning after a leisurely ride along the Garden Route.

For more details contact the Blue Train reservations (South Africa ☎ 12-334 8459, 🖷 12- 334 8464, 🖳 www.bluetrain.co.za).

very relaxed atmosphere pervades the lounges and bar: it wouldn't be unusual for one guest decked out in black tie to be having a drink with another guest still in shorts. Ellerman House has its own gym and sauna on the premises and will also arrange any health or beauty treatments you should want.

THE GARDEN ROUTE
This stretch of land, along the coastal highway between Cape Town and Port Elizabeth, is renowned for its spectacular scenery and equally good hotels. Kilometre after kilometre of glorious coastline is met by mountains covered in indigenous forest, with only the occasional dolphin or whale to break up the monotony of the view. Allow four or five days to do the journey at an easy pace, and give yourselves plenty of time to get off the road and explore.

The best section of the coast is between **Mossel Bay** and **Storms River**. The area is known for its lakes and forests as well as its two national parks (**Tsitsikamma Forest** and **Tsitsikamma Coastal Park**), both of which are worth visiting. This is also where the most famous coastal resorts of the Garden Route are found, where South Africa's affluent families come for their own summer holidays.

Plettenberg Bay, known simply as Plett, **Wilderness** and **Knysna** all offer excellent accommodation at very affordable prices, and some really élite hideaways at greater expense. Outside December and January, the peak summer months, accommodation prices drop and the whole place becomes a great deal quieter, but in the peak season, the beachside bars buzz constantly.

When you get to **George**, one of the route's major ports, take the road off the main highway which loops north over the mountains of the **Great Karoo**: the views on top of the mountains are incredible and are forever changing colour depending on the movement of the sun. The road takes you on to **Oudtshoorn**, famous for its ostriches and home to the **Kango Caves**.

Recommended hotels

Hunter's Country House (☎ 44-532 7818, 🖹 44-532 7878, 🖳 www.hunter hotels.com, PO Box 454, Plettenberg Bay 6600) nestles in the heart of the Garden Route between the **Tsitsikamma Mountains** and the Indian Ocean, overlooking magnificent rainforests. A member of Relais & Chateaux and voted South Africa's Hotel of the Year 2000, this is an exclusive retreat with 23 luxurious suites in idyllic thatched country cottages. Beautiful manicured gardens and almond orchards enable you to really relax into the incredibly mellow atmosphere, and the chapel in the forest is very popular for weddings.

All the cottages and public rooms are furnished in beautiful old country house style with chintz cushions, polished brass, wooden beams and antiques. Each suite has a fireplace and private patio and is individually decorated. The opulent Forest Suite is really secluded, looks on to the forest and has a private pool, an enormous master bedroom with a four-poster and a separate lounge and dining room.

Only a short drive from Plettenberg Bay and in the middle of the Garden Route, Hunter's is the perfect place to stop off for a few days. Doubles cost from US$93/R740 for an Orchard Suite; US$210/R1680 for the Forest Suite per person per night including breakfast and VAT, but excluding US$1.25/R10 tourist levy per night. Book through Relais & Chateaux numbers worldwide (see p12) or in the UK through African specialists Carrier or ITC Classics (see pp12-13).

Plettenberg Park (☎ 44-533 2030, 🖹 44-533 2074, 🖳 www.plettenberg.com, Robberg Road, Plettenberg Bay 6600) is a very special place. It is also rather expensive. Situated on a rocky outcrop overlooking a magnificent shoreline, the setting of this exclusive hotel is quite spectacular.

From the inside, almost every window seems to look down over the dramatic cliff edge to the surf pounding below and the two swimming pools seem to merge with the ocean. The Plettenberg has just 40 rooms and suites. The luxurious Bay Suites in the Blue Wing and the self-contained Beach House Suite all have their own sun deck and small pool. The interiors are a designer's dream, awash with the colour of the sun, broken up by sea grass rugs, fine oak antique furniture, verdigris tables and huge comfy sofas and armchairs. Nothing is overdone.

There's lots to do when you've had enough of lazing by the swimming pool or on the private beach: water-skiing, hobie-cat sailing, diving, dolphin watching, golf, walking in Tsitsikamma Forest or shopping in Plettenberg Bay. As a member of Relais & Chateaux, you don't need to worry about the food. The Plettenberg recruited Greg Coleman from the Mount Nelson a couple of years ago and has set about making its menu the best in the Bay.

Doubles cost from US$118/R500 to US$250/R2000, suites from US$250/R2000 to US$425/R3400 not including service. Book through Three Cities Hotels (UK ☎ 020-7225 0164, 🖹 020-7823 7701).

The **Lodge on the Bay** (☎ 44 533 4724, 🖹 44 533 2681, 🖳 www.thelodge.co.za, 77 Beachyhead drive, Plettenberg Bay, 6600) is a small, privately-owned house right on pretty Robberg Beach and the leader of a new generation of 'zen' hotels in South Africa. Offering 'comfort for the soul' in minimalist surrounds of white linen and dark wood, it is a luxurious alternative to the grand country-house style.

The Lodge on the Bay accommodates a maximum of 12 guests at a time in three suites and three standard rooms. All the rooms have CD player, satellite TV and video player, mini-bar and underfloor-heated bathrooms with Molton Brown toiletries and kimonos.

The three suites have private balconies, and bathrooms are designed by none other than Philip Starck. The 'Indochine' suite has a mahogany four-poster bed, Chinese antiques and a limestone bathroom whereas the open-plan 'Zen' garden suite has a secluded deck with a plunge pool. If you want a sea view, go for the 'Mercer' suite, which has a combination of limestone, pure white walls and dark wood furniture inspired by the sensual designs of Christian Liagre.

The lodge currently offers just breakfast and lunch, so you can enjoy the best of both worlds by strolling down to Plettenberg for dinner. It also has a swimming pool and lots of personal pampering in the spa.

Doubles cost from US$93/R750, Indochine suite from US$130/R1050, Mercer and Zen suites from US$179/R1450 per room with breakfast and VAT. Book direct or through Cazenove & Loyd Safaris (UK ☎ 020-7384 2332, 🖳 www.caz-loyd.com).

GAME RESERVES

South Africa has more than 700 reserves, parks and game farms so, wherever your itinerary takes you, it should be possible to see some game. For many people the game parks of Transvaal to the east of Johannesburg epitomise the 'real' Africa. This was once frontier country where the pioneering Voortrekkers fought against the British and the countryside to forge a life for themselves. This is where **Kruger National Park** is found: it's a world unto itself, with more animal species than any other wildlife park on the whole of the African continent.

Londolozi Private Game Reserve

Londolozi, particularly famous for its leopards, has consistently been recognized as the best game camp in South Africa. This world-renowned game reserve has set the standards that all its competitors strive for: the camps are small, intimate and incredibly luxurious. The original camp has been run by the same family for over 75 years and is the flagship of the celebrated Conservation Corporation Africa.

There are five self-contained camps in Londolozi; each has its own swimming pool,

---

LONDOLOZI PRIVATE GAME RESERVE

(☎ 013-735 5653, 🖹 013-735 5100, 🖳 londolozi@relaischateaux.com), PO Box 6, Skukuza 1350, South Africa
Reservations: Through Conservation Corporation Africa (South Africa ☎ 11 809 4300, 🖹 11 809 4514, 🖳 www.ccafrica.com), Relais & Châteaux toll-free numbers worldwide (see p12) and leading tour operators to Africa
Getting there: The camp provides daily air transfers from the nearest airport, Skukuza; there are daily scheduled flights from Jo'burg to Skukuza; direct shuttle flights are available daily from Johannesburg International Airport to the lodge; private air charters are also available on request
Accommodation: Tree Camp has six luxurious suites; Founders has five chalets and one suite; Pioneer has three exclusive suites and three chalets; Bateleur Camp has eight chalets and four suites; Safari Lodge has six chalets
Amenities: Each camp has a 'boma', swimming pool, lounge, balcony, bar, plus game drives in Land-Rovers and nature walks with trackers; Tree Camp and Bateleur Camp rooms all have private plunge pools
Dress code: Casual
Weddings: Can be arranged
Minimum stay: None
Rates: Doubles from US$600 to US$650 per person full board including game drives
Credit cards: Most major
Taxes and service charge: Skukuza Airport tax and tourism levy additional charges

boma (thatch roof, open-air African dining area), deck and an impressive lounge and bar area with a suspended balcony overlooking the Sand River. The original Bush Camp has now been divided into the secluded Founders Camp which offers five chalets and one suite with views over the river; and Pioneer Camp which has three exclusive suites and three lavish chalets, decorated in colonial style. In a secluded spot, they conjure up the old days of safari with elevated private balconies, pristine en suite bathrooms, outdoor showers and views over the river.

Bateleur Camp houses the main reception and curio shop and has eight chalets and four suites, all with elevated balconies and plunge pools. From the pristine bathrooms are magnificent views of the surrounding bush. Then there is Tree Camp, where guests can dine on a balcony suspended 20m above the river in an ancient ebony tree with, of course, breathtaking views. Each Tree Camp room is beautifully decorated with a plunge pool and private deck and the en suite bathrooms, with their fluffy white towels, remind you that you may be in the bush but you're far from roughing it. The fifth camp, Safari Lodge, is known as 'the secret place' and has six intimate chalets for the ultimate in exclusivity and privacy.

On your doorstep are 16,500 hectares of prime game land literally teeming with wildlife. You'll see the Big Five here along with a dazzling array of other wildlife amongst the beautiful and diverse bushveld of the Kruger National Park.

Being a member of Relais & Châteaux, you can expect the food at Londolozi to be excellent. Each camp has its own bar and superb catering facilities: the staff greet you with lavish breakfasts as you return from early morning game drives and prepare picnics for you to eat in the bush. Their delicious dinners under the stars in the 'boma' are the perfect way to round off the day.

Other recommended hotels

Conservation Corporation Africa also owns several other fabulous safari camps including **Ngala** and **Phinda**, both of which are highly recommended, and the intimate **Singita** (☎ 11 234 0990, 🖻 11 234 0535, 🖳 singita@relaischateaux.com) also a member of Relais & Chateaux. The camp is newer but its luxury is on a par with Londolozi, and it also offers one of the finest safari experiences in Africa.

If you're looking for a great safari experience but are worried about breaking the bank, **Tanda Tula Bush Camp** (☎ 21 794 6500, 🖻 21 794 7605, 🖳 res@ilink.co.za) in the heart of Timbavati Nature Reserve, straddling the boundary of Kruger National Park, is a great choice, and one of the best places to see the big five. There are many activities to be enjoyed at Tanda Tula including walks, drives in open 4x4 vehicles (at night too), game and bird watching from hides, relaxing on your veranda whilst thirsty visitors come to drink from the water hole or simply cooling off in the swimming pool. You may see cheetah, leopard, elephant, giraffe, zebra, various antelope and possibly even the white lions of Timbavati. As there are no fences between the National Park and private reserves, the game-viewing possibilities are endless whilst the chance of meeting other game-viewing vehicles is nil.

With a maximum of 16 guests in eight charming tents with en suite bathrooms and private patios overlooking the river bed, you will be treated like personal guests at Tanda Tula. If you're feeling adventurous, it may be possible to 'sleep-out' at one of the hides overlooking a waterhole. Doubles cost from R2348/US$212 per person per night including all meals and game activities. Book through UK tour operator Cazenove & Loyd Safaris (☎ 020-7384 2332, 🖳 www.caz-loyd.com).

BENGUELA ISLAND

Although it's not actually in South Africa, most visitors to **Benguerra Lodge** (☎ 11 483 2734, 🖻 11 728 3767, PO Box 87416, Houghton, 2041) use it as a coda to a South African holiday. Situated off the coast of **Mozambique**, Benguerra Lodge is set on a secluded island surrounded by the warm waters of the Indian Ocean so it is the perfect place if you fancy a beach holiday at the end of a tour of South Africa. It offers bare-foot luxury and fantastic diving and watersports among totally unspoilt and uncluttered surroundings.

Nestled in the indigenous forest, the lodge's accommodation is in thatched bun-galows on stilts. There are en suite bathrooms and private balconies from which you can watch the magnificent sunsets and diverse birdlife: the island is home to over 115 varieties of bird including the rare Olive Bee-Eater and the Crab Plover. However, only two of the 13 chalets have a double bed (No 1 and No 13) so book early and make sure you emphasize this request.

Transfers to the island are on Mondays and Fridays only from Jo'burg International Airport. A three-night package, including flights, all meals, use of wind-surfers and hobie-cats, and taxes costs around US$865 per person, plus US$450 each for the return flights from Johannesburg. Book through UK tour operators, Cazenove & Lloyd Safaris (☎ 020-7384 2332, 🖳 www.caz-loyd.com).

Dubai
(BEST TIME: OCTOBER TO MAY)

Like all good weddings, the spirit of desert-fringed Dubai in the United Arab Emirates is found in the combination of something old and something new: a taste of Arabia mingled with futuristic technological wonder. In the Arab souks the air is thick with frankincense and spices, all that glitters *is* gold, and you can haggle all you like. In the glitzy new malls – one even shaped like a pyramid – the shopping is legendary. Hotels are out of this world and being treated like the Queen of Sheba or an Arabian prince may be just what you need for a few nights.

If you can tear yourself away from the exclusive beach clubs and rooftop plunge pools, the fun never stops in Dubai. From water parks to world-class golf, nightclubs to revolving restaurants – there is something for everyone. Everywhere is open late, and alcohol is served in most hotels. There are plenty of opportunities for romance – a dhow cruise to see the city illuminated at night, alfresco eating on balmy evenings, a night sleeping in the desert in a Bedouin tent. And if you want more action and adventure, there are desert safaris past palm-fringed oases, mountain streams and goats, dune driving and sand-skiing.

Burj Al Arab

Burj Al Arab is the cream of a cluster of exclusive hotels creating a paradise on earth in the fashionable area of Jumeirah. The tallest hotel in the world, it nests on its own man-made island, its stunning billowing sail-shape an unforgettable technological wonder. What's more, its accommo-

---

DUBAI

Dubai offers year-round sunshine and white sand beaches, desert adventure and shopping with luxurious hotels and a buzzing night-life

When to go: October to May. June to September are very hot, but off season hotel rates drop to the ridiculous

Average maximum temperatures °C

JAN	FEB	MAR	APR	MAY	JUN	JUL	AUG	SEP	OCT	NOV	DEC
23	24	26	30	36	39	40	39	40	35	34	25

Flight times to Dubai from:

New York (via London) 6¾ hours

LA (via London) 10 hours

London: 7-9 hours

Sydney: 8 hours

Approx exchange rates: UAE Dirham (Dh); £1 = Dh5.8, US$1 = Dh3.67, A$1 = Dh1.94

Time difference: GMT plus 4 hours

Voltage: 220/240AC, 50Hz

Combine with: Maldives or Sri Lanka, Kenya

Country dialling code: ☎ +971 4

Further information: Tourist board website: 🖥 www.dubaitourism.co.ae and www.dubaicity guide.com for ideas. For night-life, pick up a copy of *What's On* magazine in your hotel lobby

---

BURJ AL ARAB
(☎ 301 7777, 🖨 301 7000, 💻 reservations@burj-al-arab.com, www.burj-al-arab.com) Jumeirah Beach Road, Jumeirah Beach, Dubai
Reservations: Leading Hotels of the World toll-free numbers (see p12) or through tour operators such as Carrier, Elegant Resorts, ITC Classics (see p11)
Getting there: 25 minutes by taxi transfer or 15 minutes by helicopter from the airport, 5km away; Honeymooners are swept from the airport in a Rolls-Royce Silver Shadow.
Accommodation: 202 luxury suites
Amenities: Six restaurants and lounges including Al Mahara underwater seafood restaurant and top floor restaurant Al Muntaha. Spa and health club on the 18th floor. Free access to the Wild Wadi Waterpark. Dune driving, balloon trips, sand boarding, water-skiing and sailing all available by arrangement.
Dress code: Smart
Weddings: Yes, large receptions catered for
Minimum stay: None
Rates: US$905/Dh3300 for de luxe suites to US$6850/Dh25,000 for Royal Suite.
Credit cards: Most major
Taxes and service charge: 10% tax and 10% service

---

dation and service are so over-the-top that it exceeds the hotel star-rating scale. Serious pampering awaits you.

Being swept up to the entrance in a white Silver Shadow is definitely a fitting start to a honeymoon; once there you are greeted by fuschia-pink-clad girls who sprinkle your hands with rosewater, feed you plump dates and wish you a nice stay. An aquarium lines the walls of the escalator up to the mezzanine.

Generous and tasteful, the real gold, the thick pile carpet and décor may smack of excess to some. But others will love the suites, two floors of unadulterated luxury where a mirror hangs above the silk-swathed bed in a room that can only be described as a boudoir. A private gilt staircase leads to the bedroom, from the spacious dining and sitting room. And Cleopatra would have happily allowed herself to bathe in the circular Jacuzzi, scented by a range of complimentary Hermés products.

Floor-to-ceiling and wall-to-wall windows mean wherever you are, you have a fabulous view across the city and the Arabian Gulf. Handmade sweetmeats and stuffed dates linger on the tables, and quality toiletries and robes adorn the bathroom. With pools, palms and a personal butler, you won't feel like venturing anywhere. Even staying in the cheapest room, Burj Al Arab is out of this world.

If you do get out of your room, the lavishly decorated spa on the 18th floor has his-and-hers Roman-style pools which give spectacular views over the city. A pianist tinkles gently in the palm-fringed cocktail bar, and gracious staff wash your hands in rosewater when you arrive in the bar. It may be hard to choose between the underwater **Al Mahara** restaurant, reached by 'submarine' (an underwater shuttle), which boasts vast Gulf prawns and local snapper, and the **Al Muntaha** restaurant at the top of the sail, suspended 200 metres above the sea.

The sun really sets over the ocean, turning the sky first peach, then pink and finally a perfect raspberry ripple over a silver sea. And it is warm enough even in winter to kick off your sandals and dangle your feet in the sparkling phosphorescence by the shore.

Other recommended hotels

The exclusive **Jumeirah Beach Club** (☎ 344 5333, 🖨 344 6222, 💻 www.jumeirahinternational.com) is popular with the rich and famous. With 50 private suites set in lush tropical gardens, the Beach Club offers the perfect place to relax, whether enjoying the well-equipped health club or watching the sun set at the romantic beach bar. Junior suites from US$260/Dh900 plus tax and service. Book through tour operator ITC Classics (see p12).

For a more private option, the villas at **The Jumeirah Beach Hotel** (☎ 480 000, 🖨 482 273, 💻 www.jumeirahinternational.com), sister hotel of Burj Al Arab and built in the shape of a braking wave, are the perfect hideaway. Each of the 19 Arabian-style villas has its own plunge pool and private beach view terrace where you can dine outside to the sound of cicadas and the sea lapping on the shores. Villas are from US$905/Dh3300 a night excluding tax and service, but the rate ensures that a butler is at your beck and call 24 hours a day. Book through Leading Hotels of the World reservation numbers worldwide (see p12) or tour operators Harlequin (UK ☎ 01708-850 300, 📠 01708-854 952), or Abercrombie & Kent or ITC Classics (see p11).

Just 45 minutes' drive from Dubai city, the **Al Maha** (☎ 303 4222, 📠 343 9696, 🖥 www.al-maha.com, Sheikh Zayed Road, Dubai), a member of Leading Hotels of the World, is a very different option. It is an exclusive, tranquil desert

'The blue sky, balmy air, pale sand, azure sea and incredible flora make this tropical paradise much more relaxed than we had imagined. You really can do anything here within reason and the weather in December is perfect.' **Joanna and Ian Parfitt**

resort which may give you the best taste of the romance of Arabia. The 30 lavish Bedouin-style suites have tented ceilings, traditional antiques, private pools and most importantly, air-conditioning. Activities such as camel, horse and four-wheel drive safaris in the surrounding conservation area make a great contrast to the glitz of the city. Opened in 1999, Al Maha is probably the most expensive hotel in Dubai, but as you dine alfresco on the tranquil dunes at dusk watching an Arabian oryx or shy gazelle go by, you may well think it's worth it. Suites are from US$1100 inclusive. Book through Leading Hotels of the World reservation numbers worldwide (see p12) or tour operators Abercrombie & Kent, Elegant Resorts or Sunset Travel (see p11).

India
(BEST TIME: OCTOBER TO APRIL)

There is nowhere quite like India; that heady concoction of all that is beautiful in the world and the harsh reality of a continent that is home to around one billion people.

To paint India only as a romantic destination would be painfully superficial. There are such extremes of poverty and wealth in this vast sub-continent that it would be callous just to talk of the incredible sunrises and sunsets over the **Taj Mahal**. A honeymoon in India would undoubtedly take in fabulously romantic sights but no visit to India can

---

INDIA
A startling kaleidoscope of religions, culture, heritage and people, amongst incredibly diverse landscapes – not for the faint-hearted
When to go: India's climate varies from region to region, the coolest weather on the plains is between November and March; head to the hills between April and June when it is hot and dusty on the plains, avoid July to September when the rains come
Average maximum temperatures °C

	JAN	FEB	MAR	APR	MAY	JUN	JUL	AUG	SEP	OCT	NOV	DEC
Goa	29	30	30	30	30	29	27	27	27	29	31	31
Udaipur	23	26	30	34	36	34	29	27	29	30	27	25
Darjeeling	9	9	13	16	16	18	18	18	18	16	13	11

Capital: Delhi
Flight times: to Delhi from:
      New York: 18 hours
      LA: 25½ hours
      London: 9 hours
      Sydney: 10 hours
Approximate exchange rates: Rupees (Rs) – £1 = Rs66.80, US$1 = Rs47, A$1 = Rs24.38
Time difference: GMT plus 5½ hours
Voltage: 220v AC, 50 Hz; two and three round-pin plugs
Combine with: Maldives, Nepal, Sri Lanka, Singapore
Country dialling code: ☎ 91
Further information: Government of India Tourist Office at 🖥 www.indiatouristoffice.org

gloss over the shocking filth, poverty, continual hassle and throngs of people that is part of life here. Despite all this, perhaps even because of all the difficulties, people still fall deeply in love with this fascinating country and long to return again and again.

The subcontinent has a life of its own – from the haggling buyers and sellers to the passionately revered cows in the streets, along with the vibrant colours and fragrant aroma of the flower garlands and the mounds of exotic spices piled up in the markets. It is also steeped in a complex history stretching back over 4000 years, during which the philosophies, religions and languages of its people have expanded to produce the immense wealth of culture, heritage and tradition that exists here today.

There is no doubt that India's landscapes are overwhelmingly beautiful in their variety. They range from the harsh barren deserts of **Rajasthan** to the network of waterways and lagoons in **Kerala**; from the snow-capped eastern Himalaya to the tranquil palm groves and lush paddy fields of the south, to say nothing of the long unspoilt beaches beside the Indian Ocean. You can stay in former palaces, explore hilltop forts in Rajasthan, haggle for an auto-rickshaw in Delhi, escape the heat in the hill station of **Shimla**, go spiritual in **Rishikesh** or just relax for a few days on a palm-fringed beach in **Goa**.

And then there is religion. Apart from the continually contrasting landscapes and the colourful pageant of its people, at the very heart of India is a religious spirit which more than anything else is responsible for making the continent so magical, so captivating. The very essence and indeed, the poignant romance, of India is religion and the strength of Hinduism and Buddhism, both of which originated there.

RAJASTHAN

Rajasthan's traditions and heritage make it one of those places that is romantic to the core. The state is known as the Land of the Kings, and the story of the Rajputs, its native warriors, is the stuff of legends. While chivalry and honour formed a quintessential part of the Rajputs' thousand-year rule, the individual clans' pride and zeal for independence also caused them to come into conflict with each other just as much as with their alien aggressors. As a result Rajasthan is littered with forts, palaces and temples and today, due to the pecuniary constraints on the 20th-century maharajas, many of them have

THINGS TO SEE AND DO IN RAJASTHAN

No visit to Rajasthan would be complete without a trip to **Jaipur**, known as the 'Pink City' because of the pale pink hue of the old walled city. Built in 1727 by the great warrior and zealous astronomer Maharaja Jai Singh II, all seven of the city's gates remain and the old part of the town with its jewellery market and camel-drawn carts is fascinating. Take a deep breath and jostle your way through the incessant wave of hurrying bicycles, rickshaws, Ambassador taxis and people to the various bazaars and the **Palace of the Winds**. Not far outside Jaipur is **Amber Fort**, which was built in the late 16th century and epitomises Rajput architecture. Ride up together on the back of an **elephant**.

Udaipur is without doubt one of the most romantic cities in India, and not just because of the famous Lake Palace. There are scores of wonderful palaces and temples in Udaipur, both great and small but all with that noble character that imbues the whole of this incredible city. Make sure you visit the huge and exquisitely

beautiful **City Palace**. For sunset pictures of the Lake Palace go to **Sajjan Niwas Gardens**, and then follow it up with a drink in one of the bars in the old town which screen *Octopussy* nightly.

One of the greatest experiences in India is the **Palace on Wheels** train tour around Rajasthan. This luxury train leaves Delhi every Wednesday from September to April and takes you on a tour of Jaipur, Chittorgarh, Udaipur, Ranthambhore National Park, Jaisalmer, Jodhpur, Bharatpur and Agra. The train's 14 luxurious carriages named after former royal kingdoms have in-room minibars, bathroom toiletries, a beauty parlour, and cream saloons. The week-long tour costs from US$295 per person per night, but does include everything – tours en route, entry fees and all meals. Book well in advance through Rajasthan Tourism Reception Centre (📧 jaipur@palaceonwheels.net, www.palaceonwheels.net) in Delhi, or through tour operators specializing in India (see p11).

been converted into spectacular hotels. Because of the Rajputs' glorious heritage, Rajasthan is very much India at its best for visitors: the extraordinarily colourful clothes; the almost comic moustaches of the men and their continued romantic sense of chivalry; and the crumbling palaces all make this a truly magical place, quite unlike anywhere else in the sub-continent. The best time to visit Rajasthan is between mid-October and mid-March.

Rambagh Palace Hotel

Rambagh Palace Hotel is one of the best known and most romantic palaces in all Rajasthan. Staying there will take you back to the land of the Maharaja when the building was used for royal house parties. Everything about the palace is old world ostentation; with its over the top palatial grandeur you'll never forget the experience.

Built in 1835 as a hunting lodge, in the 1920s it was transformed into a palace at the cost of Rs4 million for the use of Prince Man Singh, the Maharajah of Jaipur. In 1957 he decided to turn this glorious residence into a hotel: the first public guest was Count Artaza, the Spanish Ambassador to India.

Entering the Rambagh Palace takes you into another world. Archways and cool corridors connect rooms filled with the most incredible Rajasthani ornaments and furniture. The five Royal Suites are absolutely amazing and many of the luxury rooms are definitely worth paying the extra for as the standard rooms are a bit characterless and often have twin-beds, though they are spacious: ask if

RAMBAGH PALACE HOTEL
(☎ 0141-381 919, 🖷 0141-381 098, 🖳 rambagh@jpl.vsnl.net.in), Bhawani Sing Road, Jaipur 302 005, Rajasthan, India
Reservations: Through the Taj Group's website (🖳 www.tajhotels.com), or through specialist tour operators such as Western & Oriental, Abercrombie & Kent (see pp9-11)
Getting there: 11km from the airport, the hotel can arrange transfers
Accommodation: 113 rooms including five Royal Suites
Amenities: Suvarna Mahal restaurant, Panghat open-air restaurant (Oct to Apr), Barbeque exotica (Oct to June), Neel Mahal coffee shop, Polo Bar, indoor swimming pool, fitness centre, beauty parlour, travel desk, shopping arcade, currency exchange, in-room safes, tennis, squash, badminton, jogging track, astrologer(!), cultural theatre (October to April); golf and horse-riding on request
Dress code: Elegant casual
Weddings: Receptions can be arranged in the hotel's two banquet halls which can cater for between 30 and 200 people, the lawns can also be used
Minimum stay: None
Rates: Standard doubles cost from US$150, but go for one of the superior rooms which start at US$165, luxury rooms from US$190, Historical Suite from US$240, the Maharaja Suite from US$375 and the Grand Maharani and Prince's Suite cost from US$525; ask about the 2-night romantic package which includes transfers and loads of perks from US$280 per couple
Credit cards: Most major
Taxes and service charge: 10% expenditure tax, 10% luxury tax

you can have a look at a few before deciding. With their abundance of precious art, silk embroideries, golden dragons, elaborately-framed European canvasses, exquisite blue pottery and beautifully laid-out rooms the Royal Suites are literally fit for a king. The Prince's Suite even has a mosaic fountain in the middle of the drawing room, with huge glass doors leading onto a private terrace, while the Maharani suite has the most exquisite mirrored bathroom.

Once the only private residence in the world with its own polo field, the Rambagh Palace maintains its grand colonial feel with the help of the 200-year-old **Polo Bar** which is furnished with the late Maharaja's polo trophies. The Palace has a lovely indoor swimming pool in the grounds, surrounded by loungers to relax on.

Rajvilas

From the moment the Rajvilas town car meets you from Jaipur Airport with drinks and cold towels, you are enfolded in luxury. Rajvilas was not named *Tatler*'s Hotel of the Year 2001 for nothing. *Tatler* called it 'spiritual, calm and extraordinary in design, with a dreamy spa, immaculate service and thoughtful food'. Once you've stayed in

RAJVILAS
(☎ 0141-680 101, 🖨 0141-680 202, 💻 reservations@rajvilas.com), Goner Road, Jaipur 303 012, Rajasthan, India
Reservations: Direct, or through Small Luxury Hotels of the World numbers worldwide (see p12) or tour operators such as Western & Oriental, Elegant Resorts, Abercrombie & Kent (see pp10-11)
Getting there: From Delhi it is a one hour flight to Jaipur; Rajvilas' complimentary luxury car will meet you on arrival to transport you to the hotel (about 30 mins drive/13km)
Accommodation: 71 rooms including, de luxe rooms and luxury Rajasthani tents
Amenities: Restaurant serving both Indian and International cuisine with music and dance performances; spa, fitness centre, swimming pool, croquet, floodlit tennis courts, elephant and camel safaris, horse-riding, trekking, golf, picnics; complimentary shoe shine, hairdresser, boutique, library and library bar, 24-hour room service
Dress code: Smart casual
Weddings: Receptions for up to 30 people are possible
Minimum stay: None
Rates: De luxe doubles from US$350, Luxury Tents from US$400, Villa tent from US$650, Royal villas from US$980 to US$1200 per night; special honeymoon package available on request
Credit cards: Major credit cards
Tax and service: 10% tax

this oasis in the pink city of Jaipur, other hotels will pale in comparison. And strolling in the 32 acres of grounds, surrounded by orchids, herb gardens, pools and fountains, you'll feel like a true Maharajah.

The de luxe bedrooms, in clusters of four and six around tranquil courtyards, are adorned with beautiful wooden four-poster beds, and have bathrooms with sunken marble baths – perfect for the rose-petal baths run for you both each evening. The air-conditioned Rajasthani Luxury Tents have lavish bathrooms and teak floors and the romantic villas have private swimming pools, some with walled gardens. The modern CD and laser disk player sits next to time-honoured traditions of fruit and fresh flowers, and in case you arrive in the monsoon, or the heat of summer, an umbrella.

Everything about Rajvilas is luxurious, even the handmade cotton duvets, which are hard to resist buying to pop in your suitcase along with the beautiful candlestick which flanks the bath. Honeymooners staying at Rajvilas can arrange a private dinner, sampling the delicious Indian and International cuisine – don't miss the onion bhaji!

In the day, relax by the beautiful swimming pool or be pampered in the spa which has ayurvedic and Western treatments. Then there is Jaipur, a fusion of palaces – including the City palace, one of the best museums in India – forts, festivals and bazaars – perfect for picking up handicrafts. If none of these things excite you, Rajvilas is able to arrange adventures such as elephant or camel rides or trekking.

The Lake Palace Hotel

The legendary Lake Palace Hotel will always be at the forefront of people's minds when they think of India. This incredible white palace, famous as the location for James Bond's *Octopussy*, seems to float in the middle of the still blue waters of Lake Pichola.

Once the summer retreat of the rulers of Mewar, the Palace was built two and a half centuries ago by Maharana Jagat Singh II and covers the whole 1.5 hectare island. It is now owned and managed by the HRH Hotel Group. The Palace is so astonishingly beautiful that you couldn't possibly visit Udaipur without crossing the lake to visit it for lunch or dinner (all that non-residents are allowed to do), but to actually stay here is a total privilege.

What really makes the Palace is its gardens, around which the hotel is built so that what you see from the water is in fact largely a shell, enclosing the most magnificent array of lily ponds, marble terraces, formal garden beds and fountains. As you sit on one of the terraces taking afternoon tea you get this incredible feeling of being cocooned by a huge expanse of pure white marble. Whichever direction you look, there is wonderfully ornate masonry with slender carved columns, filigreed screens, domed chattris and ornamental fountains.

Inside is just as grand. The walls are frescoed with ancient water colours inlaid with miniature paintings and painfully intricate mirror mosaics. Black and white floor tiles contrast with brightly coloured stained-glass windows through which the shimmering waters of the lake are reflected, and the balconies are larger than many of the hotel's bedrooms. All the suites are decorated in different styles, but all are unquestionably ornate.

When you book, do make a point of emphasizing that it is your honeymoon and stress that you want a reasonably-sized room or a suite because some of the rooms are very compact and ordinary.

Shiv Niwas Palace

There is an ongoing battle between Shiv Niwas Palace and the Lake Palace Hotel as to which is the better. I believe it all comes down to the matter of the view.

While some argue that *the* view to have is from the lakeside Shiv Niwas Palace looking down over Lake Pichola and the Lake Palace Hotel, there are those for whom nothing other than actually staying in the Lake Palace, and gazing back at the shoreline, will do.

The residence of the Maharana of Udaipur, part of this incredible 400-year-old city complex has now been converted into a heritage hotel. Shiv Niwas is undoubtedly more exclusive, attracting less attention from tour operators, and a wonderful place to experience the splendour of the maharajas in less claustrophobic surroundings.

The whole hotel is charming, from the staff who couldn't be more friendly, to the old world décor all around you. The 31 rooms, including 17 suites, are spacious with bits and pieces from the Royal collection of the house of Mewar scattered around as a reminder of where you are. They are all air conditioned and have an in-room safe and

---

THE LAKE PALACE
(☎ 0294-527 961 to 973, 🖹 0294-527 974), PO Box 5, Pichola Lake, Udaipur 313 001, Rajasthan, India
Reservations: Through the Taj Group's website (💻 www.tajhotels.com) or through specialist tour operators in the UK, such as Elegant Resorts, Abercrombie & Kent, Worldwide Journeys (see p11)
Getting there: 26km from the airport, the hotel can arrange transfers
Accommodation: 81 rooms including 13 suites
Amenities: Jharokha 24-hour coffee shop, Amrit Sagar bar, Neel Kamal restaurant, swimming pool, mini-gym, travel desk, car rental, shopping arcade, currency exchange, in-room safes
Dress code: Elegant casual
Weddings: The hotel can arrange outdoor receptions for up to 60 people by the lily pond, or on the lake in its barge *Gangaur*
Minimum stay: None
Rates: Doubles from US$175, suite from US$300 to US$400 for a Historical Suite; ask about the two-night romantic package which includes a lake-facing room, loads of perks, taxes and transfers from US$750 per couple
Credit cards: Most major
Taxes and service charge: 10% luxury tax, 10% expenditure tax

---

SHIV NIWAS PALACE
(☎ 0294-52 8016/19, 🖹 0294-52 8006), City Palace, Lake Palace Drive, Udaipur 313001, Rajasthan, India
Reservations: Direct or through HRH hotels (UK ☎ 020-7792 8562, 💻 www.hrhindia.com) and specialist tour operators such as Cox & Kings (see p11)
Getting there: Local taxi from the airport
Accommodation: Nine suites, eight de luxe suites, 18 standard rooms
Amenities: Live band, swimming pool, travel desk, squash, table tennis, billiards, boating, riding, holistic health centre, room service, restaurant and bar
Dress code: Informal
Weddings: The Palace can perform weddings, costs depend on location (whether you choose the hotel or Jagmandir Island) and whether you want a Royal procession, fireworks, cocktail menu etc
Minimum stay: None
Rates: Standard rooms cost US$125, super de luxe are US$300, historic suites US$375, Royal Suite US$475, Imperial Suite US$600
Credit cards: Most major
Taxes and service charge: 3.8% food and beverage tax, 10% expenditure tax on final bill

a minibar. Although most of the rooms are very comfortable, if you're looking for extravagance on a grand scale opt for one of the two 'Imperial' honeymoon suites, one overlooking the lake with cherubs painted on the ceiling.

Spend lazy afternoons around the swimming pool or take a wander down to the City Palace which is just a few minutes away and has now been converted into a museum, before returning to have drinks on the balcony and admire the marvellous views of Lake Pichola and the Lake Palace. Some suites have two balconies, one of which has a table and chairs and is where breakfast is served, while the one on the other side is tailor-made for very private sun-bathing.

Neemrana Fort Palace

Built originally as a fort, Neemrana Fort Palace seems to rise out of the vast expanse of the Rajasthan desert from nowhere, and even when you are close enough to detect the mighty fort from the outside, it would be hard to guess the elegance and luxury that lies within.

Hidden among the folds of the **Aravalli** desert mountains, this historic fort, built in 1464, is India's oldest heritage hotel. The property sprawls over a 10-hectare hillside, while the stepped palace covers as much as a hectare: so while I feel that the word spacious is linked too readily with hotel rooms, these rooms definitely deserve the epithet.

The transformation of this incredible fort effectively turned the former ruins into 42 individually-styled rooms and suites. What makes Neemrana so special is the unique way in which each suite is decorated: each has been given a different name evocative of the room's style, hence there is the Palace of Mirrors, the Moon Palace, the Palace of Breezes and the French colonial suite.

Most rooms have balconies, terraces, courtyards or at least an area where guests can sit out and admire the incredible views. Even the bathrooms have been designed to afford the best views of the surrounding countryside.

All the rooms are furnished with Indian fabrics and an eclectic mix of colonial and Indian furniture, and the sort of Rajasthani artefacts that Western city dwellers pay fortunes for today. Lots of the rooms have wide pillars, impressive arches, and stained-glass windows – the effect is simply stunning.

> **NEEMRANA FORT PALACE**
> (☎ 01494-60007/8, 🖷 01494-60005), Port Neemrana, District Alwar, Rajasthan 301 705, India
> **Reservations**: Direct or through specialist tour operators in the UK, such as Western & Oriental, Abercrombie & Kent (see pp10-11)
> **Getting there**: 122km from New Delhi Domestic and International airports, the hotel will arrange transfer on prior notice
> **Accommodation**: 42 rooms and suites
> **Amenities**: Bar, restaurant serving French and Indian dishes, morning tea served in your room, buffet breakfast in the restaurant; swimming pool, health club, massage, indoor games room, camel and camel cart rides; treks in the nearby hills; cultural evenings at weekends
> **Dress code**: Informal
> **Weddings**: The Palace can conduct Indian weddings and cater for receptions for up to 250 people
> **Minimum stay**: None
> **Rates**: Doubles from US$43/Rs2000; suites from US$106/Rs5000 with afternoon tea
> **Credit cards**: American Express, Visa, MasterCard
> **Taxes and service charge**: There is no tax on rooms, but there is a 10% tax on food and beverages

Other recommended hotels

Samode Haveli (☎ 01423-4113/4, 🖷 01423-4123, 🖳 www.samode.com, Samode, Jaipur 303806), a 19th-century palace tucked away in the north-east corner of Jaipur, is still owned and run by the Samode royal family. It is a wonderful old building with masses of character: exquisite inlay work and frescoes, antique furnishings, a lovely terrace for a sundowner and a pretty painted dining room. With just 20 beautifully decorated and individual rooms, and two incredible suites, although often frequented by groups it remains a lovely place to stay. A night costs from US$66 for an ordinary double, and from US$95 for a de luxe suite. Ask about the two-night 'Affairs of the Heart' honeymoon package, US$940 for loads of romantic and adventurous perks. Book through specialist tour operators such as Western & Oriental, Cox & Kings (see pp10-11).

Devi Garh (☎ 2953-89211 to 20, ▤ 2953-89357, 💻 www.devigarh.com, PO Box No 144, Delwara, Udaipur 313001, Rajasthan) is an 18th-century fort nestled in the Aravalli Hills, recently transformed into an all-suites luxury hotel. The 23 suites are individually designed and styled, and several have beautiful balconies where you can take in the views of Rajasthan's most romantic city. Devi Garh has a fully-equipped fitness centre and spa and a beautiful black marble heated swimming pool. Udaipur looks as if it has been lifted from a fairytale story, so you're bound to want to explore. Anything can be arranged at Devi Garh from sightseeing to horse-riding or trekking, a game of croquet or a massage. Suites from US$170 to US$320 plus tax and service. Book through specialist tour operators such as Cox & Kings, Western & Oriental.

Deogarh Mahal (💻 www.deogarh.com), not far from Udaipur, was converted from a 17th-century palace three years ago and is incredibly romantic. It was listed by Condé Nast *Traveller* as the best hotel under £100 (US$142) in 1999, and lies just a few hours drive from Udaipur.

The tiny town of Deogarh is a wonderful example of traditional Indian life – this is the real India, and Deogarh Mahal the place to experience regal Rajasthani hospitality. The family who own it welcome guests as friends. Horse safaris, bird-watching, jeep drives, rural rail trips can all be arranged and the hotel has a swimming pool and Jacuzzi, and offers open-air roof-top ayurvedic massages. This unique yellow and white palace has 30 rooms, each reflective of a different era – just two are air-conditioned suites with a minibar. Airy terraces provide a splendid view of the surrounding mountains and lakes, and the food is excellent: home-grown fruits and vegetables, in-house milk products and oils provide a delectable and distinct freshness. Gala evenings are often featured in the evening entertainment, as well as folk music and dancing. Let the owners take you on a trip to a beautiful lake for sunset and to visit the holy caves. I have yet to meet anyone disappointed with their stay here.

Suites from US$84/Rs3950, plus taxes. Book through specialist tour operators such as Abercrombie & Kent, Cox & Kings, or Western & Oriental.

THE HIMALAYA

When you've had enough of the heat it is time to retire, just as the British used to, to get some fresh, mountain air. What better place to retreat to than to the foothills and hill stations of the mighty Himalayan mountains where you can experience breathtaking scenery, active days and cool nights.

The Indians believe that spirits live in the mountains: the town of **Rishikesh** is the birthplace of yoga and ayurveda, and famed for its spiritual teachings. The hill station, **Shimla**, a gateway to the Himalaya, was a favourite in colonial times and makes a great base for exploring the mountains, cedar forests and ancient monasteries.

Mandarin Oriental Ananda

The Mandarin Oriental Ananda is a peaceful boutique hotel in the foothills of the majestic Himalayas overlooking the holy Ganges near Rishikesh. Ananda comes from the Sanskrit word for 'peace and contentment' and here the emphasis is on relaxation and rejuvenation using the traditional methods of ancient India within a world-class spa, just what you need after the big day.

As you approach Ananda, it looks like the white tiers of a wedding cake. Set in beautifully landscaped gardens and 100 acres of virgin forest, it is built around the fabulous Palace of the Maharajah of Tehri-Garhwal who still lives there. A restored Viceroy's Palace forms part of the hotel, and each of Ananda's 75 spacious rooms and

MANDARIN ORIENTAL ANANDA, THE HIMALAYA

(☎ 01378-27500 📠: 01378-27550, 💻 anandaspa@vsnl.com), the Palace Estate, Narendra Nayar, District Tehri–Garhwal, Uttaranchal, 249175, India

Reservations: Through Mandarin or the Leading Hotels of the World reservation numbers worldwide (see pp10-11) or tour operators such as Elegant Resorts, Abercrombie & Kent

Getting there: 260km north of Delhi, it is a 40-minute flight from to Dehradun's Jolly Grant Airport (Tuesday, Thursday and Saturday only) followed by a one-hour drive or a four-hour train journey to Haridwar (several daily) or six and half hours by car

Accommodation: 70 rooms, 5 suites

Amenities: 2 restaurants and 2 snack bars: the Restaurant for signature 'Ananda Rejuvenation' cuisine, the Winter Garden for traditional Indian meals, the Pavilion for light, healthy snacks, the Palace Lounge for afternoon tea and light refreshments; heated, outdoor pool; 21,000-sq-ft spa with sauna and steam room and offering rejuvenation and relaxation therapies Swedish, Thai, ayurvedic and jet massage, shiatsu, body wraps and hydrotherapy; tennis and squash courts; Aveda beauty institute; other activities include meditation, yoga and cookery classes, trekking in the Himalayas, fishing, biking, tennis, whitewater rafting, and squash; billiards salon and games room; library; boutique

Dress code: Smart casual in the evenings

Weddings: Receptions for up to 150 guests

Minimum stay: None

Rates: Doubles from US$290, suites from US$650 to US$1200 with breakfast, lunch and dinner (American Plan); three-night spa packages cost from US$1020 and include breakfast, transfers and spa treatments

Credit cards: Most major

Taxes and service charge: 5% Government tax

luxurious suites set along the mountain ridge offer magnificent views of the Ganges river, valley of Rishikesh or the Maharajah's palace from their balconies. Each suite has its own garden, and the Palace Suite has a wrap-around terrace with outdoor Jacuzzi. Inside, they are decorated with refined richly coloured silks, hand-crafted period furniture and art reminiscent of the days of the Raj. The floors are of polished teak and the bathroom has a separate shower, and great views from the bathtub. Air conditioned and heated in the winter, all the rooms are decked out with a mini-bar, TV, telephone, safe, tea and coffee making facilities.

The Mandarin Oriental Hotel Group is renowned for its high standards of service. A civilized afternoon tea is taken in the Palace Lounge and the Pavilion, with turn of the 20th-century art deco furnishings, serves light refreshments and hot drinks throughout the day. In season, you can dine alfresco by candlelight in the wonderful amphitheatre, which holds special gala and theme evenings, music and theatre performances.

You can't help but feel healthy on the food in Ananda. The restaurant serves a fusion of Oriental and California cuisine made from organic herbs and vegetables grown in Ananda's garden, or ayurvedic food for your specific 'type'. The Maharajah even founded springs in the vicinity of the palace to tap the rich Himalayan spring water which is still served today.

The Kama Suite at the spa is the place for couples' massage, and has a Jacuzzi and sauna. As well as the many treatments on offer there is a heated outdoor swimming pool and morning yoga and meditation in the open-air Music Pavilion.

Other natural pursuits include opportunities to explore the exotic local scenery with treks into the Himalayan foothills, whitewater rafting, visits to the banks of the Ganges to witness evening prayers, and trips to the holy city of Rishikesh. After a few days at Ananda, you'll feel ready to tackle the rest of India.

Other recommended hotels

Most people combine Ananda with the fabulous Oberoi hotels in nearby Shimla, both members of Leading Hotels of the World. The luxurious **Oberoi Cecil** (☎ 0177-204 848, 📠 0177-211 024, 💻 reservations@thececil.com) is situated at one end of Shimla's

(Opposite) Top: A perfect crescent of sand: Palolem Beach, Goa (see p274), India.
Bottom: Devotee performing early morning ritual ablutions in the River Ganges, Rishikesh, India.

famous mall and has fabulous views from all its richly decorated rooms. Doubles cost from US$175, suites from US$290 including breakfast and dinner, excluding 10% tax.

The new **Wildflower Hall** (☎ 0177-480 808, 🖹 0177-480 909, 🖳 reserva tions@wildflowerhall.com), named after the beautiful acres of wildflowers that surround it, nestles in cedar woods in the Himalayan mountains 8000 feet above sea level. It has a wide variety of activities including parasailing and winter sports so makes an ideal contrast to the relaxation of Ananda, and being an Oberoi resort it doesn't compromise on luxury: a private butler service is available. Doubles cost from US$240, suites from US$450 room only, excluding 28% tax. Talk to tour operators Abercrombie & Kent (see p11) who can arrange a Himalayan itinerary for you.

AGRA AND THE TAJ MAHAL

Agra was a former capital of India and as such has a whole host of magnificent monuments and buildings dating back to the 16th and 17th centuries when the Mughals ruled the country. However, the town is hard work to look around owing to the persistence of the salesmen, touts and beggars. Nevertheless, people flock to Agra for its most famous monument, the Taj Mahal, and are not disappointed.

The Taj is quite incredible: built by Emperor Shah Jahan in memory of his wife, Mumtaz Mahal, who died in childbirth in 1631, it is the world's most extravagant monument to love and took 23 years to complete. The most poignant aspect of the story is that the emperor was later deposed by his son, who then sentenced his father to lifelong imprisonment in Agra Fort, where it is said he spent his remaining days looking out over the river at the tomb he'd built for his wife.

It's easy to get from Delhi to Agra and visit the Taj in just one day, if that's all you've got time for. But you can only fully appreciate the beauty of this vast white mausoleum when you've seen it at varying times of the day, largely because of the effect the light has on the building but also because it is majestically peaceful and far less crowded at dawn and sunset, so I'd recommend staying at least one night.

Recommended hotels

Amarvilas (☎ 562-231 515, 🖹 562-231 516, Taj East Gate Road, Taj Nagri Scheme, Agra 282 001, Uttar Pradesh) offers views of the Taj Mahal from all its guest rooms so it makes a perfect honeymoon hotel. Built in the Mughal style, the intricate painting in all the rooms and the inlaid marble give the most breathtaking overall effect. Each elegantly-appointed room has the rich green and blue colours so often seen in Rajasthan, marble bathrooms with *Amarvilas is simply the most incredible hotel I have ever visited* separate shower and a walk-in wardrobe. All the suites and many rooms have private terraces, and the stunning hotel grounds comprise terraced lawns, fountains, reflection pools and pavilions. The swimming pool is designed so you swim through pillars into a more private pool away from the sun, and the spa offers wonderful traditional ayurvedic massage, indigenous to India.

A member of Small Luxury Hotels of the World, it offers the same standards of comfort and elegance as Rajvilas in Jaipur: butler service, fruit and flowers and 24-hour dining. The excellent Indian chef creates irresistible regional Rajasthani dishes and as the Oberoi group keeps incredibly clean kitchens, Delhi Belly becomes an unnecessary worry. In Amarvilas you'll simply be left speechless by the detail and innovative thought that has gone into creating this most luxurious, spectacular hotel.

Doubles cost from US$345 to US$368, suites from US$518 per night, including tax and chauffeur transfer from Agra airport. Book through Oberoi or Small Luxury Hotels of the World reservation numbers worldwide (see pp12-13).

(Opposite) The Taj Mahal: a monument to love, Agra, India.

GOA

Goa is a wonderful place to go for an exotic sun-drenched beach honeymoon that won't cost you the earth. The palm-fringed coastline with its magnificent sandy beaches has drawn travellers for years but it has only been in the last decade that the world's travel industry has really started to realize the potential that lies in Goa. There are hundreds of decent hotels along the coast offering comprehensive facilities and comfortable accommodation. You'll also find a lively night-life as the dance culture has moved into this long-established hippie enclave.

Because of its Portuguese roots – Goa was a Portuguese colony until 1961 – the architecture has unmistakably Mediterranean tones in the white-washed churches and colonial facades, while the influence of Catholicism also ensures that the state differs markedly from the rest of India.

I have included a few exceptional hotels here, but also talk to tour operators such as Kuoni, British Airways Holidays and Sunset Travel (see pp9-10) for competitive packages if you've set your heart on Goa.

Recommended hotels

The Leela Palace (☎ 832-746 363, ▤ 832-746 352, ▦ www.theleela.com, Cavelossim Village, Salcette, Mobor, Goa 403 731) is the most stylish resort in southern Goa. Lying amidst lotus-flower lagoons, exotic tropical greenery and just a stone's throw from beautiful Mobor beach on the Arabian Sea, it is designed to reflect an ancient, grandiose summer palace.

The 159 Portuguese-style, air-conditioned rooms and suites are arranged as a small village. Each has a balcony with a lagoon or ocean view and the villas have their own private plunge pool. Luxuriously appointed, all rooms have a king-size bed, CD player, wide-screen TV and video, and marble bathrooms with huge power showers with room enough for two. You can dine on a variety of delectables in the alfresco and indoor restaurants here; Jamawar Restaurant serves innovative Indian cuisine.

Bordered by the lively fishing villages on the River Sal, there are plenty of places to visit nearby when you're not lazing around the free-form swimming pool, being pounded in the alfresco hot spa or lying between the swaying palms of the beach. Ayurvedic treatments are a speciality, and there is tennis (floodlit) and a gym and nine-hole golf course, and in season, water-skiing, windsurfing and sailing. A large space is available for receptions should you want to get married here.

Doubles cost from US$235, suites from US$375 room only, excluding 22% tax. The Leela Palace is affiliated to the Kempinski Group and can be booked through

---

THINGS TO SEE AND DO AROUND GOA

Rent a car, for a week, or alternatively hire a motorbike: much more fun and just as easy in Goa. You can even get an old Enfield for a week. Always carry all your documentation with you and remember that in India a highway code is virtually non-existent.

One of Goa's major attractions is **Anjuna flea market** on Wednesdays between October and March: tourists flock to see the Tibetan and Kashmiri traders, the Indian women in traditional tribal dress and, of course, the resident hippies. Anjuna is one of Goa's truly exotic places where 'serious travellers' ensconce themselves for months on end just soaking up the scene.

The moated ruins of **Fort Aguada** are also worth visiting. The fort was built by the Portuguese in 1612 and its hilltop location means the views are great. Another great place is **Terekhol Fort**, a small Portuguese fort way up in the north of Goa on the border with Maharashtra.

All the hotels mentioned in the Goa section and many other good hotels have their own private beaches, the best of which are **Aguada, Bogmalo, Varca** and **Cavelossim**. If you want to get away from the tourist beaches head to **Arambol, Betui** or **Palolem**. Although you'll find these beaches colonized by a handful of hardy, seasoned travellers the coast is stunning and the local fishermen are friendly.

Leading Hotels of the World (see p12 for reservation numbers worldwide) or tour operators such as Elegant Resorts, Cox & Kings, Abercrombie & Kent (see p11).

Nilaya Hermitage (☎ 832-276 793, 🖹 832-276 792, 🖳 www.nilaya hermitage.com, Arpora Bhati, Goa 403518), set high in the hills overlooking the paddy fields and the sea, is Goa's smartest hotel. It's small, with only 11 stunning, spacious rooms with domed roofs which give it a Moorish feel. Decorated with calm pastel colours and Indian furniture, some rooms have alfresco bathrooms. Each is designed individually around a theme – stars, sun, moon and sky – which is reflected in the inlaid stone floors.

An informal retreat, 'Nilaya' means heaven and in this hotel you'll find it hard to move, even to the beach, just 15-minutes' drive away. Most people hang around the pool, play tennis, listen to music, take a massage or steam bath. The European chef prepares dishes from around the world, and you can dine under the stars on the veranda listening to the gentle sound of waterfalls from the pool, in the open-sided dining room, or in the privacy of your own room. Doubles start from US$110 in the rainy season with breakfast, US$255 in high season, half board, includes airport transfers. Book through specialist tour operator Western & Oriental (see p10).

KERALA

If you've had enough of beach and want to head inland, Kerala is one of India's most stunning areas. Magnificent hills, the Western Ghats, rise from the coast and offer breathtaking scenery and Kerala's small, hideaway hill station hotels make a great contrast to the heritage hills of the north. Also worth exploring are the 'Backwaters', a network of fascinating waterways and lagoons which wind their way through paddy fields, tropical fruit trees and settlements, with Christian churches alongside temples and fishermen at the water's edge.

Recommended hotels

Tranquil: A Plantation Hideaway (☎ 493-620 244, 🖹 493-622 358, 🖳 ivorytow er@vsnl.com, 🖳 www.plantationhideaway.com, Kolagapara, Western Ghats, North Kerala) is an eight-bedroom bungalow amidst the coffee, cardamom and tea plantations, rolling hills and tropical jungle of northern Kerala. Beautifully restored with a generous use of wood and planters' furniture that take you back to plantation times. The rooms are individually decorated and have modern bathrooms and verandas, and peaceful courtyards.

This is a real homestay with great food and a hearty breakfast, served whenever you get up. Miles away from the hassle of the city, you can walk in the rolling hills or trek to the Edakal Caves nearby or simply lie in a hammock beside the pool. Doubles cost from US$250 which includes all meals, non-alcoholic beverages, taxes and local sightseeing. A bottle of champagne and 'a handsome discount' is offered to honeymooners booking direct, or book through specialist tour operator Western & Oriental (see p10).

Treehouses (☎ 471-330437, 🖹 471-331407, 🖳 www.richsoft.com/tourindia, Wynad National Park, Western Ghats, North Kerala), deep in the virgin jungle, is a place that will appeal to closet Tarzan and Jane's, as well as those who don't want to be that adventurous. Four eco-friendly lodges and three treehouses suspended 80-90 metres above the ground and reached by ropeways, nestle amidst a gurgling stream, colourful birds, tropical vegetation and misty mountains.

Although Treehouses is reached in two hours by road from Calicut, the last part is a rugged jeep ride. All the rooms have electricity, mosquito nets, running water, a flushing loo and 'telephone' shower, a carpeted veranda and a sitting room. As well as experiencing the different moods of nature – the misty winds, the first rays of sun through the trees, the magic of the monsoon, and the magnificence of birds, butterflies and occasional other wildlife – elephant or jeep safaris are arranged, as well as trekking expeditions through tribal areas or to the Edakkal caves, full of prehistoric paintings.

Staying here is really getting back to nature; bamboo poles and mats adorn the ethnically-designed rooms, some of the energy comes from cow dung, and organic vegetarian food is served on banana leaves. Treehouses US$150 per couple, full board, eco-lodges US$110, taxes included. Book through specialist tour operator Western & Oriental (see p10).

Thailand
(BEST TIME: ALL YEAR ROUND)

There are few countries that offer Thailand's beauty and diversity and make such an ideal honeymoon for couples wanting to combine a beach holiday with some oriental culture and maybe a little adventure.

What makes Thailand so exotic is its wonderful concoction of islands, vibrant night-life, mountainous jungles offering all sorts of adventures, delicious cuisine, incredibly fascinating culture and glittering temples – and above all the charming Thai people who help to make Thailand such a hassle-free place to travel around.

Thailand has some of the finest beaches in the Orient, and with 2500km of coastline there's no shortage of romantic hideaways to discover. Although some of the major beaches on the islands of **Phuket** and **Koh Samui** have become over-developed, there are still plenty of beautiful beaches to be found there, and more at **Krabi.**

These coastal resorts are home to Thailand's most romantic hotels, offering the kind of first-class accommodation and service that has helped the area develop its reputation for superb luxury resorts. While many hoteliers tend to think a four-poster bed defines romance, the Thais have taken it one step further and given the world Jacuzzi baths on outdoor decks, open-air showers, and chilled face-towels brought to your lounger on the beach. They really have got service down to a fine art, and even at the cheaper places in these beach areas you'll be looked after very well.

THAILAND
An exotic combination of islands, culture, night-life, shopping, wonderful food and first-class hotels
When to go: February to September (Koh Samui); November to April (Krabi and Phuket), November to March (Chiang Mai)
Average maximum temperatures °C

	JAN	FEB	MAR	APR	MAY	JUN	JUL	AUG	SEP	OCT	NOV	DEC
Bangkok	32	33	34	35	34	33	33	33	32	32	32	31
Chiang Mai	29	32	35	36	34	32	32	31	31	31	30	28
Koh Samui	29	30	31	32	33	32	32	32	32	31	30	29
Phuket/Krabi	33	34	34	34	32	32	31	31	30	31	31	31

Capital: Bangkok
Flight times: to Bangkok from:
New York: 18 hours
LA: 15 hours
London: 13 hours
Sydney: 9 hours
Approximate exchange rates: Baht (B) – £1 = B64.72, US$1 = B45.52, A$1 = B23.62
Time difference: GMT plus seven hours
Voltage: 220v AC, 50 Hz, US and European-style two flat-pin plugs
Combine with: The Eastern & Oriental Express from Bangkok to Singapore via Malaysia; but there is plenty to occupy you in Thailand for two or three weeks
Country dialling code: ☎ 66
Further information: 🖳 www.tourismthailand.org

Just north of Bangkok is **Chiang Mai**, Thailand's second largest city. While Chiang Mai itself is a bit of a dump, it's the place to go if you're looking for easily accessible culture and adventure. This highland city is the gateway to the north: if you hire a four-wheel drive you can discover ancient hill-tribe villages with their intricate costumes and age-old customs, or do an exhilarating trek through the jungle on an elephant, and whitewater raft along the river.

The absolute ultimate in luxury and old-world charm, the famous and fabulously elegant **Eastern & Oriental Express** makes the 1932km rail journey between Bangkok and Singapore about three times a month (see 🖳 www.orient-express trains.com for more information.

BANGKOK

Entering this river city has to be one of the most exciting experiences imaginable. Bustling, throbbing, dirty, smelly, chaotic but at the same time quite magical, Bangkok epitomises Thailand's blend of old and new and is an exhilarating city to visit. With several truly first-class hotels it is also a great place to unwind from your flight, shop for tailored suits and silks, and explore some of the fascinating temples and palaces.

The Oriental

Located right on the edge of the city's **Chao Phraya River**, the Oriental has long been Bangkok's most legendary hotel and for years has fully merited its position as one of the world's greatest hotels. When we first arrived we struggled to see what all the fuss was about but by our second day the buzz of this cosmopolitan hotel had wooed us.

All the 362 rooms and 34 suites are beautifully furnished with the kind of luxuries as standard that you'd expect in a hotel of this calibre, and all have river views. The amenities are all there: air conditioning, hairdryer, phone, radio, television with in-house video films, in-room safe, and even umbrellas to weather the usual Bangkok thunderstorms.

A particular favourite is the Noel Coward Suite: sumptuously decorated, it is situated in the original wing of the hotel and is stashed full of photographs of the man and his books. The bedroom has two four-poster single beds upholstered in turquoise blue raw silk. The bathroom is huge and divided, with wardrobes and a large basin in one part and a lovely large bath in the other. There are all the usual bathroom goodies, plus two very thick bathrobes and slippers.

The service at the Oriental is legendary and deservedly so. Each suite has a dedicated butler: he arrives at your door every evening at 6pm armed with tiny tempting canapés and sandwiches which you can indulge in as you get ready for your evening out. He also appears at random times to ask if you have any laundry, or need your shoes shined, while at the same time managing to remain very discreet. He explains on arrival that if you put the huge brass 'Do Not

THE ORIENTAL
(☎ 2-659 9000, 🖷 2-659 0000, 🖳 bscor bkk@loxinfo.co.th), 48 Oriental Avenue, Bangkok 10500, Thailand
Reservations: The Leading Hotels of the World toll-free reservations numbers worldwide (see p12)
Getting there: The hotel can arrange to collect you from the airport – a 25-minute drive – in one of their white Mercedes
Accommodation: 362 rooms and 34 suites
Amenities: Seven restaurants: Normandie, China House, Lord Jim's, Sala Rim Naam, Riverside Terrace, Veranda, and Ciao; Bamboo Bar; two outdoor pools, tennis, squash, saunas, gym, jogging; the Oriental Spa; river cruises, 24-hour room service, fully air conditioned
Dress code: Jacket and tie are required for dining in the Normandie Grill; no shorts or slippers are allowed in the hotel
Weddings: Can be arranged
Minimum stay: None
Rates: Double rooms from US$250; suites US$380 to US$2000; ask about promotional packages which offer discounts on these rates
Credit cards: Most major
Taxes and service charge: 10% tax and 10% service charge

Disturb' sign on the door he'll leave you alone for as long as you want. Apart from the immaculate and unobtrusive service, it's the little details that really make the Oriental so special. You'll find a bottle of champagne and red roses in your room on arrival, wonderfully posh writing paper and postcards contained in a very smart wallet and a continual stream of fresh flowers.

All the rooms were overflowing with beautiful flowers which were changed daily, and a very fragrant white flower was put on our pillows each night. There was an incredible thunderstorm the first night, and it was bliss to be able to open the windows and watch. It was also very funny to see two of the hotel staff punting their way past our window on a makeshift raft as the gardens had completely flooded.
Katie and Philip Stockton

The hotel's food is also good and with seven restaurants, you'll be spoilt for choice. Either dine at the renowned **Normandie Grill**, which serves French cuisine, or **Ciao** Italian restaurant in the hotel's garden. Alternatively, take the boat across the river to the other side of the hotel where the fabulous health spa is found, and the equally wonderful **Sala Rim Naam** restaurant adjacent to it. The boat ride is great – instead of normal seats it has large wooden dining room chairs down each side, to make you feel that little bit extra special.

The Oriental's spa, with its 50 different Thai treatments, is one of the most heavenly places on earth – there can be no better way of reviving your bodies after a long flight than this. As well as the sports complex and stunning spa facilities, the Oriental has two outdoor pools.

Other recommended hotels
The Peninsula (☎ 2-861 2888, 🖹 2-861 2355, 🖳 pkb@peninsula.com, 333 Charoennakorn Road, Klongsan, Bangkok 10600), directly facing the Oriental across the Chao Phraya River, has created a stir. While the Oriental is undoubtedly the Grand Dame of Bangkok, the Peninsula has a fresh modern style with fabulously big, bright airy rooms looking over the river and a selection of lovely suites including 60 one-bedroom and five themed suites. Blending the old with the new, it manages to be Oriental-pretty whilst discreetly offering state of the art technology. The rooms all have luxuri-

---

THINGS TO SEE AND DO IN BANGKOK

It is now possible to enter Bangkok on a **water taxi** straight from the airport; the journey takes about an hour and it is definitely the best way to arrive in this incredible city because the river is the centre for all the activity and at the same time you avoid the appalling traffic jams on the city's crowded streets.

The best way to see Bangkok and the surrounding region is also by river so, even if you don't get a boat from the airport, try to leave time for a cruise up **Chao Phya River**, which for 700 years was Thailand's main communication artery. A two-day, one-night cruise aboard the *Mekhala*, a traditional teak rice barge converted into a comfortable hotel, costs around US$178/£125 per person. Each of the six air-conditioned cabins has a king-size bed, dressing table and wardrobe as well as a private bathroom with a shower. As you slip out of Bangkok in the early afternoon you'll pass the Grand Palace and the Temple of Dawn, before the *Mekhala* docks at **Wat Kai Tia**, a Thai temple set in a tranquil rural village, for a candlelit dinner on the main deck. The next day you visit the

ancient capital of **Ayuthaya**, and lunch in a riverside restaurant, before returning to Bangkok in a private air-conditioned minibus. The cruises can be booked before you leave through tour operator Magic of the Orient (UK ☎ 01293-537 700).

The basic 'must see' sights in Bangkok are the **Grand Palace, Wat Phra Kaew, Wat Po, Wat Arun, Chatuchak Park's Weekend Market** open on Saturday and Sunday, and the **Floating Market**.

If you can cope with getting up early there are great photo opportunities to be had watching the Buddhist monks delivering alms outside **Wat Benjamabophit** at around 6.30am, before going onto Phak Klong Talad, Bangkok's largest floating market, near the foot of the Memorial Bridge and the flower market at nearby Chakkapet Road.

From the Oriental you can also rent a boat and cruise through Klong Bangkok Noi and along the smaller canals to **Klong Bangkok Yai** for a better insight into everyday life for the residents of this mind-blowing city.

ous bathrooms with the Peninsula signature no-condensation TV built into the marble walls above the huge bath. The hotel has its own pier where you can cross the river in a few minutes to the Oriental, or even check-in if you want a romantic arrival. If you want to transfer in more style, the hotel is the only one in Bangkok with its own helipad.

The pretty terraced, landscaped outdoor pool means you can watch the boats go by from your sunlounger, and in the evening you can enjoy every type of food in the six fashionable restaurants, with diverse entertainment including a court jester. De luxe doubles cost from US$200, double room with balcony US$240, suites from US$280 to US$2600, plus 10% service charge and prevailing government tax. Book through Leading Hotels of the World reservation numbers worldwide (see p12) or tour operators in the UK such as specialist tour operator Magic of the Orient (see p11).

NORTHERN THAILAND

The cool mountainous landscapes of northern Thailand make a welcome change from steamy Bangkok and are well worth visiting for the hill tribes and their exquisite handicrafts. Situated in a broad river valley 305m above sea level, Chiang Mai is now a modern city but there is still plenty of evidence of its former days of glory when it reigned for seven centuries as the capital of the Lanna ('million rice fields') kingdom. Chiang Mai can be reached by a one-hour internal flight from Bangkok.

The Regent Chiang Mai Resort & Spa

The Regent Chiang Mai is just 20 minutes outside the city centre, and definitely the most lavish and beautiful place to stay in northern Thailand. Located in the beautiful **Mae Rim Valley** amongst eight hectares of gardens filled with lily ponds, two small lakes and terraced rice paddies, the Regent epitomises everything that is luxurious and sensuous about this chain.

Wherever you walk or look there are tiny details of perfection, from the decorative paper lanterns hanging from the lobby ceiling and the local elephant carvings in the pavilion's secluded gardens, to the stencilled cabinets and string harps sitting on lacquered tables.

The designers have managed to combine the beauty of the traditional style of Thai architecture with just about every luxury that you could possibly imagine, striving to remain true to the local culture in every aspect of the hotel's design – even the horticulture is indigenous. Instead of creating a tropical atmosphere with sprawling bougainvillaea, they planted plumeria.

The 64 Pavilion Suites reflect the style of the Lanna Kingdom, when back in 1296 King Mengrai established his kingdom in northern Thailand. The houses were a blend of several influences in style: Burmese, Indian,

THE REGENT CHIANG MAI RESORT & SPA
(☎ 53-298 181, 🖷 53-298 189, Guest 🖷 66 53-298 190), Mae Rim-Samoeng Old Road, Mae Rim, Chiang Mai 50180, Thailand
Reservations: The Regent Resorts' toll-free reservation numbers worldwide (see pp11-12) and most major tour operators and travel agents offering holidays in Thailand (see pp11-12)
Getting there: Thai Airways operates seven flights a day to Chiang Mai Airport from where transfers can be arranged, a private limo round trip costs approximately US$50
Accommodation: 64 Pavilion suites and 13 Residence Suites
Amenities: 24-hour room service, daily laundry, CD players, satellite TV, VCRs for in-room use available on request, library, the Regent Boutique, two restaurants and 2 bars, tennis and health club, the Lanna Spa housing seven palatial treatment suites; five international golf courses close to the resort, tour desk, outdoor 20m swimming pool and covered heated Jacuzzi, mountain bikes, shuttle service to Chiang Mai
Dress code: Smart casual
Weddings: Weddings and receptions can be arranged at the Regent
Minimum stay: None
Rates: Garden view pavilion suites from US$310; rice terrace view pavilion suites from US$386; one bedroom Residence Suite from US$750, Two bedroom with private plunge pool from US$1230
Credit cards: Most major
Taxes and service charge: 18.5% will be added to your bill

THINGS TO SEE AND DO AROUND CHIANG MAI

Chiang Mai, although not the unspoilt hilltop town it once was, does have many glittering gold Buddhist temples, a good covered market and is a definite must if you are keen to explore a little of this country's fascinating culture and history. Its surrounding countryside has a totally distinct flavour compared to the rest of the country, owing to its relative isolation until the 1920s when the railway linking it with Bangkok was completed.

Chiang Mai is certainly rich in history, with relics of the ancient kingdoms and their artistic achievements that preceded the founding of the first Thai capital at **Sukhothai** in the 13th century. Even in the city itself there are scores of temples, known as 'wats', with wonderful teak carvings and intricate decorations inspired by the area's Burmese neighbours. Make sure you visit **Wat Doi Suthep**, the massive temple sitting on a hill looking down over the city, at sunset when the panoramic views of the Chiang Mai valley are breathtaking. Other temples worth looking at are **Wat Chiang Man**, **Wat Phra Singh** (particularly the small **Phra Viharn Laikam** which is probably the best example of Lanna architecture), and **Wat Suan Dok**, where the ashes of the royal family of Chiang Mai are found.

In the streets of Chiang Mai you'll see people from the **northern hill tribes**, driven to the city in the hope of selling their crafts. These fabulously dressed people, with their clanking jewellery, heavily embroidered dresses and silver turbans, are such a cultural curiosity because their relative isolation – some villages in the north are five or six days' walk away from the nearest town – means that they live today in pretty much the same way as they have for centuries. The best place to find their handiwork is on **Borsang Road**, where all the handicraft shops have now congregated. Here you can buy a large range of crafts which are still original and not machine made, including delicate silver bowls, hand-woven cottons, gold leaf on black lacquerware, expertly carved teak, Thai celadon ceramics, embroidered handbags and paper umbrellas with their ornate hand painted designs.

Most tourists spend a few days here visiting the temples before heading further north to explore the hill tribes, trek in the mountains, whitewater raft or visit elephant camps. **Mae Hong Son**, one of the prettiest hill towns in Thailand, can be reached either by a 40-minute flight from Chiang Mai, directly from Bangkok, or by renting a car or a four-wheel drive jeep in Chiang Mai, driving to Hot, spending time in Mae Hong Son and then returning via the northern route through Pai, which is still incredibly remote, and back to Chiang Mai along the picturesque winding road. In Mae Hong Son drive along the mountain roads to the villages of the Hmong and Lisu hill tribes to see the beautiful women in their traditional costumes.

There are hordes of adventure expeditions leaving from Chiang Mai daily, most of which can be organized on arrival in the city: you might try a three-day **Golden Triangle Tour** which departs from **Chiang Rai** (you can fly to Chiang Rai from Bangkok or Chiang Mai) and includes trips in long-tail boats, elephant rides as well as visits to some of the ancient and more remote hilltop towns such as Chiang Saen, one of the oldest towns in Thailand.

A good day trip from Chiang Mai takes you out to **Lamphun**, just 26km south of the city, along one of the most beautiful tree-lined roads in the north. Lamphun, the former seat of the Haripunchai Kingdom, is home to the 9th-century **Wat Prathat Haripunchia**, one of the oldest and most magnificent wats in northern Thailand.

Chinese, and the groups which were powerful in the region at that time. The Lanna theme is even incorporated in the staff uniforms, right down to their silver accessories and the buttons on their sleeves.

The vaulted ceilings tower loftily above polished teak floors, while rich Thai cottons, cream rugs and walls and beautiful Siamese art produce an air of tranquillity. The pavilions are extremely spacious, covering 70 sq metres, and comprising a bedroom with an attached bathroom with deep soaking tub and glass panels looking onto the lush foliage outside. Each Pavilion also features a Thai 'sala', a private outdoor living space, which adds to the resort's village style. The in-pavilion facilities are impressive: there's absolutely everything here, from CD players to Thai cotton robes, slippers, and even a toaster so you don't get soggy room-service toast for breakfast.

The most luxurious suites of all are the Residences, thirteen units with either one, two- or three-bedrooms. The suites cover a magnificent 350 to 524 sq metres, featuring individual plunge pools on the terrace, gabled buttresses styled to imitate ancient temples, fireplaces and polished wood floors. We're talking seriously pukka stuff.

The hotel will arrange a great variety of activities for you, tailor-made to your individual requirements: exhilarating treks into the jungle; visits to elephant training camps or orchid and butterfly farms; trips around the city's ancient temples, handicraft villages and to the night bazaar, or you can merely relax in the hotel's own extensive health club or play a game of tennis. They'll even arrange massages in the comfort of your own room, leaving you with a petal-strewn bath to wallow in afterwards.

Guests can enjoy cocktails in the **Terrace Lounge**, before having traditional Thai cuisine in the **Sala Mae Rim**, the resort's fantastic Thai Restaurant. The restaurant serves mouthwatering dishes like fresh sea bass with tamarind juice and coriander root and favourites like Thom Yum soup. Alternatively, lunch and dinner can be taken at the pool-side restaurant, or even in the privacy of your own terrace for those times when you don't feel like dressing for dinner. We loved staying in this tranquil hotel and found it the perfect place to unwind at the start of our holiday.

PHUKET
Phuket is Thailand's largest island and of course its most famous since it was used as a location in the James Bond film *The Man with the Golden Gun*. Linked to the mainland via **Sarasin Bridge**, Phuket has become very commercialized over the last ten years and is now served by direct flights from destinations as diverse as Vienna, Sydney, Hong Kong and Singapore. However, if you stay in any of the hotels listed below all you'll see are deserted beaches fringed by lush tropical scenery and the emerald waters of the Andaman Sea.

The Banyan Tree Phuket
The Banyan Tree in Phuket has received high critical acclaim from the world's glossy travel magazines, largely because of its incredibly lavish spa facilities. So if you fancy really winding down after your wedding in a pampered paradise, this is the place for you.

Opened in 1994, the Banyan Tree is set on a beach in **Bang Tao Bay** and has every kind of facility you could need from the first-class spa to the championship golf course, tennis courts, squash, sailing and windsurfing. There are also two swimming pools, one aimed at encouraging lap-swimming to keep you active and the other, a free-form pool with its own bubble mats, rapid water canal, Jacuzzi and swim-up bar, to relax in.

The hotel's luxury accommodation is in two kinds of traditional Thai-style villas surrounded by lush tropical gardens and Asian water courts. Each villa has its own private garden and Thai sala (terrace). The villas come complete with their own open-air sunken baths, while the 58 Spa Pool villas, which cover 270 sq metres including dining area, open-air sunken bath, patio, and the most wonderful nine by three-metre swimming pool, are quite simply the ultimate experience. The villas have everything from tea- and coffee-making facilities to stereos and air conditioning.

THE BANYAN TREE PHUKET
(☎ 76-324 374, 🖷 76-324 375), 33 Moo 4, Srisoonthorn Road, Cherngtalay, Amphur Talang, Phuket, 83110, Thailand
Reservations: Small Luxury Hotels of the World toll-free reservations numbers worldwide (see p12)
Getting there: 25 minutes from Phuket International Airport, the hotel can arrange transfers
Accommodation: 108 villas, including 50 villas and 58 Spa Pool villas
Amenities: Four Spa Pavilions offer saunas, steam rooms, loofah areas, Jacuzzis, beauty treatments and massage, five rejuvenation rooms offering body and beauty treatments such as facials, and the Beauty Garden for make-overs; Fitness Pavilion, championship golf course, tennis courts, two swimming pools, Watercourt Café, Saffron Restaurant, Banyan Café, Spa Lounge, Scala Terrace Restaurant, Terrace Bar, Pool Bar, Banyan Tree Gallery and bicycles for guest use
Dress code: Casual smart in the restaurants
Weddings: The hotel hosts receptions for up to 150 people
Rates: Villas from US$330; Spa pool villas from US$1100
Credit cards: Most major
Taxes and service charge: Not included

Dining can either be on your own terrace or at one of the Banyan Tree's five restaurants: the intimate **Watercourt** offers a variety of dishes with a Mediterranean touch, **Saffron** has award-winning Thai cuisine, the **Banyan Café**, overlooking the golf course, is informal and open and features international and Asian favourites, **Scala Terrace** specializes in fusion seafood, while the **Spa Lounge** offers meals for the health-conscious. This hotel is the kind of place that makes you feel so cossetted it's difficult to summon the energy to leave its gates. I loved every minute of being here.

Amanpuri

Amanpuri, situated on Pansea beach on the island's west coast, is a very exclusive hotel and definitely one of the best in Phuket.

When it opened in 1988 Amanpuri was the first of the Amanresorts, a small hotel chain now widely regarded as having the world's most exclusive and luxurious properties. The word Amanpuri means 'region of tranquillity' in Sanskrit and with just 40 rooms this small hotel is a total haven for escapists.

The bedrooms, or pavilions as they are known, are arranged across eight hectares of coconut-studded hillside, with the most wonderful views of the bay and beach below. They are connected by elevated walkways with colonnades.

Each pavilion covers 115 sq metres and offers unrivalled luxury with a large separate bedroom, dressing room and bathing area. The beds are king-size and there is also air conditioning, a minibar, electronic in-room safe, stereo system, a luxurious bathroom with a sumptuous sunken bath and separate shower, and a wonderful outdoor terrace or 'sala' ideal for sunbathing or dining alone together. All the rooms have sleek teak wood furnishings, and cream walls and bed linen: extremely simple but wonderfully elegant. Pavilions No 103 and No 105 are the best located because of their ocean views, though the three de luxe pavilions have partial ocean views.

Amanpuri has two restaurants, both of which are open air. The **Terrace** offers casual Thai and European meals, while the **Restaurant** specializes in Mediterranean dishes; the Bar, which overlooks the sea, offers poolside drinks and snacks. There is, of course, also 24-hour room service, and between November and April barbecues are held on the beach.

Facilities include an amazing black-tiled freshwater pool, six floodlit tennis courts, windsurfing, water-skiing, diving, a gym on the beach, a sauna and a teak-panelled library with an impressive array of books and music. Golf can easily be arranged as Amanpuri has membership of the private Blue Canyon Golf & Country Club – one of the premier courses in South-east Asia; for the less active, massage and beauty treatments will be conducted in the privacy of your own pavilion or at the salon. Golf carts are provided for moving around the hotel.

Amanpuri also has a terrific scheduled cruise programme offering guests a variety of boats and excursions from day and night-time cruises to **Phang-Na Bay** where the

---

AMANPURI
(☎ 76-324 333, 🖹 76-324 100, 🖳 www.amanresorts.com), Pansea Beach, Phuket 83000, Thailand
Reservations: Through Sterling Hotels and Resorts reservation numbers worldwide (see p12) and most major tour operators/travel agents worldwide (see pp9-10)
Getting there: Frequent hour-long flights from Bangkok land at Phuket Airport each day; Amanpuri is 20 minutes from the airport via private limousine transfer
Accommodation: 40 pavilions, 30 villas
Amenities: Freshwater pool; six floodlit tennis courts; watersports facilities include windsurfing, sailing, snorkelling, water-skiing, diving, as well as cruises on any of its many charter boats; hair, massage and beauty salon; golf nearby; shop; two restaurants, a pool-side bar; 24-hour room service; beachfront gym; library
Dress code: Smart casual
Weddings: No
Minimum stay: None
Rates: Pavilions from US$420, villas from US$1150
Credit cards: Most major
Taxes and service charge: All rates are subject to 8.2% government tax and 10% service charge

limestone cliffs and islands provide truly dramatic scenery, to a traditional Chinese sailing junk, which takes guests to **Koh Wah** for a day's swimming, snorkelling and lunch on the deserted beaches north of **Bangtao**.

Other recommended hotels

The **Chedi** (☎ 76-324 017/20, 🖹 76-324 252, 🖵 www.chedi-phuket.com, Pansea Bay, 118 Moo 3, Choeng Talay, 83110 Phuket) is a pretty cottage-style hotel overlooking the most beautiful beach in Phuket, adjacent to Amanpuri. It is the perfect place for honeymooners looking for sophisticated solitude. All the 110 Thai-style thatched cottages have separate dressing area and bathroom, as well as a minibar, electronic in-room safe, satellite TV, hairdryer, air conditioning, tea and coffee-making facilities and phone. The serene décor is of panels of woven palm fronds and earth-coloured fabrics. There are two restaurants at the Chedi: the main dining room which serves a good selection of both local and international dishes, and Rim Lay, an alfresco restaurant on the beach, which specializes in freshly-caught fish. Snacks are served by the hotel's large hexagonal swimming pool. As well as the pool, which has its own wading pond, there is a spa and two floodlit tennis courts, and a wide variety of watersports are available free of charge. Only scuba diving and water-skiing cost extra.

One bedroom cottages on the hillside from US$160; on the beachfront from US$290 per couple including breakfast and transfers, plus 10% service charge, 10% VAT and 0.2% provincial tax.

KOH SAMUI

Koh Samui is one of Thailand's most beautiful resorts – a small island totally covered by coconut plantations which still provide the mainstay of the island's economy. If you don't want to spend a fortune on a hotel, Koh Samui's roots as a backpackers' paradise mean that you can find a rustic beach hut for around US$10 a night on any of the island's dozen beaches. However, if you fancy a little luxury, Koh Samui is also home to some of the most beautiful and romantic hotels ever built.

Le Royal Méridien Baan Taling Ngam

Le Royal Méridien Baan Taling Ngam has the kind of fantastic rooms and really first-class service that inspires everyone who's been there to come home raving about it.

Located on Koh Samui's secluded and tranquil western coast, this wonderful hotel's name means 'your home on a beautiful cliff', which just about summarizes the ethos of this wildly romantic place.

This is one of those hotels that makes you feel excited as soon as you set your eyes on it. The view from the stunning open-plan reception area out to sea with the little green dots of islands below you is mesmerizing.

There are 73 Thai-style rooms with teak wood interiors. You will be accommodated in either a de luxe room, a beach villa or a cliff villa, all of which overlook the neighbouring islands of **Ang Thong Marine National Park**. The rooms are a clever mix between traditional wooden materials and essentially very modern Thai designs. All the rooms have satellite TV, DVD player, CD and stereo system, air conditioning, in-room safes, minibar and phones, tea- and coffee-making facilities as well as luxury bathrooms and spacious balconies.

The cliff-side villas are the best of all. Set on two storeys, the bedroom and bathroom are downstairs, while a centrally-placed staircase takes you upstairs into a stunning open-plan lounge with the most incredible views and furnished with Thai silks, rugs and chunky wooden furniture. The cliff villas have a pantry and dining table, a balcony running right along the length of the front of the villa and the added luxury of a

The suite was so spacious and beautifully decorated it was the sort of place you dream about living in, if only we could have brought it back to Britain.
Martin and Meea

LE ROYAL MERIDIEN BAAN TALING NGAM

(☎ 77-423 019, 🖷 77-423 220), 295 Moo 3, Taling Ngam Beach, Surathani 84140, Koh Samui, Thailand

Reservations: Le Méridien reservation centres: UK toll-free (☎ 08000 282840); USA, Canada, Mexico toll-free (☎ 1 800 543 4300); Australia toll-free (☎ 1 800 622240); Japan toll-free (☎ 0120 094040)

Getting there: There are regular flights from Bangkok and Phuket to Samui; arrange your 50-minute limousine transfer from airport to hotel at the time of booking (US$134 per person)

Accommodation: 40 de luxe rooms; 23 cliff villas, 7 beach villas, 2 de luxe suites, 1 Royal Villa 'Baan Napa'

Amenities: Three restaurants, the Veranda bar, pool deck bar, PADI-licensed diving school, two main swimming pools plus five shared pools for the cliff villas, cruises to nearby islands and beaches, general watersports, gym, two tennis courts, mountain bikes, beauty salon and spa, boutique, 24-hour room service, jeep rental and shuttle bus to town

Dress code: Elegant casual

Weddings: Can be arranged

Minimum stay: None

Rates: Doubles from US$300/B13,500 to US$550/B24,750

Credit cards: Most major

Taxes and service charge: 7% tax and 10% service charge

TONGSAI GRAND VILLAS

(☎ 77-425 015 🖷 77-425 462), 84 Moo 5, Bo Phut, Koh Samui, Surat Thani 84320, Thailand

Reservations: Small Luxury Hotels of the World toll-free reservations numbers worldwide (see p12)

Getting there: The hotel will collect you from Koh Samui Airport

Accommodation: 15 private cottages

Amenities: Large free-form swimming pool, small beach for swimming, windsurfing and snorkelling, tennis, piano bar, Thai restaurant, pool-side bar, 24-hour room service

Dress code: Very relaxed

Weddings: Can be arranged

Minimum stay: None

Rates: Villas from US$440/B20,000 to US$1099/B50,000

Credit cards: Most major

Taxes and service charge: Included

beautiful horizon-style swimming pool shared between six villas, with its own Jacuzzi and a swim-up bar. Alternatively, go for one of the de luxe suites which have huge balconies off both the lounge and the bedroom, an extremely funky black-slate toilet, a four-poster bed made out of chunky wooden posts, and the most wonderful black-slate bathroom where a round window allows you to lie back in the sunken bath and gaze out to sea.

As one of the two Le Royal Méridien resorts in Thailand, you'll find the service and facilities at Baan Taling Ngam very definitely up to scratch. Choose from the three main restaurants – the **Lom Talay** serving Asian and International dishes, **Baan Chantra Restaurant** for Royal Thai cuisine, or the **Promenade Restaurant** by the beach, serving Eastern and Western seafood. The **Veranda Bar** in the lobby with its wonderful view also makes the perfect spot for a cocktail as the sun drops on the Gulf of Thailand. Bar snacks and drinks can also be enjoyed all day long on the Pool Deck.

There are seven outdoor swimming pools, a whirlpool, lots of watersports including PADI instruction, ocean kayaks, sailing and windsurfing, as well as cruises to nearby islands on the hotel's own speedboats or long-tail boat for picnics à deux, or snorkelling. Other facilities include a beauty salon & spa, 24-hour room service, boutique, jeep rental, gym, two tennis courts and mountain bikes, so there's plenty to do.

Tongsai Grand Villas

Tongsai Grand Villas, perched high above its own private beach, is undoubtedly one of the best in Koh Samui. Located a good drive away from any local bars, shops or restaurants, Tongsai Grand Villas best suits those who really do want to relax and do nothing.

The 15 secluded honeymoon cottages, an abundance of bamboo and wicker surrounded by tropical gardens, are just superb. On entering the room you are shown the bedroom area with its four-poster bed shrouded in mosquito netting, off which there is a small shower room with a basic shower. You then follow a bamboo and wicker staircase down to a sitting room where champagne and flowers await you. Everything up until now is very attractive but quite basic, but when you go through the French windows and see the dark wooden deck with its Jacuzzi, outdoor shower, vanity unit, two sun loungers and table, you know you've stumbled upon a little slice of paradise!

The deck is surrounded by lush green plants and foliage so that while you lie in the bath staring out at the turquoise sea, no one can see in. We were exhausted from the wedding and found it a great place to vegetate, eat, swim and relax; it was absolutely fabulous.
Anthony and Deborah Clifden

A visit to Tongsai Grand Villas is full of welcoming touches like the freshly-sliced papaya waiting for you in your room each afternoon, and the way the pink and blue cotton robes are changed daily; fresh white towels are also left by the Jacuzzi. The rooms have a full selection of luxury amenities from air conditioning and minibar, to a TV with in-house videos and a phone.

One of the nicest things about staying at Tongsai is the incredibly relaxed atmosphere. There only ever seems to be about ten couples staying in the hotel and no one's bothered what you wear for dinner – if you want to eat in shorts and T-shirts that's fine, but if you feel like dressing up you won't feel out of place. The restaurant beside the pool serves great stir-fries during the day and lots of good European dishes in the evening. Upstairs the Thai food is terrific and it's a lovely place to eat outside by lamp light with the staff fussing around you.

There isn't much of a beach at Tongsai Grand Villas so don't think that this is going to be a major water-sporting hotel. The nearest water-sport facilities, like the bars, are a 15-minute bus ride away. But don't let this put you off as Tongsai Grand Villas is a wonderfully relaxing hotel with a lovely free-form swimming pool and that tremendous deck to get back to.

Other recommended hotels

If all of the above sound too extortionate, don't worry because there's lots of more moderately-priced accommodation in Koh Samui. Talk to the major UK tour operators such as Tropical Places, Kuoni Travel, BA Holidays and Hayes and Jarvis (see pp9-11 for details): they get amazingly good deals on lovely hotels because of the sheer bulk they book in. For example, Tropical Places was recently offering ten days at **Paradise Beach Resort**, a great Thai-style resort hotel overlooking **Maenam Beach**, for US$994/£699 per person including flights, bed and breakfast and transfers, with complimentary upgrade, fruit, flowers, honeymoon cake and bottle of sparkling wine for honeymooners on arrival.

Wherever you're booking from, it's worth giving these companies a call as you might find the price of an international call from the US or Australia could save you a small fortune, or even easier of course, check the Internet.

KRABI

This stunning peninsula, close to the Malaysian border, has so far escaped the commercialization of its sister Thai beach resorts, a situation perhaps largely due to its remote location. This spectacularly beautiful province with its dramatic limestone rock protrusions and sweeping palm-fringed beaches overlooks countless offshore islands, one of which, Phi Phi Island, was the setting for *The Beach*.

Rayavadee Premier Resort

Rayavadee Premier Resort is two hours from Phuket. The journey there can be by speedboat; whizzing through those classic 'James Bond' islands is a great way to arrive. Situated on a peninsula 19km south-west of Krabi, the Rayavadee has access to three white sandy beaches. The 98 delightful two-storey circular pavilions and two villas are scattered around the grounds. Some have their own private Jacuzzi downstairs, and all of them have a good-sized living area connected via a spiral staircase to the bedroom and bathroom above. All the pavilions are equipped with air conditioning,

RAYAVADEE PREMIER RESORT
(☎ 75-620 740, 🖹 75-620 630, 💻 rayavadee@rayavadee.com), 67 Moo 5, Sai Thai-Susan Hoy Road, Tambon Sai Thai, Amphur Muang, Krabi 81000, Thailand
Reservations: The Leading Hotels of the World reservations numbers worldwide (see p12) and most major tour operators/travel agents worldwide
Getting there: The hotel will arrange complimentary transfers from Phuket Airport which take about two hours by bus or speedboat, or you can request a limo
Accommodation: 98 pavilions, 2 villas
Amenities: Krua Phra-Nang restaurant for traditional Thai dishes and fresh seafood, Raya Dining Restaurant, Terrace and Lounge for Asian and continental fare, poolside snack bar and beach bar; Large swimming pool with whirlpool, two floodlit tennis courts, air-conditioned squash court and fitness centre, sauna, massage and Jacuzzi, watersports, snooker and table tennis, video and CD library, boutique, and book and magazine library
Dress code: Elegant casual
Weddings: Can be arranged
Minimum stay: None
Rates: Pavilions from US$490 to US$725; villas from US$1635
Credit cards: Most major
Taxes and service charge: 10% tax and 10% service charge added to your bill

minibar, tea and coffee-making facilities, satellite TV, hi-fi system with CD and cloakroom. Up the spiral staircase the second floor has a king-size bed, double bath, separate shower, hairdryer, bathrobes and slippers, in-room safe, a second TV with satellite and video player. Best of all, the bathroom and bedroom are separated by a wardrobe which cunningly opens on both sides, so you can see the bed from the bath and vice versa. All the restaurants have sea views.

The Rayavadee Premier Resort has had so much publicity since it opened, you'll probably get there and realize you recognize the pool from fashion shoots and travel articles in glossy magazines – the way the freshwater pool floats seamlessly into the sea is now one of the world's classic honeymoon images.

Watersports are rather limited largely because all motorized watersports are banned in order to maintain Krabi's atmosphere of tranquillity. However, snorkelling and scuba diving, windsurfing, dinghy sailing and canoeing are readily available and the beauty of staying here is not really to dash around doing lots of activities, but just to relax in the heavenly surroundings.

The beaches are fantastic and because, because beaches in Thailand are public there's always lots of local action to soak up.

Malaysia
(BEST TIME: ALL YEAR ROUND)

If you are looking for something off the beaten track with unspoilt national parks, very accessible wildlife and an element of adventure, Malaysia is the perfect destination. Malaysia borders Thailand in the north, Singapore and Indonesia to the south and the Philippines to the east. It comprises Peninsular Malaysia and the states of Sabah and Sarawak. Once a British Protectorate, Sarawak and Sabah on the island of Borneo form Eastern Malaysia. Here is South-east Asia at its most untouched, where vast areas of virgin rainforest are sanctuary to some of the world's rarest flora and fauna.

Although Malaysia is blessed with some fabulously luxurious hotels, you have to expect quite basic accommodation in the jungle. The advantage of going to some of the more basic hotels is that you stay in traditional-style buildings, right in the heart of rainforest with wildlife all around, and while the accommodation might be simple, you can expect to find truly delicious local dishes. The local guides are usually great – really informative about the flora and fauna of the region – and take tremendous pride in their country. Most visitors to Malaysia try to take in the mysterious **Mt Kinabalu**, a visit to the **Sepilok Orang-utan Rehabilitation Centre**, a few nights in the jungle and some well-earned rest on one of Malaysia's islands.

MALAYSIA

An area of outstanding natural beauty, exhilarating adventure and luxury hotels – the perfect honeymoon combination

When to go: Malaysia is pretty much a year-round destination: it is almost always warm and humid and has sporadic rainfall

Average maximum temperatures °C

JAN	FEB	MAR	APR	MAY	JUN	JUL	AUG	SEP	OCT	NOV	DEC
32	33	33	33	33	33	32	32	32	32	32	32

Capital: Kuala Lumpur

Flight times: to Kuala Lumpur from:
New York: 19$^{1}/_{2}$ hours
LA (via Sydney): 23 hours
London: 12 hours
Sydney: 8$^{1}/_{2}$ hours

Approximate exchange rates: Ringgit (MYR) (the Ringgit is often referred to as the Malaysian dollar) – £1 = MYR5, US$1 = MYR3.80, A$1 = MYR1.97

Time difference: GMT plus eight hours

Voltage: 220v AC, 50 Hz, square three-pin plugs

Combine with: Singapore and Thailand

Country dialling code: ☎ 60

Further information: 🖳 www.malaysiamydestination.com

PANGKOR ISLAND
Pangkor Laut

A couple of honeymooners I spoke to recently described Pangkor Laut as 'heaven on earth, the ultimate in luxury'. This wonderful island hideaway has certainly built up quite a following over the last few years.

Undoubtedly one of the world's most luxurious and spectacular hotels, Pangkor Laut is set on a private 120-hectare island, where guests are accommodated either in beautifully crafted over-the-water villas, hillside villas with glorious views, or 'estates' – two, three of four bedroom villas each with a private secluded garden. Built like a village, the hotel's architecture is Malaysian in style and exquisitely designed.

Throughout the suites there is superb detailing, but nothing is over the top or overdone: instead the simplistic beauty of wooden floors and locally-made furniture creates a wonderfully tranquil atmosphere making your room the perfect place to retreat to at the end of a day on the beach.

The bathrooms in the hill villas are quite incredible; the reconstituted stone bath is big enough for two and you can lie back in it and look out to sea – if you shut your eyes all you can hear are the sounds of the jungle – and beside the bath is a stone slab just big enough for two gin and tonics.

Whether you stay in an over-the-water villa, an 'estate villa', or up on the hillside,

PANGKOR LAUT
(☎ 05-699 1100, 🖷 05-699 1200), c/o Pangkor Laut Island, Lumut Post Office, 32200 Lumut, Perak, Malaysia

Reservations: Small Luxury Hotels of the World toll-free reservation numbers worldwide (see p12) and most leading tour operators and travel agents

Getting there: The hotel can arrange limo transfers from Kuala Lumpur Airport (US$125/MYR475 per car; three hours), or from Ipoh Airport (US$66/MYR250; one hour) and Penang Airport (US$125/MYR475; three hours); guests are then taken to the island from Lumut by ferry – there are several ferries a day

Accommodation: 125 guest rooms and three suites

Amenities: Fitness centre, hot spa and cold plunge bath, massage, sauna, three swimming pools, two squash courts, three tennis courts, resort boutiques, golf nearby, indoor board games, jungle treks, fishing trips, kayaks, sailing, windsurfing, watersports centre, boating, charter cruises, sunset cruises, TV lounge

Dress code: Smart casual

Weddings: The hotel can host wedding receptions

Minimum stay: None

Rates: Villas from US$184/MYR700 to US$575/MYR2185; Estates from US$8000/MYR30,400

Credit cards: Most major

Taxes and service charge: Included

the suites all have a good-sized area for sitting out on, wooden loungers with really comfortable mattresses and a panoramic view of the bay. For those staying in the hill villas there's a timber tower with a lift that takes you up to your level: the lift stops at the jungle walkway for the semi-detached apartments.

All the restaurants overlook the sea and there's a wide variety to choose from. There is no fixed menu in the Chinese restaurant, just a board with various meats and fish listed: it's up to you to tell the waiter how you'd like it cooked. Breakfasts are absolutely huge and are buffet style.

Most guests spend their days either lying by one of the island's three swimming pools or down at the beach ensconced on a lounger, but there's plenty to do if you feel like being active. Get a map from reception and head off on one of the many walks on the island, or have a game of tennis.

Whatever you choose to do the staff are ready to help you: if you want to go to the beach they immediately radio for a driver who will take you to the other side of the island where the beach is. Once there you are met by one of the beach boys who will take your towels to whichever pair of loungers you choose and will keep your glasses replenished all day long.

At the back of the beach, in amongst the palm trees, there's an octagonal beach bar which does amazing satay and other traditional Malay snacks. Everything about the resort is carefully conceived and perfectly executed, so much so that you'll never want to leave.

LANGKAWI

The Datai

THE DATAI
(☎ 04-959 2500, 🖷 04-959 2600), Jalan Teluk Datai, 07000 Langkawi, Kedah, Malaysia
Reservations: Leading Hotels of the World toll-free reservation numbers worldwide (see p12)
Getting there: The hotel does arrange transfers from Langkawi Airport, costing US$33/MYR125 one way for a limousine
Accommodation: 108 guest rooms: 54 de luxe rooms, 40 villas and 14 suites
Amenities: The Pavilion Thai restaurant, the Beach Club, the Dining Room, lobby lounge, duty free boutiques, beauty salon, car rental, library, white sand beach, two swimming pools, health club with spa, two tennis courts, bicycles, jungle treks, windsurfing, sailing, snorkelling, golf; boat charters and scuba diving can be arranged
Dress code: Elegant casual
Weddings: Can be arranged
Minimum stay: None
Rates: Doubles from US$320/MYR1260; villas from US$380/MYR1450; suites from US$515/MYR1850
Credit cards: Most major
Taxes and service charge: Included

Tucked away on the north-western tip of Langkawi, between the majestic Macincang mountains and the Andaman Sea, is a sumptuous and beautifully-designed hotel, the Datai.

Adrian Zecha, the man behind the fantastic Amanresorts chain, is partly responsible for making this such an amazing resort through his investment and the fact that it is currently run by General Hotel Management, his own management company. The resort certainly has all the Aman hallmarks of perfect design, simple but elegant furnishings made from expensive solid materials – minimal interior decoration and stunning exterior layout.

The hotel's interiors are dominated by the deeply polished red hew of local balau timber, set off by subtle, low-voltage spotlighting and beautiful rustic ornaments. Each room is equipped with luxury mod cons such as air conditioning, king-size bed, humidity controls, satellite TV, private bar and separate shower and bath.

The hotel's cheapest accommodation is in the main building itself, de luxe rooms are 500 metres from the beach, while the 40 villas are scattered up the hillside under the tropical rainforest canopy. Each has its

(Opposite) Top: Camping in style, Amanwana, Moyo Island, Indonesia (see p67). **Bottom:** Tying the knot on the beach, the Philippines. Planning to get married abroad? See p307.

own elevated veranda and sun terrace and is connected to the public facilities via a series of pathways.

Like any truly first-class resort, the Datai's dining and leisure facilities are extremely impressive. During the day you can work up an appetite by swimming in one of the two beautiful pools, sailing, windsurfing or snorkelling from the resort's perfect white sandy beach, or playing tennis or golf. The Datai is a very quiet hotel, with little in the way of evening entertainment apart from the top quality cuisine. The **Pavilion** offers authentic Thai cuisine, while the **Dining Room** serves delicious Malaysian and Western dishes.

We were looking for a mixture of adventure, wildlife and luxury and we got an abundance of all three! Malaysia is still relatively unspoilt which enabled us to feel like true explorers as we were whizzed up tiny rivers in boats, surrounded by thick rainforest, and watched monkeys playing in the trees. The food is delicious, a mixture of Chinese, Indian and Malay – the only negative point is that the alcohol is heavily taxed. Rice wine is lethal but a cheaper option! Accommodation can be basic but this is in true jungle style and if you have a week at Pangkor Laut planned at the end you can put up with anything! One word of advice: don't climb Mt Kinabalu immediately you get there, getting married tends to zap your energy reserves and getting to the peak of Mt Kinabalu requires all the energy you could possible muster!

Charlotte and Ian Cross

Hong Kong
(BEST TIME: ALL YEAR ROUND)

Handing the former colony back to the Chinese hasn't altered the hotel scene in Hong Kong. Hardly a haven for cheap accommodation, it's rather a case of five-star or bust. However, if you are booking your holiday through a tour operator they can often wangle you a spectacular deal for a couple of days' stopover.

Taxis are numerous and readily available, and fares are much lower than in most cities. Red taxis serve Hong Kong Island and Kowloon; the green taxis in the New Territories and the blue ones on Lantau Island are even cheaper. The drivers speak limited English, but the best way to get around the language barrier is have your destination written in Chinese characters.

HONG KONG
A heady mixture of Chinese culture with its temples, markets and tea shops as well as crowded streets, gleaming skyscrapers and luxurious hotels
When to go: All year round, but May to September is hot and humid
Average maximum temperatures °C

JAN	FEB	MAR	APR	MAY	JUN	JUL	AUG	SEP	OCT	NOV	DEC
19	19	21	25	29	30	31	31	30	28	24	21

Airport: Kai Tak International Airport
Flight times: to Hong Kong from:
  New York: 18¾ hours
  LA: 16½ hours
  London 12 hours
  Sydney: 7¾ hours
Approximate exchange rates: Hong Kong dollar (HK$) – £1 = HK$11.09, US$1 = HK$7.80, A$1 = HK$4.05
Time difference: GMT plus eight hours
Voltage: 200v/220v AC, 50 Hz
Combine with: Australia, New Zealand, Malaysia, Thailand, Philippines, India, Singapore
Country dialling code: ☎ 852

(Opposite) Exotic bathrooms on different sides of the globe. **Top:** View from the bath in the De luxe Harbour View suite, Peninsula Hotel, Hong Kong (see p290). **Bottom:** The bathtub is just a step away from the bed in your tent at the luxurious Il Moran Governor's camp, Masai Mara, Kenya (see p233).

It is worth noting that any trip through cross-harbour tunnel has a surcharge, which includes the driver's return toll. Taxi drivers do expect to be tipped, but just round up the fare to the nearest dollar. Note that they cannot pick you up if you're standing on a restricted street (marked by yellow lines).

The **Star Ferry**, which has connected Hong Kong and Kowloon since 1898, runs regularly between 6:30am and 11:30pm and must be one of the cheapest and most scenic ferry rides in the world. It's almost a disappointment that it takes only eight minutes!

The Peninsula

There are scores of top quality hotels in Hong Kong, all with really first-class accommodation and service, but somehow the legendary Peninsula, first opened in 1928, still manages to stand head and shoulders above them all in the romance stakes. For around US$90 the Peninsula will meet you at the airport in one of its fleet of 13 green Rolls-Royce Silver Spurs, which somehow symbolizes everything that is elegant and outrageously decadent about this hotel.

The Peninsula is immaculate and seriously lavish, boasting some of the most incredible skyline views anywhere in the world and a sense of design and opulence that will continually make your mouth drop open. Despite its recent refurbishment, which brought many technological innovations to the hotel, it still retains the colonial elegance and character that its competitors somehow lack. The only disadvantage is its location on the **Kowloon** side, making it not quite so accessible to the night-life of **Central** and **Wan Chai**, but the Star Ferry (see above) and MTR underground run until about midnight. After that you'll have to resort to a taxi: they are pretty cheap but communication can sometimes be tricky (see p289)!

Because the hotel gets so many honeymooners and couples celebrating anniversaries it has now put together what it calls its 'Romance Packages'. These vary in content and price throughout the year, but usually comprise a de luxe room at a special rate of around US$481/HK$3700 including all sorts of glamorous extras such as champagne, breakfast in bed, round trip from the airport in one of the hotel's green Rollers, and even flowers presented by one of the Peninsula's bell boys.

The Peninsula has 246 guest rooms and 54 suites, all of which are equipped with so many mod cons and luxury gadgets there's no point in listing them all.

Suites range in size from the spacious 85 sq metre junior suites to the awesome 370 sq metre Peninsula Suite. Go for one of the De luxe Harbour View Suites which are located in both corners of the hotel's new tower: you get ceiling to floor glass walls on two sides of the bedroom providing panoramic views over Victoria Harbour, and the bathroom's Jacuzzi is strategically placed to make the most of the magnificent

---

THE PENINSULA
(☎ 2920 2888, 🖹 2722 4170), Salisbury Road, Kowloon, Hong Kong
Reservations: The Leading Hotels of the World toll-free reservation numbers worldwide (see p12)
Getting there: Hong Kong International Airport is just 40 minutes by car, the hotel can arrange transfers in one of its green Rolls-Royce Silver Spurs for around US$90/HK$700, or by helicopter for US$962/HK$7500
Accommodation: 246 guest rooms and 54 suites
Amenities: 24-hour currency exchange, florist, hairdresser and beauty salon, health club and spa, helicopter sightseeing tours, fleet of Rolls-Royce Silver Spurs, shopping arcade with 89 shops, sightseeing tours, swimming pool, valet parking service, eight restaurants and two bars
Dress code: Guests are requested not to wear shorts or flip flops in public places
Weddings: The Peninsula caters for both weddings and receptions for a minimum of 80 and a maximum of 120 people
Minimum stay: None
Rates: Doubles cost from around US$442/ HK$3400 for a De luxe Room; Junior suites from around US$727/ HK$5600
Credit cards: Most major
Taxes and service charge: Tax 3%, service charge 10%

THINGS TO SEE AND DO IN HONG KONG

If you're not staying on Hong Kong Island, take the Star Ferry from Kowloon across to the island and the Peak Tram from Central up to **Victoria Peak**. One of the most advanced tram systems in the world, the climb takes only eight minutes and costs HK$20, or HK$30 for a return. The walk around the top is really worth doing for the views, then stop off for lunch or dinner at the *Peak Café* which has excellent food, reasonable prices (for Hong Kong!) and a really good atmosphere – sit in the garden if possible. Or you could try *Café Deco*, which is also good and has awesome views of the city.

A trip to **Stanley**, on the south side of Hong Kong Island, to visit the market is well worth while. There's also a good selection of places to stop for lunch: particularly recommended are *Stanley's Oriental*, *Stanley's French* and *Lucy's*.

There are lots of organized harbour cruises but just as good, a lot more authentic, and significantly cheaper is the ferry journey to **Lantau**, which departs from one of the piers by Central.

All the major designer shops are crammed into Central's **shopping centres** – the Landmark, Prince's Building, Pacific Place and the Galleria. Look out for the World of Joyce in the Galleria, which is Hong Kong's Conran shop and is great for homeware and designer clothes; Shanghai Tang in the Pedder Building is a beautifully laid-out shop and is well worth a visit for its traditional Chinese clothes which have been reworked in amazing fabrics; BeBe, On Lan Street, is a great place to pick up some designer bargains; and Lane Crawford in both Pacific Place and Ocean Terminal is the Harrods of Hong Kong!

If you need to refuel, *Phi-B* on Petticoat Lane and *Antidote* in Soho, are the most happening bars in Central. In the evening, *Blue* on Lyndhurst terrace is the place to see and be seen. Still in Central, there are some good bars on D'Aguilar Street; try *Shermans*, or if you fancy

a bit of live music head for the *Jazz Club* which is open until late.

For antiques and a slightly more Oriental experience Hollywood Road, Cat Street, Western Market and the 'Lanes' in and around Central are all really worth a look.

In terms of markets, **Temple Street Market**, in Tsim Sha Tsui (TST) District, is *the* place to pick up that fake Rolex or Chanel hand-bag, while **Stanley Market** is good for just about everything from tourist junk to good-value clothing. While you're in TST you could eat at *Tutto Bene* on Knutsford Terrace which, although fairly pricey, is a good trendy Italian. Again, make sure you sit outside.

If you're not staying at the Peninsula you must go up to *Felix*, the rooftop restaurant designed by Philippe Starck; it is worth visiting even if it's just for a drink.

If you're on the look out for authentic Chinese food, the *American Peking Restaurant* on Lockhart Road, Wan Chai, is very reasonable and popular with gweilos (Westerners working in Hong Kong) and, better still, the waiters actually speak and understand English! Try the *Chinese Thai Restaurant* in Shek O for a really authentic South-east Asian eating experience. If you want upmarket Cantonese head for *Number 1 Harbour Road* at the Grand Hyatt Hotel: it's probably the best in town though it's painfully expensive.

Macau

Macau, situated on a tiny peninsula at the mouth of the Pearl River, is linked to mainland China by a narrow isthmus, and is only 55 minutes away from Hong Kong by jet foil. This Portuguese colony has some fantastic hotels and a totally different atmosphere from Hong Kong.

For more information on what to do in Hong Kong, visit the Tourist Board's website: 🖳 www.hkta.org

---

harbour and Kowloon city vistas. The views are totally captivating by day and even more so at night as thousands of lights glitter on the island.

One of the best things about the Peninsula is the fantastically designed **Felix** rooftop restaurant, located right up on the 28th floor. Designed by Philippe Starck, the décor is about as incredible as the views making it one of the most superbly romantic places to enjoy cocktails and dinner. And if you find yourselves slightly overdoing it, don't worry, you can always recuperate in the distinctly Venetian-looking health spa and swimming pool, or on the sundeck.

Other recommended hotels

The bathrooms in the de luxe suites of the **Regent Hong Kong** (☎ 2721 1211, 📄 2739 4546, 🖳 www.fourseasons.com, 18 Salisbury Road, Tsim Sha Tsui, Kowloon) have the ultimate view from their Jacuzzi baths: you can lie back sipping champagne as the sun sets behind the myriad of skyscrapers and over Victoria Harbour. It's the bell boys in spotless white uniforms, the vast fleet of gleaming Daimlers, the knowledge that your every wish is being taken care of by a 24-hour butler, that makes the Regent such a slick hotel. Almost two-thirds of its 602 bedrooms overlook the harbour, while ultimate hedonists gravitate towards the De Luxe Terrace suites featuring outdoor Jacuzzis which look straight on to the harbour. Otherwise there is Hong Kong's largest private outdoor swimming pool to relax in, three outdoor spa pools which are set in granite with glass walls to maximize the views, and the most fantastic indoor spa. Doubles cost from US$481/HK$3750 city view, US$609/HK$4750 harbour view.

The **Mandarin Oriental** (☎ 2522 0111, 📄 2810 6190, 🖥 www.mandarinorien tal.com, 5 Connaught Road Central, Hong Kong) has the sort of solid reputation that the colonial Far East was built on.

For over 30 years this hotel has been among the best of the luxury hotels in Hong Kong. It is without doubt the most wonderful refuge from the madness that is Hong Kong, a place of utter indulgence and sophistication. Set in the middle of the business centre it also boasts wonderful harbour views. With a ratio of two staff to each guest you'll be looked after admirably. Double rooms cost from US$256/HK$1999 for a city view and from US$346/HK$2699 for a de luxe harbour view.

Australia
(BEST TIME: ALL YEAR ROUND)

Australia, the world's largest island and its smallest continent, is increasingly popular as a honeymoon destination. It is a land of dramatic contrasts which has, quite simply, got the lot. A honeymoon in Australia will allow you to experience the outback, listen to the thrilling sounds of tropical rainforests, sail among offshore islands or in coastal waterways, dive on the world's largest coral reef, or just lie on deserted beaches in some of the most luxurious resorts imaginable. Australia also has one of the world's most vibrant, beautiful and cosmopolitan cities. When you land in Sydney and see the sun shining on the distinctive white sails of the Opera House with the harbour glistening before you, you'll know you've picked the right place for your honeymoon.

Two weeks is plenty of time to see lots of Australia but, because the country is so huge, I suggest you break down your trip to three or four 'must see' areas. Most travellers to Australia have three principal sights in mind: the Great Barrier Reef and Queensland's Gold Coast, Sydney, and Ayers Rock. But you could quite easily forget all about Ayers Rock: it's a long way out and do you really want to be shepherded around somewhere sandy and rocky with the blistering heat burning down on you, as part of a group of

---

AUSTRALIA

Big sunshine, crashing surf, sandy beaches, diving and snorkelling on the Great Barrier Reef, stunning Sydney, and vast tracts of untouched tropical rainforest and rugged outback
When to go: The climate ranges from temperate in the south to tropical in the north, so there is year-round sunshine in Queensland (although May and September are the driest months), while November to March is the best time to visit Sydney
Average maximum temperatures °C

	JAN	FEB	MAR	APR	MAY	JUN	JUL	AUG	SEP	OCT	NOV	DEC
Sydney	26	26	25	22	19	17	16	18	20	22	24	25
Cairns	31	31	30	29	28	26	26	27	28	29	31	31

Capital: Canberra
Flight times:
    to Sydney from:
        New York: (via LA) 17½ hours
        LA: 12 hours
        London: (via LA) 24 hours
    to Cairns from:
        New York: (via LA) 23½ hours
        LA: 18 hours
        London: 19 hours
Approximate exchange rates: Australian dollar (A$) – £1 = A$2.54, US$1 = A$1.82
Time difference: Queensland: GMT plus nine hours
Voltage: 240v/250v AC, 50 Hz, three-pin plugs
Combine with: Los Angeles, Malaysia, Singapore, Hong Kong, Thailand, New Zealand, Fiji
Country dialling code: ☎ 61
Further information: Australian Tourist Commission 🖳 www.australia.com

tourists, on your honeymoon? It's far better to concentrate your time experiencing the beautiful islands off the Great Barrier Reef, or on the Sunshine Coast in the popular resort of Noosa, combined with a few days in Sydney, perhaps also fitting in a brief stay in the nearby Blue Mountains to give you some experience of the Australian bush.

SYDNEY

After Olympic-fever gave it world exposure, it would be hard to miss out Sydney. Situated on a magnificent natural harbour, a few days here is a great way to start your holiday. In just three days you can see a lot but if you're feeling too tired to do much sightseeing, hop on a ferry and cross the harbour to one of the city's beaches.

The Park Hyatt Sydney

Since it opened in 1990, the Park Hyatt Sydney has become established as a hotel with a view. Whether you are in the award winning, theatre-style harbour-kitchen restaurant enjoying an informal lunch or sitting gazing at the harbour lights from your balcony at night, the view is just staggering. The hotel is situated in the fashionable Rocks District and is so close to the water you can virtually reach out and touch it.

A classic boutique hotel with 158 recently refurbished rooms and suites, the Park Hyatt Sydney is a great deal more intimate than most of the neighbouring international hotels and it was cleverly designed to maximize its greatest asset – the view of the harbour and the Opera House. The four-storey hotel follows the contours of the harbour wall nestled beneath the Harbour Bridge, so from the moment you walk into the 'lobby' – where instead of a traditional reception you check in at an antique desk – you'll be utterly mesmerized by the view. The vast expanse of polished granite, marble and sandstone run up to sheet-glass windows and doors beyond which everything is blue – it's almost like being on a ship.

Most of the rooms have balconies, all have air conditioning, separate dressing rooms, wide-screen TVs, VCRs, and personal butler service as well as hordes of other impressive gadgets such as remote control curtains. Understated elegance is the theme of the décor with light hues and stylish, contemporary furniture.

As a result of the numerous requests received from guests insisting on having a room with a harbour view, the Park Hyatt Sydney's rooms are now ranked in four different categories, so you know in advance what you are getting. De luxe Harbour rooms have floor to ceiling windows leading to a private balcony, with views of Campbells and Sydney Cove – without an opera house in sight! De luxe Opera Rooms, as you'd expect, have perfect picture postcard views of Sydney's most

---

THE PARK HYATT SYDNEY
(☎ 2-9241 1234, 🖷 2-9256 1555), 7 Hickson Road, The Rocks, NSW 2000, Australia
Reservations: Hyatt Reservation numbers worldwide (see p13), or in the UK through tour operator Elegant Resorts (see p13)
Getting there: 25 minutes by taxi from Sydney International Airport, the hotel can arrange private transfers for you by limousine or taxi
Accommodation: 158 guest rooms, most with balconies: 122 rooms, 31 Executive Studios, three Premier Suites, Diplomatic Suite and Governor Suite
Amenities: 24-hour butler service, wardrobe storage service for travelling guests, daily laundry and dry-cleaning service, harbourkitchen&bar, the Club Bar, Rooftop Terrace, the Spa including sauna, steam room, fitness centre, outdoor Jacuzzi and rooftop swimming pool and sundeck
Dress code: Smart casual
Weddings: The Park Hyatt caters for weddings big and small and has all sorts of packages on offer, such as a reception for a minimum of 40 guests in the Rooftop Terrace including welcome canapés, a gourmet buffet and drinks, wedding night in a harbour-view room with champagne on arrival and breakfast for the bride and groom the following morning
Minimum stay: None
Rates: Harbour view rooms from US$329/A$600; Opera House view rooms from US$357/A$650
Credit cards: Most major
Taxes and service charge: Included

famous building, while the Executive Harbour Studios are junior suites with an open-plan living area and bedroom, plus two private balconies looking out over the harbour.

There can be few more invigorating ways to start your day than swimming in the hotel's roof-top pool or just lounging in the outdoor Jacuzzi, before enjoying breakfast on the sun-drenched terrace looking out over the harbour. The famous yellow ferries shuttle commuters in from the north side, and the incessantly tacking sail boats remind you that this is a city where leisure is taken seriously. The Park Hyatt may be the most expensive five-star hotel in Sydney but, if you can afford it, it's worth the extra for the views and service, especially if you are not going to be in the city for long.

The Observatory Hotel

The Observatory is just around the corner, slightly set back from the harbour. Although it doesn't have the views of the Opera House, it is a splendidly luxurious town house hotel with a warm atmosphere and was voted one of the five best city hotels by Andrew Harper's 'Hideaways of the Year'. The hotel is in the fashionable Rocks District and

within easy walking distance of Sydney Harbour Bridge, the Opera House, and Circular Quay. It is widely regarded as the most comfortable hotel in Sydney.

An Orient-Express Hotel, each room in the Observatory lives up to the fastidious standards set by this hotel group. All are spacious, elegant and beautifully decorated with fine antiques, paintings and tapestries, and feature first-class facilities including television, two phones, in-room safe, hairdryer, fully-stocked minibar, CD and video player with remote control. The Observatory is one of those hotels where everything looks new and extremely plush, from the heavy curtains in the bedroom to the thick carpeting underfoot and the properly fluffy towels. It all feels marvellously expensive!

The fabulous marble bathrooms have the kind of baths, with lashings of bath salts and other goodies, that ensure you look forward to getting ready to go out each evening. They also have huge walk-in showers where the jets spray you from every angle, and lovely Molton Brown toiletries.

But the biggest luxury of all at the Observatory is the swimming pool and spa facilities. Above the 20m pool is a ceiling of fibre-optic lights, designed to recreate the constellations of the Southern Hemisphere. Adjacent to the pool is a Jacuzzi, sauna and

> **THE OBSERVATORY HOTEL**
> (☎ 2-9256 2222, 🖷 2-9256 2233), 89-113 Kent Street, Sydney, NSW 2000, Australia
> **Reservations**: Through Orient-Express Hotels (🖳 www.orient-expresshotels. com), the Leading Hotels of the World reservation numbers worldwide (see p12), or UK tour operators such as ITC Classics, or Elegant Resorts (see p13)
> **Getting there**: Approximately 25 minutes from the airport by local taxi, or the hotel can arrange collection in a limousine at a cost of US$46/A$90
> **Accommodation**: 100 rooms: 79 de luxe rooms, 8 junior suites, 12 executive suites, and the Observatory Suite
> **Amenities**: Drawing room, Globe bar, Galileo Restaurant offering modern Australian cuisine with an Italian influence, 20m star-lit pool, gymnasium, massage, sauna, steam room, flotation tank, tennis court, valet parking, 24-hour room service
> **Dress code**: Smart casual
> **Weddings**: The hotel does cater for weddings with a marriage celebrant present and can host pretty much any kind of reception you want
> **Minimum stay**: None
> **Rates**: De luxe doubles from US$323/ A$630, suites from US$421/US$821
> **Credit cards**: Most major
> **Taxes and service charge**: Included

steam room, as well as massage rooms and float-tank facilities – guaranteed to ease jet lag or the after-effects of a night on the town.

Although you probably won't be staying in to make the most of them, the Observatory's dining facilities are also good: the formal **Galileo Restaurant** was designed to resemble the famous Venetian restaurant, Harry's Bar. If you are just after a drink then the club-like atmosphere of the **Globe Bar** with its cedar panelled walls is a good place to sit for a pre-dinner gin and tonic. There is also a drawing room with an open fireplace.

THINGS TO SEE AND DO IN SYDNEY

For the best views of the **Opera House** stop for lunch, or just a drink at the Park Hyatt – even if you can't afford to stay there it's worth popping in because the views are just awesome and a constant reminder of where you are! Whether you stay there or not, go to the **Rocks**: it's a great place to cruise around, shop and sit in pavement cafés, especially at weekends when you'll often find live bands playing on the streets. It is the oldest part of Sydney, but the whole area has undergone substantial gentrification over the last decade and, as well as being a cool place to wander about, it also has the best city views. You can climb to the top of the **Sydney Harbour Bridge** for spectacular 360-degree views with BridgeClimb (ticket hotline ☎ 2-8274 7777, ⌨ www.bridgeclimb.com); open 7am to 7pm. If you want a bird's eye view consider a scenic flight over the harbour and city with Sydney Harbour Seaplanes.

If you are even half-way interested in opera, then attending a performance at the Opera House is a must. Walking up the steps, all dressed up, with those famous white peaks towering above you and a faint breeze lifting off the harbour, has to be one of the most magical experiences in the world. Contact **Sydney Opera House Tourism Services** (☎ 2-9250 7870, ▤ 2-9252 2085; ⌨ soh.nsw.gov.au) about a dinner and performance package.

If you just want to look around this magnificent building but aren't so keen on opera, do one of the **guided tours** which leaves the lower forecourt level between 9am and 4pm daily.

Without doubt the best way to get a sense of the real Sydney is to hop on a yellow **ferry**, or an organized cruise, from Circular Quay – you get the best views of the Opera House and Harbour Bridge from the water. Head for one of the harbour beaches, such as **Balmoral** or **Camp Cove**, or **Palm Beach** which is further north but is easy to get to via seaplane from Rose Bay, on the south side of Sydney Harbour.

One of the best things to do on a sunny day in Sydney is to take a ferry trip out to **Watson's Bay**, over the other side of the Harbour, for lunch on the beach at *Doyle's*, the renowned seafood restaurant at 11 Marine Parade. Get the concierge at your hotel to book you a table on the beachfront.

On Saturdays the market at **Paddington** is definitely worth a visit: spend the morning there looking around the many stalls which have everything from candles to clothes made by young local designers; remember to take cash with you as very few stalls take credit cards. Once you're done in the market pop into *Bistro LuLu*, (☎ 2-9380 6888) 257 Oxford Street, owned by one of Australia's most popular chefs and serving modern French-style dishes.

Bibliophiles should go to **Berkellouws Book Sellers**, (☎ 2-9560 3200) 70 Norton Street, Leichardt, where there is a great coffee shop amongst the second-hand books. The food is scrummy and there are all sorts of interesting looking people and books there.

No visit to Sydney would be complete without an afternoon on **Bondi Beach**, or its smaller neighbour, **Tamarama**. Bondi was cleaned up after the city council realized that one of their hottest tourist attractions was actually turning into a bit of a dump. There are still more beautiful beaches in the world but it is a fun place to stroll around and of course, great for a bit of body surfing. If you're feeling peckish on the way back from the beach in the early evening, stop for a beer and some delicious snacks at *Bondi Tratt*, 34 Campbell Parade, or for modern Australian cuisine try *Hugo's* (☎ 2-9300 0900 – book ahead, 70 Campbell Parade).

For other hip haunts head back into town to *SALT* (☎ 2-9332 2566) 229 Darlinghurst Rd, Darlinghurst, which won Good Food Awards' 'Best new restaurant 2000', and on to *Lime Bar*, 114 Darlinghurst Rd, to taste a bit of Sydney's hot dance culture. Alternatively, if you can't get into Hugo's in Bondi, *Hugo's Lounge* at Level 1, 33 Bayswater Road, Kings Cross, also serves modern Australian food.

For other ideas check out the honeymoon section at ⌨ www.visitnsw.com.au or ⌨ www.australia.com.

Other recommended hotels

Nestled in the picturesque Rocks district, the five-star **ANA Harbour Grand Hotel Sydney** (☎ 2-9250 6000, ▤ 2-9250 6250, ⌨ www.anahotels.com.au, 176 Cumberland Street) is opulent and gracious: Venetian crystal chandeliers, exquisite décor and an enviable collection of fine art set the tone. But people come here for the unparalleled views – it is the only harbour hotel where every room has an uninterrupted view over the water. It also boasts the largest rooms in town.

The 'Romance at the Rocks' package costs from US$232/A$453 per couple and includes accommodation in a de luxe Corner View Room, Australian bubbly on arrival, breakfast in your room and late check-out.

THE BLUE MOUNTAINS

Just over an hour directly west of Sydney are the Blue Mountains, named after the blue haze which perpetually hangs over these vast craggy mountains, allegedly produced by the combination of oil from the thousands of eucalyptus trees and the sunlight. The principal recreation in the Blue Mountains is bush walking: impressive sandstone cliffs soaring up to 5000ft, thundering waterfalls, Aboriginal heritage and abundant native wildlife are just some of what you'll see on the 100km of walks. Abseiling, horse-riding and other outdoor activities are all available. For the less energetic, the mountains can be seen to equal effect on horseback or with any of the many tour companies operating four-wheel drive, cycling and train tours in the area, or even on the back of a Harley Davidson.

With a spectacular view over the famous **Three Sisters** from the front-facing windows, the Orient-Express-owned **Lilianfels Blue Mountains** (☎ 47-801 200, 🖹 47-801 300, 🖳 reservations@lilianfel.com.au, Lilianfels Avenue, Echo Point, Katoomba, NSW 2780) won't let you down. Having won several awards for its service and food, it is rated as one of Australia's foremost hotels.

Lilianfels is a lovely place to spend a few days of your honeymoon taking in the invigorating mountain air and enjoying the hotel's fantastic health facilities. It is equally popular for weddings which are held in the immaculately-kept gardens with the most magical of backdrops.

If you can, opt for one of the five suites as they have more character than the bedrooms. Prettily furnished in strong colours, they have Jacuzzi baths, beautiful antique furniture and staggering views over the mountains.

Double rooms cost US$176/A$343 and suites from US$240/A$468; book through Orient-Express Hotels (🖳 www.orient-expresshotels.com), or Small Luxury Hotels of the World toll-free reservation numbers (see p12).

There are also a few small and lovely boutique hotels. **Cleopatra** (☎ 02-4787 8456, 🖹 02-487 6092, 🖳 cleopat@ozemail.com.au) is a five-bedroomed, 19th-century, listed homestead turned luxury hideaway in a dramatic garden designed by Paul Sorensen. Listed in *Tatler*'s 101 Best Hotels 2001, it offers the best modern Australian cuisine for miles. Doubles cost from US$85/A$167, suite from US$142/A$278. **Whispering Pines by the Falls** is a beautiful old wooden heritage building in the woods, just minutes from the start of the best walking trails. One of UK tour operator Bridge the World's 'Little Gems' (☎ 020-7734 7447). Doubles cost from US$87/£170.

Fur further information visit 🖳 www.bluemountaintourism.org.au.

Quay West Apartments (☎ 2-9240 6000, 🖹 2-9240 6060, 🖳 www.mirvac hotels.com.au, 98 Gloucester Street, The Rocks) are a luxurious alternative to a traditional hotel room – villa living on the harbour. Quay West offers all the comfort and services of a world-class hotel but with more privacy and independence. Next to the ANA on Circular Quay, harbour-view apartments offer similarly stunning views.

All apartments have a spacious sitting room, bathroom and well-equipped kitchen and guests have use of a swimming pool, spa and sauna, restaurant and room service. A one-bedroom harbour view apartment costs from US$246/$A480 per couple. Book through UK tour operator Tailor Made Travel (☎ 01386-712 046).

QUEENSLAND

A honeymoon in Queensland can be as lazy, exhilarating, tranquil, glitzy, laid-back or sophisticated as you want. You can choose between spending long days lounging around on the beach, scuba diving amongst the coral and tropical fish of the Great Barrier Reef, walking through the noisy jungle, living it up at the casinos or even exploring the beautiful Whitsunday Islands with the privacy afforded by your own chartered yacht.

Queensland, the state where kangaroos outnumber people, is absolutely huge. But despite its size it is relatively easy to explore thanks to the great network of internal flights from Sydney, as well as a number of direct international flights flying straight into Queensland's 'gateway' towns of **Cairns**, **Townsville** and **Brisbane**.

The Sunshine Coast

Outside Australia, people only think of the islands of the Great Barrier Reef when they think of Australia's coast, but native Australians are just as fond of the Sunshine Coast below **Fraser Island** and, in particular, **Noosa**. A cosmopolitan village of restaurants, boutiques and sidewalk cafés, the real beauty about Noosa is that it is also just minutes away from beaches, rainforest, bushland, everglades and lakes. The best time to visit this vibrant coastal town is between October and April and make sure you stay on the river or on the bay. Noosa is brimming over with great restaurants but do go to **The Salt Water**, which is known for its amazing seafood.

If you want to really pamper yourselves the **Sheraton Noosa Resort** (☎ 7-5449 4888, 🖹 7-5449 2230, 🖳 www.sheraton.com, 14-16 Hastings Street, Noosa Heads) is most luxurious. This lovely caramel-coloured hotel, with its blue balconies overlooking the swimming pool, provides a stylish base on Noosa's Hastings Street. All the rooms are spacious with private balconies and well equipped with either a king-size or two double beds, kitchenette and spa baths in addition to all the usual luxuries. Apart from Noosa's many restaurants on the doorstep, the Sheraton also has **Cato's**, its own speciality grill and seafood restaurant, a beachfront restaurant, pool and cocktail bar. Doubles cost from US$128/A$250 for a Noosa view room to US$141/A$275 for a pool view; pool side villa from US$182/A$355. Call toll-free from the US (☎ 800-325 3535) and from the UK (☎ 800-325 353535) or visit 🖳 www.sheraton.com for international reservation numbers.

ISLANDS OF THE GREAT BARRIER REEF

The **Whitsunday Islands**, once the tips of ancient mountains scattered either side of **Whitsunday Passage**, are among the safest and most scenic sailing waters in the world. This group of 74 hilly and wooded islands, many of them fringed with reefs, were originally named by Captain Cook in 1770. Today only nine of the 74 have been developed for tourism.

Further up the coast, are the **Family Group** of islands of which **Bedarra** and **Dunk** are particularly famous resorts, and much further still is **Lizard**, Australia's northernmost island.

Hayman Island

Hayman Island is without doubt the best known of the Whitsunday Islands, and arguably the most celebrated, exclusive and luxurious hotel in Australia. A totally self-contained resort, Hayman has been owned and operated by Ansett Australia since the late 1980s when the company totally redeveloped the island with the aim of creating a resort that would rank among the finest in the world. They have succeeded in creating an extremely swanky resort – it is the only one of Australia's island resorts that has been invited to become a member of the Leading Hotels of the World. A holiday at Hayman is all about indulgence, pleasure, elegance and the most attentive service imaginable, on an island no bigger than 8km in circumference.

The most northerly of the Whitsunday Islands, Hayman is also one of the closest to the Great Barrier Reef, so the opportunities for diving are really first rate.

The hotel is a 50-minute boat trip away from Hamilton Island – easily accessible from Sydney, Brisbane or Cairns. From the moment you are handed a glass of chilled champagne aboard *Sun Goddess*, one of the hotel's private luxury launches, for the trip to Hayman itself, you'll know you are in for a treat. The resort's unique architectural style comprises three-storey modern buildings with tiered white terraces, so that from the side they resemble a cruise ship. Each tier has a succession of balconies overlooking the most fantastic array of swimming pools, joined by jetty-like walkways and interspersed with lofty palms and lush tropical foliage. The overall effect is just like something out of a James Bond movie.

To complement the island's extraordinary natural beauty – two white coral beaches and glistening clear blue waters as far as the eye can see – the hotel has six restaurants serving exquisite food from casual Italian to formal French, and Oriental seafood. The range of sporting facilities is equally impressive, including a large saltwater swimming pool, two freshwater pools, a golf target range, a state of the art health club, tennis and squash courts as well as a huge range of watersports. Nothing is done on a small scale at Hayman; the West Wing Pool – after massive refurbishment in 2000 it's now known as the Pool Wing – is seven times the size of an Olympic pool!

Inside, soft neutral colours and the cooling honey-coloured marble produce a restful air, while the bedroom furnishings are extremely plush incorporating floral designs and pastel plaids. The 203 rooms and suites and 11 penthouses are all luxuriously appointed with air conditioning, ceiling fans, phones, television and videos, radio, tea and coffee-making facilities, in-room safe, hairdryers, minibars, plus beautiful marble bathrooms with toiletries and bathrobes. Each room also has a private balcony or terrace overlooking either the swimming pools, the tropical gardens, or southwards over the beach across the Whitsunday Passage.

The staff will arrange day trips taking the two of you out to nearby **Bali Hai** and **Langford Reef**, two popular picnic and snorkelling spots, leaving you all alone to wallow in your private island paradise. Or else charter one of the island's fully crewed yachts and explore these stunning blue seas and islands under your own steam for a few days.

HAYMAN ISLAND
(☎ 7490 1234, 🖷 7490 1567, 💻 www.hayman.com.au), Great Barrier Reef, North Queensland 4801, Australia
Reservations: The Leading Hotels of the World toll-free reservation numbers worldwide (see p12)
Getting there: 50 minutes by luxury launch from Hamilton Island, which is reached by flights from Cairns, Brisbane, Sydney and all major Australian cities on a daily basis
Accommodation: 170 rooms, 33 suites and 11 penthouses overlooking the pools, grounds, and beaches
Amenities: 24-hour room service, six restaurants and three bars, three swimming pools, boutiques, information centre and activities desk, weekly activities programme including bush-walking, a huge selection of watersports including para-sailing, waterskiing, windsurfing, diving courses, sailing aboard the resort's yachts, six floodlit tennis courts, squash, putting green, table tennis, Hayman Health Club, Hernando's night-club
Dress code: Smart casual attire for all restaurants except La Fontaine where a jacket is required for men
Weddings: Weddings are so popular on Hayman that they've built a Wedding Chapel called Stella Maris, which is used in addition to the Swan Pond, the formal garden and the beach as a wedding venue; ask about the 'Pure Indulgence Wedding' package which costs around US$1537/A$2995 and includes everything from arrival in a Silver Cloud Rolls-Royce to being dropped off on an island with champagne at sunset.
Minimum stay: None
Rates: Palm-garden view double from US$283/A$544 to US$437/A$852; suite from US$762/A$1485, penthouse from US$960/A$1870 with buffet breakfast; special extra package for honeymooners
Credit cards: Most major
Taxes and service charge: Included

Lizard Island

Lizard Island is Australia's most northerly island resort located 240km north-east of Cairns and, as such, continues to be one of the most unspoilt and naturally beautiful of the islands on the Great Barrier Reef.

Lizard is so far north that even after landing at Cairns you'll have a further one-hour flight to the island. Once you get there you'll know it was worth it. If you are seeking a tropical island and underwater paradise, but don't want to share it with hordes of other tourists, it's worth making the effort to get up to Lizard. And following an A$14 million total refurbishment which finished in July 2000, you'll be seeing Lizard at its best.

The island, named after its first inhabitants, the monitor lizards, is blessed with 24 pristine white sandy beaches, 1000 hectares of environmentally protected woodland, and

LIZARD ISLAND
(☎ 7-4060 8999, 🖷 7-4060 3991), Lizard Island, Great Barrier Reef Resort, North Queensland 4870, Australia
Reservations: Through P&O (🖥 www.poresorts.com) or UK tour operator Tailor Made Travel (see p13)
Getting there: One hour from Cairns in a private plane or with Macair; the planes land on the island
Accommodation: 40 guest rooms: 16 Sunset Point villas, two family rooms, 18 Anchor Bay suites
Amenities: Freshwater swimming pool, full range of watersports including sailing, fishing and scuba diving, glass-bottom boat cruises, dining room, lounge, bar, tennis, room service
Dress code: Casual
Weddings: Both ceremonies and receptions are occasionally catered for
Minimum stay: None
Rates: From US$323/A$630 per person per night including all meals and many island activities
Credit cards: Most major
Taxes and service charge: Included

some of the most incredible diving available anywhere along this coast: the diverse underwater attractions include 150-year-old clams and the ridiculous-looking potato cod fish.

The 40 guest rooms, set among coconut palms on the wonderfully sheltered **Anchor Bay**, come in three different styles. The 18 Anchor Bay suites have magnificent views, while the two family rooms have separate living areas and are superbly comfortable. All the suites have a balcony with views of the bay, private facilities, air conditioning, ceiling fans, one king or twin double beds (so make sure that you state that you want a king-size bed), minibar, writing desk, phone, iron/ironing board, hairdryer and bathrobes.

Lizard is an all-inclusive resort where meals, bush walks and many watersports are included in the basic tariff. You won't have to pay for dinghies, paddle-skis, waterskiing, fishing gear and bait, catamarans, sailboards or snorkelling equipment, but you do have to pay for scuba-diving lessons and equipment hire, game-fishing charters, Great Barrier Reef trips, all refreshments and alcohol.

The hotel's bar and restaurant have a very relaxed club-like atmosphere, where guests often join each other for drinks, though you don't have to worry about your privacy being invaded too much – there is plenty of space on this lovely remote island.

Other recommended hotels

Bedarra Island (☎ 7-4068 8233, Bedarra Island 4854, Great Barrier Reef, North Queensland) is a very luxurious and equally expensive all-inclusive private island retreat. Twenty minutes in a private launch from Dunk Island, Bedarra is unashamedly elitist; no children under 16 years of age are allowed, nor are day-visitors, so the entire island is reserved for the privileged 31 guests housed in the luxuriously appointed 15 beachside villas.

The rooms, either split-level or two-storey, have beautifully polished wood floors and walls, elegant pine and rattan furniture, a king-size bed covered in warm tones of salmon pink, and all mod cons such as TV/VCR, minibars and air conditioning. A week of this kind of luxury, with the champagne and vintage wines flowing from the 24-hour bar, will set you back a pretty substantial US$410/A$800 per person per night including all meals, open bar, accommodation and all island activities.

Following an A$8million refurbishment completed in 2000, **Dunk Island** (☎ 70-688 199, 🖥 www.poresorts.com, Brammo Bay, Dunk Island 4810, North Queensland), a truly beautiful hideaway, has been given a contemporary look and a new spa.

Tracts of virgin rainforest, sweeping arcs of golden sand and lush green gardens full of soaring palm trees cover the island. One of only three true rainforest islands on the coast, Dunk is a lush home to native fauna and flora, cool walking trails, a real Australian farm, and some fantastic big-game fishing. Dunk is an island offering lots of activities, but a word of warning – it is not child-free.

Just 5km off the mainland's Mission Beach, midway between Cairns and Townsville, Dunk is reached by either a 30-minute flight from Cairns or a 45-minute flight from Townsville. With four grades of accommodation, from Banfield Units set in the gardens to the superb Bayview villas, the island offers a wide range of prices: a five-night Dunk Island package starts from US$377/A$735 per person per night which includes breakfast, dinner with nightly entertainment and lots of activities.

The **Beach Club** (🖳 www.hamiltonisland.com.au), a couples-only five-star boutique resort on Hamilton Island opened in 2000, now offers a reason to go for active couples who like to have the best of both worlds. Scenic and romantic walks through forests and pristine, secluded beaches co-exist with plenty of activities should you want them. Hamilton is one of the most easily accessible islands by air from Sydney, Brisbane and Cairns and a good-value alternative to some of the other islands. The 55 minimalist, designer rooms all have private balconies with spectacular views of the Coral Sea and Whitsunday Islands. It also has a private swimming pool, music room, library and exclusive Club Lounge.

The 'Honeymoon & Indulgence' package from US$1207/A$2352 per couple includes champagne and chocolates on arrival, four nights' accommodation, breakfast buffet, three-course dinner in Hamilton Island's signature restaurant, the Beach House, and a twilight sail. Book direct, or through UK tour operators Travel Portfolio (☎ 01284-762255, 🖳 tpuk@globalnet.co.uk), or Kuoni or Bridge The World (see pp9- 13).

Into the rainforest

Silky Oaks (☎ 7-4098 1666, Daintree Rainforest, Mossman River Gorge, North Queensland), owned by P&O, is located 80km north of Cairns which makes it a great base from which to explore **Cape Tribulation National Park**. Perched high up in the mountains above the Mossman River Gorge, Silky Oaks' guests stay in tree houses, which are en suite and have some luxuries including a fan, tea and coffee-making facilities and a hairdryer. The hotel offers four-wheel drive wilderness safaris to **Daintree River** and **Cape Tribulation**, as well as day trips to the Great Barrier Reef. Doubles cost from US$219/A$426.

The **Daintree Ecolodge and Spa** (☎ 7-4098 6100, 🖹 7-4098 6200, 🖳 www.dain tree-ecolodge.com.au, 20 Daintree Road, Daintree Village, North Queensland 4873), also deep in the rainforest has managed to incorporate satellite TVs as well as Jacuzzis

---

THE GREAT BARRIER REEF

The Great Barrier Reef, one of Queensland's three **World Heritage** sites, is the largest marine park in the world and a scuba diver's paradise. Extending along Queensland's coastline from Cape York at the tip of mainland Australia to Gladstone in the south, the reef is more than 2000km long and comprises 2900 individual reefs and 74 coral islands. It was formed 10,000 years ago and today supports an incredibly diverse and dense population of 10,000 species of sponge, 350 different species of coral, 4000 species of molluscs, and 1500 species of fish and mammals from swarming pelagics to massive humpback whales.

The reef also has some of the **best wall diving in the world**, especially in the outer sections of the Barrier Reef, the Coral Sea or Oceanic Reefs, where sheer walls of coral disappear into the sea floor hundreds of metres below. It is not uncommon to find yourself swimming alongside sea snakes measuring about two metres long, reef sharks, giant Potato Cod, Manta Rays and turtles.

You can dive in Queensland all year round, but the most consistently good weather is between August and January. The variety of diving on offer is quite astounding. While many of the best reef dives are reached by charter boat, on some coral cays and islands you can literally walk off the beach and dive into a coral world. There are also many excellent locations for beach and river diving. If you prefer to stay dry, you can view the coral and fish through underwater observatories.

Yacht charter operator, the **Moorings** runs sailing charters on a wide range of boats around Hamilton Island and through the Whitsundays. Charters can be booked either through the Moorings' office in Australia toll-free (☎ 1-300 363 300), with the UK office (☎ 01227-776 677, 🖹 01227-776 670), in the US toll-free (☎ 800-835 7742) or through 🖳 www.moorings. com.

For more ideas visit the Queensland Tourism site: 🖳 www.queenslandholidays. com.au.

THE GREAT SOUTH PACIFIC EXPRESS

The **Great South Pacific Express** (GSPE) is the first five-star hotel on wheels in the Southern Hemisphere and is a great way to see some of the expansive countryside.

The GSPE, Australia's first long-distance luxury train, began scheduled services in April 1999 and offers a year-round service from Brisbane to Cairns and Brisbane to Sydney. Since January 2001, Brisbane to Sydney services go via the Hunter Valley vineyards, the Blue Mountains west of Sydney (see box p297) and the capital city, Canberra.

A Pullman/State compartment Sydney to Brisbane for three days/two nights costs US$920/A$1200. Book a trip on the GSPE through Orient-Express (🖳 www.orient-express.com).

For further information see *Australia by Rail* by Colin Taylor (Trailblazer, see p318).

---

in its 15 air-conditioned 'treehouses', set high in the rainforest canopy. It has a solar-heated undercover swimming pool, spa treatments that earned it a recent recommendation as one of the top five spas in the South Pacific, and river tours, reef dives, fishing and horse-riding all nearby. Luxury villa from US$251/A$476.

Three-night 'Daintree Dreaming' package with accommodation in a luxury villa with cooked breakfast, champagne and chocolates, massage, heavenly body treatment, interpretive rainforest walk with local guide, and transfers to and from Cairns/Port Douglas costs from US$1139/A$2220. Reservations toll-free within Australia (☎ 1800-808 010) or book through UK tour operator ITC Classics (☎ 0870-751 9310) or Tailor Made Travel (☎ 01386-712 073).

New Zealand
(BEST TIME: NOVEMBER TO MARCH)

New Zealand is the place if you are looking for a little more from your honeymoon than spending two weeks on a lounger – adventure in a truly unspoilt wilderness. Few visitors to New Zealand stay in one place because there's so much to see and do: build your itinerary around the key sights and hotels I've covered in this chapter.

You'll find such a staggering mix of scenery in New Zealand that you won't believe you have only visited one country: ancient glaciers; smouldering volcanoes; azure lakes fringed with lush green pines and surrounded by a backdrop of craggy snow-capped mountains; fertile grasslands stretching out as far as the eye can see, and everywhere the unrelenting surf crashing down on vast empty beaches.

This country is also heaven for animal lovers. You can swim with huge packs of dusky dolphins, watch awesome 12m sperm whales surfacing and diving, visit the Fjordland crested penguin, one of the rarest varieties of penguin in the world, and sea-kayak past fur seal colonies.

But New Zealand is perhaps best known for its adventure activity, from bungee jumping, whitewater rafting and jet boat racing through narrow gorges, to heli-skiing, parapenting, and trail biking along challenging mountain paths. You can experience more exhilarating adventure in one day in **Queenstown** than a normally sporty person will see in a lifetime.

New Zealand is a land of rugged beauty, of hugely diversified landscapes, and of activities. Most of the main sights are located near enough to each other so that once there, you won't have to do much travelling around. But perhaps the country's best attribute is its space and remoteness. If you are looking for peace and tranquillity – somewhere to rediscover each other away from hordes of other honeymooners, then this is the place for you.

NEW ZEALAND

A truly unspoilt wilderness of ancient glaciers, smouldering volcanoes, azure lakes fringed with lush green pines, crystal clear mountain streams and craggy snow-capped mountains, with lots of opportunity for adventurous pursuits from bungee jumping to swimming with dolphins

When to go: November to March are the summer months, but skiing is best in August

Average maximum temperatures °C

	JAN	FEB	MAR	APR	MAY	JUN	JUL	AUG	SEP	OCT	NOV	DEC
Auckland	23	23	22	19	17	14	13	14	16	17	19	21

Capital: Auckland

Flight times: to Auckland from:

New York: (via LA) 17¾ hours

LA: 12 hours

London: 28 hours (via LA/Far East)

Sydney: 3 hours

Approximate exchange rates: New Zealand Dollar (NZ$) – £1 = NZ$3.40, US$1 = NZ$2.39, A$1 = NZ$1.24

Time difference: GMT plus 12 hours

Voltage: 230v, slanted three-pronged plugs

Combine with: Australia, Bali, Fiji and anywhere else in the South Pacific, Hawaii, Los Angeles, Hong Kong, Thailand, Malaysia or Singapore

Country dialling code: ☎ 64

Further information: 🖳 www.purenz.com

In honeymoon terms, New Zealand's South Island has more to offer than the North Island; a contentious statement I'm sure, but most travel agents would agree. It really depends on how much time you have: if you are going for two weeks or less, I would concentrate all your time on seeing the South Island because the best sights and places are in a fairly compact area: the ever-changing landscapes of the South Island offer some of the most spectacular and unspoilt scenery the world has to offer. However, there are some good hotels and places to visit in the North Island, so if you have three weeks spend the first one in the North Island and then move to the South Island for the remaining two weeks.

The best way to see the South Island is to fly into **Christchurch**, the island's main city, and hire a car. Driving in New Zealand is an absolute pleasure, the roads are in good condition, the sign posts are clear, efficient and easy to map-read by, and the highways are so empty that you'll very rarely have a car both in front and behind you! Besides, the surrounding countryside is invariably so beautiful, and constantly changing, that even a four-hour drive will be positively enjoyable.

SOUTH ISLAND

The one place that you won't want to miss out on in New Zealand's South Island is **Queenstown**. Now becoming famous throughout the world for its bungee jumping and numerous other dare-devil activities, Queenstown is indisputably the adventure capital of the Southern Hemisphere. Because Queenstown is right down the bottom of the South Island, it might pay to fly there direct from Christchurch. The only problem with flying is the huge expense: return tickets from Christchurch will set you back around NZ$570 each with Air New Zealand (🖳 www.airnewzealand.co.nz) – New Zealand is one of the most expensive places for domestic flights in the world. But flying does avoid a six-hour drive from Christchurch, allowing you to conserve your energy for the numerous activities that await you, not to mention the extra time in this wicked resort. **Blanket Bay** (see p304), near Queenstown, is also the hottest place to stay in New Zealand.

If you're not flying in to Queenstown, then the drive along the rugged west coast, taking in the **Fox** and **Franz Josef** glaciers and on through the **Haarst Pass** via lakes **Hawea** and **Wanaka** is the best way to get there. On the return journey make sure you

---

THINGS TO SEE AND DO IN QUEENSTOWN

Queenstown feels just like an Alpine ski-resort with traditional wooden chalets overhanging bustling streets filled with four-wheel drive wagons, and numerous cafés and bars with pavement tables, all surrounded by a backdrop of vast rocky mountains. Uniquely, Queenstown is a year-round resort, where skiing in the winter is just as popular as all the waterborne activities of the summer.

Here you can attempt the ultimate challenge, the **Awesome Foursome**. For around US$158/NZ$378 you can hurl yourself off a pipeline into Skipper's canyon – the **world's** largest **bungee jump**; catch a **helicopter** swooping 225kph down the Canyon; **whitewater raft** the furious rapids through a 170m disused mining tunnel, and finish off by rocketing through the Canyon's thin gorge, hurtling past rocks just millimetres away from you in the 340hp boats run by **Shotover Jet**. You'll need a drink after all that.

Queenstown is also a great base from which to see **Milford Sound** and walk the stunning **Milford Track**, though be warned that it is very popular with tourists which does rather detract from the area's outstanding natural beauty.

---

take a different route, driving via **McKenzie Country** to see the magnificent snow-covered **Mt Cook**, the country's highest mountain.

Recommended lodges

Timara Lodge (☎ 3-572 8276, ▤ 3-572 9191, ▢ www.timara.co.nz, Dog Point Road, RD2, Blenheim), in the heart of the largest wine-producing area of New Zealand, renowned for its fine food and impressive wine cellars, is the perfect place to relax and look back on your day's adventures. It's well placed for touring the Marlborough wineries, visiting the Marlborough Sounds and Golden Bay area, or even to go whale-watching at nearby Kaikoura.

Set in beautifully-kept formal gardens where swans swim in the mill pond, the Lodge was built in 1923 as a private country manor and is now run along the lines of a country house hotel, accommodating just eight guests. Timara hosts wedding receptions, for a maximum of 160 people.

Only two of the lodge's four rooms are doubles so prior booking is essential, and it costs US$419/NZ$1000 per couple inclusive which includes the best local wines. The bedrooms are really lovely and well-equipped with clock radio, hairdryer, heated towel rails, complimentary toiletries, bathrobes, ironing board and a phone. There are pleasing personal touches too, from the freebie chocolates and bottle of mineral water left out for you, to the fresh flowers in every room.

Days at Timara are spent touring the surrounding countryside on the lodge's mountain bikes, or on foot. There are 72 hectares of walks to be discovered and a rowing boat on the lake making it the perfect spot for a picnic. If all you want to do is relax for a day there's a lovely outdoor swimming pool and a grass tennis court.

Blanket Bay (☎ 3-442 9442, ▤ 3-442 9441, ▢ www.blanketbay.com, PO Box 35, Glenorchy, near Queenstown), a member of Small Luxury Hotels of the World (toll-free reservations see p12) is the new hot place in New Zealand. Sheltered by the high peaks of the spectacular Southern Alps, and mirrored in Lake Wakatipu, this luxury all-inclusive lodge was on Brad Pitt and Jennifer Aniston's honeymoon list. Described as 'wilderness with parmesan wafers and truffle oil' in *Tatler*'s 101 Best Hotels 2001, this lodge is heaven for the design-conscious.

Vast is the scale here – both inside and out. The heart of the lodge is the 30ft high Great Room with vaulted timber beams and panoramic windows. The five guest rooms and three spacious suites are finished in the rich textures of restored native timber and local schist stonework. All have open log fires, super king-size beds, sumptuous sofas and chairs and spectacular lake views from their private balconies. The Paradise room, with its cathedral ceiling, underfloor heating, steam room and vast private terrace, lives up to its name.

THINGS TO SEE AND DO AROUND BLENHEIM

Blenheim, about two hours from Kaikoura up the one road north is the South Island's **wine capital**, made famous by the prolific Montana winery which is accountable for one in every two bottles of New Zealand wine produced.

Many of the wineries in the Marlborough region are open to visitors. The best way to see them is to drive north, from Nelson through Richmond to Motueka (on the SH60 Coast Road) and do the loop back round on the Moutere River road, stopping off for the odd tasting en route.

The best place to stop for lunch, or better still dinner, is the world famous *Hunter's Winery*. Make sure you have time to sample the winery's famous Sauvignon and Chardonnay on the terrace before having dinner: looking out through the vines to the sun setting over the surrounding mountains is wonderful.

In many ways it makes sense to head straight on up to Blenheim after Kaikoura as you won't want to spend more than a couple of days in Christchurch and there's lots more to see and do around the very top of the South Island.

From Blenheim you'll be ideally placed to visit both the convoluted waterways of the **Marlborough Sounds** and **Nelson**, a small seaside town right on the top of the island, which boasts some of the best beaches and more sunshine than any other part of the South Island. The place to stay around Blenheim is **Timara Lodge**, see p304.

After a few days in either place you should be ready to hit the adventure trail again. A couple of hours' drive further up the coast will take you to the **Abel Tasman National Park**, where the coastline of unspoilt and protected native forest makes for a spectacular five-day walk or, arguably better still, great sea kayaking trips. **Abel Tasman Kayaks** (☎ 3-527 8022, 🖳 3-527 8032, 🖳 www.kayaktours.co.nz) offer all sorts of packages from one-day guided trips to five-day remote coastal trips, and they even allow you to head off on your own if you've got some experience.

You don't need any experience of canoes if you're going on one of the guided trips, however, just a love of water and thirst for adventure. We did the three-day trip which I think was just about the right length of time to really get into it, but not too long to miss our bed.

The kayaks are very easy to handle and definitely afford the best views of this breathtakingly unspoilt coastline, not to mention the chance to get to beaches only accessible from the sea. You'll also have plenty of chance to see lots of local wildlife from colonies of frolicking fur seals to plummeting gannets dive-bombing for their supper in the clear waters around you.

Although you'll be in a group of six, plus a guide, you'll find you can get all the privacy you want, paddling along at your leisure and pitching your tent in your own private, secluded spot at night. Sitting on those beautiful, remote sandy beaches, the colour of golden honeycomb, watching the sun go down over the water at night is a must. Life simply can't get much more romantic, or heavenly, than that.

Blanket Bay is perfectly positioned to experience this beautiful region, by speed boat from the private jetty, windsurfing or sailing on the lake, heli excursions to Milford Sound and of course, walking in the alpine scenery. If you want a lazy day, just drink in the alpine air from the side of the swimming pool or beach, soak in the spa or perhaps take a stroll under the starry southern skies. Doubles cost US$456/NZ$1090, suites from US$707/NZ$1690 per couple inclusive (all drinks except wine).

A less expensive option is UK tour operator, Bridge the World's Little Gems collection (☎ 0870-444 7474, 🖳 www.bridgetheworld.com) launched in 2001. This is a collection of mainly privately-owned bed and breakfast properties, guesthouses, lodges and boutique hotels ranging from gourmet homesteads to a converted retreat for nuns, with an average of seven rooms. The most costly – **Tongariro Lodge** – costs just US$168/NZ$282 per person per night.

NORTH ISLAND

Even if you only have a few days to spare for North Island, try to make it to **Auckland**. Commonly known as the City of Sails, the picturesque harbour provides great entertainment both on the water and around it. Explore the underworld at **Kelly Taltons**, or stand on top of one of the 48 extinct volcanoes to get a 360° panoramic view of the city. Take the bus downtown to **Parnell Village**, a cluster of colonial shops all painted in bright colours with an endless choice of food. To enjoy something a little quieter take a boat ride out to **Waihete Island**.

Beyond Auckland is the breathtaking **Bay of Islands** district extending for more than 805km of indented coastline with over 150 small islands. An idyllic setting, relaxed and wonderfully peaceful, you can hire a Laser if you're into sailing which will get you out to some of the islands on your own, or for some real action do one of the deep-sea fishing trips, or try some surfing. If you go beyond **Paihia** to **Waihangi** you can visit the village where the treaty was signed between the colonials and the Maoris in 1840. A good round trip starts at **Russell** up the eastern coast and through **Opononi** and down the west side through the tropical nature reserve, or the bush as it's known locally. Here you'll see the huge Kauri trees – one tree trunk takes at least six men's arms linked together to circle it.

South of Auckland in **Maramarua** is Hôtel du Vin (☎ 9-233 6314, 🖺 9-2336215, 🖳 reservations@duvin.co.nz), a lovely 46-room hotel situated in its own vineyard – De Redcliffe Winery – and an idyllic spot to stop for a night en route to **Cambridge** and **Rotorua**, famous for its hot mud pools and geysers which spray water as high as 18m in places.

Then move on to **Hawkes Bay** to sample some of the world famous wine and munch your way through endless orchards of apples, nectarines and peaches. Finally, drive on down through the many dairy and sheep farms to windy **Wellington**, which does have some great sights, fantastically hip bars and beautiful gardens to visit, before heading back to Auckland, or to Huka Lodge near **Lake Taupo** (see below) or across to the South Island.

Recommended hotels

Huka Lodge (☎ 7-378 5791, 🖺 7-378 0427, 🖳 www.hukalodge.co.nz, PO Box 95, Taupo), a member of Small Luxury Hotels of the World and Leading Hotels of the World (toll-free reservations for both see p12) is one of the most exclusive retreats in the Southern Hemisphere. Built in 1920 as a fishing lodge, it lies beside Huka Falls which feeds down to huge Lake Taupo, created by volcanic eruption and home to some of the world's best freshwater trout.

The 20 guest suites are each set in private bush just metres from the Waikato River, and plenty of activities are on offer, including horse-riding, jetboating, rafting, bush-walking, skiing, fly fishing and hunting. It's expensive to stay here at US$503/NZ$1204 per couple, but this includes breakfast, a five-course dinner and cocktail hour (excludes tax).

STAYING IN LODGES IN NEW ZEALAND

Hotels in New Zealand are in scarce supply in tour operators' brochures these days. The 'in-places' to stay, and just perfect for honeymooners, are lodges; these are small, intimate, luxurious places and are set amidst idyllic scenery. The blazing log fires match the warmth of local hospitality, and the fine food and wines along with the heady fresh air can't help but make you feel good.

These distinctive properties offer some of the finest five-star country house style accommodation in the Southern Hemisphere so they don't come cheap – expect to pay around US$419/NZ$1000 per couple per night (excluding 12.5% tax). However, with breakfast, a delicious dinner, drinks, and all activities and facilities included, once you get there you won't have

to worry about a thing. You can be as active as you like – horse-riding, sailing, fishing or bush walking – or simply laze by the lake or pool, or soak in the spa.

For those who want to get married in the wilderness, Huka Lodge (see above), Timara Lodge and Blanket Bay (see p304) host weddings.

Tour operator Tailor Made Travel (UK ☎ 01386-712000, 🖺 01386-712071, 🖳 www.tailor made.co.uk) in association with the New Zealand Lodge Association (🖳 www.lodge sofnz.co.nz) offers the widest choice of lodges, including the ones listed in this guide. Tour operators ITC Classics, Elegant Resorts, Abercrombie & Kent, and Bridge the World also offer lodges in New Zealand (see p13).

GETTING MARRIED ABROAD

According to British tour operator Kuoni, weddings abroad have increased by 40 percent in the last two years and every year, more and more couples decide to get married abroad. They are motivated by several considerations, the first and last of which is romance. It is also usually a great deal less expensive than having a big wedding at home, and lots of couples prefer to take their vows alone, or with a few close friends. As a result the number of places where you can be married abroad has grown.

Hotels all over the world are now geared up for weddings and can provide as many or as few extra trappings as you want. Whether you choose a secluded cove in Jamaica, a jungle lodge in Costa Rica, a hot-air balloon floating above the African plains of the Serengeti or a French château, there are certain legal requirements that you must fulfil in order to make your marriage a binding one. These vary considerably from country to country, so check *exactly* what you need when booking, and to avoid any confusion check everything with the embassy in your country before you depart.

Most countries request the following:
• your birth certificates
• valid 10-year passports and valid visas
• an affidavit confirming your marital status
• your previous spouse's death certificate if you are widowed
• a decree absolute if you are divorced
• a minimum residency requirement (anything from one to seven days)
• that you are both over 18 years old, or in some countries over 21 years old (in Bali men must be over 23 and women over 21)
• some countries require that you adhere to certain religious requirements

Many of the large tour operators, such as JMC, Kuoni and Tradewinds in the UK, produce dedicated wedding brochures with detailed country and hotel information. Even specialist tour operators, such as Elite Vacations for the Seychelles and Olympic Holidays for Greece, produce special information packs.

Useful websites to browse through for ideas include: 🖥 www.weddingsworld. co.uk and 🖥 www.weddings-abroad.com, or specific country sites such as 🖥 www. gettingmarriedinitaly.com or 🖥 www.new-zealand-weddings.co.nz which can help once you've decided on the location for your dream wedding.

In this book we've indicated hotels that specialise in arranging complete weddings. Page references for these hotels are given below. If a hotel isn't listed below that doesn't necessarily mean that they can't arranged for you to get married: contact the hotel directly.

ISLANDS OF THE WORLD
The Caribbean Islands
Sandals resorts 19

Fiji
Yasawa Island Lodge 59
Vatulele Island Resort 60
Turtle Island Resort 61
The Wakaya Club 62

The Philippines
Amanpulo (non legally-binding ceremony only) 64
El Nido Lagen Island 65

Indonesia
Begawan Giri Estate 68
Four Seasons Jimbaran 69
Kupu Kupu Barong 70
The Oberoi Lombok 71

Sri Lanka
Saman Villas 73
Hotel Kandalama 75

The Maldives
Four Seasons Resort Maldives 78

The Seychelles
Le Meridien Fisherman's Cove 81
Sunset Beach 82
Charming Lady 83
L'Archipel 84
Lemuria 85
La Digue Island Lodge 87
Denis Island Lodge 88

Mauritius
Le Saint Géran Hotel 91
Le Touessrok & Ile aux Cerfs 92
Royal Palm 93
Paradise Cove Hotel 94

EUROPE

England
Cliveden 101
The Devonshire Arms 103
The Lygon Arms 105
Chewton Glen 107
Combermere Abbey Cottages 109
Samling 109

Scotland
The Scotsman 110
The Gleneagles Hotel 112
Skibo Castle 117
Myres Castle 117
Dundas Castle 117

Wales

Ireland

France

Spain

Italy

Greece

Cyprus

NORTH AMERICA

USA

Mexico

Mexico (cont'd)
Hacienda Katanchel 200
Hacienda Tomozon 200
Camino Real 201
La Casa de la Marquesa 202

Costa Rica
Finca Rosa Lanca 206
Lapa Rios 207
Hotel Villa Caletas 209

SOUTH AMERICA

Brazil
Copacabana Palace 218

AFRICA

Morocco
La Mamounia Hotel 224

Kenya
Wilderness Trails at Lewa Downs 231
Little Governor's Camp 232
Ol Donyo Wuas 233
Galdessa 234
Hemingways 235
The Funzi Keys 236

Tanzania
Klein's Camp 239
Grumeti River Lodge 239
Selous Safari Camp 239
Sand Rivers Selous 240
Ras Kutani Beach Resort 241
Ras Nungwi 242
Mnemba Island Lodge 243
Kinasi Camp 244

Zimbabwe
Sanyati Lodge 246
The Victoria Falls Hotel 247
Tongabezi 248

Botswana
Sandibe Safari Lodge 251
Jack's Camp 252

South Africa
The Mount Nelson 254
The Cellars-Hohenort 255
Ellerman House 256
Hunter's Country House 259
Londolozi Private Game Reserve 260

ASIA

Dubai
Burj Al Arab 263

India

Shiv Niwas Palace 269
Neemrana Fort Palace 270

Thailand
The Oriental 277
The Regent Chiang Mai 279
Le Royal Méridien Baan Taling Ngam 283
Tongsai Grand Villas 284
Rayavadee Premier Resort 285

Malaysia
The Datai 288

Hong Kong
The Peninsula 290

AUSTRALASIA

Australia
The Park Hyatt Sydney 294
The Observatory Hotel 295
Lilianfels 297
Hayman Island 298
Lizard Island 299

New Zealand
Timara Lodge 304
Blanket Bay 304
Huka Lodge 306

TRAILBLAZER

The Blues Highway – New Orleans to Chicago
A travel and music guide *Richard Knight*
1st edition, 304pp, 50 maps, 30 colour photos
ISBN 1 873756 43 7   £12.99, Can$29.95, US$19.95
The first travel guide to explore the roots of jazz and blues in the USA.
❑ Detailed city guides with 40 maps ❑ Where to stay, where to eat
❑ The best music clubs and bars ❑ Who's who of jazz and blues
❑ Historic landmarks ❑ Music festivals and events ❑ Exclusive interviews
with music legends Wilson Pickett, Ike Turner, Little Milton, Rufus Thomas,
Honeyboy Edwards and more. *'This book is vital.'–* ***Sam Phillips***

Sahara Overland – a route & planning guide *Chris Scott*
1st edition, 544 pages, 24 colour & 150 B&W photos
ISBN 1 873756 26 7   £19.99, Can$44.95 US$29.95
Covers all aspects Saharan, from acquiring documentation to vehicle
choice and preparation; from descriptions of the prehistoric art sites of
the Libyan Fezzan to the ancient caravan cities of southern Mauritania.
How to 'read' sand surfaces, using GPS – it's all here along with 35
detailed off-road itineraries covering over 16,000kms in nine countries.
*"THE essential desert companion for anyone planning a Saharan trip
on either two wheels or four.'* ***Trailbike Magazine***

Adventure Motorcycling Handbook *Chris Scott*
4th edition, 288 pages, 28 colour, 100 B&W photos
ISBN 1 873756 37 2   £12.99, Can$29.95, US$19.95
Every red-blooded motorcyclist dreams of making the Big Trip – this book
shows you how. Choosing a destination, bike preparation, documentation
and shipping, trans-continental route outlines across Africa, Asia and Latin
America, and back-country riding in SW USA, NW Canada and Australia.
Plus – first hand accounts of biking adventures worldwide. *'The closest thing
to the Bible for overland adventure motorcyclists...'* ***BikeNet***

The Inca Trail, Cuzco & Machu Picchu *Richard Danbury*
2nd edition, £10.99, Can$24.95, US$18.95
ISBN 1 873756 64 X, 288pp, 45 maps, 24 colour photos
The Inca Trail from Cuzco to Machu Picchu is South America's most
popular hike. This practical guide includes 20 detailed trail maps,
plans of eight Inca sites, plus guides to Cuzco and Machu Picchu.
'Danbury's research is thorough...you need this one'. ***Sunday Times***

Trekking in the Pyrenees *Douglas Streatfeild-James*
2nd edition, £11.99, Can$27.95 US$18.95
ISBN 1 873756 50 X, 320pp, 95 maps, 55 colour photos
All the main trails along the France-Spain border including the GR10
(France) coast to coast hike and the GR11 (Spain) from Roncesvalles to
Andorra, plus many shorter routes. 90 route maps include walking times
and places to stay. Expanded to include greater coverage of routes in Spain.
'Readily accessible, well-written and most readable...' ***John Cleare***

Trekking in the Dolomites *Henry Stedman*
256 pages, 52 trail maps, 13 town plans, 30 colour photos
ISBN 1 873756 34 8, *1st edition,* £11.99, US$17.95
The Dolomites region of northern Italy encompasses some of the most
beautiful mountain scenery in Europe. This new guide features selected
routes including Alta Via II, a West-East traverse and other trails, plus
detailed guides to Cortina, Bolzano, Bressanone and 10 other towns.
Also includes full colour flora section and bird identification guide.

TRAILBLAZER

Trekking in Corsica *David Abram*
256pp, 53 maps, 48 colour photos
ISBN 1 873756 63 1, £11.99, Can$27.95 US$18.95 *1st edition*
A mountain range rising straight from the sea, Corsica holds the most arrestingly beautiful and diverse landscapes in the Mediterranean. Among the many trails that penetrate its remotest corners, the GR20, which wriggles across the island's watershed, has gained an international reputation. This new guide also covers the best of the other routes. With 44 route maps and 9 village plans. Includes full colour flora guide.

Trekking in Ladakh *Charlie Loram*
288pp, 75 maps, 24 colour photos
ISBN 1 873756 30 5, £10.99, Can$22.95, US$18.95 *2nd edition*
Fully revised and extended 2nd edition of Charlie Loram's practical guide. Includes 70 detailed walking maps plus information on getting to Ladakh.
'Extensive...and well researched'. **Climber Magazine**
'Were it not for this book we might still be blundering about...'
The Independent on Sunday

West Highland Way *Charlie Loram*
224pp, 48 maps, 10 town plans, 40 colour photos
ISBN 1 873756 54 2, £9.99, Can$22.95, US$16.95 *1st edition*
Scotland's best-known long distance footpath passes through some of the most spectacular scenery in all of Britain. From the outskirts of Glasgow it winds for 95 miles (153km) along the wooded banks of Loch Lomond, across the wilderness of Rannoch Moor, over the mountains above Glencoe to a dramatic finish at the foot of Britain's highest peak – Ben Nevis. Includes Glasgow city guide.

Trans-Siberian Handbook *Bryn Thomas*
432pp, 48 maps, 32 colour photos
ISBN 1 873756 42 9, £12.99, Can$28.95 US$19.95 *5th edition*
First edition short-listed for the **Thomas Cook Guidebook Awards**. New fifth edition of the most popular guide to the world's longest rail journey. How to arrange a trip, plus a km-by-km guide to the routes. Updated and expanded to include extra information on travelling independently in Russia. New mapping.
'Definitive guide' **Condé Nast Traveler**

Australia by Rail *Colin Taylor*
288 pages, 50 maps, 30 colour photos
ISBN 1 873756 40 2, *4th edition*, £11.99, US$19.95
Re-researched and expanded to include 50 strip maps covering all rail routes in Australia plus new information for rail travellers. Includes 14 town plans and six city guides: where to stay, where to eat and the most interesting places to stop off along the way.
Full of friendly advice, and spiced with humour – **Network**

Trans-Canada Rail Guide *Melissa Graham*
240 pages, 31 maps, 24 colour photos
ISBN 1 873756 39 9, *2nd edition*, £10.99, US$16.95
Expanded 2nd edition now includes Calgary city guide. Comprehensive guide to Canada's trans-continental railroad. Covers the entire route from coast to coast. What to see and where to stay in the cities along the line, with information for all budgets.
'Invaluable' – **The Daily Telegraph**

January

Argentina, Australia, Bahamas, Belize, Brazil, Canada, Caribbean, Chile, Costa Rica, Cuba, Dubai, Ecuador, Egypt, Hawaii, Hong Kong, India, Kenya, Malaysia, Maldives, Mexico, Morocco, New Zealand, Philippines, South Africa, Tanzania, Thailand, Turks & Caicos, USA, Venezuela

February

Argentina, Australia, Bahamas, Belize, Brazil, Canada, Caribbean, Chile, Costa Rica, Cuba, Dubai, Ecuador, Egypt, Hawaii, Hong Kong, India, Kenya, Malaysia, Maldives, Mexico, Morocco, New Zealand, Philippines, South Africa, Sri Lanka, Tanzania, Thailand, Turks & Caicos, USA, Venezuela

March

Argentina, Australia, Bahamas, Belize, Brazil, Canada, Caribbean, Chile, Costa Rica, Cuba, Dubai, Ecuador, Egypt, French Polynesia, Hawaii, Hong Kong, India, Kenya, Malaysia, Maldives, Mexico, Morocco, New Zealand, Philippines, South Africa, Sri Lanka, Tanzania, Thailand, Turks & Caicos, USA, Venezuela

April

Australia, Bahamas, Belize, Brazil, Britain, Canada, Caribbean, Costa Rica, Cuba, Cyprus, Dubai, Ecuador, Egypt, France, French Polynesia, Greece, Hawaii, Hong Kong, Indonesia, Ireland, Italy, Malaysia, Maldives, Mauritius, Mexico, Morocco, Spain, South Africa, Sri Lanka, Thailand, Turks & Caicos, USA, Venezuela, Zimbabwe

May

Australia, Bahamas, Belize, Botswana, Brazil, Britain, Canada, Caribbean, Cyprus, Dubai, Ecuador, Fiji, France, French Polynesia, Greece, Hawaii, Hong Kong, Indonesia, Ireland, Italy, Malaysia, Maldives, Mauritius, Mexico, Morocco, Seychelles, Spain, South Africa, Sri Lanka, Thailand, Turks & Caicos, USA, Venezuela, Zimbabwe

June

Australia, Bahamas, Brazil, Botswana, Britain, Canada, Caribbean, Cyprus, Ecuador, Fiji, France, French Polynesia, Greece, Hawaii, Hong Kong, Indonesia, Ireland, Italy, Malaysia, Maldives, Mauritius, Morocco, Peru, Seychelles, Spain, Tanzania, Thailand, USA, Venezuela, Zimbabwe